Strategic Management

Cases

Competitiveness and Globalization

8th Edition

Michael A. Hitt
Texas A&M University

R. Duane Ireland
Texas A&M University

Robert E. Hoskisson
Arizona State University

Australia • Brazil • Canada • Mexico • Singapore • Spain • United Kingdom • United States

Strategic Management: Competitiveness and Globalization (Cases) 8th Edition

Michael A. Hitt, R. Duane Ireland, and Robert E. Hoskisson

VP/Editorial Director: Jack W. Calhoun

VP/Editor-in-Chief: Melissa Acuña

Senior Acquisitions Editor: Michele Rhoades

Developmental Editor: Rebecca Von Gillern—Bookworm Editorial Services

Executive Marketing Manager: Kimberly Kanakes

Marketing Manager: Clint Kernen

Marketing Coordinator: Sara Rose

Senior Content Project Manager: Colleen A. Farmer

Technology Project Editor: Kristen Meere

Manufacturing Coordinator: Doug Wilke

Production Service: LEAP Publishing Services, Inc.

Compositor: ICC Macmillan, Inc.

Senior Art Director: Tippy McIntosh

Photo Manager: Sheri I. Blaney

Photo Researcher: Marcy Lunetta

Printer: Transcontinental

Internal & Cover Designer: Craig Ramsdell, Ramsdell Design

Cover Image: © Don Hammond/Design Pics/Corbis

Library of Congress Control Number: 2007940878
Student Edition ISBN 13: 978-0-324-58113-3
Student Edition ISBN 10: 0-324-58113-0

Instructor's Edition ISBN 13: 978-0-324-58122-5
Instructor's Edition ISBN 10: 0-324-58122-X

Concepts and Cases ISBN 13: 978-0-324-65559-9
Concepts and Cases ISBN 10: 0-324-65559-2

South-Western Cengage Learning
5191 Natorp Boulevard
Mason, OH 45040
USA

Cengage Learning products are represented in Canada by Nelson Education, Ltd.

For your course and learning solutions, visit **academic.cengage.com**

Purchase any of our products at your local college store or at our preferred online store **www.ichapters.com**

Printed in Canada
1 2 3 4 5 6 4 11 10 09 08 07

Preface

Our goal in writing each edition of this book is to present a new, up-to-date standard for explaining the strategic management process. To reach this goal with the 8th edition of our market-leading text, we again present you with an intellectually rich yet thoroughly practical analysis of strategic management.

With each new edition, we are challenged and invigorated by the goal of establishing a new standard for presenting strategic management knowledge in a readable style. To prepare for each new edition, we carefully study the most recent academic research to ensure that the strategic management content we present to you is highly current and relevant for organizations. In addition, we continuously read articles appearing in many different business publications (e.g., *Wall Street Journal, BusinessWeek, Fortune, Financial Times,* and *Forbes,* to name just a few); we do this to identify valuable examples of how companies use the strategic management process. Though many of the hundreds of companies we discuss in the book will be quite familiar to you, some companies will likely be new to you as well. One reason for this is that we use examples of companies from around the world to demonstrate how globalized business has become. To maximize your opportunities to learn as you read and think about how actual companies use strategic management tools, techniques, and concepts (based on the most current research), we emphasize a lively and user-friendly writing style.

Supplements

Instructors

IRCD (0-324-58118-1) Key ancillaries (Instructor's Resource Manual, Instructor's Case Notes, Test Bank, ExamView™, PowerPoint® and Case Analysis Questions Using Business & Company Resource Center) are provided on CD-ROM, giving instructors the ultimate tool for customizing lectures and presentations.

Instructor Case Notes (0-324-58121-1) All new expanded case notes provide details about the 29 cases found in the second part of the main text. These new expanded case notes include directed assignments, financial analysis, thorough discussion and exposition of issues in the case and an assessment rubric tied to AACSB assurance of learning standards that can be used for grading each case. The case notes provide consistent and thorough support for instructors, following the method espoused by the author team for preparing an effective case analysis. The case notes for the 8th edition have been written in great detail and include questions and answers throughout along with industry and company background and resolutions wherever possible.

Instructor's Resource Manual (0-324-58124-6) The Instructor's Resource Manual, organized around each chapter's knowledge objectives, includes teaching ideas for each chapter and how to reinforce essential principles with extra examples. The support product includes lecture outlines, detailed answers to end-of-chapter review questions, instructions for using each chapter's experiential exercises, and additional assignments.

Certified Test Bank (0-324-58126-2) Thoroughly revised and enhanced, test bank questions are linked to each chapter's knowledge objectives and are ranked by difficulty and question type. We provide an ample number of application questions throughout and we have also retained scenario-based questions as a means of adding in-depth problem-solving questions. With this edition, we introduce the concept of certification, whereby another qualified academic has proofread and verified the accuracy of the test bank questions and answers. The test bank material is also available in computerized ExamView™ format for creating custom tests in both Windows and Macintosh formats.

ExamView™ (Available on IRCD: 0-324-58118-1) Computerized testing software contains all of the questions in the certified printed test bank. This program is an easy-to-use test creation software compatible with Microsoft Windows. Instructors can add or edit questions, instructions, and answers, and select questions by previewing them on the screen, selecting them randomly, or selecting them by number. Instructors can also create and administer quizzes online, whether over the Internet, a local area network (LAN), or a wide area network (WAN).

All-New Video Program (0-324-58129-7) You spoke and we listened! For our 8th edition we have a selection of 13 brand-new videos that relate directly to chapter concepts. Provided by Fifty Lessons, these new videos are a comprehensive and compelling resource of management and leadership lessons from some of the world's most successful business leaders. In the form of short and powerful videos, these videos capture leaders' most important learning experiences. They share their real-world business acumen and outline the guiding principles behind their most important business decisions and their career progression.

PowerPoint® (0-324-58118-1) An all-new PowerPoint presentation, created for the 8th edition, provides support for lectures emphasizing key concepts, key terms, and instructive graphics. Slides can also be used by students as an aid to note-taking.

WebTutor™ WebTutor is used by an entire class under the direction of the instructor and is particularly convenient for distance learning courses. It provides Web-based learning resources to students as well as powerful communication and other course management tools, including course calendar, chat, and e-mail for instructors. See http://webtutor.thomsonlearning.com for more information.

Product Support Web Site (academic.cengage.com/management/hitt) Our product support Web site contains all ancillary products for instructors as well as the financial analysis exercises for both students and instructors.

The Business & Company Resource Center (BCRC) Put a complete business library at your students' fingertips! This premier online business research tool allows you and your students to search thousands of periodicals, journals, references, financial information, industry reports, and more. This powerful research tool saves time for students—whether they are preparing for a presentation or writing a reaction paper. You can use the BCRC to quickly and easily assign readings or research projects. Visit http://academic.cengage.com/bcrc to learn more about this indispensable tool. For this text in particular, BCRC will be especially useful in further researching the companies featured in the text's 29 cases. We've also included BCRC links for the Strategy Right Now feature on our Web site, as well as in the Cengage NOW product. Finally, we have incorporated data from BCRC into the exercises for financial analysis to facilitate students' research and help them focus their attention on honing their skills in financial analysis (see Web site).

Resource Integration Guide (RIG) When you start with a new—or even familiar—text, the amount of supplemental material can seem overwhelming. Identifying each element of a supplement package and piecing together the parts that fit your particular needs can be time-consuming. After all, you may use only a small fraction of the resources available to help you plan, deliver, and evaluate your class. We have created a resource guide to help you and your students extract the full value from the text and its wide range of exceptional supplements. This resource guide is available on the product support Web site. The RIG organizes the book's resources and provides planning suggestions to help you conduct your class, create assignments, and evaluate your students' mastery of the subject. Whatever your teaching style or circumstance, there are planning suggestions to meet your needs. The broad range of techniques provided in the guide helps you increase your repertoire as a teaching expert and enrich your students' learning and understanding. We hope this map and its suggestions enable you to discover new and exciting ways to teach your course.

Students

Financial analyses of some of the cases are provided on our product support Web site for both students and instructors. Researching financial data, company data, and industry data is made easy through the use of our proprietary database, the Business & Company Resource Center. Students are sent to this database to be able to quickly gather data needed for financial analysis.

Acknowledgments

We express our appreciation for the excellent support received from our editorial and production team at South-Western. We especially wish to thank Michele Rhoades, our Senior Acquisitions Editor; Rebecca von Gillern, our Development Editor; Kimberly Kanakes and Clinton Kernan, our Marketing Managers; and Colleen Farmer, our Content Project Manager. We are grateful for their dedication, commitment, and outstanding contributions to the development and publication of this book and its package of support materials.

We are highly indebted to the reviewers of the seventh edition in preparation for this current edition:

Brent Allred,
The College of William and Mary

Jame Bronson,
University of Wisconsin, Whitewater

Daniel DeGravel,
California State University, Los Angeles

Steve Gove,
University of Dayton

Peggy Griffin,
New Jersey City University

Franz Kellermans,
Mississippi State University

Frank Novakowski,
Davenport University

Finally, we are very appreciative of the following people for the time and care that went into the preparation of the supplements to accompany this edition:

Brian Boyd,
Arizona State University

Judith Gebhardt,
Catholic University

Steve Gove,
University of Dayton

Dana Gray,
Rogers State University

Michael A. Hitt
R. Duane Ireland
Robert E. Hoskisson

Case Title	Manufacturing	Service	Consumer Goods	Food/ Retail	High Technology	Transportation/ Communication	International Perspective	Social/ Ethical Issues	Industry Perspective
3M Cultivating Core Comp.	●		●		●		●		
A-1 Lanes	●						●		●
Abercrombie & Fitch				●				●	●
AMD vs Intel	●				●				●
Boeing	●						●		●
Capital One		●							
Carrefour in Asia				●			●		
Dell	●		●		●				●
Disney		●						●	●
Ford	●		●						●
GE Welch & Immelt	●	●			●			●	
Home Depot		●		●			●		
China's Home Improvement				●			●		
Huawei	●				●		●		
ING Direct		●		●					
JetBlue		●				●	●		●
Corp. Gov. at Knight Trans.		●				●			
Lufthansa		●				●	●		
Microsoft		●			●				
Nestlé	●		●	●				●	
Netflix		●		●					
PenAgain	●		●						
PSA Peugeot Citroën	●		●				●		
Sun Microsystems		●			●		●		
Teleflex Canada	●				●				
Tyco International	●							●	
Vodafone		●			●	●	●		
Wal-Mart Stores				●			●	●	
WD-40	●		●				●		

Case Title	Chapter 1	2	3	4	5	6	7	8	9	10	11	12	13
3M Cultivating Core Comp.			●				●						●
A-1 Lanes								●					●
Abercrombie & Fitch					●					●		●	
AMD vs Intel					●								●
Boeing				●	●			●	●				
Capital One				●		●	●						
Carrefour in Asia		●						●					
Dell		●		●		●							
Disney						●				●		●	
Ford				●	●							●	
GE Welch & Immelt							●					●	●
Home Depot				●	●							●	
China's Home Improvement	●				●			●					
Huawei					●			●					
ING Direct				●								●	●
JetBlue		●		●	●								
Corp. Gov. at Knight Trans.										●		●	
Lufthansa								●	●		●		
Microsoft					●	●							
Nestlé	●						●				●		●
Netflix		●	●		●							●	
PenAgain									●				●
PSA Peugeot Citroën			●						●				
Sun Microsystems	●			●				●					
Teleflex Canada						●						●	●
Tyco International						●				●	●	●	
Vodafone	●		●				●	●					
Wal-Mart Stores	●	●	●	●									
WD-40			●	●				●					●

About the Authors

Michael A. Hitt

Michael A. Hitt is a Distinguished Professor and holds the Joe B. Foster Chair in Business Leadership at Texas A&M University. He received his Ph.D. from the University of Colorado. He has co-authored or co-edited 26 books and 150 journal articles.

Some of his books are *Downscoping: How to Tame the Diversified Firm* (Oxford University Press, 1994); *Mergers and Acquisitions: A Guide to Creating Value for Stakeholders* (Oxford University Press, 2001); *Competing for Advantage* 2nd edition (South-Western College Publishing, 2008); and *Understanding Business Strategy* (South-Western College Publishing, 2006). He is co-editor of several books including the following: *Managing Strategically in an Interconnected World* (1998); *New Managerial Mindsets: Organizational Transformation and Strategy Implementation* (1998); *Dynamic Strategic Resources: Development, Diffusion, and Integration* (1999); *Winning Strategies in a Deconstructing World* (John Wiley & Sons, 2000); *Handbook of Strategic Management* (2001); *Strategic Entrepreneurship: Creating a New Integrated Mindset* (2002); *Creating Value: Winners in the New Business Environment* (Blackwell Publishers, 2002); *Managing Knowledge for Sustained Competitive Advantage* (Jossey-Bass, 2003); *Great Minds in Management: The Process of Theory Development* (Oxford University Press, 2005), and *The Global Mindset* (Elsevier, 2007). He has served on the editorial review boards of multiple journals, including the *Academy of Management Journal, Academy of Management Executive, Journal of Applied Psychology, Journal of Management, Journal of World Business,* and *Journal of Applied Behavioral Sciences.* Furthermore, he has served as Consulting Editor and Editor of the *Academy of Management Journal.* He is currently a co-editor of the *Strategic Entrepreneurship Journal.* He is president of the Strategic Management Society and is a past president of the Academy of Management.

He is a Fellow in the Academy of Management and in the Strategic Management Society. He received an honorary doctorate from the Universidad Carlos III de Madrid and is an Honorary Professor and Honorary Dean at Xi'an Jiao Tong University. He has been ackowledged with several awards for his scholarly research and he received the Irwin Outstanding Educator Award and the Distinguished Service Award from the Academy of Management. He has received best paper awards for articles published in the *Academy of Management Journal, Academy of Management Executive,* and *Journal of Management.*

R. Duane Ireland

R. Duane Ireland holds the Foreman R. and Ruby S. Bennett Chair in Business from the Mays Business School, Texas A&M University where he previously served as head of the management department. He teaches strategic management courses at all levels (undergraduate, masters, doctoral, and executive). His research, which focuses on diversification, innovation, corporate entrepreneurship, and strategic entrepreneurship, has been published in a number of journals, including *Academy of Management Journal, Academy of Management Review, Academy of Management Executive, Administrative Science Quarterly, Strategic Management Journal, Journal of Management, Strategic Entrepreneurship Journal, Human Relations, Entrepreneurship Theory and Practice, Journal of Business Venturing,* and *Journal of Management Studies,* among others. His recently published books include *Understanding Business Strategy, Concepts and Cases* (South-Western College Publishing, 2006), *Entrepreneurship: Successfully Launching New Ventures* (Prentice-Hall, Second Edition, 2008), and *Competing for Advantage* (South-Western College Publishing, 2008). He is serving or has served as a member of the editorial review boards for a number of journals, including *Academy of Management Journal, Academy of Management Review, Academy of Management Executive, Journal of Management, Journal of Business Venturing, Entrepreneurship Theory and Practice, Journal of Business Strategy,* and *European Management Journal,* and more. He has completed terms as an associate editor for *Academy of Management Journal,* as an associate editor for *Academy of Management Executive,* and as a consulting editor for *Entrepreneurship Theory and Practice.* He is the current editor of *Academy of Management Journal.* He has co-edited special issues of *Academy of Management Review, Academy of Management Executive, Journal of Business Venturing, Strategic Management Journal, Journal of High Technology and Engineering Management,* and *Organizational Research Methods* (forthcoming). He received awards for the best article published in *Academy of Management Executive* (1999) and *Academy of Management Journal* (2000). In 2001, his co-authored article published in *Academy of Management Executive* won the Best Journal Article in Corporate Entrepreneurship Award from the U.S. Association for Small Business & Entrepreneurship (USASBE). He is a Fellow of the Academy of Management. He served a three-year term as a Representative-at-Large member of the Academy of Management's Board of Governors. He is a Research Fellow in the National Entrepreneurship Consortium. He received the 1999 Award for Outstanding Intellectual Contributions to Competitiveness Research from the American Society for Competitiveness and the USASBE Scholar in Corporate Entrepreneurship Award (2004) from USASBE.

Robert E. Hoskisson

Robert E. Hoskisson is a Professor and W. P. Carey Chair in the Department of Management at Arizona State University. He received his Ph.D. from the University of California-Irvine. Professor Hoskisson's research topics focus on corporate governance, acquisitions and divestitures, corporate and international diversification, corporate entrepreneurship, privatization, and cooperative strategy. He teaches courses in corporate and international strategic management, cooperative strategy, and strategy consulting, among others. Professor Hoskisson's research has appeared in over 90 publications, including the *Academy of Management Journal, Academy of Management Review, Strategic Management Journal, Organization Science, Journal of Management, Journal of International Business Studies, Journal of Management Studies, Academy of Management Executive* and *California Management Review.* He is currently an Associate Editor of the *Strategic Management Journal* and a Consulting Editor for the *Journal of International Business Studies,* as well as serving on the Editorial Review board of the *Academy of Management Journal.* Professor Hoskisson has served on several editorial boards for such publications as the *Academy of Management Journal* (including

Consulting Editor and Guest Editor of a special issue), *Journal of Management* (including Associate Editor), *Organization Science*, *Journal of International Business Studies* (Consulting Editor), *Journal of Management Studies* (Guest Editor of a special issue) and *Entrepreneurship Theory and Practice*. He has co-authored several books including *Understanding Business Strategy* (South-Western/Thomson), *Competing for Advantage*, 2nd edition (South-Western College Publishing, 2008), and *Downscoping: How to Tame the Diversified Firm* (Oxford University Press).

He has an appointment as a Special Professor at the University of Nottingham and as an Honorary Professor at Xi'an Jiao Tong University. He is a Fellow of the Academy of Management and a charter member of the Academy of Management Journals Hall of Fame. He is also a Fellow of the Strategic Management Society. In 1998, he received an award for Outstanding Academic Contributions to Competitiveness, American Society for Competitiveness. He also received the William G. Dyer Distinguished Alumni Award given at the Marriott School of Management, Brigham Young University. He completed three years of service as a representative at large on the Board of Governors of the Academy of Management and currently is on the Board of Directors of the Strategic Management Society.

To Shawn and Angie. I have been blessed to have two wonderful children. You have always been highly important to me; I love you very much and I am proud of your accomplishments.

—***Michael A. Hitt***

To my beloved Grandmother, Rowena Steele Wheeler Hodge (1905–2007). You have been such a strong beacon of guiding light for me for so long. You are a treasured blessing. Rest in peace. I love you, Grandma.

—***R. Duane Ireland***

To my dear wife, Kathy, who has been my greatest friend and support through life, and I hope will remain so into the eternities.

—***Robert E. Hoskisson***

Case Studies

Preparing an Effective Case Analysis

What to Expect From In-Class Case Discussions

As you will learn, classroom discussions of cases differ significantly from lectures. The case method calls for your instructor to guide the discussion and to solicit alternative views as a way of encouraging your active participation when analyzing a case. When alternative views are not forthcoming, your instructor might take a position just to challenge you and your peers to respond thoughtfully as a way of generating still additional alternatives. Often, instructors will evaluate your work in terms of both the quantity and the quality of your contributions to in-class case discussions. The in-class discussions are important in that you can derive significant benefit by having your ideas and recommendations examined against those of your peers and by responding to thoughtful challenges by other class members and/or the instructor.

During case discussions, your instructor will likely listen, question, and probe to extend the analysis of case issues. In the course of these actions, your peers and/or your instructor may challenge an individual's views and the validity of alternative perspectives that have been expressed. These challenges are offered in a constructive manner; their intent is to help all parties involved with analyzing a case develop their analytical and communication skills. Developing these skills is important in that they will serve you well when working for all types of organizations. Commonly, instructors will encourage you and your peers to be innovative and original when developing and presenting ideas. Over the course of an individual discussion, you are likely to form a more complex view of the case as a result of listening to and thinking about the diverse inputs offered by your peers and instructor. Among other benefits, experience with multiple case discussions will increase your knowledge of the advantages and disadvantages of group decision-making processes.

Both your peers and instructor will value comments that contribute to identifying problems as well as solutions to them. To offer relevant contributions, you are encouraged to think independently and, through discussions with your peers outside of class, to refine your thinking. We also encourage you to avoid using "I think," "I believe," and "I feel" to discuss your inputs to a case analysis process. Instead, consider using a less emotion laden phrase, such as "My analysis shows. . . ." This highlights the logical nature of the approach you have taken to analyze a case. When preparing for an in-class case discussion, you should plan to use the case data to explain your assessment of the situation. Assume that your peers and instructor are familiar with the basic facts included in the case. In addition, it is good practice to prepare notes regarding your analysis of case facts before class discussions and use them when explaining your perspectives. Effective notes signal to classmates and the instructor that you are prepared to engage in a thorough discussion of a case. Moreover, comprehensive and detailed notes eliminate the need for you to memorize the facts and figures needed to successfully discuss a case.

The case analysis process described above will help prepare you effectively to discuss a case during class meetings. Using this process results in consideration of the issues required to identify a focal firm's problems and to propose strategic actions through which the firm can increase the probability it will outperform its rivals. In some instances, your instructor may ask you to prepare either an oral or a written analysis of a particular case. Typically, such an assignment demands even more thorough study and analysis of the case contents. At your instructor's discretion, oral and written analyses may be completed by individuals or by groups of three or more people. The information and insights gained by completing the six steps shown in Table 1 often are of value when developing an oral or a written analysis. However, when preparing an oral or written presentation, you must

Table 1 An Effective Case Analysis Process

Step 1: Gaining Familiarity	a. In general—determine who, what, how, where, and when (the critical facts of the case). b. In detail—identify the places, persons, activities, and contexts of the situation. c. Recognize the degree of certainty/uncertainty of acquired information.
Step 2: Recognizing Symptoms	a. List all indicators (including stated "problems") that something is not as expected or as desired. b. Ensure that symptoms are not assumed to be the problem (symptoms should lead to identification of the problem).
Step 3: Identifying Goals	a. Identify critical statements by major parties (for example, people, groups, the work unit, and so on). b. List all goals of the major parties that exist or can be reasonably inferred.
Step 4: Conducting the Analysis	a. Decide which ideas, models, and theories seem useful. b. Apply these conceptual tools to the situation. c. As new information is revealed, cycle back to substeps a and b.
Step 5: Making the Diagnosis	a. Identify predicaments (goal inconsistencies). b. Identify problems (discrepancies between goals and performance). c. Prioritize predicaments/problems regarding timing, importance, and so on.
Step 6: Doing the Action Planning	a. Specify and prioritize the criteria used to choose action alternatives. b. Discover or invent feasible action alternatives. c. Examine the probable consequences of action alternatives. d. Select a course of action. e. Design an implementation plan/schedule. f. Create a plan for assessing the action to be implemented.

Source: C. C. Lundberg and C. Enz, 1993, A framework for student case preparation, *Case Research Journal*, 13 (Summer): 144. Reprinted by permission of NACRA, North American Case Research Association.

consider the overall framework in which your information and inputs will be presented. Such a framework is the focus of the next section.

Preparing an Oral/Written Case Presentation

Experience shows that two types of thinking (analysis and synthesis) are necessary to develop an effective oral or written presentation (see Exhibit 1). In the analysis stage, you should first analyze the general external environmental issues affecting the firm. Next, your environmental analysis should focus on the particular industry (or industries, in the case of a diversified company) in which a firm operates. Finally, you should examine companies against which the focal firm competes. By studying the three levels of the external environment (general, industry, and competitor), you will be able to identify a firm's opportunities and threats. Following the external environmental analysis is the analysis of the firm's internal organization. This analysis provides the insights needed to identify the firm's strengths and weaknesses.

As noted in Exhibit 1, you must then change the focus from analysis to synthesis. Specifically, you must synthesize information gained from your analysis of the firm's external environment and internal organization. Synthesizing information allows you to generate alternatives that can resolve the significant problems or challenges facing the focal firm. Once you identify a best alternative, from an evaluation based on predetermined criteria and goals, you must explore implementation actions.

In Table 2, we outline the sections that should be included in either an oral or a written presentation: strategic profile and case analysis purpose, situation analysis, statements of strengths/weaknesses and opportunities/threats, strategy formulation, and strategy implementation. These sections are described in the following discussion. Familiarity with the contents of your book's thirteen chapters is helpful because the general outline for an oral or a written presentation shown in Table 2 is based on an understanding of the strategic management process detailed in those chapters. We follow the discussions of the parts of Table 2 with a few comments about the "process" to use to present the results of your case analysis in either a written or oral format.

Exhibit 1 Types of Thinking in Case Preparation: Analysis and Synthesis

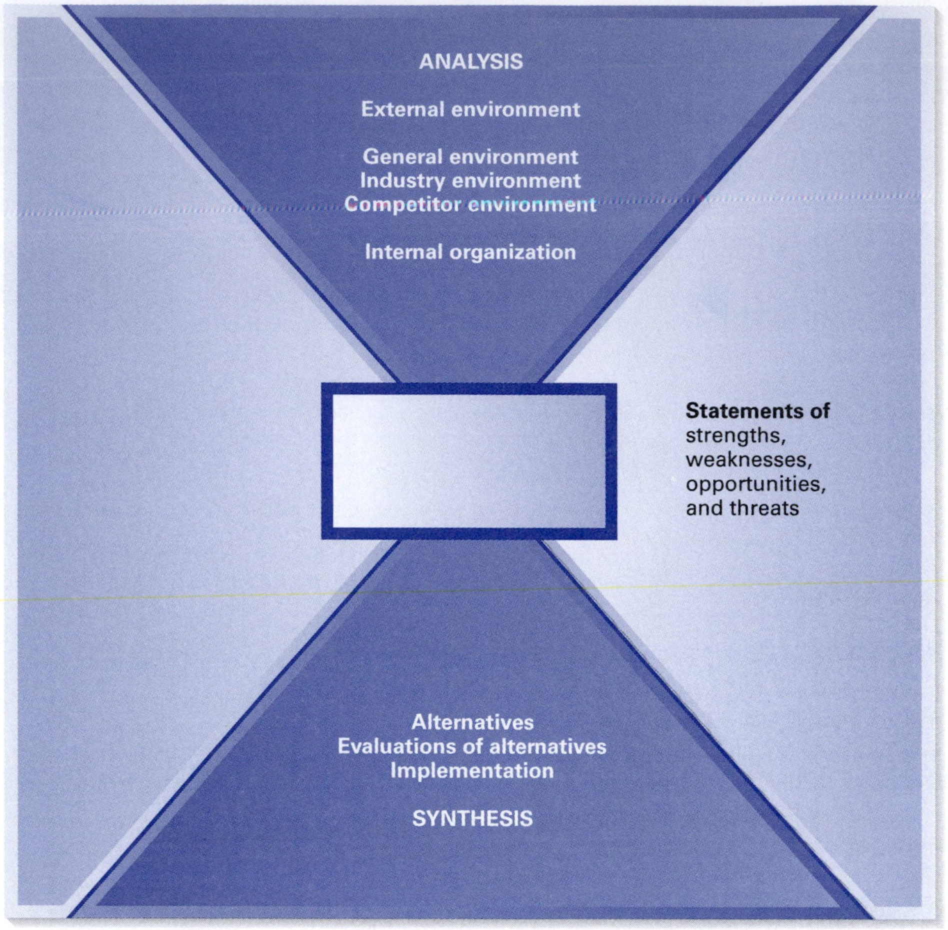

Table 2 General Outline for an Oral or Written Presentation

I. Strategic Profile and Case Analysis Purpose

II. Situation Analysis
   A. General environmental analysis
   B. Industry analysis
   C. Competitor analysis
   D. Internal analysis

III. Identification of Environmental Opportunities and Threats and Firm Strengths and Weaknesses (SWOT Analysis)

IV. Strategy Formulation
   A. Strategic alternatives
   B. Alternative evaluation
   C. Alternative choice

V. Strategic Alternative Implementation
   A. Action items
   B. Action plan

Strategic Profile and Case Analysis Purpose

You will use the strategic profile to briefly present the critical facts from the case that have affected the focal firm's historical strategic direction and performance. The case facts should not be restated in the profile; rather, these comments should show how the critical facts lead to a particular focus for your analysis. This primary focus should be emphasized in this section's conclusion. In addition, this section should state important assumptions about case facts on which your analyses are based.

Situation Analysis

As shown in Table 2, a general starting place for completing a situation analysis is the general environment.

General Environmental Analysis. Your analysis of the general environment should focus on trends in the six segments of the general environment (see Table 3). Many of the segment issues shown in Table 3 for the six segments are explained more fully in Chapter two of your book. The objective you should have in evaluating these trends is to be able to *predict* the segments that you expect to have the most significant influence on your focal firm over the next several years (say three to five years) and to explain your reasoning for your predictions.

Table 3 Sample General Environmental Categories

Technological Trends
- Information technology continues to become cheaper with more practical applications
- Database technology enables organization of complex data and distribution of information
- Telecommunications technology and networks increasingly provide fast transmission of all sources of data, including voice, written communications, and video information
- Computerized design and manufacturing technologies continue to facilitate quality and flexibility

Demographic Trends
- Regional changes in population due to migration
- Changing ethnic composition of the population
- Aging of the population
- Aging of the "baby boom" generation

Economic Trends
- Interest rates
- Inflation rates
- Savings rates
- Exchange rates
- Trade deficits
- Budget deficits

Political/Legal Trends
- Antitrust enforcement
- Tax policy changes
- Environmental protection laws
- Extent of regulation/deregulation
- Privatizing state monopolies
- State-owned industries

Sociocultural Trends
- Women in the workforce
- Awareness of health and fitness issues
- Concern for the environment
- Concern for customers

Global Trends
- Currency exchange rates
- Free-trade agreements
- Trade deficits

Industry Analysis. Porter's five force model is a useful tool for analyzing the industry (or industries) in which your firm competes. We explain how to use this tool in Chapter 2. In this part of your analysis, you want to determine the attractiveness of an industry (or a segment of an industry) in which your firm is competing. As attractiveness increases, so does the possibility your firm will be able to earn profits by using its chosen strategies. After evaluating the power of the five forces relative to your firm, you should make a judgment as to *how* attractive the industry is in which your firm is competing.

Competitor Analysis. Firms also need to analyze each of their primary competitors. This analysis should identify competitors' current strategies, strategic intent, strategic mission, capabilities, core competencies, and a competitive response profile (see Chapter 2). This information is useful to the focal firm in formulating an appropriate strategy and in predicting competitors' probable responses. Sources that can be used to gather information about an industry and companies with whom the focal firm competes are listed in Appendix I. Included in this list is a wide range of publications, such as periodicals, newspapers, bibliographies, directories of companies, industry ratios, forecasts, rankings/ratings, and other valuable statistics.

Internal Analysis. Assessing a firm's strengths and weaknesses through a value chain analysis facilitates moving from the external environment to the internal organization. Analysis of the primary and support activities of the value chain provides opportunities to understand how external environmental trends affect the specific activities of a firm. Such analysis helps highlight strengths and weaknesses (see Chapter 3 for an explanation and use of the value chain).

For purposes of preparing an oral or a written presentation, it is important to note that strengths are internal resources and capabilities that have the potential to be core competencies. Weaknesses, on the other hand, are internal resources and capabilities that have the potential to place a firm at a competitive disadvantage relative to its rivals. Thus, some of a firm's resources and capabilities are strengths; others are weaknesses.

When evaluating the internal characteristics of the firm, your analysis of the functional activities emphasized is critical. For instance, if the strategy of the firm is primarily technology driven, it is important to evaluate the firm's R&D activities. If the strategy is market driven, marketing functional activities are of paramount importance. If a firm has financial difficulties, critical financial ratios would require careful evaluation. In fact, because of the importance of financial health, most cases require financial analyses. Appendix II lists and operationally defines several common financial ratios. Included are tables describing profitability, liquidity, leverage, activity, and shareholders' return ratios. Leadership, organizational culture, structure, and control systems are other characteristics of firms you should examine to fully understand the "internal" part of your firm.

Identification of Environmental Opportunities and Threats and Firm Strengths and Weaknesses (SWOT Analysis). The outcome of the situation analysis is the identification of a firm's strengths and weaknesses and its environmental threats and opportunities. The next step requires that you analyze the strengths and weaknesses and the opportunities and threats for configurations that benefit or do not benefit your firm's efforts to perform well. Case analysts and organizational strategists as well, seek to match a firm's strengths with its opportunities. In addition, strengths are chosen to prevent any serious environmental threat from negatively affecting the firm's performance. The key objective of conducting a SWOT analysis is to determine how to position the firm so it can take advantage of opportunities, while simultaneously avoiding or minimizing environmental threats. Results from a SWOT analysis yield valuable insights into the selection of a firm's strategies. The analysis of a case should not be overemphasized relative to the synthesis of results gained from your analytical efforts. There may be a temptation to spend most of your oral or written case analysis on results from the analysis. It is important, however, that you make an equal effort to develop and evaluate alternatives and to design implementation of the chosen strategy.

Strategy Formulation-Strategic Alternatives, Alternative Evaluation, and Alternative Choice. Developing alternatives is often one of the most difficult steps in preparing an oral or a written presentation. Developing three to four alternative strategies is common (see Chapter 4 for business-level strategy alternatives and Chapter 6 for corporate-level strategy alternatives). Each alternative should be feasible (i.e., it should match the firm's strengths, capabilities, and especially core competencies), and feasibility should be demonstrated. In addition, you should show how each alternative takes advantage of the environmental opportunity or avoids/buffers against environmental threats. Developing carefully thought out alternatives requires synthesis of your analyses' results and creates greater credibility in oral and written case presentations.

Once you develop strong alternatives, you must evaluate the set to choose the best one. Your choice should be defensible and provide benefits over the other alternatives. Thus, it is important that both alternative development and evaluation of alternatives be thorough. The choice of the best alternative should be explained and defended.

Strategic Alternative Implementation-Action Items and Action Plan. After selecting the most appropriate strategy (that is, the strategy with the highest probability of helping your firm in its efforts to earn profits), implementation issues require attention. Effective synthesis is important to ensure that you have considered and evaluated all critical implementation issues. Issues you might consider include the structural changes necessary to implement the new strategy. In addition, leadership changes and new controls or incentives may be necessary to implement strategic actions. The implementation actions you recommend should be explicit and thoroughly explained. Occasionally, careful evaluation of implementation actions may show the strategy to be less favorable than you thought originally. A strategy is only as good as the firm's ability to implement it.

Process Issues. You should ensure that your presentation (either oral or written) has logical consistency throughout. For example, if your presentation identifies one purpose, but your analysis focuses on issues that differ from the stated purpose, the logical inconsistency will be apparent. Likewise, your alternatives should flow from the configuration of strengths, weaknesses, opportunities, and threats you identified by analyzing your firm's external environment and internal organization.

Thoroughness and clarity also are critical to an effective presentation. Thoroughness is represented by the comprehensiveness of the analysis and alternative generation. Furthermore, clarity in the results of the analyses, selection of the best alternative strategy, and design of implementation actions are important. For example, your statement of the strengths and weaknesses should flow clearly and logically from your analysis of your firm's internal organization.

Presentations (oral or written) that show logical consistency, thoroughness, and clarity of purpose, effective analyses, and feasible recommendations (strategy and implementation) are more effective and are likely to be more positively received by your instructor and peers. Furthermore, developing the skills necessary to make such presentations will enhance your future job performance and career success.

Appendix I Sources for Industry and Competitor Analyses

Abstracts and Indexes	
Periodicals	ABI/*Inform* *Business Periodicals Index* *InfoTrac* Custom Journals *InfoTrac* Custom Newspapers *InfoTrac* OneFile EBSCO Business Source Premiere Lexis/Nexis Academic *Public Affairs Information Service Bulletin* (PAIS) *Reader's Guide to Periodical Literature*
Newspapers	*NewsBank—Foreign Broadcast Information* *NewsBank-Global NewsBank* *New York Times Index* *Wall Street Journal Index* *Wall Street Journal/Barron's Index* *Washington Post Index*
Bibliographies	*Encyclopedia of Business Information Sources*
Directories	
Companies—General	*America's Corporate Families and International Affiliates* *Hoover's Online: The Business Network www.hoovers.com/free* D&B *Million Dollar Directory (databases:* http://www.dnbmdd.com*)* *Standard & Poor's Corporation Records* *Standard & Poor's Register of Corporations, Directors, and Executives* (http://www.netadvantage.standardandpoors.com *for all of Standard & Poor's)* *Ward's Business Directory of Largest U.S. Companies*
Companies—International	*America's Corporate Families and International Affiliates* *Business Asia* *Business China* *Business Eastern Europe* *Business Europe* *Business International* *Business International Money Report* *Business Latin America* *Directory of American Firms Operating in Foreign Countries* *Directory of Foreign Firms Operating in the United States* *Hoover's Handbook of World Business* *International Directory of Company Histories* Mergent International Manual Mergent Online (http://www.fisonline.com—for "Business and Financial Information Connection to the World") Who Owns Whom
Companies—Manufacturers	*Thomas Register of AmericanManufacturers* U.S. Office of Management and Budget, Executive Office of the President, *Standard Industrial Classification Manual* U.S. *Manufacturer's Directory, Manufacturing & Distribution, USA*
Companies—Private	*D&B Million Dollar Directory* *Ward's Business Directory of Largest U.S. Companies*

Companies—Public	Annual Reports and 10-K Reports *Disclosure*(corporate reports) *Q-File* Security and Exchange Commision Filings & Forms (EDGAR) *http://www.sec.gov/edgar.shtml* *Mergent's Manuals*: • *Mergent's Bank and Finance Manual* • *Mergent's Industrial Manual* • *Mergent's International Manual* • *Mergent's Municipal and Government Manual* • *Mergent's OTC Industrial Manual* • *Mergent's OTC Unlisted Manual* • *Mergent's Public Utility Manual* • *Mergent's Transportation Manual* Standard & Poor Corporation, *Standard Corporation Descriptions: http://www.netadvantage.standardandpoors.com* • *Standard & Poor's Analyst Handbook* • *Standard & Poor's Industry Surveys* • *Standard & Poor's Statistical Service*
Companies—Subsidiaries and Affiliates	*America's Corporate Families and International Affiliates* *Ward's Directory* *Who Owns Whom* *Mergent's Industry Review* *Standard & Poor's Analyst's Handbook* *Standard & Poor's Industry Surveys* (2 volumes) U.S. Department of Commerce, *U.S. Industrial Outlook*
Industry Ratios	Dun & Bradstreet, *Industry Norms and Key Business Ratios* *RMA's Annual Statement Studies* *Troy Almanac of Business and Industrial Financial Ratios—*
Industry Forecasts	International Trade Administration, *U.S. Industry & Trade Outlook*
Rankings & Ratings	Annual Report on American Industry in *Forbes* *Business Rankings Annual* *Mergent's Industry Review http://www.worldcatlibraries.org* *Standard & Poor's Industry Report Service* http://www.netadvantage.standardandpoors.com *Value Line Investment Survey* *Ward's Business Directory of Largest U.S. Companies*
Statistics	*American Statistics Index (ASI)* Bureau of the Census, U.S. Department of Commerce, *Economic Census Publications* Bureau of the Census, U.S. Department of Commerce, *Statistical Abstract of the United States* Bureau of Economic Analysis, U.S. Department of Commerce, *Survey of Current Business* Internal Revenue Service, U.S. Treasury Department, *Statistics of Income: Corporation Income Tax Returns* *Statistical Reference Index (SRI)*

Appendix II: Financial Analysis in Case Studies

Table A-1 Profitability Ratios

Ratio	Formula	What It Shows
1. Return on total assets	$\frac{\text{Profits after taxes}}{\text{Total assets}}$ or $\frac{\text{Profits after taxes + Interest}}{\text{Total assets}}$	The net return on total investments of the firm or The return on both creditors' and shareholders' investments
2. Return on stockholder's equity (or return on net worth)	$\frac{\text{Profits after taxes}}{\text{Total stockholder's equity}}$	How profitably the company is utilizing shareholders' funds
3. Return on common equity	$\frac{\text{Profits after taxes − Preferred stock dividends}}{\text{Total stockholder's equity − Par value of preferred stock}}$	The net return to common stockholders
4. Operating profit margin (or return on sales)	$\frac{\text{Profits before taxes and before interest}}{\text{Sales}}$	The firm's profitability from regular operations
5. Net profit margin (or net return on sales)	$\frac{\text{Profits after taxes}}{\text{Sales}}$	The firm's net profit as a percentage of total sales

Table A-2 Liquidity Ratios

Ratio	Formula	What It Shows
1. Current ratio	$\frac{\text{Current assets}}{\text{Current liabilities}}$	The firm's ability to meet its current financial liabilities
2. Quick ratio (or acid-test ratio)	$\frac{\text{Current assets − Inventory}}{\text{Current liabilities}}$	The firm's ability to pay off short-term obligations without relying on sales of inventory
3. Inventory to net working capital	$\frac{\text{Inventory}}{\text{Current assets − Current liabilities}}$	The extent to which the firm's working capital is tied up in inventory

Table A-3 Leverage Ratios

Ratio	Formula	What It Shows
1. Debt-to-assets	$\frac{\text{Total debt}}{\text{Total assets}}$	Total borrowed funds as a percentage of total assets
2. Debt-to-equity	$\frac{\text{Total debt}}{\text{Total shareholders' equity}}$	Borrowed funds versus the funds provided by shareholders
3. Long-term debt-to-equity	$\frac{\text{Long-term debt}}{\text{Total shareholders' equity}}$	Leverage used by the firm
4. Times-interest-earned (or coverage ratio)	$\frac{\text{Profits before interest and taxes}}{\text{Total interest charges}}$	The firm's ability to meet all interest payments
5. Fixed charge coverage	$\frac{\text{Profits before taxes and interest + Lease obligations}}{\text{Total interest charges + Lease obligations}}$	The firm's ability to meet all fixed-charge obligations including lease payments

Table A-4 Activity Ratios

Ratio	Formula	What It Shows
1. Inventory turnover	$\frac{\text{Sales}}{\text{Inventory of finished goods}}$	The effectiveness of the firm in employing inventory
2. Fixed-assets turnover	$\frac{\text{Sales}}{\text{Fixed assets}}$	The effectiveness of the firm in utilizing plant and equipment
3. Total assets turnover	$\frac{\text{Sales}}{\text{Total assets}}$	The effectiveness of the firm in utilizing total assets
4. Accounts receivable turnover	$\frac{\text{Annual credit sales}}{\text{Accounts receivable}}$	How many times the total receivables have been collected during the accounting period
5. Average collecting period	$\frac{\text{Accounts receivable}}{\text{Average daily sales}}$	The average length of time the firm waits to collect payment after sales

Table A-5 Shareholders' Return Ratios

Ratio	Formula	What It Shows
1. Dividend yield on common stock	$\frac{\text{Annual dividend per share}}{\text{Current market price per share}}$	A measure of return to common stockholders in the form of dividends
2. Price-earnings ratio	$\frac{\text{Current market price per share}}{\text{After-tax earnings per share}}$	An indication of market perception of the firm; usually, the faster-growing or less risky firms tend to have higher PE ratios than the slower-growing or more risky firms
3. Dividend payout ratio	$\frac{\text{Annual dividends per share}}{\text{After-tax earnings per share}}$	An indication of dividends paid out as a percentage of profits
4. Cash flow per share	$\frac{\text{After-tax profits + Depression}}{\text{Number of common shares outstanding}}$	A measure of total cash per share available for use by the firm

Case 1

3M: Cultivating Core Competency

Mridu Verma

ICFAI Business School

One of the keys to sustainable success is unfettered and well-directed innovation. Innovation is not just about a process, it's also about imagination and people.

GEORGE W. BUCKLEY[1]

—3M CHAIRMAN, PRESIDENT, & CEO

Introduction

In 2006, the $21.2 billion 3M was the epitome of a high-technology/low-technology business with over 50,000 products ranging from Post-it Notes and Scotch tape to transdermal patches of nitroglycerin and optical films. 3M owed its formidable strength to its unusual corporate culture, which comfortably fostered innovation and inter-departmental cooperation, backed by a massive research and development budget, which typically exceeded $1 billion annually. Because of this, the company was a leader in—and in many cases a founder of—a number of important technologies, including pressure-sensitive tapes, sandpaper, protective chemicals, microflex circuits, reflective materials, and premium graphics. 3M operated in electronics, telecommunications, industrial, consumer and office, health care, safety, and other markets. It owned popular brands such as Post-it, Scotch-Brite, and 3M Scotchshield. Because the end-user segment for the products was diverse, the company did not fall under any of the normal industry classifications. In December 2005, the company recorded a net profit of $3.2 billion, an increase of 7 percent from 2004.

When George Buckley joined 3M as the CEO in December 2005, the company was facing criticism from analysts and investors over anemic revenue growth that had slowed to between 1 and 5 percent through parts of 2004 and 2005, even while the broader markets had been expanding. Buckley realized that he needed to generate growth, maintain premium margins, and strategically manage the company's portfolio—all without driving out 3M's culture of innovation on which both the company's fame and its long history of success rested. He needed to develop a growth strategy that was based on and enhanced 3M's core competency. What could he do to ensure that?

Background Note

Minnesota Mining and Manufacturing Company (nicknamed 3M) was formed in 1902 by five businessmen. The company's initial venture to mine a rare mineral and market it as an abrasive was unsuccessful. In 1907 and 1909, William L. McKnight[2] and A. G. Bush joined 3M and soon designed an aggressive, customer-oriented brand of salesmanship. Sales representatives, instead of dealing with a company's purchasing agent, were encouraged to proceed directly to the shop where they could talk with the people who used the products. In so doing, 3M salesmen could discover both how products could be improved and what new products might be needed. This contact resulted in some of 3M's early innovations. For instance, when Henry Ford's newly motorized assembly lines created too much friction for existing sandpapers that were designed to sand wood and static objects, the concerned 3M salesman informed the company of the customer's problem. The company devised a tougher sandpaper, and thus captured much of this niche market within the growing auto industry.

Another salesman noticed that dust from sandpaper use made the shop environment extremely unhealthy. Around the same time, a Philadelphia ink manufacturer named Francis G. Okie wrote McKnight with a request for mineral grit samples. Prompted by curiosity, McKnight approached Okie and found that he had invented a waterproof, and consequently dust-free, sandpaper. In 1921, after purchasing the patent and then solving various defects, 3M came out with Wetordry sandpaper and significantly expanded its business. It also hired the inventor as its first full time researcher, making the creation of one of the first corporate research and development (R&D) divisions in the United States.

In 1923, a salesman in an auto body painting shop noticed that the process used to paint cars in two tones worked poorly. In response, 3M developed a successful masking tape—Scotch tape—which prevented the paints from running together. The company immediately began to develop different applications of its new technology and the transparent Scotch tape was created. Another salesman invented a portable tape dispenser, and 3M had its first large-scale consumer product. During the 1930s, it funneled 45 percent of its profits into new product research and tripled in size.

3M continued to grow during World War II by concentrating on understanding its markets and finding a niche to fill, rather than shifting to making military goods, as many U. S. corporations had done. Among the new products debuting in the immediate postwar period was Scotch magnetic audiotape, which was introduced in 1947. Under McKnight,[3] 3M grew almost 20-fold. By 1952, it had surpassed the $100 million mark and was employing approximately 10,000 people.

The new president Richard Carlton kept the company focused on product research leading to further innovations in the 1950s: the first dry-printing photocopy process, ThermoFax (1951), Scotchgard fabric and upholstery protector (1956), and Scotch-Brite scouring pads (1958). In 1959 the company marked its 20th consecutive year of increased sales. 3M doubled in size between 1963 and 1967, becoming a billion-dollar company in the process. During the 1970s, a number of obstacles interfered with its growth and the company also lost the cassette tape market to two Japanese companies, TDK and Maxell, who were engaged in price-cutting. 3M stuck to its tradition of abandoning markets where it could not set its own prices, and backed off. During the 1980s, major competitors seemed to threaten the company on all fronts. The major product innovation of the decade was Post-it—a low-tech marvel.

L. D. DeSimone[4] who became the CEO in 1991, pushed research staff to work more closely with marketers and transform existing technology into commercial products. Product turnaround time was slashed; product development rivaled basic research. Customer-driven products such as Never Rust Wool Soap Pad made from recycled plastic bottles and a laptop computer screen film that enhanced brightness without heavy battery drain were invented. In 1992, international sales accounted for aver 50 percent of total 3M sales. In 1994, more than $1 billion of the $15 billion in total sales came from first-year products. By 1997, 30 percent of total sales were generated from products introduced within the past four years. Declines in both revenues and profits in 1998 prompted restructuring, including a workforce reduction of about 5,000. 3M also reorganized into six business segments in 1999.[5] Highlighting the company's continued commitment to innovation, nearly 35 percent of revenues in 2000 came from products that had been introduced within the previous four years. Many of these products fell within higher technology areas. DeSimone's stewardship of 3M ended at the close of 2000 with his retirement.

McNerney's Balancing Act

When W. James McNerney[6]—the first outsider at the helm in the company's nearly 100 years of existence—took over as chairman and CEO in early 2001, he found 3M underperforming and relatively directionless. Its vaunted research facilities were turning out fewer and fewer commercial hits, and quarterly results were not meeting shareholders' and analysts' expectations. Though it still drew many of the world's best chemical engineers, the company's labs had not had a major breakthrough for over two decades.

One of McNerney's first initiatives was to launch Six Sigma,[7] a quality control and improvement initiative to cut costs by reducing errors or defects. During his first year, he saved more than half a billion dollars through various efforts, including the layoff of 6,500 of the company's 75,000 workers and a major streamlining of purchasing functions. Another initiative, dubbed 3M Acceleration, involved channeling more of product development funds on the most promising ideas, dropping weaker ideas earlier in the process, and in this way getting the best products to market much faster. In implementing this and other initiatives, most of which focused on making the company more efficient, McNerney had to be careful not to drive out 3M's culture of innovation. Nevertheless, one apparent victim of McNerney's efficiency drive was 3M's revered 15 Percent Rule.[8] Although the rule still existed in theory, it was increasingly difficult to act upon it within the evolving culture at 3M, which was seemingly becoming more short-term oriented.

Early in 2002 the company officially became the 3M Company. In addition to organic growth, McNerney also decided to look at acquisitions to generate growth. In December 2002, he purchased Corning Precision Lens, Inc., for $850 million. Renamed 3M Precision Optics, Inc., the acquired unit was the world's leading supplier of optical lenses used in projection televisions. In 2002, revenues increased marginally, while net income increased by about 20 percent. In early 2003, 3M reorganized yet again, this time attempting to gain improved access to larger, higher-growth markets. 3M's largest division—transportation, graphics, and safety—was split into display and graphics; safety, security, and protection services; and transportation. The specialty material segment was split up, with consumer-related products shifted to the consumer and office unit and industrial products shifted to the industrial unit. Health care became the largest unit.[9]

In October 2003, 3M implemented a major realignment of its R&D operations. Fourteen separate technology centers were closed, with the scientists at these centers shifted either to a newly formed Corporate Research Laboratory or to the company's 40 divisions, where they would be able to work closely on products within those divisions. The main goal of this R&D shakeup was to move more of 3M's R&D resources to the divisions where the products were actually developed and thereby bring the scientists closer to customers. This latest initiative was McNerney's attempt to turn a slightly ossified manufacturing company into a nimbler growth machine. In 2003, 3M posted an increase in sales and operating margin. In June 2005 McNerney resigned from 3M to become Boeing's CEO. In December 2005, George Buckley, an engineer, became the company's CEO. He was entrusted with the task of revitalizing 3M's competitive advantages.

Evaluating 3M

Buckley conducted a detailed study of the company and found that it was a highly capable scientific, engineering, and manufacturing company with deeply conservative values, participating in many successful niche markets. 3M had incredible intersegment technology sharing, where new markets were continually built through a virtual "adjacency machine"—technology sharing and transfer across products and markets. For example, Scotch-Brite Sponges, 3M Respirators, Filtrete Filters, and Thinsulate Insulation along with dozens of other 3M products, drew on nonwoven materials technology—one of more than 32 3M technology platforms (see Exhibit 2).

3M had a strong R&D capability. Its strong knowledge and understanding of technologies such as adhesives, materials science, light management, micro replication, and nonwoven materials had resulted in several innovative products. Furthermore, the company had the ability to manufacture these innovative products efficiently and consistently, on a global basis. The company had reduced cycle time to commercialization substantially from four years to two and a half years in order to realize sales faster. R&D expenses totaled $1.2 billion in 2005, $1.19 billion in 2004, and $1.14 billion in 2003. R&D expenditure as a percentage of sales stood at 6.3 percent in 2003, 5.9 percent in 2004, and 5.9 percent in 2005.

3M had diversified operations in terms of the number of industries and geographic regions served. The company's revenues were spread across its six key businesses, with health care (the largest contributor) and industrial accounting for about 21 percent and 18 percent of the total revenues, respectively. Other businesses included display and graphics; consumer and office; electro and communications; and safety, security, and protection services. The group had also maintained a regional balance in operations, with the United States accounting for 39.1 percent, Asia Pacific

Exhibit 1 How 3M Invention Machine Goes to Market

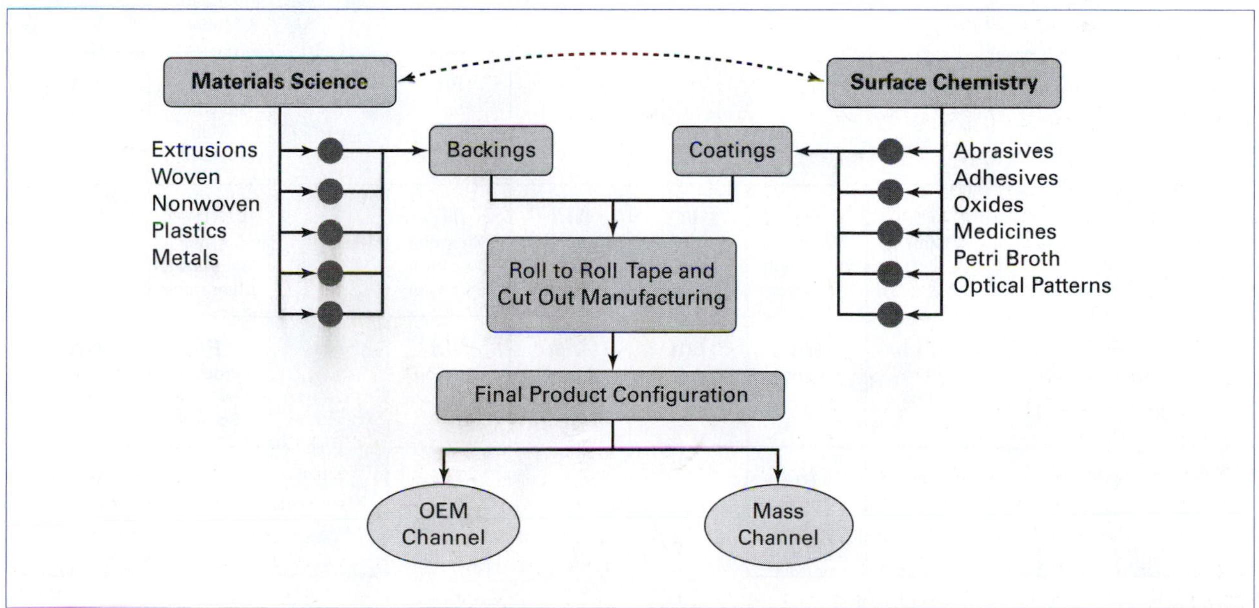

Source: George Buckley's presentation to investors in May 2006; http://www.3m.com.

27.1 percent, Europe, Middle East, and Africa 24.7 percent, and Latin America and Canada 8.9 percent of total revenues. This diversity across industries and regions enabled the company to protect itself against demand fluctuations in industry segments and regions.

The industrial division, whose products included tapes, coated and nonwoven abrasives, adhesives, specialty materials, and supply chain execution software solutions, showed a strong performance in fiscal 2005. The acquisition of Cuno,[10] along with continued demand for industrial adhesives and tape were the growth drivers for this division. Its revenues increased by 10.5 percent from 2004 to $3.8 billion. The personal care segment was witnessing sales declines in three areas: personal care-related products,[11] drug delivery, and pharmaceutical. Sales of certain products within 3M's pharmaceuticals business, primarily comprising prescription drugs designed for inhalation, women's health, and cardiovascular, also declined due to price pressure in Europe and decreased demand for some of these older products.

Buckley observed that 3M's history was rooted in an "invent and experiment" approach or "make a little, sell a little," which had led to an incremental approach to capacity and strategic planning, with complex supply chains evolving quite naturally—extrusion processes at one plant, coating in another plant, and final conversion at yet another. Though individual plants were run with superb efficiency, interconnecting logistics were often complicated and costly, resulting in higher inventory. Buckley believed that chronic underinvestment in core capacity had led to many lost upside growth opportunities. In fact, this underinvestment in core markets had made readily available growth hard to capture. The company's strategic planning capability seemed underdeveloped, but this deficiency did not diminish the fact that the company possessed world-class manufacturing capability.

3M's world-class materials science and surface chemistry capability was built over many years. It had often entered markets only after privileged intellectual property (IP) positions were built. In early days scale was not considered important and demand and capacity were often underestimated. 3M had focused on making risk-free capital investments by using highly flexible machine tools capable of making many products in plants that served multiple businesses. The cross-business use of central technologies was encouraged by the earlier leadership, which in turn led to 3M's participation in many high-margin niche areas such as reflective material (3M Scotchlite) and sealing ground

Exhibit 2 3M Lattice : The 32 Technology Platforms

Ad Adhesives	**Am** Advanced Materials	**Bi** Biotech							**Rf** Reclosable Fasteners
Ab Abrasives	**Dd** Drug Delivery						**Mr** Micro-replication	**Pe** Predctive Engineering & Modeling	**Rp** Radiation Processing
Ac Acoustics	**Dm** Display Materials					**Nt** Nano Technology	**Nm** Nonwoven Materials	**Pm** Polymer Melt Processing	**Sm** Specialty Materials
As Application Software	**Do** Dental & Orthodontic Materials	**Fi** Films	**Fs** Filtration, Separation, Purification	**Is** Integrated Systems Design	**Md** Medical Data Mgmt	**Mi** Microbial Detection & Control	**Pc** Precision Coating	**Po** Porous Materials & Membrane	**Su** Surface Modification
Ce Ceramics	**Ep** Electronic Packaging	**Fl** Fluoro-materials	**Im** Imaging	**Lm** Light Mgmt	**Me** Metal Matrix Composites	**Mo** Molding	**Pd** Particle & Dispersion Processing	**Pr** Process Design & Control	**Wo** Wound Mgmt
Cp Chemical Power Sources	**Fc** Flexible Converting & Packaging	**Fo** Fiber Optics	**Ip** Inks & Pigments				**Pp** Precision Processing		**Vp** Vacuum Processing

Source: George Buckley's presentation to investors in May 2006; http://www.3m.com.

connections (3M Scotchcast), among others. A high degree of conservatism had become the norm. Though 3M's inward focus brought margin benefits, it often hindered growth and long-range planning.

Buckley realized a need to demystify 3M and understand the workings of the 3M Lattice. In understanding 3M, it was important to realize that the company was not a conglomerate with siloed independent business units. It was a unique model of a technology and manufacturing *adjacency lattice* that shared basic technologies and manufacturing processes across multiple businesses, markets, and product lines. Almost all of 3M's basic businesses were connected to each other in this way, from water filtration to Scotch brand tape. He opined, "In network theory, the power of a network (or lattice) is proportional to the square of the number of users.[12] It is this lattice that makes 3M so powerful and enduring as an industrial competitor. But . . . the lattice can also make 3M difficult to organize for optimal growth"[13] (see Exhibit 2).

As noted above, to encourage innovation, perhaps to deal with "latticing" the company used the 15 Percent Rule, which allowed its employees to spend up to 15 percent of company time on independent projects, a process called "bootlegging" or "scrounging."

Defining 3M's Core Competency

3M is an invention and manufacturing company. Its major strength lay in solving and delivering unique solutions for original equipment manufacturers (OEM) and mass channel customers. Its technologies could be extended into multiple markets. 3M's technology portfolio and process capability were at the core of its unique business model. This strength included technologies such as adhesives, materials science, light management; microreplication and nonwoven materials; and its ability to not only develop unique products, but also to manufacture them efficiently and consistently around the world. By sharing technologies, manufacturing operations, brands, and other resources across its businesses and geographies, it increased speed and efficiency. These technology platforms were the thread that wove together the company's diverse businesses. It was their interlocking and sometimes overlapping nature that set 3M apart from other companies. Industry observers pointed out that 3M's remarkable breadth of technologies, along with its ability to combine them to create a steady stream of groundbreaking products, made it unique.

The range of a single technology application could be seen in many areas. On one end of the adhesion spectrum were the Post-it Products—a universal communication tool that could stick practically anywhere, yet could be repositioned time and again—and on the other end was 3M Scotch-Weld Structural Adhesive that had taken the place of metal fasteners in the production of airplanes, helping make aircraft lighter and more fuel-efficient. In the electronics industry, 3M Form-in-Place Gaskets (nonwoven technology product), were widely used in computer hard disk drive covers. This resilient, ultra-clean, adhesive-based material sealed out contaminants, while also increasing manufacturing productivity. Thinsulate Insulation—another nonwoven product—offered warmth without bulk. It was incorporated into jackets, boot, gloves, and sleeping bags. A companion product—Thinsulate Acoustic Insulation—helped in reducing road noise inside vehicles. Yet another 3M product based on nonwoven technology—3M Nomad Floor Matting—helped in keeping floors clean longer.

In applying coatings, 3M had developed world-class competencies. It modified the shapes and patterns of surface coatings in a process called microreplication, which in turn altered the fundamental behavior of a product. This micromanufacturing competency, leveraged across many markets made it difficult for 3M's competitors to beat it. For example, the technology made road signs return nearly twice as much reflected light to drivers as the brightest materials previously available. In the automotive industry, the technology (3M Paint Replacement Film) eliminated the need for paint on door pillars, window sashes, and other body trim. When combined with high-performance abrasives and fasteners, the microreplication technology enabled diapers to hold more securely and comfortably. It was also used to create channels that directed fluids across a surface using capillary action as in biotechnology products (see Exhibit 3).

According to Buckley, 3M's fundamental core competency lay in applying coatings to backings. Both the coatings and the backings were traditionally developed inside 3M. The backings could either be woven or nonwoven fabrics, paper, cloth, plastics, or metal while coatings were adhesives, abrasives, medicines, nano particles, or imprinted optical patterns. 3M applied coatings to backings in a highly precise manufacturing approach that involved the large-scale unwinding, winding, and splitting of tapes. 3M sometimes sold its coatings and backings separately configured as other products, such as face masks, Thinsulate thermal and acoustic insulation, and roofing granules. In developing backings and coatings competencies, broad know-how in adjacent technologies was built in areas such as microreplication of surface patterns, optics and light management, nanotechnology, and ceramics adhesives. 3M extended this adjacent knowledge across multiple markets in less obvious applications such as Post-it Notes (the adhesive was microreplicated) and adhesives (on which 3M's dentistry competency was based).

Interestingly, the same precision machining and materials science capabilities had also been applied in market adjacencies such as dentistry. Though experts cited

Exhibit 3 Technology Market Architecture

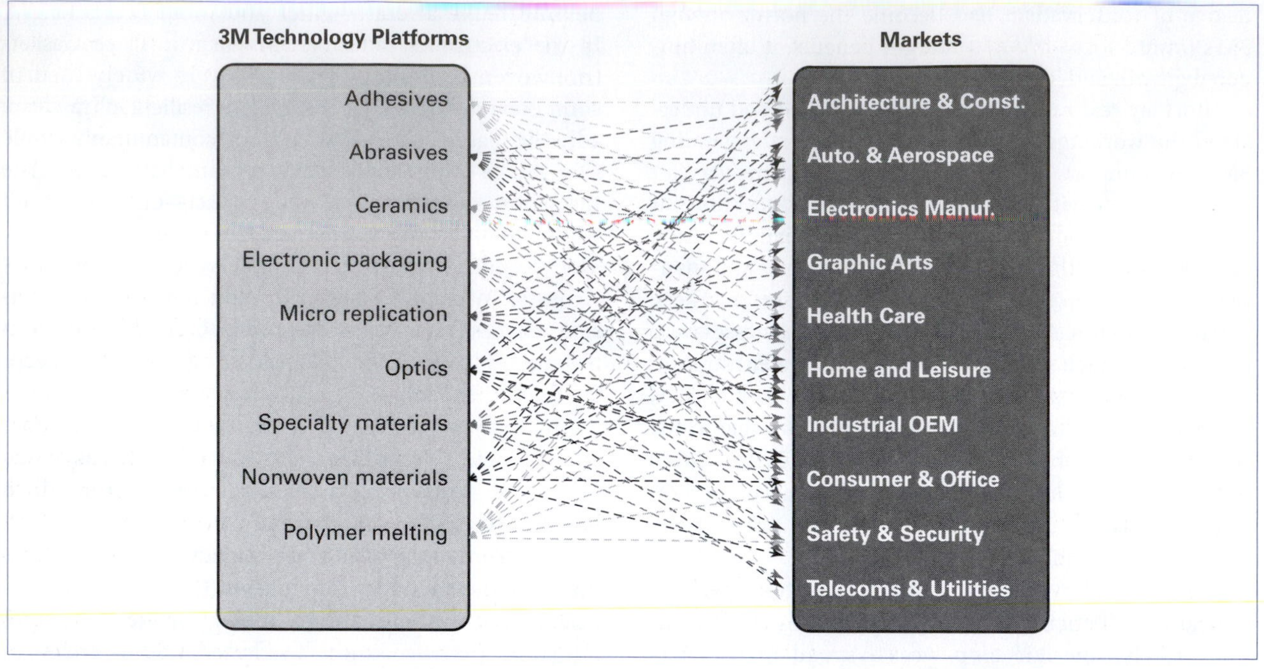

Source: George Buckley's presentation to investors in May 2006; http://www.3m.com.

innovation as 3M's main strength, Buckley felt that the company's superior manufacturing capability and know-how was equally important and a significant barrier to entry. He believed that one source of the next wave of growth would come from reinvention of the space science materials with nanotechnology. In addition to its core, 3M had six competitive platforms: low cost, which gave it a considerable edge over competition; scale share; relative share; customer value chain; pristine service; and premium brands.

Buckley's Strategy

Technology and innovation had played a key role throughout 3M's illustrious history. Buckley recognized that it was also the engine of 3M's future growth. He stressed the uniqueness of the company's shared technology model. For future growth, the company was searching for disruptive technologies as well as logical developments and extensions of its existing products. It would increasingly prospect for "just out of the garage" technology developments, which would be the key to building its core competency. The heart and soul of 3M's approach would remain technological differentiation and application across multiple lines of business. It would add digital-oriented competencies over time.

To grow its core business, the company intended to build on 3M's strengths through constant reinvention, even stronger key customer partnerships, customization, solving customers needs, entering niche segments, and capturing new segments. Buckley intended to build scale, increase market share, emphasize localization, and build long-term competency. The idea was to defend created markets against new entrants, using dual branding in the upper middle market; emphasizing product localization using a mixture of brands and local acquisitions; thoughtfully extending private labeling, and accurately planning capacity. The core product categories he had identified for building scale included Scotch-branded industrial and office tapes, abrasives, automotive, optical films, face masks and respirators, medical tapes and drapes, Post-it Notes, and traffic signage. It would aim for a relative share in areas such as dentistry, orthodontics, office supplies, roofing granules, commercial graphics, and adhesives.

3M's core strategy focused on developing and growing the existing market by using its technological prowess to invent natural substitute technology. He intended to ensure that the 15 Percent Rule was followed. To aid speed, 3M went for strategic licensing of technology, investment in small technology companies, greater university support and liaison, and encouraging the use of imagination and invention extensively. A renewed focus on innovation would encourage new products and continued international expansion and penetration with greater emphasis on localization. In mid-2006, 3M was generating more than 60 percent of its sales from outside the United States with more than 20 percent coming from emerging markets. For international growth the company was concentrating on BRICP (Brazil, Russia, India, China, and Poland), Eastern Europe, Western

Europe, Japan, and Australasia. Over time 3M intended to divest or close those businesses where it could not, over time, build scale or good relative share, or differentiate through technology. It also intended to divest in areas where the base technology was at "end of life" and could not be refreshed, or the risk profile suggested another owner could extract more value than 3M. As a part of this strategy, in November 2006, 3M sold the pharmaceutical business for $2.1 billion.

It was decided that the majority of acquisitions would closely reflect and support its strategic plan and adjacencies. Trends showed that adjacency would evolve in areas such as electronics and software, RFID/Wireless/global positioning service (GPS), minerals extraction, oil and gas, food safety, border crossing and security, and consumer electronics. The company intended to build new business through enhanced focus on emerging business opportunities with high growth potential such as filtration, track and trace, energy and minerals extraction, and food safety. The concept would be used where capability existed with ready adjacencies but no focus. Buckley outlined a clear acquisition strategy driven by a determination to quickly add value. Soon after joining the company, he told analysts that acquisitions would be one way he would grow the top line. In 2006, 3M announced 16 acquisitions, which equaled the number of acquisitions the company had made in the previous four years combined. However, these deals were smaller than many purchases made in the past years. Alfred Marcus, professor of strategic management and organization at the University of Minnesota's Carlson School of Management applauded the small "tuck-in" acquisition strategy as he felt that small buys were more likely to be successful than big ones. Big deals required a lot of time and money to integrate and took longer to pay off, he said.

No clear pattern emerged among the kind of businesses that 3M has purchased. The company made at least two acquisitions in each of its six business units. While some of the deals provided access to new geographic markets, like the UK-based Security Printing & Systems passport-printing business it bought in July 2006; other deals were just filling in capacity in channels 3M already understood, such as the acquisition of Nylonge Corp., an Elyria, Ohio-based maker of household cleaning products. Additionally, other small deals focused on acquiring new technology, such as the $95 million purchase of Brontes Technologies Inc. announced in October 2006. Brontes developed a digital tool for dentists that mapped dimensions to facilitate design of crowns, bridges, and orthodontic appliances.

Looking Ahead

In April 2006, 3M reported record first-quarter sales and profits with local-currency sales growth of over 10 percent and earnings per share increase over 20 percent. The company also raised its 2006 revenue growth guidance, and expected full-year, organic local-currency growth between 5.5 and 8 percent, up from a previous expectation of 4 to 7 percent. However in June 2006, Buckley surprised Wall Street when he announced that the company would miss its earnings target for the second quarter, sending the company's stock tumbling from a 52-week high of $88 per share in May 2006 to a 52-week low of $67 in July 2006. 3M said the problems stemmed from its display and graphics business, which had difficulties launching a new optical-film factory. It also misread demand for LCD TVs in advance of the World Cup soccer tournament. But by fall 2006, investor confidence in Buckley was restored, thanks to a convincing third-quarter turnaround that beat analysts' estimates. In the third quarter, 3M's sales increased 7.3 percent compared to the same period a year earlier. Not including acquisitions, organic sales were up 6.5 percent. Buckley was projecting 8 percent growth by 2008 and 10-plus percent by 2011.

3M's acquisitions were expected to contribute $350 million to $400 million to its expected $22.8 billion in 2006 sales. But at the end of year one, Buckley's record was exactly as advertised. Revenue growth was up, and the number of acquisitions was way up. John Roberts, an analyst at Buckingham Research believed that investors were still waiting to see growth accelerate at 3M's core businesses. Mark Henneman, a principal analyst at St. Paul-based Mairs and Powers Funds, which invested in 3M stock, credited Buckley for slowly reinvigorating 3M's engineering culture and technological foundation. "He's focusing investments on where the core competencies are, and I think that increases the chance for success going forward."[14]

Other industry observers also opined that Buckley had sparked more innovation and boosted morale. Art Fry, a retired 3M scientist who had invented Post-it Notes opined that the acquisitions were a quick way of building and adding technology to the company. But like in product development, some ventures would fail, he said. "I think basically he's more like an old-school-type 3M leader in that he's focused both on building the company and operating it. The [improved] morale is palpable; you can just feel it around 3M," Fry mentioned.[15] Fry opined that circumstances Buckley had to face due to underinvesment in growth platforms under former CEO James McNerney Jr. and an emphasis on boosting profits was "like you walk in after the feast and you have to clean up all the dirty dishes."

Buckley still had to take care of other problems also. Retailers such as Wal-Mart, Target, Staples, and Office Depot were increasingly offering branded goods (better known as private labels) at affordable prices. An increasing number of 3M's customers, particularly in the consumer and office business, had been shifting to private label products. This migration prompted 3M to target lower price points through the launch of secondary brands. Compared to margins of about 45 percent from premium-priced products, lower-priced products would only yield maximum of 20 percent. The private label products of mass market retailers lowered margins of the company. Meanwhile, higher oil prices resulted in price increases and supply limitations of several oil-derived raw materials (see Appendixes 1–9).

As 2006 drew to a close, Buckley decided to evaluate his strategy to determine whether it would yield desired results. Would his initiatives succeed in building 3M's core competency? What else could he do?

Appendix 1 The World's Most Innovative Companies 2005

Asia	Europe	North America	Global
1. Apple	1. Apple	1. Apple	1. Apple
2. Google	2. Google	2. Google	2. Google
3. 3M	3. Nokia	3. P&G	3. 3M
4. Samsung	4. Microsoft	4. 3M	4. Toyota
5. Microsoft	5. 3M	5. Toyota	5. Microsoft
6. IBM	6. Toyota	6. GE	6. GE
7. GE	7. Virgin	7. Starbucks	7. P&G
8. Toyota	8. BMW	8. Microsoft	8. Nokia
9. Nokia	9. GE	9. IBM	9. Starbucks
10. infosys	10. eBay	10. Dell	10. IBM
11. Virgin	11. IKEA	11. Wal-Mart	11. Virgin
12. P&G	12. RyanAir	12. IDEO	12. Samsung
12. Dell	12. Sony	12. Target	13. Sony
14. Sony	14. Intel	14. Samsung	14. Dell
15. Intel	15. Porsche	15. Southwest	15. IDEO

Source: George Buckley's presentation to investors in May 2006; http://www.3m.com.

Appendix 2 3M Innovation: Process, Imagination, People

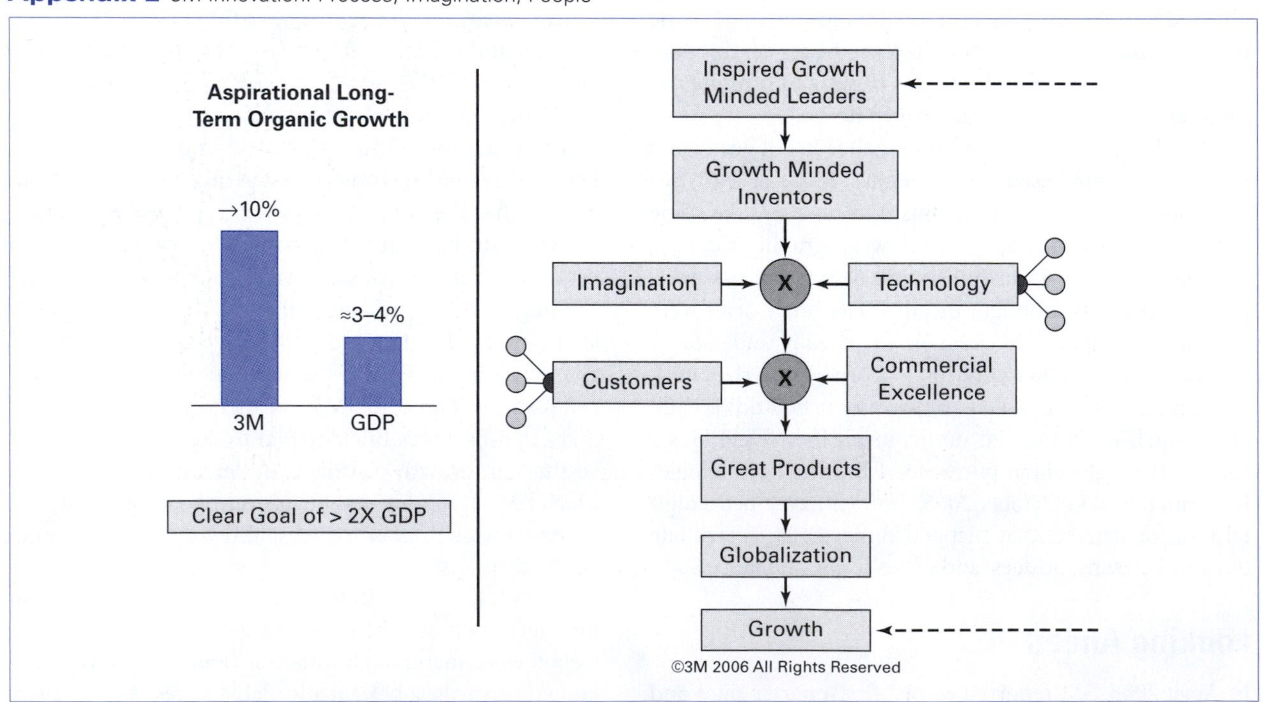

Source: George Buckley's presentation to investors in May 2006 at 3M Investor Meeting; http://www.3m.com.

Appendix 3 Some Breakthrough 3M Products

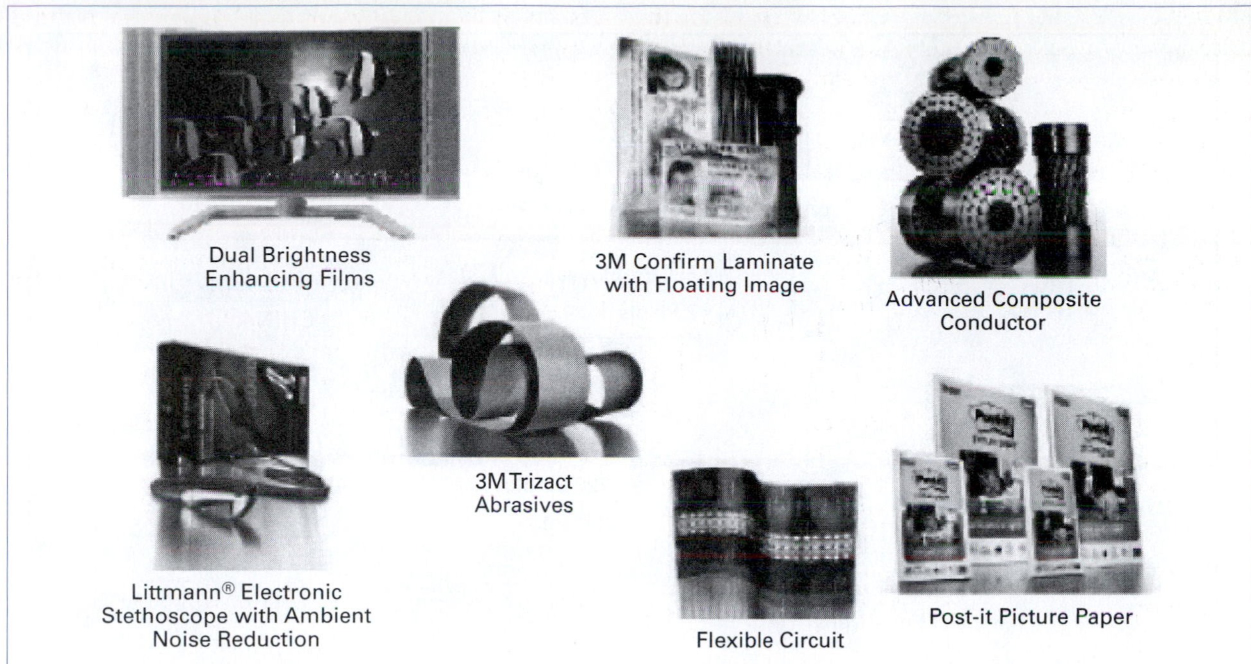

Source: George Buckley's presentation to investors in May 2006; http://www.3m.com.

Appendix 4 3M Patent Portfolio

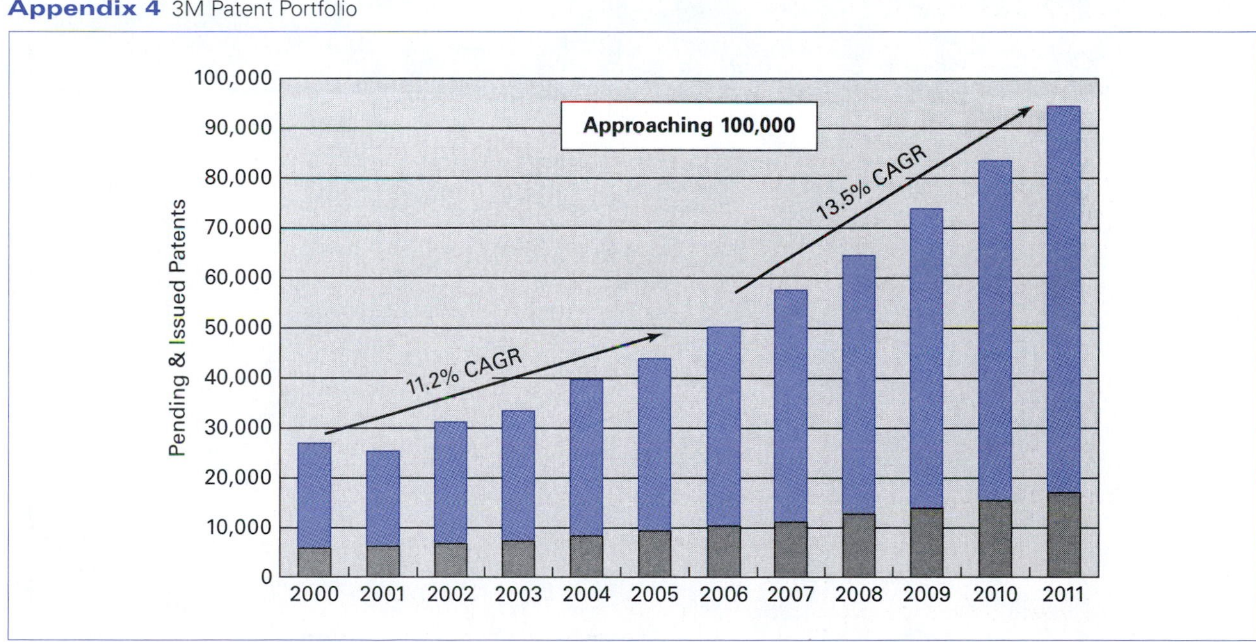

Source: George Buckley's presentation to investors in May 2006; http://www.3m.com.

Appendix 5 Building Emerging Country Capacity, End 2006

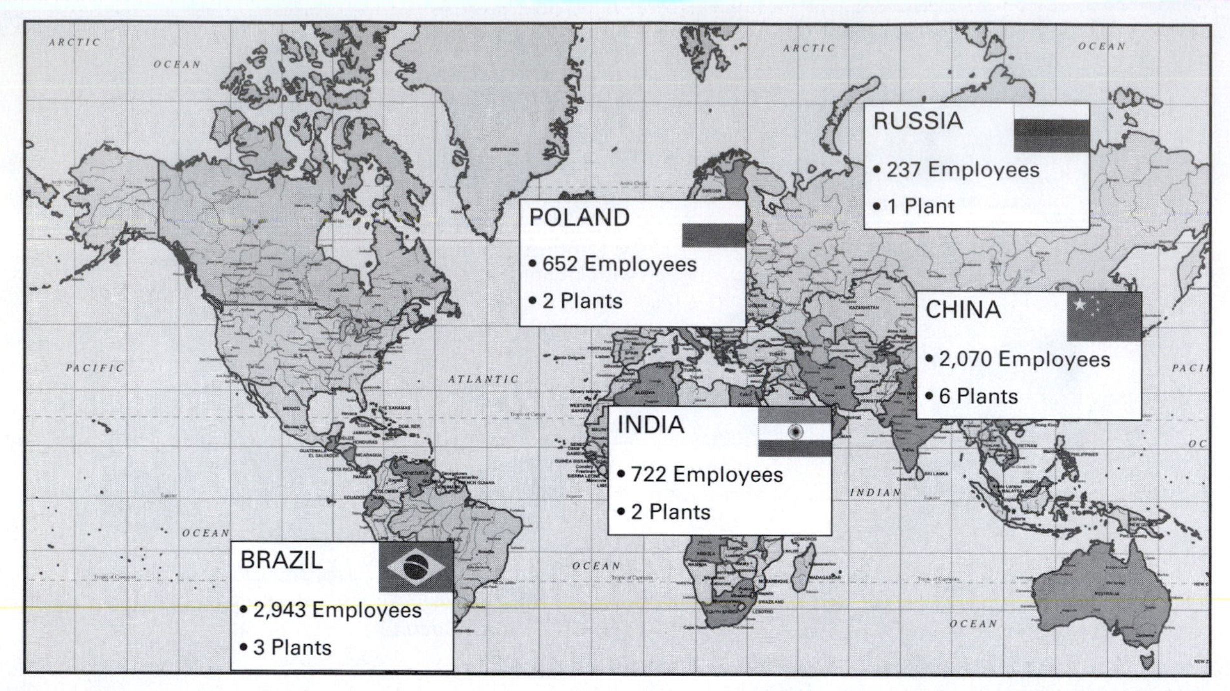

Source: George Buckley's presentation to investors in May 2006; http://www.3m.com.

Appendix 6 3M vs. Peers—Du Pont Analysis

Net Income / Sales × Sales / Assets × Assets / Equity = ROE%

	Net Income Margin % ×	Asset Turn ×	Leverage =	ROE
3M	**15.3%**	**1.03x**	**2.03x**	**32.0%**
ITW	11.6%	1.13	1.52	19.8%
Danaher	11.4%	0.87	1.80	17.8%
IR	10.0%	0.90	2.04	18.3%
Emerson	8.8%	1.04	2.18	20.0%
Tyco	8.3%	0.64	1.92	10.1%
UTX	7.4%	0.93	2.70	18.6%
Eaton	7.2%	1.09	2.70	21.3%
HON	5.7%	0.86	2.87	14.0%
Textron	5.1%	0.61	5.04	15.8%
ITT	4.2%	1.05	2.59	11.5%

Source: George Buckley's presentation to investors in May 2006; http://www.3m.com.

Appendix 7 Financial Information

(In $ millions, except per share amounts)	2005	2004	2003	2002	2001
Years ended December 31:					
Net sales	**$21,167**	$20,011	$18,232	$16,332	$16,054
Income before cumulative effect of accounting change	**3,234**	2,990	2,403	1,974	1,430
Per share of common stock:					
Income before cumulative effect of accounting change—basic	**4.23**	3.83	3.07	2.53	1.81
Income before cumulative effect of accounting change—diluted	**4.16**	3.75	3.02	2.50	1.79
Cash dividends declared and paid	**1.68**	1.44	1.32	1.24	1.20
At December 31:					
Total assets	**$20,513**	$20,708	$17,600	$15,329	$14,606
Long-term debt (excluding portion due within one year) and long-term capital lease obligations	**1,368**	798	1,805	2,142	1,520

Source: 3M Annual Report 2005.

Appendix 8 3M SWOT Analysis

Strengths	Weaknesses
Strong R&D capability	Weak personal care segment
Diversified business portfolio	Low margins in the United States
Robust industrial business	
Opportunities	**Threats**
Growing demand for LCDs	Growth in private labels
Acquisition of brands	Higher oil prices
International expansion	Exchange rate fluctuations

Source: 2006, Datamonitor Company Report, July.

Appendix 9 A Few 3M Brands

Source: George Buckley's presentation to investors in May 2006; http://www.3m.com.

Notes

1. S. Black, Buys defines 3M CEO's first year, *Minneapolis/St. Paul Business Journal,* December 1, 2005.
2. McKnight ran 3M between 1914 and 1966, serving as general manager from 1914 to 1929, president from 1929 to 1949, and chairman of the board from 1949 to 1966. He created the general guidelines of diversification, avoiding price cuts, increasing sales by 10 percent a year, high employee morale, and quality control that fueled the company's growth and created its unique corporate culture. In some ways, the sales system overshadowed the guidelines.
3. In 1949, McKnight became chairman of the board (with A. G. Bush also moving from daily operations to the boardroom).
4. DeSimone joined 3M in 1958 as a manufacturing engineer and moved into management while working in international operations.
5. The six segments were Industrial Markets; Transportation, Graphics, and Safety; Health Care; Consumer and Office Products; Electro and Communications; and Specialty Material.
6. McNerney was a 19-year veteran of General Electric Company (GE)—like 3M a diversified, manufacturing-oriented corporation—having most recently served as head of GE Aircraft Engines. McNerney had lost out in a three-way battle to succeed legendary GE leader John F. (Jack) Welch, Jr.
7. Six Sigma was a quality control and improvement initiative that had been pioneered by Motorola, Inc., and AlliedSignal Inc. and then adopted by GE in the late 1990s. The aim of the statistics-driven program was to cut costs by reducing errors or defects.
8. The 15 Percent Rule allowed 3M employees to spend up to 15 percent of company time on independent projects, a process called "bootlegging" or "scrounging" to encourage innovation.
9. Health Care became the largest unit in terms of both revenues (22% of the total) and earnings (27%).
10. In August 2005, 3M acquired Cuno, a manufacturer of a comprehensive line of filtration products for the separation, clarification, and purification of fluids and gases. 3M and Cuno had complementary sets of filtration technologies, which enabled them to bring an even wider range of filtration solutions to customers around the world.
11. The personal care diaper closure business continued to experience significant price increases due to raw material increases. However, 3M has been unable to raise its prices sufficiently to cover raw material inflation, owing to a competitive environment in the diaper market. The company chose to manufacture lower volumes rather than suffer losses in the end.
12. Robert Metcalfe, Inventor of the Ethernet.
13. George Buckley's presentation to investors in May 2006; http://www.3m.com.
14. S. Black, Buys defines 3M CEO's first year.
15. Ibid.

Additional Readings and Reference

1. J. Webern, 2000, 3M's big clean-up, *BusinessWeek,* June 5, 96–98.
2. D. Little, 2000, 3M: Glued to the Web, *BusinessWeek,* 3708, November 20, EB64.
3. M. Arndt, 2002, 3M: A lab for growth, *BusinessWeek,* January 21, 50–51.
4. J. Useem, 2002, Jim McNerney thinks he can turn 3M from a good company into a great one—with a little help from his former employer, General Electric, *Fortune,* (3), August 12, 127–132.
5. M. Overfelt, 2003, 3M, *Fortune Small Business,* 13 (3), April, 36.
6. M. Arndt & D. Brady, 2004, 3M's rising star, *BusinessWeek,* April 12, 62–74.
7. 2004, Innovation is job one, *BusinessWeek,* April 12, 120–120.
8. M. Arndt, 2005, The new skipper at 3M's helm, *BusinessWeek,* December 19, 12.
9. H. David, 2006, Creativity pays. Here's how much, *BusinessWeek,* April 24, 76–76.
10. 2006, 3M CEO outlines strategy for growth, company press release, http://www.3m.com, May 2.
11. 2006, Tamper-indicating security seals from 3M, *Business & Commercial Aviation,* 98(6), June, 88.
12. 2006, 3M CEO outlines long-term strategy for growth, *Filtration + Separation,* 43 (5).
13. 2006, 3M puts emphasis on convenience in bandage packaging, *Drug Store News,* June 26, 48.
14. T. B. Jensen, 2006, Meeting environmental demands with pressure-sensitive tapes, *Adhesives & Sealants Industry,* 13 (7), 27–30.
15. 2006, 3M completes OMNII acquisition, *Proofs,* 89 (3), June, 46–48.
16. 2006, 3M'S Post-it sortable cards, *OfficeSolutious,* July–August, 46.
17. 2006, 3M SWOT analysis, *Datamonitor,* July.
18. A. DeRosa, 2006, 3M investing in film projects, *Plastics News,* July 17.
19. 2006, Products and services by category Hardware, *Computers in Libraries,* July–August, 12–13.
20. 2006, I. Brat, At 3M, stock slide stirs criticism, *Wall Street Journal,* July 24.
21. 2006, Quaker fabric launches safer Scotchgard fabric, *Home Textiles Today,* September 18, 10.
22. 3M Annual Report 2006.
23. 3M Annual Report 2005.
24. http://www.3m.com.
25. http://www.wikipedia.com.
26. http://www.hoovers.com.
27. http://www.fundinguniverse.com.
28. CEO Buckley's presentation to analysts in May 2006, Investor relations, http://www.3m.com.
29. Company presentation to analysts in 2003, http://www.3m.com.
30. http://www.yahoofinance.com.

Case 2

A-1 Lanes and the Currency Crisis of the East Asian Tigers

Phil E. Stetz, Stephen F. Austin State University
Todd A. Finkle, The University of Akron
Larry R. O'Neil, Stephen F. Austin State University

On July 2, 1997, Rick Baker, the president and founder of A-1 Lanes (a manufacturer and an international supplier of wood and synthetic bowling lanes) was having his morning coffee when he was devastated to learn that Thailand had devalued its currency, the baht, by 11 percent. Baker had an uneasy feeling about the potential domino effect across all countries in Asia because their economies were interrelated. If that happened, Baker wondered, how would it affect the future of his company?

Baker realized that the company faced several critical issues. First, 80 percent of A-1's sales were derived from countries in and around the Asian Pacific Rim. Second, the company had more than $1 million in accounts receivable from this region. Third, in 1996 the company had taken out a loan for $500,000 on a new manufacturing facility to capitalize on the popularity and growth of bowling centers in Korea, China, and Taiwan.

The combination of these issues in conjunction with the cut-throat competition within the bowling equipment industry placed Baker in a position to make a critical decision about the future of his company. He had narrowed his decision to three options: (1) liquidate his company, (2) sell the company, or (3) stay in business and try to weather the impending storm.

Company Background

In 1985, Baker and two investors founded A-1 Lanes in a chicken house and barn in Rusk, Texas. The company's main products were high-grade wood and technologically advanced synthetic bowling lanes for domestic and international markets. According to Baker, "The key to our success is the quality of the wood and the advanced synthetic design of our bowling lanes supported with responsive service, operational efficiencies and proven accomplishments at penetrating international markets."

Although the company began with high expectations, A-1 Lanes quickly discovered that locally owned bowling centers across the United States did not have the financial resources to replace existing lanes. Instead, owners would simply sand the lanes. To complicate matters, competitors within the industry developed a synthetic overlay for existing lanes. For example, Brunswick developed a cost-effective way of refurbishing worn and damaged wood lanes that prolonged their service life by as much as 10 years. Rather than tearing out and replacing existing lanes, bowling centers could sand them down and overlay the wood with a synthetic resin, thereby restoring the old lanes to industry standards.

Because of the weakened demand for wood replacement of bowling lanes, A-1 began to concentrate on new bowling lane sales in international markets. According to Baker, "We pursued international markets because the margins were better, receivables were more reliable, and the additional volume meant a healthier bottom line." As a result, A-1 grew and moved operations into a vacant 34,000-square-foot metal building in 1987.

In the same year, A-1 Lanes began to establish relationships with distributors in other parts of the world (e.g., Mendes, a Canadian marketer of bowling lanes). In 1988, Baker and his investors forged a partnership with a company called Dacos, an established distributor of bowling equipment and accessories that was based in Europe and Korea. With a source for U.S. manufactured lanes, Dacos could offer a complete turn-key package to bowling center owners and developers all over the world. In turn, the arrangement enabled A-1 to compete directly with the largest firms in the industry, Brunswick and American Machine Foundry (AMF). It also gave A-1 an

This case is intended to stimulate class discussion rather than to illustrate the effective or ineffective handling of a managerial situation. *The company, names, events, and financials are all real.*

advantage over smaller competitors in the United States because those firms lacked similar distribution channels and presence in Europe and Asia.

The Bowling Industry

Archeologists discovered that bowling dates back to ancient Egypt when they found pins in a child's tomb. The sport expanded into Europe in the early 1900s, but its popularity in the United States did not thrive until after World War II. In the 1950s, television embraced bowling and the automatic pin spotter was invented. The game grew dramatically in the United States and eventually peaked in the 1960s. New markets emerged in Australia and Mexico, as well as in other Latin American countries. By the mid-1970s, the bowling boom had spread into Japan. Russia followed suit by opening its first bowling center in 1976. Interest in bowling also grew in China. The bowling boom spread into Thailand and the Asia Pacific regions during the early 1990s.

By the 1990s, bowling comprised two main industries. One involved the ownership and operation of bowling centers. The other was the manufacture of bowling equipment used in bowling centers or by bowlers. These manufactured items included automatic pin spotters, computerized automatic scoring systems, wood and synthetic bowling lanes, lane maintenance systems, masking panes, ball returns, seating, bumper bowling systems, replacement and maintenance parts, and operating supplies such as spare parts, pins, lane oils, bowling balls, bowling shoes, and other bowling accessories.

In 1996, estimates were that more than 100 million people in more than 90 countries bowled at least one game a year and bowlers in the United States spent approximately $4 billion annually on lane fees, equipment and supplies, uniforms, and food and beverage purchased within bowling centers.[1] More than 53 million Americans patronized the country's bowling centers every year, making tenpin bowling the number one indoor participation sport in the United States.[2]

The Bowling Industry in the United States

During bowling's peak years in the 1960s and early 1970s, bowling centers were being constructed almost overnight across the country. During the early to mid-1970s white American blue-collar workers (the primary clientele of the bowling industry) moved to the suburbs, away from the city neighborhoods where most of the bowling centers had been built. Bowling began to open facilities in the suburbs while maintaining their existing centers in the cities. This strategy was not successful due to the lifestyle changes of the blue-collar workers.[3] They were simply less interested in bowling than they had been.[4]

As a result, the new suburban bowling centers were not as successful, while existing bowling centers in the cities became only marginally profitable. The number of bowling centers gradually declined, but the number of lanes increased due to the construction of large new centers and the remodeling of surviving ones.[5] Exhibit 1 shows the historical relationship between the number of centers, lanes, and population in the United States.[6]

In response to the decreasing popularity of bowling, many bowling operators started differentiating their image by renovating their alleys into entertainment centers in the early 1990s.[7] Their strategy was to market to families with children and teenagers by offering childcare, video games, laser lights, lightweight neon-glowing bowling balls, and fog machines. They also devised bumper bowling, in which gutters are filled with plastic tubes to keep the balls on the lane. This strategy proved to be profitable and operators were able to restore their revenues to the levels of the 1960s.[8]

Many analysts thought operators had created a "double-edged sword" by pampering one market segment and alienating another. The upgraded facilities with flashy, loud, and

Exhibit 1 U.S. Bowling Centers, 1955–1995

				Population	
Year	Centers	Lanes	Lanes per Center	Total (000)	Per Center
1955	7,062	60,648	8.6	165,275	23,403
1965	11,363	165,601	14.5	193,460	17,025
1975	8,974	144,829	16.1	215,973	24,046
1985	8,629	159,394	18.5	237,950	27,575
1995	7,331	144,187	19.7	262,755	35,841

Source: A-1 Lanes company literature.

modern atmospheres were the opposite of the dark, quiet, smoky lanes to which league bowlers were accustomed. Evidence indicated that league bowlers, a steady source of revenue for bowling centers, further dwindled due to these changes.[9] A league bowler commented, "The centers have all of these great gimmicks and are giving financial breaks to families and people that really do not bowl that much. Meanwhile, they're raising the prices for league bowlers, the true loyal customers, and driving them away."[10]

The U.S. bowling center industry (see Exhibit 2) was highly fragmented. The top eight operators, including AMF, accounted for less than 10 percent of U.S. bowling centers. The two largest, AMF and Brunswick Corporation ("Brunswick") owned approximately 340 and 111 U.S. bowling centers, respectively.[11] Four medium-sized chains together accounted for 70 bowling centers. More than 5,300 bowling centers were owned by single-center and small-chain operators, which typically owned four or fewer centers.

By 1997, the U.S. bowling center industry was considered mature and was characterized by a continual contraction in the number of bowling centers. Nevertheless, the decreasing lineage (games per lane per day) was offset by an increasing average price per game and by revenue from ancillary sources. Bowling centers derived their revenues from bowling (60.2%), food and beverage (25.4%)[12], and other sources such as rentals, amusement games, billiards, and pro shops (14.4%).[13]

According to the 1997 Economic Census, 619 establishments existed with 17,109 employees in the hardwood dimension and flooring mills classification (NAICS 321912).[14] However, only a few companies operated in the bowling lane and equipment supply business (see Exhibit 3).[15] Some of the competitors

Exhibit 2 Operators of U.S. Bowling Centers in 1997

Operator	Number of Bowling Centers	Percent of Total
AMF	370	6.3
Brunswick	111	1.9
Bowl America	23	0.4
Active West	16	0.3
Mark Voight	16	0.3
Bowl New England	15	0.2
Subtotal:	551	9.4
Single-center & small-chain operators	5,302	90.6
Total	5,853	100.0%

Source: AMF Bowling Worldwide Inc. (1997). Annual Report: 10-K, Period ending December 31.

Exhibit 3 Major Competitors in the Bowling Equipment Industry in 1997

Company Name	Product Line	Total Employees	Estimated Sales ($M)	Headquarters
Brunswick Corp.	Bowling Equipment*	1,000	$350.0	Lake Forest, IL
AMF	Bowling Equipment*	635	$250.0	Richmond, VA
Heddon Bowling Corporation	Synthetic Lanes	50	$ 40.0	Tampa, FL
Hodge Lumber Company	Wood Lanes	40	$ 30.0	New Knoxville, OH
Mendes	Synthetic Lanes	40	$ 30.0	Quebec City, Canada
Murrey International	Synthetic Lanes	35	$ 30.0	Los Angeles, CA
A-1 Lanes	Wood & Synthetic Lanes	35	$ 12.5	Rusk, TX

*Equipment includes bowling lanes, automatic pinsetters, ball returns, computerized scoring equipment, business systems, and other industrial equipment and supplies sold to bowling centers in addition to resale products, such as bowling balls, bags, shoes, and other bowlers' aids, sold primarily through pro shops.

Source: From A-1 Lanes 1997 company estimates.

Exhibit 4 Selected Markets in the International Bowling Industry in 1997

Country	Centers	Lanes	Lanes per Center	Population Total (000)	Population Per Lane*
Japan	1,123	32,200	29	125,000	3,900
Korea	1,104	16,300	15	45,350	2,800
Taiwan	370	11,567	31	21,120	1,800
United Kingdom	210	4,400	21	58,160	12,900

*The population per lane is an industry statistic that enables a bowling lane distributor to get an idea of the number customers per lane per city or area. This statistic is better than "bowling centers" because it gives an idea of literally how many people can actually bowl and a good indication of a saturation point for bowling centers in a given area.

Source: From A-1 Lanes company literature.

manufactured a broad range of products; others produced only a specific line of equipment. All competitors were active in both the domestic and international markets.

Foreign-based competition in the bowling lane manufacturing industry was almost nonexistent due to the lack of key raw materials. For example, lane construction required the use of specific types and grades of maple and pine. The necessary maple is found only in the United States and the preferred southern yellow pine is found only in the southeastern region of the United States. Furthermore, Asian bowling operators showed little interest in purchasing bowling lanes or other bowling products and accessories manufactured outside the United States. They considered bowling an American sport and the equipment had to be manufactured in the United States.

Bowling in Asia

In the late 1980s, because of the saturation of bowling lane markets in the United States and Europe, Brunswick and AMF began to expand into the Asian Pacific Rim by developing bowling centers throughout the region. The pivotal event that triggered Asian interest was the inclusion of bowling as a trial event in the 1988 Olympics in Seoul, South Korea.[16] After the Olympics, a bowling boom began in East Asia.

U.S. bowling exports increased by 27 percent from 1988 through 1993, and sales to China accounted for almost one-third of sales. An estimated 15,000 lanes were already in use in China, and most industry analysts expected this demand to blossom into a 100,000+ lane market. With a population of 1.3 billion, 100,000 lanes would amount to approximately one lane per 13,000 people, much lower than the United States rate of one lane per 1,800 people. Exhibit 4 estimates the population per lane for selected international markets in 1997.[17]

Asian Cultures

Asian cultures reflected numerous influences. Their business practices differed in many ways from those in the United States. Conducting business in Asia required a long-term perspective through the formulation of strong bonds and ties with potential business partners. Patience was important and connections were crucial. Asia, particularly China, was a gift-giving culture and the giving of gifts was a means to solidify personal ties.[18]

Many social and cultural demographics helped to explain the popularity of bowling in Asia. Half the Asian population was younger than 25, an optimal age range for introducing the sport to new bowlers. A bowling enthusiast and Asian market analyst, Mort Luby Jr., explained bowling's popularity:

Bowling is popular in the Asian market because many young urban people complain there isn't much to do with their leisure time (and increased disposable income). Disco is dead, the nightclubs are intimidating, the bars are full of AIDS, and foreign movies are expensive and largely incomprehensible. There are very few mid-price restaurants. Bowling has filled this recreational void with a vengeance.[19]

Asian Economies

Following the rapid growth in the 1980s of Taiwan, Korea, Singapore, and Hong Kong, the so-called Four Tigers, a new wave of economic growth swept across Asia. This wave was driven primarily by the newly industrializing economies of Malaysia, Thailand, Indonesia, and others. Thailand's growth was especially noticeable. The *Nation,*

Bangkok's independent newspaper, predicted that Thailand would become known as the "Fifth Tiger" during the 1990s. The Asian Development Bank predicted that Asia's economy would grow at a pace twice as fast as other world regions. Some suggested that the new millennium would begin the "Asian Century."[20]

The early 1990s also marked the globalization of financial markets. With slow growth and competitive home markets, private capital flows turned to these emerging markets that offered higher interest rates and robust economic growth.[21] From 1990 to 1997, capital flows to developing countries rose more than five-fold. While world trade grew by about 5 percent annually, private capital flows grew annually by 30 percent. The most mobile forms of flow, commercial bank debt and portfolio investments, set the pace,[22] with East Asia absorbing nearly 60 percent of all short-term capital.[23]

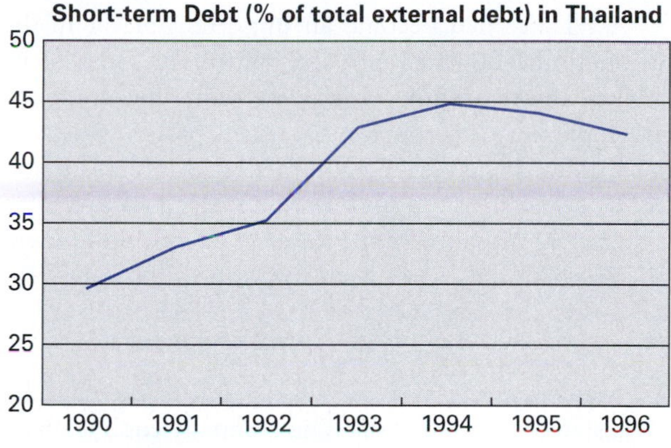

Source: World Bank, 2002[24]

Thailand attempted to "become the regional financial hub" for neighboring economies. The government enacted policies in 1993 that allowed some foreign and local banks to make loans in U.S. dollars and other currencies through what was called the Bangkok International Banking Facilities (BIBF).[25] However, with the Thai government continuing to maintain high interest rates on baht-denominated loans to keep inflation in check,[26] the policy was in reality a conduit by which local Thai companies could obtain special foreign loans at far lower interest rates than could be borrowed in baht.[27]

For example, in the mid-1990s, an investor could borrow yen at nearly 0 percent interest and invest in Bangkok skyscrapers, where the expected annual return was 20 percent.[28] With access to low-interest loans and readily available capital, and high demand, foreign capital flowed into the region and accounted for as much as 13 percent of Thailand's GDP, reaching a peak of $25.5 billion in 1995. Nearly 75 percent of these foreign capital inflows were from international banks in the form of bank loans with maturities of less than one year. The majority of these loans were made to Thai banks and finance companies, which in turn made domestic loans of much longer duration.[29]

The dramatic influx of cheap capital spurred investment in the domestic infrastructure, such as chemical and steel plants. Developers counted on the continuation of strong growth. Luxury hotels and high-rises became plentiful as development companies borrowed and invested at a breakneck pace.[30]

The year 1996 marked the beginning of an economic downturn in Thailand.[31] Exports began to stagnate and growth slowed.[32] The Asian Development Bank attributed the decline in exports to several factors, including a slump in the electronic sector, tight monetary policies in other countries, and the appreciation of the U.S. dollar against the Japanese yen.[33]

The appreciation of the U.S. dollar had a serious effect on Thailand's economy because the Thai baht was "pegged" to a basket of currencies with strong ties to the U.S. dollar.[34] As the dollar strengthened, so did the baht. Meanwhile Japanese exports, priced in yen, became more attractive to consumers in the United States.[35] Another disadvantage of letting the baht remain on par with the U.S. dollar was that Thai interest rates were far above U.S. rates, which caused distortion of the real worth of the baht. Nevertheless, the combination of exchange-rate stability and high interest rates continued to attract vast capital inflows.[36]

In light of an economic slowdown and the accumulation of aggressive investment, heavy borrowing, and wasteful use of resources, the International Monetary Fund (IMF), on September 1996, warned that several Southeast Asian economies "current growth rates may be above their sustainable long-term trends." The report also suggested that a key economic problem confronting the developing countries was how to prevent big foreign-capital inflows from fueling inflation, blowing out their current accounts and producing a repeat of Mexico's financial-market crunch. The report also stated that the rapid growth of spending on real estate—a classic sign of speculative excess—in Indonesia, Malaysia, and Thailand and the appearance of skilled-labor bottlenecks in the region were early signs of overheating.[37] Following the IMF's warning of impending peril, senior Asian central bankers met on November 20, 1996, at the World Economic Forum to discuss how to prevent a "financial crisis from hitting the region."[38]

In the first and second quarters of 1997, Thailand's banks experienced a net $6 billion outflow of foreign investment. Short-term loans were not being renewed by foreign banks. During this time, Baker watched the exchange rate and was confident the Thai government would be able to maintain the value of the baht, therefore preserving the existing dollar/baht pegged exchange rate. However, the Bank of Thailand began to run out of reserves in its attempt to maintain the baht's value. On July 2, 1997, the Thailand government devalued its currency.[39]

Because the Asian Pacific economies were interconnected,[40] this event was likely to affect the currencies of the whole Asian Pacific region.[41] For American bowling manufacturers exporting to East Asia, the baht devaluation was a major concern on three accounts. First, U.S. firms feared that their Asian customers would be unable to pay off their accounts (usually payable in U.S. dollars). Second, a significant devaluation would make U.S. exports substantially more expensive across the entire region. Finally, governments usually raise interest rates in conjunction with any devaluation to assist in the stabilization of their currency. Manufacturers worried that the higher prices of capital equipment and higher interest rates could quash Asian investment in bowling centers (and new bowling equipment) almost overnight, especially if governments acted quickly.

A-1's International Expansion

Following the 1988 Olympics, A-1 began shipping lanes to Taiwan. From 1990 to 1992, the company concentrated on developing contacts through Dacos' Asian networks. Increasing sales to Korea and Taiwan more than offset A-1's declining sales to Europe, where the market was saturated. Baker saw a distinctive Asian business mind-set: "They were much more aggressive than we are in the West," he said, "They would actually build a bowling alley next to an existing one to drive out a local competitor."

By the end of 1992, Taiwan and South Korea were also reaching a saturation point for new wood bowling lanes; however, China had a growing interest in bowling. AMF and Brunswick had already developed centers in China. A-1 was able to penetrate this market in 1993 and 1994, mainly through its partnership with Dacos. A-1 had developed a synthetic lane called UltraLane, a popular substitute for wood flooring. As a result of this innovation, A-1 Lanes was one of only three companies in the world to supply both wood and synthetic lanes. By 1995, Asia was the company's main market. In 1996, A-1's sales increased to $12.4 million, 33 percent above the previous year.

In 1995–1996, AMF attempted to consolidate the highly fragmented bowling equipment industry by slashing the prices of its capital equipment, especially wood and synthetic flooring. The aggressive move drove down prices and profitability across the industry. A-1 matched AMF's pricing, but its profits suffered substantially.

In spite of the region's problems, Baker and his Asian distributors saw increasing interest in bowling in Singapore and Malaysia. They thought these markets were promising, and the additional volume could possibly offset the smaller profit per unit and thereby restore net income to its 1995 level. At this time, A-1 had 80 percent of its sales volume in the Asian markets and 20 percent in the United States.

A-1's Situation

As Rick Baker contemplated the changes in the international market, he could not help but think about his own firm's viability. A-1's domestic sales were primarily of synthetic overlay systems. He wondered how A-1 could survive an Asian crash and continue to make a profit, or at the very least, generate a positive cash flow. To understand his company's financial health he began to assess its activities, assets, and capabilities.

A-1 Lanes had become an important player in the international bowling industry within 10 years of its chicken-house origin. In Baker's view, his company strived to provide competitively priced, premium-quality bowling lanes and related equipment to the domestic and international markets, and this had earned a favorable industry reputation. More than 30 capital equipment distributors used A-1 as a source for bowling lanes.

Manufacturing Facilities

A-1 was operating at about 60 percent of the capacity of its state-of-the-art plant. The company could expand production quickly to meet the demand in Singapore and Malaysia. More than 160 companies supplied the materials A-1 used to produce its bowling lanes and complementary components and accessories, such as gutters, capping, and return tracks. Rusk, Texas, was an ideal location because of its proximity to southern yellow pine. In Baker's mind, its location gave A-1 a distinct advantage over rivals in the northern states due to low inbound costs of lumber and easy access to the mills.

Products and Innovation

Wood lanes were constructed of the highest quality southern yellow pine and hard maple boards, which were routed and milled to specification, and shipped either pre-nailed or loose to be installed by the ultimate buyer. According to Baker:

The specifications for building wood lanes are very strict concerning the orientation and grain of the wood. Some wood is not appropriate, so there are many rejected boards. To aid in lowering the rejection rate and our costs, we have trained graders in local sawmills to grade lumber for use in our manufacturing process.

Exhibit 5 Breakdown of A-1's Sales in 1996

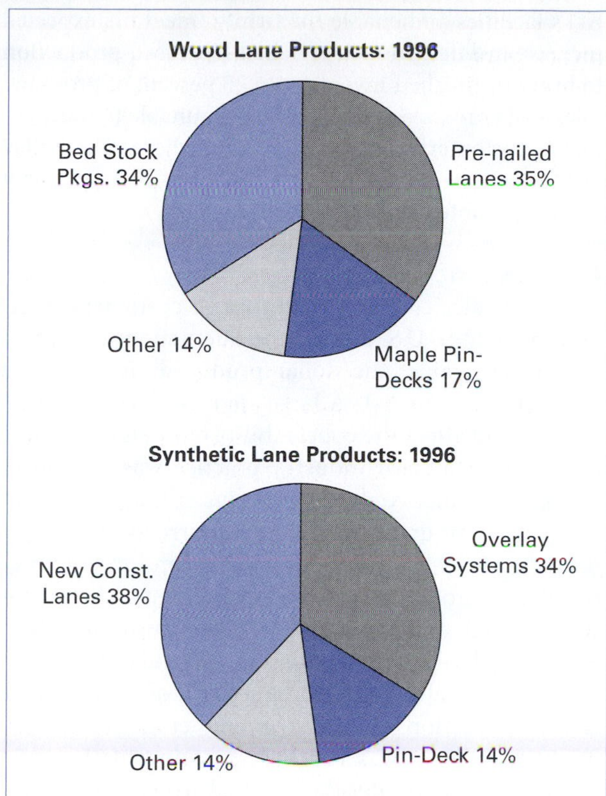

Once purchased, the lanes were shipped from the plant and assembled on site by highly skilled carpenters who specialized in the installation of bowling lanes.

Wood lanes and various derivatives accounted for 58 percent of A-1's revenues in 1996. Each wood lane cost $6,250 including accessories. A breakdown of revenue from the company's various products is shown in Exhibit 5.

To address some of the shortcomings associated with wood lanes, such as marring and gouging (deep etching), synthetic lanes were introduced during the 1980s. However, A-1 did not introduce its first synthetic flooring, UltraLane, until 1992. Baker was especially proud that this innovation was developed within the company and that the resin could be used not only for the construction of new lanes, but also for refurbishing existing wood lanes (overlay system). He elaborated,

The advantage of UltraLane is its improvement to the approach surface. Our competitors' synthetic flooring used the same product on the approach and the lane. The lane material was not slick enough for the approach. Bowlers' shoes stubbed on the material, and some lawsuits have been filed over injuries. UltraLane's approach has an orange peel texture that is very slick to the bowling shoe and allows it to slide properly.

By 1996, synthetic sales accounted for 42 percent of A-1 Lanes' total revenue, up from 25 percent of total sales in 1994. New synthetic lanes sold by the company were typically shipped in sections, installed on site, and cost $7,000 per lane. Exhibit 5 shows the breakdown of revenue from various synthetic lane products sold by A-1 Lanes.

In addition to UltraLane, Baker and his team continuously developed innovative products to complement or improve their existing products. For instance, A-1 developed a unique "snap on" ball return capping system and engineered changes in lane components that made the system less costly to manufacture. The capping system, made of high-impact plastic, covers (caps) the gutter dividers (A) and ball returns (B) that are positioned alternately between lanes.

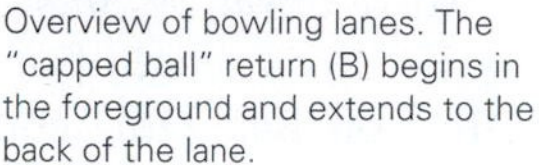
Overview of bowling lanes. The "capped ball" return (B) begins in the foreground and extends to the back of the lane.

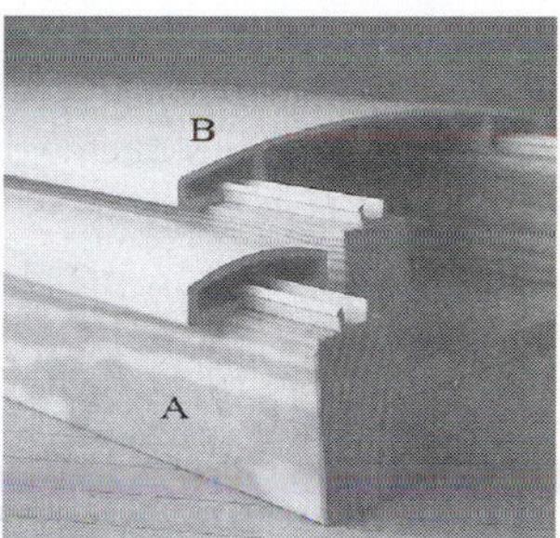

Close-up of Capping System. A divider (A) and a ball return system (B) are made of wood and then covered (capped).

Baker believed that continuously improving A-1's products was crucial to being competitive, even survival. Technological enhancements could alter the entire bowling equipment industry, bringing changes that could accelerate the development of bowling in foreign markets. Baker thought it ironic that the entire industry could be undermined by the recent currency devaluation rather than by a radical innovation.

Marketing

"We need to do little advertising because the coverage of our company in trade publications is very positive due to our quality of products and reputation," Baker said. However, to stay in continual contact with its customers, A-1 bought display space at trade shows and at regional and international meetings of national bowling associations.

A-1's ongoing relationship with Dacos was a "win-win situation," he thought. It allowed Dacos to offer a complete bowling center package that included pinsetters and bowling lanes supplied by A-1. By 1996, 50 percent of A-1's sales were channeled through this partnership. Dacos was formulating plans for developing bowling centers in Malaysia and Singapore, thereby enabling A-1 to be at the forefront of bowling's continuing growth in Asia.

Service and Sales

A-1's sales force was smaller than those of most competitors. The company's top three executives were its sales force and had been with the company since its inception. Baker thought that its sales force was an advantage for A-1 because competitors' sales forces were generally not very experienced. Furthermore, because of the knowledge and experience of its sales team, A-1 was able to provided consistent and reliable service. In Baker's mind, such service was especially important because business in Asia was primarily based on relationships.

Being small brought another advantage, he believed. Asians were insulted when larger companies sent middle managers to negotiate deals. Because A-1 was so small, all encounters with the company were with executives. Baker remembered that when he gave his Asian customers his business card and introduced himself as the president of A-1 Lanes, they would respond as if he were the president of AMF. When Baker traveled to Asia, he was treated "like royalty."

Performance Metrics

According to Baker, "It is amazing how a small firm in a rural community could sell millions of dollars of product to customers halfway around the world." Even so, Baker felt helpless in the currency crisis. Feeling a sense of urgency in his company's financial situation, Baker thought, "I wonder what story the financial statements might tell me?" (See Exhibits 6 through 8.)

A-1 Lanes' net profit reached an all-time high in 1995. Baker was sure that his decision to cut prices had hurt the bottom line, but he surmised that everyone in the industry was experiencing the slimmer margins. The real question, he figured, was how long AMF would pursue its price-cutting policy.

Another troublesome aspect of the financials was the increase in operating expenses as a percent of sales. Baker knew that these expenditures were needed to modernize A-1's facilities and enable the firm to meet the expected increase in sales. In fact, A-1 had increased production to bring its finished inventory to 25 percent of projected sales. Baker reasoned that if A-1 were unable to meet demand, customers could easily go elsewhere. The outlay of $554,000 to modernize the plant was financed by a 10 percent note payable over 10 years.

Credit and Currency Risk

Although sales contracts with foreign customers specified payment in U.S. dollars, the fluctuations of foreign currencies against the dollar produced risk for both the customer and A-1. A large appreciation in the U.S. dollar could affect the collectability of foreign accounts receivable. Standard industry practice was to ship to foreign customers only after receipt of full payment in U.S. dollars, or upon presentation of irrevocable letters of credit. However, Baker did make exceptions for long-standing customers that were key accounts. The exception applied to several major Asian customers, and Baker wondered whether this decision had been a smart one. He thought that hedging techniques to reduce A-1's transaction exposure would entail too much work; already he was too busy growing his business and filling orders. Besides, he had irrevocable letters of credit.

A-1's Future

Although Baker knew he did not fully understand the story within A-1's financials, he was growing uncomfortable with how the crash in Asian currency markets could affect his company. Should he have monitored the Asian economic environment more closely? Should he have expanded manufacturing operations in 1996? Should he have extended credit to his selected foreign customers? How could he have protected his company?

Exhibit 6 A-1 Lanes Income Statement, 1994–1996

	1996	1995	1994
Sales	$12,359,561	$9,326,649	$7,781,131
Cost of Goods Sold	9,887,649	6,460,768	6,035,549
Gross Profit	**2,471,912**	**2,865,881**	**1,745,582**
Operating Expenses	1,680,900	1,325,557	742,081
Earnings Before Interest and Taxes	**791,012**	**1,540,324**	**1,003,501**
Interest Expense	111,340	45,113	70,322
Income Tax Expense	203,902	447,779	317,281
Net Income	**$ 475,770**	**$1,047,432**	**$ 615,898**

Exhibit 7 A-1 Lanes Balance Sheet, 1994–1996

	1996	1995	1994
Cash	$ 296,603	$ 114,847	$ 73,411
Accounts Receivable	2,101,125	1,416,523	950,180
Inventory	2,050,636	2,418,940	1,571,758
Other Current	84,622	58,752	25,000
Total Current Assets	**4,532,986**	**4,009,062**	**2,620,349**
Fixed Assets	1,121,783	567,877	462,939
Accumulated Depreciation	(496,993)	(301,163)	(258,981)
Net Fixed Assets	624,790	266,714	203,958
TOTAL ASSETS	**$5,157,776**	**$4,275,776**	**$2,824,307**
Accounts Payable	$1,382,526	$1,440,354	$1,043,776
Short-Term Notes Payable	0	0	249,000
Taxes Payable	11,711	271,529	336,905
Other Current Liabilities	38,008	56,083	227,957
Total Current Liabilities	**1,432,245**	**1,767,966**	**1,857,638**
Long-Term Notes Payable	1,289,400	547,449	72,740
Common Stock	15,000	15,000	15,000
Excess of Par	60,000	60,000	60,000
Retained Earnings	2,361,131	1,885,361	818,929
Total Equity	**2,436,131**	**1,960,361**	**893,929**
TOTAL LIABILITIES & EQUITY	**$ 5,157,776**	**$4,275,776**	**$2,824,307**

Exhibit 8 A-1 Lanes Cash Flow Statement, 1994–1996

	1996	1995	1994
Cash Flow from Operating Activities			
Net Income	$475,770	$1,047,432	$615,898
Depreciation	195,830	42,182	55,108
(Increase) Accounts Receivable	(684,602)	(466,343)	(350,218)
Other Current	(25,870)	(33,752)	(31,654)
(Increase) Decrease Inventory	368,304	(847,182)	(355,916)
Increase (Decrease) Accounts Payable	(57,828)	396,578	115,530
Taxes Payable	(259,818)	(65,376)	(32,126)
Net Cash from Operating Activities	**11,786**	**73,539**	**48,276**
Purchase of Fixed Assets	**(553,906)**	**(104,938)**	**(74,136)**
Financial Proceeds			
Decrease Short-Term Notes	0	(249,000)	(250,000)
Increase Long-Term Debt	741,951	474,709	434,742
(Decrease) Other Current Liabilities	(18,075)	(171,874)	(91,279)
Total Proceeds (Payments)	**723,876**	**53,835**	**19,327**
Net Change in Cash	**$181,756**	**$ 22,436**	**$ 28,949**

Exhibit 9 A-1 Lanes Financial Ratios versus Industry[1] Averages

	A-1 Lanes			Industry[2]			1996[4] Sales $10–$25 M
	1996	1995	1994	1996	1995	1994	
1. Firm Liquidity **Current Ratio**	3.16	2.27	1.41	1.80	1.70	1.70	1.8
Average Collection Period for Accounts Receivable	62.05	55.44	44.57	NA	NA	NA	NA
2. Operating Profitability **Operating Income Return on Investment**	15.34%	36.02%	35.53%	7.20%	11.10%	9.30%	10.00%
Operating Profit Margin	6.40%	16.52%	12.90%	3.60%	4.63%	4.43%	5.56%
Total Asset Turnover	2.40	2.18	2.76	2.00	2.40	2.10	1.8
Accounts Receivable Turnover	5.88	6.58	8.19	13.00	12.50	12.20	12.9
Inventory Turnover	4.82	2.67	3.84	5.10	6.30	5.90	7.00
Fixed Assets Turnover	19.78	34.97	38.15	7.20	6.60	6.50	6.80
3. Financing Decisions **Debt Ratio**	25.00%	12.80%	2.58%	20.10	20.30%	20.80%	15.6%
Times Interest Earned	7.10	34.14	14.27	3.10	4.50	6.00	14.6
4. Return on Equity **Return on Equity[3]**	32.47%	78.57%	112.26%	17.31%	25.06%	23.13%	18.28%

1. SIC 2426; NAICS 321918 Manufacturing, Other Millwork (including Flooring).
2. Source: Robert Morris & Associates (1996). *Annual Statement Studies: Financial Ratio Benchmarks.* Philadelphia, PA.
3. RMA does not report net income (after taxes) nor stockholders equity. Therefore, a derivative was used (Profit before taxes/net worth) as an indicant for return on equity.
4. This information is reported for the current year (1996) of firms with sales of $10–$25 million.

Baker recalled that his old management professor at college once told him that behind each set of financial statements is a story—especially when you compare your company with the industry averages. Baker visited the library and collected the ratios pertaining to his industry. Now he laid them on a table next to A-1's financial statements (see Exhibit 9). He grabbed an ice cream bar from the freezer and sat down to ponder his next move.

1. C. Pezzano, 1996, The push is on for olympic status, *The Record* (New Jersey), January 7: S17.
2. 1997, AMF Bowling looks to equity markets going public, *The IPO Reporter,* September 1, Securities Data Publishing.
3. C. Stooksbury, 1998, Bowling boasts lengthy history as popular pastime, *Amusement Business,* May: 20.
4. Bowling centers. *Encyclopedia of American Industries,* 2001: 2.
5. N. King, 1997, Bowling must learn by its mistakes, *The Ledger* (Lakeland, Florida), July 20: C2.
6. A-1 Lanes company literature.
7. S. Hansell, *Overview of the Bowling Industry.* http://www.ltfun.com/documents/hansell_article.pdf (accessed January 7, 2006).
8. M. Matzer, 1996, Bowling for dollars, *Brandweek,* August: 18.
9. S. Hansell, 1998, A double-edged sword, *International Bowling Industry,* July: 37.
10. I. P. Murphy, 1997, Bowling industry rolls out unified marketing plan, *Sports Marketing,* January: 2.
11. 1997, AMF Bowling Worldwide Inc., 1997 Annual Report: 10-K, Period ending December 31.

12. Food and beverage includes bar sales. On average, bar sales would account for 55 percent of these sales.
13. I. P. Murphy, 1997, Bowling industry rolls out unified marketing plan, *Sports Marketing,* January: 2.
14. 1997 Economic Census: Bridge Between NAICS and SIC Manufacturing. http://www.census.gov/epcd/ec97brdg/E97B1321.HTM#321918 (accessed August 25, 2004).
15. From A-1 Lanes 1997 company estimates.
16. M. Cooper, 1998, On the shining paths of tenpin, *The Nation,* 267, August 10: 35.
17. From A-1 Lanes company literature.
18. M. Luby, Jr., 1998, Asia's malaise is only temporary, *Bowler's Journal International,* January: 12. http://www.census.gov/epcd/naics/NAICS32A.HTM#N321918.
19. Ibid.
20. 1990, Wave of growth sweeping across Asia, Jiji Press Ltd., June 7.
21. M. N. Baily, D. Farrel, & S. Lund, 2000, The color of hot money, *Foreign Affairs,* 79(2), March/April: 99–110.
22. 1998, East Asia: The road to recovery, World Bank, Washington, DC.
23. WEO, cited in East Asia: The road to recovery, 1998, World Bank, Washington, DC.
24. World Development Indicators on CD-ROM, 2002, World Bank.
25. B. Einhorn & R. Corben, 1997, One tired tiger, *Business Week* (International Edition), March 24.
26. 1997, Thailand finally lets its currency float, *Wall Street Journal,* July 3.
27. J. Sapsford, 1997, Asia's financial shock: How it began, and what comes next, *Wall Street Journal,* November 26.
28. World Development Indicators on CD-ROM, 2002, World Bank.
29. M. N. Baily, D. Farrel, & S. Lund, 2000, The color of hot money, *Foreign Affairs,* 79(2), March/April: 99–110.
30. C. Lebourgre, 1997, Thailand: "Tis an ill wind that blows nobody any good," *Banque Paribas Conjoncture,* May.
31. Thailand, http://www.infoplease.com/ipa/A0108034.html.
32. C. Lebourgre, 1997, Thailand: "Tis an ill wind that blows nobody any good," *Banque Paribas Conjoncture,* May.
33. 1997, Asia-Pacific to grow at slower pace in '97 and '98, Japan Economic News Wire. *Kyodo News Service,* April 17.
34. H. Sender, 1997, Get a grip: Can Thailand's Central Bank handle the baht crisis? *Far Eastern Economic Review,* 160(13): March 27.
35. 1997, Several European bourses float at lofty levels: Tokyo shares rise following pause for holiday, *Wall Street Journal,* January 17.
36. H. Sender, 1997, Get a grip: Can Thailand's Central Bank handle the baht crisis? *Far Eastern Economic Review,* 160(13): March 27.
37. P. Kandiah, 1996, Malaysia warned over possibility of Mexico-style crash, *The Nikkei Weekly,* September 30, *http://web.lexis-nexis.com/universe/document* (accessed April 23, 2003).
38. S. Kohli, 1996, Bankers fear Asian "Mexico" crisis, *South China Morning Post,* November 21, *http://web.lexis-nexis.com/universe/document* (accessed April 10, 2003).
39. M. N. Baily, D. Farrel, & S. Lund, 2000, The color of hot money, *Foreign Affairs,* 79(2), March/April: 99–110.
40. R. Y. C. Wong, 1999, Lessons from the Asian financial crisis, *Cato Journal,* 18(3), Winter: 391–398.
41. A. Brummer, 1996, East Asian tigers are endangered, *The Guardian* (London), October 16. *http://web.lexis-nexis.com/universe/document* (accessed April 1, 2003).

Case 3

Abercrombie & Fitch: An Upscale Sporting Goods Retailer Becomes a Leader in Trendy Apparel

Janet L. Rovenpor, Professor
Manhattan College

On November 10, 2005, Abercrombie & Fitch (A&F) celebrated the opening of a new 36,000-square-foot, four-level flagship store on Fifth Avenue and 56th Street in Manhattan. The timing was perfect—right ahead of the busy Christmas shopping season during which the retailer hoped to sell large quantities of cashmere sweaters, Henley long-sleeved fleeces, hand-knit wool sweaters, polo shirts, and jeans. The Fifth Avenue store, considered a prototype for other flagship stores, featured dark interiors, oak columns, bronze fixtures, and a central staircase with frosted glass-block flooring. A mural of muscular, skin-showing rope climbers in a setting from the 1930s by the artist Mark Beard was prominently displayed. "We're really excited to be back on Fifth Avenue. We're really trying to build the character of the brand. We had a little store in Trump Tower that closed in 1986, and we have been looking on Fifth Avenue for a few years. This is a prestige location and great for the positioning of the brand," commented CEO Michael Jeffries.[1]

In an attempt to gauge customer reaction to the opening of the new store, *New York Magazine* surveyed 75 teenagers asking them what the A&F brand meant to them. Answers were varied: "It's gross." "It's overpriced." "It's stylish and sleek." "It's very logotistical." "It projects the typical image of the perfect American male—good at school and masculine." "It was cool up until we were 16. Then it got this dumb-jock-meathead image."[2] Perhaps such contradictory statements were just what A&F's senior executives wanted. Consumers either loved or hated the company, its products, and its image. Part of the trendy retailer's competitive strategy, in fact, was to stir up controversy, go against convention, and appeal emotionally to its youthful customers.

A&F's Fifth Avenue store symbolized the values the retailer held: sensuality, a youthful lifestyle, a love for the outdoors and fun with friends. It was the culmination of the retailer's creative endeavors to design and implement an exciting store format that drew shoppers in and captivated them. The loud music, appealing visuals, and perfumed interiors encouraged teenagers to "hang out" and "browse." A&F had come a long way from its early beginnings in 1892. Back then, A&F was considered a luxury sporting goods retailer with conservative tastes that appealed to affluent clients, including adventurers, hunters, presidents, and heads of royal families. President Theodore Roosevelt, for example, purchased snake-proof sleeping bags for a 1908 African safari at an Abercrombie store. Admiral Richard Byrd bought equipment for his 1950 expedition to Antarctica.

A&F's competitive strategies seemed to be working. By February 2007, the retailer operated 944 stores in 49 states, the District of Columbia and Canada. It had 8,500 full-time and 77,900 part-time employees (including temporary staff hired during peak periods such as the back-to-school and holiday seasons). Its fiscal 2006 revenues were \$3.32 billion and its net income was \$422.2 million. It opened its first European store, in London, in March 2007. It expects to open a store in Tokyo in late 2009. *Apparel Magazine* ranked A&F number three in terms of profitability (net income as a percentage of sales) among apparel retailers in 2007 (up from number four in 2006).[3] In March 2007, A&F joined the S&P 500 stock index (replacing Univision Communications, Inc., which had been acquired by an investor group).

At the same time, questions existed regarding the retailer's long-term success. Would teenagers, A&F's primary target market, remain loyal to the company and its products? Could A&F bring back some of the shoppers it had alienated because of its treatment of minority employees and its racy slogans on its t-shirts? Would A&F be able to maintain its competitive advantage in a fragmented industry in which new entrants from both the United States as well as from overseas markets were intent on imitating A&F's strategies? Should CEO Jeffries be concerned with the exodus of talented senior executives from his top management team? Who would eventually succeed Jeffries? Would the retailer's new corporate governance and diversity initiatives pay off?

The U.S. Specialty Apparel Industry

A&F was considered a "specialty retailer." Retailers in this category sold products in specific merchandise categories (e.g., apparel, footwear, office supplies, home furnishings, books, jewelry, or toys). Numerous small to midsized firms existed. They survived by catering to local tastes and preferences. Sometimes their financial performance was adversely affected when a competitor entered their niche or when the preferences, lifestyles, and demographics of their target markets changed. As young people became interested in electronics and began spending more and more time playing video games, for example, the fortunes of retailers such as Best Buy rose at the expense of retailers that included Toys "R" Us.[4]

Specialty apparel retailers opened stores in shopping malls and constructed free-standing units along major roadways. The firms enhanced their capabilities to sell products via directing mailings of catalogs and through Web sites equipped with shopping cart technologies. To compete with mass merchandiser and department stores, they tried to (a) maintain high prices and high-quality merchandise; (b) cultivate customer loyalty through various membership programs; and (c) promote their own private-label brands. J. Crew, for example, offered high-end, limited edition items (e.g., crocodile sling backs and silk wedding dresses), which created excitement and enticed consumers to buy early at full prices. Chico's FAS Inc. offered a customer loyalty program, Passport Club, which gave customers discounts and other benefits when their purchases exceeded $500.

In 2007, consumer spending tightened as the economy slowed. Individuals spent more on gasoline and food and began to cut back on other purchases amid lower consumer confidence and a slump in the housing market. Retailers saw declines in customer traffic and sales in July, the start of the usually brisk back-to-school shopping season.[5] July same-store sales (i.e., sales dollars generated by stores that have been open more than one year) at A&F, American Eagle Outfitters (AEOS), and the Gap fell 4 percent, 6 percent, and 7 percent, respectively.

Demographics began to shift; the baby boom generation was aging. Those specialty apparel retailers who appealed mostly to teenagers realized that they needed to hold on to their consumers as they entered their twenties. A&F, AEOS, and even the Gap began to open, with varying degrees of success, stores that targeted an older demographic. Rivals who already catered to an older consumer group, such as Ann Taylor Loft and Express LLC, were equally eager to lure such young adults away.[6] Specialty apparel retailers also faced increased competition from such department store chains as JCPenney and Kohl's, which started offering more fashionable and exclusive private label goods.

A&F faced some threat of being an acquisition target. Many private equity transactions were completed in 2007. Apollo Management LP acquired Claire's Stores Incorporated (a teen accessory retailer) for $3.1 billion; Golden Gate Capital acquired a 67 percent stake in The Limited's Express clothing chain. Private equity firms saw an opportunity to turn around struggling businesses and get them ready for resale. When retailers went private, they no longer had to report comparable same-store sales or quarterly earnings to investors; they could concentrate on improving their business operations.[7]

Believing that "trend transcends age," A&F catered to cool, attractive, fashion-conscious consumers by offering products to meet their needs through different life stages—from elementary school to post-college.[8] The retailer managed four brands:

- A&F: This brand was repositioned in 1992. It offered apparel that reflected the youthful lifestyle of the East Coast and Ivy League traditions for 18- to 22-year-old college students. In February 2007, the A&F brand operated 360 stores in the United States (close to its capacity of 400 stores).
- abercrombie: A brand that was launched in 1998 targeted customers aged 7–14 with fashions similar to the A&F line. In early 2009, Abercrombie operated 177 stores.
- Hollister Company: Launched in 2000, this brand targeted 14-to 18-year-old high school students with lower-priced casual apparel, personal care products, and accessories. It promoted the laid-back, California surf lifestyle in its 393 stores by early 2007 (with potential for many more).
- Ruehl: This brand was launched in 2004, and grew to include 14 stores by 2007. It sold casual sportswear, trendy apparel, and leather goods to post-college consumers in 22–35 age group. Its line of clothing was inspired by the lifestyle of New York City's Greenwich Village. The merchandise was more upscale and more expensive than the A&F line.

A fifth store concept was on its way. A&F refused to reveal details, although Jeffries remarked that accessories—hats, totes, fragrances and jewelry—were a growing and important part of the business.[9] Rumors circulated that the retailer would launch either an accessories brand or an intimate apparel line with its own store locations.

A&F had three main competitors. Two were the publicly held firms of American Eagle Outfitters (AEOS) and the Gap. A third firm, J. Crew, had been a privately held firm until June 2006. For basic comparative financial data, see Exhibit 1 (five-year data for J. Crew are not

Exhibit 1 Basic Comparative Financial Information for Abercrombie & Fitch (A&F), American Eagle Outfitters (AEOS), and the Gap

	A & F					AEOS					GAP				
	2006	2005	2004	2003	2002	2006	2005	2004	2003	2002	2006	2005	2004	2003	2002
Operating Revenues (in millions $)	3,318.2	2,784.7	2,021.3	1,707.8	1,595.8	2,794.4	2,309.4	1,881.2	1,520.0	1,463.1	15,943.0	16,023.0	16,267.0	15,854.0	14,454.7
Net Income (in millions $)	422.2	334.0	216.4	204.8	194.8	387.4	293.7	224.2	60.0	88.7	778.0	1,113.0	1,150.0	1,030.0	477.5
Return on Revenues (%)	12.7	12.0	10.7	12.0	12.2	13.9	12.7	11.9	3.9	6.1	4.9	6.9	7.1	6.5	3.3
Return on Assets (%)	20.9	21.3	15.8	17.2	22.1	21.6	20.3	20.8	7.5	12.6	9.0	11.8	11.3	10.2	5.4
Return on Equity (%)	35.2	40.1	28.3	25.5	29	30.1	27.7	27.9	9.8	16.4	14.7	21.5	23.7	24.4	14.3
Current Ratio	2.1	1.9	1.6	2.4	2.8	2.6	3.0	3.3	2.8	3.0	2.2	2.7	2.8	2.7	2.1
Debt/Capital Ratio (%)	0	0	0	0	0	0	0	0	2.1	2.8	3.5	8.6	27.6	34.2	44.2
Debt as a % of Net Working Capital	0	0	0	0	0	0	0	0	4.1	5.7	6.8	15.6	46.4	59.3	96.1
Price/Earnings Ratio (High-Low)	17–10	19–12	20–10	16–10	17–8	19–9	18–10	15–5	28–16	25–8	23–17	18–13	20–14	20–10	31–15
Earnings Per Share—Basic ($)	4.79	3.83	2.33	2.12	1.99	1.74	1.29	1.03	.28	.41	.94	1.26	1.29	1.15	.55
Share Price (High-Low, $)	79.42–49.98	74.10–44.17	47.45–23.07	33.65–20.65	33.85–14.97	33.01–14.83	22.69–12.97	15.92–5.28	7.79–4.40	10.15–3.25	21.39–15.91	22.70–15.90	25.72–18.12	23.47–12.01	17.14–8.35

Source: Standard & Poor's Industry Surveys: Retailing Specialty, August 2007.

reported because the retailer had operated at a loss when it was privately held; ratios, such as return on revenues and return on equity, are not meaningful).

Based in Warrendale, Pennsylvania, AEOS sold lower-priced casual apparel and accessories to men and women aged 15–25. The Schottenstein family (who held interests in Value City Department and Furniture Stores) owned 14 percent of the retailer. AEOS operated more than 900 stores in the United States and Canada with approximately 40 percent of its stores located west of the Mississippi River. Revenues in fiscal 2006 were $2.8 billion (an increase of 21% from fiscal 2005); net income reached $387 million (an increase of 31.9% from fiscal 2005).

AEOS launched two new store concepts in 2006. Martin + Osa was a clothing store selling denim and active sportswear targeting men and women aged 24–40. It did not perform as well as expected. Efforts that included replacing its president with a former Liz Claiborne executive were underway in 2007 to make the women's merchandise more feminine, less outdoorsy, less expensive, and of better quality. Aerie was an intimate apparel sub-brand that was launched adjacent to existing AEOS stores and as stand-alone stores. It was successful and plans were in place to expand upon its merchandise with fragrance and personal care items.

J. Crew operated 227 retail and outlet stores in the United States. With a joint venture partner, it also had 45 stores in Japan. Millard "Mickey" Drexler, former CEO of the Gap, headed the retailer. He promised that J. Crew would "be the best, not the biggest."[10] Revenues in fiscal 2006 were $1.15 billion (up 20.9% from fiscal 2005). Net income (applicable to common shareholders) in fiscal 2006 was $71.6 million (or $1.49 per diluted share) compared to a net loss of $9.7 million (or a loss of 39 cents per diluted share) in fiscal 2005. J. Crew launched Madewell, a casual clothing store for women, which sold merchandise at prices that were 20–30 percent lower than J. Crew merchandise. Its initial public offering of common stock in June 2006 raised $402.8 million. At the time, it was the third largest apparel retailing IPO in history.

Whereas J. Crew was the smallest of A&F's direct competitors, the Gap was the largest with 3,000 stores worldwide. The Gap sold basic casual clothing and accessories for children, men, and women. Revenues in fiscal 2006 were $15.9 billion (a decrease of 0.5% from fiscal 2005); net income was $778 million (a decrease of 30.1% from fiscal 2005). It operated Banana Republic (high-quality fashionable apparel) and Old Navy (low-priced trendy clothing). Its most recent entry, Forth & Towne (stylish apparel for women over 35), was open for 18 months before being shut down.

The Gap was struggling to turn around its performance, which began to decline in 2000 when it overexpanded, assumed too much debt, and made a few fashion-related miscalculations. Under pressure from the board of directors, CEO Paul Pressler resigned in January 2007. Glenn Murphy, who had been the CEO of a large Canadian drug store chain, was hired to replace him. The firm also hired Goldman Sachs to explore strategic options for the retailer. Rumors circulated that the company intended to put itself up for sale or to spin off one of its divisions, most likely Banana Republic.

A&F's Early Beginnings

A&F was founded in 1892 by David T. Abercrombie (see Exhibit 2 for key milestones in A&F's history). Abercrombie was a civil engineer, topographer, and colonel in the Officers Reserve Corps. He was also an avid hunter and fisherman. The first store was located on Water Street in lower Manhattan. Ezra Fitch, a lawyer and one of Abercrombie's best customers, became a partner in 1900. The two men frequently argued. Fitch continued to run the company after Abercrombie resigned in 1907.

A&F's 12-story building on Madison Avenue and 45th Street opened in 1917. It featured a log cabin and casting pool on the roof and a rifle range in the basement. The store's location was excellent. By 1923, Madison Avenue and 45th Street had become the "heart" of the "specialized shop trade."[11] Near A&F's flagship store were Brooks Brothers, Tiffany Studios, Eastman Kodak, and Maillard's. The Roosevelt Hotel was just undergoing construction. Abercrombie died in 1931 at the age of 64; Fitch died of a stroke aboard his yacht in Santa Barbara, California, in 1930 at the age of 65.

A&F's managers promoted it as "The Finest Sporting Goods Store in the World." An early advertisement announcing the opening of a new store on 36th Street appears in Exhibit 3. A&F was known for its expensive and exotic goods as well as for its affluent clientele. It was possible to buy an antique miniature cannon for $300, a custom-made rifle for $6,000, or a Yukon dog sled for $1,188. Presidents William Taft and Warren Harding purchased golf clubs at A&F. President Dwight Eisenhower bought hunting boots for $55 for his walks in the woods at Camp David. Other famous customers included Amelia Earhart, Greta Garbo, Charles Lindbergh, Clark Gable, the Duke of Windsor, Howard Hughes, and Ernest Hemingway.

A&F was not just a place to purchase sporting goods and rugged apparel. It was also a place where individuals could learn new skills and get involved in the community. In 1923, the Adirondack Club held its annual meeting in A&F's log cabin. Its members discussed whether an open season should be declared on beavers whose dam-building activities were causing floods, damaging timber, and ruining trout streams. In 1966, A&F held a lecture on

Exhibit 2 Key Milestones in A&F's Early History

1892:	A&F was founded by David T. Abercrombie, an engineer, topographer, outdoorsman, and colonel.
1900:	Ezra Fitch, a lawyer from Kingston, New York, became Abercrombie's business partner.
1907:	Abercrombie resigned from the company.
1917:	A&F's 12-story building on Madison Avenue and 45th Street opened.
1928:	Ezra Fitch resigned as president. He was succeeded by James S. Cobb.
1929:	A&F acquired an interest in Von Lengerke & Detmold, a gun, camp, and fishing chain based in Chicago.
1935:	A&F earned a net profit of $148,123 up from $123,424 in the previous year.
1940:	Otis Guernsey was elected president and CEO.
1943:	A&F earned a net profit of $286,694.
1958:	A store in San Francisco opened.
1961:	John H. Ewing became president and CEO, succeeding Guernsey. Earl Angstadt became the president and CEO in the mid-1960s.
1962:	A&F opened a store in Colorado Springs, Colorado.
1963:	A&F's opened a store in Short Hills, New Jersey.
1967:	A&F acquired the Crow's Nest, a nautical supply store with a national mail order business.
1968:	Sales peaked at $28 million and net income rose to $866,000.
1970:	Angstadt resigned. He was replaced by William Humphreys. Henry Haskell, a major shareholder, soon replaced Humphreys as CEO. A&F lost money every year until 1977.
1972:	A store in a Chicago suburb opened.
1977:	A&F declared bankruptcy.
1978:	A&F was acquired by Oshman's Sporting Goods Incorporated.
1988:	The Limited acquired A&F from Oshman's.
1989:	Sally Frame-Kasaks was named president and chief executive of A&F. She left in 1992.
1992:	Michael Jeffries became president and chief executive of A&F.
1996:	A&F was spun off from The Limited.
1999:	The company operated 186 A&F stores and 13 abercrombie stores.
2001:	A&F opened a new 260,000-square-foot corporate office and a 700,000-square-foot distribution center in New Albany, Ohio. It cost $130 million.

how to capture a musk ox bare-handed without harming it. In 1967, A&F ran a fishing clinic in which experts discussed tackle, knot tying, and trout angling techniques. In 1973, A&F served flambé quail, prepared in the log cabin's fireplace, in celebration of a talking cookbook it had produced. The cookbook contained two 40-minute cassettes and a booklet of recipes printed on waterproof and grease-proof plastic.

Throughout its early history, A&F did a good job keeping up with its customers and with changing fashions. During World War II, when activities such as parlor skeet and military board games were popular, A&F sold a wooden box that could be filled with water and used to blow sailboats from side to side. In the 1940s, barbeque picnics in fields outside country homes became the latest fad arriving from the West. A&F sold high-quality BBQ equipment and insulated canvas bags to keep drinks cold. In 1964, A&F made a splash when it developed the capacity to sell a cashmere sweater, with a lifelike reproduction of a color photograph of one's pet embroidered on it. It sold resort wear with a fruit motif in the 1940s and Bermuda-length culottes in the 1960s. A&F had a clearly defined target market. CEO Anstadt said, "We aren't out for the teenage business. Our customers are on the go and have the time and the money to enjoy travel and sport."[12]

A&F had its share of problems. Some were typical of all retailers throughout the decades and some were atypical. During the early 1940s, A&F stores were low on inventory. Commerce had been disrupted by the

Exhibit 3 An Early A&F Advertisement in the *New York Times*, 1912

Opening

We Cordially Invite You to Inspect Our New Store

We maintain at this address, the finest Sporting Goods Store in the world. We want you to visit the establishment—we are proud of it, and we are proud of the stock we have to show you. It comprises everything for the Great Out of Doors, each article the BEST for its purpose and most of them exclusive. You can't get them elsewhere.

For a good many years, this concern, The Abercrombie & Fitch Co., occupied a small, exclusive store at 57 Reade Street, in the dingy downtown district where buyers came only because they HAD to—because they could not buy elsewhere the things they bought from us. We have been known the world over not only as the one place where the big Nimrods, Explorers, Hunters, Trappers, Fishermen,—the whole Out-of-Door Brotherhood were outfitted, but as a sort of informal clearing house of information for them. We outfitted Col. Roosevelt for his trip into Africa—Stewart Edward White speaks of our outfits in his textbooks—our peculiar specialty of having the RIGHT thing, the CORRECT thing and finally the EXCLUSIVE thing was recognized by the adept many years ago. Our business grew by word of mouth—by talks over camp fires and at club tables, because when once a man or woman found us, they had found the ONLY one there was and took a pride in passing on the good news. We outgrew our store—we outgrew the building—and now we have our own building on 36th Street. So long as we had to move, we moved to a place where you could get at us—right in the centre of your shopping district.

We have the finest store of its kind in the world. We have not merely the finest stock of our sort in the world, but we carry the ONLY correct things for the purpose. We have broadened our business and to bring this about, we have manufactured in quantities impossible before because of the restrictions of space in our old quarters. All the economies due to manufacturing and buying on a wholesale plan are reflected in the very low prices of the goods we offer you.

We want you to see our Out-of-Door Clothing for Men and Women and for Boys. We want you to see our complete outfits for camping, for canoeing, for fishermen, for golfers, for every one of the sports. We want you to see to what lengths we have gone to provide not only the best, but the exactly RIGHT and the EXCLUSIVE thing for your favorite sport, the thing you have always wanted but couldn't get elsewhere because it didn't EXIST elsewhere.

EZRA H. FITCH, President

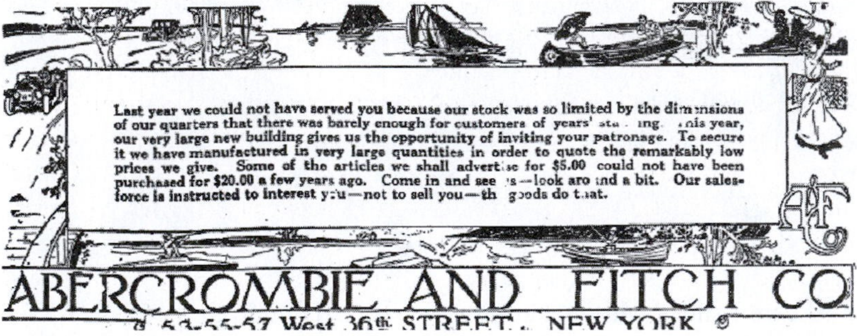

Last year we could not have served you because our stock was so limited by the dimensions of our quarters that there was barely enough for customers of years' standing. This year, our very large new building gives us the opportunity of inviting your patronage. To secure it we have manufactured in very large quantities in order to quote the remarkably low prices we give. Some of the articles we shall advertise for $5.00 could not have been purchased for $20.00 a few years ago. Come in and see us—look around a bit. Our salesforce is instructed to interest you—not to sell you—the goods do that.

A&F

ABERCROMBIE AND FITCH CO

53-55-57 West 36th STREET, NEW YORK

wartime effort. It was difficult to import goods from abroad. Manufacturers were busy making binoculars, field glasses, saddles, and marine clocks for use by the army and navy. A&F wrote to its customers, asking them if they would like to sell optical or sporting goods in satisfactory condition back to the retailer so that the items could be refurbished and resold to new customers. One year, the Office of Price Administration placed limitations on civilian consumption of rubber products, which caused a rush on golf balls sold by A&F. A&F joined other retailers in asking customers to do their Christmas shopping early in November. A lack of available labor had overwhelmed the postal services and caused delays.

At least twice in A&F's history, a customer used one of the guns on display in an A&F shop to commit suicide. The first shooting occurred in 1932, when the son of a famous horse breeder killed himself. The second shooting occurred in 1968 when an immigrant from Czechoslovakia killed himself. Subsequently, extra care was taken to ensure that every gun was fitted with a trigger lock and kept in locked show cases. Customers were no longer handed guns or ammunition over the counter; upon purchase, the firearms were delivered to their homes.

Employee theft and shoplifting occurred. In 1915, for example, Gustave Touchard, Jr., a champion tennis player, was charged with stealing 48 dozen golf balls worth $288 from an A&F store on 36th Street. He had worked at the store as a manager of its sporting department. In 1923, a well-dressed woman was caught with 21 yards of Scotch tweed cloth hidden in the ulster (i.e., a bulky overcoat) she was wearing. The theft occurred a few weeks after two sisters who shopped at Macy's while carrying small dogs in their arms were caught with stolen items in their wide sleeves. In 1969, inventory shrinkage (from bookkeeping errors, internal theft, and shoplifting) totaled $1 million (up from between $600,000 and $700,000 the previous year). This problem contributed to the retailer's pretax loss for the year.[13]

Between 1970 and 1976, A&F continued to incur financial losses. In the fiscal year ending January 31, 1976, A&F incurred a net loss of $1 million on sales of $23.8 million.[14] The loss followed annual deficits ranging from $287,000 to $540,000 every year since 1970.[15] A&F's best year had been in 1968 when it reported pretax earnings of $866,000 on sales of $28 million.[16] Managers began to search for a possible buyer of the firm. No one was seriously interested.

In August 1976, A&F filed for bankruptcy. It held a sale to liquidate its inventory of $8.5 million. A sign in the retailer's Madison Avenue store read: "They say we're stuffy so we're moving the stuff out at tremendous reductions on all floors."[17] After the sale, the stores were closed. A&F's difficulties were attributed to competition from mass marketers (e.g., Hermann's World of Sporting Goods) who sold discounted merchandise, to the lack of professional managers and leadership turnover (the retailer had three different CEOs in the preceding six years), to high overhead costs, and to fewer customers who could afford its exotic, high-priced items.

In 1978, Oshman's Sporting Goods of Houston acquired A&F's name, trademark, and mailing list for $1.5 million. A&F's slogan was changed from "The Finest Sporting Goods Store in the World" to "The Adventure Goes On." The new owners had studied A&F's business model for two years. According to its president, Jerry L. Nanna, "We examined the original business, took it apart and retained the good qualities. We also retained some of the legendary old products that Abercrombie had and expanded their variety. But we dropped most of the tailored clothing that proved to be a drain."[18] The owners believed that they could bring A&F up-to-date to the styles of the 1980s. The chain expanded to 12 stores; sales of $20 million were expected in 1982.

In 1988, The Limited acquired 25 A&F stores and its catalog business for $47 million from Oshman's. Two additional stores were closed. At the time, The Limited operated a chain of 3,100 stores that sold women's apparel. In 1992, Michael Jeffries became president and chief executive of A&F, a retailing unit of The Limited. A new format was introduced. The chain began to carry casual, classic American clothes for men and women in the twenties. A&F became one of The Limited's fastest-growing divisions. The number of stores grew from 40 in 1992 to 113 in 1996. Its sales increased at a compounded annual rate of 40.3 percent during those same years.[19] In 1996, The Limited spun off A&F. Jeffries stayed on as CEO.

Senior Executives and Corporate Governance

Michael Jeffries got his start in retailing at an early age when he helped his father select the toys that were sold in the family's chain of party supply stores. He also enjoyed organizing and designing the window and counter displays. Born in 1944, Jeffries received a BA in economics from Claremont McKenna College and an MBA from Columbia University. He entered the management training program of Abraham & Straus (a New York department store that belonged to Federated) in 1968. From there, he went on to start a women's clothing store, Alcott & Andrews, which later failed. He worked in merchandising at Paul Harris, which also went bankrupt.[20]

In his flip-flops, polo shirt, and torn jeans, Jeffries embodied the casual look of A&F more than anyone else. He made sure that A&F's apparel reflected the lifestyles of college students. Teams of designers, merchandisers and marketers visited college campuses once a month to talk to students and find out what they like and how they spend their time. On one of those visits in 1998, Jeffries saw someone wearing nylon wind pants. A&F was quick to make its own version of the pants. Tom Lennox, A&F's director of corporate communications and investor relations once said, "We just believe that it is our job to position Abercrombie & Fitch as the coolest brand, the brand with the greatest quality, the aspirational brand of college students."[21]

A&F's success did not make Jeffries complacent. He was quoted as saying, "Every morning I'm scared. I'm superstitious. I come in every morning being afraid to look a yesterday's figures, and I want everyone else to have that same kind of fear."[22] He worked hard and constantly traveled from store to store. He was always thinking of ways to extend the A&F brand. Jeffries had a few eccentric habits. He went through revolving doors twice, parked his black Porsche at an odd angle in the company's parking lot, and wore the same lucky shoes when he reviewed financial reports.[23] It was almost as if he felt that his firm's good fortune could change at any time. Perhaps he realized that his primary target audience—teenagers—was fickle and that trendy apparel quickly became outdated.

Between 2003 and 2006, A&F had three different chief financial officers and two different chief operating officers. The latter position remained unfilled. In July 2003, Wesley McDonald, who had been A&F's CFO for four years, left to become CFO of Kohl's Corporation. He was replaced in February 2004 by Susan Riley who had held CFO positions at Mount Sinai Medical Center, Dial Corporation, and Tambrands Incorporated. In August 2005, Riley resigned for family reasons and returned to her home in New York City. Michael Kramer became A&F's new CFO. He had been the CFO of the retail unit of Apple Incorporated. He also had retail experience working for Gateway Inc., The Limited, and Pizza Hut. He had a BA in business administration and accounting from Kansas State University and was a certified public accountant.

Seth Johnson was A&F's COO between 2000 and 2004. Before that, he had been its CFO. Johnson was credited with keeping costs down by reducing payroll and travel expenses. He was responsible for installing computer systems to help A&F's distribution system run more efficiently. He had aspired to a CEO position and was offered such an opportunity at Pacific Sunwear of California, Inc. Robert Singer, the former CFO of Gucci, became the next president and COO in 2004. After 15 months on the job, Singer resigned to become the CEO of Barilla Holding SpA. Disagreements about international expansion were cited as the reason for his departure. Singer's duties were divided between John Lough (executive vice president of logistics and store operations) and Michael Kramer (CFO). Search for a replacement began.

Unlike other retailers, A&F did not have division presidents for its brands. Merchants from different businesses reported directly to the CEO. They did not work within a particular brand. Instead, they led categories (e.g., denim or outerwear). They were responsible for these brands across each of the company's divisions. That way, their expertise and knowledge could best be leveraged and exploited.

A&F encountered criticism from shareholders regarding executive compensation and the composition of its board of directors. In February 2005, shareholders charged A&F directors with wasting corporate assets by paying CEO Jeffries $22.9 million in salary, bonus and stock options. The company settled the law suit and Jeffries agreed to reduce his $12 million bonus to $6 million and to forgo new stock options for two years. The bonus was contingent on meeting specific earnings targets. Jeffries would receive the full $6 million bonus if A&F's earnings per share increased by 13.5 percent between February 1, 2005, and January 31, 2009.[24]

Shareholders also expressed concern over the independence of A&F's board of directors. John W. Kessler, chair of the compensation committee, had financial ties to the retailer. As chair of a real estate development firm owned by The Limited's CEO Wexner (Jeffries former boss), Kessler sold the land upon which A&F built its headquarters in 1999. He received a fee for finding the site. Kessler's son-in-law, Thomas D. Lennox, was A&F's director of investor relations and communications. Samuel Shahid, president and creative director of the advertising agency that received $2 million a year from A&F for its services, was a board member until May 2005. He was replaced by Allan A. Tuttle, an attorney for the luxury goods maker, Gucci Group. Although Tuttle did not have financial ties to A&F, he was a friend of Robert Singer, who at the time was A&F's president and COO.

A&F denied wrongdoing and settled the lawsuits to "avoid the uncertainty, harm and expense of litigation."[25] As part of its agreement with shareholders, A&F promised to provide more public information about executive compensation and to add independent members to its board and compensation committee.

A&F faced a formal investigation by the U.S. Securities and Exchange Commission regarding insider selling of stock. In June and July of 2005, when A&F's stock price was high, Jeffries sold 1.6 million shares worth $120 million. In August, share prices declined after the company announced it would miss Wall Street expectations regarding its second quarter earnings. A&F was also sued for making false and misleading statements of monthly and quarterly sales figures and for failing to disclose that profit margins were declining and inventory rising. The company announced that it was cooperating with the SEC and that the shareholder lawsuit had no merit.

Store Concept and Marketing Strategies

When customers walked into an original A&F clothing store in a local mall and they were often greeted by a young, handsome salesperson wearing the latest fashion in casual attire. The store's lights were dimmed and posters of attractive models wearing its trademark cargo pants and polo shirts adorned the walls. In some stores, chandeliers made of fake deer antlers or whitewashed moose antlers hung from the ceilings. Apparel was neatly folded and placed on long wooden tables. The retailer's hip, trendy, and "All-American" look was reinforced by the playing of loud dance music and the spraying of men's cologne. The intent was to provide a sensual experience that appealed to a shopper's sense of sight, smell, and sound. According to marketing expert, Pam Danziger, "Shoppers are rejecting the old concept of 'hunting and gathering' shopping in favor of a more involved, interesting, dynamic retail experience."[26] A&F was able to successfully implement an exciting store format.

Every A&F store was designed according to one of several specific models created at company headquarters. The retailer wanted complete control over its brand and to communicate a consistent message in all stores across the nation. Jeffries himself made sure the model stores were "perfect."[27] The prototypes were photographed and sent to the store managers of the individual outlets for replication. Jeffries was known for paying attention to every detail. He visited stores and made sure that the clothes were folded correctly. He approved the background music to be played in the stores and selected the appropriate volume level for all locations. He even gave suggestions on how mannequins could be made to look more rugged and masculine.

A&F's Web site (http://www.abercrombie.com) was created to match the feel and aura of its stores as much as possible. It featured striking black-and-white images of young people in outdoor settings. Many of the male models were shirtless, and the female models wore skimpy shorts. Web surfers could view film clips and download wall paper while listening to sensuous music. According to Forbes magazine, the Web site's best feature was the photo gallery showing images of the models that made A&F famous. Its worst feature was that its line of clothing was not shown by the models.[28]

A&F extended its successful store concept and marketing ideas to its newer brand name stores, Hollister Company and Ruehl. Hollister stores were designed to look like beach houses with faux porches and house style layouts. The name came from a span of gated coastal property north of Santa Barbara where surfers liked to hang out. Surfboards leaned against the store walls. Fans blew constantly to mimic the breeze coming in from the ocean. Shoppers could sit in comfortable chairs and read surfing, skateboarding, and snowboarding magazines.

Ruehl (rhymes with "cool") stores imitated the architecture of Greenwich Village with red-brick facades, iron fences, flowerboxes, and small windows. They looked like brownstones. Ruehl was the name of a fictitious German family who had come to America in the 1850s and opened a leather-goods shop in Greenwich Village. Couches and armchairs were available for lounging. Copies of the *Village Voice* and *New York Times* were found on coffee tables. Jazz music played. Signs were not posted outside. The shopper was expected to stumble upon the store just as if he or she were walking in a city neighborhood; the great "find" would be spread via word-of-mouth.[29] Experts reported that young people want to be part of a brand story.[30]

A&F had an enviable target market. It catered to teenagers, whose population in the United States was expanding. In 2003, 32 million teens lived in the United States. This number was expected to rise to 35 million by 2010. Moreover, teens spent approximately $170 billion on goods and services in 2002, with one-third going toward apparel.[31] Spending in 2005 was lower at $159 billion.[32] Teen retailing was considered to be somewhat recession-proof. Although teens worked for low wages, they had multiple revenue streams—babysitting, paper routes, part-time jobs, and assistance from parents.[33] They usually did not have financial obligations (no mortgages or bills to pay.) Parents, too, were more likely to spend money on their children than on themselves.

A&F's busy seasons were spring and fall. Forty percent of its sales were realized in the spring and 60 percent in the fall (during the back-to-school and holiday season periods). It hired extra employees during those times. A&F was able to maintain its high prices without resorting to sales and discounts. It was afraid that cutting prices for a big sale would cheapen its brand. A&F saved money on promotions, relying frequently on word-of-mouth advertising. The retailer claimed that it spent less than 2 percent of net sales on marketing in 2004.[34] It also kept down its administrative expenses and negotiated lower fees from its suppliers. High prices and low costs comprised a formula that clearly worked.

In its A&F stores, the retailer tried to introduce two or three new items in its stores every week. It launched a new men's line, Ezra Fitch, which featured high-quality apparel made from cashmere, velvet, and leather. A&F cultivated brand loyalty. Shoppers could join Hollister's Club Cali and receive gift cards based on how much they spent. Invitations to after-hours parties with new bands at the stores were also available. Instead of marking down items the day after Thanksgiving in 2004 (the start of the busy Christmas shopping season), preferred customers who spent $1,000 a year or more were invited to a live concert given by Ryan Cabrera. The concert was also shown on big screen televisions in 50 other Hollister stores around the nation.

A&F generated controversy. Adults often reacted negatively to its catalogues, revealing clothes, and racy slogans (for some examples, go to http://www.nytimes.com/2004/03/23/national/23WVA.html?ex=1395378000&en=824d455730751a9c&ei=5007&partner=USERLAND, http://news.bbc.co.uk/1/hi/world/asia-pacific/1938914.stm, and http://www.sptimes.com/2005/11/05/Floridian/It_s_grrrl_power_vs_A.shtml). Some teenagers, however, might have responded positively to its advertising in a show of rebellion against the traditional values and lifestyles of their parents. Teens were reluctant to shop in the same stores as their parents. Some observers believed that A&F purposely created controversy and engaged in risky practices to attract attention, draw in shoppers, and sell more products. As an analyst with Midwest Research in Cleveland remarked, "Abercrombie is not a company that really cares about backing away from controversy. They use controversy as a free advertising gig and are successful in driving traffic into the stores."[35]

Here is a list of A&F's controversial moves:

- In July 1998, a story entitled, "Drinking 101," appeared in an A&F Fall back-to-school catalog. It featured recipes for alcoholic beverages and a game for helping students decide which drink to mix. After being criticized by Mothers Against Drunk Driving (MADD), A&F deleted the story and sent postcards to students who received the publication by mail reminding them to "be responsible, be 21, and don't ever drink and drive."[36]
- In April 2002, A&F sold a line of T-shirts with Asian cartoon characters and matching ethnic slogans: "Wong Brothers Laundry Service, Two Wongs Can Make It White": "Wok-N-Bowl"; "Buddha Bash, Get Your Buddha on the Floor." The retailer took the T-shirts off store shelves after protests from college students from campuses around the country. A&F's spokesperson, Hampton Carney apologized, saying "It is not, and never has been, our intention to offend anyone. These were designed to add humor and levity to our fashion line. Since some of our customers were offended by these T-shirts, we removed them from all our stores."[37]
- In May 2002, A&F sold thong underwear for girls 10 years and over with sexual phrases such as "eye candy" and "wink, wink" printed on the front. Family-advocacy groups and Christian organizations protested. The line was recalled in Washington, D.C., area stores.[38]
- In December 2003, under heavy criticism from parents and consumer groups, A&F decided to stop publishing its provocative catalog, *A&F Quarterly*. Its holiday issue featured nude models and articles about group sex and masturbation.[39]
- In March 2004, Bob Wise, governor of West Virginia asked A&F to pull from its shelves T-shirts with the slogan, "It's All Relative in West Virginia." Wise explained that the slogan was offensive because it referred to a stereotype that West Virginia was a state that condoned incest.[40]
- In October 2004, officials of USA Gymnastics sought the immediate removal of a T-shirt depicting a male gymnast performing on the still rings alongside the phrase, "L is for Loser." They wrote a letter to Jeffries saying its members would be encouraged to withdraw their support of the chain.[41]
- In May 2005, A&F quietly pulled a line of T-shirts from its stores with slogans that read: "I Brews Easily," "Candy Is Dandy But Liquor Is Quicker," and "Don't Bother I'm Not Drunk Yet." The company was criticized for glorifying underage drinking and promoting a lifestyle that was illegal for its target audience. Pressure came from the International Institute for Alcohol Awareness, a public advocacy group that worked to reduce underage drinking. This time, A&F responded to criticism before the issue was reported in national newspapers.[42]
- In November 2005, 24 participants in the Allegheny County Girls as Grantmakers program, organized a "girlcott" of A&F stores to protest its "attitude t-shirts" that featured such slogans as: "Who needs brains when you have these?"; "Blondes Are Adored, Brunettes Are Ignored"; "All Men Like Tig Old Bitties." Other groups, such as Peace Project, an antidiscrimination student club in Norwalk, Connecticut, and the Women & Girls Foundation of Southwestern Pennsylvania, joined in. A&F pulled two of the more offensive T-shirts and its executives agreed to meet with several of the protestors. The girls suggested that the retailer print more appropriate slogans such as: "All This and Brains to Match" and "Your Future Boss." They hoped the firm would launch such a line and donate a portion of revenues to groups like theirs.[43]

Logistics and Supply Chain Management

A&F operated solely as a retailer. It assumed responsibility for creating and managing its brands. Unlike other businesses, A&F did not distribute its apparel and accessories through wholesale channels, through licensing, or through franchising. Abercrombie clothing could not be purchased in department stores or in discount stores. It could, however, be purchased online via the A&F's Web site. E-commerce transactions generated more than $100 million in business a year. [44]

During 2005, A&F purchased merchandise from approximately 246 factories and suppliers located around the globe, primarily in Southeast Asia and Central and South America. It did not source more than 50 percent of its apparel from any single factory or supplier. The design and development process for a garment took between six weeks to three months.[45] Retailers struggled to reduce this time so as not to get stuck with inventory of merchandise that lost its fashion appeal. A&F made the process more efficient by centralizing its design services at its New Albany headquarters, which reduced overseas travel of executives.

A&F also operated a distribution center in New Albany, Ohio. Merchandise was received and inspected and then distributed to stores via contract carriers. It was here that concepts for new divisions were created and prototypes for new stores were constructed. The new formats were kept secret until their launch dates.

A&F launched an anticounterfeiting program in an effort to protect its brand and prevent low-cost manufacturers in Asian factories from making imitations of its products. Local authorities seized 300,000 pairs of fake Abercrombie jeans (worth $20 million) in a raid of a Chinese warehouse in 2006. The retailer hired a former FBI agent to head a 10-person department to conduct investigations overseas and to work with foreign authorities.[46]

A&F began experimenting with radio frequency identification (RFID) technology in its Rhuel stores that sold higher-priced and higher-quality merchandise. Tags that could be monitored electronically were sewn into the seams of garments. The location of the garments could be tracked, enabling an employee to quickly return to the shelves garments that had been left in dressing rooms or placed in the wrong spots on the floor. The technology could be used to prevent theft and to differentiate between authentic products and counterfeit goods.

A&F's Financial Performance

In fiscal 2006, A&F achieved revenues of $3.32 billion, an increase of 19 percent from fiscal 2005. Its net income rose to $422.2 million, an increase of 26.4 percent from fiscal 2005 (see Exhibit 4). Earnings per share rose to $4.59 from $3.66. A&F opened 93 new stores and added 11,000 employees to its payroll. It had no long-term debt. It repurchased 1.8 million shares of common stock for $103.3 million in fiscal 2005, but it did not make additional purchases in fiscal 2006. It paid dividends of 70 cents a share for a total of $61.6 million.

Managers at the retailer considered Abercrombie & Fitch to be a maturing brand with opportunities for expansion in prime locations in the United States and with greater potential overseas. The abercrombie brand might grow to 250 stores and seek locations in Canada. Hollister was seen as the fastest-growing brand while Ruehl was building a strong customer base but still needed to prove itself (see Exhibit 5 for sales by brand).[47]

Exhibit 4 Five-Year Summary of A&F's Financial Performance

	2006*	2005	2004	2003	2002
Operating Revenues (in thousands)	$3,318,158	$2,784,711	$2,021,253	$1,707,810	$1,595,757
Gross Profit (in thousands)	$2,209,006	$1,851,416	$1,341,224	$1,083,170	$980,555
Operating Income (in thousands)	$658,090	$542,738	$347,635	$331,180	$312,315
Net Income (in thousands)	$422,186	$333,986	$216,376	$204,830	$194,754
Earnings per Share—Diluted	$4.59	$3.66	$2.28	$2.06	$1.94
Dividends Declared per Share	$.70	$.60	$.50	0	0
Total Assets (in thousands)	$2,248,067	$1,789,718	$1,386,791	$1,401,369	$1,190,615
Capital Expenditures (in thousands)	$403,476	$256,422	$185,065	$159,777	$145,662
Long-Term Debt (in thousands)	0	0	0	0	0
Shareholders' Equity (in thousands)	$1,405,297	$995,117	$669,326	$857,764	$736,307
Number of Stores	944	851	788	700	597
Gross Square Feet	6,693,000	6,025,000	5,590,000	5,016,000	4,358,000
Number of Employees (average)	80,100	69,100	48,500	30,200	22,000

*Fiscal 2006 is a 53-week year.

Sources: 2203–2007, A&F 10-K.

Exhibit 5 Three-Year Summary of A&F's Financial Performance by Brand

	2006*	2005	2004
Net Sales by Brand (in thousands)	**$3,318,158**	**$2,784,711**	**$2,021,253**
Abercrombie & Fitch	$1,515,123	$1,424,013	$1,210,222
abercrombie	$ 405,820	$ 344,938	$ 227,204
Hollister	$1,363,233	$ 999,212	$ 579,687
Ruehl**	$ 33,982	$ 16,548	$ 4,140

	2006*	2005	2004
Increase (Decrease) in Comparable Store Sales ***	**2%**	**26%**	**2%**
Abercrombie & Fitch	(4)%	18%	(1)%
abercrombie	10%	54%	1%
Hollister	5%	29%	13%
Ruehl**	14%	N/A	N/A

	2006*	2005	2004
Net Retail Sales per Average Store (in thousands)	**$3,533**	**$3,284**	**$2,569**
Abercrombie & Fitch	$3,945	$3,784	$3,103
abercrombie	$2,251	$1,957	$1,241
Hollister	$3,732	$3,442	$2,740
Ruehl**	$3,248	$2,903	$1,255

*Fiscal 2006 is a 53-week year.

**Data for Ruehl reflect the activity of 14 stores open in fiscal 2006, 8 stores open in fiscal 2005, and 4 stores open in fiscal 2004. Year-to-year comparisons may not be meaningful.

***A store is included in comparable store sales when it has been open as the same brand at least one year and its square footage has not been expanded or reduced by more than 20 percent within the past year.

Sources: 2005–2007, A&F 10-K.

A&F's Socially Responsible Practices

A&F held fund-raising activities that benefited local charities and communities. Every Christmas holiday season, shoppers were invited into its stores to have their picture taken with its models. The $1 fee was matched by the retailer and the proceeds donated to foundations such as Toys for Tots or the Juvenile Diabetes Research Foundation. It held the A&F Challenge, an action-packed outdoor event at its headquarters in New Albany, Ohio. Participants, who paid an entry fee of $25, went on a 20-mile cycling tour, a 5K inline skating tour, and a 5K run. They heard live music from a band, enjoyed food and drinks and received a T-shirt. All proceeds went to the Center for Child and Family Advocacy in Columbus, Ohio. Its largest donation—$10 million—went to a Children's Hospital in

Columbus in June 2006. The hospital's new trauma center would bear the A&F name.

A&F also sometimes got involved in issues at the supplier end of its business. In 2004, it joined a boycott of Australian merino wool in an effort to force ranchers to end their cruel procedure of "mulesing" that protected lambs from flies. Even though A&F did not purchase much Australian wool, wool producers feared that the retailer would set a precedent and that other retailers would soon join the boycott. They agreed to end the practice by 2010 or sooner.[48]

Organizational Culture and Human Resource Management

A&F's core corporate values were "nature, friendships, and having fun."[49] The values were reflected in everything from the decor of the retailer's stores and the casual attire of its employees to the layout of A&F's headquarters in New Albany, Ohio, and to the firm's advertising messages. If no customers were in the store to serve, employees might throw a football to one another in the store. The retailer's homepage on the World Wide Web featured a treehouse that could be downloaded as wallpaper.

A&F's headquarters, built in 2001, was situated in the woods along Blacklick Creek in New Albany, Ohio. Its campus-like setting served as a continual reminder to employees that the firm's target audience was college students. It was also designed to encourage team work and creativity. Instead of using desks in individual cubicles, employees engaged in collaborative work situated at long tables in doorless conference rooms. Employees could walk along paths in the woods to relax, think, or seek inspiration for a new idea. The headquarters had no executive suite. Jeffries had no desk or office. He also worked in a conference room with a view of the grounds from large windows.

Employees enjoyed healthy meals that included roast chicken, international dishes, salads, fruit juices, and gourmet coffees in the full-service cafeteria. They traveled from building to building on scooters and were allowed to bring their skateboards. A bonfire pit provided the atmosphere of an outdoors summer camp. Employees worked out in the gym. One of the architects said, "A&F wants to give back to the people who work there. That's why they can go to that rusty barn the first thing in the morning, or get sweaty in the gym and then go to work, have a great meal and then go back to work again. It reinforces the idea that this is community."[50]

Store managers visited nearby fraternities and sororities to recruit sales people or "brand representatives." They were encouraged to ask attractive shoppers in their stores if they wanted to apply for a sales position. Lennox, A&F's investor relations and communications director, acknowledged that the firm liked to hire job candidates who looked great. "Brand representatives are ambassadors to the brand. We want to hire brand representatives that will represent the Abercrombie & Fitch brand with natural classic American style, look great while exhibiting individuality, project the brand and themselves with energy and enthusiasm, and make the store a warm, inviting place that provides a social experience for the customer," he said.[51] The company ran a manager-in-training program for seniors and graduates. Promotion to store manager could occur one year after completing the training.

Brand representatives were expected to adhere to a dress code outlined in an Abercrombie Associate's Handbook. Hair was to be neatly combed and attractive; makeup was to be worn to enhance natural features and create a fresh, natural appearance; fingernails were not to extend more than 1/4 inch beyond the tip of the finger and nail polish was to be a natural color; mustaches, goatees and beards were unacceptable; jewelry was to be simple and classic (only women were allowed to wear earrings as long as they wore no more than two earrings in each ear and each earring was no larger than a dime and did not dangle).[52]

In 2000, the California Department of Industrial Relations received complaints from several A&F employees who said that they were forced to buy and wear the company's clothes on the job. One woman in another part of the country later claimed that she spent more on clothes for work than she earned at the store. Such company policy might have violated a state work uniform law that required employees to supply the clothing when they wanted workers to wear specific apparel. In 2003, A&F settled the lawsuit in California for $2.2 million without admitting wrongdoing. Employees received reimbursements ranging from $180 to $490 depending on their job status and the amount of money spent on clothing.[53] The case spurred other similar lawsuits across the state and the rest of the nation against The Limited, The Gap, Chico's, and Polo Ralph Lauren. In some states, lawyers used the federal Fair Labor Standards Act that required employers to pay minimum wage to argue that sales associates ended up with less than minimum wage after spending their earnings on store clothing.

A&F's legal problems were only just beginning. In July 2003, two former A&F employees filed a lawsuit accusing the company of failing to pay overtime wages when they were required to work 50–60 hours a week. The plaintiffs claim that they were sales associates, with no management responsibilities, but were classified as managers so that the retailer could avoid paying overtime. According to the Federal Fair Labor Standards Act and the Ohio Minimum Fair Wage Standards Act, nonexempt employees must be paid time and a half for work in excess of 40 hours a week.

Exhibit 6 Summary of Workplace Discrimination Acts in the United States

a. Title VII of the Civil Rights Act of 1964 makes discrimination based on race, color, religion, sex, and natural origin, illegal. It applies to employers with 15 or more employees. Before a plaintiff can file a lawsuit, he or she must file a charge with the Equal Employment Opportunity Commission within 180 days of the discriminatory act. The EEOC will conduct an initial investigation and will attempt to reconcile the parties. If the EEOC decides not to sue, it will issue a right-to-sue letter, giving the complaining party 90 days to file a lawsuit on her own. A charging party can request the EEOC to issue a right-to-sue letter 180 days after filing the charge with the EEOC.

b. The Americans with Disabilities Act of 1990 prohibits discrimination against the disabled. It applies to employers with 15 or more employees. *Disability* is broadly defined. The same EEOC procedures must be followed under this act as with a Title VII action as discussed in part (a).

c. The Age Discrimination in Employment Act of 1967 prohibits discrimination against employees who are more than 40 years old. It pertains to employers with 20 or more employees. The complainant must file a charge with the EEOC but can file a lawsuit after waiting only 60 days after filing with the EEOC.

d. The Civil Rights Act of 1866, 42 U.S.C. Section 1981, protects against racial discrimination. This statute does not require any filing with the EEOC and applies to all employers, regardless of number of employees. An employer's practice is illegal if it treats one protected group of employees more harshly than others, unless the employer can prove the practice was justified because of "business necessity." This act allows for unlimited compensatory and punitive damages as well as reimbursement of legal expenses.

Source: D. Kolber, 2005, Knowledge of discrimination laws vital, *Atlanta Business Chronicle,* http://atlanta.bizjournals.com/atlanta/stories/2005/05/30/smallb7.html, May 27. For more information, go to http://www.eeoc.gov/.

In June 2003, lawyers for nine plaintiffs filed a lawsuit against the retailer for discriminating against minorities in its hiring practices and job placement. It allegedly cultivated an "overwhelmingly white work force" and steered minority applicants into less visible jobs.[54] Former A&F employees appeared on CBS's television program *60 Minutes* and said that A&F was interested in hiring employees who fit a certain look. Anthony Ocampo worked at an Abercrombie store during his Christmas break from Stanford University. When he returned to get a summer job, he was told that he could not be rehired because the store already had too many Filipinos working there. Eduardo Gonzalez, another Stanford University student who was Latino, was told that he could only work as in the store's stock room or as part of the overnight crew. At Banana Republic, he was asked if he was applying for a management position. Carla Grubb, an African-American student at California State University at Bakersfield, felt she was not treated fairly because she was scheduled to work only during closing times and was asked to wash the front windows, vacuum, and clean the mannequins.

In November 2003, another lawsuit was filed against A&F on behalf of a New Jersey woman who claimed that her application for a sales-associate position was denied because she was African-American. A&F denied that it discriminated against minorities. It claimed that minorities represented 13 percent of all its store associates (which exceeded national averages). The U.S. Equal Employment Opportunity Commission also initiated a lawsuit, claiming that A&F violated parts of the Civil Rights Act of 1964 (see Exhibit 6 for a summary of relevant laws and legal procedures). Store managers reported that they were instructed to discard job applications if the candidates did not possess the right look.

In November 2004, A&F paid $50 million (including legal fees) to settle the discrimination lawsuits. It agreed to hire a vice president of diversity; provide training in diversity and inclusion to its employees and managers; increase the number of minority employees in sales and store management positions; enhance its compliance and oversight processes; and use more minority models in its advertising. The retailer promised that within two years its sales force would be 9 percent African-Americans; 9 percent Latinos; its current percentage of Asians; and 53 percent women.[55] A&F was told to stop recruiting from predominantly white fraternities and sororities. It agreed to hire 25 full-time diversity recruiters who would seek new hires from historically black colleges, minority job fairs, and minority recruiting events. Michael Jeffries issued a statement: "We have, and always have had, no tolerance for discrimination. We decided to settle this suit because we felt that a long, drawn-out dispute would have been harmful to the company and distracting to management."[56]

Todd Corley became A&F's new vice president of diversity. Due to his efforts, A&F established a $300,000 grant for scholarships for the United Negro College Fund; became a sponsor of the Organization of Chinese Americans' College Leadership Summit; became a sponsor of the National Black MBA Association; and offered internships for minority college juniors seeking retail-management careers through Inroads, Incorporated.

A&F's Future

Looking ahead, A&F was likely to face increased competition. One of its direct rivals, American Eagle Outfitters, was able to outperform A&F in terms of profitability and assume the number one rank (compared to A&F's third rank) among U.S. publicly traded apparel companies in 2007 as listed by *Apparel Magazine*. Newcomers to the specialty apparel industry, as well as large department stores, sought to imitate A&F's product offerings. Metropark, for example, a West Coast chain for 20- to 35-year-old shoppers, opened its fifteenth store in Atlanta, Georgia. It planned to open an additional 50 stores by 2007. The retailer sold brand name casual apparel made by such designers as True Religion and Joe's Jeans. It also tried to create a night club-like atmosphere in its stores with flat screen televisions playing music videos and a lounge offering energy drinks and magazines.

Department stores, too, began to diversify their lines by stocking merchandise from new suppliers and by promoting their own in-house labels. Oved Apparel launched Company 81 in 2005 as "an Abercrombie for department stores."[57] It began to sell distressed denim, chinos, shorts, golf jackets, blazers, and graphic t-shirts at the wholesale level. It provided department stores with in-store signage and imagery from its advertising campaign to complement its merchandise. Federated Department stores, which operated Macy's and Bloomingdales, created an in-house label called, "American Rag." Its merchandise was similar in style to A&F's but priced more moderately.

As if sensing the encroachment of competitors, A&F began an unusual effort to improve its customer service. In the past, brand representatives acted more like models than salespeople. They were known for their snobbish disregard of shoppers. They did not talk to customers until they were within five feet of each other.[58] Some customers felt intimidated. Under COO Singer, store greeters were positioned in the entrance to each store and salespeople were posted in every section. A vice president of training was hired to work with store staff. The number of employees was increased, and hours of store operations were extended. The added attention helped reduce shrinkage of merchandise.[59] Nonetheless, progress in customer service may have been derailed by the departure of Singer from the company.

A&F also needed to be ever vigilant regarding the needs and preferences of its target markets. Teenagers were perceived as being fickle. According to experts on the reactions of millennials to pop culture, they were difficult to influence because they thought more independently and changed their minds more frequently than previous generations. They would find the "emphasis on the physicality of models" in A&F advertisements unappealing.[60] The emerging trend toward ethical consumption was also something to be watched. Young people began to purchase food products and clothing with "Fair Trade" labels. They were committed, for example, to purchasing coffee that was organically grown from suppliers who paid bean pickers higher wages than the going rate. They bought T-shirts that were not made in overseas sweatshops.

The challenges for A&F executives in 2007 and beyond were to anticipate competitor moves, to improve customer service, and to maintain consumer loyalty. They needed to hire talented top managers who could work well alongside CEO Jeffries. These domestic imperatives came at a critical time for the retailer. It was about to expand further into the European and Asian markets by opening stores in Italy, France, Germany, Spain, Denmark, Sweden, and Japan. Pamela Quintiliano, a WR Hambrecht retail analyst, gave the expansion plan a nod of approval: "Abercrombie is an incredibly strong brand name, and there's a hunger for American brands around the world."[61]

Notes

1. J. E. Palmierie & D. Moin, 2005, A&F hits Fifth Avenue fray, *DNR 35*, November 14, 4.
2. D. Penny, 2005, The Abercrombie report, *New York 38*, November 21, 6.
3. 2007, The Apparel top 50, *Apparel Magazine*, 48(11), July, 12, 20.
4. M. Souers & M. Normand, 2006, Specialty retailers demonstrate resilience in face of adversity, *Standard & Poor's Industry Surveys: Retailing: Specialty*, January 12.
5. J. Covert, 2007, Shoppers held back in July; retailers' weak sales show impact of tumult in the housing market, *Wall Street Journal*, August 10, A2.
6. M. Souers & J. DeFoe, 2007, Specialty retailers experience mixed results in 2007, *Standard & Poor's Industry Surveys: Retailing: Specialty*, August 2.
7. Ibid.
8. A&F, 10-K; J. Sheban, 2006, Oh, Canada! *Knight Ridder Tribune Business News*. February 26, 1.
9. J. Sheban, 2006, Abercrombie & Fitch plans fifth concept, *Knight Ridder Tribune Business News*, November 18, 1.
10. D. Molin, 2007, J. Crew mission: Being best, not biggest, *WWD*, 193(125), June 13, 2.
11. 1923, Rapid growth in specialized shop trade Madison Avenue in the Forties The Centre, *New York Times*, February 18. Retrieved April 21, 2006, from ProQuest Historical Newspapers database.
12. 1965, New face for fashion at Abercrombie & Fitch, *New York Times*, September 11, 14. Retrieved April 21, 2006, from ProQuest Historical Newspapers database.

13. 1970, Changes weighed for Abercrombie, *New York Times*, September, 70. Retrieved April 21, 2006, from ProQuest Historical Newspapers database.
14. 1976, Abercrombie reports loss of $1 million in fiscal year, *New York Times*, August 26, 68. Retrieved April 21, 2006, from ProQuest Historical Newspapers database.
15. R. Hanley, 1976, Abercrombie & Fitch Put Up for Sale, *New York Times*, July 20, 1976. Retrieved April 21, 2006, from ProQuest Historical Newspapers database.
16. I. Barmash, 1976, Abercrombie & Fitch in bankruptcy step, *New York Times*, August 7, 47. Retrieved April 21, 2006, from ProQuest Historical Newspapers database.
17. C. G. Fraser, 1976, "Stuffy" Abercrombie's gets sale relief, *New York Times*, August 29, 47. Retrieved April 21, 2006, from ProQuest Historical Newspapers database.
18. I. Barmash, 1982, New guise for Abercrombies, *New York Times*, November 9, D1. Retrieved April 21, 2006, from ProQuest Historical Newspapers database.
19. D. Canedy, 1996, After unbuttoning its image, a retail legend comes to market, *New York Times*, September, F3.
20. R. Berner, 2005, Flip-flops, torn jeans—and control, *BusinessWeek*, May 30, 68.
21. M. Cole, 2004, Facing a brave new world, *Apparel*, 45, July, 22.
22. M. Pledger, 1999, Abercrombie & Fitch focuses on American college audience, *The Plain Dealer*, June 22, 2S.
23. Berner, Flip-flops.
24. 2005, Abercrombie CEO benefits settlement OKd, *Los Angeles Times*, June 15.
25. 2005, Abercrombie CEO benefits.
26. M. Wilson, 2006, The "pop" factor, *Chain Store Age*, 82, April, 78.
27. B. Denizet-Lewis, 2006, The man behind Abercrombie & Fitch, *Salon*, http://www.salon.com/mwt/feature/2006/01/24/jeffries/index_np.html, January 24.
28. Web site reviews: Abercrombie & Fitch, Forbes.com, accessed May 1, 2006, from http://www.forbes.com/bow/b2c/review.jhtml?id=6833.
29. J. Verdon. 2004, Abercrombie targets 20-somethings with coffeehouse-style store in Paramus, N.J., *Knight Ridder Tribune Business News*, September 17, 1.
30. C. Collins. 2006, Status of U.S. brands slips globally among teens, *The Christian Science Monitor*, February 16, 13.
31. J. Ablan, 2003, Trend setter, *Barron's*, 83, March 31, 21.
32. P. B. Erikson, 2006, Companies focus on youthful influence for prosperity, *Knight Ridder Tribune Business News*, April 16, 1.
33. J. Ablan, Trend setter; P. B. Erickson, Companies focus on youthful influence for prosperity.
34. Presentation at the Merrill Lynch Retailing Leaders & Household Products & Cosmetics Conference, March 25, 2005; accessed April 22, 2006, from http://www.abercrombie.com.
35. T. Turner, 2004, Retailer Abercrombie & Fitch angers West Virginia residents with new T-shirt, *Knight Ridder Tribune Business News*, March 24, 1.
36. 1998, Abercrombie & Fitch plans to delete drinking section, *Wall Street Journal*, July 30, 1.
37. G. Kim, 2002, Racism doesn't belong on T-shirts, *Knight Ridder Tribune Business News*, April 28, 1.
38. D. DeMarco, 2002, Abercrombie & Fitch pulls children's thong, *Knight Ridder Tribune Business News*, May 23, 1.
39. J. Caggiano, 2003, Abercrombie & Fitch drops racy publication, *Knight Ridder Tribune Business News*, December 11, 1.
40. T. Turner, Retailer Abercrombie & Fitch angers West Virginia residents with new T-shirt.
41. 2004, USA Gymnastics upset with Abercrombie & Fitch, *The Washington Post*, October 8, D2.
42. K. S. Shalett, 2005, Shamed off shelves, *Times-Picayune*, May 20, 1.
43. M. Haynes, 2005, "Girlcott" organizers meet with Abercrombie & Fitch execs over T-shirts, *Knight Ridder Tribune Business News*, December 6, 1.
44. 2005, Abercrombie & Fitch Co. at Banc of America Securities Consumer Conference, *Fair Disclosure Wire*, March 17.
45. K. Showalter, 2005, A&F readies $10 million expansion, *Business First of Columbus*, http://columbus.bizjournals.com/columbus/stories/2005/03/14/story5.html, March 11.
46. J. Sheban, 2006, Fighting fakes: Abercrombie enlists expert to help it combat counterfeiting, *Knight Ridder Tribune Business News*, February 3, 1.
47. 2006, A&F 10-K, 31.
48. J. Sheban, 2004, Abercrombie & Fitch's wool boycott helps end "mulesing" practice, *Knight Ridder Tribune Business News*, November 12, 1.
49. D. Gebolys, 2001, Inside Abercrombie & Fitch, *The Columbus Dispatch*, May 24, 1F.
50. K. Showalter, 2001, Abercrombie & Fitch: Campus reflects the true nature of New Albany firm's culture, *Business First of Columbus*, http://columbus.bizjournals.com/columbus/stories/2001/08/27/focus1.html?page=3, August 24.
51. S. Greenhouse, 2003, Going for the look, but risking discrimination, *New York Times*, July 13, 12.
52. B. Paynter, 2003, Don't hate me because I'm beautiful, *Kansas City Pitch Weekly*, September 4.
53. 2003, Abercrombie & Fitch settles dress code case, *Houston Chronicle*, June 25, 2.
54. T. Turner, 2003, Cincinnati suit charges Abercrombie & Fitch with failing to pay overtime, *Knight Ridder Tribune Business News*, July 9, 1.
55. J. Sheban, 2005, Abercrombie & Fitch: The face of change, *The Columbus Dispatch*, July 31, F1.
56. S. Greenhouse, 2004, Abercrombie & Fitch bias case is settled, *New York Times*, November 17, A16.
57. L. Bailey, 2005, The New South: Young men's & streetwear, *DNR*, 35, August 22, 94.
58. Paynter, Don't hate me because I'm beautiful.
59. S. Kang, 2005, Abercrombie & Fitch tries to be less haughty, more nice *Wall Street Journal*, June 17, B1.
60. V. Seckler, 2006, Brands' challenge: Bridging gap with young people, *WWD*, 77, April 12.
61. Sheban, Oh Canada!

Case 4

AMD vs. Intel: Competitive Challenges

Siddhartha Paul
ICFAI Business School

What can still hurt us the most, frankly, is Intel's antitrust practices. That's the largest obstacle for us to get where we need to go.

—Hector Ruiz,
Chairperson and CEO of AMD[1]

The competitive challenges between the top two chip makers Intel and AMD took on a new dimension due to different strategic initiatives of both companies. AMD, the second largest chip maker, challenged the market leader Intel with its server chips. Intel had faced stiff competition from the Opteron chip manufactured by AMD ever since its launch in 2003. AMD's revenue increased from $3.5 billion in 2003 to $5.8 billion in 2005 (see Exhibit 1). Moreover, in 2006, AMD announced its plan to acquire Array Technologies Incorporated (ATI) for $5.4 billion. The merger between AMD and ATI posed a threat and challenge to Intel. Still, AMD was worried about Intel's antitrust practices. AMD blamed Intel for its illegal discount program that resulted in AMD's PC market share drop in Japan. Therefore, analysts were skeptical about whether AMD could overcome Intel's monopolistic practices (see Appendix 1).

Company Background

AMD

AMD was founded by Jerry Sanders and seven friends on May 1, 1969. During its early years, the company's major products were outsourced from other companies that were redesigned and upgraded for better speed and efficiency. In 1975, AMD launched its first memory product—a random access memory (RAM)[2] chip known as Am9102. In the same year the company developed a reverse-engineered[3] version of 8080A standard processor. This product brought AMD into the microprocessor[4] arena. The company's business grew to $168 million by the end of 1975. During the 1980s, AMD ventured into the overseas market with the establishment of facilities in Singapore and Thailand. Since the rise in the personal computer industry, in the early 1980s, AMD played an important role by providing high-quality x86 processors.[5] In 1986, AMD launched the industry's first 1-million bit EPROM (erasable programmable read-only memory).[6] In the following year the company merged with Monolithic Memories,[7] the pioneer in field-programmable logic.[8]

Exhibit 1 Net Sales of AMD (in $ billions)

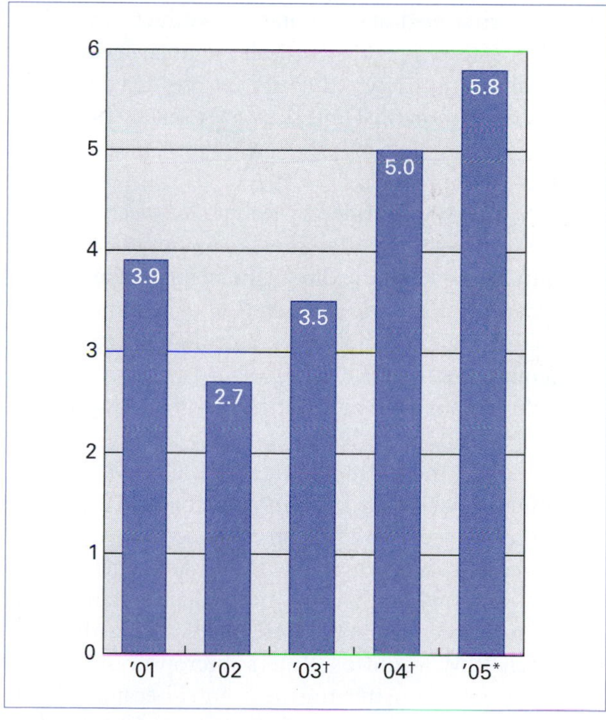

Source: http://annualreport.amd.com.

Since the early 1990s, AMD introduced various products, including microprocessors compatible with IBM computers, networking and communication chips, programmable logic devices, and high-performance memory. During the same period, AMD introduced new products in the microprocessor category including the AM386 and AM486. During the same period (1990), flash memory[9] took over the EEPROM (electrically erasable programmable read-only memory) market by serving as a nonvolatile[10] memory solution. AMD launched the first economically viable single-voltage flash memory device and, in 1993, established a joint venture with Fujitsu Limited[11] and formed Fujitsu AMD Semiconductor Limited, or Spansion. In 1994, AMD formed an alliance with Compaq Computer Corp. under which AMD's microprocessors were part of Compaq computers. The company released its AMD-K6 processors in 1997 and AMD Athlon processors in 1999. In February 2002, AMD acquired Alchemy Semiconductor,[12] which designed microprocessors for personal connectivity. In the following year, the company formed a new flash memory semiconductor joint venture with Fujitsu. Both the companies offered their flash memory solutions under the global brand name Spansion. In 2005, AMD introduced the dual core processor for desktop PCs. AMD achieved sales of $5.8 billion in the year 2005, which was an increase of 17 percent compared to 2004. AMD's business divisions consisted of computation products (microprocessors), memory products (flash memory devices), and personal connectivity solutions (embedded microprocessors for commercial and consumer markets).

INTEL

In 1968, Intel was founded by Robert Noyce and Gordon Moore as Integrated Electronics Corporation. During its initial years the company manufactured semiconductor[13] memory for mini computers and mainframe computers. In 1969, it launched the world's first metal oxide semiconductor (MOS)[14] static RAM, followed by the Schottky[15] bipolar 64-bit[16] static random access memory (SRAM)[17] chip. By 1970 the company became the market leader in the highly competitive DRAM,[18] SRAM, and ROM[19] market. In 1971, Intel introduced the world's first microprocessor. The company continued with its improvements and came up with the 8086 microprocessors in 1978, which became the industry standard. In 1981, Intel entered into a strategic alliance with IBM,[20] in which IBM would use Intel's microprocessor for its desktops models. After this deal, Intel became a dominant player in the desktop PC segment. In 1982, Intel continued to develop innovative products and launched the high-performance 16-bit microprocessor (80286). Further developments led to the 386 microprocessors and then the 486 microprocessors in 1989. Beginning in 1991, Intel started its brand building with the slogan "Intel Inside" to connect personal computers with the Intel microprocessor in users' minds. According to Dataquest,[21] Intel became the largest semiconductor supplier in 1992. The company changed the industry standard the following year by launching the Pentium processors (Pentium I), which were 300 times faster than the microprocessors used in IBM desktops. Intel continued its strategy of upgrading the models of the Pentium processors and launched Pentium-II, Pentium-III, and Pentium-IV. In 1998, the company segmented its product portfolio according to customer profile. The company introduced the Celeron processor for the household PC segment, and the Pentium II Xeon processor for workstations[22] and servers.[23] During the same time, it introduced high-performance StrongARM technology[24] for handheld computing and communication devices. In 2003, the company came up with its Centrino[25] mobile technology for laptop PCs.

In 2005, Intel recorded revenue of $38.8 billion, and the company's product portfolio included microprocessors, chipsets, motherboards, and flash memory. It also had communications infrastructure components, network processors, applications and cellular baseband processors, and products for network storage.

Chip Industry Overview

The chip industry's major customers were manufacturers of computers, digital consumer appliances, and mobile communications. This industry experienced growing demand due to the increasing semiconductor content of electronic products. World Semiconductor Trade Statistics (WSTS)[26] estimated that the global chip revenue would rise by 10.1 percent in 2006 over its 2005 mark of $227.5 billion.[27] Analysts predicted that the chip industry would reach a new height during the next three years due to the growth of wireless and consumer electronics and computers. WSTS predicted that the global chip industry would accelerate to 11 percent in 2007 and 12.8 percent by 2008.[28]

Computers were the biggest user of semiconductor chips and would continue to drive demand in the semiconductor industry. According to analysts, about 41 percent of all semiconductors produced were consumed by computers (see Exhibit 2). But the demand for chipsets in other sectors also grew. Jean-Philippe Dauvin, chief economist for semiconductor supplier STMicroelectronics,[29] stated, "Cell phones, laptops, DVD players and automotive electronics are traditional applications for semiconductors and those applications are in a renewal mode in the United States, Europe and Japan." He was also of the opinion that the electronics market in China, India, and Eastern Europe was growing and would boost the semiconductor demand.

Exhibit 2 Where Semiconductors Are Consumed

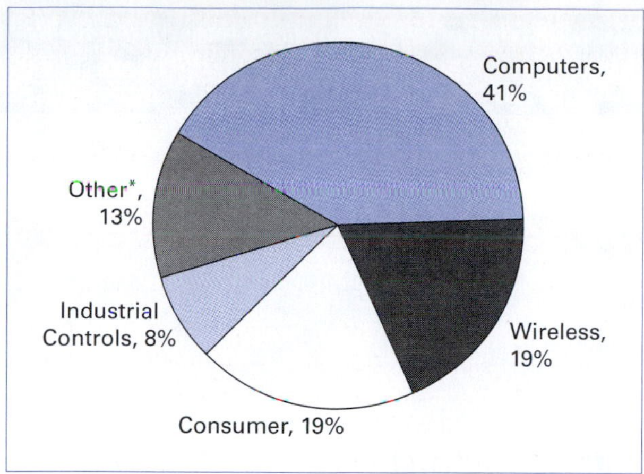

*"Other" includes automotive, wired components, and multichip packages.

Source: http://www.purchasing.com/article/CA6361157.html.

Exhibit 3 Gartner's Worldwide PC Vendor Unit Shipment Second Quarter 2006

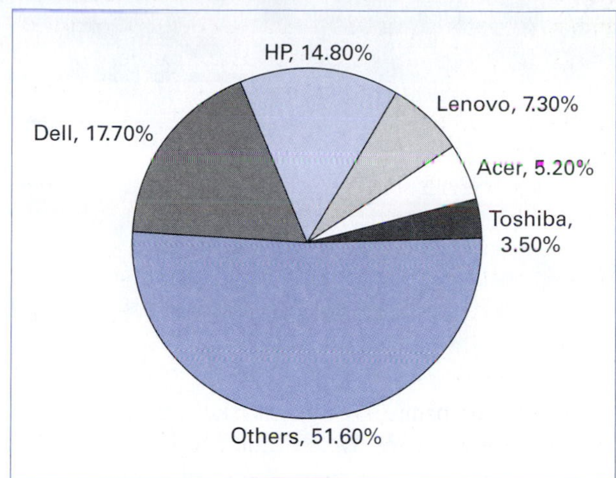

Note: Percentages include desktop PCs, mobile PCs, and x86 servers.

Source: http://computers.tekrati.com/research/news.asp?id=7475.

Analysts expected chip demand within the computer industry to increase due to Vista, Microsoft's new operating system.[30] Vista required that the computers be equipped with more DRAMs. Analysts opined that due to Vista, the amount of DRAM in a PC would double. Therefore, according to Tom Trill, director of DRAM marketing for Samsung Semiconductor, "Overall, Vista is good news for everyone in the PC industry. PC growth is robust, and megabytes of DRAM per system is growing"[31] Moreover, analysts also felt that cell phones, MP3 players, and personal digital assistants (PDAs) would drive demand for chipsets due to more innovative features. The number of chips in mobile phones was increasing as more functions were added. According to Dauvin of STMicroelectronics, the voice-centric phones had about $12 of semiconductor content whereas the 3G phones equipped with camera, video, and audio features had about $65 of chip content. The chip companies manufacturing NAND flash[32] would benefit the most due to increased usage of NAND in the cell phones. Analysts predicted that the NAND market was expected to grow from $10.5 billion in 2005 to $14.8 billion in 2009.

According to WSTS, the Asia-Pacific market would be the largest and fastest-growing regional market in chip revenue with 12.4 percent in 2006 and 12.8 percent in 2007. WSTS predicted that the Asia-Pacific segment would rise by 15 percent to $150 billion in 2008.[33]

Battle Intensified: AMD vs. Intel

Intel, the world leader in making chipsets, faced intense competition from its competitor AMD. The company achieved its biggest victory when Dell, the largest PC maker worldwide (see Exhibit 3), announced in May 2006 that it would start using AMD's server chips. This announcement was a major setback for Intel; Dell had been its largest customer. Dell opted for AMD's Opteron chips in the high-end server segment. In view of Technology Business Research[34] analyst, Martin Kariithi, this was a major blow to Intel. As Intel's largest customer, Dell accounted for almost one-fourth of Intel's processor shipment per quarter. Hewlett-Packard (HP), the world's second-largest PC manufacturer, used AMD chips in their machines. Whereas Lenovo, the third-largest manufacturer and already a strong AMD customer in China, planned to use AMD chips in its business desktop PCs for the United States.

Intel began losing market share. According to the analysts, the company's market share declined from 74.3 percent in the first quarter of 2006 to 72.9 percent in the third quarter. Whereas, AMD's share grew by half a point from 21.1 percent in the first quarter of 2006 to 21.6 percent in the third quarter. However, from 2005 onward, AMD followed a more aggressive approach that ate away at Intel's market share until Intel's share of the chip market was 72.9 percent (2006), down from 82.2 percent a year earlier (2005), according to Mercury Research.[35] AMD's third quarter sales increased by 9 percent in 2006 from its previous quarter, and by 32 percent from the prior year (see Exhibit 4). At the same time, Intel's revenue declined by 12 percent to $8.74 billion from $9.96 billion a year earlier (2005). However, Intel's CFO Andy Bryant felt that the company had been recovering market share from AMD.

Exhibit 4 AMD's Third Quarter Results, 2006

				Change	
	Q3 2006	Q2 2006	Q3 2005	Q3 2006 vs. Q2 2006	Q3 2006 vs. Q3 2005
Net Sales (billions)	$1.33	$1.22	$1.01	9%	32%
Operating Income (millions)	$119	$102	$129	17%	(8)%
Gross Margin	51.4%	56.8%	55.4%	(5.4)%	(4.0)%

Source: http://www.amd.com/us-en/Corporate/VirtualPressRoom/0,,51_104_543~113657,00.html.

According to him, "We lost market share and were under price pressure. We still have to live with tough year-over-year comparisons . . . but we think the worst is behind us." The company was in a restructuring mode that included the elimination of 10,500 jobs through layoffs, attrition, and the sale of underperforming business groups. This elimination was about 10 percent of its total workforce. Intel expected that this restructuring would save the company $5 billion by 2008. As Intel lost market share to AMD, it slashed prices of many products. In July 2006, Intel dropped the price of its Pentium 4 desktop chip to $84 from $218. The company also reduced its price for the expensive Pentium D desktop chip by 40 percent, which had been priced at $530 to $316. According to an analyst at the Enderle Group,[36] both AMD and Intel were hit massively hard by the price war. Intel's average selling price revenue of its processor was lower even though the total processor unit sales were high in the third quarter (2006). AMD also faced the same consequence of the price war—the higher desktop microprocessor sales reflected a lower average selling price during the same period.

AMD's Opteron chip aimed for the corporate server market was launched in 2003. This chip boosted AMD's revenue from $3.5 billion in 2003 to $5.8 billion in 2005. The company also kept the momentum going for its Opteron processors as its market share rose from 22.1 percent in the first quarter of 2006 to 25.9 percent in the second quarter of 2006, according to Mercury Research. But Intel reacted by its release of Xeon 5100 chip for servers. Intel claimed that its Xeon chip was 71 percent better than AMD's Opteron and also had an 84 percent improvement over AMD's power consumption. Moreover, Intel launched its Core 2 Duo processor in July 2006 and planned to release a microprocessor that had four computing engines on a single chip (Core 2 Extreme quad-core). The company felt that its restructuring in addition to its new product development would win back market share from AMD.

Intel's Antitrust

AMD had been in the growth stage of its product life cycle with its Opteron processors, which boosted the company's revenue. But still AMD was worried about Intel's exclusionary practices in Britain, Germany, and Japan. Especially in Japan, AMD began to lose market share, beginning in 2002. According to Gartner Dataquest, AMD's unit share slid from 25 percent in mid-2002 to 9 percent in mid-2004 (see Exhibit 5). AMD's portion of Sony's business dropped from 23 percent in 2002 to zero by 2004, and its total share of NEC[37] business dropped by 35 percent during the same period. During early 2004, AMD brought these figures to the notice of the Japan Fair Trade Commission,[38] and in April of the same year, the commission's agents raided Intel's Japan office. In the next year, the commission ruled that, since May 2002, Intel had violated Japanese law by offering rebates to computer manufacturers upon the purchase of a high percentage of Intel processors.

According to Tom McCoy, AMD executive vice president of legal affairs, "Intel went into Japan and just blew us out as a matter of sheer exercise of monopoly power." He believed that Intel gave Japanese computer makers millions of dollars in rebates for exclusivity. He felt that this rebate sometimes amounted to 100 percent. Therefore, in June 2005, AMD filed a historic antitrust suit against Intel. AMD accused Intel of illegally preserving its monopoly on x86 processors through an illegal discounting program. According to McCoy, "Our customers were telling us, 'The only thing that prevents us from buying more technology from you is the fact that we don't think we can withstand the punishment Intel will put on us.' What the industry needed was antitrust cover to try to back Intel off its practices. With the regulatory spotlight being turned on bright, the industry would be more courageous in building market share with us."

Analysts explained the so-called rebates offered by Intel: If a computer maker bought 100 chips in the last

Exhibit 5 AMD Share in Japanese PC Market

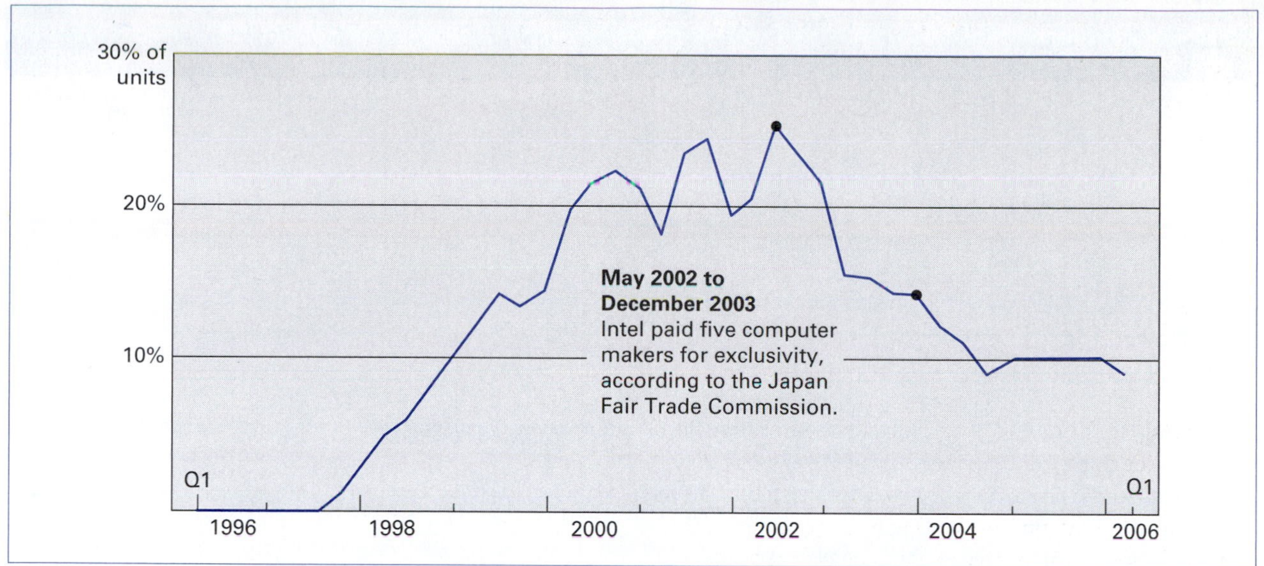

Source: Roger Parloff, Intel's Worst Nightmare, *Fortune,* September 4, 2006.

quarter, of which 90 units were supplied by Intel and the rest from AMD, then in the new quarter AMD might bid for 20 units to increase its share. But Intel might dash AMD's hopes by offering illegal discounting. According to the analysts, if the price per processor was $90, then Intel would offer it at $80 if the computer maker was buying more than 80 percent of its processors from Intel. Moreover, the rebate was not only applied to the processors over the 80 percent target but to every processor that the company was buying from Intel in that quarter. According to AMD's outside lawyer, "Effectively, what Intel's saying is, if you don't buy those ten incremental units from AMD, we'll give you them for free." He explained that 80 processors at $90 each cost the same as 90 processors at $80 each and so he felt that "AMD has to give away product for free. It's pretty axiomatic that you can't stay in any business if you're giving away your product free to pick up the market share." But Intel reacted by labeling it as a simple discounting program that was a part of its trade promotion. If a computer manufacturer purchased less than 20 percent of its chips from Intel, a discount price was not offered, but if it bought between 20 and 40 percent, then a discount price was offered. However, if this figure rose to 80 percent to 100 percent, then the company enjoyed the highest discount rate. In Intel's view, this arrangement was a traditional discount program that increased with volume.

Analysts opined that the case against Intel would not be tried before 2008 because the findings for the case would be monumental; but in September 2006, a federal judge dismissed a major portion of AMD's antitrust lawsuit against Intel. According to him, AMD could not sue Intel in the U.S. courts for its monopolistic tactics in other countries. Moreover, the judge ruled that AMD could not prove that Intel's illegal tactics abroad had an effect on AMD's operations in the United States. However, the judge also ruled that AMD could ask the court to reconsider its decision by presenting foreign evidence that would be a part of the domestic trial. Intel was happy with the proceedings and its spokesperson Chuck Mulloy said, "We are pleased that the judge understood and agreed with our argument and analysis of the law. Nonetheless, we plan to vigorously defend ourselves on the remaining portions of this case." Tom McCoy, on the other hand, felt that "Intel cannot escape antitrust scrutiny for its conduct. As this U.S. litigation is joined by global antitrust investigations, it is clear that Intel cannot escape the consequences of its illegal monopoly abuses." Therefore, the conflict continued between the top two chip makers and analysts were undecided about who would emerge as the winner in this legal war (see Appendix 2).

The Road Ahead

AMD has grown steadily in the server market with its Opteron chips. According to IDC, the global server market was expected to grow by 11 percent per year with 11.8 million unit shipments by 2010.[39] Marty Seyer, AMD vice president and head of the server chip division, said that the company was aiming for a 40 percent global market share for server chips by 2009, which was already 26 percent in the second quarter of 2006, according to IDC analyst Shan Rau. Moreover, AMD

Appendix 1 Market Share Ranking of the Top 20 Semiconductors, 2005

Rank 2005	Rank 2004	Company	Country of origin
1	1	Intel	United States
2	2	Samsung Semiconductors	South Korea
3	3	Texas Instruments	United States
4	7	Toshiba Semiconductors	Japan
5	6	STMicroelectronics	Europe
6	4	Infineon (spin-off from Siemens Semiconductors)	Europe
7	5	Renesas (merger of Mitsubishi and Hitachi Semiconductors)	Japan
8	8	NEC Semiconductors	Japan
9	9	Philips Semiconductors	Europe
10	10	Freescale (ex Motorola Semiconductors)	United States
11	14	Hynix	South Korea
12	13	Micron Technology	United States
13	15	Sony Semiconductors	Japan
14	12	Matsushita Semiconductors	Japan
15	11	AMD (1)	United States
16	17	Qualcomm (3) (fabless)	United States
17	16	Sharp Semiconductors	Japan
18	19	Rohm	Japan
19	20	IBM Microelectronics (2)	United States
20	22	Broadcom (3) (fabless)	United States

Source: http://en.wikipedia.org.

has aggressively challenged Intel by diversifying into the graphics chip category with its acquisition of ATI Technologies in a $5.4 billion deal. Still, AMD's alleged antitrust suit against Intel continued to worry AMD when it considered what effects Intel's practices might have on AMD's growth in other countries, but especially in Japan. Because AMD felt that this practice by Intel was anticompetitive, it filed an antitrust law suit against Intel. Analysts felt that if these claims were proven, then AMD would have a winning hand. However, the same analysts were skeptical that AMD would win the legal battle against Intel based on AMD's setback that happened when a federal judge dismissed a major portion of AMD's antitrust lawsuit against Intel.

Appendix 2 Intel and AMD: Parallel Time Lines

AMD's product introductions followed carefully behind Intel's—until the Athlon arrived.
Today, AMD is in the enviable position of having Intel clone its 64-bit x86 extensions.

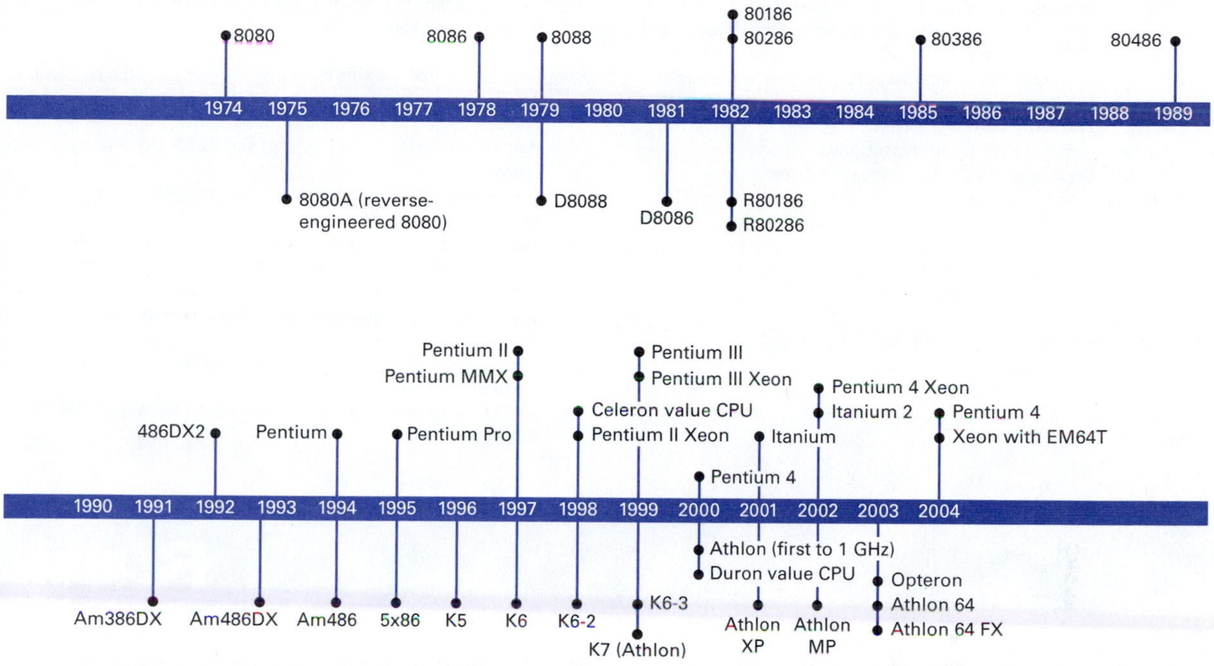

Year	Above the time line	Below the time line
1974	8080	
1975		8080A (reverse-engineered 8080)
1976		
1977		
1978	8086	
1979	8088	D8088
1980		
1981		D8086
1982	80186, 80286	R80186, R80286
1983		
1984		
1985	80386	
1986		
1987		
1988		
1989	80486	
1990		
1991		Am386DX
1992	486DX2	
1993		Am486DX
1994	Pentium	Am486
1995	Pentium Pro	5x86
1996		K5
1997	Pentium II, Pentium MMX	K6
1998	Celeron value CPU, Pentium II Xeon	K6-2
1999	Pentium III, Pentium III Xeon	K6-3, K7 (Athlon)
2000	Pentium 4	Athlon (first to 1 GHz), Duron value CPU
2001	Itanium	Athlon XP
2002	Pentium 4 Xeon, Itanium 2	Athlon MP
2003		Opteron, Athlon 64, Athlon 64 FX
2004	Pentium 4, Xeon with EM64T	

Source: http://www.infoworld.com/infoworld/img/35FEamd-in.gif.

Notes

1. R. Parloff, Intel's worst nightmare, *Fortune*, September 4, 2006.
2. Random access memory (RAM) refers to data storage formats and equipment that allow the stored data to be accessed in any order—that is, at random, not just in sequence.
3. Reverse engineering (RE) is the process of discovering the technological principles of a mechanical application through analysis of its structure, function, and operation.
4. A microprocessor is a digital electronic component with transistors on a single semiconductor integrated circuit (IC). One or more microprocessors typically serve as a central processing unit (CPU) in a computer system or handheld device.
5. x86 is the generic name of a microprocessor architecture. The architecture is called x86 because the earliest processors in this family were identified by model numbers ending in the sequence "86": the 8086, the 80186, the 80286, the 386, and the 486.
6. EPROM, or erasable programmable read-only memory, is a type of computer chip that retains its data when its power supply is switched off. In other words, it is nonvolatile.
7. Monolithic Memories, Inc. (MMI), produced bipolar PROMs, programmable logic devices, and logic circuits. MMI invented Programmable Array Logic (PAL) devices. MMI was eventually acquired by AMD.
8. The company produces a family of programmable logic device semiconductors used to implement logic functions in digital circuits.
9. Flash memory ash is a form of nonvolatile computer memory that can be electrically erased and reprogrammed.
10. Nonvolatile memory retains its contents even if power is turned off.
11. Fujitsu is a Japanese company specializing in semiconductors, computers (supercomputers, personal computers, servers), telecommunications, and services, and is headquartered in Tokyo.
12. This privately held company designed microprocessors for personal connectivity devices.
13. A semiconductor is a material with an electrical conductivity and acts as an intermediate between an insulator and a conductor.
14. A metal oxide semiconductor (MOS) structure is obtained by depositing a layer of silicon dioxide (SiO2) and a layer of metal (polycrystalline silicon is actually used instead of metal) on top of a semiconductor die.
15. A Schottky barrier is a metal-semiconductor junction.
16. A bit refers to a digit in the binary numeral system (base 2).
17. Static random access memory (SRAM) is a type of semiconductor memory. The word *static* indicates that the memory retains its contents as long as power remains applied, unlike dynamic RAM (DRAM) that needs to be periodically refreshed.
18. Dynamic random access memory (DRAM) is a type of random access memory that stores each bit of data in a separate capacitor.
19. Read-only memory (ROM) is a class of storage media used in computers and other electronic devices that can only be read.
20. IBM (International Business Machines Corporation) manufactures and sells computer hardware, software, infrastructure services, hosting services, and consulting services.
21. Dataguest is a leading provider of market research, statistical, and forecasting data to IT vendors, manufacturers, and investors.

22. A workstation (Unix workstation, RISC workstation, or engineering workstation) is a high-end technical computing desktop microcomputer designed primarily to be used by one person at a time, but can also be connected remotely to other users when necessary.
23. A server is a computer system that provides services to other computing systems—called clients—over a network.
24. StrongARM technology was designed to accelerate the development of advanced handheld computing products, enable new classes of low-power, high-performance Internet access devices, and enhance Internet backbone products.
25. Centrino is a platform marketing initiative from Intel for a particular combination of CPU, main board chipset, and wireless network interface in the design of a laptop personal computer.
26. WSTS Inc. is a nonprofit mutual benefit corporation whose charter and bylaws define services for the world semiconductor industry, including management of the collection and publication of trade net shipments and semiconductor industry forecasts. WSTS headquarters are incorporated and located in San Jose, California.
27. Global chip growth forecast for 2006 revised up, http://www.webwereld.nl, May 31, 2006.
28. Ibid.
29. STMicroelectronics is a leading international supplier of semiconductors.
30. Microsoft Windows Vista is the next major version of Microsoft Windows, the proprietary operating system developed by Microsoft.
31. Chip growth reaches new heights, http://www.purchasing.com/article/CA6361157.html, August 17, 2006.
32. Flash memory is a form of nonvolatile computer memory that can be electrically erased and reprogrammed.
33. Global chip growth forecast for 2006 revised up, http://www.webwereld.nl, May 31, 2006.
34. Technology Business Research is an information and market research organization that analyzes computer and networking equipment companies.
35. Mercury Research is a small, focused research firm that provides detailed information for PC-related semiconductor and components markets.
36. This research organization provides perspectives for the technology leaders.
37. NEC, part of the Sumitomo Group, provides information technology (IT) and network solutions to business enterprises, communications services providers, and government. Their business is divided into the three principal segments: IT Solutions, Network Solutions, and Electronic Devices.
38. Fair Trade Commission is the name for the government unit charged with ensuring the fairness of trade.
39. AMD aims for 40 percent of server market, http://news.com.com, August 22, 2006.

References

R. Parloff, 2006, Intel's worst nightmare, *Fortune,* September 4.

J. Robertson, 2006, Judge dismisses key part of AMD lawsuit, http://www.businessweek.com, September 27.

J. Robertson, 2006, AMD earns 27 cents per share in 3Q, http://www.businessweek.com, October 18.

Intel shares up after beating street, http://www.businessweek.com, October 18, 2006.

Ahead of the Bell: Intel, http://www.businessweek.com, October 18, 2006.

R. Konrad, 2006, Intel plans quad-core chip in late 2006, http://www.businessweek.com, September 26.

HSBC sees limit on AMD's sales, http://www.businessweek.com, October 9, 2006.

M. Kanellos, 2006, AMD, Intel trim processor pricing, http://news.com.com, October 25.

J. Davis, 2006, AMD, Intel margins suffer on price war, http://www.edn.com, October 24.

S. Hillis, 2006, AMD profit margins fall amid Intel price war, http://news.yahoo.com, October 18.

J. G. Spooner, 2006, AMD, Intel brace for third-quarter showdown, http://www.eweek.com, August 1.

AMD reports third quarter results, http://www.amd.com, October 18, 2006.

AMD's third quarter earnings were good, but the stock took a hit as its competition with Intel heats up, http://www.tmcnet.com, October 18, 2006.

Intel profit plunges by 35% in third quarter, http://www.finfacts.com, October 17, 2006.

Intel shows signs of chip comeback, http://cnnmoney.com, October 17, 2006.

A. Hesseldahl, 2006, Intel's AMD troubles continue, http://www.businessweek.com, October 17.

M. Andrejczak, 2006, AMD quarterly profit up 77% on chip demand, http://www.newsalert.com, October 18.

A. Hesseldahl, 2006, AMD's race for server space, http://www.businessweek.com, August 22.

AMD shoots for 40 percent of server market, http://money.cnn.com, August 22, 2006.

Chip sales may increase by 10 percent, WSTS says, http://www.taipeitimes.com/News/biz/archives, May 31, 2006.

D. Goodin, 2006, AMD to buy chip-maker ATI for $5.4B, http://www.businessweek.com, July 24.

http://en.wikipedia.org.

http://www.amd.com.

http://www.intel.com.

Case 5

Boeing: Redefining Strategies to Manage the Competitive Market

Ryan Gust, Brandon Barth, Joey O'Donnell, Drew Forsberg, Robin Chapman

Arizona State University

Introduction

In 1992 Boeing and Airbus parent, EADS, agreed to conduct a joint study on the prospects for a superjumbo airplane. With a forecasted 5 percent annual growth in air travel, both companies saw the need for a new aircraft large enough to support this growth. However, the world will not be permitted to see what the brain trust of the two aerospace industry giants could have produced. Airbus and Boeing reached different conclusions concerning market trends, and the joint effort was called off.

The average size of aircraft grew until the late 1990s; however, this trend began to change as carriers shifted their primary focus to profits as opposed to market share. Strong competition among airlines prompted ticket prices to fall in recent years. As a result, carriers dramatically reduced costs and aggressively expanded their networks. The assumption reached by many carriers was that in order to become more flexible, a smaller aircraft must be used to reach many regional airports rather than larger aircraft that can only access hub airports in major cities.[1]

As both companies considered which options to pursue in order to satisfy the growing market, Airbus speculated that the hub-and-spoke system would prove to be the future for airlines and decided to launch the A-380 project in December 2000. Boeing's aircraft, dubbed the 787, was launched in 2005. This aircraft represents a fundamentally different vision, one anchored in the belief that the point-to-point system is the most sensible growth platform.

What is at stake for Boeing and Airbus? Boeing invested more than $8 billion in development for the 787, while Airbus went over budget, investing more than $14 billion and experienced a two-year delay in delivery to its customers. Boeing received solid orders for the midsized 787 and is determined to deliver the 787 in May 2008 as promised to avoid the problems that have plagued its competitor. Some manufacturing problems threatened to delay delivery, however, and are minimizing Boeing's margin for error.[2]

This case discusses the history of Boeing and the salient industry forces affecting the company, leading to the critical decisions faced by both competitors. The key strategic issues driving Boeing's competitive strategies are also outlined along with a discussion of strategies used to manage the competitive environment by both Boeing and Airbus, and the challenges facing both companies.

Boeing's History

William E. Boeing originally worked in the timber industry, and his knowledge of wooden structures led him to design and build an airplane, the B&W Seaplane. When the B&W was ready to fly, the test pilot was late and Mr. Boeing grew impatient, which prompted him to pilot the aircraft himself.[3] This example illustrates Mr. Boeing's level of determination, a key quality of his character, which was incorporated into his airplane manufacturing company.

Established on July 15, 1916, the company was originally called Pacific Aero Products Company. A year later Mr. Boeing changed the name to what is now the Boeing Airplane Company. Edgar Gott, William Boeing's first cousin, became president of the company in 1922.[4] Gott helped Boeing Co. obtain business contracts with the military; succeeding presidents, Philip G. Johnson and Clairmont L. Egtvedt, maintained this relationship with the government throughout WWII. Boeing became a powerhouse in large part due to its war effort, essentially because the military ordered numerous B-17 Bombers.

After the war many of the Bomber orders were canceled, so Boeing's management team tried to recover by

The authors would like to thank Professor Robert E. Hoskisson for his support and under whose direction the case was developed. The case solely provides material for class discussion. The authors do not intend to illustrate either effective or ineffective handling of a managerial situation. This case was developed with contributions from Hal Hardy and Emily Little.

diversifying its product offerings. Boeing began selling a luxurious four-engine commercial aircraft known as the Stratocruiser.[5] However, this aircraft was not the commercial success Boeing had hoped for and as a result, Boeing once again found itself at the drawing board.

William M. Allen took control of Boeing in 1945 and oversaw the building of the United States' first commercial jet airliner, the 707. The 707 had capacity for 156 passengers and helped the United States become a leader in commercial jet manufacturing. The 720 jet plane, which was faster, soon followed, but it had a shorter flying range. A demand for planes capable of flying long routes led Boeing to develop the 727.[6] This aircraft utilized one less engine than previous models and was thought to be significantly more comfortable and reliable than competitors' products.[7] Because most models are eventually discontinued to allocate resources to "new and improved models," the 727 was discontinued in 1984; however, by the beginning of 2000 almost 1,300 of these planes were still in service. Boeing achieved additional commercial success in 1967 and 1968 with the production of the 737 and 747. The 737 would become the best-selling commercial jet aircraft in history while the 747 would hold the passenger seating capacity record for 35 years. The 747 utilizes a double-decker configuration, allowing for a maximum of 524 passengers on board.[8]

In 1994, under the leadership of Frank Shrontz, Boeing developed the 777. This aircraft would actually be the first aircraft designed entirely by computer. "Throughout the design process, the airplane was 'pre-assembled' on the computer, eliminating the need for a costly, full-scale mock-up."[9] This aircraft became the longest range twin-engine aircraft in the world.

Thornton "T" Wilson became president of Boeing in 1968 and continued as CEO until 1986. Malcolm T. Stamper became president in 1972 and, in collaboration with Mr. Wilson, he led Boeing's development of the single-aisle 757 and the larger twin-aisle 767 in the wake of a new European competitor, Airbus. During these years Boeing also participated in space programs and military projects, such as the International Space Station and the development of new sophisticated missiles. Today, "Boeing is organized into two business units: Boeing Commercial Airplanes and Boeing Integrated Defense Systems," with the latter making Boeing the world's second-largest defense company.[10]

Philip M. Condit took over in 1996 but was quickly relieved of his position in 1997 because he underestimated Airbus's ability to compete with Boeing. Harry Stonecipher succeeded Condit and faced even more intense rivalry with Airbus. By 2003, Airbus had become the market leader, sending Boeing scrambling frantically to pursue new projects, such as the Sonic Cruiser. The Sonic Cruiser aimed to please customers with a faster, more comfortable ride for long-distance travel. The Cruiser would cut an hour off traditional travel time by flying at a higher elevation and a Mach speed of .98 (most aircraft fly at Mach .80).[11] When Lew Platt became board chair in December of 2003, Boeing abandoned the Sonic Cruiser project in order to focus its efforts on the 787 Dreamliner. Airlines were favoring planes that boasted fuel efficiency over those that offered faster speed. The Dreamliner, slated to fly in May 2008, is popular in the industry because of its potential fuel economy, one-piece composite fuselage sections, and eco-friendliness. It will cost slightly more than half of Airbus's complementary product, and currently has more than twice as much order-book value.[12]

Although each of Boeing's leaders sought to improve the organization during his tenure (for additional biographical information on Boeing's previous leadership, please refer to Exhibit 1), the rivalry with Boeing's key competitor is still intense.

Airbus: Boeing's Key Competitor

The industry for large commercial aircraft (LCA) is a duopoly composed of Boeing Co. and Airbus Industries. These two manufacturing giants have emerged in an unsteady industry whose fortune is based upon strategic timing and luck. Market share is overwhelmingly the most important consideration for each company when making strategic decisions. Essentially, market share determines success. Airbus, once considered a small player, swiftly emerged as an industry giant by focusing on the needs of the market, a standard product line, efficient production methods, and successful marketing ploys. Other players such as Douglas Aircraft Corporation and Lockheed Martin, who were successful and competitive corporations, fell from their positions due to failure in their demand forecast strategies and they merged with other competitors; especially significant was the merger between McDonnell Douglas and Boeing.[13]

Airplanes are grouped into families based on size, range, and technology. At the low end of the market are two single-aisle airplanes; the Boeing 737 and the Airbus A-320, which both seat about 190 people. These planes have each been extremely successful in generating sales, but fall short as revenue earners for both companies. The most profitable market segment has been the middle market, filled with the medium-sized aircraft, which seat from 200 to 300 passengers. Boeing's 757 and Airbus's A330-200 are the most popular planes in this segment. High-end jumbo airplanes fill the remaining segment of the market and are characterized by long-range flight capability, 300+ seats, and maximum use of technology. Each company attempts to develop its products to match the forecasted market demands by producing an airplane

Exhibit 1 Biographical Information on Boeing's Previous Leadership

Walter James McNerney Jr.
President, Chief Executive Officer, and Chairman of the Board of Directors of The Boeing Company, 2005–Present
McNerney received a BA from Yale University in 1971 and an MBA from Harvard in 1975. While receiving his education, McNerney played varsity baseball and hockey. McNerney started his executive career at General Electric in 1982. Over the next 19 years he held many positions including president and CEO of GE Aircraft Engines, GE Lighting, and GE Electrical Distribution and Control. He also spent time as president of GE Asia-Pacific and GE Information Services, and executive vice president of GE Capital. In 2001 McNerney joined 3M as CEO. After turning down two offers in two years, 3M CEO McNerney finally accepted the position as CEO and chairman of The Boeing Company in June of 2005. McNerney had already been a member of the board of directors at Boeing since 2001. He is the chair of the U.S.-China Business Council and serves on the World Business Council for Sustainable Development.

James A. Bell
Interim Chief Executive Officer of the Boeing Company, March 2005–June 2005; Chief Financial Officer, 2004–Present
James A. Bell received a BA in accounting from California State University. Mr. Bell started his career as an accountant at The Rockwell Company. He advanced through management at Rockwell, holding positions as senior internal auditor, accounting manager, and manager of general and cost accounting. When Rockwell's aerospace division was acquired by Boeing in 1996, Bell moved with it. At Boeing, Bell held positions as the vice president of contracts and pricing for the company's space and communications division, as well as senior vice president of finance and corporate controller. In 2004, following the firing of Michel M. Sears (due to a government contract scandal), Bell accepted the position as the chief financial officer of The Boeing Company. Bell also served as an interim CEO for a few months in 2005 between the time that Harry Stonecipher was forced to resign and James McNerney Jr. accepted the position.

Harry C. Stonecipher
President; 1997–2005; Chief Executive Officer of The Boeing Company, 2003–2005
Harry C. Stonecipher received a BS in physics from Tennessee Technological University in 1960. He began his career as a lab technician at General Motors. He then moved to GE's large engine division and worked his way up to become a vice president and then a division head. He left GE to go to Sundstrand where he became president and CEO after two years. After that he served as president and CEO of McDonnell Douglas until the merger with Boeing in 1997. At Boeing he served as the president and COO until 2003 when he filled the shoes of Philip M. Condit as CEO. In 2005, however, Stonecipher resigned at the request of the board after news of a "consensual relationship" with a female board member surfaced (violating Boeing's Code of Conduct).

Philip Murray Condit
Chief Executive Officer, 1996–2003; Chairman of the Board, 1997–2003 of The Boeing Company
Condit earned a Bachelor's degree in mechanical engineering from the University of California, Berkley; a master's degree in Aeronautical Engineering from Princeton; an MBA from the MIT Sloan School of Management; and a PhD in engineering from Science University of Tokyo. Condit started at Boeing in 1965 as an aerodynamics engineer, he then advanced to a lead engineer and soon after became a marketing manager. After a short break to earn his MBA he returned to Boeing, working through a myriad of leadership positions until he ascended to CEO in 1996 and board chair in 1997. His time as CEO and chairperson was characterized by a number of mergers and acquisitions as well as a struggle with increasing competition with Airbus. Condit was forced to resign in 2003 amidst corruption charges involving his freezing of a contract with the U.S. Air Force in 1997.

Thornton "T" A. Wilson
President, 1968–1972; Chief Executive Officer, 1969–1986; Chairman of the Board, 1972–1987; Chairman Emeritus of The Boeing Company, 1987–1993
Wilson received an aeronautical engineering degree from Iowa State University in 1943 and a master's degree in aeronautical engineering from the California Institute of Technology in 1948. Wilson begins his career with Boeing in 1943 and advanced rapidly. His first assignment of note was as project engineer on the B-52 and then was general manager of the proposal team for the Minuteman intercontinental ballistic missile program. Wilson became a vice president in 1963 and was put in charge of planning the Boeing corporate headquarters in 1964. He was named executive vice president in 1966 and president in 1968. Wilson became the CEO in 1969 and board chair in 1972.

Louis Gallois
Chief Executive Officer of Airbus, 2006–Present
Gallois graduated from both the Ecole Des Hautes Etudes Commerciales (where he received an education in economic science) and the Ecole Nationale de l'Administration. In 1972 Gallois started with the Treasury Department of the French government. During1982–1987, Gallois worked his way up at the Cabinet Office of the Ministry of Research. His appointment as the Head of Civil and Military Cabinet Office of the French Ministry of Defense took place in 1988. It was in 1989 that Gallois shifted his career from government to the private sector when be became board chair and CEO of SNECMA, an airplane engine manufacturer. He then moved to Aerospatiale, another aerospace manufacture, as board chair and CEO. Gallois was chair of the French National Railways from 1996 to 2006. In October 2006, Gallois became CEO of Airbus.

Source: Executive Biographies, Wikipedia, http://en.wikipedia.org; http://www.boeing.com.

that offers the appropriate size, range, fuel efficiency, and technology. These forecasts are based on huge uncertainties, such as what size of airplane will airlines need in order to carry an unknown amount of people to and from large hub airports or smaller regional airports. These variables make accurate short-term projections and assumptions key to long-term success in an industry that is constantly changing.[14]

Airbus became a competitive global manufacturer of LCAs with the help of "launch aid," a form of government subsidies implemented to help a company, such as Airbus, compete and survive in industries where competitive giants such as Boeing have established distribution networks and economies of scale. Airbus was able to establish a significant market share and a brand name by making airplanes that addressed the needs of the market. Airlines had been "crying" for midsized cost efficient airplanes, and Airbus answered by building the A-320. The "commonality" that the A-320 had with other Airbus airplanes was attractive to airlines because of its potential to reduce pilot and attendant training costs as well as improve airplane turnaround time.[15]

Despite Airbus's strategy, Boeing had not embraced commonality among its products because of the changes and high costs that would be incurred at its current stage. As a result, the manufacturing giant fell from its number one position. In order for Boeing to survive its newfound misfortune, it needed to make serious changes in its strategy and business processes. The first aspect considered for business-process change would be its relationships with suppliers.

Suppliers

The importance of suppliers to aircraft manufacturers has shifted with advancements in technology. Chuck Agne, a former director of supplier management for Boeing's Integrated Defense Systems, said in 2004 that Boeing's strategy was to "move up the value chain," meaning that Boeing was going to focus less on the many details and more on their core competence, integration, and assembly. As part of this strategy, Boeing consolidated its supplier list and managed relationships only with those that provide quality products with the best value. Agne said, "What we have found is, the suppliers we're sticking with are the ones who are able to move up that value chain with us."[16]

Traditionally, most manufacturers similar to Boeing completed all research and production in-house. Technological research and development is seen as a competitive advantage that must be closely guarded within the airplane production industry. Boeing's key technical expertise—such as wing technology and new lightweight materials such as composites—are considered its core competencies. Boeing traditionally believed that outsourcing these components to suppliers would give the suppliers control over manufacturing and ultimately place the supplier in control when determining its share of revenue. However, it is no longer a sensible option for Boeing to keep an entire production line in-house. Thus, a new trend emerged in the production of new aircraft, such as the 787 Dreamliner. For the first time Boeing announced it would "offload" (Boeing's term for *outsourcing*)[17] the design of it wings and parts of its fuselage to Japan, and also outsource its fuselage panel work to an Italian company. It is estimated that now 70 percent of the components of a given airplane are outsourced. As such, Boeing is responsible for plane assembly, assuming the title of "Systems Integrator."[18]

Boeing also sought strategic partnerships globally in an effort to reduce costs and perhaps generate sales. By outsourcing to countries such as China and India, Boeing entered what is called an "offset agreement," such that they obtain aircraft sales in return for manufacturing work. This arrangement allowed Boeing to gain more substantial entry into two of the largest and fastest growing airplane markets (China and India).[19]

One of the main attractions for establishing strategic partnerships is the ability to distribute some of the risk associated with the large investment required to build an airplane. By outsourcing, LCA manufacturers are able to share risks and focus their efforts on marketing and supplier relationships. By developing components of the 787 Dreamliner in Japan, Boeing also acquires support from Asian Airlines through the purchase of planes, aided by Japanese government incentives. Another indirect financial benefit to Boeing is the fact that the Japanese and Italian companies are all subsidized by their governments. If successful, the projects present multiple opportunities for Boeing to develop and market their product in an entirely new way.[20] However, risk sharing also equates to profit sharing.

In addition to diminished profits, other implications related to outsourcing are worth noting. First of all, many Boeing employees, including the engineers, are against the outsourcing for obvious reasons; they feel that their jobs are at stake and believe that Boeing has lost sight of its larger interests.[21] Former CEO Harry Stonecipher countered outsourcing concerns by stating, "We have to understand that the go-it-alone approach doesn't work in today's world. Companies will increasingly focus on their core competencies. As they do, they will outsource (a) where the markets are, and (b) where the best people to do the job are."[22] Eventually union leaders and employees were able to acknowledge that outsourcing is about more than just cutting jobs, it is about competing efficiently in a global industry.[23]

Additional controversy centers on whether Boeing is transferring knowledge vital to U.S. military security and commercial competitiveness. The United States has given Boeing's aerospace and defense divisions many subsidies to develop technology. Some of this technology has presumably been transferred to Boeing's aircraft manufacturing division. Japanese suppliers may use the technology shared by Boeing to eventually design their own airplanes. Over the past three years, "The Japanese government and its heavy industrial firms have openly sought to establish Japan as an aerospace power for generations."[24] A Japanese aerospace giant would pose a huge threat to both Boeing and Airbus because it would be able to capitalize on political and trade ties with the flourishing Asia-Pacific markets.[25]

Comparatively, Airbus has kept tighter control over the knowledge it shares with suppliers. In fact, in late 2005 Airbus tightened control over tier one suppliers, directing them to outsource only minimal amounts of work to Asian countries.[26] As such, most of their suppliers are associated with European Union countries, most of which have some ownership in Airbus's parent, EADS. Airbus models its relationship with suppliers after Wal-Mart and utilizes JIT, just-in-time delivery. To further develop efficiencies it follows the approach of the auto industry and requests that its suppliers deliver all components in prepackaged trays that can be loaded onto carts similar to a chest of drawers. Assembly line workers are able to get everything they need without having to leave their stations. As a result, some of Airbus's assembly lines have nearly doubled their efficiency in the past two years.[27]

Clearly, Airbus and Boeing are utilizing relatively different strategies concerning value chain logistics. Consequently, the question remains: Which strategic approach to value chain management will provide better efficiency and long-run strategic advantage? Boeing must continuously monitor and evaluate over time these key concerns in order to maintain positive relations with its stakeholders, specifically its customers and employees.

Customers

Boeing's mission statement signifies that one of its core competencies lays in "detailed customer knowledge and focus."[28] Customers have the choice of buying new or used planes and to license them or purchase them entirely. The customers for Boeing's commercial division are the airlines of the world, and governments are the customers for the defense division. For the commercial division, carriers in China and India are becoming valuable overseas customers, as income rises in these countries along with a forecasted air traffic growth of 8.8 percent in China through the year 2024, and 25 percent growth yearly in India.[29] Half of the orders for the Boeing 787 Dreamliner are from Asia-Pacific clients. Although it is early in the process, the Airbus A-380 currently has not been purchased by any American carriers, which may suggest that Boeing will dominate the superjumbo aircraft market within the United States.[30] Australia's carrier, Qantas, has indicated it will purchase 115 of its 787 Dreamliners valued at more than $14 billion.[31]

United Airlines has traditionally been Boeing's largest domestic customer,[32] and low-cost airlines have also been key clients for Boeing. However, successful sales campaigns by Airbus resulted in some lost sales for Boeing with the low-cost airlines. JetBlue, when it first emerged in the low-cost industry, announced its decision to purchase Airbus's A-320 over Boeing's 737.[33] JetBlue liked the wider seats, more leg room, and more overhead storage that the A-320 could offer its passengers.

Through early 2004, a major problem seemed to lay in the fact that Boeing had a weak sales force and Airbus was consistently pricing its products below Boeing's prices.[34] These factors, coupled with superior technology in the A-320, won Airbus a considerable amount of Boeing's previous contracts. Boeing's list of lost deals was getting longer and longer, with notable losses to Airbus from United Airlines, AirBerlin, Air Asia, and Southwest. The situation became extremely alarming to Boeing, and in the latter half of 2004 and the beginning of 2005, numerous changes were made in Boeing's sales force. Senior executives and board members were sent into the field to garner sales, decision making was sped up, and the salespeople were empowered to take more risks in pricing.[35]

Frustration with the two-year delay in delivery of the Airbus A-380 (as discussed later in the case) allowed Boeing to acquire some valuable customers from Airbus, including FedEx. FedEx is experiencing growing demand for international freight shipments and needs more planes in its fleet sooner than Airbus can deliver, which resulted in a $2.3 billion loss for Airbus and a $3.6 billion gain for Boeing in new orders.[36] Virgin, also frustrated with the Airbus delays, canceled its order for the A-380 and partnered with Boeing, ordering 15 of its 787s.[37]

In addition to the battle for sales, Boeing and Airbus have been engaged in an ongoing dispute concerning the role that governments play in the success of the two companies.

Government Issues

Boeing attributes much of Airbus's success to its extensive financial support through subsidies called "launch aid" from Spain, France, Germany, and Great Britain, the four member countries that have ownership interests in EADS, the parent of Airbus. During the 1980s Airbus was able to create its multitude of products because of the financial support it relied on from these countries. Airbus still receives a debatable amount, thought to be $1.7 billion for the year 2005.[38]

Boeing was able to further its case against "launch aid" when Airbus released plans to develop the A-350 in response to Boeing's 787, which suspiciously will be developed despite the huge financial losses Airbus accumulated due the problems associated with its A-380 superjumbo jet.[39] Boeing sought protection from the World Trade Organization from these subsidies because they threaten its competitiveness in the global economy. Conversely, Airbus fired back, claiming that Boeing also receives subsidies from the U.S. government. This financial aid comes in the form of "federal research and development contracts from NASA and the Pentagon and, more recently, tax breaks from Washington State."[40] Those in support of Boeing counter with the argument that these contracts are business deals associated with its defense business (not its commercial airlines business) and for which other companies can compete and therefore are not defined as subsidies.[41] Nonetheless, Airbus argues that the government funded technology assists in commercial plane development because such technology is transferable.

For example, about half of the 787 will consist of composites of which knowledge can be directly drawn from Boeing's experience with the B-2 stealth bomber program. However, Airbus also has the ability to draw on military technology from its parent company EADS, so the true validity within this argument is uncertain. Both companies decided to file complaints with the WTO in 2004. The acceptance of government subsidies by global corporations, known as "extraterritorial income," is deemed illegal by the WTO. In reality both companies receive almost equal support from their governments, and tracking or even ending these funds is difficult. The WTO has little judicial power and really only provides leverage to settle disputes.

It is understood that WTO cases are fraught with risk and have uncertain outcomes and often last for years. Also, the European Union and the United States, the two sides in this dispute, are the strongest members in the WTO. The outcome is yet to be determined, but the ultimate conclusion is likely to have an impact on the finances of both firms.[42]

Financials

Boeing's revenue increased nearly 15 percent from 2005 to 2006 ($53,621 million to $61,530 million). In part, this extraordinary growth can be attributed to the record-breaking number of orders and a one-third increase in production capacity. Boeing's net profit on this revenue more than doubled from $464 million in 2005 to $980 million in 2006. This jump equates to net change of 111.2 percent. For investors it is great news. It allowed Boeing to increase its earnings per share (EPS) from $0.59 in 2005 to $1.28 in 2006 (see Exhibits 2, 3, and 4).

Boeing's financial margins indicate how well the organization is utilizing sales dollars. Boeing's gross margin increased at the end of 2006 to 17.6 percent from 14.6 percent in 2005. Gross margin provides insight into the profit available from the sales dollars. Generally, the higher the percentage of gross margin, the more flexible the organization can be in its operating decisions. The gross margin for the industry average is 13.8 percent for 2006 (see Exhibits 2, 3, and 4). Due to its increased flexibility Boeing increased its spending for R&D by nearly $1 billion.

Operating margin (or operating profit margin) increased 2.7 percentage points in 2006 from 2005, moving from 3.9 percent to 6.6 percent. This ratio is useful in determining the earnings before taxes (EBIT) on each dollar. The stronger the ratio, the better, and when coupled with growth year over year, this ratio equates to a favorable analysis. Net margin also increased from 2005 (3.3%) to 2006 (5.6%) for a net change of 2.3 percentage points, indicating that Boeing is doing a better job at controlling its costs and converting its revenue dollars into profit (see Exhibits 2, 3, and 4). Cash flow grew to be 12 percent of revenues, up $.5 billion from $7 billion in 2005 (see Exhibit 7).

Boeing is heavily leveraged compared to its industry; its debt-to-equity ratio is 2.01, compared to the industry average of 0.96. However, when building products with budgets discussed in terms of billions of U.S. dollars, leveraging perhaps allows for better use of assets. This rationale can be seen in Boeing's 2006 credit rating of A3, as provided by Moody's Investors Service.[43] Despite the positive credit rating it is especially important for Boeing to contain its debt levels and use its financial resources wisely in order to come out on top with its strategy versus Airbus's strategy. (For a broader picture of Boeing's financial condition and a comparison of Airbus's financials please refer to Exhibits 5, 6, 7, and 8.)

Opposing Strategies

In comparing the strategies of Boeing and Airbus, one analyst concluded the following: "In today's marketplace, distinct differences in the way competitive products work have become increasingly rare. But functional product differentiation is exactly what the rivalry between the Airbus A-380 and the Boeing 787 Dreamliner is all about: Two companies with fundamentally different products, based on diametrically opposite visions of the future."[44] Boeing maintains that increased fragmentation in the form of point-to-point travel will not only solve the problem of airport congestion, but also appeal to travelers. Airbus on the other hand believes that hub-to-hub travel, especially between major cities will continue to grow—with an emphasis on the Asian markets.

Exhibit 2 Boeing Financial Ratios with Contrast

Growth Rates %	Company	Industry	S&P 500
Sales (Qtr vs year ago qtr)	26.20	16.40	13.60
Net Income (YTD vs YTD)	–14.00	28.10	24.40
Net Income (Qtr vs year ago qtr)	111.20	57.40	80.80
Sales (5-Year Annual Avg.)	1.12	8.39	13.12
Net Income (5-Year Annual Avg.)	–4.83	58.28	22.42
Dividends (5-Year Annual Avg.)	12.03	11.41	9.95

Price Ratios	Company	Industry	S&P 500
Current P/E Ratio	33.1	22.2	21.9
P/E Ratio 5-Year High	65.3	88.0	61.3
P/E Ratio 5-Year Low	9.0	20.9	14.8
Price/Sales Ratio	1.20	1.28	2.77
Price/Book Value	15.63	7.46	4.06
Price/Cash Flow Ratio	19.80	16.10	14.80

Profit Margins %	Company	Industry	S&P 500
Gross Margin	18.0	13.8	36.8
Pre-Tax Margin	5.2	5.1	19.1
Net Profit Margin	3.6	2.7	13.4
5Yr Gross Margin (5-Year Avg.)	15.3	14.5	35.6
5Yr PreTax Margin (5-Year Avg.)	4.3	5.5	17.2
5Yr Net Profit Margin (5-Year Avg.)	3.5	4.0	11.8

Financial Condition	Company	Industry	S&P 500
Debt/Equity Ratio	2.01	0.96	1.32
Current Ratio	0.8	1.2	1.2
Quick Ratio	0.5	0.8	1.0
Interest Coverage	12.5	11.1	24.7
Leverage Ratio	10.9	5.5	4.6
Book Value/Share	6.01	18.51	19.14

Investment Returns %	Company	Industry	S&P 500
Return On Equity	27.9	24.5	21.6
Return On Assets	3.9	5.5	8.0
Return On Capital	8.2	9.8	10.5
Return On Equity (5-Year Avg.)	20.8	16.5	20.2
Return On Assets (5-Year Avg.)	3.5	4.0	6.6
Return On Capital (5-Year Avg.)	6.1	6.5	8.7

Management Efficiency	Company	Industry	S&P 500
Income/Employee	14,325	18,312	104,736
Revenue/Employee	399,546	315,545	856,844
Receivable Turnover	11.7	19.5	17.5
Inventory Turnover	6.3	9.6	8.9
Asset Turnover	1.1	1.1	0.8

Source: Boeing Company Financial Ratios, *Reuters,* http://stocks.us.reuters.com/stocks/ratios.asp?symbol=BA&WT.

Exhibit 3 Boeing Performance Summary, 10 years

	Avg P/E	Price/Sales	Price/Book	Net Profit Margin (%)
12/06	28.20	1.14	14.79	3.6
12/05	19.50	1.05	5.08	4.8
12/04	21.30	0.82	3.82	3.5
12/03	39.50	0.68	4.36	1.4
12/02	13.90	0.50	3.43	4.3
12/01	15.10	0.55	2.86	4.9
12/00	19.90	1.12	5.01	4.1
12/99	16.50	0.66	3.15	4.0
12/98	37.70	0.57	2.48	2.0
12/97	–286.40	1.04	3.68	–0.4

	Book Value/Share	Debt/Equity	Return on Equity (%)	Return on Assets (%)	Interest Coverage
12/06	$6.01	2.01	46.5	4.3	12.0
12/05	$13.82	0.97	23.2	4.3	9.3
12/04	$13.56	1.08	16.1	3.2	5.7
12/03	$9.67	1.77	8.4	1.3	NA
12/02	$9.62	1.87	29.8	4.4	10.9
12/01	$13.57	1.13	26.1	5.8	10.7
12/00	$13.18	0.80	19.3	5.0	6.7
12/99	$13.16	0.59	20.1	6.4	7.3
12/98	$13.13	0.57	9.1	3.0	3.6
12/97	$13.31	0.53	–1.4	–0.5	–0.4

Source: Boeing Company Financial Ratios, *Reuters,* http://stocks.us.reuters.com/stocks/ratios.asp?symbol=BA.

The solution for Boeing is the 787 Dreamliner, a midsized twin-engine airplane with long-haul capabilities, longer than any of Boeing's previous models. Boeing has championed the 787 as "revolutionary," encompassing major changes in all aspects of the airplane including design, production, and finance. Based on a decade of focus groups and scientific studies, the objective for the 787 has been to offer the passenger the most comfortable point-to-point travel experience with as few intermediate stops as possible. The 787 will have more standing room, larger windows and bathrooms, ambient light settings in the cabin to adjust to the time of day, and the cabin will also be set at a higher humidity level. For the airlines it is an attractive product because it is fuel efficient (burning 27 percent less fuel per passenger than the A-380[45]), made from lightweight composite materials, and simple to operate.[46]

Airbus's offering is dubbed the A-380, or commonly referred to as the "superjumbo." The A-380 will be the largest aircraft in the world, 35 percent larger than the current largest, the Boeing 747-400. The A-380 is 239 feet long and stands over 80 feet tall.[47] It can be configured with bars and specialty boutiques. With a wing span of almost 300 feet, the A-380 can transport 550 passengers in a typical three-class layout.[48] Airbus claims the A-380 will allow 10 million additional passengers per year to fly between airports with no increase in flights.[49] Despite a size that provides boasting rights, it also creates challenges because the A-380 will only be able to utilize the largest airports—most facilities are unable to accommodate this aircraft. Airports are having to spend millions of dollars to accommodate this new superjumbo plane. For example, London's Heathrow airport has already spent $909 million for upgrades to prepare for the A-380.[50] Thus, Boeing has the opportunity to exploit smaller airports. The success of Boeing's strategy will depend largely upon its marketing approach. (See Exhibits 9 and 10 to view the differences in features and success between the 787 and A-380.)

Marketing Approach

As a result of the billions of dollars already spent, and the future of the firm at stake, Boeing has marketed the 787 extensively. Boeing recognized that as its products became more sophisticated, it needed to revamp its marketing approach. Rob Pollack, vice president of branding at Boeing, said, "We realized that if you have the most

Exhibit 4 Financial Highlights

Financial Highlights			
Sales	61.53Bil	Revenue/Share	78.68
Income	2.21Bil	Earnings/Share	2.85
Net Profit Margin	3.59%	Book Value/Share	6.01
Return on Equity	27.93%	Dividend Rate	1.40
Debt/Equity Ratio	2.01	Payout Ratio	43.00%

Revenue–Quarterly Results (in Millions)	FY (12/06)	FY (12/05)	FY (12/04)
1st Qtr	14,264.0	12,681.0	12,903.0
2nd Qtr	14,986.0	14,684.0	13,088.0
3rd Qtr	14,739.0	12,355.0	13,152.0
4th Qtr	17,541.0	13,901.0	13,314.0
Total	61,530.0	53,621.0	52,457.0

Earnings Per Share–Quarterly Results	FY (12/06)	FY (12/05)	FY (12/04)
1st Qtr	$0.91	$0.68	$0.77
2nd Qtr	–$0.21	$0.71	$0.75
3rd Qtr	$0.90	$1.28	$0.56
4th Qtr	$1.30	$0.62	$0.24
Total	$2.90	$3.29	$2.32

Qtr. over Qtr. EPS Growth Rate	FY (12/06)	FY (12/05)	FY (12/04)
1st Qtr	47%	183%	—
2nd Qtr	NA	4%	–3%
3rd Qtr	NA	80%	–25%
4th Qtr	44%	–52%	–57%

Yr. over Yr. EPS Growth Rate	FY (12/06)	FY (12/05)
1st Qtr	34%	–12%
2nd Qtr	NA	–5%
3rd Qtr	–30%	129%
4th Qtr	110%	158%

Source: Boeing Company Financial Highlights, *Reuters*, http://stocks.us.reuters.com/stocks/financialHighlights.asp?symbol=BA.

state-of-the-art products in the world, how you represent yourself has to be done with state-of-the-art marketing techniques." The new strategy presents Boeing as not just a manufacturer, but a "life cycle partner," providing its customers with business solutions through the full lifespan of its products.[51] "Trade shows are now more about creating an immersion than a spectacle. Media is designed to bring the brand to life. Press events strive to stamp an indelible message."[52] Prospective clients are now invited to Boeing's Customer Experience Center, a 30,000-square-foot facility that allows an interactive experience in which Boeing's sales force can address the needs, concerns, and challenges of its customers. "The studio is facilitating discussions that might never have taken place between Boeing and its clients."[53]

The effort taken to improve its marketing and sales approach will hopefully prove to benefit Boeing as it strives to overcome the challenges that lay ahead.

The Challenges Ahead

As previously mentioned, Airbus has experienced significant delays and other problems surrounding the A-380 project. Not only has Airbus run 50 percent over budget, but they also face hundreds of millions of dollars in penalties for delays. EADS's earnings will decrease by $6 billion over the next four years, and the share price has declined 21 percent in the past year (2006). Additionally, Christian Streiff was forced to quit after only three months in his position as CEO.[54] The problems started when mechanics spent weeks routing 348 miles of bundled electrical wiring in each plane, but came up short when attempting to connect one section to another. The cause was determined to be the fact that engineers in Hamburg were drawing on two-dimensional computer programs whereas engineers in Toulouse were using three-dimensional programs.[55]

Multiple redesigns of the proposed A-350 model intended to compete with Boeing's 787 Dreamliner have been delayed as well, resulting in more bad press for Airbus. Six years ago, Airbus executives said the company would need to sell 250 A-380s to break even on the investment. This number has now risen to more than 400 due to delays and cancelations. The company has ramped up production of its A-320 model, the single-aisle aircraft purchased by many low-cost carriers, in an effort to earn badly needed cash. This tactic could prove disastrous if suppliers are not able to keep up with Airbus's schedule.

Exhibit 5 Boeing Income Statement

Boeing	2006	2005	2004	2003	2002
Period End Date	12/31/2006	12/31/2005	12/31/2004	12/31/2003	12/31/2002
Period Length	12 Months	12 Months	12 Months	12 Months	12 Months
Stmt Source	10-K	10-K	10-K	10-K	10-K
Stmt Source Date	2/16/2007	2/16/2007	2/16/2007	2/28/2005	2/28/2005
Stmt Update Type	Updated	Reclassified	Reclassified	Restated	Restated
Revenue	61,530.00	53,621.00	51,400.00	50,256.00	53,831.00
Total Revenue	**61,530.00**	**53,621.00**	**51,400.00**	**50,256.00**	**53,831.00**
Cost of Revenue, Total	50,437.00	44,984.00	43,968.00	44,150.00	45,804.00
Gross Profit	**11,093.00**	**8,637.00**	**7,432.00**	**6,106.00**	**8,027.00**
Selling/General/Administrative Expenses, Total	4,171.00	4,228.00	3,657.00	3,200.00	2,959.00
Research & Development	3,257.00	2,205.00	1,879.00	1,651.00	1,639.00
Depreciation/Amortization	0	0	3	0	0
Interest Expense (Income), Net Operating	–146	–88	–91	–28	49
Unusual Expense (Income)	571	0	0	892	–2
Other Operating Expenses, Total	226	–520	–23	–7	–44
Operating Income	**3,014.00**	**2,812.00**	**2,007.00**	**398**	**3,426.00**
Interest Income (Expense), Net Non-Operating	–240	–294	–335	–358	–320
Gain (Loss) on Sale of Assets	0	0	0	0	0
Other, Net	420	301	288	460	37
Income Before Tax	**3,194.00**	**2,819.00**	**1,960.00**	**500**	**3,143.00**
Income Tax, Total	988	257	140	–185	847
Income After Tax	**2,206.00**	**2,562.00**	**1,820.00**	**685**	**2,296.00**
Minority Interest	0	0	0	0	0
Equity In Affiliates	0	0	0	0	0
U.S. GAAP Adjustment	0	0	0	0	0
Net Income Before Extra Items	**2,206.00**	**2,562.00**	**1,820.00**	**685**	**2,296.00**
Total Extraordinary Items	9	10	52	33	–1,804.00
Accounting Change	0	17	0	0	–1,827.00
Discontinued Operations	9	–7	52	33	23
Net Income	**2,215.00**	**2,572.00**	**1,872.00**	**718**	**492**
Total Adjustments to Net Income	0	0	0	0	0

Source: Boeing Company Financial Statements, *Reuters*, http://stocks.us.reuters.com/stocks/incomeStatement.asp.

Exhibit 6 Boeing Balance Sheet

Boeing	2006	2005	2004	2003	2002
Period End Date	12/31/2006	12/31/2005	12/31/2004	12/31/2003	12/31/2002
Stmt Source	10-K	10-K	10-K	10-K	10-K
Stmt Source Date	2/16/2007	2/16/2007	2/28/2006	2/28/2005	2/27/2003
Stmt Update Type	Updated	Restated	Restated	Restated	Updated
Assets					
Cash and Short-Term Investments	6,386.00	5,966.00	3,523.00	4,633.00	2,333.00
Cash & Equivalents	6,118.00	5,412.00	3,204.00	4,633.00	2,333.00
Short-Term Investments	268	554	319	0	0
Total Receivables, Net	5,655.00	5,613.00	5,269.00	5,522.00	6,296.00
Accounts Receivable—Trade, Net	5,285.00	5,246.00	4,653.00	4,466.00	5,007.00
Accounts Receivable—Trade, Gross	5,368.00	5,336.00	0	0	0
Provision for Doubtful Accounts	–83	–90	0	0	0
Notes Receivable—Short-Term	370	367	616	857	1,289.00
Receivables—Other	0	0	0	199	0
Total Inventory	8,105.00	7,878.00	6,508.00	5,338.00	6,184.00
Prepaid Expenses	0	0	0	0	0
Other Current Assets, Total	2,837.00	2,449.00	2,061.00	3,798.00	2,042.00
Total Current Assets	**22,983.00**	**21,906.00**	**17,361.00**	**19,291.00**	**16,855.00**
Property/Plant/Equipment, Total—Net	7,675.00	8,420.00	8,443.00	8,597.00	8,765.00
Goodwill, Net	3,047.00	1,924.00	1,948.00	1,913.00	2,760.00
Intangibles, Net	1,426.00	671	955	1,035.00	1,128.00
Long-Term Investments	4,085.00	2,852.00	3,050.00	646	0
Note Receivable—Long-Term	8,520.00	9,639.00	10,385.00	10,057.00	10,922.00
Other Long-Term Assets, Total	4,058.00	14,584.00	14,082.00	11,447.00	11,912.00
Other Assets, Total	0	0	0	0	0
Total Assets	**51,794.00**	**59,996.00**	**56,224.00**	**52,986.00**	**52,342.00**
Liabilities and Shareholders' Equity					
Accounts Payable	16,201.00	16,513.00	14,869.00	13,514.00	13,739.00
Payable/Accrued	0	0	0	0	0
Accrued Expenses	0	0	0	0	0
Notes Payable/Short-Term Debt	0	0	0	0	0
Current Port. of LT Debt/Capital Leases	1,381.00	1,189.00	1,321.00	1,144.00	1,814.00
Other Current Liabilities, Total	12,119.00	10,424.00	6,906.00	3,741.00	4,257.00
Total Current Liabilities	**29,701.00**	**28,126.00**	**23,096.00**	**18,399.00**	**19,810.00**
Total Long-Term Debt	8,157.00	9,538.00	10,879.00	13,299.00	12,589.00
Long-Term Debt	8,157.00	9,538.00	10,879.00	13,299.00	12,589.00
Deferred Income Tax	0	2,067.00	1,090.00	0	0

(continued)

Exhibit 6 Boeing Balance Sheet *(continued)*

Boeing	2006	2005	2004	2003	2002
Minority Interest	0	0	0	0	0
Other Liabilities, Total	9,197.00	9,206.00	9,873.00	13,149.00	12,247.00
Total Liabilities	**47,055.00**	**48,937.00**	**44,938.00**	**44,847.00**	**44,646.00**
Redeemable Preferred Stock	0	0	0	0	0
Preferred Stock—Non Redeemable, Net	0	0	0	0	0
Common Stock	5,061.00	5,061.00	5,059.00	5,059.00	5,059.00
Additional Paid-In Capital	4,655.00	4,371.00	3,420.00	2,880.00	2,141.00
Retained Earnings (Accumulated Deficit)	18,453.00	17,276.00	15,565.00	14,407.00	14,262.00
Treasury Stock—Common	−12,459.00	−11,075.00	−8,810.00	−8,322.00	−8,397.00
ESOP Debt Guarantee	−2,754.00	−2,796.00	−2,023.00	−1,740.00	−1,324.00
Other Equity, Total	−8,217.00	−1,778.00	−1,925.00	−4,145.00	−4,045.00
Total Equity	**4,739.00**	**11,059.00**	**11,286.00**	**8,139.00**	**7,696.00**
Total Liabilities & Shareholders' Equity	**51,794.00**	**59,996.00**	**56,224.00**	**52,986.00**	**52,342.00**
Total Common Shares Outstanding	788.74	800.17	832.18	841.48	799.66
Total Preferred Shares Outstanding	0	0	0	0	0

Source: Boeing Company Financial Statements, *Reuters,* http://stocks.us.reuters.com/stocks/balanceSheet.asp.

However, Airbus executives insist that losses will be recouped by 2010.[56]

Boeing also invested heavily in its 787 project and faced criticism over weight issues and composite construction materials. Although both firms experienced setbacks, Airbus has taken the brunt of these setbacks, as already noted. Boeing's challenges have more to do with potential production delays and meeting its massive order-backlog on time. In 2007, Boeing had already announced some delays. Boeing officials noted that "it is possible to overcome a nearly four-month delay in the 787 Dreamliner program and deliver the first jet on time in May [2008]."[57] However, "Industry observers and a number of the plane's suppliers say it would be the aerospace equivalent of hitting a hole in one on a golf course." The complexity of producing an aircraft is significant, but when you have to simultaneously bring together a large array of suppliers and the various parts that they produce to meet a deadline, the possibilities for error increase geometrically.

In the long term, Boeing must wonder whether it is going to create a new competitor in Japan and eventually in China, given its outsourcing strategy. Also, Airbus countered Boeing's 787 product strategy with the A-350 in addition to the A-380 (Boeing does not have a comparable product, unless they can effectively update the 747). Thus, both Boeing and Airbus face significant strategic challenges.

Conclusion

Both Boeing and Airbus spent billions of dollars in developing their unique strategies. Airbus bet that the way to cope with increased customer demand is to offer a platform, namely the A-380, capable of moving mass amounts of people using the hub system. Alternatively, Boeing focused on the 787 to offer consumers long-range capabilities while at the same time using direct connections. Initial trends indicate support for Boeing strategies based on accumulated orders for the 787, numbering nearly 500, whereas Airbus's A-380 has not received the amount of orders originally forecasted. Airbus also experienced major setbacks with the two-year delivery delay while running nearly 50 percent over budget[58] and losing orders from frustrated customers. Thus, Boeing currently holds the lead in the aerospace

Exhibit 7 Boeing Statement of Cash Flows

Boeing	2006	2005	2004	2003	2002
Period End Date	12/31/2006	12/31/2005	12/31/2004	12/31/2003	12/31/2002
Net Income/Starting Line	2,215.00	2,572.00	1,872.00	718	492
Depreciation/Depletion	1,445.00	1,412.00	1,412.00	1,306.00	1,362.00
Amortization	100	91	97	94	88
Non-Cash Items	1,552.00	1,807.00	1,538.00	1,737.00	2,907.00
Discontinued Operations	–14	12	–51	63	76
Unusual Items	344	–437	102	1,068.00	2,723.00
Other Non-Cash Items	1,222.00	2,232.00	1,487.00	606	108
Changes in Working Capital	2,187.00	1,118.00	–1,415.00	–1,079.00	–2,513.00
Accounts Receivable	–244	–592	–241	357	–155
Inventories	444	–1,965.00	535	191	1,507.00
Prepaid Expenses	–522	–1,862.00	–4,355.00	–1,728.00	–340
Other Assets	718	600	–425	–1,321.00	–2,038.00
Accounts Payable	–744	1,147.00	1,321.00	–132	–441
Accrued Expenses	114	30	214	311	67
Taxes Payable	933	628	1,086.00	320	322
Other Liabilities	1,677.00	3,086.00	705	876	–978
Other Operating Cash Flow	–189	46	–255	47	–457
Cash from Operating Activities	**7,499.00**	**7,000.00**	**3,504.00**	**2,776.00**	**2,336.00**
Capital Expenditures	–1,681.00	–1,547.00	–1,246.00	–836	–1,001.00
Purchase of Fixed Assets	–1,681.00	–1,547.00	–1,246.00	–836	–1,001.00
Other Investing Cash Flow Items, Total	–1,505.00	1,449.00	–200	896	–381
Acquisition of Business	–1,854.00	–172	–34	289	–22
Sale of Business	123	1,709.00	194	186	157
Sale of Fixed Assets	225	51	2,285.00	95	0
Sale/Maturity of Investment	2,850.00	2,725.00	1,323.00	203	140
Purchase of Investments	–2,815.00	–2,866.00	–4,142.00	–102	–505
Other Investing Cash Flow	–34	2	174	225	–151
Cash from Investing Activities	**–3,186.00**	**–98**	**–1,446.00**	**60**	**–1,382.00**
Financing Cash Flow Items	395	70	23	0	0
Other Financing Cash Flow	395	70	23	0	0
Total Cash Dividends Paid	–956	–820	–648	–572	–571
Issuance (Retirement) of Stock, Net	–1,404.00	–2,529.00	–654	18	67
Issuance (Retirement) of Debt, Net	–1,680.00	–1,378.00	–2,208.00	18	1,250.00
Cash from Financing Activities	**–3,645.00**	**–4,657.00**	**–3,487.00**	**–536**	**746**
Foreign Exchange Effects	38	–37	0	0	0
Net Change in Cash	**706**	**2,208.00**	**–1,429.00**	**2,300.00**	**1,700.00**
Net Cash, Beginning Balance	5,412.00	3,204.00	4,633.00	2,333.00	633
Net Cash, Ending Balance	6,118.00	5,412.00	3,204.00	4,633.00	2,333.00

Source: Boeing Financial Statements, *Reuters*, http://stocks.us.reuters.com/stocks/cashFlowStatement.

Exhibit 8 Airbus Select Financials

(Euro, million)	2006	2005	2004	2003
EBIT	(572)	2307	1919	1353
Total Revenue	25190	22179	20224	19048
Assets	33958	33226	35044	29290
Goodwill	6374	6987	6883	6342
Liabilities	24096	20553	17019	17501
Provisions	6272	4205	0	0
Capital Expenditures	1750	1864	2778	2027
Depreciation, Amortization	1140	1131	1088	1628
R&D	2035	1659	1734	1819
Exchange Rate	0.757855	0.844589	0.738788	0.793869

(U.S., million)	2006	2005	2004	2003
EBIT	(433)	1948	1418	1074
Total Revenue	19090	18732	14941	15122
Assets	25735	28062	25890	23252
Goodwill	4831	5901	5085	5035
Liabilities	18261	17359	12573	13894
Provisions	4753	3551	0	0
Capital Expenditures	1326	1574	2052	1609
Depreciation, Amortization	864	955	804	1292
R&D	1542	1401	1281	1444

Source: 2006, 2005, 2004, *EADS Annual Reports*, www.eads.com/1024/en/investor/Reports/Archive/Archives.html.

Exhibit 9 Dreamliner (787) vs. Superjumbo (A-380)

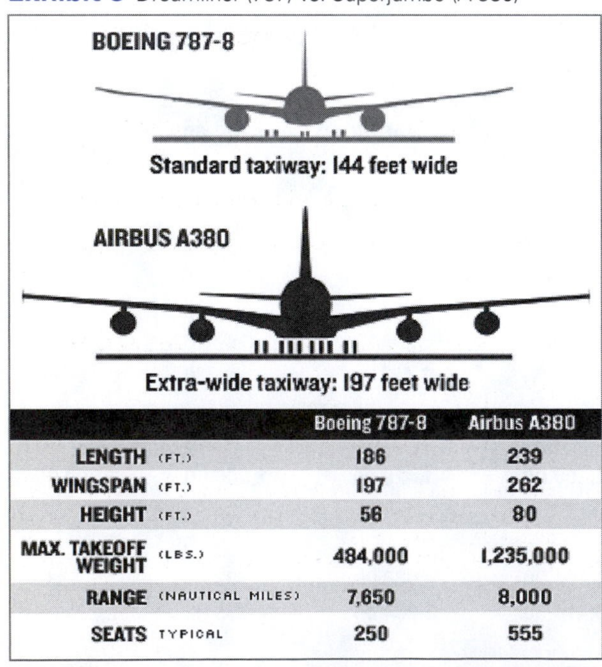

	Boeing 787-8	Airbus A380
LENGTH (FT.)	186	239
WINGSPAN (FT.)	197	262
HEIGHT (FT.)	56	80
MAX. TAKEOFF WEIGHT (LBS.)	484,000	1,235,000
RANGE (NAUTICAL MILES)	7,650	8,000
SEATS TYPICAL	250	555

Source: 2007, Dissecting the A-380's troubles, *Fortune*, http://www.fortune.com, March 5.

Exhibit 10 Boeing vs. Airbus Orders

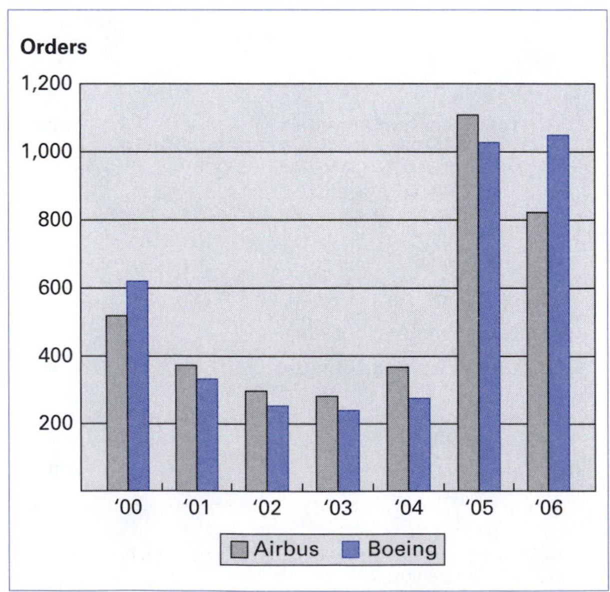

Source: 2007, Dissecting the A-380's troubles, *Fortune*, http://www.fortune.com, March 5.

industry. However, the Asian markets are growing, and demand for large aircraft to meet air traffic increases is also likely to grow. Boeing may be confident in its strategy, but recent minor delays serve as a reminder that Boeing cannot get too comfortable. The first A-380 is slated to be delivered to Singapore Airlines on October 15, 2007.[59] Will this aircraft become a sensation? Will Airbus be able to recoup its costs by 2010 and flourish in the industry? Will Boeing realize continued strategic success, given Airbus's A-350 program, which was established to compete with the 787?

Notes

1. 2001, Aviation competition: Regional jet service yet to reach many small communities, United States General Accounting Office, http://www.gao.gov, February, 5–10; D. Schlossberg, 2007, FAA fights proliferation of small planes, http://www.consumeraffairs.com, August 23.
2. J. L. Lunsford, 2007, Boeing's 787 faces less room for error: Dreamliner flight tests pushed by months; sticking to delivery date, *Wall Street Journal,* September 6, A13.
3. 2007, Boeing, *Wikipedia,* http://en.wikipedia.org/wiki/Boeing.
4. 2007, Boeing History, http://www.boeing.com/history/chronology.
5. 2007, Boeing History, http://www.boeing.com/history.
6. 2007, Boeing History: Beginnings—Building a company, *Aviation History,* http://www.wingsoverkansas.com/history/article.asp?id=404.
7. R. J. Gordon, 1983, Energy efficiency, user cost change, and the measurement of durable goods prices, The U.S. national income and product accounts: Selected topics, Chicago: University of Chicago Press, 235.
8. 2007, Boeing, *Wikipedia,* http://en.wikipedia.org/wiki/Boeing_747-8.
9. 2007, Boeing history, http://www.boeing.com/history/boeing/777.
10. 2007, Boeing, http://www.careerbuilder.com.
11. 2001, Boeing's Sonic Cruiser skirts the edge of the sound barrier, *Popular Mechanics,* http://www.popularmechanics.com, October.
12. L. Laurent, 2007, Boeing's Dreamliner, Airbus's nightmare, *Forbes,* http://www.forbes.com, July 9.
13. J. Newhouse, 2007, *Boeing Versus Airbus,* Toronto, Canada: Alfred A. Knopf.
14. Ibid.
15. Ibid.
16. J. Destefani, 2004, A look at Boeing's outsourcing strategy, *Manufacturing Engineering,* March.
17. Ibid.
18. Ibid.
19. 2006, Boeing's global strategy takes off: The aerospace titan is taking a measured approach to outsourcing, with help from local teams, *BusinessWeek,* http://www.businessweek.com, January 30.
20. Ibid.
21. Ibid.
22. Harry C. Stonecipher, 2004, Outsourcing, the real issue, Orange County Business Council Annual Meeting and Dinner, http://www.boeing.com/news/speeches, June 2.
23. 2006, Boeing's global strategy takes off.
24. E. F. Vencat, 2006, A Boeing of Asia? It could happen, now that Airbus and Boeing build planes in global factories, *Newsweek International,* http://www.msnbc.msn.com, May 15.
25. Ibid.
26. J. Newhouse, *Boeing versus Airbus.*
27. C. Matlack & S. Holmes, 2007, Airbus revs up the engines; to generate badly needed cash, it's boosting output of its popular A-320 to record levels, *BusinessWeek,* March 5, 4024: 41.
28. 2004, There where they're needed, *Boeing Frontiers,* http://www.boeing.com, December.
29. V. Kwong & A. Rothman, 2006, Boeing vs. Airbus: The next bout, *International Herald Tribune,* http://www.iht.com, February 16.
30. L. Wayne, 2007, Airbus superjumbo takes a lap around America, *New York Times,* http://www.nytimes.com, March 20.
31. A. Burgos, 2005, Qantas sets $14 billion order for Boeing planes, *Forbes,* http://www.forbes.com, December 14.
32. J. Newhouse, *Boeing versus Airbus.*
33. 1999, JetBlue chooses the Airbus A-320, Press Releases, http://www.jetblue.com, July 14.
34. L. Timmerman, 2004, Boeing sales to get new leadership, *The Seattle Times,* http://www.seattletimes.com, December 4.
35. D. Drezner, 2005, Competition has been good for Boeing, http://www.danieldrezner.com, April 13.
36. M. Schlangenstein, 2007, FedEx dumps Airbus for Boeing, *The News Tribune* (Tacoma, WA), http://www.thenewstribune.com, September 25.
37. P. Olson, 2007, Branson turns his back on Airbus, *Forbes,* http://www.forbes.com, April 25.
38. D. Ackman, 2005, Boeing, Airbus showdown at 40,000 feet, *Forbes,* http://www.forbes.com, May 31.
39. M. Adams, 2006, Airbus announces new jet to rival Boeing Dreamliner, *USA Today,* http://www.usatoday.com, July 18.
40. D. Ackman, Boeing, Airbus showdown at 40,000 feet.
41. Ibid.
42. J. Audley & K. Saleh, 2004, Boeing vs. Airbus: Trade fight could prove costly for everyone, *The Seattle Times,* http://www.seattletimes.com, December 6.
43. 2006, Moody's boosts Boeing's credit rating, *International Business Times,* http://in.ibtimes.com, March 15.
44. M. E. Babej & T. Pollak, 2006, Boeing versus Airbus, *Forbes,* http://www.forbes.com, May 24.
45. P. Olson, Branson turns his back on Airbus.
46. M. E. Babej & T. Pollak, Boeing versus Airbus.
47. 2007, Anatomy of an A-380, *Fortune,* March 5, 101–106.
48. J. Newhouse, *Boeing versus Airbus.*
49. Ibid.
50. R. Stone, 2007, Airbus A-380 promises less for big airports, *Wall Street Journal,* September 5, D7.
51. 2007, Ground Control, *Event Marketer,* http://www.eventmarketer.com, February 11.
52. Ibid.
53. Ibid.
54. N. D. Schwartz, 2007, Big plane, big problems, *Fortune,* March 5, 95–98.
55. 2007, Anatomy of an A-380.
56. G. Parkinson, 2006, Crisis at Airbus as chief quits after only 100 days, The *(London) Independent,* http://www.findarticles.com, October 10.
57. J. L. Lunsford, 2007, Boeing's tall order: On-time 787, suppliers say Dreamliner delivery could hit may target—if all goes right, *Wall Street Journal,* September 17, A8.
58. D. Michaels, 2007, More super, less jumbo for this carrier, *Wall Street Journal,* September 25, B8.
59. Ibid.

Case 6

Capital One: The American Credit Card Company's Growth Strategies

Susmita Nandi, Sumit Kumar Chaudhuri

ICFAI University

In consumer lending, every product is evolving in the same direction as credit cards—toward large, national-scale consolidators replacing local, face-to-face lending. That evolution has happened in credit cards. It's well under way in auto finance, mortgages, and home equity. Its coming more slowly in installment lending. So consumer lending, a major part of the asset side of banking, is all flowing toward national consolidators like Capital One.

—RICHARD D. FAIRBANK,
CEO AND CHAIRMAN,
CAPITAL ONE FINANCIAL CORPORATION[1]

Capital One Financial Corporation is a diversified bank holding company, with a 2005 market value of $18.92 billion. It provides a gamut of financial services through its main subsidiaries—Capital One Bank, Capital One F.S.B. (which offers consumer and commercial lending and consumer deposit products), and Capital One Auto Finance Inc (COAF). From a small local bankcard issuer in 1995, the company has transformed itself into one of the largest financial institutions in the United States by continually introducing a steady stream of products. It features one of the most recognized brands in the industry, which it leverages along with its strategies of direct marketing, risk analysis, and information technology to grow and diversify into other businesses. Ranked 206th in the *Fortune* 500 list in 2005,[2] the company has been gradually transforming itself from a credit card company to an institution that provides banking and other financial services to consumers. By January 2005, it was the 31st largest deposit institution in the United States with $25.6 billion[3] in interest-bearing deposits.

Capital One has been on the path of diversification from the late 1990s and has made three acquisitions between 2004 and 2005: Onyx Acceptance Corporation, eSmartloan, and Hibernia National Bank. It has also acquired a home equity brokerage company in the United Kingdom, the Hfs Group, to strengthen its Global Financial services (GFS) subsidiary in the British market. As of April 2005, it possessed sufficient liquidity ($21 billion) and capital ($9.2 billion)[4] to enable its famous brand to expand into new markets and seize the right opportunities for profitable growth. Although the company's acquisition of Hibernia in March 2005 provided it an opportunity to enter the fast-developing Texas markets of Houston and Dallas, it might face stiff competition from other large credit companies, such as Citigroup and J.P. Morgan.

Capital One: The Background

Capital One is the fifth largest credit card provider in the United States[5] and one of the largest issuers of MasterCard and Visa credit cards. It was founded as a wholly owned subsidiary of Virginia-based Signet Bank when Richard D. Fairbank, CEO and chairman of Capital One, was invited by the bank to head its bankcard division. It began its operations in 1953, the same year MasterCard International was formed. Fairbank and the former vice chairman of Capital One, Nigel Morris, realized that traditional banks offered loans without focusing on the customers—like analyzing their risk characteristics. They decided that by using technology and data mining techniques in the decision-making process of providing credit, the bank could charge the appropriate interest rates more accurately and earn greater profits. In 1994, Capital One was spun off from Signet as a public credit card company and established itself in McLean, Virginia. It had an initial public offering of 7,125,000 shares of common stock in the United States and Canada, at a price of $16 per share,[6] which was managed by J.P. Morgan Securities Inc., Goldman, Sachs & Co. and Barney Inc. It is a part of the S&P 500 index, and also trades on the New York Stock Exchange with the symbol COF.

Between 1994 and 2004, the company grew at an annual compound rate of 29 percent,[7] both in terms of its EPS and the number of customers. In 2004, its earnings were $1.5 billion, and the EPS was at $6.21.[8] At the end of 2004, the company and its subsidiaries held 48.6 million accounts and $79.9 billion[9] in managed loans outstanding, which grew by 12 percent ($8.6 billion) over the previous year (see Exhibit 1). It had 17,760 employees in March 2005. The bank offers 7,000[10] variations of its MasterCard and Visa cards, each one is customized to appeal to different customer preferences and needs by combining product features such as different backgrounds and colors, along with varied annual percentage rates, credit limits, fees, and rewards programs. Capital One's pricing strategy is based on the risk level of its customers. It offers platinum and gold cards to its preferred customers with excellent credit history and a wide range of secured and unsecured cards to customers with limited or poor credit history. The company also provides a range of consumer products like auto financing, mortgage services, credit insurance, and home-equity loans.

Customizations of credit cards at Capital One are made with the support of its Information-Based Strategy (IBS), which uses sophisticated data-mining techniques to match its credit cards (its combination of interest rates, fees, rewards, and other conditions) with targeted customers based on their credit scores, credit uses, and other parameters. IBS is the fusion of one of the world's largest databases, information systems, a well-trained team of analysts and statisticians, and advanced scoring models. The company's decision-making process is made efficient by bringing together marketing, credit, risk, and information technology. It selects its most profitable customers and the appropriate rate by using the rigorous testing of econometric and time series models. The credit ratings of customers is based on the Fair Isaac Corporation (FICO) scores, which are used to predict payment risk by looking at several variables, including credit history. The IBS system uses FICO scores to divide its customers into three groups of super-prime (with excellent credit history), prime (average credit history), and sub-prime (with poor or very little credit history). Through the use of IBS, the company has been able to locate a group of students who were not included in the mailing lists of other credit card companies because these students, mostly unemployed and little or no credit histories, were considered high risk. Capital One's strategy of sending credit card applications, which were tailored to the needs of these students, proved effective, as 70 percent of the applications were filled and mailed back, thus creating a new market for the company. IBS has also helped Capital One avoid customers who do not pay interest charges on loans. The charge-off rate (for bad debt) of Capital One is the industry's lowest, and for 2004 was at 4.37 percent, compared to 5.32 percent in the previous year.[11]

Capital One's GFS segment offers a portfolio of diverse products to both domestic and international consumers. In the domestic market, the GFS segment includes installment lending, health care finance, mortgage lending services, and small business lending services. GFS has been on a growth curve and in 2004, it accounted for 27 percent of Capital One's total managed loans, which are comprised of reported loans and off-balance sheet securitized loans. It also accounts for 14 percent of its earnings. Its international portfolio primarily consists of credit card business in the United Kingdom and Canada, valued at $8.2 billion and $2.4 billion,[12] respectively. Capital One is the United Kingdom's seventh largest credit card issuer, and among the top ten of the same in Canada. In January 2005, the company completed the formalities to acquire a British equity brokerage firm called Hfs Group to strengthen its position in the United Kingdom. Although Capital One had holdings in France and South Africa, it exited these markets due to lack of growth opportunities.

Growth Strategies

Capital One generated strong earnings and loan growth again in 2004, as it has each year since its initial public offering ten years ago. The company is well positioned for continued success in 2005 in both our U.S. credit card and our growing and profitable diversification businesses.

—Richard D. Fairbank,
Chairman and CEO,
Capital One Financial Corporation[13]

Capital One grew at 30 percent[14] (see Exhibit 2, on page 68) between 1994 and 2004 by issuing credit cards at attractive interest rates. Most of its business is conducted via direct mail (junk-mail solicitations), although it also markets its products through television and Internet (http://www.capitalone.com). It expanded its credit card operations in Canada, Europe, and South Africa in the late 1990s. At the same time, the company also made strategic moves toward diversifying its portfolio by entering into financing of automobiles and other motor vehicles, mortgage and home equity loans, insurance, and other consumer lending products. Although 60 percent of its total managed loans is in its credit cards business (see Exhibit 3, on page 68), the company is gradually increasing its operations in other business segments.

In 1998, Capital One bought *Amerifee*, a company that provided financing for elective surgeries such as orthodontic, vision, and cosmetic procedures. It became a wholly owned subsidiary of Capital One in May 2001. *Amerifee* is a market leader known for introducing Orthodontists Fee and Dental Fee plans in 1993 and 1998, respectively. These fee plans are the largest patient payment plans in

Exhibit 1 Capital One Income Statement Data, 2004

(dollars in millions, except per-share data)	2004	2003	Percent Change
Income Statement Data:			
Interest income	$ 4,794.4	$ 4,367.7	9.77%
Interest expense	1,791.4	1,582.6	13.20
Net interest income	3,003.0	2,785.1	7.82
Provision for loan losses	1,220.9	1,517.5	–19.55
Net interest income after provision for loan losses	1,782.1	1,267.6	40.59
Non-interest income	5,900.2	5,415.9	8.94
Non-interest expense	5,322.2	4,856.7	9.58
Income before income taxes and cumulative effect of accounting change	2,360.1	1,826.8	29.19
Income taxes	816.6	676.0	20.79
Income before cumulative effect of accounting change	1,543.5	1,150.8	34.12
Cumulative effect of accounting change, net of taxes of $8.8	–	15.0	–100.00
Net income	$ 1,543.5	$ 1,135.8	35.90
Dividend payout ratio	1.66%	2.14%	
Per Common Share:			
Basic earnings per share	$ 6.55	$ 5.05	29.70
Diluted earnings per share	6.21	4.85	28.04
Dividends	0.11	0.11	0.00
Book value as of year-end	33.99	25.75	32.00
Selected Year-End Reported Balances:			
Liquidity portfolio	$ 10,384.1	$ 7,464.7	39.11
Consumer loans	38,215.6	32,850.3	16.33
Allowance for loan losses	(1,505.0)	(1,595.0)	–5.64
Total assets	53,747.3	46,283.7	16.13
Interest-bearing deposits	25,636.8	22,416.3	14.37
Borrowings	9,637.0	14,812.6	–34.94
Stockholders' equity	8,388.2	6,051.8	38.61
Selected Average Reported Balances:			
Liquidity portfolio	$ 10,528.6	$ 6,961.2	51.25
Consumer loans	34,265.7	28,677.6	19.49
Allowance for loan losses	(1,473.0)	(1,627.0)	–9.47
Total assets	50,648.1	41,195.4	22.95
Interest-bearing deposits	24,313.3	19,768.0	22.99
Borrowings	8,520.2	12,978.0	–34.35
Stockholders' equity	7,295.5	5,323.5	37.04
Reported Metrics:			
Revenue margin	19.08%	21.95%	
Net interest margin	6.44	7.45	
Delinquency rate	3.85	4.79	
Net charge-off rate	3.78	5.74	
Return on average assets	3.05	2.76	
Return on average equity	21.16	21.34	
Average equity to average assets	14.40	12.92	
Operating expense as a % of average loans	11.63	13.04	
Allowance for loan losses to consumer loans	3.94	4.86	
Managed Metrics:			
Revenue margin	12.89%	14.65%	
Net interest margin	7.88	8.64	
Delinquency rate	3.82	4.46	
Net charge-off rate	4.41	5.86	
Return on average assets	1.73	1.52	
Operating expense as a % of average loans	5.41	5.94	
Average consumer loans	$ 73,711.7	$ 62,911.91	17.17
Year-end consumer loans	79,861.3	71,244.8	12.09
Year-end total accounts	48.6	47.0	3.26

Source: Compiled by ICFAI Business School Case Development Centre from http://www.capitalone.com.

the sectors of Orthodontics and Dentistry. In 2001, it pioneered the Family Fee plan, which was specifically designed for treatment of infertility and are offered through Reproductive Endocrinologists and infertility clinics.[15] The subsidiary formally became Capital One Healthcare Finance in April 2005.

Exhibit 2 Capital One Financial Summary, 2004

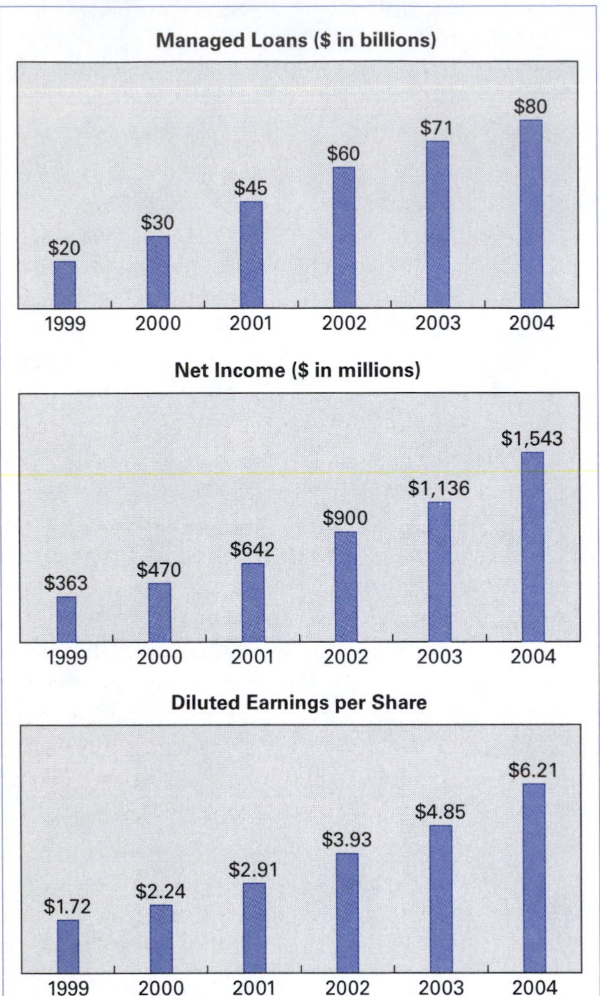

Source: Compiled by ICFAI Business School Case Development Centre from http://www.capitalone.com.

Capital One soon realized that the auto financing market is double that of the credit card market, and therefore it has a strong growth potential in that segment. This market is highly fragmented and no company holds more than 20 percent[16] of the market share. It provided an opportunity to Capital One Auto Finance Inc. (COAF) to introduce innovative offers and increase its market share. COAF added $163.8 million[17] to the company's earnings in 2004, and has continued to be on a high growth curve. To strengthen its market position in the automobile finance segment, the company acquired *ONYXAcceptance Corporation* (Onyx) for $191 million[18] (in an all cash transaction) on January 11, 2005. It also acquired InsLogic, an insurance brokerage firm, from Onyx's management team. The purchase strengthened the Auto Finance subsidiary of Capital One and enhanced its dealer relationships, coast-to-coast market penetration in the United States, and its product line among the prime borrowers. Onyx is based in Foothills, California, and provides automobile loans to certain independent and franchise dealerships all over the United States. Onyx claims to have purchased and securitized $10 billion[19] in auto loans since its inception in 1993, and will add 12,000 new dealerships to Capital One's list. According to David R. Lawson, Capital One's executive vice president, and president of COAF, "This transaction combines two strong franchises with complementary strengths. Onyx's significant and long-standing presence with California dealerships coupled with its strong prime product offering fills out both COAF's product line and geographic footprint. Together, we expect to realize significant revenue and cost synergies."[20] This acquisition may make COAF the second largest auto lender in the United States.

COAF has announced that it has raised its car loan limit to $100,000[21] (previously $75,000) for direct-to-consumer vehicle loans that have originated from its Web

Exhibit 3 Capital One Loan Portfolio

Business Segment	% of Total Loans, 1996	% of Total Loans, 2000	% of Total Loans, 2002	% of Total Loans, 2003	% of Total Loans, 2004
Credit Cards	100%	78%	68%	63%	60.75%
Auto Loans	0	2	13	13	12.5
International Operations	0	20	19	24	26.75
Total	100	100	100	100	100

Source: Compiled by ICFAI Business School Case Development Centre from http://www.capitalone.com.

site (http://capitaloneautofinance.com) in February 2005. This move was made in response to the growing demand for luxury cars such as Corvette by Chevrolet, so that the company can get more business from this customer segment. This extension is limited to only those with excellent credit histories (super-prime customers). The vice president of COAF, Brian Reed, said, "Car buyers have more choices than ever today at the higher end of the car spectrum, so we've adjusted our limit to offer consumers greater flexibility."[22] The competitive advantage of COAF is that the loan process takes place on the Internet and requires no legacy fees. Also, its IBS system allows it to charge varying interest rates depending on the customer's risk levels.

In February 2005, Capital One purchased eSmartloans .com for $155 million,[23] one of the largest online providers of home equity loans mortgages in the United States. Headquartered in Overland Park, Kansas, the company offers a variety of products that are marketed and delivered directly to homeowners. The purchase is meant to broaden Capital One's offering of consumer loans and deepen its position in the growing U.S. home equity market. Larry Klane, Capital One's executive vice president of Global Financial Services, said, "eSmartloan has succeeded in building a scalable technology platform, a highly skilled sales team, and an outstanding reputation for customer service and speed to close. By combining these strengths with Capital One's powerful national brand, access to 47 million accounts, and expertise in direct marketing, we will enhance the growth of our home equity lending business."[24]

In early March 2005, Capital One announced its decision to purchase Hibernia National Bank. Hibernia is the largest bank in Louisiana,[25] with 316 branches in Louisiana and Texas, and $17.4 billion[26] in deposits. It provides a wide assortment of financial products and services through its banking and non-banking subsidiaries that ranges from deposit products, small business, commercial, mortgage, private and international banking, to trust and investment management, brokerage, investment banking, and insurance. Capital One paid a 24 percent premium over Hibernia's closing stock price of $26.57 as on March 4, or $33 per share,[27] and a total of $5.3 billion for the purchase. The merger is expected to cost $175 million in restructuring expenses and result in near-term synergies of $135 million.[28] According to Fairbank, "This acquisition is a natural extension of the diversification strategy we have been pursuing for some time. The transaction brings together two financial companies with complementary strengths and represents a compelling long-term value proposition for shareholders of both companies. Hibernia's leading market share in Louisiana and its promising Texas branch expansion create not only a solid growth platform as we continue to expand, but also an additional source of lower cost funding. Additionally, we believe our national brand, 48 million accounts, broad product offerings, asset generation capabilities, and market expertise will drive profitable growth in branch banking." [29]

Capital One wanted to purchase a commercial bank with a strong management team and a large local market share. Hibernia has both these qualities as well as the potential to expand extensively into Texas markets. Currently it has only 109 branches in Texas, but the cities of Dallas and Houston are number 2 and 3 in terms of fastest growing markets in the metro cities, a seemingly untapped potential for capturing market share in that region.[30] The main advantage of purchasing Hibernia is that Capital One gains access to a lower cost of funding at 1.38 percent against a rate of 4.24 percent.[31] One third of Capital One's funding is obtained from the deposits in its fully owned Internet bank at 4 percent, which is higher than that paid by any of its rivals. The rest of it comes from securitization, which is risky as well as costlier than its other avenues of sourcing funds. It can increase ratio of funding from deposits from the previous 30 percent to 40 percent,[32] to support its lending operations in the areas of credit cards, auto finance and mortgages. Acquiring Hibernia is also expected to increase its profit margins due to decreased interest expenses and bring stability to its businesses of consumer lending and other financial products. It now has the ability to use Hibernia's brick-and-mortar branches as a launching pad to market its range of offerings in combination with its IBS techniques. The deal also provides Capital One with the opportunity to enter the debit-card market and also introduce its own home equity credit line.

Potential Challenges

Early in the twenty-first century, the U.S. credit card industry witnessed a high level of competition and was also going through a phase of consolidation. For example, J.P. Morgan merged with Chase in 2000, and the combined group merged with Bank One in July 2004 to form the second largest U.S. bank holding company with a combined asset base of $1 trillion[33] and 19.1 percent of the total credit card market share. The U.S. consumer debt amount of $2.1 trillion (Federal Reserve Bank data) in January 2005 was mostly due to the top ten credit card companies, which held 85 percent of the market share.[34] Market share of Capital One in the credit card segment fell from 7.2 percent in 2003[35] to 6.8 percent (see Exhibit 4) in 2004. Capital One was left with no innovative ideas such as being the first bank to offer automatic balance transfers, which could grab business from other banks. The rise in personal bankruptcies and the economic recession between 2001 and 2004, coupled with the saturation of the credit card market diminished growth opportunities for Capital One in that market. This

Exhibit 4 Top Ten U.S. Bank Credit Card Issuers, Third Quarter 2004

Rank/Issuer	Outstandings ($ billions)	Market Share
1. JPM Chase	$ 131.5	19.1%
2. Citigroup	112.0	16.3
3. MBNA	81.5	11.8
4. Amer. Exp.*	63.9	9.3
5. Bank of Amer.	55.4	8.0
6. Discover**	47.1	7.2
7. Capital One	46.1	6.8
8. HSBC	20.1	2.9
9. Providian	17.9	2.6
10. Wells Fargo	8.2	1.2
TOTAL	$ 583.7	85.2%

*Includes $25.2 billion in nonrevolving outstandings.
**As of August 31, 2004.
Source: Compiled by ICFAI Business School Case Development Centre from http://www.cardweb.com.

Appendix 1 David Spade in a Capital One Advertisement

Source: http://www.capitalone.com.

necessitated its diversification into other consumer lending operations through different distribution channels such as Hibernia.

Capital One has been bombarding the Internet, radio, and television with its advertisement, "What's in your wallet?" with one of the versions featuring the famous Hollywood comedian David Spade (Appendix 1). It spent $285 million on advertisements, a total marketing expense of $1.3 billion[36] in 2004 and $5.4 million in January 2005,[37] which was more than competitors such as American Express. In a consumer survey conducted by *USA Today's* weekly poll, 30 percent of the people "disliked" the advertisement, while 12 percent liked it "a lot," suggesting that it did not receive the popularity it wanted. It was opined that the advertisement expense has been eating into Capital One's profits.

Another potential hurdle for Capital One is its potentially risky source of funding from securitization. It pools together the loans it originates and invests pieces from that collection in different securities. Because the investment is dependent on the stock market price fluctuations, this source of funding involves a great deal of uncertainty and risks of monetary loss. It has also amassed a large portfolio of sub-prime customers as it relies on its IBS system to guide it toward greater profit margins (related to greater risk), without incurring heavy losses. Due to federal regulations and a great many of its customers defaulting on their loans, Capital One had to shift away from sub-prime to a greater proportion of prime and super-prime customers. This change led to smaller margins as the company offered an introductory rate of 9.9 percent to its super-prime customers vis-à-vis a rate of 25.9 percent[38] charged to sub-prime customers who are associated with

Appendix 2 Capital One Financial Corporation (COF) Year Movement of Stock Price and Volume

Source: Compiled by ICFAI Business School Case Development Centre from http://www.capitalone.com.

high probability of delinquency. In July 2002, the company disclosed its decision to tighten controls over its loan disbursements (mainly to sub-prime lenders) to meet the banking regulators' demands, leading to a 40 percent decline[39] in its shares in one day (Appendix 2).

Management of Hibernia's branch banking and its non-consumer lending operations, after the merger is complete, might pose a challenge for Capital One because it lacks experience in those fields. The non-consumer lending portfolio consists of commercial and industrial loans (C&I) and commercial real-estate (CRE) loans. Hibernia's combined portfolio of C&I and CRE is worth \$4 billion,[40] and its small business portfolio is valued at \$3.2 billion. The challenge will be to efficiently integrate Hibernia into its system and strategy, which includes incorporation of its retail branch banking, and review of its business and asset integration plans. For the short term, it might need to rely on Hibernia's management team in making any strategic decisions.

Part of the strategic long-term vision, as announced by the company is to expand further into the state of Texas, especially in Dallas and Houston, and establish new branches there. In expanding in that direction, Capital One is likely to face stiff competition from several major players in the credit card and banking industry such as JP Morgan, Citigroup, Bank of America, and American Express. It may be difficult for Capital One to steal any business away from these giants, even with its innovative ideas and products, because the bigger players have strong presence in that region. Analyst and credit rating agencies like Fitch have warned that Capital One's growth depends on its ability to aggressively defend and maintain market positions in the states of Louisiana and Texas. Fairbanks said, "We're well positioned to continue our profitable growth. Financially, we've never been stronger. Our flagship credit card business is thriving. We're successfully taking IBS, the strategy that made Capital One a winner in credit cards and auto finance, to new businesses. And, we have a powerful brand and huge customer base to fuel our growth and diversification. Our people have pulled together to make Capital One the strong, diversified company it is today. And I am confident that they will sustain our momentum as we enter our second decade as a public company."[41]

Notes

1. M. McNamee, 2005, Capital One's concrete step, http://www.businessweek.com, March 11.
2. http://www.fortune.com.
3. http://www.capitalone.com.
4. Ibid.
5. N. Slaughter, 2005, Capital One shells out, http://www.fool.com, March 7.
6. 1994, Capital One financial corporation completes initial public offering, http://www.businesswire.com, November 15.
7. http://www.fortune.com.
8. Ibid.
9. 2005, Capital One to acquire Hibernia Corporation for $5.3 billion in stock and cash, http://biz.yahoo.com, March 6.
10. M. McNamee, 1999, Capital One: Isn't there more to life than plastic?" http://www.businessweek.com, November 22.
11. http://www.capitalone.com.
12. Ibid.
13. http://www.capitalone.com.
14. 2005, A capital idea, http://www.economist.com, March 10.
15. http://www.capitalonehealthcarefinance.com.
16. Ibid.
17. http://www.capitalone.com.
18. Ibid.
19. http://www.onyxacceptance.com.
20. http://www.capitalone.com.
21. 2005, Capital One announces new online auto loan limit of $100,000, http://www.pwrebdirect.com, February 25.
22. Ibid.
23. http://www.mccollpartners.com.
24. http://www.capitalone.com.
25. Louisiana is one of the southern-most states in the U.S. and is located between Texas and Mississippi.
26. A capital idea, op. cit.
27. 2005, Capital One buying Hibernia for $5.3B, http://www.cnnmoney.com, March 7.
28. http://www.Capitalone.com.
29. Capital One to acquire Hibernia Corporation for $5.3 billion in stock and cash, op. cit.
30. Capital One's concrete step, op. cit.
31. A capital idea, op. cit.
32. Ibid.
33. T. Locke, 2005, Bank One, JPMorgan merger ups the ante in Colorado banking game, http://www.bizjournals.com, March 25.
34. A capital idea, op. cit.
35. K. Maguire, 2005, Capital One rolls with the punches, http://news.yahoo.com, March 21.
36. http://www.capitalone.com.
37. M. McCarthy, 2005, Capital One's 'What's in your wallet?' ads filling airwaves, http://www.usatoday.com, March 13.
38. S. Maranjian, 2005, How to owe $40,000 by doing nothing, http://www.fool.com, February 11.
39. R. Barker, 2003, Who's minding the store at Capital One? http://www.businessweek.com, March 24.
40. 2005, Fitch places Capital One on rating watch positive; Hibernia on watch negative, http://www.bloomberg.com, March 7.
41. http://www.capitalone.com.

Case 7

Carrefour in Asia

Claudia Gehlen, Neil Jones, Philippe Lasserre

INSEAD

"China represents a huge market and now it has acquired its WTO membership. But there is no easy way to stand out a winner here. China is nearly as big as Europe and all areas differ from each other," declared Jean-Luc Chereau, president of Carrefour China, at the opening of the first Carrefour store in Urumqi, Xinjiang province. The Urumqi hypermarket was the forty-second to be opened by the company in China where Carrefour was the leading mass retailer, despite mounting competition.

History

In 2003 Carrefour was the second-largest mass retailer in the world with net sales totaling €70.5 billion (US$84 billion) and net profits of €1.6 billion. It operated 10,378 stores in 29 countries and employed more than 410,000 people.

Although primarily known as a hypermarket pioneer, Carrefour also operated supermarkets, hard discounts and other formats, such as convenience stores (see Exhibits 1 and 2).

Exhibit 1 Carrefour's Key Figures

Year	Revenue (in million euros)	Net Income (in million euros)	Net Profit Margin (%)	Employees	Sales Area (m²)	Annual Sales/m² in Euros
2003	70,486	1,629	2.3%	410,000	13,207	5,337
2002	68,728	1,347	2.0	396,662	9,767	7,037
2001	69,486	1,265	1.8	382,821	9,151	7,593
2000	64,802	1,065	1.6	330,247	8,130	7,971
1999	51,948	898	1.7	297,290	6,569	7,908
1998	27,408	647	2.4	132,875	3,721	7,366
1997	25,804	546	2.1	113,289	3,075	8,392
1996	23,615	476	2.0	103,600	2,727	8,660
1995	22,046	539	2.4	102,900	2,378	9,271
1994	20,778	324	1.6	95,900	2,129	9,760
1993	18,708	448	2.4	81,500	1,920	9,744

Exhibit 2 Carrefour Formats Worldwide

Format	Number of Stores	Sales (incl. taxes in million euros)	Sales % of Total	Sales Area (1000 m²)	Sales Incl. Taxes/m² in Euros
Hypermarkets	823	51,060	57.60%	6,985	7,310
Supermarkets	2,380	22,592	25.50	3,394	6,656
Hard discounts	4,456	6,692	7.60	1,459	4,586
Other stores	2,718	8,229	9.30	1,369	6,010
Total	10,378	88,572	100.00	13,207	

Note: Those figures relate to all stores operated under Carrefour's banner, including the franchises.
Source: Carrefour Annual Report, 2003.

This case was written by Claudia Gehlen, Research Associate, under the supervision of Neil Jones and Philippe Lasserre, both professors at INSEAD. It is intended to be used a basis for class discussion rather than to illustrate either effective or ineffective handling of an administrative situation.

It has always been significantly more international than most of its competitors (see Exhibit 3). Carrefour's international operations are located in three major geographical zones: Europe and the Middle East, Latin America, and Asia. In 2003, 49 percent of its hypermarket revenues were derived from markets outside France (see Exhibit 4). In Europe and China, Carrefour is the number one retailer in terms of size.

Carrefour developed the hypermarket concept of bringing nearly all types of consumer goods under one roof in 1959, when the Defforey and Fournier families created their first hypermarket in the suburbs of Paris. It built a reputation as the retailer that offered the most variety and freshness at low prices. For years its claim to fame was to offer a massive array of quality goods in one place, at reasonable prices rather than bargain-basement value.

The retailer operated exclusively in France until the late 1960s before expanding into Spain, where under the name of Pryca, it became the country's second-largest retailer. It then successfully entered Portugal, Argentina, and Brazil. However, in more mature markets its results were not so conclusive and it had to pull out of the United Kingdom, Switzerland, the United States, and Belgium (although it was later to reenter Switzerland and Belgium).

As in France during the 1960s, Carrefour was generally successful when it entered new markets that had seen dramatic changes in consumer buying habits, coupled with high growth in *per capita GNP*, suburbanization, greater participation of women in the labor force, and a large increase in the ownership of cars and refrigerators.

During the 1980s and 1990s, Carrefour continued its international expansion through a combination of organic growth and acquisitions, extending its reach into Latin America. The 1990s were characterized by a move into Asia, starting with Taiwan in 1989 and a few years later expanding to Malaysia, China, South Korea, Thailand, Singapore, Indonesia, and Japan. In all the Asian markets, hypermarkets emerged as the winning format (see Exhibit 5).

In France, due to regulatory constraints, Carrefour merged in 1999 with rival Promodès, the number two in the French market. The merger may also have been motivated by Wal-Mart's acquisition of Asda in the United Kingdom that same year. From 2000 to 2003 Carrefour wrestled with integrating Promodès' businesses into its existing operations. As a result, its performance and organic growth rate slipped during this period. Carrefour focused intensely on integration and repairing weak domestic sales and by the end of the year it had successfully repositioned itself to continue its international expansion at its historically fast pace.

Carrefour also has a foothold in the Middle East. In the United Arab Emirates (UAE), the joint venture company between Majid al Futtaim and Carrefour was the most dynamic and fast-moving hypermarket chain, with a total of eight stores in 2004. Thanks to its massive buying power, Carrefour could guarantee low prices while permanently offering about 50,000 items in stock.

In February 2004 shares in Carrefour SA jumped in value, renewing market speculation that its larger rival, Wal-Mart, was planning a bid. Wal-Mart had coveted the French market for years but its attempts to buy a French subsidiary had been stymied since its abortive courtship of the Auchan and Carrefour chains in 1999.

Adding to the speculation over Carrefour's future was the death in a plane crash in December 2003 of a member of the Halley family group, Carrefour's largest shareholder with an approximate 11.5 percent stake. Such speculation highlighted that Carrefour was vulnerable to a takeover, or at least to increased competition from international competitors like Wal-Mart and Tesco that were posting stronger domestic growth. In 2003 Carrefour's hypermarkets

Exhibit 3 Level of Internationalization of Global Retailers in 2003

Retailer	Number of Countries	Net Sales (in million US$)	Foreign Sales %
Carrefour	29	84,000	50
Metro	22	46,900	45
Ito-Yokado	12	27,238	41
Tesco	11	39,521	18
Aeon	10	24,677	17
Costco	7	37,993	16
Wal-Mart	11	205,500	16
Daiei	3	17,717	1

Source: http://www.siamfuture.com; companies reports.

Exhibit 4 Carrefour Worldwide Operations

Region	Number of Stores	Net Sales (in million euros)	Sales (% of total)	Investments Million€	%/Sales	Operating Million €	Margin %
France	1,448	35,704	50.65%	818	2.3%	2144	6.0%
Europe	3,606	25,526	36.21	1169	4.6	952	3.7
Latin America	814	4,619	6.55	295	6.4	13	0.3
Asia	199	4,637	6.58	436	9.4	143	3.1
Total	6,067	70,486	100.00	2717	3.9	3251	4.6

Source: Carrefour Annual Report, 2003.

Exhibit 5 Carrefour Formats by Region

Sales Incl. Taxes in 2003 (in million euros)					
	Hypermarkets	Supermarkets	Hard Discounts	Others	Total
France	23,948	13,151	2,037	5,576	44,912
Europe	17,900	8,302	4,405	2,453	33,060
Latin America	4,059	1,139	245	–	5,444
Asia	5,152	–	4	–	5,157
	51,060				–
Total	50,509	22,592	6,692	2,719	88,572

Number of Stores in 2003					
	Hypermarkets	Supermarkets	Hard Discounts	Others	Total
France	216	1,005	588	1,766	3,575
Europe	315	1,121	3,381	953	5,770
Latin America	147	254	432	–	833
Asia	145	–	55	–	200
Total	823	2,380	4,456	2,719	10,378

Sales Area in 2002 (thousand m²)					
	Hypermarkets	Supermarkets	Hard Discounts	Others	Total
France	1,864	1,577	343	945	4,729
Europe	2,584	1,367	959	425	5,335
Latin America	1,316	449	141	–	1,907
Asia	1,220	–	16	–	1,236
Total	6,985	3,393	1,459	1,370	13,207

Source: Carrefour Annual Report, 2003.

had a 13.9 percent share of the "fast-moving consumer goods" category in its French home market (which included food as well as household goods and health and beauty products), down from 14.4 percent in 2002. The company might have considered a defensive merger with another European retailer had Wal-Mart set its sights on Carrefour, although any merger or takeover might well run into culture clashes, integration headaches, and antitrust concerns. As CEO Daniel Bernard put it, "Hostile bids in a 'people' sector simply don't work."

Another threat came from the growth of hard-discounters like Aldi from Germany that sold goods at rock-bottom prices. In order to fight back against the hard-discounters, Carrefour expanded its own hard discount chain, ED.

Carrefour's Approach

The basics of Carrefour's concept are (1) one-stop shopping, (2) low prices, (3) self-service, (4) quality products, (5) freshness, and (6) free parking.

Before entering a new international market, local conditions are analyzed against a set of socio-economic criteria. The size and maturity of the market, the legal framework and the openness to foreign investors are major aspects. For instance, Carrefour postponed its entry into India due to a lack of clarity on direct foreign investment. Basic figures regarding population, per capita GDP, transport networks, the level of motorization, urbanization, real estate prices, and so forth are also taken into account. However, Carrefour does not believe only in extensive market research, as Jean-Michel Arlaud, head of its Romanian operations, put it in an interview:

When we decided to set up stores in Romania, it was more an instinctive feeling than the results of a market study. If we had based our decisions on studies, we would never have come.

Once the feasibility study is conclusive, Carrefour focuses on selecting the format best suited to the particular market and adapting that format to local needs. Unprecedented in its history, Carrefour has opted in many Asian countries for an urban location for its stores due to the population density, and has positioned its hypermarkets as proximity stores rather than suburban stores, offering a limited product range but producing greater volume.

Carrefour tries to establish as many stores as possible in major urban areas in order to achieve economies

Exhibit 6 Carrefour's Virtuous Circle

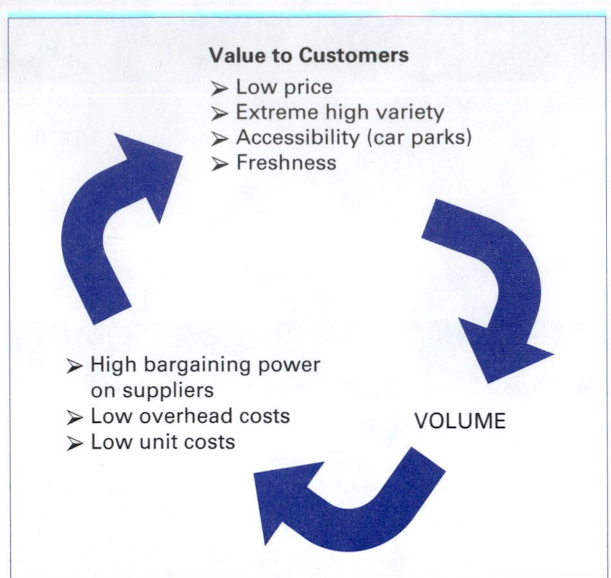

Source: Carrefour Annual Report, 2003; EIU Data Services.

of scale. Its challenge in each new market is to recreate the virtuous circle of "freshness + variety + low prices → high volume → high bargaining power → low costs → low prices" (see Exhibit 6).

For Carrefour, price is not simply a competitive advantage but an essential means of survival. In order to drive down prices in response to competition while maintaining high-quality brands, Carrefour advertises new promotions and discounts every day, reminding customers that they will be refunded if they find the same product cheaper elsewhere.

Taking local constraints into account, Carrefour has added new services in developing markets, such as free shuttle services for customers and play areas for children, as well as home delivery. In some markets, such as China, Carrefour has launched its own product line in home appliances and spices.

Because Carrefour operates on tiny margins (6.9 percent gross margin and 2.5 percent net margin), the slightest improvement in these translates into significant growth for the bottom line.

One important factor in cost management is its sourcing strategy. In China, for instance, more than 95 percent of its merchandise is locally sourced and the remainder is sourced through local importers or the trading office in Hong Kong. Carrefour has built big global procurement centers coordinated through Shanghai and Hong Kong.

The centralization of its IT systems and administrative procedures achieves further savings. Shared processes and systems increase operational efficiency and the introduction of international product ranges complements its locally sensitive strategy. In order to increase its profitability, in 2000 Carrefour created the GNX online supply platform with Oracle and Sears, whereby suppliers and retailers can exchange information via the Internet and optimize the flow of merchandise, thus reducing their administrative costs. Other retailers have since joined GNX including Metro (Germany), Sainsbury's (U.K.), Kroger (U.S.) and Coles Myer (Australia).

Carrefour also works actively with local governments and nonprofit organizations to protect the environment. In 2002 Carrefour and the Chinese Packaging Corporation initiated actions to globally reduce pollution from packaging. Worldwide, Carrefour requested that its stores make less use of plastic in packaging, thereby gaining a reputation as a model in the retailing industry.

While venturing into new markets, Carrefour's human resource policy has relied on a small number of expatriates. In 2002 Carrefour employed about 200 expatriate executives with solid experience of adapting Carrefour's retailing concept to local contexts. They were mainly recruited in France but also in countries that were considered Carrefour strongholds, such as Taiwan.

When opening a new market, Carrefour operates a dual system for employing expatriates and local executives. Initially, store and department heads are experienced expatriates. Local managers receive six months' training in a country of the region where Carrefour is already successfully operating. Thereafter they work hand-in-hand: the expatriates contributing their expertise and experience and the local executives sharing their know-how of the local business environment. Carrefour's aim is to eventually promote local talent to top management.

As early as 1969 Carrefour was the first mass retailer to measure performance on the return on invested capital instead of the classic concept of gross profit margin used in traditional trade. In terms of remuneration it has a reputation for paying employees well: Department heads earn 20 percent more than they would with other supermarkets, and can earn a bonus linked to the results of the department. The pressure for sales and profit is put on department heads, as each store is a profit center. In Asia, department heads are much more autonomous than in France and are also in charge of recruiting employees and negotiating salaries.

In China, Carrefour employs 95 percent of local Chinese managers and invests heavily in their training. In 2002 Carrefour employed a total of 18,000 local employees, and 1,000 Chinese department heads were trained in retail techniques and business management.

Carrefour in Asia

In 2003 Carrefour was present in eight Asian markets, operating 144 hypermarkets and 55 hard discount stores (see Exhibits 7 and 8). The Asian zone represented

Exhibit 7 Carrefour's Asian Presence

	Year of Entry	Sales in 2002 (in million euro)	Sales growth (%)	GDP Growth in 2002 (%)	Population (millions) in 2002	Urban population (%)
Taiwan	1989	1,381.00	1.6	3.0	22.50	n.a.
Malaysia	1994	225.90	–1.7	3.5	24.00	58.7
China	1995	1,369.50	6.1	7.5	1,282.10	33.1
South Korea	1996	1,242.90	1.7	6.3	48.10	83.0
Thailand	1996	416.40	21.0	4.5	63.40	22.4
Singapore	1997	86.00	6.0	2.2	3.60	100.0
Indonesia	1998	313.20	48.6	3.5	217.10	42.9
Japan	2000	156.90	6.1	0.9	127.20	79.1
Total		**5,191.80**				

Exhibit 8 Carrefour in Asia

	Expansion of Stores and Surface												Tesco	Macro	Wal-Mart
	1993	1994	1995	1996	1997	1998	1999	2000	2001	2002	2003	Surface (1000 m²)	2002	2002	2002
China			2	3	7	14	20	24	24	36	**95**	**337**	12	5	25
Hypermarkets											40	321			
Hard Discounts											55	15			
South Korea				3	3	6	12	20	22	25	27	**253**	20		9
Hong Kong				1	2	4	4								
Indonesia						1	5	7	8	10	**11**	**73**		12	
Japan								1	3	4	**7**	**65**			
Malaysia		1	1	2	3	5	6	6	6	6	**7**	**69**	1	8	
Singapore					1	1	1	1	1	1	**2**	**15**			
Taiwan	7	8	10	13	17	21	23	24	26	28	**31**	**243**	3	8	
Thailand				2	6	7	9	11	15	17	**19**	**172**	41	21	
Total	7	9	13	24	39	59	80	94	105	126	**199**	**1228**	**77**	**54**	**34**
Hypermarkets											144	1212			
Hard Discounts											55	15			

13 percent of the group's hypermarket sales and 6.7 percent of the total. Net sales revenues totaled €4,637 million and profits €143 million (4.7 percent of the total).

When first moving into Asia, Carrefour opted for joint ventures and partnerships to make up for its lack of knowledge of the Asian market. Later on it worked with financial or industrial partners only when national regulations made it necessary, as in China, Thailand, Malaysia, and Indonesia.

With the exception of Japan, Carrefour chose those countries that, despite their low GDP, had reached a sufficient level of maturity to make the transition to mass consumption. Timing was crucial to Carrefour's success because it entered these markets earlier than its competitors, who had delayed entry due to the Asian crisis. Local competition was also slow to react to this new phenomenon and was often thwarted by the onset of the Asian crisis, especially in Korea, Thailand, and Indonesia.

According to Gérard Clerc, the vice president who led Carrefour's Asian expansion, the Asian crisis did not affect the company; on the contrary, Carrefour benefited, thanks to its low price policy and emerged even stronger from the crisis with a higher market share than expected. Until the year 2000 international competition had been rather timid but was now progressing fast. International players such as Makro, Metro, Tesco, and Wal-Mart had shown a big appetite for the region.

Even though Asian customers still tended to shop daily at wet markets or "mom & pop" stores, buying patterns were slowly changing and a certain degree of Westernization of local tastes was apparent in most countries. Moreover, impulse buying was on the rise and replacing necessity purchasing. Shopping as a form of leisure was an increasing phenomenon: a visit to the French hypermarket had turned into a Sunday outing.

Carrefour in Taiwan

"It was as if the Huns had arrived in Taiwan," Gérard Clerc said of the reaction of local retailers in Taiwan to Carrefour's arrival.

In 1987 Carrefour selected Taiwan as the entry point into the vast, mainly untapped market space for hypermarkets. As René Brillet, director of the Asia region, put it: "This explains why we have roots on this continent, offering us the potential for tremendous growth, because of its size, its cultural diversity and its enormous population." Another advantage of the Taiwanese experience was that it served as a human resource hub for other Asian markets, especially China.

However, Carrefour did not have an easy start in Taiwan and it was almost two years before it finally set up a hypermarket in 1989. Carrefour, with Makro, was the first foreign retailer to establish the hypermarket concept in Taiwan. The retailer entered a partnership with a local food and retailing conglomerate, the President Group, which held 40 percent of the shares. The President Group is a dominant figure on the Taiwanese business landscape, ranking number two in size. Right from the start it accepted the role of a dormant partner but played a big role in introducing Carrefour to the political and economic establishment.

During this period real estate prices skyrocketed, making some adaptation of Carrefour's policy necessary. Traditionally, Carrefour had set up much bigger stores in suburban areas. Instead of buying the sites, Carrefour rented space to operate hypermarkets in Kaohsiung and Taipei on a much smaller scale (3,500 m^2) in urban centers on two stories instead of the classic one-floor layout. In addition, in urban areas some kind of "protection" from the local secret societies had to be negotiated.

All stores consistently had pilot departments to introduce new product ranges. Study conclusions were then introduced on a national scale across all Carrefour stores in Taiwan. This cross-learning was vitally important as it spread the know-how within the company. Subsequently, Carrefour increased the size of its new stores.

In certain cases Carrefour chose industrial and commercial parks to develop the hypermarkets. Wholesale stores or "green stores" were built in industrial areas, and general retailing or "blue stores" in residential areas. By adopting this strategy Carrefour could capture both big and small accounts and grow much faster than its rival Makro.

Carrefour is pronounced Jia Le Fu in Chinese, which means "luck and happiness for the whole family." This fortunate phonetic translation unexpectedly contributed to Carrefour's success in Taiwan and later in China, where foreign names often remain unpronounceable.

However, Carrefour still had to tackle different business approaches, especially to negotiation. "For Europeans, Chinese are known to be difficult negotiators. They consider the negotiation process as a refined art which they master with intelligence and patience," Gerard Clerc explained. Managing the supply chain was another major challenge. Taiwanese suppliers lacked rigor, organization, equipment, and aggressiveness, but they were much more flexible than their Western counterparts. They sold products, not services, and often lacked information regarding basic data on their sales, inventory level, and even internal accounting.

Communication was another challenge. In Taiwan, all documents were written in Chinese while Carrefour's documentation was in English. Corporate culture, training, and company goals, among other factors, were difficult to communicate to all staff members, and promotions were only possible for English-speaking staff.

The cultural gap was also a source of misunderstanding amongst management. Rather than sharing their knowledge with their staff, local managers had the tendency to withhold information. According to one French local store manager, Philippe Ravelli, the French and the Chinese cultures do not give the same priority to the three basic elements in daily life. For the Chinese, emotion (quing) comes first, followed by reason (li), and law (fa). For the French, law comes first (the company policy), reason second, emotion last. Despite such differences, thanks to its adaptive capabilities Carrefour became the largest mass retailer on the island.

Fortunately, Taiwan was relatively spared by the Asian crisis and consumption levels continued to increase. Carrefour continued to reinforce its lead over Makro, sometimes opening new stores near existing Makro stores. By 2003 Carrefour was operating 31 stores in Taiwan, which continued to be its most important Asian market with net sales of €1,322 million.

Carrefour in South Korea

Since the liberalization of the Korean retail market in 1996, local and foreign retailers, such as Carrefour, Makro, Costco, Wal-Mart, and Metro, had struggled to stake out their territory. Local conglomerates raised the stakes and invested massively to protect the local industry. But the Asian crisis forced these local retailers to freeze their expansion plans, and some even had to file for bankruptcy. As a consequence, Carrefour further reinforced its position and recorded its first profit in 1997. Restructuring and modernization of existing stores started in 2001. Carrefour introduced a new feature with the creation of cultural centers in two stores in partnership with Korea's leading newspaper. These offered women and children weekly courses in English, dance, cooking, drawing, and other subjects. In 2003 Carrefour, now the number four food retailer, operated 27 stores, posting net sales of €1,149 million.

Carrefour in Thailand

As with Korea, Thailand seemed to present all the conditions for Carrefour to succeed and the crisis offered an opportunity to expand while costs were lower and the competition reduced. Carrefour opened two stores there in 1996. However, unlike Korea, the chain operated with two local partners and this postponed their expansion plans for a year and reduced the number of stores to be opened from five to two in 1999.

Foreign ownership laws in Thailand allowed foreign companies—except American companies—to hold no more than 49 percent of the shares. Carrefour argued that this law would favor its rival, Wal-Mart. When the Central Retail Corp. sold its 40 percent shareholding in 1998, this law made it impossible for Carrefour to purchase the shares.

In 2002 Carrefour introduced a number of sales innovations that proved successful. The fresh product concept was redesigned in order to reproduce the atmosphere and merchandising style found in street markets, while emphasizing hygienic conditions. As an example, the "pork quality line" covered the entire cycle from breeding selection and reproduction to stocking the shelves. In 2003 Carrefour Thailand counted 19 stores with net sales of €392 million.

Carrefour in Indonesia

With a population of 202 million, Indonesia was an attractive market for retailers, which Carrefour entered in 1998 at the peak of the Asian crisis. Just before the merger with Carrefour, Promodès had opened two stores in the country in 1998 and 1999, and these were subsequently integrated.

Indonesia's recovery from the Asian crisis had not been swift, unlike Korea and Thailand. The country was still facing major problems of financial sector fragility and private sector debt. Carrefour took advantage of the Indonesian crisis with its low prices. In order to offer a larger section of the population its first opportunity to purchase durable household goods, Carrefour organized two "free credit" campaigns in 2002, which were a resounding success, given that the household appliance segment represented 21 percent of total sales revenues.

In 2003 Carrefour was Indonesia's leading foreign hypermarket with 11 stores and net sales of €286 million. In addition to consolidating its position in Jakarta, Carrefour also planned to enter other provinces in 2003.

Carrefour in Malaysia

When Carrefour entered the Malaysian market in 1994 it met with little competition. Before the Asia crisis Malaysia had experienced one of the strongest growth rates of all the Asian nations. The strong contraction of the economy after 1998 did not jeopardize Carrefour's expansion. In 1999 it opened its sixth store, and in 2003 its seventh. In 2004 it planned to open a hypermarket in Kepong, Kuala Lumpur, on three stories with 46,450m^2 of floorspace.

Illustrating the local adjustments necessary for this market, all products within its stores were "halal" in compliance with prevailing food requirements. Nevertheless, in order to cater to the large ethnic Chinese community it also operated a separate "non-halal" store outside its catchment zone. Alcoholic beverages received a distinct label clearly indicating the alcohol content.

In 2003 Carrefour was the number three food retailer in Malaysia but was facing increasing competition from strong local and foreign retailers, such as Tesco. Carrefour's net sales represented €226 million in 2003.

Carrefour in Singapore

Since entering this mature and sophisticated market in 1997, Carrefour succeeded in modifying both shopping habits and price expectations among the small population of 4 million Singaporeans. However, local competition remained strong and professional (NTUC) and local suppliers resisted Carrefour's methods. Singapore was not overly affected by the Asian crisis, posting a rise of more than 2 percent in GDP in 1999.

Backed by a dynamic commercial strategy with frequent and original promotional campaigns, Carrefour, No. 5 in food retail, adapted well to the local economic environment. Monthly theme promotions were introduced (French Week, Wine Fair, Japanese Week, Bicycle Week, etc). In particular, products imported from France, both fine foods and fresh produce, recorded continuing success. Its hypermarket in Suntec City registered significant sales growth, and a second store was opened in Plaza Singapura in December 2003. Net sales in 2003 amounted to €83 million (see Exhibit 9).

Carrefour in Hong Kong

Initially, Carrefour thought Hong Kong would help it penetrate the Chinese market. In contrast to Taiwan, Hong Kong's retail industry was hard hit by the Asian crisis and had yet to return to strong growth. The price slump and

Exhibit 9 Carrefour Advertisement in Singapore

suppliers' concerns over retailers' insolvency worked in Carrefour's favor and the company opened four stores by 1998. But in 1999 it experienced fierce competition and had to modify its activity. Despite its efforts, Carrefour failed to find large sites suitable for developing its hypermarket concept and to acquire a significant market share. It disposed of its four stores in 2000.

Carrefour in China

Based on the lessons learned in Taiwan, Carrefour moved into China in 1995 with its first store opening in Shanghai. In 2003 it was ranked the top foreign retailer with net sales of €1,031 million, operating 40 hypermarkets and 55 hard discount stores in all major cities. The continental Chinese market is quite different from those of Taiwan and Hong Kong because urbanization, consumption and purchasing power are steadily increasing (see Exhibit 10).

Exhibit 10 Per Capita Annual Disposable Income of China's 10 Richest Cities, 2002–2003

	Income (in US$)	Population (in million)
Shenzhen	2,887	1.3
Guangzhou	1,812	7.1
Shanghai	1,796	13.3
Ningbo	1,724	5.4
Beijing	1,677	11.3
Xiamen	1,560	1.3
Hangzhou	1,557	6.3
Jinan	1,330	5.7
Tianjin	1,246	9.2
Nanjing	1,231	5.5

Sources: National Statistics Bureau; Ministry of Public Security.

As in Taiwan, Carrefour had to deal with a different negotiation culture and at first used Taiwanese negotiators for its suppliers in China. Since 1992, foreign participation in retailing had been permitted through joint ventures with Chinese companies. At first, Carrefour's strategy was to look for a strong local partner who could help it overcome the hurdles while keeping the majority stake and assigning a non-operational role to the partner. Its relationship with Lianhua, one of the two major local retailers, helped Carrefour to establish its leadership in China. In different provinces it used different partners.

In 1999 China's central government ruled that foreign companies could not own more than 65 percent of any retailing enterprise in China. Carrefour, which wholly owned many of its stores, was subsequently ordered to sell its excess shares (above the regulatory 65 percent limit) and in 2002 signed a deal to sell stakes to local partners.

China's retail scene differs substantially from one store type to another as well as geographically. Convenience stores and supermarkets are dominated by domestic chains such as Lianhua, whereas hypermarkets are in the firm hands of big international players. In the Shanghai region, foreign retailers such as Carrefour, Makro, Wal-Mart, and Metro generate about a third of total supermarket sales. Because most retailers concentrate their efforts in this part of China, competition is steadily increasing. As a result, Royal Ahold, which operated 46 stores until 2002, withdrew from China and eventually divested all its activities in the Asian region.

In 2000 Carrefour experienced legal tribulations due to the intricate network of central, provincial, and local authorities that resulted in lengthy negotiation procedures at many different levels. "Sometimes, we may have problems in understanding Chinese laws and regulations, but we always respond positively to the government's requirements when problems arise, by rectifying our operations to make sure that the law is fully observed," commented Jean-Luc Chereau. Even though China is officially a centralized country, local authorities seek to enforce their own sphere of influence. In its rush to achieve economies of scale, Carrefour set up hypermarkets and operated stores based on licenses obtained from local authorities, which were not approved by the central authorities. Subsequently, the SETC (State Economic and Trade Commission) threatened to shut down all the stores if Carrefour did not comply with central government regulations. As a result Carrefour had to re-apply to obtain proper licenses from the central regulator, a delay that enabled its closest foreign competitor, Wal-Mart, to make inroads into the market.

Thus from 2000 to 2002 Carrefour was not allowed to open any new stores until it had first restructured its existing outlets. "Through two-and-a-half years of effort, we have completed our revamp in China, and now we are heading into a fast growth period in the country," said Chereau. Legal restructuring was performed in collaboration with the Chinese authorities and allowed expansion to resume. In this respect, the Chinese authorities were pragmatic with regard to legislation, having first evaluated the benefits an industrial player could bring to the country.

In 2002 and 2003 Carrefour stepped up its expansion in a bid to move faster than its competitors. It opened more hypermarkets in existing and new cities as well as 55 new Dia discount stores.

In 2004 Carrefour opened its forty-second hypermarket in one of the most remote regions in China. The new Urumqi store in Xinjiang province in the northwestern part of the country shared a 6,500 m^2 shopping center with five other stores. For religious reasons it could not sell fresh pork, but focused on beef and lamb. This shopping center was the first to be built by a retail chain in a province earmarked by the authorities as a development priority. The store was served by 17 different bus lines. Carrefour's aim had always been to pioneer urban centers that had been ignored by competitors, as with Wuhan and Shenyang, where it opened hypermarkets in 1999 despite a 30 percent rate of unemployment.

Carrefour opened its first Champion store in Zhongguancun Beijing. This was its fifth store in Beijing, and regarded as Carrefour's flagship store in Asia after three years of dormancy in the capital. Located in an area dubbed Beijing's Silicon Valley, the outlet has floorspace of 11,600 m^2, much bigger than any other Carrefour store in the country. As an area lacking big shopping centers and supermarkets, Zhongguancun is attracting foreign retailers such as PriceSmart, one of Carrefour's major rivals. In the wake of the Zhongguancun store opening, Carrefour planned to open one or two more stores in Beijing in 2004 as well as a store in Jinan, the capital of east China's Shandong Province.

Carrefour is one of the world's major exporters of Chinese products. It purchased US$1.6 billion worth of goods in China in 2002 and US$2.15 billion in 2003. Since 2002 a new organization within the group has aimed to expand market outlets for its suppliers and enhance its product offering in its European stores. An "export service" was established in Shanghai, and 10 liaison offices were set up with the objective of doubling export volumes by 2005.

Carrefour also sought to participate in public welfare projects and to contribute to local communities, while cooperating closely with local authorities. Among other things, the company set up Hope primary schools, donated to disaster-hit areas, and contributed face masks during the SARS outbreak.

In 2004 China announced that it would honor its pledges to open the booming retail sector to foreign players such as Wal-Mart and Carrefour, abolishing joint-venture requirements before the end of the year. Beijing also promised to end restrictions on the location and number of foreign-owned chain stores.

With China's entry into the WTO, its main trade barriers such as import taxes had to be abolished, but nontariff trade barriers might still be put in place. Although officially welcomed, the press often blames foreign retail operations for destroying jobs and killing the local retail industry. In recent years Shanghai-based major retailers have started to defy foreign competition.

In 2004 the Bailian Group, which controlled Lianhua Supermarket Holdings, announced plans to merge with Hualian into China's largest retailer, the Brilliance Group, with the aim of creating a local giant with assets of US$721.4 million.

Carrefour has only just started making profits in all its stores, while Wal-Mart is still witnessing losses in some outlets. The company's aim is to operate 70 hypermarkets in a few years' time, but political risk remains high in China.

Carrefour in Japan

Being a different market in cultural and economic terms, Carrefour postponed entering Japan until 2000. By then, compared to the 1990s, real estate prices had become more affordable, loans more attractive, and the traditional clout of wholesalers was slowly being reduced to a more logistic function.

Compared to other Asian markets many differences still remain. Although Japan's GDP and purchasing power are much higher, refrigerators and storage space in Japanese homes are limited, so housewives tend to go shopping more often. They make it their daily routine to visit a nearby supermarket where other friends congregate, rather than to drive to a hypermarket to stock up on groceries for a week.

In addition, the Japanese have a sound marketing culture and are perfectionists. Japan is a much more advanced market with established consumer trends, local brands, and supplier networks. Consumers are sophisticated and look for quality and service.

Despite the spectacular bankruptcies of local players such as Mycal in 2002, Japan's retail sector has remained overcrowded and competition quite fierce. Japan was left with five major general merchandise store chains, namely Ito-Yokado, Aeon (parent company of Jusco), Daiei, Uny, and Seiyu, of which Wal-Mart was the largest shareholder in 2002 (see Exhibit 11).

Ito-Yokado, Japan's largest supermarket chain, had no plans to copy Carrefour or to open hypermarkets because land costs remained too high. Ito-Yokado did not reduce prices but instead emphasized higher quality. Aeon, the parent company of Jusco, was Japan's second-largest supermarket chain and took a more aggressive and innovative approach. It operated 368 stores in 2002. Daiei, for years Japan's largest retailer, had been on the edge of bankruptcy for some time. Uny, the smallest of the four, had not been able to keep up with the rapid expansion pace of Jusco and Ito-Yokado.

Exhibit 11 Main Japanese Retailers, February 2003

	Revenue (in million US$)	Net income (in million US$)	Net Profit Margin %	Employees
Ito-Yokado	28,435.50	178.80	0.6	125,400
Aeon	24,274.40	436.00	1.8	42,376
Daiei	18,692.20	1,151.60	6.2	26,589
Uny	8,736.90	106.70	1.2	25,095

Source: Hoover's Online.

One concrete barrier to entry into the Japanese market was the close network of multiple layers of intermediaries. Carrefour fell short of its original plan to persuade all of its Japanese suppliers to adopt the Carrefour direct-purchasing system, which was revolutionary by Japanese standards. Instead, local distributors launched lawsuits against Carrefour as the company opted to purchase directly rather than conform to the long-established distribution channels. After the Japanese distributors lost their case, Carrefour resumed its expansion.

When Carrefour opened its first megastore in a Tokyo suburb in December 2000, so many shoppers poured into the store that managers had to restrict entry. Two other stores, set up in Tokyo and Osaka, were similarly clogged. Junichi Kanamori, a retail analyst at Société Générale Securities Ltd. in Tokyo, explained that Carrefour's arrival was portrayed as "a foreign attack on the Japanese retail market. That made people think something French was going to arrive. Then they discovered it wasn't different from other supermarkets." It was not surprising, therefore, that after a month customers evaporated because shoppers had initially shown up purely out of curiosity.

Like other Western megastores, Carrefour had apparently swept into the Japanese market with much fanfare and little sensitivity to Japan's retail culture. The company did not adequately adjust its business to the purchasing patterns of Japanese consumers, nor did it capitalize on the curiosity of local consumers regarding products hailing from France.

There was some misconception that Carrefour was a general merchandise store that competed on price alone. Japanese supermarkets chains began slashing prices in anticipation of the "foreign threat." Thus its three stores were showing major losses and Carrefour had to review its ambitious plans to expand to 13 stores by 2003.

In 2003 Carrefour continued its adaptation to the specific requirements of the local market. Along with demonstrating its professionalism in fresh produce, the company established its first sales space specializing in French household goods at its fully renovated store in Chiba Prefecture. Named "La Maison," the 110m^2 store-within-a-store offered 1,000 items ranging from fragrant soaps to trendy tableware and other sundry goods, all made in France. The French-themed corner came into being after a pilot sales space in Carrefour's fourth hypermarket store at Saitama Prefecture was well received by housewives. The corner was established to grow consumer interest in certain categories of French products that were not available in Japanese supermarkets, and bring the "French touch" loved by the Japanese.

This approach was a clear departure from Carrefour Japan's existing policy of localizing its merchandise and the highly successful store would serve as a benchmark for future store openings. In 2003 Carrefour's stores recorded net sales of €225 million. However, rumors circulated in October 2004 in the *Asian Wall Street Journal* that, according to a consultant, Carrefour was planning to sell its eight stores in Japan due to "difficulties in acquiring real estate for new stores and the lack of touch with Japanese consumers' tastes."

Notes

1. *EuroMonitor.*
2. *Asian Wall Street Journal,* March 2004.
3. CSFB report, October 10, 2003.
4. INSEAD case Carrefour's Entry into Asia (A1), (A2), 10 years later.
5. Interview Gérard Clerc, *Reflets ESSEC* magazine.
6. Carrefour Worldwide.
7. *China Business Weekly,* March 2004.
8. Comparative Study of Asia Strategy: Wal-Mart versus Carrefour.
9. *Forbes,* March 2004.
10. *China Online,* March 2004.
11. *International Herald Tribune,* 2001.
12. *Retail Asia Online,* March 2000.

Case 8

Dell: From a Low-Cost PC Maker to an Innovative Company

Abhijit Sinha

ICFAI Business School

If you ask, Okay, is Dell in the penalty box? Yeah, Dell is in the penalty box. Then we will use this opportunity to fix everything.[1]

—Michael Dell,
Chairman, Dell Inc.

There is no perfect linear path to success. I think the stock market overreacted.[2]

—Michael Dell,
Chairman, Dell Inc.

No, the sky is not falling at Dell.[3]

—Kevin B Rollins,
Chief Executive Officer, Dell Inc.

Dell had a humble beginning at a dorm room of the University of Texas, Austin, in 1984, where 18-year-old Michael Dell started a part-time business of computer peripherals. The company became the number one PC maker of the United States in 1999. The company's revenue grew from $546 million in 1991 to $32 billion in 2001 and $56 billion in 2005.[5] Dell and its founder, Michaell Dell, earned many laurels from both analysts and investors. When Dell became a publicly listed company in 1989, its founder became the youngest CEO in the *Fortune* 500. The company emerged as the world's number one PC seller, enjoying strong brand equity and high customer satisfaction ratings. Its unique Dell Business Model[6] however became a debatable topic among both academicians and industry experts (see Exhibit 1).

After enjoying a heady growth since Dell's inception, both the chairperson and the CEO probably wished to hide behind a mask before announcing the company's second quarter financial performance, for FY 2006–2007. Dell's second quarter revenue and profit failed to match the expectations. Though the company posted revenue of $55.9 billion (February 3, 2006), the company failed to achieve its own forecasted target for revenue growth during the second quarter for FY 2006–2007. August 2006 was difficult month and the second quarter of FY 2006–2007 was the harshest quarter for the company. Its bottom line was its lowest ever—51 percent down, compared to the same period of the previous financial year (see Exhibit 2). Faltering on its own forecasted revenue growth target was not new for Dell. During the second quarter for FY 2005–2006, the company's revenue grew

Exhibit 1 Direct Business Model of Dell

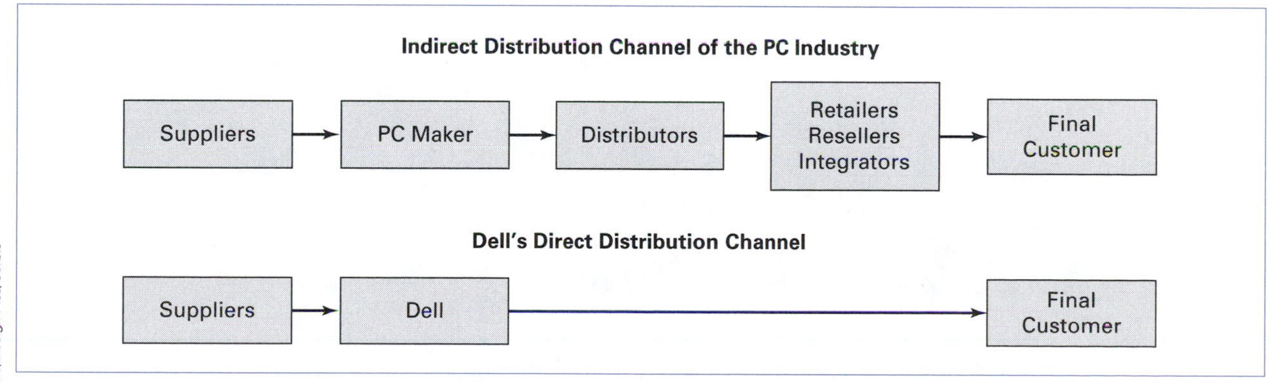

Source: 2003 Competing in Network Era, http://www.oft.osd.mil, December.

Exhibit 2 Dell's Financial Highlights (in $ million)

	August 2006	May 2006	July 2005
Net Revenue	$ 14,094	$ 14,216	$ 13,428
Cost of Revenue	11,904	11,744	10,929
Gross Margin	**2190**	**2472**	**2499**
Selling and Administrative Expenses	1457	1394	1204
Research Expenses	128	129	122
Total Operating Expenses	**1585**	**1523**	**1326**
Operating Income	605	949	1173
Income from Investment and other Income	53	50	61
PBIT	**658**	**999**	**1234**
Income Tax Provision	156	237	214
PAT	**502**	**762**	**1020**

Source: http://www.dell.com.

by 14.7 percent to $13.4 billion compared to its projected growth of 18 percent.[7] In the third quarter of the same financial year, Dell posted revenue of $13.9 billion instead of its targeted $14.5 billion. For a company like Dell, whose top line had grown consistently at the yearly average by 15 percent since 2001–2002, the decline in its growth raised questions over the success of its strategy and business model.

Following its sluggish growth, Dell's customer satisfaction rating declined in the survey conducted by the University of Michigan in 2005. The company had to write off $450 million for the installation of defective capacitors[8] in a large number of computers. In August 2006, it also had to recall 4.1 million lithium batteries that were manufactured by Sony and were used in Dell's laptops. To add to its woes, for the first time in the history of Dell Inc., the company hinted at layoffs—what it called "workforce realignment"—and the Security and Exchange Commission (SEC) launched an informal investigation against the company's accounting practices. Investors who enjoyed more than 28,000 percent gains since Dell went public 17 years ago, and the Wall Street[9] analysts who were accustomed to high revenue, increasing market share, and rocketing profits of the company, suddenly became skeptical about Dell's future. In the second quarter of FY 2006–2007, the company's stock was already down by 25 percent and had been falling further (see Exhibit 3). Before the recent setbacks in 2005 and 2006, the company had also experienced hurdles in 1989 and 1993[10] and was certainly put to a disadvantage when the NASDAQ[11] fell in 2000. Yet, during 2000–2004, the company was able to dominate the PC market. But in August 2006, it announced a 51percent decline in its revenue for the second quarter of FY 2006–2007 compared to the same period of the previous year. Dell's top line growth, though positive, had

Exhibit 3 Declining Stock Price

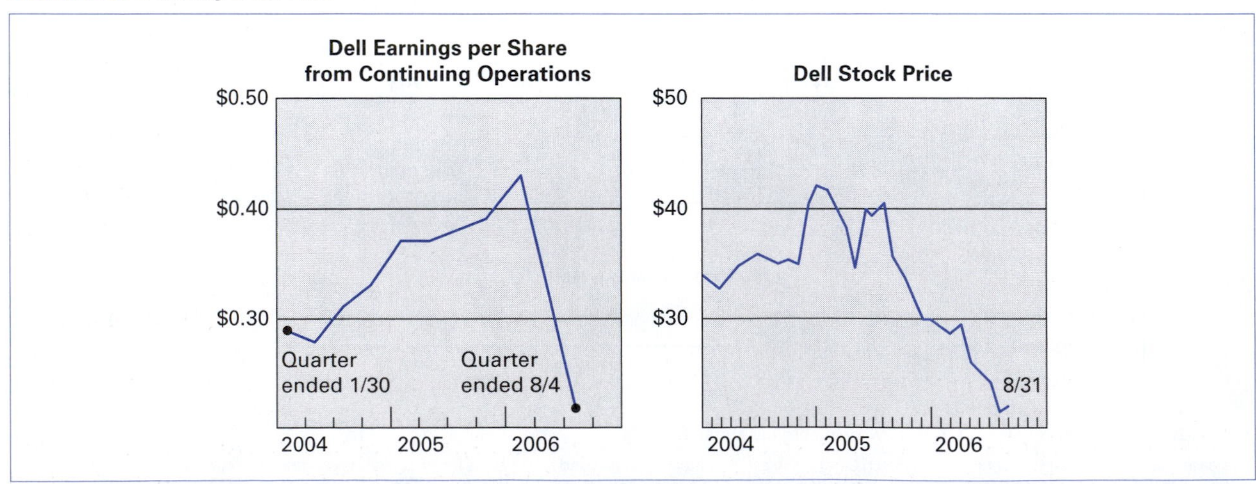

Source: http://www.fortune.com.

declined continuously during the past six quarters. The fact that the company could not meet its own modified and modest targets raised an awkward question among the stakeholders, "Could this be the end of Dell as we know it?"

Company Background

In 1984, 18-year-old Michael Dell, a student at the University of Texas, Austin, set up PCs Limited as a part-time business in his dorm room to sell IBM compatible computers built from stock components. Michael Dell started formatting hard disks for personal computers, added additional memory, disk drives, and modems with IBM clones and sold them for 40 percent less than that of the IBM machines. In 1985, the company moved up the value chain and started to assemble Dell branded PCs ("Turbo PC") instead of upgrading the machines of other manufacturers. Within one year of its operation, the company posted revenue of $6 million. Inspired by the success of the company, Michael Dell dropped out of college in 1986, to run the business full time. During this time, he renamed the company Dell Computer Corporation.

In 1984, when Michael Dell started the company (PCs Limited), the PC industry had vertically integrated companies like IBM (hardware) and software developers like Microsoft. Dell presumed that customization, fast delivery and low price would give his company a higher profit margin over IBM and HP. Contrary to the existing trends of displaying the products in retail stores or selling them through intermediaries, the company delivered its products directly to the consumers. Dell sourced the components directly from the manufacturers, assembled them according to the customer specifications and delivered them free of cost. Initially, it took orders over the telephone, followed by advertisements in magazines and dailies and later from its e-commerce platform, *www.dell.com.*

In 1989, as noted above, the company issued an IPO. In 1992, *Fortune* 500 included Dell Computer Corporation among the world's best 500 companies. In the same year, Michael Dell was also featured in *Fortune* 500 as the youngest CEO. The company forayed into the United Kingdom, and then into Australia and Japan in 1993. It set up its own manufacturing facilities in Limerick, Ireland (to serve European, Middle East, and Africa), Penang, Malaysia (1996), Xiamen, China (1998), Eldorado do Sul, Brazil (1999, to serve Latin America), and Texas and Tennessee in the United States. In 1999, Dell Computer Corporation overtook Compaq and became the largest PC seller in the United States.

Along with setting up manufacturing facilities in different markets, the company tried to improve its products according to industry trends and consumer preferences. In 1989, it launched the notebook computer, followed by the network server (1996), workstation systems (1997), network switches (2001), and projectors and printers (2002). In 2003, the company extended its product portfolio to the consumer electronics market by launching flat panel TVs, Dell Digital Jukebox, USB key drives, and Windows mobile-powered PDAs. In the same year, in recognition of its efforts at product extension, the company's name was changed to Dell Inc. The company marketed its products under different brand names to different consumer segments. OptiPlex, Latitude, and Precision were targeted at medium-sized and large consumers, whereas students and small offices were identified as the target audience for Dimension, Inspiron, and the XPS Brand.

In January 2004, Dell entered into a technology partnership with Fuji, Xerox, Kodak, and Samsung, followed by a strategic partnership with Microsoft Corporation and Oracle Inc. It set up the Dell Enterprise Command Center to support the server and storage customers in the region. In January 2005, the company entered into a contract with Bombardier Recreational Products to supply technology products and services throughout the global IT network.

U.S. PC Industry in 2006

During the 1980s IBM and Apple Computer were the leading PC manufacturers, and Microsoft, Lotus, and IBM, were the major software firms of the United States. By the end of the 1990s, the U.S. PC market had matured due to high penetration in the traditional market and stagnation in the replacement market. According to a survey conducted by U.S. Consumer Electronics Association in 2005, more than 90 percent of households in the United States had at least one PC, 36 percent had two or more PCs, and 52 percent were reluctant to purchase a new PC.[12] In the United States, PC sales surpassed 190 million in 2005 and were growing at 5 percent annually.

During 2000–2001, the U.S. PC market accounted for 34 percent of the global PC sales. However, after the slump in the industry during 2000–2001, PC sales consistently declined. For instance, the PC shipments dropped by 11 percent from 128 million in 2001 to 114 million in 2002. Between 1996 and 1999, the average growth of PC sales in the United States was 16 percent, which reduced to 3.6 percent between 2000 and 2004. Its average price also declined by 17 percent, thereby reducing industry revenue by 4 percent. Moreover, its average selling price, which had long been near $2,000, dropped down to $1,500 for both household and business segments. Analysts feared that the growth in the industry was stagnating after showing an upward trend from 1995 to 2000.

Because the PC market had matured, companies tried different strategies to improve sales. HP[13] stressed the household mass market; Gateway Computers[14] focused on semiprofessionals; and Apple and Dell sought business customers. Various sales promotion tools (discounts, easy installment plans, free gifts) were offered to attract customers. Leading PC manufacturers such as Dell, HP, and Apple offered freebies—scanners and printers—along with PCs and huge discounts to reduce the inventory. Analysts felt that consolidation was the right measure to deal with overcapacity. In 2002, the PC industry experienced the most expensive merger between HP and Compaq, valued at $25 billion. The scenario, however, did not improve. Dell, who had recorded a high profit margin previously, began to reduce prices. After the dot.com bubble burst, many corporate companies were reluctant to invest in IT, thereby reducing the profit of HP and Dell, and pushing Gateway Computers into the red.

The industry leaders realized that the PC market had matured, leaving little room for growth, so they started diversifying into other areas and new markets. While HP provided e-business services and Web site management, Dell and Apple[15] diversified into the consumer electronics business and launched music systems as well as digital and flat televisions. Dell also started working as an Internet service provider. PC makers realized the potential of developing countries (India, China, Brazil, and Russia) and forayed into these markets. HP, which first entered the Chinese market, registered a 40 percent revenue growth from the developing market in 2004. Lyle Hurst of HP commented, "The wealthest 1 billion people in the world are pretty well served and we are targeting the next 4 billion." In 2001, only 670 million people who constituted 11 percent of the global population used PCs. Considering the increasing potential of developing markets, analysts felt that PC sales would touch 1 billion in 2010.[16]

In 1984, when Michael Dell started his company, IBM and HP were ranked as the United States's number one and number three most admired companies, respectively. In those days, nobody knew Michael Dell and his company. Commodore, with $1.1 billion PC sales and a 27 percent market share in the United States, was the market leader followed by IBM, Apple, and Tandy (see Exhibit 4). But in 2006, the scenario changed. Dell topped the list of the top 10 most admired U.S. companies, while HP and IBM found no place in this list (see Exhibit 5). Dell controlled 33 percent of the U.S. market share (see Exhibit 6) (one out of three PCs shipped was of Dell) and 19 percent of the global market (see Exhibit 7). Besides being the most admired computer company in the United States (see Exhibit 8), Dell was also the number one brand in Britain, Canada, and Ireland. In 2006, the company's earnings increased to $55 billion from a modest $80,000 in its inception year (1984). Further, its

Exhibit 4 U.S. PC Companies, 1984

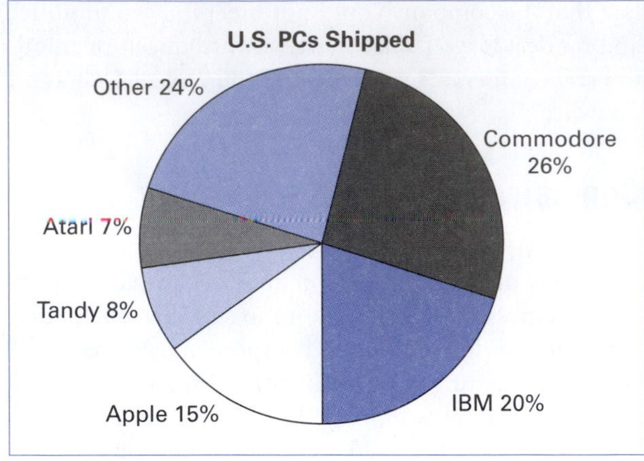

Source: http://www.fortune.com.

Exhibit 5 The Most Admired Companies, 2005

Rank	Most Admired Companies in U.S.	Most Admired Companies Globally
1.	Dell Inc.	GE
2.	GE	Wal-Mart
3.	Starbucks	Dell Inc.
4.	Wal-Mart	Microsoft
5.	SouthWest Airlines	Toyota Motor
6.	Fed Ex	Procter & Gamble
7.	Berkshire Hathaway	Johnson & Johnson
8.	Microsoft	Fed Ex
9.	Johnson & Johnson	IBM
10.	Procter & Gamble	Berkshire Hathaway

Source: http://www.fortune.com.

Exhibit 6 U.S. PC Industry, 2005

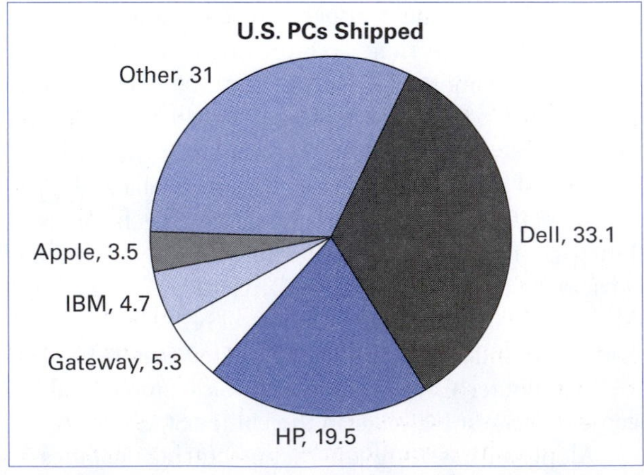

Source: http://www.fortune.com.

Exhibit 7 Top PC Makers (Global market share, first quarter 2005)

Rank	Company	Location	Market Share
1.	Dell Inc.	Texas, US	19%
2.	HP	California, US	15
3.	IBM/Lenevo	NewYork/ HongKong	7
4.	Fujitsu/ Siemens	Japan/ Germany	5
5.	Acer	Taiwan	4
6.	Toshiba	Japan	4
7.	NEC	Japan	3
8.	Apple	California, US	2
9.	Gateway	California, US	2

Source: http://www.idc.com.

Exhibit 8 The Most Admired Computer Companies in the U.S.

YEAR			
2005	2004	Company	Score (out of 10)
1	1	IBM	7.61
2	2	Dell	7.46
3	4	Apple	6.84
4	3	Xerox	6.67
5	8	Pitney Bowes	6.52
6	6	Canon	6.49
7	7	HP	5.91
8	9	Sun Microsystems	5.81
9	10	NCR	4.92
10	5	Gateway	4.86

Source: http://www.fortune.com.

investors experienced a 28,000 percent jump in stock prices since the company went public 18 years earlier. Dell's direct business model created ripples among both the academicians and industry experts.

Dell: Facing Challenges

In 2005, the U.S. PC industry experienced many changes. IBM, the company that invented the desktop computer, sold its PC business to Lenovo in 2004; Gateway, merged with eMachines[17]; and the biggest merger in the PC industry between HP and Compaq happened in 2002. In 2003, Dell surpassed HP and emerged as a global leader with 17.6 percent market share. During 2001–2004, its average global revenue increased 19 percent, while the industry average was 12 percent. However, in 2005, after leading for almost two decades, Dell started facing problems.

During the second quarter of 2006, Dell announced that it would fall short of both its expected revenue and earnings. Though the company's bottom line was growing sluggishly, its top line growth was experiencing a decline for the last six quarters (see Exhibit 9). Between 1995 and 1999, Dell's earnings doubled on each quarter, but during the last 20 quarters, it increased by only 43 percent. It was an amazing rate according to industry standards, but a slower one when compared to its past performance. Though analysts admitted that with a turnover of $56 billion and being positioned as number 25 in the *Fortune* 500, the company was too large to replicate its previous growth rate.

In the second quarter of 2006, the company's earnings were reduced by only 1 percent, compared to the previous quarter of 2006, and it recorded revenue of $14 billion, lower than its projected $16 billion. Thus, Dell, the company that once grew more than the industry average, failed to even maintain its projected growth. In fact, it even experienced negative growth. Stakeholders felt that the shortfalls portrayed that Dell might be struggling to slash costs in order to maintain its profitability, while

Exhibit 9A Dell's Bottom Line

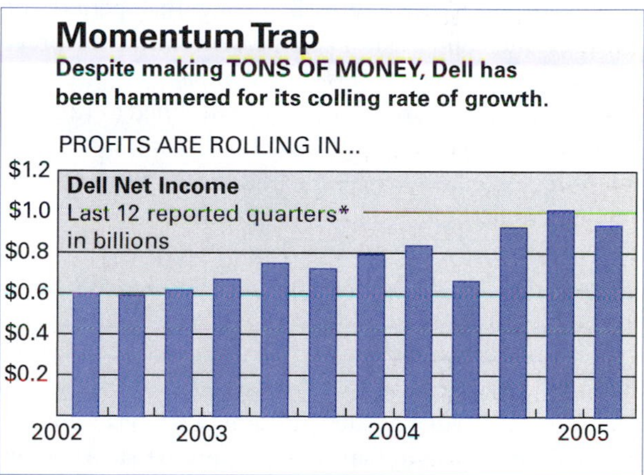

Source: http://www.fortune.com.

Exhibit 9B Dell's Top Line

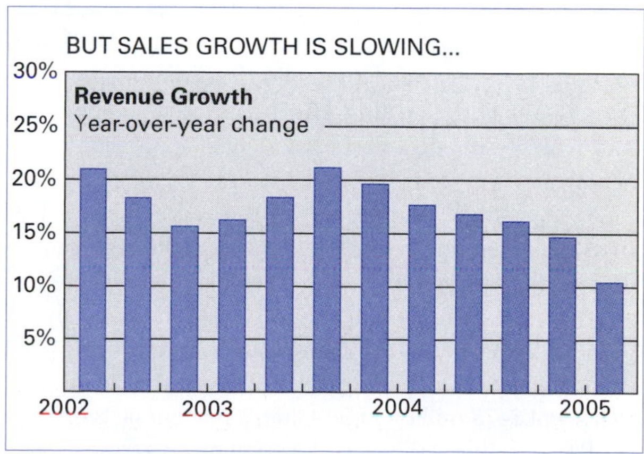

Source: http://www.fortune.com.

Exhibit 9C Dell's Revenues and Net Income (in $ million)

	2006	2005	2004	2003	2002
Revenue ($)	$55,908	$49,205	$41,444	$35,404	$31,168
Net Income ($)	3,572	3,043	2,645	2,122	1,246

Source: Compiled by the author from *Dell Annual Report* 2006.

also trying to reduce prices to increase its market share along with maintaining its top line growth. Michael Dell and Kevin Rollins, Dell's CEO, confessed that the company tried to increase its market share by reducing prices. Although the price cut helped the company to increase its shipments by 6 percent, its operating income declined by 48 percent.[18] Kevin Rollins termed the plan as a "one-time pricing and miscalculation problem" when the sales of PCs did not increase as expected. Analysts opined that Dell also failed to replace Intel chips with cheaper and better quality chips from AMD.

Apart from its top line and bottom line, Dell's growth rate in unit shipments also declined. While competitors like Acer and Fujitsu increased their global shipments in 2005, Dell's growth during that period was 17.8 percent, compared to 23.7 percent during the previous year. According to IDC, the company's unit growth rate in 2005 in the United States also declined to 12.2 percent from 16.3 percent in the 2004.[19]

Industry analysts and stakeholders felt that in the recent quarters, the company's aggressive cost cutting to meet its financial targets had compromised other performance measures, including customer support and product quality. As Jason Maxwell[20] commented, "The way is to keep customers happy in an efficient manner. Not getting the processes right can really snowball through the system quickly."[21] Michael Dell and Kevin Rollins were also worried about the unhappy customers most. Although the company once boasted its excellence in customer service, its after-sales service declined during the past couple of years. During those years, the company relocated its call centers to support its after-sales service team in India, Philippines, and Taiwan. Criticizing Dell's outsourcing strategy, Nick Donatiello, CEO of Odyssey, a San Francisco–based consulting firm commented, "They put a knife in their own heart."[22] Michael Dell also confessed, "The team was managing costs instead of managing service and quality."[23] Employees at the call centers of Dell were evaluated on the time taken to handle each call instead of the satisfaction level of the customers. Therefore, customers remained unhappy and called back angrily.

Dell also spent less on research and development (R&D) compared to HP and IBM. For instance, in 2005, Dell spent $475 million or less than 1 percent of its revenue on R&D, while HP and IBM spent 6 percent each. Meanwhile, the companies with innovative products like Apple (with its iPod) were growing at a faster pace. Apple's stunning success with its products, iMac and the MacBook models, iPod, and the iTunes Music store virtually changed the dynamics of the industry. Dell failed to lure its customers by a traditional box slapped with Intel processors and Microsoft operating system. Even in the second quarter of 2006, HP grew faster than Dell. HP's unit growth rate was 17.9 percent, whereas Dell's was 17.8 percent. HP also proved to be more innovative than Dell. MediaSmart TV, the latest offerings from HP, could work both as conventional TV and wireless monitor for a PC, and could display photos, music, and video. HP also became more appealing and innovative than its competitors in marketing. HP's recent advertisements focus less on product features and more on the emotional aspects of using the product, feelings of the users, and the way the products changed the users' lives. Compared to its innovative competitors, Dell still positioned itself as a "value for money" PC supplier. Most of its products were alike with minor changes in configurations. Aaron Goldberg, PC industry expert of consulting firm Ziff-Davis commented, "Competitors are selling the use, the solution. But Dell's still selling products, the BQS31-S273."[24] But in a mature and consolidated industry like the PC industry, premium products, and not the basic products, contributed mostly to the company's top line and bottom line.

In the mature PC industry, the low-cost, low-style approach that made Dell number one in the PC industry seemed outdated. Contrary to cheap PCs, product design and branding also played a key role. But Dell did not have core competence in either branding or innovative product design. Analysts perceived that Dell's brand consisted of "a man and a business model." Industry analysts opined that Dell lacked in innovation and development of new businesses. Undoubtedly, for 10 years, the company's direct business model helped it to perform flawlessly, but it was a seemingly impossible approach to continue.

In 2005, Dell, which was famous for its operational efficiency, had to write off $300 million. In its shipments, most of the computers had faulty capacitors. Hence, besides $300 million for replacing them, the company had to pay $150 million extra to cover the costs associated with its recent global layoffs ("workforce realignment" according to Dell management) and the excess inventory of machine parts that Dell would not use anymore. According to a survey conducted by the University of Michigan in 2005, Dell's customer satisfaction rating fell by 6.3 percent to 74 points.

Exhibit 10 Customer Satisfaction Rating of Dell, 2005

Company	2004 (Rating)	2005 (Rating)	% Change
Apple	81	81	0%
HP (HP Brand)	71	74	2.8
Dell	79	74	-6.3
Gateway	74	72	-2.7
HP (Compaq brand)	69	67	-2.9
Others	71	74	+4.2
Industry Avg	74	74	0

Source: http://www.fortune.com.

Exhibit 11 Brand Valuation of Global Top Five Computer Companies

Rank 2005	Rank 2004	Company	Brand Value 2004	Brand Value 2005	% Change	Country of Ownership
3	3	IBM	$ 53,791	$ 51,767	4%	United States
5	5	Intel	33,499	31,112	8	United States
12	12	HP	20,978	19,860	6	United States
29	25	Dell	11,500	10,367	11	United States
43	50	Apple	6,871	5,554	24	United States

Source: http://www.interbrand.com.

However, Apple, with its innovative products, such as iPod,[25] led the list with a score of 81(see Exhibit 10). Along with the customer satisfaction rating survey, Dell received a negative ranking in the Interbrand's survey of 2005 (see Exhibit 11).

Dell faced challenges in the corporate market as well. Due to an increase in Internet traffic, the enterprising customers shifted to more powerful servers, instead of assembling lower-end models where Dell had its competence. For instance, both IBM and HP offered high-tech servers called Blade Servers, which required more sophisticated software than the stand-alone Dell machines. Dell was the only major server maker that used Intel chips in its servers. But the preference of the corporate customers was high-speed servers based on Advance Micro Devices (AMD) Opteron chip. Thus, Dell was losing out to IBM and HP. Greg Papadopoulos, chief technology officer of Sun Microsystems, commented, "Dell is stuck with only Intel, and Intel is just not competitive right now."[26]

To add to its worries, Dell experienced sluggish sales growth in Britain, where the company was the number one PC seller. According to IDC, in the Asia-Pacific region, the fastest-growing PC market (see Exhibit 12), Dell ranked third with only 7.8 percent market share. The Chinese PC group, Lenevo, which acquired IBM's PC business and had 20.4 percent market share, led the market, followed by HP with 14 percent market share. Analysts commented that because Dell could not replicate its direct selling business model in China, it failed to gain a significant market share in the largest emerging market of the Asia-Pacific region (see Exhibit 13). Chinese customers preferred to see and examine the products before purchasing, which meant Dell's business model was not effective in China.

Moreover, the lithium battery controversy further added to the worries of Michael Dell and Kevin Rollins. On August 14, 2006, the company announced that it would recall 4.1 million laptop computer batteries sold from April 2006 to July 2006. The batteries fitted in Dell laptops had the possibility of overheating and, in rare cases, catching fire. The lithium-ion (Li-ion) batteries used by Dell were manufactured by Sony Energy Devices Corporation. Earlier, these Li-ion batteries caused several incidents of Dell product recalls. In 2001, Dell recalled 284,000 laptop batteries and in 2005, it recalled 22,000 batteries. However, the recall of 4.1 million was the largest product battery recall in the history of the consumer electronics industry. Though Dell claimed that the recall process did not affect the Dell brand negatively, or affect the company financially, analysts had a different opinion. Analysts believed that the recall would cost the company $450 million and would have a negative impact on "Brand Dell."

Dell was no longer the high-flying company it used to be. It was not possible for a $50 billion company to

Exhibit 12 Emerging Markets

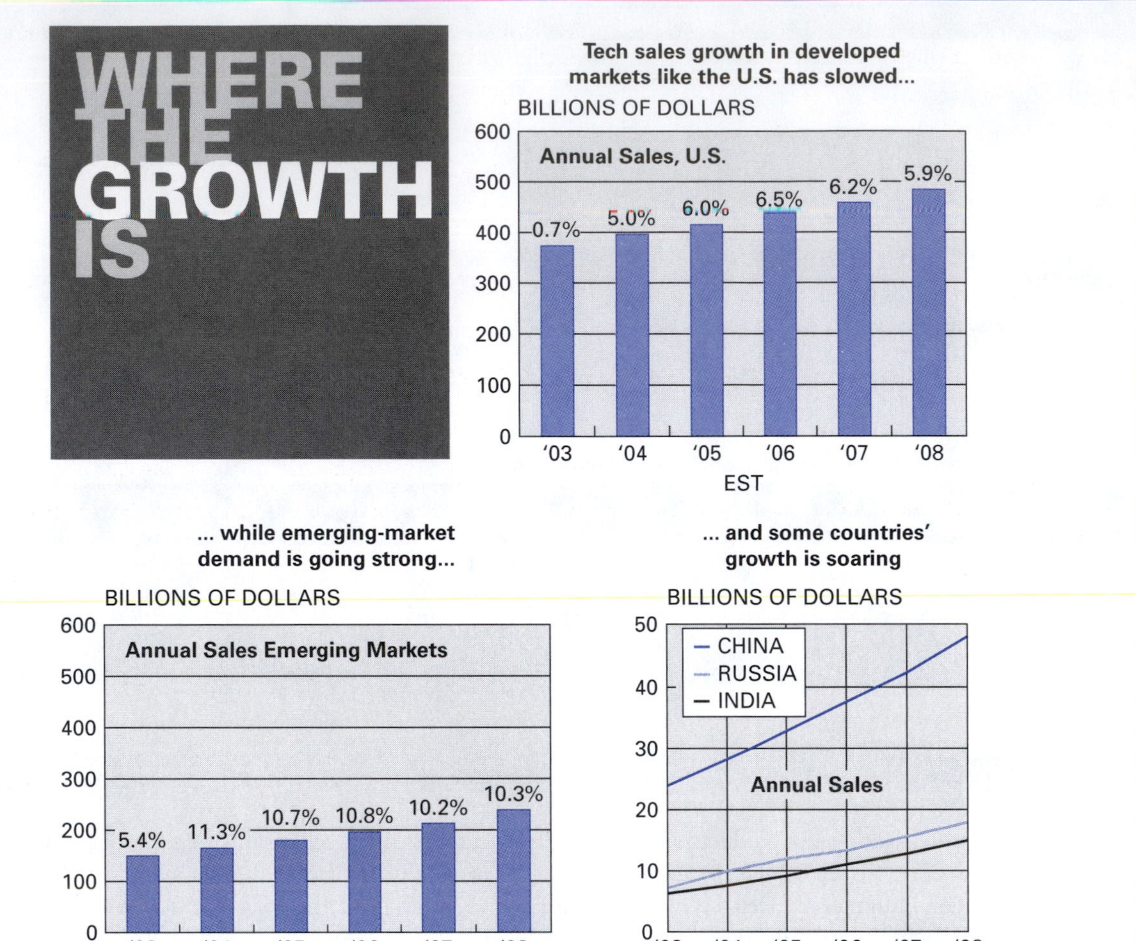

Source: http://www.fortune.com.

Exhibit 13 U.S. and Worldwide PC Market Growth

	1975	1980	1985	1990	1995	2000	2003	2005	2010
U.S. PC Sales ($ million)	$0.04	$0.76	$ 6.6	$ 9.5	$ 21.4	$ 46	$ 48.3	$ 56.6	$ 66.7
U.S. PC Revenues ($ billion)	0.05	1.50	17.2	24.5	56.8	869	78.1	84.5	86.1
Global PC Sales ($ million)	0.05	1.10	11.0	24.2	70.1	130	149.0	181.0	249.0
Global PC Revenues ($ billion)	0.06	3.60	29.5	71.3	155.0	247	243.0	270.0	302.0

Source: http://www.etforecasts.com.

ensure double-digit growth every year. The law of large numbers would eventually affect any business model, regardless of its uniqueness. "What Dell did was really brilliant,"[27] commented Phil Asmundson.[28] By developing a direct sales structure for customized PCs, Dell eliminated all kinds of inventory and intermediaries, which resulted in its phenomenal success. But even in the sluggish PC industry, this structure alone could not trigger continuous growth. In an era where every company needed to challenge and reinvent itself, the industry analysts pondered on how Dell would do this. (See Appendixes 1, 2, and 3.)

Appendix 1 Dell Products and Services

Servers Dell's PowerEdge line of servers includes rack and tower servers for enterprise customers and aggressively priced tower servers for small organizations and workgroups/remote locations.

Storage Dell/EMC and Dell's PowerVault lines of storage products offer hardware and software products to store, serve, and protect customer data.

Printing and Imaging Systems Dell offers a wide array of printers, from photo printers for consumers to large multifunction lasers for corporate workgroups.

Workstations Dell Precision desktop and mobile workstations are intended for professional users who demand exceptional performance to run sophisticated applications, such as three dimensional computer-aided design, digital content creation, geographic information systems, computer animation, software development, and financial analysis.

Notebook Computers Dell offers two lines of notebook computer systems, namely Latitude and Inspiron.

Desktop Computers Dell has two lines of desktop computer systems. The OptiPlex line is designed for corporate, institutional, and small-business customers. The Dimension line is designed for small businesses and home users requiring fast technology turns and high-performance computing.

Networking Products Dell's PowerConnect switches connect computers and servers in small- to medium-sized networks.

Electronics and Accessories Products Dell offers a range of electronics and accessories, including monitors, printers, handhelds, notebook accessories, networking and wireless products, memory, projectors, and scanners.

Managed Services Dell also offers a wide range of IT management services, including on-site and other related services. Apart from these, Dell offers various services such as Professional Services, Deployment Services, Support Services, Training, and Certification Services.

Source: http://www.dell.com.

Appendix 2 Market Share of Top 5 PC Vendors Worldwide (Shipments in thousand units)

Rank	Company	2005 Shipments	Market Share (%)	2004 Shipments	Market Share (%)
1.	Dell	37,732	18.1	31,769	17.7
2.	HP	32,525	15.6	28,101	15.7
3.	Lenovo	12,995	6.2	4,183	2.3
4.	Acer	9,803	4.7	6,368	3.6
5.	Fujitsu/ Siemens	8,489	4.1	7,187	4.0
	Others	107,041	51.3	101,573	56.7
	Total	208,586	100.0	179,181	100.0

Source: http://www.idc.com.

Appendix 3 Market Share of Top 10 Notebook Vendors Worldwide

Rank	Company	2005 Shipments (in thousand units)	Market Share (%)
1.	Dell	11,290	17.29
2.	HP	10,250	15.70
3.	Toshiba	7,156	10.96
4.	Acer	6,626	10.15
5.	Lenovo	5,376	8.23
6.	Fujitsu/Siemens	4,089	6.26
7.	Sony	2,560	3.92
8.	NEC	2,447	3.75
9.	Apple	2,171	3.32
10.	Asustek	1,552	2.38

Source: Compiled by the author from http://macdailynews.com/index.php/weblog/comments/84.

Dell's Turnaround Strategy

Until recently, Dell's business model revolved around the world's most efficient assembly and distribution of Wintel Technology. If a customer wanted a PC with an Intel chip and Microsoft software, Dell was the optimal choice for the customized PC at the lowest price. Though Dell's core business of manufacturing and selling customized PCs was a relatively low-margin commodity business, the "Wintel vendor" label had worked for the company. But growth in the PC business was slowing down, particularly in the mature U.S. market. Michael Dell understood that the company would need new growth drivers to add or move incremental business lines into profitable business lines. For instance, the markets for servers and printers, which were still relatively new to Dell, had higher margins than those of PCs. Dell moved into servers and storage, mobility products, services, software peripheral categories, and printers, thereby, becoming a diversified IT company.

In 2003 Dell introduced multifunction flat panel TVs, DJ music players, an online music download service, digital music players, and projectors. Analysts commented that the product extension into the consumer electronics market was a natural fit for the company. New products such as plasma TVs, MP3 players, and digital cameras were still in their infancy. Along with these growing lines, entertainment had become increasingly digital, making music, movies, and photos an extension of the PC. Dell's PCs ran on Intel Pentium 4 processors and the Microsoft's Windows XP Media Center System. These PCs enabled live-TV viewing and included DVD players, TiVo-style personal video recorders, and software for digital music downloading and photo management. "We are here to confirm our entry into the consumer electronics category. We are expanding our line up, even as our PC business is profitable in every segment,"[29] commented Michael Dell. The media PC occupied a middle ground between standard PCs and consumer electronics. These models were considered by the PC giants to have immense potential. Dell's Media Center PCs were a combination of PC and entertainment systems with the ability to play music, edit, play, and record videos, besides having Internet compatibility. In 2006, the company launched XPS, a high-end subbrand in the media PC segment. It also purchased gaming PC maker Alienware to strengthen its position in the media PC segment. The recently launched XPS M2010 was positioned as "A unique luggable multimedia computer designed to be carried from room to room, complete with large screen, high-quality speakers and an easy-to-access DVD player."[30]

Analysts felt that with its proven business model in the PC industry, Dell would also be able to gain a significant share in the consumer electronics industry, not only because these two segments had similar products, but also the same buying process and target customer groups. Besides the supply side, Dell was able to source components at a lower price, because a large number of OEMs were identical and in the same low cost production countries, operating in a similar industry. The fundamental difference between Dell and its competitors was that while other companies produced to match sales forecasts, Dell produced every single machine for a specific order. This approach helped Dell to reduce its inventory and prices. For instance, Dell carried only four days of inventory, compared to IBM's 20 days and HP's 28 days. The company also urged its suppliers to build raw-material inventory bases close to Dell's factories for cost sharing.

In addition to expanding its consumer electronics business, the company improved its products and launched innovative product lines to match the industry trends and tastes of its customers. With the advent of computer networking technology, the company entered into the network server market in 1999, followed by workstation systems market and storage products (2001). It also introduced network switches, projectors, and printers for corporate and consumer markets. In 2005, Dell launched new consumer PC lines. The company introduced desktop models in the $250–350 price bracket, notebooks at $500–750, midsized and business PCs at $350–400. In the PC industry, Dell waged a war against HP's printer business. Because printing was an installed base business, the revenue came from the demand of cartridges from the established customers, who would buy them for years. In 2002, Dell began to sell both inkjet and laser printers, and within three years it managed to grab 20 percent of the U.S. inkjet printer market. Analysts felt that the margins from printers were not as great as from its other businesses, but that the product with its low price had the potential to be a significant business for Dell within a few years.[31]

A new move of Dell that was appreciated by analysts was the Robins decision to use AMD microprocessors in its products. Michael Dell and Kevin Rollins also admitted that the move, though necessary, took a long time to implement. Michael Dell commented, "We overestimated Intel and under estimated AMD in prior periods."[32] Since 2004, AMD had developed processors that were faster and more energy efficient than Intel's. AMD's prices were also lower than Intel's. Despite these reasons, until May 2006, Dell was the only manufacturer who refused to use AMD's product. Michael Dell commented that Dell was an "equal opportunity processor user" and it would not restrict the use of AMD recovers to two types of server and one desktop line only, but would use AMD chips more extensively.

To improve the customer satisfaction rating, Dell took some innovative measures. Analysts felt that the customers expected a low-priced PC, along with better customer service. Stephen Dukker, founder of eMachines Inc., commented, "Customers want to have their cake and eat it too. They want a PC at $300 but expect the same support that came with a machine 10 years ago and cost $2,500."[33] The company planned to offer a one-year membership to customers so that they could opt for various levels of assistance at varied prices. For instance, one of the options was a quarterly PC tune-up, where the company personnel would clean the hard drive and check security software. The company also opened kiosks (57 kiosks in 9 states of the United States) in 2003 to enable the shoppers to acquaint themselves with its products.

For the corporate customers, the company also improved its services. In 2005, the company introduced its Premier Page Web site. This Web site was customized according to the specific needs of the corporate customers. Each company's Premier Page provided specific information about the Dell products and services it used. Orders placed through a company's Premier Page, were routed to Dell for approval and processing. The Web page helped the customers to track records of inventories and assignments through detailed purchasing reports, on the basis of geographic location, product, average unit price, and total dollar value.

In the overseas markets, Dell started taking some new initiatives. For instance, in China, the company launched the Smart PC in 2002. The Smart PC was a low-cost, high-memory basic PC, without any value-added service. It was offered at a price lower than $579, compared to the Chinese-made Tongxi PC that was priced at $628. Because most of the Chinese customers were not confident about electronic transactions, Dell worked with Chinese banks to receive payments. These innovative initiatives and products helped the company to increase its market share to 7.8 percent by 2005 from 4 percent in 2002.

If product recalls are handled properly, a company not only can keep damage to a minimum but also may find opportunities to reap unexpected benefits.[34]

Nevertheless, analysts were not convinced by the company's claims. They thought Dell, and not the battery manufacturer Sony, would face bad publicity because of the recall. According to them, in order to save its reputation among customers Dell had to be more strategic. From the perspective of industry analysts, the recall would have a bigger impact on Dell's reputation with individual customers than corporate customers. They asserted that institutional buyers "will probably take a balanced view of this." An analyst commented, "If Dell handles this well, and everything comes together with the right message, I think corporate buyers will shrug it off over time and it will be a forgotten issue a year from now."[35] On the other hand, experts warned, individual customers were expected to form a negative opinion of the company and it would be difficult for the company to change customer perceptions.

Some industry watchers felt that Dell's voluntary recall of faulty batteries would boost its efforts to improve its customer service and win back the goodwill of the customers. They pointed out that the recall was a great opportunity for Dell to prove that it acted voluntarily to protect its customers. Moreover, industry insiders said that Dell would not have any serious financial implication because Sony (the battery manufacturer) was sharing the cost of the recall with Dell. They also mentioned that the fact that Dell announced the recall first and others (Apple and Matsushita) followed, would go on to show that Dell was a company with foresight.

Despite these odds, Dell was able to retain its number one position in the PC industry across the globe. In July 2006, in a survey jointly conducted by *Investor's Business Daily* and TIPP, Dell still topped the list (50 percent of U.S. consumers who planned to buy PCs opted for Dell as their first choice). Dell had more market share in the United States (45 percent) than the combined market share of HP, Gateway, and Apple. Even though the dominance in the domestic PC market was difficult to improve dramatically, the company experienced success in selling related products and services to businesses. In the quarter ending in July 2006, the company experienced 36 percent growth in its storage business and 21 percent in its service business (see Exhibit 14).

Turnaround Strategy: Will It Do Wonders?

Dell's stakeholders were worried about the threats that its initiatives faced. Their foremost concern was the failure of Dell's business model in the consumer electronics division, which the company thought would work. According to David Naranjo of DisplaySearch, in the $130 billion consumer electronics industry, Dell was ranked number 10 in LCD TV shipments (with 2.4 percent market share) and number seven in plasma screen shipments (with 3.3 percent market share) in 2005. The much-hyped Media Center PC segment also failed to act as a growth driver. HP's HP-z500 Windows XP-based PC and Apple's Macintosh Mini were more innovative products than Dell's Media PC; hence HP and Apple were the market leaders. Though Dell offered its products at competitive prices, its business model failed to replicate the success of Dell's PCs in the consumer electronics business. The customers of the consumer electronics category preferred to compare various brands displayed in the retail stores, thereby judging the product quality before making purchasing decisions. But Dell did not have enough shelf space in its retail outlets to display its products. Dell's customers could buy only through catalogs and the Web site, which did not provide adequate demonstration value and

Exhibit 14 Dell's Net Revenue by Product Category (in $ billion)

	August 2006	April 2006	July 2005	Growth Rates	
				Sequential	Year to Year
		Net Revenue by Product Category			
Desktop PC	$ 4.9	$ 5.1	$ 5.1	6%	4%
Mobility	3.7	3.7	3.4	1	8
Server	1.4	1.3	1.3	0	1
Storage	0.5	0.5	0.4	12	36
Enhanced Services	1.4	1.4	1.2	2	21
Software	2.2	2.2	2.0	2	10
		Percentage of Total Net Revenue			
Desktop PC	35%	36%	37%		
Mobility	26	26	26		
Server	9	9	10		
Storage	4	3	3		
Enhanced Services	10	10	9		
Software	16	16	15		

Source: http://www.dell.com.

was the main reason for Dell's failure. Thus the company overlooked the Chinese customers' preference of touching and examining the products before purchase. While the market leader Lenovo had 4,800 retail outlets in China alone, the number of Dell's retail outlets was negligible.

Analysts were skeptical about the tech companies' idea of making successful forays into consumer markets. During the 1980s, IBM made a foray into such markets with its PC Jr. Machine but was forced to withdraw in the early 1990s. Similarly, Dell was accustomed to the PC market, but the consumer electronics category would be a tougher challenge. The retail stores, however, were packed with products from entrenched companies, including Sony, Samsung, and Phillips, and aggressive new companies such as Apex Digital. Several other PC companies—Apple, Gateway, and HP—also made forays into the consumer electronics segment. For instance, Gateway introduced 100 new products, including 11 plasma and liquid crystal display televisions, digital cameras, camcorders, MP3 music players, and DVD players.

Even the struggling U.S. consumer electronics market became a problem for Dell. Though the segment accounted for only 15 percent of the company's turnover in 2005, it was considered to be a key growth driver. The analysts predicted only 4–5 percent growth ($8 billion) in the consumer electronics segment for 2006, compared to 13 percent in 2005 and 19 percent in 2004.

Kevin Rollins acknowledged that the company had emphasized selling low-end PCs. These PCs had insignificant margins and contributed negligible amounts to the company's bottom line, but Dell did not plan to abandon its most popular $500 PC segment. However, the company, with its pricing and innovative business model, was expected to find opportunities in the up-market. It needed to identify its key growth drivers from the up-market category, including printers. But analysts felt that achieving success in the PC business and doing the same in the printer business were two different things. Dell succeeded in the PC business because it, unlike that of the printer business, was commodifying. Moreover, Dell outsourced the manufacturing of printers to Lexmark, Fuji, and Kodak, who might not be capable of producing Dell-compatible printers.

With a 19 percent share (2005) of the $1.2 trillion global IT market, the CEO and the chair of Dell predicted that the company would hit $80 billion in revenue by 2010. Analysts figured out that more than 70 percent of Dell's projected revenue would be derived from corporate customers, TVs, displays, media center PCs, and other accessories and services. Due to higher profit margins, the aggregate revenue growth of these categories would be twice that of desktop computers. The company needed a yearly growth of 15 percent to meet its target. But in the fiscal year 2005–2006, the company expected only a 10 percent growth, much less than the 20–25 percent of the 1990s. However, as always, Michael Dell was relentlessly upbeat, "Our model continues to be best in the business. We would not trade ours for anyone else's. It is also important to have a little perspective. In the past ten years our sales are up about 15 times, earnings and stock prices are up about 20 times. Not too shabby!"[36] It's difficult to refute this claim, but past performance is no guarantee of future results.

Notes

1. 2006, Dell: Under siege, *Fortune,* September 18.
2. 2006, Dell's midlife crisis, *Fortune,* November 28.
3. Ibid.
4. Fatboy Slim (born on July 16, 1963, also known as Norman Cook) is a British musician in the dance music genre. His style is known as big beat, a combination of hip hop, breakbeat, rock, and rhythm and blues.
5. Dell: Under siege.
6. Dell Inc. sells all its products to both consumers and corporate customers, using a direct sales model via the Internet Internet and telephone network. It manufactures PCs according to the customer specifications.
7. 2005, Technology's Mr. Predictable, http://www.economist.com, September, 22.
8. A capacitor is a passive electronic component that stores energy in the form of an *electrostatic field.* In its simplest form, a capacitor consists of two conducting plates separated by an insulating material called the dielectric. Capacitance is directly proportional to the surface areas of the plates, and is inversely proportional to the plates' separation.
9. Wall Street is the name of a narrow street in lower Manhattan running east from Broadway downhill to the East River. Considered to be the historical heart of the Financial District, it was the first permanent home of the New York Stock Exchange. The phrase "Wall Street" is also used to refer to American financial markets and financial institutions as a whole.
10. In 1989, Dell launched a high end product named "Olympic," which was rejected by the customers and subsequently withdrawn by the company. In 1992, Dell also faced quality problems in its notebook.
11. NASDAQ (originally an acronym for National Association of Securities Dealers Automated Quotations) is a U.S. electronic stock market. It was founded by the National Association of Securities Dealers (NASD) who divested it in a series of sales in 2000 and 2001. It is owned and operated by The Nasdaq Stock Market, Inc.
12. The consumer PC market in United States, http://www.oft.gov.uk.
13. Hewlett-Packard Company, commonly known as HP, is one of the world's largest corporations. Headquartered in Palo Alto, California, United States, it has a global presence in the fields of computing, printing, and digital imaging, and also sells software and services.
14. Gateway, Inc., is an Irvine, California-based computer company founded in 1985 by Ted Waitt. Originally called Gateway 2000, it was one of the first widely successful direct order companies, utilizing a sales model similar to that of Dell.
15. Apple Computer, Inc., is an American computer technology company. Apple was a major player in the personal computer revolution in the 1970s. The Apple II microcomputer, introduced in 1977, was a hit with home users. In 1983, Apple introduced the first commercial personal computer to use a graphical user interface (GUI), the Lisa. In 1984, Apple introduced the revolutionary Macintosh. The Macintosh (commonly called the "Mac") was the first successful commercial implementation of a GUI, which is now used in all major computers. Apple is known for its innovative, well-designed hardware and software, such as the iPod and the iMac, as well as the well-known iTunes application (originally part of the iLife suite), and Mac OS X., its current operating system.
16. Kenellos Michael, 2005, A billion PC users on the way, CNET News, http://www.cnet.com, August 2.
17. On January 30, 2004, Gateway purchased low-cost PC maker eMachines, hoping that its outsourced manufacturing process would help Gateway cut costs and eMachines' profitable retail business would help its bottom line. Gateway announced its intention to keep the eMachines brand.
18. In the first quarter of 2006, the company posted an operating income of $949 million, which reduced to $605 million during the second quarter.
19. U.S.-based IT consulting firms provide information technology industry analysis, market data and insight, as well as strategic and tactical guidance.
20. Jason Maxwell is the portfolio manager of Los Angeles–based TCW Group, which owns 29 million shares of Dell Inc.
21. 2005, It's bad to worse at Dell, *BusinessWeek,* November.
22. 2006, Dell: Under siege, *Fortune,* September 18.
23. Ibid.
24. Ibid.
25. The iPod is a brand of portable digital media player designed and marketed by Apple Computer.
26. 2005, It's bad to worse at Dell, *BusinessWeek,* November.
27. 2005, Dell's midlife crisis, *Fortune,* November 28.
28. Phil Asmundson is the managing partner of Deloitte's United States Technology, Media, and Telecommunications global industry group specialists.
29. R. Shim & J. G. Spooner, Dell opens its doors to home electronics, CNET News.com.
30. http://www.dell.com.
31. Dell's color laser is almost half the price of an HP and the cartridge is 45 percent less.
32. 2006, Dell: Under siege, *Fortune,* September 18.
33. 2005, Hanging up on Dell, http://www.businessweek.com, October 10.
34. N. C. Smith, et al. A strategic approach to managing product recalls, *Harvard Business Review.*
35. L. Tucci, 2006, Battery recall has upside for Dell, http://searchtechtarget.techtarget.com, August 16, 2006.
36. 2005, Dell's midlife crisis, *Fortune* November 28.

Case 9

Governing the House of the Mouse: Corporate Governance at Disney, 1984–2006

Steve Gove

University of Dayton

Michael Eisner joined the Walt Disney company in 1984, just after the venerated icon of American animation thwarted a hostile takeover attempt. Over the next 20 years, Eisner would lead the company through a remarkable transformation during a period of rapid industry change. Disney's revenues would grow from $1.5 billion to more than $30 billion, the number of employees from 28,000 to more than 125,000, and the firm's stock would appreciate some 1,600 percent. At the heart of the company remained Disney's animated film unit. Under Eisner's revitalization, Disney churned out such hits as *The Lion King* and *Aladdin,* fell into decline, and then partnered with Pixar to transition animated film making into the digital age with *Toy Story* and *Finding Nemo* among the hits. How could this remarkable performance occur in a company whose corporate governance practices were repeatedly labeled as among the worst in corporate America?

Overview of the Motion Picture Industry

In 1946, the average person in the United States went to 28 films a year, with 4 billion tickets sold.[1] The industry's primary rival was radio. Motion picture revenues and profits came exclusively from ticket sales in theaters. By the 1950s, widespread adoption of television meant movie theaters had competition for America's eyeballs. On a Friday night in 1956, a Los Angeles television station aired the film *Thirty Seconds Over Tokyo* and local theaters experienced a 25 percent drop in ticket sales.[2] It was a sign of things to come. By 1960, television was in more than 80 percent of U.S. homes and theater attendance in steady decline.

In 1973, the motion picture industry hit rock bottom: A mere 865 million tickets sold, just 4 per person. The industry aggressively sought alternative sources of revenue. In 1980, home video was a nascent business. Films on videocassettes, then the cutting-edge technology, were typically priced from $70 to $90. By 1983, video rentals reached $625 million annually[3] and VCR penetration would soon reach 18 percent.[4] Other distribution channels, which captured revenue for studios and further increased competition for the local theater, were also growing. Launched in 1972, HBO/Cinemax, the leading player in the subscription-based, at-home syndication market, rode the growth of cable television and had 16.2 million viewers by 1984.[5]

During the 1980s the motion picture industry shifted from one focused on the quality and content of shows, to one fixated on distribution, licensing, and marketing arrangements.[6] A young executive, Michael Eisner of Paramount, noted "90 percent of our meetings used to dwell on what our movies were going to be about," but now were increasingly about release windows, pricing of home videos, software, and release for home viewing.[7] The pace of change would only increase. By 1996, Disney, for example, would delve into its film archive and re-release *Snow White* ten times, making it their most profitable feature.[8] In 2003, *Finding Nemo* would be a blockbuster with $340 million in U.S. ticket sales. Within the industry it would become famous for a different reason: Its $485 million in VCR and DVD sales eclipsed revenues from its theatrical release.[9]

The industry also started to focus attention beyond the film, targeting merchandise and licensing for revenues. The 1977 hit *Star Wars* ushered in this era of film-licensed merchandise. Films developed as "blockbusters" or "event films" had budgets exceeding $100 million and would involve equally large merchandising deals. Disney's *The Lion King,* for example, involved some 2,500 licensed products.[10] In the late 1990s and beyond, motion picture studios would expand their reach, becoming diversified entertainment behemoths embedded in the broader "entertainment" business. No firm represented this transformation more than Disney.

The author developed this case for the purpose of class discussion rather than to illustrate either effective or ineffective handling of the situation. Contact person: Steve Gove, Management / Marketing Department, University of Dayton, MH 713, 300 College Park, Dayton, OH 45469-2271, (937) 229-2239, gove@udayton.edu.

Eisner Enters the Magic Kingdom: 1984

Michael Eisner was hired away from Disney's rival Paramount Studios, having been passed over for advancement from president to chairperson. At the time, Paramount was considered among the leaders of the movement to capitalize on merchandising and alternative sources to supplement ticket sales revenue. Many who interacted with Eisner during his Paramount tenure complained he was difficult to work with, but his critics could not argue about his success.[11] Eisner was credited as a creative force in Paramount's rise to one of Hollywood's most successful studios with his contribution to the development of hit films such as *Raiders of the Lost Ark*, *Grease*, and *Terms of Endearment* and hit TV shows such as *Happy Days*, *Laverne and Shirley*, *Taxi*, and *Cheers*.

The film industry experienced rapid changes during the early 1980s, but for Disney, it was a time of crisis. The firm's stock had languished (see Figure 1). The studio released only three films in 1983. By June 1984, the situation was so bad the firm was the target of a hostile takeover attempt by investor Saul Steinberg. Disney thwarted the takeover through a series of defensive maneuvers, including the acquisition of Arvida Corporation, a property development company, principally owned by Bass Brothers Enterprises.[12] The deal provided Disney with 20,000 acres of Florida land and the Bass Brothers with $200 million in Disney stock, enough to exert influence in the company. Facing strong opposition, Steinberg's 11.1 percent interest in the company was sold back to Disney in a practice labeled "greenmail." Disney purchased the shares at $70.83 per share for a total of $325 million, a premium of some $60 million, or nearly 23 percent over market value.[13] Disney also announced an additional defensive maneuver, the acquisition of Gibson Greetings, but later abandoned the deal as the threat of Steinberg subsided and after investor Irwin Jacobs, another possible suitor, disclosed ownership of 6 percent of Disney and threatened a proxy fight unless the plans were cancelled for a purchase he berated as "flagrantly" overpriced.[14]

Figure 1 Performance of Disney for Five Years Prior to Eisner's Arrival, September 1979–September 1984

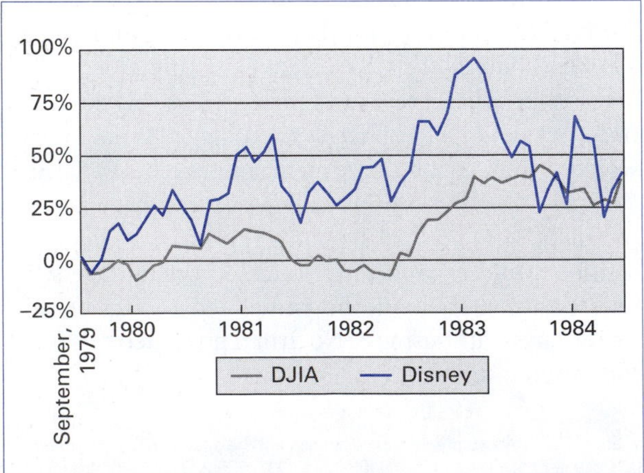

Dissatisfied with the company's performance and subjected to the humiliation of hostile takeover attempts, outside directors met to discuss the possible ouster of president and CEO Ronald Miller.[15] The son-in-law of company founder Walt Disney by marriage to Walt's daughter Diane, Miller had been with Disney for 30 years, president since 1980 and CEO since 1983.[16] Despite his rise within the company, Miller was considered to be symbolic of undermanagement of the company.[17] In a private meeting of Disney's eight outside directors, a coalition formed and agreed to bring the subject of Miller's tenure to discussion and a vote of the full board.

The next day, in a meeting of the full board, all 14 of the firms directors voted for Miller's resignation.[18] The revolt was led by director Philip Hawley[19] and Roy Disney, the nephew of company founder Walt Disney.[20] Roy Disney had resigned from the board in March 1984 following disagreements with Miller and other top managers regarding his role in the company and the firm's failure to hire first-class talent in film and television production.[21] Philip Hawley, co-chair of Disney's outside director's committee, had recently defended his own firm from a hostile acquisition. Hawley had approved Disney's buyout of Saul Steinberg's share to prevent overthrow of the company's management, but had admonished management to significantly improve earnings.[22]

The search for a new CEO was undertaken while under the threat of another takeover. Jacobs, by then controlling 7.7 percent of the company, considered launching his own unsolicited tender offer for control of the company.[23] A spokesperson for Roy Disney, whose interests controlled approximately 5 percent of the company, spurned the offer, stating "one major shareholder—whose name happens to be Disney—is firmly committed to the independence of this company."[24]

Possible CEO candidates included many Hollywood insiders, including Eisner, Frank Wells, then vice chairperson of rival Warner Bros., Dennis Stanfill, former chairman of 20th Century-Fox Film, and Fox Studios chairman Alan Hirschfield.[25] The search ended on September 23, 1984, when the board voted to hire Eisner as CEO and chairperson of the board and Frank Wells as president and chief operating officer.[26] Disney's existing chairperson, Raymond Watson, would resign as board chair but remain on as a director. At least two factions had emerged during the search. One side, including director Philip Hawley, favored the hiring of Stanfill. Another faction wanted Eisner, including members of the Disney family—Roy, Walt's widow Lillian, and

Table 1 Disney's Board Composition, 1980–2006

Unclassified Board ⇨ (1980–1986) | Classified Board Structure ⇨ (1987–2000) | Return to Unclassified Board ⇨ (2001–2006)

Last Name	First Name	Director Beginning	1980	1981	1982	1983	1984	1985	1986	1987	1988	1989	1990	1991	1992	1993	1994	1995	1996	1997	1998	1999	2000	2001	2002	2003	2004	2005	2006
Anderson	William H.	1960	■	■	■	■																							
Morrow	Richard T.	1971	■	■	■	■																							
Hawley	Phillip M.	1975	■	■	■	■	■																						
Miller	Ronald	1966	■	■	■	■	■																						
Tatum	Donn B.	1964	■	■	■	■	■	■	■	■	■	■	■	■															
Ahmanson	Caroline Leonetti	1975	■	■	■	■	■	■	■	■	■	■	■	■															
Disney Lund	Sharon	1984					■	■	■	■	■	■	■	■	■	■													
Baldwin	Robert	1983				■	■																						
Wells	Frank G.	1984					■	■	■	■	■	■	■	■	■	■	■												
Cobb	Charles E., Jr.	1984					■	■	■	■																			
Williams	Samuel L.	1983				■	■	■	■	■	■	■	■	■	■	■	■												
Walker	E. Cardon	1960	■	■	■	■	■	■	■	■	■	■	■	■	■	■	■	■	■	■									
Nunis	Richard A.	1981		■	■	■	■	■	■	■	■	■	■	■	■	■	■	■	■	■									
Lozano	Ignacio E., Jr.	1981		■	■	■	■	■	■	■	■	■	■	■	■	■	■	■	■	■	■	■	■						
Russell	Irwin E.	1987								■	■	■	■	■	■	■	■	■	■	■	■	■	■						
Disney	Roy E.	1967	■	■	■	■	■	■	■	■	■	■	■	■	■	■	■	■	■	■	■	■	■	■	■	■			
Watson	Raymond L.	1974	■	■	■	■	■	■	■	■	■	■	■	■	■	■	■	■	■	■	■	■	■	■	■	■			
Gold	Stanley P.	1987					■				■	■	■	■	■	■	■	■	■	■	■	■	■	■	■	■			
Eisner	Michael D.	1984					■	■	■	■	■	■	■	■	■	■	■	■	■	■	■	■	■	■	■	■	■	■	
Wilson	Gary L.	1985						■	■	■	■	■	■	■	■	■	■	■	■	■	■	■	■	■	■	■	■	■	■
Stern	Robert A.M.	1992													■	■	■	■	■	■	■	■	■	■	■				
Bowers	Reveta F.	1993														■	■	■	■	■	■	■	■	■	■				
Poitier	Sidney	1994															■	■	■	■	■	■	■	■	■				
Litvack	Sanford M.	1995																■	■	■	■	■	■						
Mitchell	George J.	1995																■	■	■	■	■	■	■	■	■	■	■	■
Ovitz	Michael	1995																■	■										
Murphy	Thomas S.	1996																	■	■	■	■	■	■	■	■			
O'Donovan	Leo J., S. J.	1996																	■	■	■	■	■	■	■	■	■	■	■
Van de Kamp	Andrea	1998																			■	■	■	■	■				
Estrin	Judith L.	1998																				■	■	■	■	■	■	■	■
Bryson	John E.	2000																						■	■	■	■	■	■
Iger	Robert A.	2000																						■	■	■	■	■	■
Lozano	Monica C.	2000																						■	■	■	■	■	■
Matschullat	Robert W.	2002																								■	■	■	■
Chen	John S.	2004																									■	■	■
Lewis	Aylwin B.	2004																									■	■	■
Langhammer	Fred H.	2005																										■	■
Pepper	John E., Jr.	2006																											■
Smith	Orin C.	2006																											■
Jobs	Steve	2006																											■

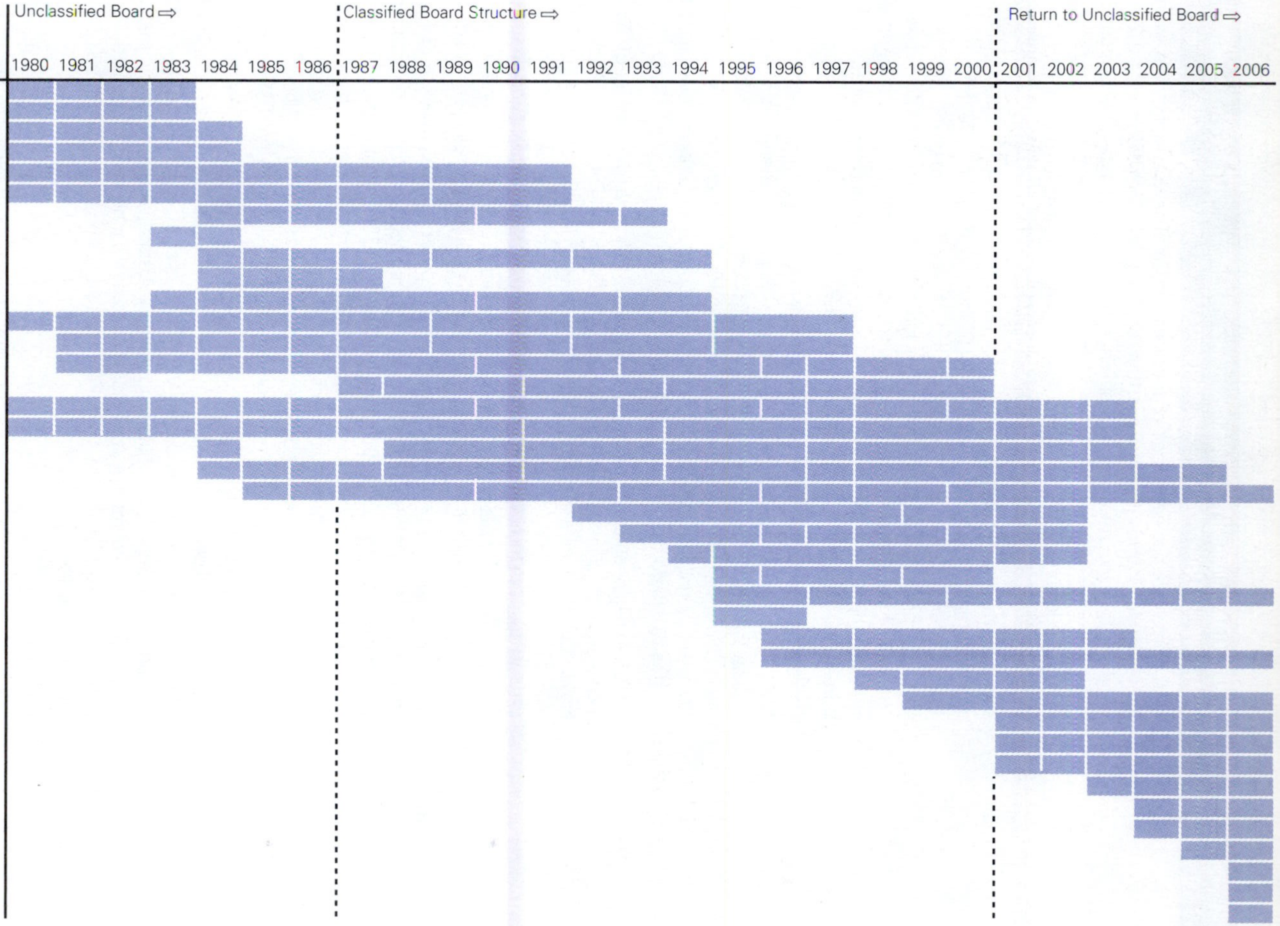

Note:

Proxies not available for all years. Directors join and depart the board at various points during the year. Missing years and inexact dates filled in with case writer's estimates.

White cell borders indicate reelection, multiple cells joined without border indicates continued multiple year term.

Table 2 Bios of Select Disney Directors

Director	Director Beginning	Brief Bio (parenthetical year indicates Disney proxy statement from which bio was adapted)
Ahmanson, Caroline Leonetti	1975	Mrs. Ahmanson has been chair of the board of Caroline Leonetti Ltd. (a women's center for self-improvement) since 1945 and has, for more than the past 20 years, been engaged in numerous civic, philanthropic, and charitable affairs. From 1982 to 1984 she was chairperson of the Federal Reserve Bank of San Francisco, of which she is currently chair emeritus, and now serves as a member of the board of directors of Flour Corporation and of Carter Hawley Hale Stores, Inc. (1988)
Bowers, Reveta F.	1993	Mrs. Bowers was elected to the board of directors on April 26, 1993, to fill the vacancy created by the death of Sharon Disney Lund. Since 1976, Mrs. Bowers, 45, has been the head of school for the Center for Early Education, an independent school for preschool through sixth grade located in Los Angeles. Mrs. Bowers is a member of the board of directors of several not-for-profit educational organizations, including the National Association of Independent Schools and Educational Records Bureau, Inc. She is also a trustee of Harvard-Westlake School, an independent high school located in Los Angeles. (1993)
Bryson, John E.	2000	Mr. Bryson served as chair of the board, president, and chief executive officer of Edison International, the parent company of Southern California Edison, since 1990. He is also a director of The Boeing Company; Pacific American Income Shares, Inc.; LM Institutional Fund Advisors, Inc.; and the Council on Foreign Relations, and a trustee of Stanford University. (2000)
Chen, John S.	2004	Mr. Chen has been chairperson, chief executive officer, and president of Sybase, Inc., a software developer, since November 1998. From February 1998 through November 1998, he served as co-CEO. Mr. Chen joined Sybase in August 1997 as chief operating officer and served in that capacity until February 1998. From March 1995 to July 1997, Mr. Chen was president of the Open Enterprise Computing Division, Siemens Nixdorf, a computer and electronics company, and chief executive officer and chairperson of Siemens Pyramid, a subsidiary of Siemens Nixdorf. (2004)
Disney Lund, Sharon	1984	Mrs. Lund, daughter of the late Walt Disney, served for more than the past five years as an officer of Retlaw Enterprises, Inc., a successor to the corporation that was originally organized by the late Walt Disney in 1952 to carry on certain of his personal business ventures. Retlaw is owned by members of his family, including Mrs. Lund. She also served as a trustee of the California Institute of the Arts, the Marianne Frostig Center of Educational Therapy, and the Curtis School Foundation. (1988)
Disney, Roy E.	1967	Mr. Disney has been vice chairperson of the board of directors of the company since 1984, and since November 1985 has also served as head of the company's animation department. In addition, Mr. Disney is chairperson of the board of Shamrock Holdings, Inc., which, through its subsidiaries, is engaged in real estate development and other investments. Mr. Disney is a nephew of the late Walt Disney. Mr. Disney's service as a director of the company began in 1967, but was interrupted in 1984. (1984)
Eisner, Michael D.	1984	Mr. Eisner is chairperson of the board of directors and chief executive officer of the company. Prior to joining the company in September 1984, Mr. Eisner was president and chief operating officer of Paramount Pictures Corp., a wholly owned subsidiary of Gulf-Western Industries, Inc. Prior to joining Paramount in 1976, Mr. Eisner was senior vice president of prime time production and development for ABC Entertainment, a division of the American Broadcasting Company, Inc., with responsibility for the development and supervision of all prime-time series programming, limited-series movies made for television, and the acquisition of talent. (1988)
Estrin, Judith L.	1998	Ms. Estrin currently serves as chief technology officer and senior vice president of Cisco Systems Inc. She was formerly president and chief executive officer of Precept Software, Inc., a developer of networking software of which she was co-founder until its acquisition by Cisco in April 1998. Ms. Estrin was a computer industry consultant from September 1994 to March 1995, and served Network Computer Devices as president and chief executive officer from October 1993 to September 1994 and as executive vice president from July 1988 to October 1993. She also serves as a director of FDX Corporation and Sun Microsystems. (1998)

Director	Director Beginning	Brief Bio (parenthetical year indicates Disney proxy statement from which bio was adapted)
Gold, Stanley P.	1984	Mr. Gold has served as president and chief executive officer of Shamrock Holdings, Inc., a company engaged in ranching, real estate, agricultural processing, and energy, and of Shamrock Broadcasting, Inc., a company engaged in the operation of radio and television stations. During this period, Mr. Gold was also vice president of the Hollywood entertainment law firm of Gang, Tyre, Ramer & Brown, Inc., and president and chief executive officer, director, and chairperson of the board of directors of Central Soya Company, Inc., an international agribusiness operation. Mr. Gold is also chairperson of the board of directors of Enterra Corporation, an energy equipment company. (1988)
Iger, Robert A.	2000	Mr. Iger has served as president and chief operating officer of the company since January 2000, having served as president of Walt Disney International and chairperson of the ABC Group. From 1974 to 1998, Mr. Iger held a series of increasingly responsible positions at ABC, Inc., and its predecessor Capital Cities/ABC, Inc., culminating in service as president of the ABC Network Television Group and president and chief operating officer of ABC, Inc. He is a member of the board of directors of Lincoln Center for the Performing Arts in New York City and a trustee of Ithaca College. (2000)
Jobs, Steve	2006	Mr. Jobs is chief executive officer and a member of the board of directors of Apple Computer, Inc. Prior to Pixar's merger with the company, he was chairperson and chief executive officer of Pixar since 1986. (2006)
Langhammer, Fred H.	2005	Mr. Langhammer is chairperson of Global Affairs for The Estée Lauder Companies Inc., a manufacturer and marketer of cosmetics products. Prior to being named chairperson, Global Affairs, Mr. Langhammer was chief executive officer of The Estée Lauder Companies Inc., president, and chief operating officer. Mr. Langhammer joined The Estée Lauder Companies in 1975 as president of its operations in Japan. In 1982, he was appointed managing director of its operations in Germany. He is also a director of The Gillette Company and Inditex S.A., an apparel manufacturer and retailer. (2005)
Lewis, Aylwin B.	2004	Mr. Lewis is president, chief multibranding and operating officer of YUM! Brands, Inc., a franchisor and licensor of quick service restaurants including KFC, Long John Silvers, Pizza Hut, Taco Bell, and A&W. Prior to being named president, chief multibranding and operating officer in 2003, he was chief operating officer of YUM! Brands since 2000 and chief operating officer of Pizza Hut since 1996. Mr. Lewis is also a director of Halliburton Co. (2004)
Litvack, Sanford M.	1995	Mr. Litvack is senior executive vice president and chief of corporate operations of the company, having served as senior vice president, general counsel, from April 1991 through June 1992 and as executive vice president for law and human resources from June 1992 to August 1994. Mr. Litvack was a litigation partner with the law firm of Dewey Ballantine from 1987 until joining the company in 1991. (1997)
Lozano, Ignacio E., Jr.	1981	Mr. Lozano is chairperson and chief executive officer of Lozano Enterprises, which publishes *La Opinion,* the largest Spanish-language newspaper in the Los Angeles metropolitan area. Mr. Lozano was publisher and editor of *La Opinion* from 1953 to 1986, except for the period from 1976 through 1977 when he was the U.S. Ambassador to El Salvador. He continues to serve as the editor-in-chief of *La Opinion.* Mr. Lozano is also a member of the board of directors of BankAmerica Corp., Pacific Lighting Corporation, and a number of public service and charitable organizations. (1988)
Lozano, Monica C.	2000	Ms. Lozano is president and chief operating officer of *La Opinion,* the largest Spanish-language newspaper in the Los Angeles metropolitan area, and vice president of its parent company, Lozano Communications, Inc. She also serves as president of the California State Board of Education. In addition, Ms. Lozano is a trustee of SunAmerica Asset Management Corporation and the University of Southern California, and is a director of the California Health Care Foundation, the Fannie Mae Foundation, the National Council of La Raza, and the Los Angeles County Museum of Art. (2000)

(continued)

Table 2 Bios of Select Disney Directors *(continued)*

Director	Director Beginning	Brief Bio (parenthetical year indicates Disney proxy statement from which bio was adapted)
Matschullat, Robert W.	2002	Mr. Matschullat is a private equity investor and served from October 1995 until June 2000 as vice chairperson of the board of directors of The Seagram Company Ltd., a global company with entertainment and beverage operations. He also served as chief financial officer of Seagram until January 2000. Prior to joining Seagram, Mr. Matschullat was head of worldwide investment banking for Morgan Stanley & Co., Inc., a securities and investment firm, and was one of six management members of the Morgan Stanley Group board of directors. He is also a director of The Clorox Company and McKesson Corporation. (2002)
Nunis, Richard A.	1981	Mr. Nunis is president of Walt Disney Attractions, a principal business of the company encompassing the company's theme parks and resorts, and is president of Disneyland, a division of the Company, and Walt Disney World Co., a wholly owned subsidiary of the company. Mr. Nunis has been a senior executive of the company or a subsidiary thereof for more than the past five years. Mr. Nunis is also a member of the board of directors of Sun Banks, Inc. (1988)
O'Donovan, Leo J., S.J.	1996	Fr. O'Donovan has served as president of Georgetown University in Washington, D.C., since 1989. He is chair of the board of the Consortium on Financing Higher Education and a member of the board of directors of The Riggs National Bank of Washington, D.C., the National Council on the Arts of the National Endowment for the Arts, the Association of Catholic Colleges and Universities, and the Consortium of Universities of the Washington Metropolitan Area. (1997)
Pepper, John E., Jr.	2006	Mr. Pepper previously served as chair of the executive committee of the board of directors of The Procter & Gamble Company, having served in various positions at Procter & Gamble, including chairperson of the board from 2000 to 2002, chief executive officer and chairperson from 1995 to 1999, president from 1986 to 1995, and director from 1984 to 2003. Mr. Pepper serves on the board of Boston Scientific Corp. and is a member of the Executive Committee of the Cincinnati Youth Collaborative. (2006)
Poitier, Sidney	1994	Mr. Poitier was elected to the board of directors on November 21, 1994, to fill the vacancy created by the death of Frank G. Wells. The actor, director, and writer is the chief executive officer of Verdon-Cedric Productions, a film production company, and a member of the board of directors of SpectraVision, Inc. Mr. Poitier has won many awards, including the Academy Award for Best Actor and the American Film Institute's Lifetime Achievement Award. He belongs to numerous civic organizations, including the Children's Defense Fund, the NAACP Legal Defense and Education Fund, and the Natural Resources Defense Council. (1994)
Russell, Irwin E.	1987	Mr. Russell is an attorney engaged in private practice specializing in the entertainment industry. Until 1986, he was senior partner in the law firm of Russell & Glickman. Mr. Russell has served as an ad hoc arbitrator for the Federal Mediation Conciliation Service and the American Arbitration Association. He is a founder and is currently a director of RAI Research Corporation. (1988)
Smith, Orin C.	2006	Mr. Smith was president and chief executive officer of Starbucks Corporation from 2000 to 2005, having joined Starbucks as vice president and chief financial officer in 1990. Prior to joining Starbucks, Mr. Smith spent a total of 14 years with Deloitte & Touche. Mr. Smith is a director of Starbucks, Nike, and Washington Mutual.
Stern, Robert A.M.	1992	Mr. Stern is a practicing architect, teacher, and writer. He is senior partner of Robert A.M. Stern Architects of New York, which he founded, and a Fellow of the American Institute of Architects. Mr. Stern is also a professor at the Graduate School of Architecture at Columbia University in New York. Mr. Stern was the architect of the Yacht, Beach Club, and Boardwalk hotels and the Casting Center at the Walt Disney World Resort, the Newport Bay Club, and the Cheyenne Hotel at the Euro Disney Resort. (1992)
Tatum, Donn B.	1964	Mr. Tatum was a senior executive of the company for more than 25 years until 1983, after which he continued to provide consulting and other services to the company until January 2, 1987. From 1971 to 1977, Mr. Tatum was chairperson of the board and chief executive officer of the company; from 1977 to 1980 he was chairperson of the board and from 1980 to 1983 he was chair of the Executive Committee. He is currently a director of Western Digital Corporation. (1988)

Director	Director Beginning	Brief Bio (parenthetical year indicates Disney proxy statement from which bio was adapted)
Van de Kamp, Andrea	1998	Ms. Van de Kamp, 55, has served as chairperson of Sotheby's West Coast, a unit of the international auction company, since 1989, and is a member of the board of directors of Sotheby's North America. She also serves as a director of City National Bank and Jenny Craig International, and as chairperson of the board of the Los Angeles Music Center, Inc. In addition, Ms. Van de Kamp is a trustee of Pomona College, in Pomona, California. (1998)
Walker, E. Cardon	1960	Mr. Walker was a senior executive of the company for more than 25 years until 1984, after which he has continued to provide consulting and other services to the company. Mr. Walker was chairperson of the board and chief executive officer of the company from 1980 to 1983. He currently serves on the board of directors of McDonald's Corporation. (1988)
Watson, Raymond L.	1974	Mr. Watson was chairperson of the board of the company until 1984. Since then, Mr. Watson has been chair and chief executive officer of Ray Watson, Inc. (real estate development). Mr. Watson was president of The Irvine Company, president of The Newport Development Co., and a former Regents Professor in the Graduate School of Management at the University of California, Irvine. He is a director of Mitchell Energy & Development Co., Pacific Mutual Life Insurance Company, and vice chairperson of The Irvine Company. (1988)
Wells, Frank G.	1984	Mr. Wells is president and chief operating officer of the company. Prior to joining the company in September 1984, Mr. Wells was president of Warner Bros. Inc., the motion picture subsidiary of Warner Communications, Inc., from 1975 to 1977; president and co-chief executive officer from 1977 through 1981; and vice chairperson from 1982 to 1984. Before his association with Warner Bros. Inc., he was a partner in the Hollywood entertainment law firm of Gang, Tyre & Brown. (1988)
Williams, Samuel L.	1983	Mr. Williams has been a senior partner in the law firm of Hufstedler, Miller, Carlson & Beardsley since July 1965. He has served as president of the State Bar of California, the Los Angeles County Bar Association and the Board of Police Commissioners of the City of Los Angeles. He is currently a member of a number of charitable and public service organizations and serves on the board of directors of the Bank of California, N.A. (1988)
Wilson, Gary L.	1985	Mr. Wilson is executive vice president and chief financial officer of the company. Prior to joining the company in July 1985, Mr. Wilson was executive vice president and chief financial officer of Marriott Corporation where he was responsible for financial management, strategic planning, and corporate development. He serves on the board of directors of Northwest Airlines, Inc. (1988)

Sharon Lund Disney, who collectively controlled about 13 percent of the company. The Bass Brothers, instrumental in thwarting the takeover, had increased holdings in the company from 5.5 to 8.6 percent[27] and also supported Eisner and Wells. In the end, the influence of ownership prevailed and the board voted unanimously to hire Eisner and Wells.

Wells, a lawyer with broader experience, was initially expected to assume the CEO position. The appointment of Eisner, with more experience in the creative aspects of production, to the position suggested that Disney would continue to be centered around movie production. Upon his appointment, Eisner solidified this expectation by stating he was mandated by the board to make Disney the equal of the best and biggest Hollywood studios. He announced ambition to increase the share of revenue and profits from Disney's entertainment divisions, from the 20 percent they constituted in 1984, to 50 percent.[28] Just a week after arriving, Eisner put this into action with the hiring of 33-year-old wonder kid Jeffery Katzenberg from Paramount as president of motion pictures and television.[29]

After their election, Eisner and Wells met with Bass Brothers and gained their commitment to support long-term changes at the company. Said Sid Bass, "We're with you for the next five years."[30] Shortly thereafter, Bass Brothers purchased Jacob's share in the company, reportedly for $61 a share, increasing ownership to some 24 percent of the company.[31] This ownership block mostly quelled the potential for another unsolicited takeover, but represented a significant change in ownership within a company that, for most of its existence, had been a family enterprise.

Following Walt Disney's death in 1966, Disney had essentially remained unchanged. The few films produced followed familiar stories, 1950s-style silly comedies, and animated cartoons. The problem was that American culture had evolved. The film fans that Disney created were left in a chasm, void of Disney films fitting their advanced age and the changed world around them. One commentator described Disney as existing in a state of "suspended animation."[32] Said Eisner, "My first week at Disney, there was an employee recognition dinner. They sang Disney songs and I realized the newest song was 20 years old. And at the theme parks, Tomorrowland was looking a bit like Yesterdayland. My real challenge is to create the new without letting 'Disneyesque' vanish from the dictionary."[33]

Disney's governance too was evolving. Possibly to thwart another takeover attempt, the firm adopted a classified structure under which directors were elected to three-year terms, with appointments staggered so that in any year only one "class," or one-third of the directors, was up for reelection. Of the directors, several were former Disney managers, including its former CEO, Raymond Watson. A number of the directors were of an advanced age, and their average tenure with the company was lengthy, which suggested a possible distance from the changing industry environment.

In short order, Eisner returned Roy Disney, who had produced and directed some 35 Disney nature films, to an active management role in the company, sharing management responsibility for Disney's animated films with Katzenberg. The animation group would increase production from one release every three years to one every 18 months.[34] Roy also rejoined the board in June along with Stanley Gold, the chief executive of Roy Disney's Shamrock holding company.

In some irony, Disney's biggest hit in 1984 was *Splash,* developed and released under Disney's Touchstone label that former CEO Miller had started. Eisner commented on Disney's move under Miller to develop entertainment for a broader audience as "the right idea" but Miller did "not have time to exercise it completely."[35] Due to the multiyear period needed to develop a motion picture, Disney's 1985 releases were also films that had commenced under Miller's direction, including *Baby, My Science Project,* and *Return to Oz. The Black Cauldron,* Disney's most complex animated film, had begun production six years prior to Eisner's arrival—prior even to Miller's appointment as president. At a cost of $25 million, it was also at the time Disney's most expensive animated film. It would be both a critical and commercial flop.[36]

The Bass Brothers recommended that Disney should increase the price of theme park admission and develop hotels within or around the parks. Gary Wilson, a seasoned veteran of hotel firm Marriott, was hired as Disney's CFO with a seat on the board to lead expansion into hotels. Wilson targeted a 20 percent earnings growth and a 20 percent gain in stock price yearly. The reshuffling of Disney's top management was also accompanied by changes within the board of directors. Stanley Gold, an ally of Roy Disney, resigned from the board to make room for Sharon Lund Disney, daughter of founder Walt Disney and sister of Diane, wife of the removed Ronald Miller. Disney announced that Philip Hawley and Robert Baldwin would not be slated by the company to stand for reelection.[37]

Details of Eisner's compensation contract became speculation in the industry. It was expected to be beyond the reported $2 million a year he was paid while at Paramount. Other Hollywood executives questioned Disney's ability to pay a CEO a rate comparable to other Hollywood studios when Disney's film volume was low. While other studios released 1,520 films in 1984, Disney released only two. Eisner commented, "We came in with deals that relate to the company as a whole without regard to any particular industry."[38]

Eisner's deal was negotiated by his personal attorney, Irwin Russell, who Eisner would invite to join the board in 1987. In an SEC filing, the full details of Eisner's and Wells's compensation contracts were disclosed. Eisner received a one-time payment of $750,000 as compensation for lost benefits upon leaving Paramount. His annual compensation would include both a base annual salary of $750,000 and two forms of incentive compensation.[39] First, Eisner was granted the right to purchase 510,000 shares of Disney stock at $57.44 per share. (Upon his hire, Disney's shared traded at $63.75.) Second, Eisner would receive an annual bonus equal to 2 percent of the amount by which the company's net income exceeds a 9 percent return on stockholders' equity.[40] This amount equated to 2 percent of profits above $100 million, the most Disney had earned in a year. Disney's return on equity for the fiscal year ending September 30, 1984, was 7.7 percent.

The compensation structure for Frank Wells was similar, including a one-time payment of $250,000, annual salary of $400,000, options for 460,000 shares of Disney stock, and an annual bonus equaling 1 percent of increases in return on stockholders' equity above 9 percent.

Katzenberg too wanted stock options similar to Eisner. During negotiations, Wells argued the board of directors would never approve it. Both Eisner and Wells agreed that incentives were appropriate, and all settled on 2 percent of profit for all projects Katzenberg successfully completed. At the time, Wells explained to Eisner it wouldn't amount to much while telling Katzenberg it would be an annuity for his kids. Wells's assessment may have been based on Hollywood's accounting system, where even the most successful movie was frequently unprofitable and where merchandising and video sales were a new phenomena. The times, however, were rapidly changing.

Building the House: 1985–1993

Eisner quickly improved performance. Disney's stock was soon trading near $120 and the firm declared a 4-to-1 stock split, its first in over a decade, and announced a $0.08 quarterly dividend. Market reaction was strong; the firms stock increased by $5.50. The next year, no longer a likely takeover target, Disney divested the assets of Arvida for $400 million.[41] The chairperson of Disney's Arvida unit, Charles E. Cobb, Jr., left the company and resigned his directorship to become U.S. assistant secretary of commerce.[42] His position on the board was filled by a returning Stanley Gold, president and CEO of Shamrock Enterprises.[43]

The value of Eisner's compensation package for 1988, including exercised options, totaled $40 million, making him the year's highest paid executive.[44] However, in 1989, Eisner fell far down on the list with a paycheck of $9.5 million. He was topped by deputy Frank Wells, whose income totaled $50.9 million and former Disney CEO Gary Wilson, at $49.9 million. This apparent pay disparity was the result of Wells's and Wilson's exercise of stock options, whereas Eisner did not exercise options in 1989, but instead retained options for 1.4 million Disney shares. His compensation agreement awarded him options for 2 million more shares. At the time, it was a record amount and drew the attention of the business press,[45] but criticisms were tempered due to its basis in the company's increasing financial performance.

In 1990, Disney adopted a stock option plan for top company executives. Disney's program would allow the company to reward top executives with a total of up to 8.5 million shares of company stock. Once awarded, 20 percent of the options would be exercisable each year. With approximately 135 million shares outstanding, the stock option program represented a significant potential dilutionary effect. To offset potential dilution, Disney also increased its stock repurchase program by 8.5 million shares. This plan allowed the company to pay executives in a tax-friendly manner, but Disney was on the hook for the cash cost of shares repurchased at market value.

In 1992, Disney reduced the size of its board of directors from 14 to 13 members. Two directors, Caroline Leonetti Ahmanson and Donn Tatum, retired from the board and one new director, Robert A. M. Stern, joined.[46] Ahmanson was chair of a women's self-improvement center and chair of the Federal Reserve Bank of San Francisco from 1982–1984 where she continued as chair emeritus. She served as a director of Carter Hawley Hale Stores, whose CEO, Phillip Hawley, had favored hiring a candidate other than Eisner. Tatum had joined Disney in 1956, served in several capacities including executive vice president of Disneyland before joining Disney's board in 1964. Stern, a professor at Columbia University, was the architect for several major Disney commissions, including the Yacht and Beach hotels, Walt Disney World's casting center, and two EuroDisney hotels. The net effect was the elimination of one independent director, decreasing the independent oversight of management and tilting the board toward Eisner.

In February 1992, Disney announced plans for a second 4-to-1 stock split due to continued stock appreciation. On the day of the announcement, Disney's shares were trading at a record $146.50 per share, which represented an overall stock increase of 1,400 percent since Eisner's appointment. In contrast, the S&P 500 Average during the same period returned roughly 300 percent. Performance was attributed to solid gains in all of Disney's operations, especially film. For the year, Disney's film business earned $508 million on revenues of $3.11 billion. Many of the company's recent releases had been hits, including *Beauty and the Beast* and *Father of the Bride.* Eisner along with the CEOs of many U.S. firms were drawing the attention of the business press, investors, and Congress with multimillion-dollar compensation packages. Many, such as Eisner's, were based on stock options. Given favorable tax treatment by Congress, the options awarded to top executives were, in the words of one commentator, "being doled out like Monopoly money."[47]

The year 1993 closed on a mixed note: The film business showed real increases, while the performance of Euro Disney hurt the company. Euro Disney had been spearheaded by Eisner and the subject of much controversy. Euro Disney's condition was so dire that the enterprise teetered on bankruptcy and required restructuring. Disney's 49 percent share in the losses reduced income by nearly $515 million.[48] This reduction was, however, offset by further increases in Disney's film business, which recorded a record operating profit of $622 million, a 22 percent increase over 1992's performance. Revenue in the unit was a record $3.67 billion, attributed to a series of successes including *Aladdin,* their most successful animated film to date.[49]

An Unraveling of Sorts: 1994 and 1995

On April 4, 1994, Disney president Frank Wells, along with two other passengers, was killed in a helicopter crash while heli-skiing in central Nevada.[50] Wells, together with Eisner, was credited as the chief architect behind Disney's emergence as a major player in the entertainment industry. Eisner was seen as the creative force with Wells, an attorney, providing the business acumen. In a decade, the two leaders had increased revenues 467 percent to

$8.5 billion, and grown market capitalization from $2 billion to $22 billion. Wells's sudden death would certainly be felt by the company, but Disney would survive. Richard Simon, analyst at Goldman, Sachs & Co. assessed the sadness of the situation and noted, "It is impossible to measure Frank's contribution to Disney's success. . . . [however,] we believe Disney's management has positioned the company for growth that is based on a broad management team."[51]

The issue of who would succeed Wells as Disney's president soon came to the forefront. Speculation was widespread that Jeffrey Katzenberg was a likely and willing candidate. However, Disney's Hollywood Pictures, under Katzenberg's leadership, was struggling. Katzenberg had recently tripled the number of pictures the unit was to release each year from 20 to 60 in an attempt to return the unit to profitability.[52]

Eisner initially divided Wells's responsibilities among Disney's existing executives, assuming the position of president himself on an interim basis. Just weeks after Wells's death, Eisner noted that serving as president gave his management team greater direct access to him.[53] Soon, Eisner announced he would hold the president title on a long-term basis, but the appointment of a future president was not ruled out.[54]

The feasibility of this structure was tested. On a Friday evening in mid-July, Eisner fell ill and underwent emergency quadruple bypass surgery. The procedure was considered routine, and Eisner was on his feet by Monday,[55] returning to work after a brief convalescence. Speculation on Wall Street was that following the recent death of Wells, succession plans had been addressed by the board. Again Katzenberg was rumored as the likely successor. In a later interview, Eisner confessed that prior to his surgery he made a handwritten list of people to be his replacement should he not survive the operation and gave it to his wife Jane.[56] Who was on the list? Did the board have a succession plan? Because succession plans make the transition between CEOs easier, they may be opposed by CEOs, who fear their job security is diminished when an acknowledged and prepared replacement exist.

Just a month later, any succession plan that may have included Katzenberg unraveled. Katzenberg announced he would leave the company when his contract expired at the end of September. Outside Disney's executive offices and outside the firm, the news came as a shock and was attributed to his not being named as Wells's replacement.[57] Katzenberg, however, insisted that he had informed Eisner and Wells a year earlier that he might leave after his contract expired. Other top managers had also departed, attributed in part to Eisner's management style. Raymond Watson, Disney director and chair of the executive committee, said the decision to bypass Katzenberg was "fully discussed in the board room,"[58] adding the position was not consistent with his skills. Watson said, "This job is a partnership in which Michael needs complementary kinds of talent. This is a different person than Jeffrey. The most important thing is to reinforce Michael."[59]

In a later interview, Eisner said Wells's death was both a tremendous personal loss and a major business problem. Katzenberg, Eisner recalled, soon began campaigning for the position of president and was told early on that he wasn't going to get it. "Jeffrey," Eisner said, "wanted a job that I wasn't prepared to give him . . . [he] wanted to be completely in the spotlight and he was no longer interested in the team unless he was the captain."[60]

News of Katzenberg's impending departure may have been tempered by relief that the production schedule of 60 films a year would be abandoned. Disney's latest animated feature *The Lion King* was also emerging as a hit. The film, costing roughly $50 million to make, had taken in a record $250 million during its first 11 weeks in theaters. By the end of the year, *The Lion King* ticket sales would total $750 million worldwide with an additional $1 billion in sales of merchandise. Still, it was feared that Katzenberg might go to a rival studio. In October, speculation ended with no sigh of relief when Katzenberg announced the formation of DreamWorks SKG with fellow Hollywood film elite Steven Spielberg and music mogul David Geffen (see "The Cost of Saying Good-Bye").

Roy Disney dismissed concerns that the new entity would be a threat to Disney, especially in animation, because it would be four to five years before the studio could put an animated film in the market.[61] Furthering Disney's advantage, Mr. Disney compared creating animated features to a great golf swing: "You see Greg Norman out there and it looks really easy," he said. "You say, I could do that. And you get out there and all the body parts seem wrong. It's just not as easy at it seems."[62] New Line Cinema's animated film *The Swan Princess* for example, created by former Disney animators, grossed less than $10 million.

Still, his departure marked a milestone: Of the fab three of Wells, Katzenberg, and Eisner, brought in to resuscitate an ailing Disney, only Eisner remained. Full replacements had not been made for Wells or Katzenberg. Was the big cheese of the mouse house being stretched too thin? Afraid to develop and promote talent that might replace him? Did Disney have, as some analysts assessed, a broad and deep bench of management talent? Or was the situation more dire? One commentary described Eisner's situation as bordering on Shakespearean: "A great leader becomes fond of shuffling executives, seems threatened by any accumulation of power beneath him, and avoids confronting the realities of mortality by failing to create a line of succession—even after undergoing emergency heart surgery at the age of 52."[63]

The Cost of Saying Good-Bye

Even before his departure, a struggle ensued about payments for future profits due Katzenberg under his contract. Still unresolved as of the announcement of Michael Ovitz as Disney president, the position Katzenberg had sought, public animosity escalated. In April 1996, Katzenberg sued Disney for $250 million, claiming his right to 2 percent of the gross receipts for projects he oversaw from 1984–1994, including such mega-hits as *The Lion King* and *Beauty and the Beast*. [Lieberman, D. 1996, Katzenberg sues Disney for $250 million, *USA Today*, 01B.] The lawsuit for $580 million alleged that Disney was refusing to provide Katzenberg with financial details necessary to put a final price tag on what he saw as compensation due.

In Hollywood the feud was a spectator sport with a central question: Why would Michael Eisner not settle the matter to quiet the bad PR? One commentator speculated on three possible scenarios, "(1) The Bad Dad script, in which Eisner supposedly takes twisted pleasure from denying his protégé of 19 years. (2) The Scrooge plot, in which the Disney chairman is simply loathe to part with a buck. (3) The Eisner Is Right scenario: Maybe Katzenberg is owed zip" (Harris, 1996).

Several attempts were made at settling up between Eisner, Katzenberg, and their intermediaries. Eisner, at several points, expressed he wasn't going to pay Katzenberg anything (Stewart, 2005, *Disney War*). An initial offer was made by the Katzenberg camp for $60 million, a subsequent agreement negotiated by Michael Ovitz, his replacement, for $100 million, was axed by Eisner and in-house counsel Litvack.

It would not be until 1999, some 5 years after Katzenberg departed the company, that the matter was finally resolved. At trial, Katzenberg's attorneys produced a letter prepared as part of negotiations for a contract extension and signed by Frank Wells, which included a discussion of future payments based on the profits for films produced. It read: "It is, of course, obvious but nonetheless worth pointing out that many of these pictures still have substantial revenues forthcoming from ancillary markets which continue to accrue to Jeffrey's benefit. . . . Of course, [these] will continue 'forever' in the sense that even if he should leave one day, there would be an arbitrated amount as to future income from the pictures." (*Financial Times,* 1999.)

The trial judge ruled in favor of Katzenberg, who was awarded $250 million in addition to $77 million paid since his departure. Disney and Katzenberg settled out of court for the remaining difference between the $325 million paid and the $580 million claimed. One newspaper reported of the trial, "Although the case drew much attention because of the colorful clash of personalities, it has also exposed again the fallibility of the Hollywood way with loosely constructed contracts, and the generosity of the film industry's compensation packages." (*Financial Times,* 1999.) Katzenberg may have gotten in a final jab: the character of Lord Farquaad in the 2001 DreamWorks SKG smash hit *Shrek* is reportedly a parody of Eisner.

Even with Disney's considerable financial success, the company was being criticized for its governance practices. CalPERS, the giant pension fund, gave the company's governance an "F+" due to lagging the General Motors Governance Guidelines, considered the industry standard.[64] The ratings did not improve with the appointment of Academy Award winning actor Sidney Poitier as president. Even though Poitier had impressive acting credentials, governance experts questioned his contribution. With its array of studios, theme parks on multiple continents, and the motion picture industry in the midst of rapid change, Disney was becoming a complex empire. Eisner's mandate to reform Disney had been largely realized.[65] The company's resort operations had grown from fewer than 3,000 rooms to more than 21,000 and would soon include a cruise line. Films, the heart of the Disney company, had once declined to less than 5 percent of income, but now contributed 40 percent. Disney, in 1994, was the first studio to ever break the $1 billion mark in combined U.S. ticket sales with the success of *The Lion King, Pulp Fiction,* and *The Santa Clause.*

Complexity soon increased dramatically: In August, a deal was announced to merge Capital Cities/ABC with Disney in a transaction valued at $19 billion,[66] which roughly doubled the size of Disney. This move positioned Disney as the second largest entertainment company in the United States, behind Time Warner. The combined company would be named Walt Disney Co. and Eisner's position as CEO and chairperson would remain unchanged. Capital Cities/ABC's chairperson, Thomas S. Murphy, would leave day-to-day operations and join the board. The merger would signal an era of integration in the industry, combining Disney's studio entertainment and film library with Capital Cities/ABC's broadcast and publishing distribution systems. The company would combine film, television, artistic, production, distribution, and broadcast under a single studio entity. Eisner noted, "The merger positions us for substantial growth worldwide and puts us in a strong competitive position in an industry which, by this transaction, we are helping to define." The two companies were considered highly complementary with executives foreseeing no staff reductions resulting from the combination. Great respect was given to the management of the Capital Cities/ABC, so much, in fact, that Murphy's lieutenant, Robert A. Iger, would continue in his position as president of ABC.

The Michael Ovitz Situation: 1995–1996

On August 15, 1995, Eisner introduced Michael Ovitz as the new president of the Walt Disney Co.[68] Considered one of the most powerful people in Hollywood, Ovitz had an inauspicious start in Hollywood as a tour guide at Universal Studios theme park[69] and rose up as an agent within the William Morris Agency. In 1975, he and four William Morris colleagues left and cofounded Creative Artists Agency (CAA). CAA created an approach in Hollywood labeled "packaging" talent and films wherein a film's creative team—the director, producer, and star(s)—is presented to a studio in a take-it-or-leave-it manner. Successes under the "packaged" formula included *Ghostbusters, Dances with Wolves,* and *Rain Man.*[70]

News of Ovitz joining Disney led to speculation of a wildly uneven distribution of power within the Hollywood establishment. Said Steve Tisch, Disney producer, "The headline in the paper should be 'Disney Reveals It Is Developing a Nuclear Arsenal.' It is an unbelievable announcement . . . this will reinvent the whole entertainment industry." Harvey Weinstein, head of the Disney's Miramax studio, predicted a bright future: "The other studios might just as well throw in the towel. At this point why bother?"[71]

Speculation outside Disney was less dire, focusing on the seeming impossibility of Ovitz and Eisner working together. One outsider noted, "Two big egos can work together, but not forever."[72] A joke began circulating Hollywood, questioning the ability of the Eisner and Ovitz, both monumentally successful and known as passionate and highly driven, to work together: "If Ovitz is God, who is Michael Eisner?"[73]

In an industry where paychecks are indicators of power and status, Ovitz's contract was the subject of much speculation. Ovitz, it was reported, had rejected prior offers from firms such as MCA/Universal for as much as $360 million over 10 years.[74] Surely he wouldn't accept a position at Disney for less? The issue was certainly pertinent as attention was once again focused on Eisner's pay. Depending on one's perspective, it was a gross excess, indicative of the excesses of Corporate America's leaders or a model system aligning leadership with shareholder interests. By any account, it was considerable; cumulatively upward of a half billion dollars. His leadership had increased return on equity and profits more than 20 percent per year for ten years[75] and his pay, while high in dollar terms, was directly linked to increases in shareholder wealth (see Figure 2). It was, in the assessment of one analyst, just like the return given to shareholders: "damned good."[76] An investment of $1,000 in the S&P 500 would have quadrupled to about $4,000 by 1995. The same investment in Disney stock would be worth some $16,500—quadruple the index. Although Eisner's compensation from options exercised was considerable (in 1993, for example, he exercised some 5.4 million options for some $200 million), holdings in the company remained significant. In 1995 Eisner held some 2 million shares of Disney stock and options worth roughly $600 million. Eisner's pay was, from this perspective, aligned with what governance advocates push for: almost entirely tied to increases in shareholder wealth.

The attention given to Eisner's pay coupled with Katzenberg's dispute over profits resulted in considerable attention to Ovitz's pay package. Ovitz's hiring and pay actually received scant attention by Disney's full board. Eisner himself was the instrumental force in hiring and structuring the pay for Ovitz. Eisner approached Ovitz and negotiated the general structure of the compensation formula, a structure including both base pay and stock options. Unlike Eisner, Ovitz was leaving his ownership position at CAA, with annual income of $20–$25 million, and faced considerable downside risk if the position at Disney did not work out. As an outsider added to Disney, the move could raise resentment of other Disney managers passed over for the appointment.[77]

Disney's corporate by-laws specified that the board was responsible for hiring the president, but Eisner and his attorney Russell, not corporate counsel Litvak, approached Ovitz and drafted a contract and compensation agreement over one weekend. Neither the board of directors nor the compensation committee was involved in its development. The details of the deal, along with analysis of its potential costs, fell

Figure 2 Performance of Disney Stock Under Eisner's Reign, September 1984–September 1995

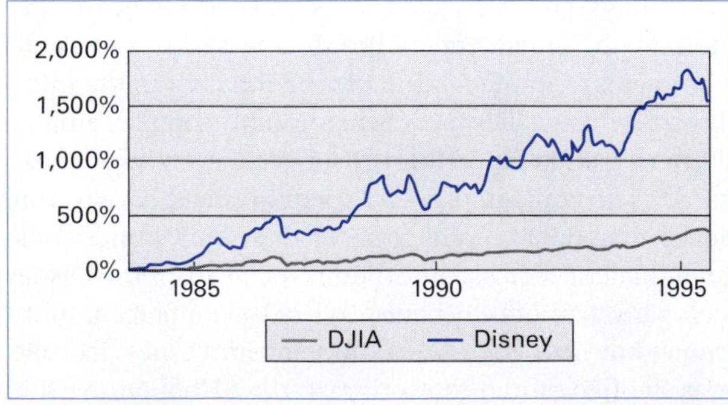

Figure 3 Reporting Structures for Disney Presidents

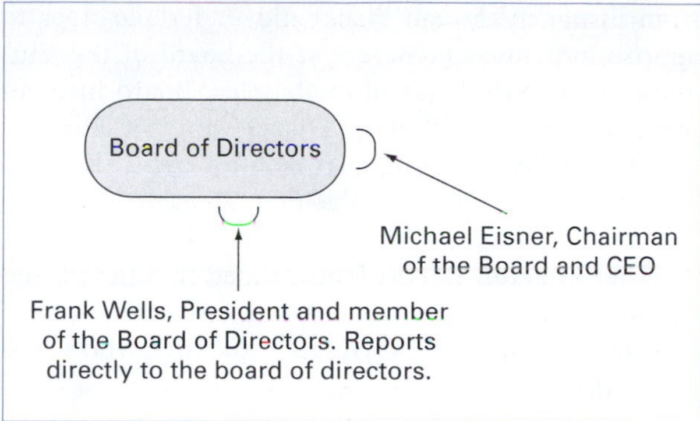

A Reporting Structure for Frank Wells

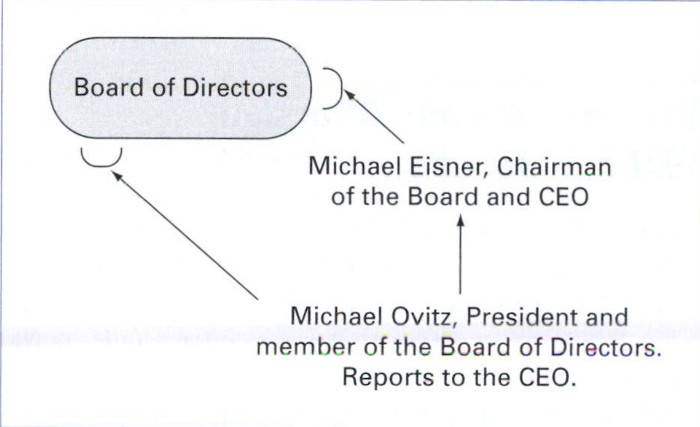

B Reporting Structure for Michael Ovitz

on Russell, the head of Disney's board compensation committee. Eventually, a deal for two tranches of options was struck: the first tranche, 1 million options per year, for years 3, 4, and 5 of his contract vesting at $57 a share, and the second tranche, an additional 2 million shares of Disney stock with immediate vesting should his contract be renewed.[78] Any not-for-cause termination would result in Ovitz receiving his remaining salary, $7.5 million a year for bonuses, immediate vesting of the first tranche of options, and a $10 million cash payout for the second tranche.

Russell cautioned that the value of the options was significant, beyond others at Disney and in corporate America. Raymond Watson, another compensation committee member, and Graef Crystal, an outside consultant who had headed Towers Perrin's executive compensation practice, assessed the arrangement. It was estimated the contract would be worth nearly $24 million a year. The boards compensation committee, including directors Russell, Lozano, and Poitier, met formally for one hour, with Ovitz's compensation as one of four items on the agenda.[79] Shortly thereafter, an executive meeting of the board commenced, finalizing the hiring of Ovitz and approving the compensation plan.[80]

Immediately upon the announcement of his addition to the company, speculation began that Ovitz's primary motivation was to become Eisner's heir at Disney. Eisner, known as a reluctant power sharer, again declined to directly address questions of succession, adding only that Ovitz "[is] the number two man and if something happens to me, he'd be a pretty good candidate."[81]

Like Wells, Ovitz was responsible for Disney's three operating divisions, but unlike Wells, would not be a co-equal of Eisner. Neither legal nor finance would report to Ovitz. In a structural arrangement resulting in a less powerful president, Ovitz would report not to the board as Wells had, but instead to the CEO, a structural arrangement insisted on by Sid Bass.[82] Ovitz would hold a seat on Disney's board of directors, but Michael Eisner would be his boss (see Figure 3). In practice, he had far less discretion and authority than had Katzenberg, and his role in the company was never fully defined or delegated by Eisner.

Immediately upon his hire, Ovitz and Eisner, along with ABC's Robert Iger, personally delved into fixing one of the company's major problems: ABC television network's sagging lineup of shows. In the years leading up to the acquisition, ABC had seen its viewership, and advertising revenues, erode. Its stable of hits, such as *Home Improvement* and *Roseanne* were considered faded gems, losing audience to the likes of rival NBC's *Friends* that would become the center of NBC's "Must See Thursday" and dominate ratings for nearly a decade. The involvement of a studio chairperson in the development and selection of shows was not unique to Disney. Both GE's chairperson Jack Welch, owner of the NBC network, and CBS chairperson Michael Jordan were involved in scheduling and production decisions.[83]

Just months into Ovitz's tenure, rumors circulated the situation was not working out. As an agent at a firm he founded, Ovitz was accustomed to considerable discretion to serve his clients. The same was simply not available given the fiduciary responsibilities of a public company. Lavish parties and gifts are standard mechanisms plied by agents, but largely impossible for the manager of a publicly traded firm. Roy Disney was asked about his transition to a position as the second in command in a publicly held company instead of the principal in a privately held one. Disney replied, "There was more culture shock than expected because he really did run a little fiefdom of his own and when he had to be the next guy down on the ladder, well egos are fragile things. But he is getting hold of it now."[84] Later reports suggested that as an executive, Ovitz was a poor fit with Disney's management philosophy. During one retreat at Walt Disney World in Orlando, Ovitz reportedly refused to participate in group activities, insisted on a limousine while other executives, including Eisner, rode a shuttle bus, and made inappropriate demands of park employees.[85]

While Disney's top managers focused on integrating Ovitz and ABC, much outside attention was focused on their governance system. In July, Disney appointed a Jesuit priest, Father Leo O'Donovan, to the board. Appointment of O'Donovan, the president of Georgetown University, was thought an attempt to satisfy the public that Disney would not stray far from their history as a purveyor of family entertainment.[86] Skeptics noted that O'Donovan was not fully independent from Eisner, because Eisner had served on Georgetown's board of directors from 1985 to 1991, Eisner's son had attended Georgetown, and Eisner had, at O'Donovan's request, made a $1 million contribution.[87]

Relationships such as O'Donovan's drew the attention of *BusinessWeek* in its inaugural Report Card on Corporate Governance, which cited Disney for having a board that was "too cozy" with the CEO.[88] The report cited Disney in particular as a paradox: high stock performance in spite of ineffective governance. Disney's board was ineffective due to what one authority would label "collective kowtowing . . . due to Eisner's desire to surround himself with yes men."[89] Relationships between Eisner and other directors were also highlighted as reducing effective governance. Irwin Russell performed personal legal services for Eisner and work for the company, a possible conflict of interest. Former U.S. Senator George Mitchell had been selected by Eisner to serve on Disney's board and subsequently rose to chairperson with annual compensation of approximately $500,000. Reveta Bowers was the administrator of a Hollywood private school that three of Eisner's children had attended. The *BusinessWeek* report admonished, "Even the smartest CEO needs skeptics on the board of directors to prevent healthy ego from becoming destructive hubris."[90]

Near year end, turmoil in Disney's executive suite peaked again when it was announced that Ovitz was leaving the company. The press described Ovitz' tenure as "tumultuous"[91] and his exit the end of a disaster. Ovitz, it seemed, was unable or unwilling to adjust to Disney's company culture, being the second in command, lacking the authority to make major decisions, and who was increasingly distrusted by fellow Disney managers.[92] Attention also focused on leadership in Disney, specifically Eisner. For some, the conclusion was that Eisner gave lip service to a strong top management team, but instead was to remove anyone who developed power and ambition equal to his own and could potentially pose a threat to his position as CEO. By some accounts, instead of shifting responsibilities, Eisner had actually increased his level of involvement in decision making that was to be under Ovitz's purview.[93]

The move to finally remove Ovitz came directly from Eisner. Although Eisner did undertake steps to apprise individual members of the board of the situation, the decision was ultimately his. Board involvement was highly limited. Disney director Richard Nunis said, "It was enough reason for me if the chief executive of the company decided he needed to make a change. I decided I would support that decision."[94] Another director, Robert Stern, stated that the payout necessary under his contract was a "wise investment" to rid the company of Ovitz, an executive who was a distraction.[95]

Even though Ovitz's exit may have reduced internal turmoil, it also reduced Disney's cash balance. The final cost for his 14 months with Disney: some $140 million in cash and stock options.

The Outcome and Aftermath: 1997 and Beyond

In the weeks leading up to Disney's February 1997 annual meeting, discontent with Disney's management culminated in the unprecedented. In the same proxy statement that disclosed Ovitz's severance payments, it was announced that Eisner signed a new 10-year employment contract, his third since joining Disney in 1984. The contract included options for 8 million more shares of Disney stock in addition to his salary and bonus and 8 million options previously awarded. The value of the new options was reported in company financial disclosures as $195.4 million. The deal drew the attention of the business media with outlets such as *BusinessWeek* labeling the deal "A (Lion) King's Ransom"[96] and reporting the details (see Table 3) *Forbes* magazine estimated Eisner's wealth as $460 million.[97] The contract also included a provision that solidified Eisner's power and reduced the board's ability, if it had any, to force changes in management. If Eisner were to lose either the chairperson or CEO title, all stock options would vest immediately and Disney would immediately pay the cash value of his salary and bonus for all future years. Any action to remove or even reduce Eisner's solo grip on power would put Disney's cash flow on the hook for hundreds of millions of dollars.

An initiative to protest the firm's handling of Ovitz's compensation, Eisner's pay, and overall governance laxities by withholding votes for the firm's slate of directors was urged by several parties, including Institutional Shareholder Services (ISS),[98] the College Retirement Equities Fund (CREF),[99] and other major investor groups. Conrad Mackerron, social research director for Progressive Asset Management commented, "We do not see how it was in the company's best interest to sign an

Table 3 Eisner's Revised Compensation[152]

A (Lion) King's Ransom Eisner's New 10-year Contract	
Base Pay:	$750,000 per year
New Options:	8 million shares, hypothetically worth $195.4 million
Existing Stock Options:	6.7 million shares, worth $358 million in 2006
Bonus:	Varies based on financial performance, but capped at $15 million a year for the first two years
Severance:	If fired without "good cause," Eisner's 8 million new shares vest immediately; he also gets salary and bonuses for the remainder of his 10-year contract, plus two years

employment agreement awarding Ovitz a vast sum of money in the event of his premature departure. . . . What is the benefit for shareholders in such an agreement?"[100] Kenneth West, director of CREF's Corporate Assessment Program stated, "In this case, the proposals for Mr. Eisner's compensation were so generous as to be completely out of line. How much incentive does someone need?"[101] Additional concerns were raised about the level of independence of directors on Disney's board. According to West, only seven of Disney's 16 directors were truly independent, the remainder are or were Disney employees.

At the shareholder meeting, Ovitz's compensation package would consume much of the discussion. Eisner apologized for his decision to hire Ovitz. "My intentions were appropriate and, I thought, wise. It just didn't work out that way." But he still defended the payout to Ovitz, "Obviously, we did not want to make [the mistake of keeping him on]. . . . The cost would have been much higher had we stayed the unstayable course."[102] When the votes were in, 13 percent of shareholders withheld their support for the five directors. *BusinessWeek* reported this event as the most sizable "just say no" vote in years, and Disney topped the list as the worst board in corporate America.[103] Despite the vote of no confidence, all five directors returned to the board. At the meeting, Warren Buffett, whose company Berkshire Hathaway owns 24 million Disney shares, expressed his support for the company.[104] "We have a fantastic board," Eisner would insist, "and I hope I'm not intimidated into changing the direction of the board."[105]

Ovitz's departure and compensation would become the subject of an extended lawsuit, marking a turning point in U.S. corporate governance. Shareholders sued to recover compensation paid to Ovitz by terming his termination as made on a "for cause" basis and the action of Disney's directors as a failing their fiduciary duty of due care (which would have been covered under the directors and officers liability insurance coverage). One reporter later noted the case rested not on managerial fraud, "just utter cluelessness and laxity"[106] of Disney's board of directors in allowing the arrangement. By simply allowing the suit to go forward, Chancellor William Chandler III signaled a time of change in corporate governance practices (see "Judgment Day").

Surprisingly, at the end of 1997, Eisner exercised options for 7.3 million shares of Disney stock at a pretax profit of some $300 million without much notice.[107] He retained stock options worth an additional $590,580.[108]

Disney's 1998 annual meeting continued as a venue for governance reform proposals. One by CREF would institute a new criterion for assessing director independence, requiring "no present or former employment of the company, or any significant financial or personal ties to the company or its management."[109] Additionally, the proposal would require the firm to reconfigure its board, including assurances that all board committees were comprised exclusively of independent directors. In CREF's view, the proposal would be a success if even 20 percent of shareholders voted for it. Disney's directors viewed the matter otherwise, with Director Litvack commenting in advance of the meeting that he wouldn't consider as significant a resolution opposed by three quarters of the shareholders.[110] Some of the reluctance may have stemmed from the company's continued performance. The stock had appreciated some 50 percent since the last shareholder meeting, increasing market capitalization some $76 billion over Eisner's tenure. (See Figure 4, on page 117.) Shortly before the meeting, Proxy Monitor, an investment advisory group, had labeled Disney's board as a "rubber-stamp" for management.[111]

The company was showing some signs of responding to governance critics. A proposal jointly crafted by management and CREF to phase out its three class directorship system, making all directors stand for election each year, passed with 60 percent of the votes. This would increase Disney's susceptibility to another hostile takeover, but was considered effective governance. The CREF resolution garnered 35 percent of the votes, more than

Judgment Day

The Ovitz case was ultimately decided in favor of Disney's management in 2005 (Court of Chancery of Delaware. 2005. *In re The Walt Disney Company* derivative litigation, 1-174: New Castle, Delaware). The price tag, less legal fees, for Ovitz's 14 months at Disney came to some $140 million, including $38.9 million in cash plus options (*Daily Variety*, 2005). In his decision, Chancellor Chandler was scathing of Disney's CEO and governance systems, noting:

By virtue of his Machiavellian (and imperial) nature as CEO, and his control over Ovitz's hiring in particular, Eisner to a large extent is responsible for the failings in process that infected and handicapped the board's decision making abilities. Eisner stacked his (and I intentionally write "his" as opposed to "the Company's") board of directors with friends and other acquaintances who, though not necessarily beholden to him in a legal sense, were certainly more willing to accede to his wishes and support him unconditionally than [would] truly independent directors. On the other hand, I do not believe that the evidence, considered fairly, demonstrates that Eisner actively took steps to defeat or short-circuit a decision making process that would otherwise have occurred (Court of Chancery of Delaware, 2005).

The Chancellor concluded that some of the deference to Eisner may have been the result of a decade of success at running the company. Chiding Eisner for his independence from board oversight, he advised:

Eisner obtained no consent or authorization from the board before agreeing to hire Ovitz, before agreeing to the substantive terms of the OLA, or before issuing the press release. Indeed, outside of his small circle of confidantes, it appears that Eisner made no effort to inform the board of his discussions with Ovitz until after they were essentially completed and an agreement in principle had been reached. . . . As a general rule, a CEO has no obligation to continuously inform the board of his actions as CEO, or to receive prior authorization for those actions. Nevertheless, a reasonably prudent CEO (that is to say, a reasonably prudent CEO with a board willing to think for itself and assert itself against the CEO when necessary) would not have acted in as unilateral a manner as did Eisner when essentially committing the corporation to hire a second-in-command, appoint that person to the board, and provide him with one of the largest and richest employment contracts ever enjoyed by a non-CEO. I write, "essentially committing," because although I conclude that legally, Ovitz's hiring was not a "done deal" as of the [original labor agreement], it was clear to Eisner, Ovitz, and the directors who were informed, that as a practical matter, it certainly was a "done deal" (Court of Chancery of Delaware, 2005).

the 20 percent expected and double the average of similar amendments at other companies. Director Sanford Litvack, who disagreed with CREF's definition of director independence, commented, "We do understand that in this area, perceptions are important."[112] Proxy monitor claimed the vote "a shot in the arm for improved corporate governance."[113] Others were less convinced. One headline read, "Status Quo: Disney Shareholders Fail to Force Reorganization" and described the vote as giving Eisner "lackluster support."

The coming years would see significant change in Disney's board and perspectives on governance. The company again made *BusinessWeek's* list of the worst boards in 2000.[114] In 2002, *BusinessWeek,* twice applauded changes in Disney's governance, noting the company's hiring of Ira Millstein, a governance consultant, restricting positions on the audit and compensation committee to independent directors, holding outside-director-only meetings on a regular basis, requiring that directors own a minimum of $100,000 of company stock, and cutting all business relationships between the company and board members.[115] George Mitchell, who had been elected as the firm's presiding director, presided over the outside-director meetings.[116]

Celebration over improved governance was, if any, short lived. Later in the year *BusinessWeek* issued, for all intents and purposes, a retraction. In its annual report, Disney revealed the previously undisclosed relationships between the company and directors. In *BusinessWeek's* calculation, this information brought the count of non-independent directors on the board to 11 of the total membership of 17.[117] Included in the disclosures was a pledge of $25 million for the construction of the Walt Disney Concert Hall, of which $20 million had been donated to date. Andrea Van de Kamp, who had been labeled as "independent," had been chairperson and CEO of the Performing Arts Center of Los Angeles, which was responsible for the project. She joined the Disney board a year after the pledge was made.[118]

Eisner would continue to make changes to further insulate himself from the governance turmoil. Eisner had previously installed Estrin and Lozano, both staunch supporters, to the nominating and governance committee to outweigh Gold's influence. Under the newly passed Sarbanes-Oxley Act, financial executives were required to personally certify their firm's financial statements. In the process of reviewing Disney's, it was discovered that Stanley Gold, by then an active and vocal critic of Eisner, had a daughter working for the firm's consumer products division, making $86,000 a year. Under Sarbanes-Oxley and New York Stock Exchange rules, the issue was murky. Yes, a family member was employed, but other board members also had ties to Disney and were to be considered independent. John Byron was to be classified as an independent director despite his wife being employed at Disney's Lifetime Network, earning $1.35 million annually. Even Mitchell was considered independent, despite his law firm having Disney as a client, and billing the company $2.5 million in fees since 2000.[119] When the issue was raised in the board, director Van de Kamp expressed exasperation. "You must be kidding. This makes no sense. Either Gold and Bryson should be considered independent, or neither should be."[120]

In an exchange chronicled in James Stewart's book *Disney War,* Eisner and Van de Kamp met in his office weeks later where he announced she would not be renominated. Eisner denounced her as a terrible director. "You are so loyal to Stanley [Gold] it's like you've carried his babies" Eisner said.

"What you're really upset about is that I don't always vote with you. That's the real issue," replied Van de Kamp.

Eisner said, "It's not that you haven't always voted with me," and proceeded to recount every instance where Van de Kamp had not voted consistent with Eisner in a board vote. She would later express amazement that the chief executive would remember each and every vote, many of which she herself had forgotten. After Eisner informed her that she would not be renominated as a director, Van de Kamp conveyed the encounter to the other directors, but received only limited support. Tom Murphy tried to talk Eisner out of it. Meeting with Van de Kamp privately, Director Mitchell said he "didn't know enough about the situation" to intervene.

In the board meeting approving the board's slate of directors, Director Gold argued for her reinstatement. Director Poitier argued for her continued service prior to the board vote. Van de Kamp recalled beginning a speech to the board with "I was asked to serve on this board to be an independent director, and now I'm not being renominated because that's exactly what I am—an independent director." Eisner prevailed, and Van de Kamp was not among the directors proposed for service by the firm.

Changes would continue. Ultimately, just over half of the directors on Disney's board in 1999 would still be serving in 2003. Disney announced sweeping changes to increase independence and reduce board size from 17 to 13, including 9 independents.[121] Van de Kamp, O'Donovan, Russell, Bowers, Stern, and Poitier were all gone. New additions to the board would include John Bryson, CEO and board chairperson of Edison International, and Robert Matschullat, a private equity investor who was vice chairperson of the board of The Seagram Company. Returning insiders Eisner and Roy Disney, and his advisor Stanley Gold, were joined by a new addition, Robert Iger, chief operating officer, who had served the company since the merger with Capital Cities/ABC.

More Unwelcome Guests at the Gate: 2004

A tumultuous 2004 began with the echoes of screams from Disney's board room. A month earlier, Roy Disney resigned his directorship with the company, followed the next day by Stanley Gold. An uprising, according to Gold's resignation letter, had been building against Eisner for years.[122] The nominating and governance committee, which allies of Eisner now controlled, had informed Roy Disney that he would not be renominated to Disney's board, having exceeded the mandatory retirement age of 72. Mandatory retirement ages are common among corporate boards. Gold and Roy Disney, however, argued that it was unclear whether Disney's rule also applied to directors employed within the firm as managers, such as Roy, who still headed the company's animation unit.[123]

Having left the board, Roy and Gold then went on the offensive in an unprecedented manner, creating the online site "savedisney.com" with an open letter urging shareholders to withhold votes for Disney's management. They then began a road show, urging institutional investors to do the same.

Eisner was likely more concerned about deteriorating relationships with Pixar. Disney had formed a five-film deal with Pixar in 1991, with Pixar responsible for creation and Disney co-financing and distributing the films. The two companies split profits. Beginning with *Toy Story* in 1995, the partnership created an extraordinary string of hits.

The heart of The Walt Disney Co. has always been its animated film business. But as the company crossed into the digital millennium, Disney's heart appeared to be on life support. Following the unparalleled success of *The Lion King* and *Aladdin,* Disney's animators struggled. In 2001, Disney's animation was breakeven: *Atlantis* was considered marginal at best, grossing just $84 million domestically while *Lilo & Stitch* was a success, costing just $80 million to produce, yet generating sales of $145 million domestically.[124] Disney reduced fourth quarter 2002 earnings by $47 million due in part to the unsuccessful film *Treasure Planet.*[125] The picture, costing upwards of $140 million to produce, grossed just $16.5 million in ticket sales over the five-day Thanksgiving holiday weekend. Other recent Disney animated films had also underperformed. Disney's hope for 2004, *Home on the Range*, would ultimately generate just $50 million domestically.[126]

While Disney's animators were struggling, Pixar's were flourishing. Pixar's earnings were up 30 percent due to higher than anticipated DVD sales of *Monsters, Inc.*[127] *Finding Nemo* opened its first weekend with ticket sales of $70.3 million, eventually generating $339 million in domestic ticket sales and more than $865 million worldwide. That exceeded Pixar's earlier successes, including *Toy Story 2* ($246 million), *Monsters, Inc.* ($226 million), *Toy Story* ($192 million), and *A Bug's Life* ($163 million).[128] Pixar was emerging as the new king of animation and a profit machine. Meanwhile, Katzenberg's Dream/Works was also becoming a potent rival. Its film *Shrek 2* would set a box office record for an animated film, exceeding *Finding Nemo's* domestic receipts on just its twenty-fifth day of release.

Negotiations to extend the relationship between Pixar and Disney were failing. Pixar, with its proven track record and no need for co-financing, could negotiate from a position of power and contract with any distributor. Disney, alternatively, controlled rights to make sequels to the films developed under the deal. One cause of the failure to reach an agreement: Reports surfaced of tensions between Eisner and Pixar's founder, Steve Jobs. Over the prior three years, Disney's share price had declined by about 50 percent.[129] In contrast to Eisner's earlier successes, Disney's recent stock performance was abysmal; its three-year appreciation lagged the Dow Jones average by nearly half.[130] In January 2004, Jobs announced that Pixar would not renew the distribution deal with Disney. Still, Disney and Eisner remained publicly optimistic that a deal could be struck.

Roy and Gold's "Save Disney" road show was indicating signs of success and the Pixar news added to the storm. Disney badly needed the Pixar deal. Just nine days after meeting with Roy and Gold, influential Institutional Shareholder Services (ISS) recommended shareholders "withhold" votes for Eisner. Their announcement noted, "It has often appeared that reconstituting the board was aimed more at quieting healthy boardroom dissent rather than creating it." The letter went on, "At the end of the day, all roads lead back to Eisner. For 20 years Disney's revolving door for board members and management has had one constant—Mr. Eisner. The boardroom battles and management departures, which predate the Disney/Gold campaign, are disappointing, expensive, distracting, and not in the best interest of shareholders. If there ever were a case for separating the roles of chairperson and CEO, this company is the poster child."[131]

Ironically, Roy and Gold's success in fighting Eisner also left the company vulnerable. On the same day of ISS's announcement, Comcast Corp., the largest cable television operator in the United States, announced an unsolicited bid of $54 billion bid to purchase Disney (see Appendix 1 for Comcast's letter to Disney).[132] The deal, Comcast argued, would benefit shareholders by combining Disney's content assets with Comcast's distribution pipelines—a strategy of vertical integration, comparable with News Corp.'s merger with DirecTV. If combined, the entity would be an industry juggernaut. Distribution assets would include 21 million cable subscribers, more than 5 million high-speed Internet subscribers, and the ABC television network, including 10 local television and 72 radio stations.[133] These assets would be in addition to Disney's content assets that included sports, such as ESPN and The Golf Channel, children's content such as the Disney channel, Disney's studio entertainment library, and Disney's parks and resorts.

Two days prior to the public announcement, Comcast's CEO Brian Roberts contacted Eisner with an informal takeover proposal. Eisner read a response prepared by Disney's board unequivocally declining the offer.[134] Director Mitchell said, "Every board member was informed that a phone call might be made. . . . Mr. Eisner responded in accordance with the wishes of the board."[135] The board had, some two years prior, reportedly put in place a procedure that required Eisner to reject anything but a formal offer. Comcast officials expressed shock that an offer would be rejected out of hand before any details were provided. "How do you as a board say no to something [when] you're not even sure [of its] value to shareholders?"[136] Comcast's Roberts then elected to pursue the unsolicited offer after attempts to enter merger talks with Disney were rejected.[137]

Ironically, Disney's annual meeting was scheduled in Philadelphia, the location of Comcast's corporate headquarters, just weeks after the offer was made. At the meeting, Gold and Roy Disney's desire to oust Eisner came true: 43 percent of shareholder votes were withheld from Eisner, 24 percent from Mitchell.[138] More punishing, 72 percent of Disney employees voting through their 401(k) retirement plan withheld votes for Eisner; 63 percent withheld for Mitchell.

The board rebuked Comcast's offer for the company, stating it was not in the best interest of Disney shareholders.

One commentator noted, "In corporate democracy, where competing candidates almost never get onto ballots for director, it is deemed embarrassing to have even 5 percent of the votes withheld. By that standard, Eisner suffered a great humiliation."[139] Another explained the situation in historical context: "Never before in Corporate America have shareholders expressed such an enormous, public loss of confidence in a chief executive."[140] Another focused more directly on the context of the situation: "Eisner has the misfortune to have been paid a lot of money to run a company that did not do very well for years, to have seen

Figure 4 Performance of Disney's Stock Under Eisner's Reign, September 1984–September 2005

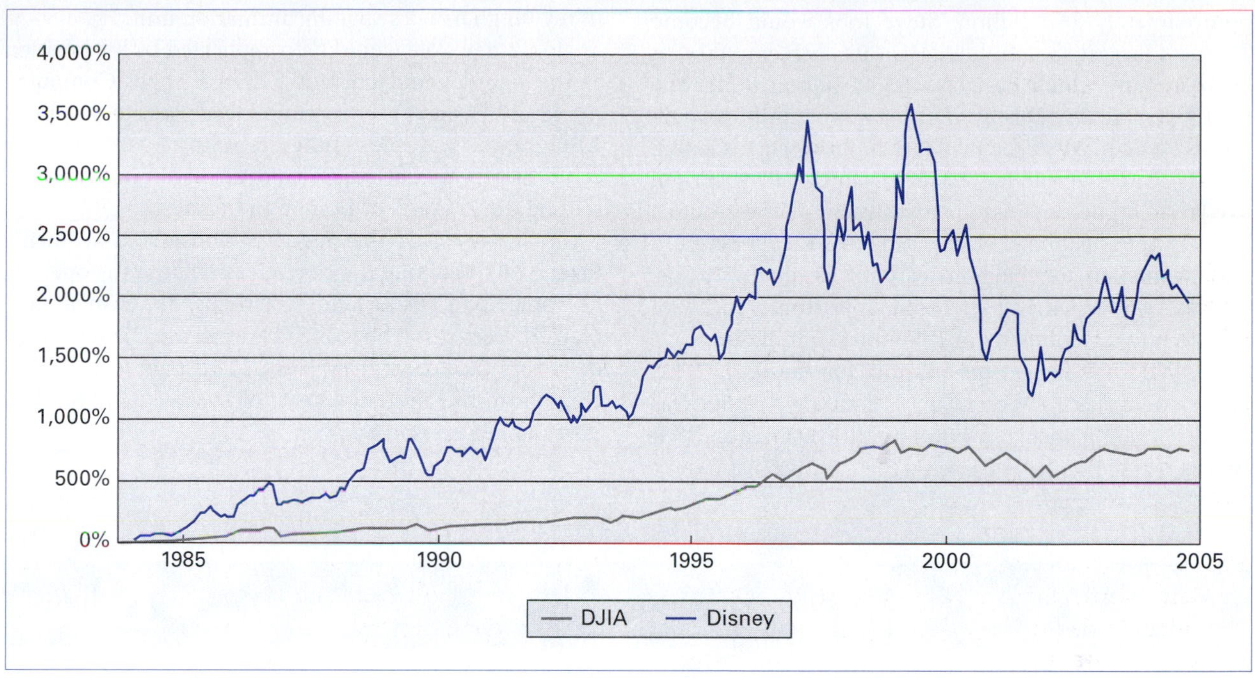

a number of top executives depart on less-than-amicable terms, and to have former board members including one whose name is Disney say the company would be better off with different management."

That evening, Disney's board issued a press release acknowledging the message from shareholders and voted to separate the positions of chairperson and CEO. Eisner would be CEO and Mitchell would be chairperson. Disney's board stated: "While making this change in governance, the board remains unanimously in support of the company's management team and of Michael Eisner, who will continue to serve as chief executive officer."[141]

Despite the vote, Eisner remained focused on running the company. "If you move toward outstanding performance in an appropriate moral and a creative way, you'll be successful," he says. "If you're not strong enough to close the door to extraneous noise, you will prove the extraneous noise to be correct. You will be paralyzed by competitors, disaffected employees, and the media."[142] However, Eisner would soon see the writing on the wall. In September, he announced his intent to resign from the company at the end of his contract in two years.

Disney president Robert Iger conceded that negotiations with Pixar had broken off. It was, he assessed, unlikely that a distribution deal between the two firms would be reached.[143] On March 14, 2005, what many had deemed impossible happened: A successor to Michael Eisner was announced. It would be Robert Iger.

Eisner's exit was much like his tenure: on his own terms. He officially stepped down as Disney's CEO on September 30, 2005, a full year earlier than his previously announced timetable. In another unexpected move, he also resigned from Disney's board one week later. Eisner's exit forced the board to extend the tenure of Chairman Mitchell to provide more time for a succession search.[144] Mitchell was slated to resign at Disney's next annual meeting, having just turned 72. Extending his tenure would require an exception to the mandatory retirement used to force Roy Disney from the board. Disney also announced the appointment of two new directors: John Pepper, former chairperson and CEO of Procter & Gamble, and Orin Smith, former president of Starbucks.

Epilogue: Enter Enfant Terrible, Pixar and Steve Jobs, 2006

In January 2006, reports surfaced in the *Wall Street Journal* that Disney was in negotiations to purchase Pixar.[145] Since taking office, Iger had reiterated that animation was at the core of the Disney brand. The acquisition of Pixar would ensure that Disney would be able to capitalize on characters such as Nemo and Buzz Lightyear and use them in their parks. Iger said the decision was about "getting a business that is vital to the future of Disney right."[146]

The success of Pixar would make the deal expensive, approximately $6.7 billion. Steve Jobs would become Disney's largest shareholder. His 50.6 percent stake in the company would be worth $3.44 billion under the deal.[147] Ironically, Disney had an opportunity to purchase Pixar in 1985 for just $15 million when George Lucas, Pixar's founder, restructured the firm. Frank Wells had argued against the investment on the grounds that Disney was not an R&D company. Katzenberg too was against it, focusing instead on producing films. Disney's waiver led, in part, to the opportunity for Steve Jobs to buy the company in 1986 for $10 million.

Roy Disney voiced his support for the deal, "This clearly solidifies the Walt Disney Company's position as the dominant leader in motion picture animation."[148] It was expected that John Lasseter, the creative inspiration behind *Toy Story* and *Cars* would take on a leading role in reviving Disney's sagging animation unit.

Jobs's new role would be complicated by his position as the founder and current CEO of Apple Computer. Apple and Disney recently announced plans to distribute ABC shows via Apple's iTunes. Jobs, as a board member, could face potential conflict of interest between representing the interests of Disney and Apple.

It was reported that Iger first considered acquiring Pixar while watching the character parade at the opening of Hong Kong Disneyland.[149] Perhaps, like Eisner more than 20 years prior, he realized that all the Disney songs, or in this case characters, were 20 years old or did not come from the animated heart of Disney at all, but had instead been created by Pixar.

Notes

1. A. Serwer, 2006, Extreme makeover: With big screens and high-def in more and more living rooms, movie theaters are taking radical new measures to woo filmgoers, *Fortune*, 153: 108–116.
2. Ibid.
3. L. Landro, 1984, Movie studios put more emphasis on home-video, pay-TV markets, *Wall Street Journal.*
4. Serwer, 2006.
5. Landro, 1984.
6. Ibid.
7. Ibid.
8. R. Olins, 1996, Disney draws on digital—Roy Disney, *The Sunday Times: London.*
9. Serwer, 2006.
10. Olins, 1996.
11. J. B. Stewart, 2005, *Disney War,* Simon & Schuster, New York.
12. A. Harmetz, 1985, The man re-animating Disney, *New York Times.*
13. Ibid.
14. R. Gibson & M. Cieply, 1984, Disney holder Jacobs weighs bid for control—His firm may make an offer or team up with others, according to SEC filing, *Wall Street Journal.*
15. Dow Jones News Service, 1984, Ronald Miller ousted as Walt Disney President, CEO.
16. S. J. Sansweet, 1984, Disney's chief is ousted; board studies 'short list' to determine his successor, *Wall Street Journal.*
17. Ibid.
18. Ibid.
19. M. Cieply, 1984a, Carter Hawley's Chairman is emerging as a force behind Disney's reshaping, *Wall Street Journal.*
20. Dow Jones News Service, 1984, Ronald Miller ousted as Walt Disney President, CEO.
21. Ibid.
22. Ibid.
23. R. Gibson & M. Cieply, 1984, Disney holder Jacobs weighs bid for control—His firm may make an offer or team up with others, according to SEC filing, *Wall Street Journal.*
24. Ibid.
25. Dow Jones News Service, 1984, Ronald Miller ousted as Walt Disney President, CEO.
26. A. Harmetz, 1984a, Board picks two new executives to head Disney, *Wall Street Journal.*
27. M. Cieply, 1984c, Disney yields to pressure from holders, names Eisner, Wells to head company, *Wall Street Journal.*
28. T. C. Hayes, 1984, New Disney team's strategy, *New York Times.*
29. A. Harmetz, 1984b, Disney names movie and TV head, *New York Times.*
30. A. Harmetz, 1985, The man re-animating Disney, *New York Times.*
31. Ibid.
32. Ibid.
33. Ibid.
34. M. Cieply, 1984b, Disney appoints co-founders son to manager role, *Wall Street Journal.*
35. T. C. Hayes, 1984, New Disney team's strategy, *New York Times.*
36. Ibid.
37. M. Cieply, 1985, Two Disney directors who helped lead takeover defense are stepping down, *Wall Street Journal.*
38. T. C. Hayes, 1984, New Disney team's strategy, *New York Times.*
39. M. Cieply, 1985, Two Disney directors who helped lead takeover defense are stepping down, *Wall Street Journal.*
40. Ibid.
41. Dow Jones News Service, 1987, Disney signs pact to sell Arvida assets to JMB Realty.
42. *Wall Street Journal*, 1987, Who's News - Walt Disney Co., *Wall Street Journal.*
43. Ibid.
44. *St. Louis Post-Dispatch*, 1990, Where salaries aren't Mickey Mouse, *St. Louis Post-Dispatch:* 5B.
45. J. A. Byrne, 1992, Executive pay—Compensation at the top is out of control. Here's how to reform it, *BusinessWeek,* 3258: 51.
46. PR Newswire, 1992, A. M. Robert, Stern nominated to Disney board of directors; Caroline Ahmanson, Donn Tatum to retire.
47. J. A. Byrne, 1992, Executive pay—Compensation at the top is out of control. Here's how to reform it, *BusinessWeek,* 3258: 51.
48. J. Daniels, 1993, Record Disney film profit stained by park's red ink, *Hollywood Reporter:* 1.
49. I. Siegel, 1993, 'Aladdin' becomes highest-grossing animated film, The Associated Press.
50. *New York Times* 1994. Frank Wells, Disney's president, Is killed in a copter crash at 62, *New York Times*: 8.
51. T. R. King, 1994, Disney taps CEO Eisner as president after death of Wells in helicopter crash, *Wall Street Journal*: B8.

52. B. Weinraub, 1994, Chairman of Disney Studios Resigns, *New York Times*: 1.
53. R. Grover & S. Toy, 1994, Life without Frank at Disney—Eisner will take on the president's duties, but it's a stopgap at best, *BusinessWeek*, 3367: 48.
54. Ibid.
55. S. Hofmeister, 1994, Disney's Chief on his feet 2 days after heart surgery, *New York Times*: 16.
56. J. Huey, 1995, Eisner explains everything, *Fortune*, 131: 44.
57. B. Weinraub, 1994, Chairman of Disney Studios Resigns, *New York Times*: 1.
58. Ibid.
59. Ibid.
60. J. Huey, 1995, Eisner explains everything, *Fortune*, 131: 44.
61. L. Adler, 1994, Roy Disney confident on animation outlook, Reuters News.
62. Ibid.
63. B. Weinraub, 1995, Clouds over Disneyland, *New York Times*: 1.
64. J. H. Dobrzynski, 1994, An inside look at CalPERS' boardroom report card: The huge investor rates the boards of the 200 biggest companies in its portfolio, *BusinessWeek*, 3394: 196.
65. J. Huey, 1995, Eisner explains everything, *Fortune*, 131: 44.
66. *Daily News Record*, 1995b, Walt Disney, Capital Cities/ABC reach an agreement to merge deal valued at about $19 billion, *Daily News Record*: 2.
67. Ibid.
68. *Daily News Record*, 1995a, Name Ovitz Disney president, *Daily News Record*.
69. *The Times*, 1995, A meeting of massive egos in Disneyland—Analysis, *The Times*.
70. Ibid.
71. Ibid.
72. Ibid.
73. Ibid.
74. Ibid.
75. J. Huey, 1995, Eisner explains everything, *Fortune*, 131: 44.
76. Ibid.
77. P. Brickley, 2005, Expert says Disney shareholders can't prove Ovitz was deceitful, Associate Press Newswire.
78. Court of Chancery of Delaware, 2005, *In re The Walt Disney Company* derivative litigation, 1–174: New Castle, Delaware.
79. Ibid.
80. Ibid.
81. *The Times*, 1995, A meeting of massive egos in Disneyland—Analysis, *The Times*.
82. Court of Chancery of Delaware, 2005, *In re The Walt Disney Company* derivative litigation, 1–174: New Castle, Delaware.
83. T. R. King & E. Jensen, 1996, Disney brings personal touch to ABC's sagging lineup—Eisner and Ovitz roll up shirtsleeves to improve ratings as soon as possible, *Wall Street Journal*.
84. R. Olins, 1996, Disney draws on digital—Roy Disney, *The Sunday Times: London*.
85. Court of Chancery of Delaware, 2005, *In re The Walt Disney Company* derivative litigation, 1–174: New Castle, Delaware.
86. *Financial Times*, 1996, Disney's new board member may be a blessing, *Financial Times*: 9.
87. Court of Chancery of Delaware, 2005, *In re The Walt Disney Company* derivative litigation, 1–174: New Castle, Delaware.
88. J. A. Byrne & R. A. Melcher, 1996, The best & worst boards: Our new report card on corporate governance, *BusinessWeek*, 3503: 82.
89. Court of Chancery of Delaware, 2005, *In re The Walt Disney Company* derivative litigation: 1–174, New Castle, Delaware.
90. *BusinessWeek*, 1996, A tough world needs tough boards, *BusinessWeek*, 3503: 190.
91. B. Orwall, 1996, Disney says Michael Ovitz is resigning as president—Decision is called mutual; Move rekindles issues of a successor to Eisner, *Wall Street Journal*: A3.
92. Court of Chancery of Delaware, 2005, *In re The Walt Disney Company* derivative litigation: 1–174, New Castle, Delaware.
93. B. Orwall, 1996, Disney says Michael Ovitz is resigning as president—Decision is called mutual; Move rekindles issues of a successor to Eisner, *Wall Street Journal*: A3.
94. N. Lipschutz, 2004, Unquestioned CEO support not director role, Dow Jones News Service.
95. *Hollywood Reporter*, 2004, Witness: Disney 'wise' to fire Ovitz, *Hollywood Reporter*.
96. R. Grover & E. Schine, 1997, At Disney, grumpy isn't just a dwarf: It's the mood of shareholders as the annual meeting nears, *BusinessWeek*, 3515: 39.
97. D. McNary, 1997a, The cost of keeping Eisner: Disney CEO gets 10-year extension, $195 million in stock, *Los Angeles Daily News*: N1.
98. *Los Angeles Daily News*, 1997, Protest Disney Ovitz package, Adviser says, *Los Angeles Daily News*: B.
99. J. Hirsch, 1997, Big pension fund joins Disney-board foes, *The Orange County Register*: C01.
100. *The Tampa Tribune*, 1997, Mouse may hear catcalls this week.
101. J. Hirsch, 1997, Big pension fund joins Disney-board foes.
102. D. McNary, 1997b, Eisner apologizes for payout to Ovitz, *Los Angeles Daily News*: B1.
103. J. A. Byrne, R. Grover & R.A. Melcher, 1997, The best and worst boards: Our special report on corporate governance, *BusinessWeek*, 3556: 90.
104. B. Orwall & J. S. Lublin, 1998, Investors take aim at Disney board again, *The Wall Street Journal*: C1.
105. J.A. Byrne, R. Grover & R. A. Melcher, 1997, The best and worst boards: Our special report on corporate governance, *BusinessWeek*, 3556: 90.
106. G. Colvin, 2005, CEO knockdown: Fear and loathing are rife among corporate board members—and that's why so many CEOs are losing their jobs, *Fortune*.
107. B. Orwall & J. S. Lublin, 1998, Investors take aim at Disney board again, *Wall Street Journal*: C1.
108. J. Reingold, R. A. Melcher & G. McWilliams, 1998, Stock options plus a bull market made a mockery of many attempts to link pay to performance, *BusinessWeek*, 3574: 2
109. B. Orwall & J. S. Lublin, 1998, Investors take aim at Disney board again, *Wall Street Journal*: C1.
110. Ibid.
111. C. Parkes, 1998, Disney shake-up urged by institutions, *Financial Times*: 17.
112. D. McNary, 1998, Status quo; Disney shareholders fail to force reorganization, *Los Angeles Daily News*: B1.
113. Ibid.
114. J. A. Byrne, 2000, The best & the worst boards from GE at the top to Disney at the bottom, *BusinessWeek* rates the panels that run Corporate America, *BusinessWeek*, 3665: 142.
115. *BusinessWeek*, 2002, Disney gets the message, *BusinessWeek*: 132; L. Lavelle 2002a. The best & worst boards: How the corporate scandals are sparking a revolution in governance, *BusinessWeek*, 3802: 104.
116. M. Roman, 2002, Disney redraws the board, *BusinessWeek*.
117. L. Lavelle, 2002b. Disney: More insiders at the castle, *BusinessWeek*, 3814: 14.
118. Ibid.
119. L. Lavelle, D. Foust, W. C. Symonds & R. Grover, 2003, Just how independent are these 'lead directors'? *BusinessWeek*, 3832: 56.
120. J. B. Stewart, 2005, *Disney War*, Simon & Schuster, New York.
121. G. Gentile, 2003, Disney cuts board by four members, strengthens independence, Associate Press Newswires.
122. R. Grover, 2003, Stalking a wily prey at Disney; By shooting for CEO Michael Eisner, Disney ex-board members Stan Gold and Roy Disney are taking on a crafty player who has lots of allies, *BusinessWeek Online*.
123. Ibid.
124. B. Orwall, 2002, Disney studios deliver a turkey for the holiday, *Wall Street Journal*.
125. M. Roman, 2002, Disney redraws the board, *BusinessWeek*.
126. D. Dunaief, 2004, Disney, Nemo not connecting; Pixar deal on the rocks, *New York Daily News*.

127. P-W. Tam, 2003, Pixar posts 30% rise in profit; Disney turning point looms, *Wall Street Journal*: B3.
128. D. Dunaief, 2004, Disney, Nemo not connecting; Pixar deal on the rocks, *New York Daily News.*
129. D. Teather, 2004, Campaign to oust Eisner intensifies: Roy Disney accuses company of squandering $25b, *The Guardian* (New York): 26.
130. Ibid.
131. J. B. Stewart, 2005, *Disney War,* Simon & Schuster, New York.
132. B. L. Roberts, 2004, Comcast's letter to Disney proposing merger, *USA Today,* February 11.
133. S. McCarthy, 2004, Comcast makes hostile $54 billion bid for Disney; Merger of cable, entertainment giants would create powerhouse, Comcast CEO says, *The Globe and Mail*: B1.
134. R. Grover, 2004, Did the mouse speak too soon? After hearing that Comcast wanted to make a bid, Disney's board scrambled to formulate a rejection—before it knew the details, *Business Week Online.*
135. Ibid.
136. Ibid.
137. *Patriot-News,* 2004, Comcast seeking takeover of Disney: Merger would reshape entertainment landscape, *Patriot-News*: A.
138. P. R. La Monica, 2004, Eisner out as Disney chair. CNN: CNN/Money.
139. F. Norris, 2004, Corporate democracy undergoes revolution, vote against Eisner signals major shift, *International Herald Tribune.*
140. R. Grover & T. Lowry, 2004, Now it's time to say goodbye; How Disney's board can move beyond the Eisner era, *BusinessWeek,* 3874: 30.
141. J. B. Stewart, 2005, *Disney War,* Simon & Schuster, New York.
142. T. Burt, 2004, It's showtime for Disney chief: Michael Eisner's 20-year management career may be judged by the court as well as the markets, *National Post*: FP3.
143. N. Yulico, 2004, Pixar-Disney not getting back together, *The Oakland Tribune.*
144. M. Marr, 2005, Disney extends Mitchell's term, *Wall Street Journal.*
145. M. Marr & N. Wingfield, 2006b, Walt Disney is in serious talks to acquire Pixar, *Wall Street Journal*: A1.
146. M. Marr & N. Wingfield, 2006a, Disney sets $7.4 Billion Pixar deal; Jobs to take seat on board and play integral role in setting creative course, *Wall Street Journal*: A3.
147. M. Marr & N. Wingfield, 2006b, Walt Disney is in serious talks to acquire Pixar.
148. M. Marr & N. Wingfield, 2006a, Disney sets $7.4 Billion Pixar deal.
149. Adapted from Grover, R. & E. Schine, 1997, At Disney, grumpy isn't just a dwarf: It's the mood of shareholders as the annual meeting nears, in *BusinessWeek*: 39.

Appendix 1 Comcast's Unsolicited Offer for Disney

Mr. Michael D. Eisner
The Walt Disney Company
500 South Buena Vista Street
Burbank, California 91521

Dear Michael:

I am writing following our conversation earlier this week in which I proposed that we enter into discussions to merge Disney and Comcast to create a premier entertainment and communications company. It is unfortunate that you are not willing to do so. Given this, the only way for us to proceed is to make a public proposal directly to you and your Board.

We have a wonderful opportunity to create a company that combines distribution and content in a way that is far stronger and more valuable than either Disney or Comcast can be standing alone. To this end, we are proposing a tax-free stock for stock merger in which Comcast would issue 0.78 of a share of its Class A voting common stock for each share of Disney. This represents a premium of over $5 billion for your shareholders, based on yesterday's closing prices. Under our proposal, your shareholders would own approximately 42% of the combined company.

The combined company would be uniquely positioned to take advantage of an extraordinary collection of assets. Together, we would unite the country's premier cable provider with Disney's leading filmed entertainment, media networks and theme park properties. In addition to serving over 21 million cable subscribers, Comcast is also the country's largest high speed internet service provider with over 5 million subscribers. As you have expressed on several occasions, one of Disney's top priorities involves the aggressive pursuit of technological innovation that enhances how Disney's content is created and delivered. We believe this combination helps accelerate the realization of that goal—whether through existing distribution channels and technologies such as video-on-demand and broadband video streaming or through emerging technologies still in development—to the benefit of all our shareholders, customers and employees.

We believe that improvements in operating performance, business creation opportunities and other combined benefits will generate enormous value for the shareholders of both companies. Together, as an integrated distribution and content company, we will be best positioned to meet our respective competitive challenges.

We have a stable and respected management team with a great track record for creating shareholder value. In fact, our shares have consistently outperformed leading stock indices by significant margins, including the S&P 500 by a margin of more than 2 to 1 since Comcast went public in 1972.

The Comcast management team greatly appreciates and is highly respectful of the Disney heritage. We know that there are many talented executives at Disney who we envision would also play a key role in managing the combined company. We also would welcome directors from your Board joining our Board.

We have analyzed the issues associated with regulatory approval and are confident that all necessary approvals can be obtained in a timely fashion. Given the landscape that has evolved in our industry over the past few years, the creation of integrated content and distribution companies is essential to increasing the level of competition. The FCC's existing program access and program carriage rules ensure that the combined company will continue to make all of its satellite-delivered national and regional cable networks available on a non-exclusive, non-discriminatory basis and that there will be no discrimination against unaffiliated programming services, all consistent with the undertakings made by News Corp. in its recent acquisition of DirecTV.

We hope that the Disney Board will pursue the opportunity that this proposed combination presents to your shareholders.

Very truly yours,
Brian L. Roberts
President and Chief
Executive Officer
Cc: Board of Directors,
The Walt Disney Company.

Case 10

Ford Motor Company

Jeff Andress, Dennis Horton, Cody Kleven,
Mike McCullar, Hollon Stevens, Robin Chapman

Arizona State University

Introduction

William Clay Ford, Jr., was staring out the window of his office in Dearborn, Michigan, lost in thought. The future of Ford Motor Company was hanging in the balance, and no one was certain how best to save this once-great company. Question after question without any easy answers kept going through his mind. . . . How much longer can Ford survive with the large losses? Will it have to sell off assets or financially restructure? Can it cut enough costs, and where should it cut? Will the union leaders realize the situation, and how much will they be willing to help? When will Chinese competitors enter the U.S. market? How can Ford develop its product offerings to adjust for higher fuel costs? How can Ford improve its product offering to reverse or at least stop the market share losses? How much more market share will it lose?

The magnitude of the situation seemed overwhelming. In order to overcome these challenges, it seemed as if Ford would have to restructure every aspect of its business. It would require improved product offerings with cutting-edge design and high quality; improved operation with more flexibility and lower costs; and improved marketing with better brand image and customer interest. Ford was at a crossroads, and the way ahead remained shrouded in fog.

History

Ford has gone through many evolutions since its humble beginnings on June 16, 1903.[1] Henry Ford began this corporation, now synonymous with the assembly line, the Industrial Revolution, and the American Dream, with 11 business associates and $28,000 in capital.[2] Ford Motor Company continued along with minimal leadership problems until the death of its president, Edsel Ford, in 1943. Intense dissension about who should succeed Edsel Ford continued until Henry Ford, at the age of 79, returned from retirement to lead the company. For the next two years under Henry Ford the company operated with massive losses of $10 million dollars per month.[3] Finally, in 1945, Henry Ford was forced to step down and Henry Ford II assumed the role of president.[4] Henry Ford II managed to successfully maneuver the company back to productivity and empowered Robert McNamara and his group (planning and financial analysis) to transform Ford's leadership style from a tyrannical dictatorship to a "powerful, professional oligarchy."[5] Over the next 20 years, Ford Motor Company's presidents and CEOs turned over 13 times.[6] The current CEO, Alan Mulally, was appointed in September 2006 to take over for William Clay Ford, Jr., who had served as both president and CEO since 2001. William Clay Ford, Jr., led Ford Motor Company to three straight years of profitability followed by a sharp decrease in profits marked by a $1.44 billion loss in the first half of 2006.[7] These losses motivated Ford Motor Company to search for a new CEO from outside the industry, Alan Mulally, formerly of Boeing Corporation. Mulally stood out as a qualified successor because he demonstrated the leadership skills Ford had established many years ago as critical to success.

Strategic Leadership

Ford Motor Company, recognizing the importance of human capital development in strengthening the company as a whole, developed a leadership training program in the late 1990s comprised of four separate courses, Capstone, Experienced Leader Challenge, Ford Business Associates, and New Business Leader. These programs were designed to instill the mind-set and vocabulary of

This case was developed with contributions from Melodie Bolin.

a revolutionary leader as well as to teach the tools necessary to steer a leadership and manufacturing revolution.[8] Ford also planned to use its Business Leaders Initiative to get all 100,000 salaried employees worldwide involved in "business-leadership 'cascades,' intense exercises that combine trickle-down communications with substantive team projects."[9] In 2000, Ford planned to guide 2,500 managers through one of its four leadership courses.[10] Yet in 2006, Ford Motor Company's leadership structure remained complex, highly bureaucratic, and comprised of a six-layered management scheme on which pay is based. The former COO for the Americas affirmed, "The company has too many layers, the company is too bureaucratic, and it takes too long to get things done."[11] (See Exhibit 1 for Ford senior leadership structure.) Ford geared up for many changes under the leadership of Alan Mulally, including the replacement of many members of the top leadership team.[12]

Alan Mulally

Alan Mulally was named CEO and president of Ford Motor Company in September 2006. He is also a member

Exhibit 1 Ford's Top Management Structure

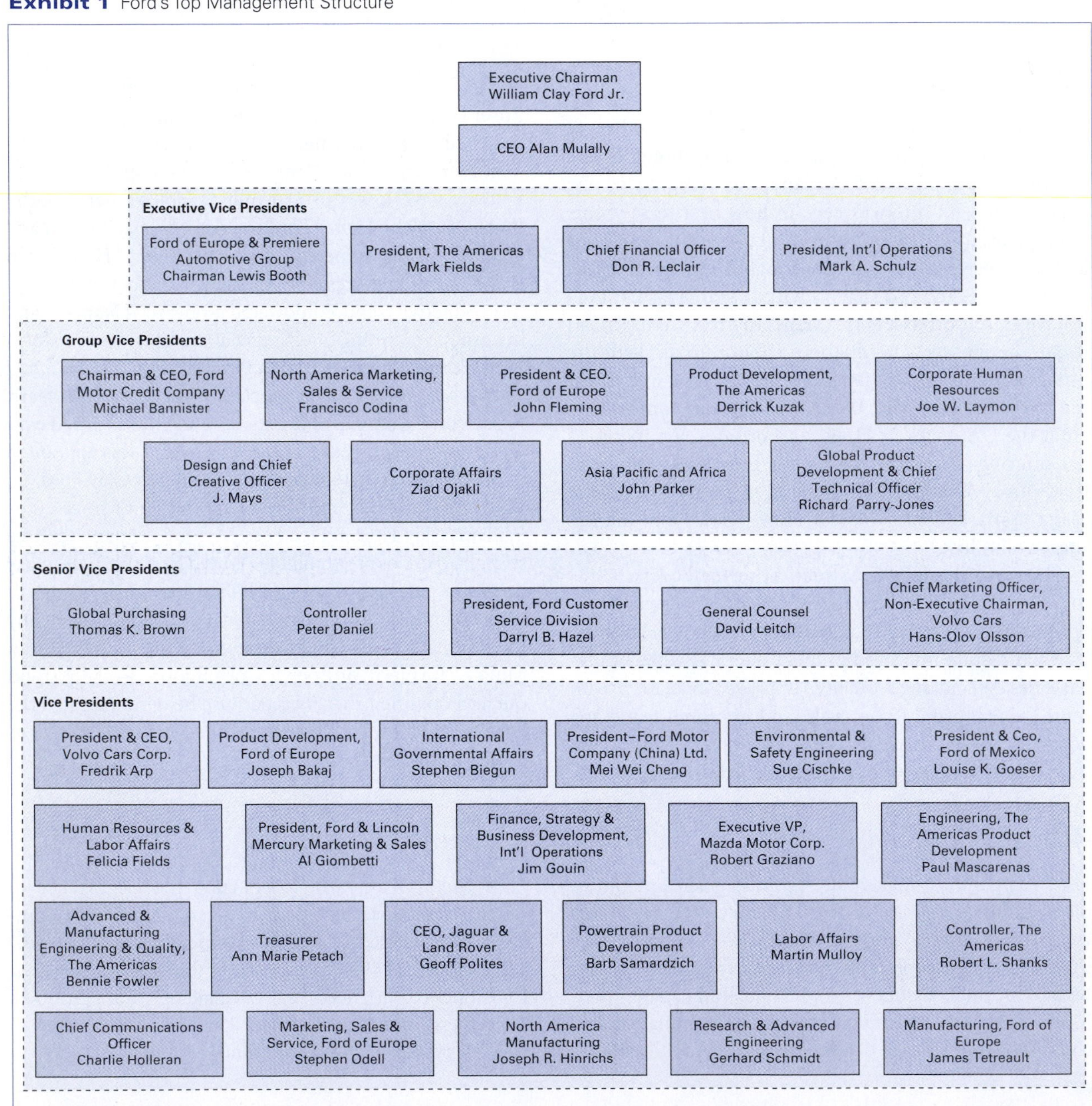

Source: 2006, Ford Company Media, http://media.ford.com.

of the board of directors. Prior to joining Ford, Mulally was an executive vice president at Boeing as well as the president and CEO of Boeing Commercial Airlines. Mulally has received many accolades throughout his career and has been recognized for his contributions and industry leadership by being named one of the "Best Leaders of 2005" by *BusinessWeek* magazine. Mulally is perhaps best known for his efforts to streamline Boeing's production system and the associated transformation of the company's commercial airplanes product line.[13] Despite his many successes in the airline industry, chiefly his turnaround of Boeing's commercial airline division, it remains to be seen whether these turnaround experiences will be applicable to the turnaround Ford is seeking.

William Clay Ford, Jr.

The current executive chairperson of Ford Motor Company is William Clay Ford, Jr. William Ford has been a member of the board since 1988, and was elected to the office of chairperson on January 1, 1999. He is also the chair of the board's Finance Committee and a member of the Environmental and Public Policy Committee. William Ford also served as chief executive officer from October 2001 to September 2006. As CEO, William Ford led the company to three straight years of profitability, after experiencing a $5.5 billion loss in 2001, by focusing on improving quality, lowering costs, and delivering new products that satisfy customers."[14] On his step back from CEO to executive chairperson, William Ford said in an interview with journalist Keith Naughton of *Newsweek*, "I've always said that titles are not important to me. This company has been part of my life since the day I was born and will be until the day I die. What's important is getting this company headed in the right direction."[15] According to Ford's Web site, William Ford continues to focus on the future of Ford Motor Company and the strategies that will move it successfully into the future. He is quoted as saying, "Innovation is the compass by which Ford Motor Company sets its direction. We want to have an even bigger impact in our next 100 years than we did in our first 100."[16]

Board of Directors

Ford Motor Company's board of directors is comprised of 13 extremely diverse members who have many different corporate and personnel backgrounds, ranging from professor of physics to publishing, banking, and auditing. Three of the directors are members of the Ford family, and six have served on the board of directors for more than 10 years (see Exhibit 2). Despite the myriad of backgrounds presented in Ford's board of directors, past decisions have shown that the Ford family retains

Exhibit 2 Ford's Board of Directors

Director	Position	Member Since
William Clay Ford Jr.	Executive Chairman, Ford Motor Company	1988
John R. H. Bond	Group Chairman, HSBC Holdings plc	2000
Stephen G. Butler	Retired Chairman and CEO, KPMG, LLP	N.A.
Kimberly Casiano	President and COO, Casiano Communications, Inc.	2003
Edsel B. Ford II	Retired Vice President, Ford Motor Company Former President and COO, Ford Credit	1988
William Clay Ford	Director Emeritus	2000
Irvine O. Hockaday, Jr.	Retired President and CEO, Hallmark Cards Inc.	1987
Richard A. Manoogian	Chairman and CEO, Masco Corporation	2001
Ellen R. Marram	Managing Director, North Castle Partners, LLC	1988
Alan Mulally	President and CEO, Ford Motor Company	2006
Homer A. Neal	Director, University of Michigan ATLAS Project, Samuel A. Goudsmit Distinguished University Professor of Physics, and Interim President Emeritus, University of Michigan	1997
Jorma Ollila	Chairman, CEO, and Chairman of the Group Executive Board, Nokia Corporation	2000
John L. Thornton	Professor and Director, Global Leadership Program, Tsinghua University, Beijing, China	1996

Source: 2006, Ford Company Media, http://media.ford.com.

most of the decision-making power and influence. It was only after Ford Motor Company began to lose billions of dollars that William Clay Ford, Jr., stepped down as CEO. Even with his resignation as CEO, it is clear that William Ford still wields most of the power at Ford, as evidenced by his renaming the board chair position, "Executive Chairman." William Ford was honored as the 2006 Automotive Industry Executive of the Year, a great honor considering the trends taking place within the automotive industry.[17]

Trends in the U.S. Auto Market

Although the U.S. auto market is large, it is not a high-growth market. The average growth rate has been less than 1 percent over the past seven years. However, competitors have experienced market share shifts. Despite the fact that GM still has the dominant market share, both GM and Ford have been losing market share to foreign competition. (See Exhibit 3 and 4 for trends related to U.S. light vehicle market share from domestic, Japanese, Korean, and European producers.) In 1995, the Big Three American auto producers held 73 percent of the U.S. market share, but by third quarter 2007, that number had dropped below 50 percent.[18] Similarly, foreign firms have steadily increased production in the United States. In 1986, U.S. firms produced about 95 percent of the cars made in the United States, but by 2005, that number had fallen to 47.7 percent.[19] The trend of increased foreign production in the United States should continue as Ford and GM continue to trim production in the United States.

Consolidation

A consolidation of auto manufacturing firms has affected both the global and domestic markets. Chrysler merged with German manufacturer Daimler-Benz in 1998 to form DaimlerChrysler, but Daimler sold Chrysler shares in 2007. Over the past several years, Ford purchased or formed agreements with Mazda, Volvo, Jaguar, and Land Rover. In 2006 GM began discussions about possible alliances with Renault and Nissan, but skeptics were relieved when these talks broke off. However, the competitive structure of the global automotive industry makes further mergers and alliances that involve firms competing in the U.S. market likely.

Market Segmentation

Another trend has been further market segmentation. With the increased number of foreign competitors and little differentiation between manufacturers, firms competing in the U.S. market have continued to target smaller customer segments, increasing the number of models each maker produces in an effort to attract each smaller customer group. Analysts predict that the number of available car models in the U.S. market will increase from 250 in 1999 to 330 by 2008. Similarly, the average annual sales of each model decreased from 106,819 to 48,626 in the years between 1985 and 2005.[20]

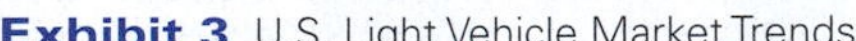

Exhibit 3 U.S. Light Vehicle Market Trends

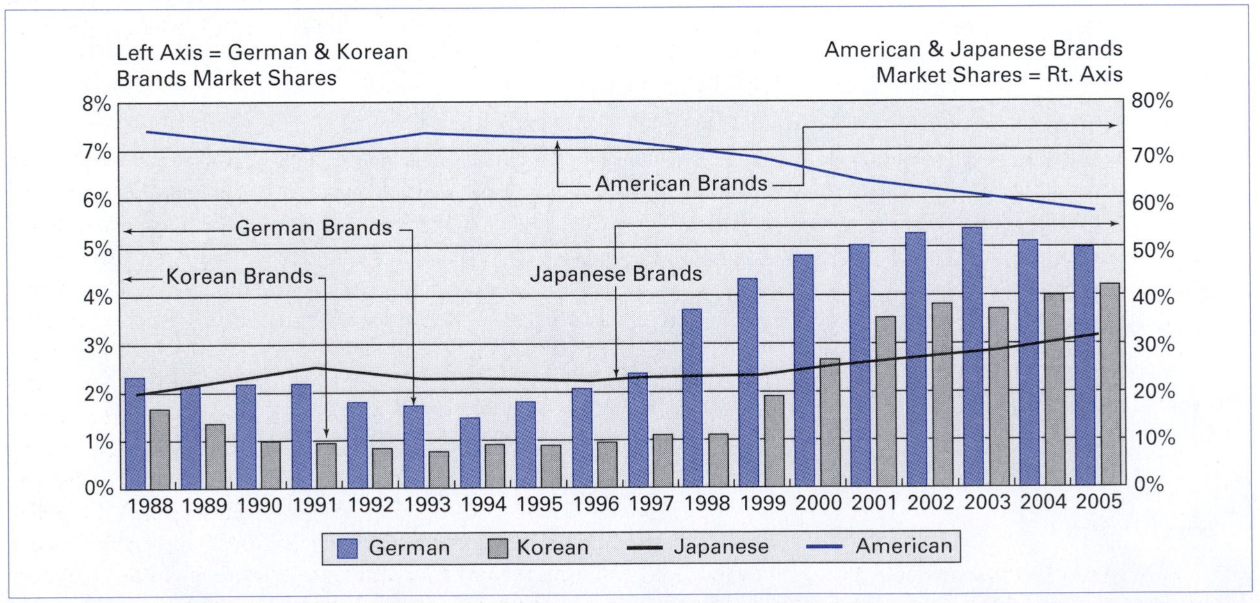

Sources: Ward's AutoInfoBank; 2006, The road ahead for the U.S. auto industry, Office of Aerospace and Automotive Industries International Trade Administration U.S. Department of Commerce, April.

Exhibit 4 North American Automotive Market Share (GM, Ford, Toyota)

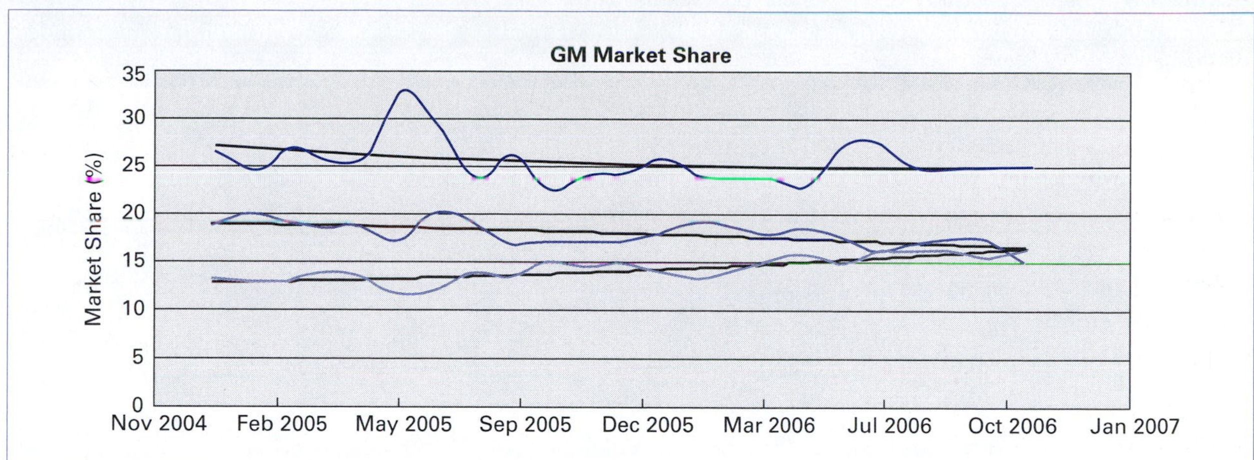

Note: Black line represents the trend of the individual automakers North American market share.

Source: 2006, North American Automotive Market Data, http://www.wardsauto.com, December 2.

Alternative Fuels

Another change is the significant trend in building cars that use alternative fuels and have higher fuel efficiency. Although hybrid cars that combine small engines with electric power currently are gaining the most attention, other alternatives such as bio diesel, electric, or hydrogen fuel cells have also been developed. Given the increasing global demand for fuel, and the recent increase in gas prices in the United States, the drive toward alternative fuels and greater efficiency should continue.

One cost-effective alternative currently being used by automakers is E85, a corn based fuel,which is a blend of 85 percent ethanol (a form of alcohol) and 15 percent gasoline. E85 provides about 25 percent less energy than traditional gasoline, but advocates argue that it will reduce U.S. dependence on foreign producers and develop a domestic industry that supports farmers.[21]

As noted previously, electric hybrid vehicles have already been commercialized and represent a significant technological change, but if hydrogen fuel cell technology can be commercialized, it would represent an even more radical technological shift. These technological innovations represent an opportunity for the auto manufacturers to differentiate themselves from the competition. Just as important as considering the current trends in the market place, automotive firms must examine the competitive environment.

U.S. Auto Industry Competitive Environment

The United States comprises the largest auto market in the world with more than 16 million vehicles sold in each of the last seven years.[22] Given its size, automakers from around the world have targeted the U.S. market for exports. Although at least 22 firms compete in the U.S. market, the four largest firms (GM, Ford, Toyota, and DaimlerChrysler) control more than 68 percent of the market and the top six firms (including Honda and Nissan) control 83.5 percent of the market.[23] See Exhibit 5 for a breakdown of light vehicle U.S. market share. General Motors (GM) and Ford are the only two domestic firms that still have a significant presence. Chrysler had been the third largest U.S. auto manufacturing firm before it merged with Daimler-Benz AG in 1998 to form DaimlerChrysler. Many of the foreign firms who compete in the U.S. market also produce vehicles in the United States. In 2006, 11 firms produced cars and light trucks in the United States (BMW, DaimlerChrysler, Ford, GM, Honda, Hyundai, Mazda, Mitsubishi, Nissan, Subaru, and Toyota).[24]

DaimlerChrysler

As mentioned, DaimlerChrysler was formed in 1998 as the result of a merger between Daimler-Benz and Chrysler. At year-end 2006 it employed approximately 360,000 people and sold almost 4.7 million vehicles (both passenger and commercial) to consumers in 200 different countries.[25] Similar to the financial struggles experienced in recent years by Ford and GM, DaimlerChrysler announced a $1.2 billion loss in 2006, a 9 percent decrease in sales, and a 0.5 percent decrease in market share to 13.5 percent.[26] The merger did not prove to be beneficial for Daimler and the majority interest of Chrysler was recently divested to a private equity group, Cerberus Capital Management (August 2007). DaimlerChrysler (to be renamed Daimler AG) continues to hold 19 percent ownership and will strive to help Chrysler succeed as a stand-alone car company.[27]

Exhibit 5 November 2006 and Year-to-Date U.S. Light Vehicle Market Share

	November 2006			YTD		
Maker	Volume	% Change	Market Share	Volume	% Change	Market Share
GM	291,061	6.0	24.3	3,698,026	(8.3)	24.5
Ford	166,397	(10.6)	13.9	2,504,151	(7.5)	16.6
Toyota	196,695	15.9	16.4	2,314,202	12.5	15.3
Chrysler	164,556	2.9	13.7	1,952,090	(7.7)	12.9
Honda	106,446	0.6	8.9	1,377,580	3.6	9.1
Nissan	76,015	(1.6)	6.3	927,474	(5.9)	6.1
Hyundai	28,417	(14.9)	2.4	418,155	1.5	2.8
BMW	25,889	(3.6)	2.2	280,186	0.7	1.9
Kia	22,203	10.5	1.9	264,298	2.8	1.7
Mazda	20,729	16.7	1.7	248,874	4.1	1.6
Mercedes	22,079	20.8	1.8	219,678	13.9	1.5
Subaru	15,800	8.8	1.3	180,090	2.3	1.2
Mitsubishi	9,256	4.0	0.8	108,648	(5.0)	0.7
Volvo	9,229	14.3	0.8	107,282	(6.3)	0.7
Suzuki	6,395	12.1	0.5	93,673	27.5	0.6
Audi	9,209	16.4	0.8	78,219	5.4	0.5
Land Rover	4,229	(7.6)	0.4	41,760	6.4	0.3
Saab	2,497	19.4	0.2	32,814	(7.8)	0.2
Porsche	2,611	(2.4)	0.2	31,377	7.9	0.2
Jaguar	1,256	(35.2)	0.1	19,130	(31.6)	0.1
Isuzu	565	(23.4)	0.0	7,977	(29.6)	0.1

Source: 2006, U.S. Light Vehicle Sales, Market Share for November.

The major brands comprising DaimlerChrysler include Mercedes-Benz, Dodge, Chrysler, Jeep, and Smart (initially only available in Europe but slated for U.S. debut). Within these brands are a wide variety of vehicle types: trucks, SUVs, sedans, compacts, and sports cars.

Like other major automobile manufacturers, DaimlerChrysler focuses on finding alternative sources of power to gasoline. The 2006 DaimlerChrysler lineup of vehicles included five E85 capable vehicles: the Dodge Durango (SUV), Dodge Ram 1500 Series (truck), Dodge Stratus (sedan), Chrysler Sebring (sedan), and Dodge Caravan. In 2007, three additional vehicles were added to the lineup. As for hybrid technology, DaimlerChrysler is far behind U.S. and Japanese competitors, but instead has focused on clean diesel power using its BLUETEC technology that reduces nitrogen oxide levels.[28]

R&D efforts are focused on fuel cell infrastructure and vehicle development and GTL (gas to liquids) diesel. Similar to Ford and GM, DaimlerChrysler is piloting fuel cell powered vehicles; it has 60 vehicles deployed worldwide.[29] Its GTL initiatives are meant to enable DaimlerChrysler's diesel product line to produce higher-quality diesel than that made from crude.[30]

General Motors

General Motors, the world's largest automaker, was founded in 1908 and currently employs approximately 284,000 people and manufactures its cars and trucks in 33 countries.[31] While Ford suffered a 7.5 percent market share loss in the last 6 years, from 22.8 percent in 2000 to about 15.3 percent in second quarter 2007,[32] GM experienced a somewhat less significant 6 percent loss, from 28.1 percent to 22.1 percent.[33] Like Ford, GM has been working to increase profitability by decreasing costs and maintaining market share.

On November 21, 2005, GM announced plant closings and the loss of jobs that resulted in an annual reduction of expenses totaling $7 billion, and a 30 percent loss in capacity. The already depleted workforce, which has been reduced by 40 percent since 2000,[34] will continue to decline by 30,000 employees by the end of 2008.

In terms of maintaining market share in future years, General Motors has focused its R&D efforts on gasoline-alternative sources of power. It currently offers 16 E85 capable vehicles which include sedans, trucks, SUVs, and vans. In September 2006 GM announced "Project Driveway," which highlighted the Chevy Equinox Fuel Cell. The hydrogen-powered Equinox is slated to be delivered to 100 customers in the fall of 2007, in three different geographic areas: California, New York City, and Washington, D.C. Drivers will be asked to report on all aspects of their driving experience. According to GM, these customers will provide the first "meaningful market test."[35]

Another aspect of GM's effort to reduce vehicle emissions and improve fuel efficiency is the research and development of hybrid vehicles. The focus has been placed on high-volume, high fuel-consuming vehicles first, but eventually GM plans to develop 12 different hybrid models The current hybrid offerings include the 2006 Chevy Silverado Classic, 2006 GMC Sierra Classic, 2007 Saturn Vue Green Line, 2008 Chevy Tahoe, and the 2008 GMC Yukon.

Toyota

Toyota Motor Company is one of the principal competitors to Ford domestically. The Japan-based automaker has made tremendous strides in increasing market share and sales volume in the North American automotive market. Since 2000, Ford's market share has continuously fallen while Toyota continues to gain ground. In 2000 Ford and Toyota had 25 percent and 10 percent of the market respectively, while at the start of 2007 they possessed 14.8 percent and 15 percent respectively.[36] Ford sold 3.05 million vehicles during 2006 while Toyota sold 2.5 million cars and trucks.[37] Toyota's success in the United States has led to a change in the "Big Three" moniker; Ford, GM, and Chrysler have instead been designated as the "Detroit Three."[38]

Toyota's appeal is based on its vehicle lineup, quality, safety ratings, and resale value. Toyota offers a vehicle lineup that spans the breadth of the automotive market from subcompact autos to full-size SUVs. Toyota currently produces seven (7) passenger cars, six (6) SUVs, two (2) truck models, and one (1) minivan, under its flagship name, with prices ranging from $11,000 to $60,000.[39] Of the vehicles in Toyota's lineup, three, one in each category except the minivan, are offered with hybrid technology. The number of available vehicles and fuel options give the consumer a great deal of flexibility when choosing an automobile.

Toyota's flagship models are considered to be high-quality vehicles and among the safest vehicles available. The National Highway Traffic Safety Administration (NHTSA) performs safety tests on each vehicle design for a given year. For the vehicle year 2006, the NHTSA rated all but one of Toyota's vehicles, the Matrix, with at least a four-star rating. Five of Toyota's vehicles received a five-star rating, the highest possible safety rating.[40]

Innovation is another of Toyota's competitive advantages over not just Ford, but the majority of the auto industry. Booz Allen, which rates companies against their peers on research and development, rated Toyota highest among major automobile producing companies.[41] In 2005, Toyota spent $7.2 billion on R&D while Ford, which spends the most on R&D within the domestic automotive industry, spent $8 billion.[42] The Booz Allen rating indicates that Toyota achieves the highest return on its R&D expenditures.

Firms within the automotive industry have had to be wise in the battle for market share by evaluating and paying attention to important factors such as suppliers, customers, possible threats, and operating costs.

Suppliers, Customers, and Other Competitive Threats

Suppliers

The auto industry obtains resources from a wide array of firms globally. Although the number of suppliers has dropped since 2001, an estimated 450 suppliers still provide output used in each automotive plant.[43] Many of these suppliers rely heavily on the auto industry for a large percentage of their revenue. For example, Gentex Corp., who supplies high-end rearview mirrors, realizes 96 percent of its sales from the auto industry.[44] Large diversified suppliers such as BASF and Dow Chemical supply plastics, foams, paint, and other basic materials to the auto industry along with many other industries. Although the large suppliers are diversified with many products in many industries, the automotive industry is still a significant customer especially for specific divisions within the large firms.

Delphi and Visteon are two key part suppliers for the auto industry. These two firms used to be the GM and Ford parts divisions until they were spun off. Since then, both firms have struggled with high debt, burdensome union contracts, and declining sales from their primary customers (GM and Ford). In fact, Delphi which was spun off from GM in May 1999 filed for Chapter 11 bankruptcy in October 2005.[45] Visteon which was spun off from Ford in 2000 has also struggled with high debt. In November 2006, Visteon's debt rating was further cut into junk bond rating by Moody's, who also lowered Visteon's credit rating from B2 to B3.[46] Although Delphi and Visteon have remained independent, financial troubles for both suppliers create concerns for GM and Ford. First, both automakers are still dependent on their spun off parts suppliers for a large amount of their parts, so supply uncertainties are a concern.[47] Second, when the parts suppliers were spun off, certain agreements where made with the unions that leave the automakers still potentially liable for labor costs. Ford, for example, has committed to the Visteon workers that they still would have jobs if Visteon folded.[48] Although Ford and GM both have financial strains of their own, they would likely have to step in if needed to ensure that their previously spun off parts suppliers remain viable.

Customers

Auto manufacturers sell their cars to a distribution network of dealerships that then sell to the general public. Additionally, the auto manufacturers sell to fleet sales firms, such as rental car companies. Although fleet sales generally are not as profitable as sales to the general public, they do account for a significant volume of sales. With production of the Taurus being discontinued, Ford is expecting fleet sales to decrease by 175,000 vehicles in 2007.[49]

Although the auto manufacturers sell to the dealerships, they have to be able to supply products that the end customer wants to purchase from the dealers, which means the auto manufacturers have to focus on the quality, design, performance, and cost desires of the general public. In addition, auto manufacturers need to recognize the emerging challenges dealers are facing. Harsh competition has minimized profit margins, especially with the current surplus of dealerships. In fact, an article in *BusinessWeek* stated, "There are too many dealers out there. If normal economic rules applied, say industry insiders, the nation's dealer population of 21,000 (three-quarters of them Big Three stores) would be cut by at least 3,000."[50] The challenges drive down margins even farther and affect compensation of car salespeople. With the explosion of information available on the Internet, the end consumers have access to more information to compare products and determine which vehicle meets their needs. Well-informed consumers are able to shop and negotiate pricing between dealerships, which diminishes a salesperson's tactical advantage.[51]

Additional Competitive Threats

Many urban areas have considered opportunities for improved public transportation via rail or bus. Salt Lake City recently implemented a mass transit system, and built the TRAX rail in time for the 2002 Winter Olympics. Phoenix is one of the most recent to begin construction of its mass transit system in the metropolitan area.

Even though factors such as capital requirements, economies of scale, need for distribution channels, and threat of retaliation make it unlikely for a new entrant to sprout up from within the United States, history has shown that new entrants can succeed in the U.S. market. Asian automakers such as Toyota and Honda have successfully entered and established themselves as key players in the market. More recent entries from Kia and Hyundai are also making progress in the United States. Automakers that are established in foreign countries have been able to gain a foothold by exporting to the United States and targeting a niche market. Once they have established a reputation and distribution channels, they then have been able to expand into the broader market. After reaching an economic scale, they typically then establish production within the United States. Chinese auto manufacturers will likely provide the next wave of new entrants into the U.S. market. China is now the second-largest auto market in the world and has a growth rate of nearly 26 percent.[52] One Chinese auto manufacturer (Greely Automotive Holding Company) recently displayed a car at the Detroit Auto Show, and they intend to begin exporting to the United States in 2008.[53]

Operating Costs

Fueled by intense competition and excess capacity within the market, automakers feel an ongoing drive to reduce costs and improve efficiencies. These desires contributed to some of the mergers and alliances already discussed, but other activities are also ongoing to reduce expenses. Ford and GM have been working to gain concessions, especially in relation to retiree medical costs, from the United Auto Workers (UAW) association, which represents many of the automaker's hourly workers. They are also striving to shed excess capacity and reduce fixed costs by closing manufacturing sites and bringing capacity more in line with their current market share. Additionally, firms are looking for more efficient ways to produce automobiles. Several firms are implementing flexible manufacturing capabilities to increase their production flexibility. For example, GM's new plant in Delta Township, Michigan, will have the new Tru-Flex system. This system will allow them to produce vehicles that have different platforms on the same assembly line.[54]

In light of the many factors associated with the automotive industry, it is wise for Ford to continue to invest heavily in R&D.

Research and Development

In addition to developing alternative fuel vehicles and associated technology, Ford Motor Company's primary engineering efforts include developing attractive safety and convenience features.

Safety Features

Ford has been working to improve the safety features of its vehicles. In an effort to reduce the probability of a rollover, Ford developed Roll Stability Control for the Volvo XC90, Lincoln Navigator, Lincoln Aviator, Ford Explorer, Mercury Mountaineer, Ford Expedition, and Ford E-Series vans. This feature detects when drivers corner too fast and applies pressure to the brakes on the outside of the turn, reducing understeer and the likeliness of a rollover. Additionally, Ford implemented what they call AdvanceTrac, which is designed to increase vehicle stability in emergency maneuver situations. Ford also developed adaptive cruise control. This feature is available in the Jaguar S-Type and uses radar to adjust the cruise control speed to the speed of the vehicle immediately in front.

Ford-engineered safety features reduce the likelihood of serious injury or death in case of a collision. One of these features is the safety canopy: In the event of an accident, airbags not only deploy in front of the driver and front passenger, but also from the sides of the vehicle to prevent passengers from being thrown into the side glass. Additionally, Ford developed what it calls an "Intelligent Safety System." The airbag inflator and steering column absorption adjust to driver variables such as seat position, body weight, and event severity.

Convenience Features

Convenience features are also a focus of Ford engineering, both as a means of product differentiation and to customer satisfaction. McKinsey & Co. estimates that electronics will comprise 40 percent of COGS by 2015 as opposed to the present 20 percent.[55] Although a large percentage of those COGS are safety related, many are convenience related, such as the integration of PDAs and cell phones for voice-activated dialing and hands-free operation, voice integration for GPS navigation, entertainment, climate control, retractable roof, and so on. For the more adventurous consumer, Ford developed a terrain response system, currently being tested in the Land Rover Range Stormer concept vehicle, which adjusts the engine, gearbox, air suspension, driveline controls, traction control functions, and brakes according to the environment and driving requirements.

Ford can get the greatest return on investment for R&D expenditures if the company's branding and marketing strategies are taken into account.

Branding and Marketing Strategies

Ford Brands

Ford markets automobiles in the United States under the Ford, Lincoln, Mercury, Mazda, Volvo, Jaguar, Land Rover, and Aston Martin brands. Because some of the brands have been acquired in recent years, some overlap occurs between target markets, but each brand tries to differentiate itself in order to appeal to a specific customer segment. Ford groups Jaguar, Volvo, Aston Martin, and Land Rover into its Premier Automotive Group (PAG).[56] Mazda, which is a Japanese auto manufacturer, and Ford started a relationship in 1979 which has continued to evolve, and in 1996, Ford took over 33.4 percent of Mazda shares.[57] The Lincoln and Mercury brands share a long history with Ford. Historically, the Ford brand included light trucks and cars targeted at the more price-conscious consumers. Lincoln targets higher-end consumers, and Mercury aims to fill the gap between the upper-end Lincolns and the lower-end Ford brand.

Marketing Strategies

In an effort to increase online traffic on dealership Web sites, and provide increased Web customization potential, in December 2006 Ford planned to implement new Web sites for 5,000 North American dealerships. The initiative focuses on bi-directional input, enabling customers to request key information such as quotes or test drives, as well as allowing Ford to push targeted advertisements and promotions out to customers. Ford strives to develop user-friendly, easy-to-operate dealer sites, which can be integrated with Ford's current corporate Web sites.[58]

Product Design and Positioning

Drastic product design transformation and advancement are critical to Ford's sustainability in the automotive market. The current leadership group is guiding designers to deliver product designs that demonstrate confidence. Ford's design director for passenger cars recognizes the need for Ford to research the market trends, desires, and expectations. As an example of the renewed design focus, in November 2006, Ford unveiled its Super Duty line of trucks planned for release in 2008, which offers increased towing capacity, improved interiors, and upgraded options packages to potential customers. For this line, Ford added MP3 capability, a superior tailgate step, and a stowable truck bed extender in its efforts to appeal to consumers. Further, the Super Duties incorporate Ford's Clean Diesel Technology, an advanced technology that equalizes diesel and gasoline emission levels.[59]

In addition to creating fresh product designs, Ford aims to further position its vehicles by offering attractive financing and discount options. In August 2006, Ford provided 0 percent financing to buyers with solid credit, and low rates even to those with mediocre credit.[60] Ford is offering bonus cash for purchases of specific 2007 models, including the Fusion, Escape, and Super Duty F-series.[61]

Ford continues its efforts to increase sales and enhance its tired brand image through a variety of approaches, ranging from participating in automotive exhibitions to marketing vehicles on film and television. At the Beijing International Automobile Exhibition, Ford will be the largest exhibitor.[62] The 2007 Ford Mondeo is driven by James Bond in the 2006 film *Casino Royale,* contributing to the positive branding of Ford as chic and powerful. Ford vehicles also appeared on the popular television show, *American Idol,* and the award-winning movie, *Crash.*[63]

Despite its efforts to differentiate and survive in an ever-intensifying competitive environment, the financial condition of the company has not been as strong as stakeholders would hope.

Financial Condition

Ford's declining economic performance can be attributed to two major factors, dwindling demand for its product and the rising cost of production and operational expenses. Rising fuel costs and increased competition, both domestic and foreign, have reduced Ford's sales and led to a loss of market share.[64] Ford's excess capacity and decrease in operating margins have put Ford at a financial disadvantage. (See Exhibits 6, 10, 11, 12, 13, and 14 for a comparison of select financial attributes for auto manufacturers.) One of the major underpinnings of its restructuring plan is to match capacity with demand.

Another financial constraint results from Ford's agreements with labor unions and its defined benefit plan, which spells out its obligations to provide post-retirement benefits for former employees. These benefits include pension benefits as well as life and health insurance in the United States and abroad. For example, in August of 2006, Ford announced plans to idle 10 of its production facilities as part of the Ford's Way Forward Plan, in an attempt to reduce inventory and production costs. This decision was required primarily due to the reductions in light truck and SUV sales. Even though the move will reduce the inventory levels and cost of machine operation, it will have a minimal effect on the cost of production personnel, hourly and salaried. Ford's agreement with the United Auto Workers union mandates that Ford continue to pay union employees the majority of their normal wage and Ford has further extended this to

Exhibit 6 Comparison of Select Financial Attributes (in $ millions)

Selected Auto Maker	Market Capitalization	Sales, TTM	Operating Income	Net Income, TTM
Ford Motor	15,187	170,425	2,842	1,575
Toyota Motor	194,505	186,677	16,668	12,176
Honda Motor	63,660	87,921	7,710	5,298
DaimlerChrysler AG	59,044	187,555	2,779	3,564

Source: 2006, Ford Motor Company, http://www.morningstar.com.

Exhibit 7 Performance of Ford Stock, January 2001 to December 2006

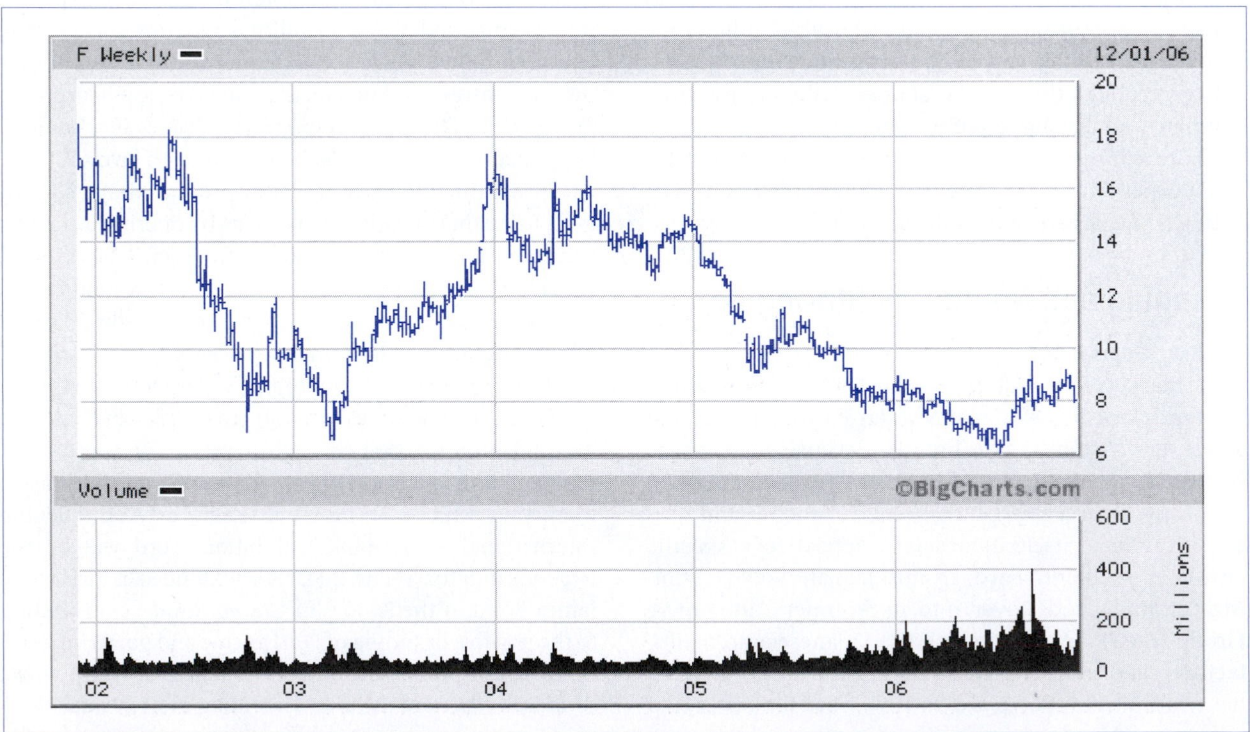

Source: 2006, Ford Motor Company, http://bigcharts.marketwatch.com/quickchart.

nonunion salaried employees.[65] These types of agreements are one of the principal causes of Ford's excessive operating costs as compared to its foreign competitors.

Ford intends to reduce operating costs through the consolidation of suppliers. To simplify its diffuse supply chain, Ford intends to consolidate the number of major parts suppliers for its automotive sector from 200 down to 100.[66] It also intends to continue to source raw materials and supplies from lower-cost geographical regions in order to improve its gross margin, which has declined 44 percent from 25.9 percent in 1996 to 14.6 percent in 2006.[67] As a comparison, the industry average is 19.2 percent,[68] representing 32 percent better performance over Ford. The narrower gross margins represent a challenge to garner adequate financial resources to mount an attack on market share against its rivals.

To further improve cash flows, Ford also stated that they will cut their dividend to shareholders of common stock in half to five cents per share and will also not be paying board member fees. Ford issued a dividend to common shareholders every year over the past 10 years, which usually yielded between 3 percent and 7 percent of earnings. The reduction in dividend payments will reduce net cash losses by $368 million per quarter.[69] (See Exhibits 7, 8, and 9 for Ford's stock performance.)

In September 2006, Ford's balance sheet showed a working capital deficit exceeding $35 billion with cash and cash equivalents balance of $25.5 billion with total current assets of $64.8 billion. In order to improve its liquidity and to allow sufficient cash reserves to fund its restructuring, Ford elected to raise an additional $18 billion. The financing includes $15 billion that is secured by current fixed assets with the balance being unsecured. In addition to funding operations, a portion of the proceeds from the new debt financing will restructure preexisting debt. It is the first time in the firm's history that Ford has been forced to secure financing with its internal assets.[70] The result of the additional debt on Ford's balance sheet resulted in further downgrades of its existing commercial paper to "junk" status. The S&P rating on Ford's senior unsecured debt was CCC-plus while Moody's assigned a Ba3 rating.[71] During the quarter ending in September 2006, Ford recorded a net loss of $5.8 billion and consumed more than $2 billion in cash.[72] Analysts anticipate that in 2007, Ford will burn through in excess of $5 billion in cash as it continues with its restructuring.[73]

An essential aspect in Ford's restructuring process is developing and understanding the corporate strategy.

Corporate Strategy

Ford's portfolio of automotive businesses includes auto manufacturers from around the world, replacement auto parts, and financial services. Ford recently hired Kenneth Leet, a former investment banker, to assist in developing a business strategy to improve business conditions. Recent

Exhibit 8 Performance of Ford Stock Versus the Dow Jones Index and GM, December 2002 to December 2006

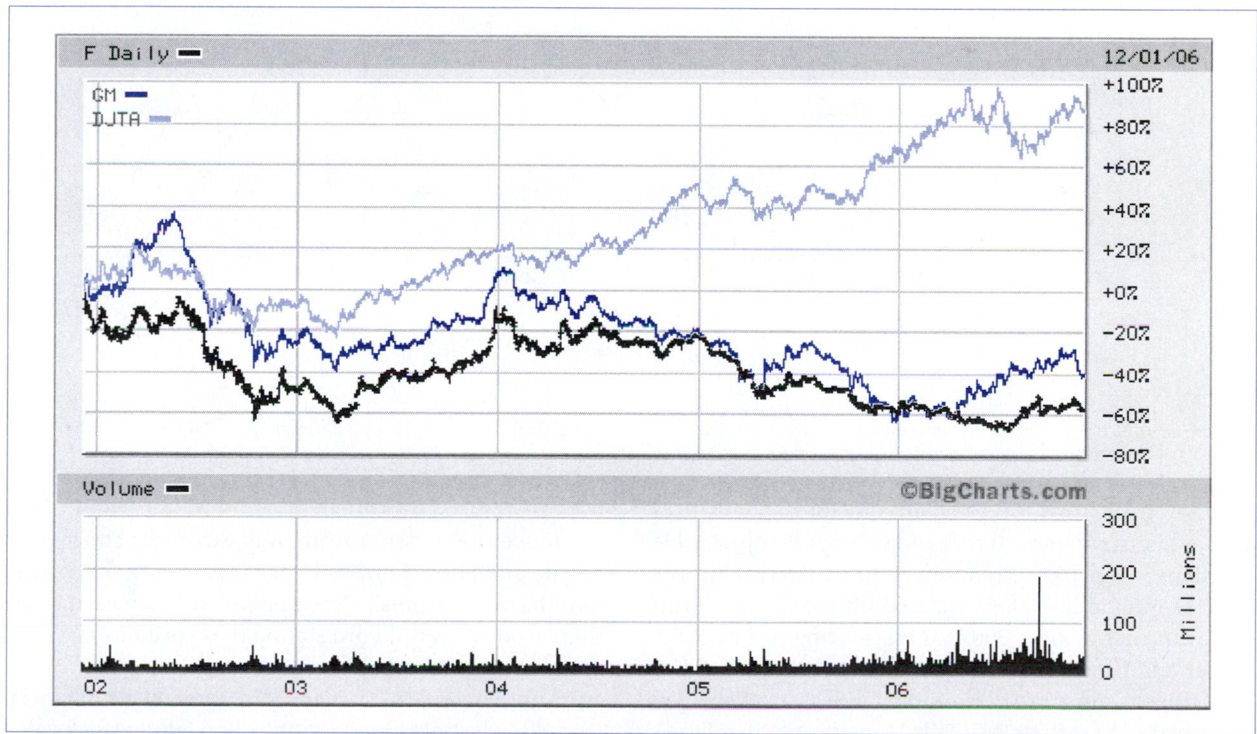

Source: 2006, Ford Motor Company, http://bigcharts.marketwatch.com/advchart/frames.

Exhibit 9 Stock Indices, 2000 to Present

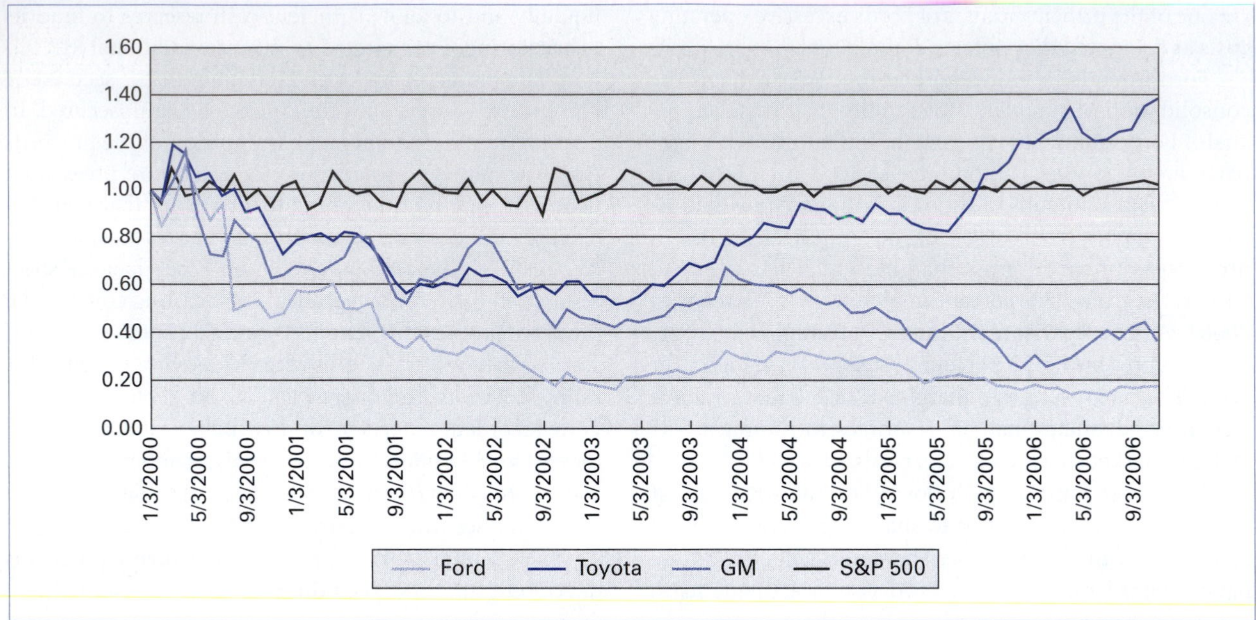

Exhibit 10 Comparative Operating Margin, 1996 to Present

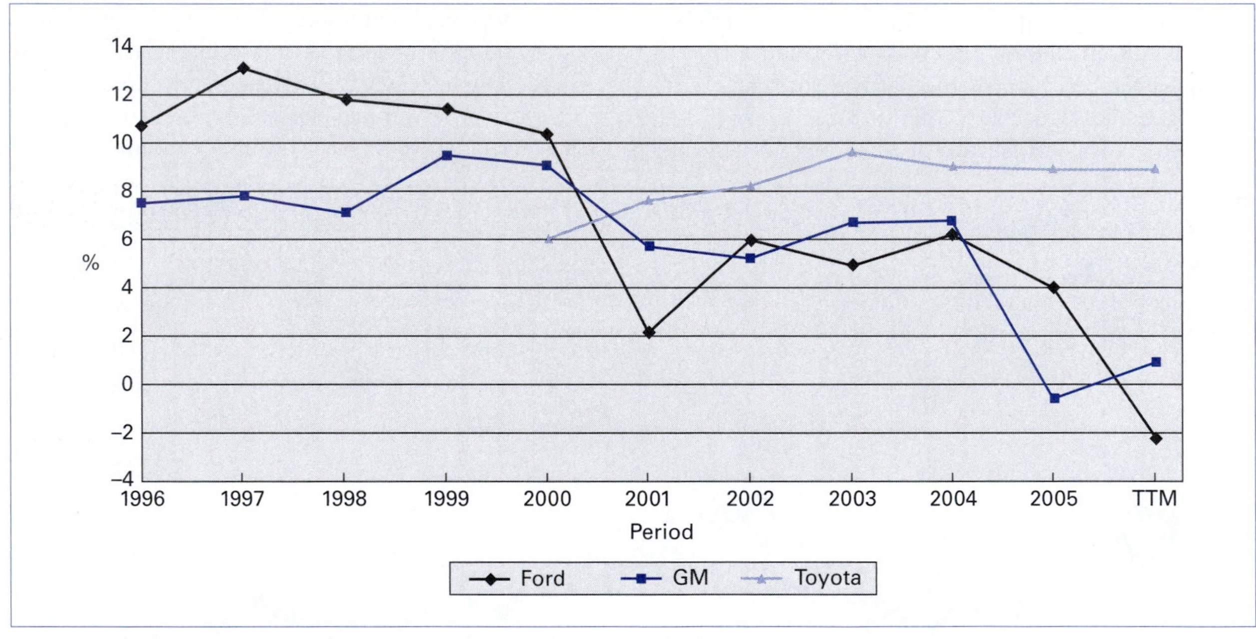

Sources: 2006, Ford Motor Company, http://www.morningstar.com; 2006, General Motors Corporation, http://www.morningstar.com; 2006, Toyota Motor Corporation, http://www.morningstar.com.

discussions include the possibility of forming alliances with other car manufacturers and selling off unprofitable divisions.[74] Due to its Premium Auto Group's pretax loss of $327 million in 2006, Ford sold off the Aston Martin brand in first quarter 2007 and is seeking to divest the Jaguar and Land Rover brands.[75]

Other rumors swirl around the idea that Ford will go private. An article in CNNMoney.com cites Ford's contemplation of going private as it restructures and tries to return to profitability.[76] This step would help to reduce the pressure from Wall Street for short-term results and allow Ford to better focus on making solid long-term decisions. However, other sources dispute this rumor with Bill Ford stating that Ford has no interest in going private.[77]

Another option to help Ford remedy its financial struggles, declining credit ratings, and falling stock value is declaring bankruptcy, but Ford asserts that bankruptcy

Exhibit 11 Financial Comparison Summary 2005 (in $ millions)

	Ford Corporation (F)	General Motors Corporation (GM)	Toyota Motor Corporation (ADR-TM)
Net revenue	$ 177,089,000	$ 192,604,000	$ 179,083,000
Cost of revenue	144,944,000	171,033,000	144,249,000
Gross profit	32,145,000	21,571,000	34,834,000
SG&A	24,652,000	22,734,000	18,844,000
Other expenses	483,000		
Operating income/(loss)	7,010,000	(1,163,000)	15,990,000
Net Income	**$ 2,024,000**	**$ (10,567,000)**	**$ 11,681,000**
Total current assets	51,712,000	99,414,000	91,387,000
Total Assets	**$ 269,476,000**	**$ 476,078,000**	**$ 244,587,000**
Total current liabilities	95,790,000	113,973,000	85,373,000
Total Liabilities	**$ 256,519,000**	**$ 461,481,000**	**$ 154,688,000**
Total Stockholders Equity	**$ 12,957,000**	**$ 14,597,000**	**$ 89,899,000**
Cash flow from operations	21,728,000	(16,856,000)	21,414,000
Cash flow from investing activities	7,408,000	8,565,000	(28,735,000)
Cash flow from financing activities	(20,651,000)	3,480,000	7,465,000
Net Change in Cash	**$ 7,989,000**	**$ (5,267,000)**	**$ 729,000**

Sources: 2006, Ford Motor Company, http://www.morningstar.com; 2006, Toyota Motor Corporation, http://www.morningstar.com; 2006, General Motors Corporation, http://www.morningstar.com.

Exhibit 12 Selected Financial Ratios for Toyota Motor Corporation

	1997	1998	1999	2000	2001	2002	2003	2004	2005	2006
Revenue ($ millions)					$118,558	$114,572	$126,232	$152,237	$173,304	$186,842
Gross margin, %					19.0	20.8	20.4	19.8	19.8	19.5
Operating margin, %					6.0	7.6	8.2	9.6	9.0	8.9
Operating income					$ 7,136	$ 8,751	$ 10,355	$ 14,672	$ 15,621	$ 16,682
Net income*					6,089	4,437	6,113	10,228	10,906	12,176
Cash flow from operations					12,887	12,265	16,978	20,096	22,148	22,341
Free cash flow					2,045	(127)	3,866	6,993	4,182	(2,271)

* Unadjusted for nonrecurring above-the-line transactions.

Source: 2007, Toyota Motor Corporation, http://www.morningstar.com.

is not an option it will consider.[78] News that Chapter 11 will not be filed has led to recent improved shareholder confidence.[79]

With the new CEO in place, other changes are slated to take place in Ford's corporate strategy. Mulally is determined to decrease the influence of the finance department, which historically had significant power in determining the final product and has too often compromised an automobile's competitiveness in order to save a few dollars.[80] Mulally believes that the key to its future success is not squeezing by with fewer resources than competitors use, but "working smarter with what it has."[81] Another component of the new strategy directed by Mulally is ridding Ford of "needless complexity."[82] Mulally stated that prior to him being on board, "The company was being managed as a collection of six or seven Fords, each

Exhibit 13 Selected Financial Ratios for General Motors Corporation

	1996	1997	1998	1999	2000	2001	2002	2003	2004	2005	2006
Revenue ($ millions)	$164,069	$178,174	$161,315	$176,558	$184,632	$177,260	$186,763	$185,524	$193,517	$192,604	$207,349
Gross margin, %	24.5	27.0	26.9	28.2	21.1	18.8	17.9	18.0	17.3	11.2	20.6
Operating margin, %	7.5	7.8	7.1	9.5	9.1	5.7	5.2	6.7	6.8	(0.6)	(3.7)
Operating income	$ 12,371	$ 13,827	$ 11,505	$ 16,797	$ 16,716	$ 10,108	$ 9,795	$ 12,445	$ 13,172	$ (1,163)	$ (7,668)
Net income*	4,963	6,698	2,956	5,922	4,342	502	1,689	3,822	2,805	(10,567)	(1,978)
Cash flow from operations	18,720	16,454	17,067	27,030	19,750	9,166	17,109	7,600	13,061	(16,856)	(11,759)
Free cash flow	(9,723)	(14,939)	(16,076)	(3,519)	(11,855)	(17,505)	(6,958)	(11,491)	(9,016)	(40,531)	(19,692)

* Unadjusted for nonrecurring above-the-line transactions.

Source: 2007, General Motors Corporation, http://www.morningstar.com.

Exhibit 14 Selected Financial for Ford Motor Corporation

	1996	1997	1998	1999	2000	2001	2002	2003	2004	2005	2006
Revenue ($ millions)	$146,991	$153,627	$144,416	$162,558	$170,064	$162,412	$163,420	$164,196	$171,652	$177,089	$170,425
Gross margin, %	25.9	29.1	27.4	26.8	25.8	20.5	23.4	20.9	20.9	18.2	6.9
Operating margin, %	10.7	13.1	11.8	11.4	10.4	2.1	6.0	4.9	6.2	4.0	(5.1)
Operating income	$ 15,707	$ 20,142	$ 17,013	$ 18,592	$ 17,718	$ 3,354	$ 9,857	$ 8,118	$ 10,681	$ 7,010	$ (8,167)
Net income*	4,381	6,866	21,964	7,222	3,452	(5,468)	(995)	495	3,487	2,024	(12,613)
Cash flow from operations	19,257	27,634	23,100	29,811	33,764	22,764	18,633	20,195	24,514	21,674	9,609
Free cash flow	10,411	18,585	14,373	21,276	25,416	15,756	11,355	12,446	17,769	14,157	2,761

* Unadjusted for nonrecurring above-the-line transactions.

Source: 2007, Ford Motor Company, http://www.morningstar.com.

pursuing its own agenda."[83] Mulally's focus is to unite the company with a single business purpose.

Additionally, Ford will concentrate more on the worldwide market and customers, and work to better utilize its global assets and capabilities.[84] The global organization will streamline operations rather than differentiating processes for different countries. Already, Ford has closed plants in Wixom, Michigan; Louisville, Kentucky; and Lorain, Ohio, and will soon close its St. Louis, Missouri, plant. Ford is also attempting to increase operational efficiency by investing $2 billion in the Rouge manufacturing plant in Dearborn, Michigan, for cutting-edge manufacturing equipment and environmental features,[85] $62 million into the Buffalo plant to increase output and widen the scope of parts production, and $240 million over the next four years at its Wayne Assembly Plant.[86] To further aid with this process, Mulally organized a global product development team.

Mulally has been working closely with labor unions in an attempt to increase contributions to the retirement plans helping to relieve the financial burden as it tries to decrease operating costs. In the effort to alleviate the financial burden of the labor agreements, Ford announced that it would be offering its 75,000 domestic union workers a buyout of their existing contracts including an option to receive lump sum payment in lieu of future pension and health care obligations.[87] Economic terms of the buyouts range from $35,000 to $140,000 and are based on current compensation, occupation level, and other post-employment compensation packages elected. Ford originally anticipated that the buyout would allow them to reduce 30,000 of its hourly positions. In late November 2006, Ford reported that the acceptance rate for the buyout had exceeded the anticipated number of 30,000 and that roughly 38,000 of its U.S. employees had opted to participate.[88] The reduction in force (RIF) buyout is expected to reduce operating expenses by between $335 million to $1.1 billion.[89] The net effect of the buyouts will increase the possibility that Ford could return to profitability in 2008.[90]

Conclusion

Ford Motor Company began with Henry Ford and his revolutionary $5-a-day minimum-wage scheme and an 8-hour work day,[91] but now, Ford Motor Company is struggling to survive. From the advent of the assembly line in 1913,[92] well-designed manufacturing has played a vital role at Ford Motor Company, but now Ford is planning to eliminate 40 percent of its workforce by 2008[93] in an effort to cut manufacturing costs. Ford is also striving to improve its competitive position by driving innovation. Successful innovation in manufacturing processes, product design, marketing approach, and business structure will be needed to improve Ford's brand image, and return Ford to profitability. The only remaining question is how and if Ford can achieve the needed improvements before time runs out.

Notes

1. 2006, Ford Company History, http://www.ford.com.
2. 2006, *Wikipedia*, http://en.wikipedia.org/wiki/Henry_Ford.
3. Ibid.
4. Ibid.
5. 2006, *Fast Company*, http://www.fastcompany.com/online/33/ford.html.
6. http://www.thehenryford.org/exhibits/fmc/chrono.asp.
7. R. Jones, 2006, Ford makes bold move, but is it enough? *MSNBC*, http://www.msnbc.msn.com/id/14687037/, September 6.
8. K. Hammonds, 2000, Grassroots Leadership—Ford Motor Co., *Fast Company*, http://www.fastcompany.com/online/33/ford.html, March.
9. Ibid.
10. Ibid.
11. S. Webster, 2006, Inside Ford: Departing exec Anne Stevens says company needs to trim at top and her job is expendable, *Detroit Free Press* (Michigan), September 18.
12. S. Webster, 2006, Change looks inevitable at Ford: Analysts expect more top rank shake-ups, *Detroit Free Press* (Michigan), September 26.
13. 2006, Alan Mulally Biography, http://media.ford.com.
14. 2006, William Clay Ford Jr. Biography, http://media.ford.com.
15. 2006, New top man at Ford, http://www.carkeys.co.uk/news/2006/september/06/11258.asp, September 6.
16. 2006, William Clay Ford Jr. Biography.
17. 2006, William Clay Ford Media Articles, http://media.ford.com/people/related_articles.
18. Ibid.; 2007, Auto sales tumble amid housing slump, http://www.msnbc.msn.com, August 1.
19. A. Halperin, 2006, Does big R&D mean big returns? *BusinessWeek*, November 26.
20. Ibid.
21. 2006, R. Vartabedian, E85 getting attention, http://www.energyrefuge.com/archives/e85_getting_attention.htm, June.
22. 2006, The road ahead for the U.S. auto industry, Office of Aerospace and Automotive Industries International Trade Administration, U.S. Department of Commerce, April.
23. 2006, U.S. light vehicle sales, market share for November, http://sg.biz.yahoo.com/061201/3/45809.html, December 2.
24. 2007, The road ahead for the U.S. auto industry.
25. 2006, DaimlerChrysler: Corporate profile, http://www.daimlerchrysler.com, December 7.
26. 2007, The road ahead for the U.S. auto industry.
27. 2007, DaimlerChrysler closes transaction on transfer of majority interest in Chrysler to Cerberus, press release, http://www.daimlerchrysler.com, August 3.
28. 2006, DaimlerChrysler: Technology & Innovation, http://www.daimlerchrysler.com, December 7.
29. Ibid.
30. Ibid.
31. 2007, General Motors: Company Information, http://www.gm.com/company/corp_info/.
32. 2007, Ford makes surprise quarterly profit, MSNBC, http://www.msnbc.msn.com, July 26.
33. D. A. McIntyre, 2007, GM's market share drives off a cliff, 24/7 *Wall Street*, http://www.247wallst.com, July 7.
34. 2006, The road ahead for the U.S. auto industry.
35. 2006, General Motors: GM Advanced Technology, http://www.gm.com/company/gmability/adv_tech/100_news/fc_fleet_launch_091806.html, December 7.
36. N. Bunkley, 2006, Ford dropped to 4th place in market share last month, *New York Times*, http://www.nytimes.com, December 2.
37. A. Taylor III, 2007, America's best car company: Toyota has become a red, white, and blue role model. How? By understanding Americans better than Detroit does, *Fortune*, http://www.cnnmoney.com, March 7.
38. Ibid.
39. 2007, Toyota Vehicle Lineup, http://www.toyota.com.
40. 2007, http://www.motortrendcars.com.
41. J. Scanlon, 2006, How to turn money into innovation, *BusinessWeek*, http://www.businessweek.com, November 14.
42. A. Halperin, 2006, Does big R&D mean big returns? *Yahoo!*, http://www.uk.biz.yahoo.com, November 11.
43. 2006, Auto industry consolidation: Is there a new model on the horizon? http://knowledge.wharton.upenn.edu/article.cfm?articleid=1365&CFID=2396121&CFTOKEN=91611858, January 25.

44. 2006, Gentex Corp Investor Information, Corporate profile, http://www.gentex.com/corp_investor.html.
45. 2006, Delphi (auto parts), *Wikipedia*, http://en.wikipedia.org/wiki/Delphi_(auto_parts).
46. Associated Press, 2006, Moody's lowers Visteon credit rating, *Yahoo!*, http://biz.yahoo.com/ap/061122/visteon_rating.html?.v=1, November 22.
47. Ibid.
48. D. Welch, 2003, Ford and Visteon: Ties that bind, *BusinessWeek*, http://www.businessweek.com/magazine/content/03_16/b3829064.htm, April 21.
49. B. Koening & A. Ohnsman, 2006, Ford's U.S. sales unexpectedly fall: Toyota gains (Update 10), *Bloomberg*, http://www.bloomberg.com/apps/news?pid=20601087&sid=aYNYk.c_jNrY&refer=home, December 1.
50. D. Welch, 2006, Death of the car salesman, *BusinessWeek*, November 27, 33.
51. Ibid.
52. 2007, China car sales rev up nearly 26%, *Asia Times*, http://www.atimes.com/atimes/china_business, July 10.
53. Ibid.
54. Ibid.
55. 2006, The road ahead for the U.S. auto industry.
56. M. Krebs, 2005, Can endangered Jaguar be saved? Edmunds.com, http://www.edmunds.com/insideline/do/Columns/articleId=104594/subsubtypeId=217, February 7.
57. 2006, Ford Motor Company, http://www.ford.com/en/company/about/brands/mazda.htm.
58. R. Kisiel, 2006, Ford dealerships get new Web site designs, *Automotive News*, November 27, 43.
59. W. Leavitt, 2006, Ford debuts '08 Super Duties, *Fleet Owner*, November 1, 101(11).
60. J. Saranow & G. Chon, 2006, The return of 0% financing; auto makers pile on deals to clear swollen inventories; some hot models excluded, *Wall Street Journal*, August 31, D1.
61. A. Wilson, 2006, Ford, GM launch year-end incentives, *Automotive News*, November 20, 3.
62. 2006, Demand for autos moves into high gear, *Financial Times Information Limited - Asia Intelligence Wire*, http://www.chinadaily.com.cn, November 18.
63. 2006, Q+A: Casino Royale reaffirms 007's bond with Ford, *Brandweek.com*, http://www.brandweek.com, November 13.
64. J. Novak, 2006, Ford arranges new financing, *Morningstar Report*, November 28, 1.
65. C. Isidore, 2006, Ford slashes production, *CNN*, http://www.money.cnn.com, August 18.
66. 2005, Ford will use fewer suppliers in attempt to cut costs, *USA Today*, http://www.usatoday.com/money/autos, September 29.
67. 2006, Ford Motor Company, http://www.morningstar.com.
68. Ibid.
69. S. Jarush, 2006, Ford halves dividend, board member fees, *The Associated Press State & Local Wire*, July 13.
70. 2006, Ford plans to obtain $18 billion financing, http://www.smartmoney.com, November 27.
71. 2006, S&P, Moody's rate Ford's new credit line, http://www.reuters.com, November 29.
72. 2006, Third quarter earnings 2006 earnings review, http://media.ford.com/article_display.cfm?article_id=24527, October 23.
73. 2006, Ford plans to obtain $18 billion financing.
74. 2006, Ford review 'may spark sell-off,' http://news.bbc.co.uk/2/hi/business/5240794.stm, August 2.
75. J. Reed, 2007, Ford selling Jaguar, Land Rover, http://www.carsguide.news.com.au, June 13.
76. 2006, Report: Ford weighs going private, *CNN*, http://money.cnn.com/2006/08/24/news/companies/ford_private/, August 24.
77. 2006, Ford CEO: Bankruptcy 'not an option,' *Fox News*, http://www.foxnews.com/story/0,2933,201563,00.html, June 29.
78. Ibid.
79. D. Kiley, 2006, Lessened bankruptcy fears lift Ford shares, *BusinessWeek*, http://www.businessweek.com, December 21.
80. D. Kiley, 2007, Mulally: Ford's most important new model, *BusinessWeek*, http://www.businessweek.com, January 9.
81. Ibid.
82. Ibid.
83. D. Levin, 2007, Think Bush has had it bad, try a day as Bill Ford, Jr., *Bloomberg*, http://www.bloomberg.com, January 11.
84. 2006, Ford Motor Company, Ford announces corporate realignment, http://www.ford.com/newsroom/pressreleases, December 14.
85. 2006, Ford Motor Company: A history of innovative thinking, http://www.ford.com/en/innovation/technology/historyOfInnovativeThinking.htm, December 3.
86. 2006, Change looks inevitable at Ford: Analysts expect more top rank shake-ups.
87. J. Rodrigues, 2006, Ford employees take deep breaths, weigh options, *Virginian Pilot*, September 16.
88. 2006, Half of Ford's U.S. factory workers accept redundancy, http://www.reuters.com., November 30.
89. Ibid.
90. 2005 Ford 10-K/A SEC filing, 23.
91. http://www.time.com/time/time100/builder/profile/ford3.html.
92. 2006, Ford Motor Company: A history of innovative thinking, http://www.ford.com/en/innovation/technology/historyOfInnovativeThinking.htm, December 3.
93. J. McCracken, S. Power, & J. White, 2006, Sharp skid: Ford and Chrysler show dark outlook for U.S. car makers; Ford will drop its dividend, cut more salaried jobs; Daimler unit's loss grows; a 'Black Friday' for Detroit, *Wall Street Journal*, http://www.wsj.com, September 16.

Case 11

Jack Welch and Jeffrey Immelt: Continuity and Change in Strategy, Style, and Culture at GE

Shirisha Regani, Saji Sam George

ICFAI Center for Management Research

I'm a different generation from Jack . . . . . I have a different view of the world.

—JEFFREY IMMELT,
CEO OF GENERAL ELECTRIC, IN 2002.[1]

The thing that makes me most proud of Jeff is his visibility in tough times.

—JACK WELCH,
FORMER CEO OF GENERAL ELECTRIC, IN 2002.[2]

An Inauspicious Beginning

Jeffrey Immelt became the chief executive officer (CEO) of the General Electric Company (GE) on September 7, 2001, drawing to a close one of the longest[3] succession planning programs in corporate America. Immelt succeeded Jack Welch, who was generally acknowledged as one of the most successful CEOs in business history for his management of GE in the 20 years he headed the company.

On September 11, 2001, just four days after Immelt stepped into the job for which he had been in training for almost a year, hijackers crashed planes into the Pentagon and the twin towers of the World Trade Center. This event shocked the world and left the U.S. economy—already in bad shape from a recession and the bursting of the dot.com bubble in 2000—battered.

It was an inauspicious beginning for Immelt. As a huge, diversified company, GE had interests in several sensitive industries, including aircraft engines, plastics, and insurance, which were sure to suffer some of the after-effects of September 11.

The terrorist attacks were a harbinger of bad times to come for GE. As of early 2006, in the four and a half years that he had headed GE, Immelt dealt with a series of problems. By 2002, GE's share price had fallen to levels much below its peak in early 2001, showing no signs of improvement by mid-2006 (refer to Exhibit 1 for GE's share price).

Background

GE's origins can be traced to 1879, when Thomas Alva Edison invented the first successful incandescent electric lamp. Edison was an entrepreneur as well as an inventor and started several small businesses dealing with power stations, wiring devices, and appliances during the late 1870s and 1880s. In 1890, he brought all these businesses together and combined them under the Edison General Electric Company (EGEC).

EGEC merged with the Thomas-Houston Electric Company[4] in 1892 to form GE. The newly formed GE was then headquartered in New York. In 1894, Edison gave way to Charles Coffin, a former shoe salesman, as the CEO of GE. Coffin licensed out the electric bulb technology to other companies, thus consolidating GE's position in the emerging lighting industry. Coffin also created a formal hierarchy at the company and organized GE's various businesses in a systematic manner, arranging each unit around a product line. Coffin was also responsible for setting up financial control systems at GE.

Coffin had a long tenure at GE and eventually stepped aside in favor of Gerard Swope in 1922. Under Swope, GE launched several progressive industrial relations initiatives, setting up new policies to give employees pensions, bonuses, stock purchase options, profit sharing, and group insurance. GE also became the first company to establish an unemployment pension plan, which guaranteed laid-off workers a stipend of $7.50 per week for a period of 10 weeks after the layoff.

In 1940, Charles Wilson became the CEO of GE. Wilson was an autocratic leader and employee relations

Exhibit 1 GE's Share Prices

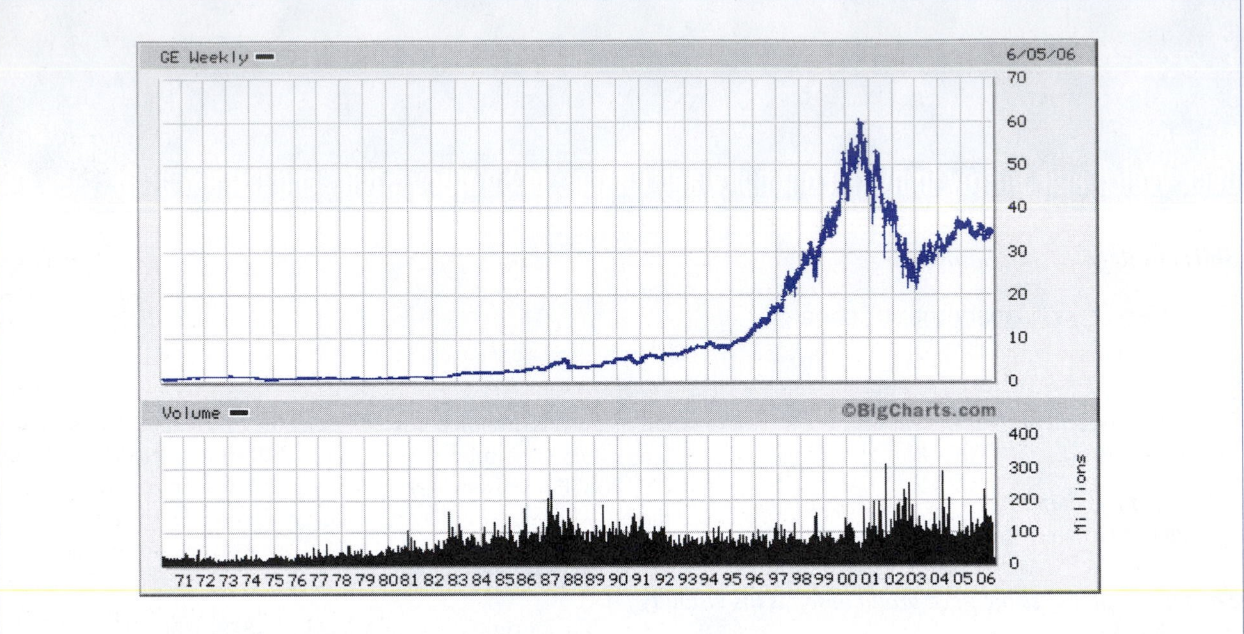

Source: http://www.bigcharts.com.

deteriorated during his tenure. After World War II (1939 to 1945), GE faced a major crisis in industrial relations due to the increasing clout of the trade unions. The crisis culminated in a major strike in 1948, which caused a rift between the blue-collar workers and the top management at the company.

By the 1950s, GE was a major industrial conglomerate with interests in a variety of businesses. But growth brought its own problems. From the beginning, GE was organized like a holding company, with a few executives at the headquarters monitoring the activities of the various businesses. Except for routine monitoring, each business unit enjoyed great autonomy. Over the years, the heads of individual businesses became powerful and began operating their units like independent businesses with little reference to GE's strategic intentions.

After Ralph Cordiner became the CEO in 1958, he embarked on a company-wide restructuring program to bring discipline to GE. To obtain more control over the various businesses, he strengthened bureaucracy within the company. Cordiner created a team of GE executives, outside consultants, and management experts to develop strategies to streamline the company's management practices. Cordiner was also responsible for setting up GE's management training center at Croton-on-Hudson in New York, popularly known as the Crotonville School,[5] to train future GE leaders.

Fred Borch succeeded Cordiner in 1964. Borch was an aggressive leader and was responsible for much of GE's growth in the 1960s. He added three new capital intensive lines to GE's portfolio: computers, nuclear power, and aircraft engines, all of which were considered risky investments, but with huge potential, at that time. Borch was also responsible for introducing the concept of strategic business units (SBUs),[6] and created 46 SBUs within the company in the late 1960s. (At that time GE's businesses were arranged around 10 groups with nearly 200 profit centers and 145 departments in all.)

Reginald Jones became the CEO in 1972. Jones accelerated GE's shift from electromechanical to electronic technology. He also emphasized the need to be responsive to the international environment and competition from overseas. Jones invested heavily in office automation in order to increase productivity and made some strategic decisions that involved strengthening promising business units, such as plastics, and divesting the unproductive computer businesses. Under Jones, GE became one of the most powerful conglomerates in the world.

A significant phase in GE's history began in 1981, when Welch became the CEO of the company.

Jack Welch

Welch, the son of a railway conductor, was born on November 19, 1935, in Salem, Massachusetts. He studied chemical engineering at the University of Massachusetts, where he graduated in 1957. He then moved to the University of Illinois, where he received his master's and PhD in chemical engineering.

Welch joined GE in 1960 as a junior engineer with an annual salary of $10,500. He was not happy with the excessively bureaucratic culture of the company. In 1961, soon after he completed his first year at GE, he resigned because he was disappointed with the $1,000 raise he received.[7] He accepted a job at a company called International Minerals & Chemicals Corporation.

But just a few days before he was due to leave GE, Reuben Gutoff, Welch's immediate superior, took him out to dinner and spent four hours trying to convince him to stay with GE. Gutoff promised Welch that he would try to create a good work atmosphere for him—one that would combine a "small-company environment, with big-company resources." He also assured Welch that he would keep him from getting entangled with GE's bureaucracy.

Welch apparently agreed to stay and see how things worked out. Gutoff presumably kept his word, because Welch stayed with GE and rapidly rose through the company's ranks. After he helped develop a new type of plastic called Noryl,[8] Welch was made general manager of GE's new plastics factory. A little later, he was made the head of GE's entire plastics division.

In 1972, Welch became vice president at GE (it was one of the fastest rises into senior management within GE). In 1977, he was made senior vice president and two years later vice chairman. In 1981, he was chosen as Jones's successor, becoming the youngest CEO in GE's history.

GE Under Welch

Welch's appointment as the CEO of GE was first greeted with skepticism. Several people thought that at 45, Welch was far too young and inexperienced for a post with so much responsibility. (GE was one of the largest companies in the world and had interests in a diverse range of businesses.) People also thought he was too flamboyant and far too aggressive to fit in with GE's staid culture.

In addition to these concerns, Jones had been a successful CEO, keeping GE profitable and growing, even during the recession of the late 1970s. He was also one of the most admired business leaders in the United States at that time. Therefore, stepping into Jones's shoes was not easy for Welch.

GE was widely regarded as one of the most profitable and well-managed companies in the world. However, Welch still felt the need for several changes that were aimed at making the company more nimble and profitable. He foresaw that GE was in danger of becoming complacent, and that this complacency would harm the company in the long run. In addition in the early 1980s, the United States was facing tough competition from the Japanese and the Europeans in several industries.

One of the first things Welch did as CEO of GE was to take steps to radically transform the company's bureaucratic culture. He created a flatter structure by trimming the company's nine management levels to six. The object of this exercise was to make GE more nimble and to improve communications within the company.

Over the years, GE had been following a matrix-based corporate planning system,[9] which was widely admired by management experts. However, Welch replaced it with what was known as his "Number One Number Two" strategy.

"Fix it, sell it, or close it" summarized Welch's approach to GE's businesses during this period. He insisted that GE should be one of the top two players in every segment in which it operated. If any business failed to meet this criterion, he closed it down or sold it. During his tenure, GE divested several businesses such as air-conditioning and housewares, and thousands of employees lost their jobs. Welch's willingness to retrench employees earned him the nickname "Neutron Jack."[10]

On the other hand, Welch acquired several other businesses he thought would add value to GE's portfolio. Some significant acquisitions in the 1980s and 1990s were Employers Reinsurance and Radio Corporation of America (RCA), including National Broadcasting Corporation (NBC). (When GE acquired RCA for $6.28 billion in December 1985, it was the biggest merger ever in the non-oil sector. It established Welch's reputation as a master of large business deals.) By the time Welch retired in 2001, he had supervised GE's acquisition of more than 600 companies.

Strategic planning was always accorded great importance at GE, and the company had been the birthplace of several new management concepts. Other companies often sent their managers to study the strategic planning process at GE. Until the 1980s, strategic planning was primarily a corporate function at the company. However, Welch made it a line function and vested the responsibility for strategic planning with individual business units. He felt that the business units understood their own markets and were better off doing their own planning.

Welch also cut the company's spending on research & development (R&D). Historically, from the time of Edison, GE had put great emphasis on R&D. The company had an active Global R&D Center in New York, assisted by more than 100 product-oriented labs around the world. By the 1980s, GE owned more patents than any other company in the world.

However, Welch felt that innovation and problem solving had to be incorporated into everyday work. To promote innovation, he launched a program called "Work Out," which encouraged employees at all levels of the organization to get involved with innovation and problem solving.

The Work Out program included a series of company retreats where a group of employees (usually 50 in number) of varying ranks and responsibilities got together to review company policies and processes and make suggestions for improvement. Employees were encouraged to argue with and criticize their superiors, and the superiors were required to respond to the issues raised by employees as soon as possible. Welch believed that organization-wide problem solving improved overall quality, which made better business sense for the company as it increased customer value. "We want to make our quality so special, so valuable to our customers, so important to their success, that our products become their only real value choice," said Welch.[11]

Welch also believed that involving all employees in the quality processes of the company had great potential benefits. He believed that human creativity was unlimited and that when this creativity was tapped, it could lead to tremendous value. "The idea flow from the human spirit is absolutely unlimited. All you have to do is tap into that well. I don't like to use the word *efficiency.* It's creativity. It's a belief that every person counts," he said.[12]

Welch's commitment to quality led to the adoption of Six Sigma at GE in the mid-1990s. Six Sigma was a quality initiative first developed at Motorola Inc.[13] in 1986. The program aimed at reducing production defects to less than 3.4 per million through continuous improvements (refer to Exhibit 2 for a note on Six Sigma).

Welch borrowed the idea of implementing Six Sigma from AlliedSignal Inc.,[14] where his friend Lawrence Bossidy had become the CEO in 1991. Welch heard from Bossidy about how the Six Sigma program was helping AlliedSignal cut costs and increase productivity. He invited Bossidy to present this idea to the top management at GE. The management was impressed with the concept and decided to implement a Six Sigma program at GE. The program was launched at the company in 1995 and was applied to 200 projects in its first year.

Launching Six Sigma was not easy. The company had to invest heavily in training employees. Employees at GE were trained in Six Sigma at three levels—green belts, black belts, and master black belts, in increasing order of proficiency. Green belts were employees who took up Six Sigma implementation responsibility along with their regular work. Black belts guided green belts in the implementation of the Six Sigma programs. Black belts were completely devoted to Six Sigma without any other job responsibilities. Master black belts supervised the black belts and were responsible for identifying the projects in which Six Sigma could be implemented.

GE made it compulsory for employees to have at least green belt training and involvement in one quality control project to be eligible for promotion to management levels. Black belts and master black belts were usually at higher levels of management, and the company ensured that the best people were trained as black belts and master black belts.

To stress the importance of the Six Sigma initiative, GE linked it with compensation. Typically, 40 percent of the annual bonus of GE's top 7,000 employees was directly related to involvement in Six Sigma. By 1996, Six Sigma was applied to 3,000 projects, and this number rose to 7,000 by 1997.

Some concerns were expressed within GE that the stress placed on Six Sigma was leading to an increase in bureaucracy within the company, and employees were rigidly following established processes and were not willing to try new things. But Welch said that he was ready to put up with a little bureaucracy if it brought improved production and greater efficiency for the company.

Exhibit 2 A Note on Six Sigma

Six Sigma is based on a combination of well-established statistical quality control techniques and simple plus advanced data analysis methods. It essentially involves the systematic training of all personnel at every level of the organization involved in the targeted activity or process. It is based on the statistical concept that the output of most of the physical processes follows a normal distribution,[36] with the processes centered at the mean. As a normal result of the manufacturing process, all manufactured items are subject to item-to-item variation. Sigma is the standardized statistical measure of the variability or the dispersion within a given population of items. Six Sigma denotes 3.4 defects per million. Other Six Sigma levels include Two Sigma, Three Sigma, Four Sigma, and Five Sigma. These levels signify 308,537; 66,807; 6,200; and 233 defects per million respectively.

Six Sigma focuses on streamlining all the processes in the organization to improve productivity and reduce capital outlays while increasing the quality, speed, and efficiency of the operations. It was originally developed to be used for physical processes—those performed in manufacturing—which are easy to observe, record, analyze, and measure. However, later on it was extended to processes that were not as explicit and encompassed business areas such as bid and proposal, procurement, and contract management. Even though Six Sigma comprised strict measurements for physical processes, it involved identifying waste in the form of delays for other processes.

Six Sigma's success is measured by the extent to which it improves the quality and profitability at all levels of an organization. At the business level, Six Sigma could be used to improve profitability and market share, and also to ensure the company's long-term viability. At the process level, Six Sigma could be used to reduce defects and variation. It could also be used to enhance process capability so as to increase profitability and customer satisfaction.

Source: Compiled from various sources.

At GE management meetings, heads of businesses were frequently encouraged to talk about the quality initiatives at their own units, so that ideas and best practices could get transferred among the company's various businesses. The business heads usually spoke about the methods they used in their units to decrease costs and/or increase efficiency, so that people from other parts of the company could borrow and adapt their ideas.

Welch stressed the importance of communication at GE. He encouraged communication at all levels and in all directions (top-down, bottom-up, and lateral) within the company. Effective communication was promoted by GE's informal culture. Welch had a unique ability to communicate with and motivate people at all levels of the organization. All the company's employees called him "Jack," and were encouraged to express their opinions candidly to their superiors or to him directly. It was said that Welch tried to create the same "small-company environment, with big-company resources," atmosphere that Gutoff had created for him at the start of his career.

Welch used GE's various meetings and review sessions to great advantage in enhancing communications at the company. GE held several company events through the year. Instead of making these events just formal company gatherings, Welch transformed them into levers of leadership. The meetings gave him a chance to interact with different people in the company, listen to their opinions, and gauge their leadership potential.

Welch also used these opportunities to make sure that all GE employees knew his opinions and ideas. At the beginning of his term as CEO, Welch had realized that a CEO of a large company could not afford to communicate only with his top people and expect things to happen. Therefore, he constantly repeated his opinions and ideas at every opportunity, to all classes of employees. In turn, the business heads followed the same behavior within their units, which ensured that the lines of communication were always active. Welch's speeches were regularly video taped, translated into local languages and sent to various GE setups across the world. This practice enabled him to make his presence felt even to employees at distant locations.

Welch believed in staying visible within GE. He regularly visited different GE departments and factories where he made it a point to interact with employees. Surprise visits were also a part of his leadership style. Analysts said that it was remarkable how, at a company of GE's size, employees at even the lowest levels in the company hierarchy seemed to know Welch and his opinions.

GE as a company lost most of its staidness under Welch. Thirty of GE's top managers met just before the close of every quarter in a meeting called the Corporate Executive Council. All the business heads were required to candidly share the new developments (particularly relating to the success or failure of new initiatives) in their departments. Welch challenged and tested his business heads constantly and pushed them to do better. Reportedly, these meetings often became heated and resulted in vigorous arguments, prompting some employees to call them "food fights" and "free for alls." However, the meetings allowed Welch to keep tabs on the happenings at the different GE businesses.

Analysts said that Welch was a master of the art of motivating people and stirring them to action. One way he made his presence felt at the company was by writing notes to employees. Welch frequently wrote notes to all levels of employees, to express appreciation for their contribution to the company, or to guide, inspire, or stir them to action. These notes were faxed directly to the employees the moment they were written, and the originals were sent later by mail. This way, Welch managed to exert a tremendous amount of influence over the GE behemoth.

Naturally, Welch did not know all the GE employees personally, but he learned about them through their bosses. Employees said that it made them feel more motivated, knowing that the CEO cared about them and bothered to get in touch personally. "We're pebbles in an ocean, but he knows about us. He's able to get people to give more of themselves because of who he is," said Brian Nailor, a marketing manager at GE's Industrial Products division.[15]

William Woodburn, an employee at GE's industrial diamonds business, recalled that when he turned down a promotion just because it would also involve a transfer and he did not want to uproot his teenage daughter from her school, he received a personal note from Welch appreciating his concern for his family. "Bill, we like you for a lot of reasons—one of them is that you are a very special person. You proved it again this morning. Good for you and your lucky family," wrote Welch.[16]

Another employee at GE's Capital Services business once spent several days preparing a report on why GE should buy AT&T's Universal Card[17] division. When this report was sent to Welch, he decided within a day that the division would not add value to GE's portfolio. However, he wrote a note to the employee appreciating the effort she had put into the presentation and complimenting her work.

Welch's charisma earned him a great reputation both within and outside GE. According to analysts, his appeal was magnified by the fact that he was a self-made man and had managed to overcome several handicaps to become a great leader. (Welch had a stutter, but was a great orator. He came from a lower middle class background, but went on to become the head of one of the greatest companies in the world.) These attributes made him a role model for many Americans.

However, Welch also had another side to him that was quite the opposite of the benevolent leader. According to GE insiders, he had a tendency to jump to conclusions about people, and formed opinions too rapidly. In addition, he was an extremely demanding boss and several employees, especially those at the lowest levels, complained about the pressure that was placed on them to perform.

Reportedly, Welch had a habit of asking people things like "What have you done for me lately?" whenever he met them. In addition, rewards and promotions at GE were based strictly on performance, and Welch routinely fired nonperformers. Several employees felt that this practice put too much pressure on them. They complained that they were never sure how much was enough.

Welch was a tough task-master who created fear in his subordinates. Nonperformers did not last at GE. Welch demanded that employees perform or be prepared to forgo their jobs. It was said that Welch was never satisfied with GE's performance even when the company was growing at more than 10 percent a year.

However, good performers were rewarded well. Analysts said that under Welch, GE functioned as a true meritocracy. Promotions at the company were mainly from within, and few outsiders were ever brought in. High performers could expect quick promotions in addition to generous bonuses, pay raises, and stock options. Bonuses and stock options were also highly differentiated with high performers being rewarded far more than mediocre ones. However, rewards came with the demand that the employee do even better the next year. "There are carrots and sticks here, and he is extraordinarily good at applying both," said Gary M. Reiner, a senior vice president at the company. "When he hands you a bonus or a stock option, he lets you know exactly what he wants in the coming year."[18]

Welch was responsible for extending the stock options program to the middle and lower levels of the organization and insisted that as many people as possible should receive options. One rule Welch made was that every time options were given, at least 25 percent of the people receiving options should be getting them for the first time, and that not more than 50 percent should get more than three grants in a row.

To determine rewards at GE, Welch devised a system where people were classified under three categories. Every department had to classify its employees as the top 20 percent, the middle 70 percent and the bottom 10 percent, based on their performance. The top performers were generously rewarded, and the middle level performers were rewarded and encouraged to emulate the top performers. The bottom 10 percent, who were considered the least effective employees, were fired. Welch believed that retaining nonperformers was detrimental to the company's health and that they would probably be better off in another company where the work was more suited to their potential and inclinations.

Among the most important events at GE under Welch were the annual "C" session meetings that started in April and lasted through May. During this period, Welch along with three senior executives traveled across the United States to meet with the top managers of each of GE's 12 businesses and to review their performance over the previous year. Three thousand senior GE employees were reviewed every year during the "C" Sessions and Welch kept close tabs on the top 500 people in the organization. The purpose of these sessions was to identify and promote leadership talent within GE.

The sessions were usually conducted with the CEO of each GE business and the senior human resource executive. Each business head was expected to identify candidates with leadership potential in their units and chalk out plans to help them realize this potential. Succession planning was also done for all key jobs within each unit, and decisions were made about who to send to Crotonville for leadership training. Welch was usually given a briefing book containing details of all the employees being reviewed along with their strengths, weaknesses, and development needs. The C sessions were a good way of identifying leadership talent within the company and planning for succession. They also served as a way to recognize good performers and assist them in developing their skills.

Leadership training and executive development were given tremendous importance at GE. Usually employees in management ranks were transferred every few years between locations. This rotation was done to enable them to learn about the various businesses and obtain an overall understanding of GE's operations.

Welch's theory of leadership later came to be known as the 4E theory. The four Es stood for Energy, Energizing, Edge, and Execute. According to Welch, successful leaders had tremendous positive energy, and the edge, or the courage, to make bold decisions. They also had the ability to energize other people, and the ability to execute, or deliver results. He connected these four Es with a P that stood for Passion. Welch said that the best leaders had the four Es as well as the P. People who had the four Es, but not the P had the potential to develop into good leaders, and were encouraged to emulate the top leaders (refer to Table 1).

Welch played an active role in leadership development at GE and taught regularly at Crotonville. He said that this gave him a chance to interact directly with the future leaders of the company. At Crotonville, managers were expected to participate actively in the leadership training, ask questions, and debate issues. Welch said interacting with the participants at Crotonville helped him understand them and their ideas about GE better. Welch

Table 1 Welch's 4Es

- **Energy:** Enormous amount of positive energy and a strong bias for action. An ability to love and adapt to change.
- **Energizing:** High level of people orientation and the ability to motivate and inspire people to maximize organizational potential.
- **Edge:** The courage to make bold decisions and the conviction to stick with them. Healthy competitive spirit.
- **Execute:** The ability to give a form to vision and deliver results.

Passion: A heartfelt, deep and authentic excitement about life and work.

Source: Compiled from various sources.

also interacted with the participants informally after the sessions at the cafeteria. Typically Welch taught one class a month at Crotonville, generally at the end of the three-week program.

Welch was also familiar with each of GE's businesses, no matter what its size, and took a keen interest in operations. It was said that when a unit was not operating up to the mark, Welch became more involved with it and asked managers to send him regular reports updating him on the situation. On the other hand, when a business was functioning well, the head of the business was given a great deal of autonomy. GE business heads who showed results were sometimes given more autonomy and power than even the heads of independent companies. "It's part of living with Jack," a former GE executive said. "If you're doing well, you probably have more freedom than most CEOs of publicly traded companies. But the leash gets pulled very tightly when a unit is underperforming."[19]

Welch promoted the idea of a boundary-less corporation at GE. Not only did he break down the boundaries separating the different departments within the company to promote the exchange of ideas, but also borrowed ideas from other companies to implement at GE. Welch believed that an organization was dependent on the external environment for its success. He created a culture at GE where people were open and curious and always ready to adopt ideas and best practices from other organizations.

Analysts said that borrowing ideas from other organizations was institutionalized at GE, and any idea that was not patented or copyrighted was adopted by the company. The adoption of Six Sigma was just one of the many examples of this practice. GE also adopted ideas such as Demand Flow Technology[20] from American Standard (a customer of GE's Motors and Industrial Systems business), Bullet Train Thinking[21] from Yokogawa (GE's partner in the Medical Systems business), and Quick Market Intelligence[22] from Wal-Mart, among others.

While most analysts agreed that Welch's successes at GE were more significant than his failures, his tenure was not without a few big missteps. One of Welch's biggest failures was GE's factory automation unit started in the early 1980s. The unit was set up to tap the nascent factory automation market by offering a collection of high-technology products. However, by 1983 it had run into serious losses due to erroneous demand projections. It was then that Welch shifted focus from manufacturing to financial services and concentrated on GE Capital Services, which remained one of the most profitable units of the company, even in the early 2000s.

Welch was also criticized for the sale of GE's appliance business to Black & Decker in 1984 and the acquisition of Thomson SA, a French medical diagnostics firm in 1987. The Kidder, Peabody & Co. (a brokerage firm that GE acquired in 1986) scam of 1994 was also a source of considerable embarrassment for GE and Welch.[23]

Welch endured some flack for the failure of GE's attempt to merge with Honeywell Inc., an aerospace and industrial-equipment group. In late 2000, Welch had learned that Honeywell's board was considering a takeover offer from GE's rival United Technologies Corporation.[24] Welch apparently did not want this deal to happen and interrupted Honeywell's board meeting with a higher offer of $43 billion.

United Technologies did not wish to enter into a bidding war with the "wild man" from GE, and refrained from further bidding. Honeywell accepted Welch's offer on the condition that he would postpone his retirement until the deal went through in late 2001. (He had previously planned to retire in April 2001). The GE-Honeywell merger was to create one of the world's largest industrial companies, until the European Union's Competition Commission refused to permit it on the grounds that it would give the merged company undue competitive advantage in the aviation industry.

Between 1981 and 2001, GE's revenues increased from about $27 billion to $129.8 billion (refer to Exhibit 3). By the time Welch retired from the company, GE was not only the biggest corporation in the world, but also one of the most profitable.

Jeffrey Immelt

Immelt was born in 1956 in Cincinnati, Ohio. His father was an employee of GE's Aircraft Engines division. As a child, Immelt was active in sports and was on the football and basketball teams at his school. He majored

Exhibit 3 GE's Revenues, 1981–2000 (in $US millions)

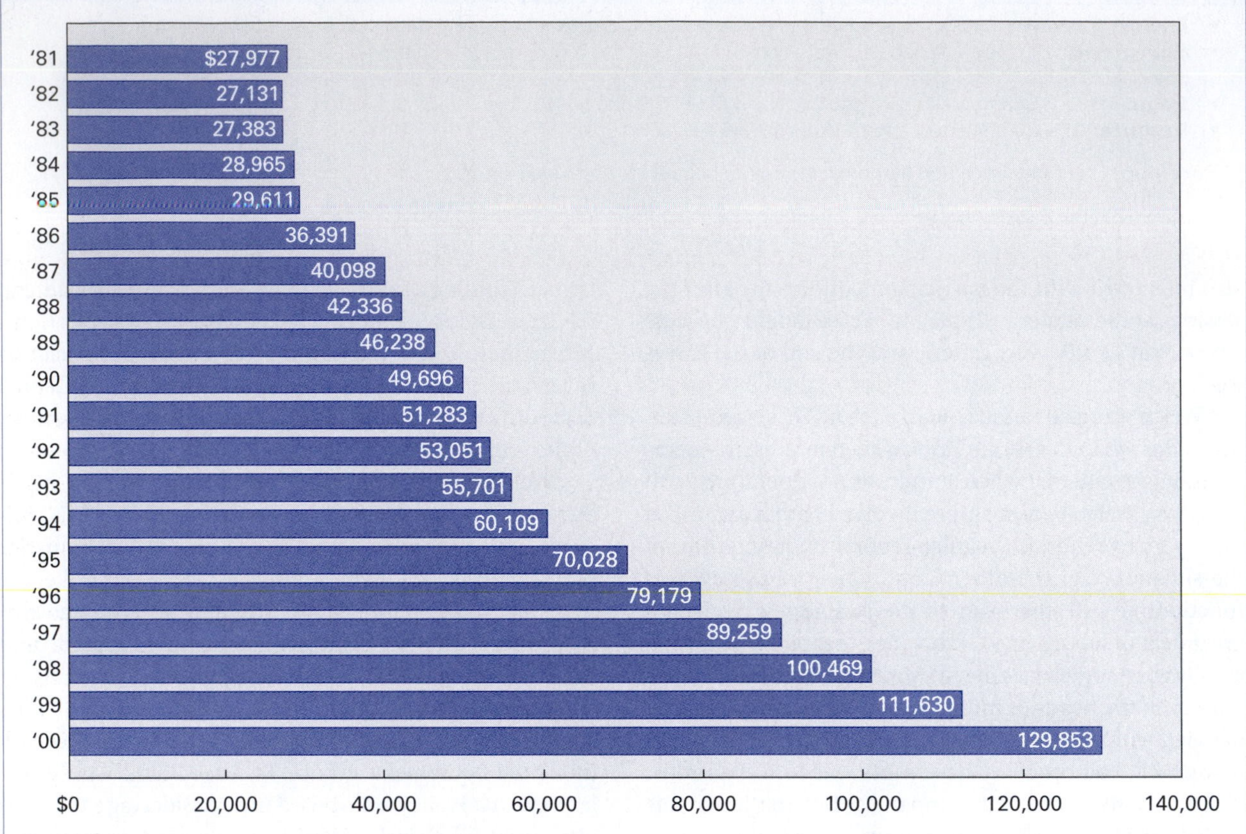

Source: http://www.ge.com.

in mathematics at Dartmouth College in the late 1970s, after which he joined Procter & Gamble Co. (P&G) as a member of its brand management team.

After about a year with P&G, Immelt enrolled in Harvard's MBA program. On finishing his degree, he joined GE as a marketing executive in 1982 at the company's headquarters in Fairfield, Connecticut. After six months, he was transferred to GE Plastics, where he continued until the late 1990s, in various marketing positions.

In the late 1990s, Immelt, along with James McNerney and Robert Nardelli, was short listed as a possible successor to Welch as GE's CEO. In November 2000, the board of GE chose Immelt as the successor. McNerney and Nardelli subsequently left GE to become the CEOs of 3M and Home Depot, respectively. Immelt was formally appointed as the CEO of GE in September 2001. Observers thought that Immelt was chosen because he was the youngest of the three contenders and therefore, likely to have the longest term. Besides, like Welch, Immelt had also spent a major part of his career at GE in the plastics division.

GE Under Immelt

Immelt became the head of GE at one of the most difficult times in American economic history. At the start of his tenure, GE lost two employees to the September 11 attacks and the company's insurance business took a $600 million hit. In addition, Aircraft Engines, one of GE's major businesses, experienced an immediate slowdown. GE Capital Aviation Services, a unit that leased aircraft to airlines, was also expected to be affected.

Immelt was in Seattle when the attacks occurred. He reacted immediately by setting up an office and command center at the small GE office in Seattle. He had to stay there for a few days because no flights were operating, so he managed through telephone and e-mail. Immelt met with investors in late September 2001 and assured them that despite the bad economic scenario, GE would still continue to post double-digit growth as it did under Welch.

However, when the New York Stock Exchange opened the week after the attacks, investors began selling their shares and the price of GE stock fell to $30 per share, 20 percent lower than the price before the attacks.

Exhibit 4 GE's Revenues and Earnings (all amounts in $US millions)

Year ended December 31	2000	2001	2002	2003	2004	2005
Revenues	130,385	126,416	132,210	134,187	151,300	148,019
Net earnings	12,735	13,684	14,118	15,002	16,593	16,353

Sources: http://www.hoovers.com; http://www.ge.com.

This lower stock price was just the beginning of a troublesome period for GE. Just a little after September 11, an anthrax[25] scare broke out when an envelope containing a brown granular substance (containing anthrax spores) was opened by NBC employee Erin O'Connor. In a few days O'Connor contracted anthrax. Over the next few months, envelopes containing anthrax spores were posted to a few prominent people in the United States, resulting in a major scare.

This incident was followed by the eruption of two of the biggest corporate scandals in U.S. business history—Enron Corporation[26] and Tyco International Corporation[27] in 2001–2002. Allegations of corporate fraud at both companies cast a shroud of doubt on all large conglomerates.

GE, being one of the largest corporations in the world, bore the full brunt of the distrust as investors started panicking and offloading their shares in the company. Investors were especially skeptical about GE's record of profitability and wanted to know how the company managed to stay profitable and fuel growth even during economic lows. They also wanted to know how much of GE's growth depended on acquisitions and how much of it was organic. The consistency that had made GE a favorite with investors now was viewed with suspicion in the early 2000s.

By early 2002, investors had started demanding more information about GE's complicated financial reports, and Immelt decided to give in to their demands. (Analysts thought that in the same situation, Welch would have ignored such rumors and demands for explanations.) GE's annual report in March 2002 was huge, giving several hitherto unknown details about the company and its financial management systems.

However, the effort did not achieve the desired outcome. In the same month, Bill Gross, the manager of Pacific Investment Management Co., which ran the largest bond fund in the world, published an article about GE's opaque finances and accused the company of inflating earnings through acquisitions and cheap debt rather than through organic growth. GE's share price fell by 6 percent after this report was published.

Investors also expressed concerns about how the company would fuel growth, when several of its units such as Aircraft Engines, Aviation Services, Plastics, and Industrial Systems were affected by the downturn in the economy. Even GE Power Systems, one of the big drivers of growth at GE, was facing large write-offs due to cancelled orders. Other concerns swirled around the debt levels of GE Capital, the company's successful financial arm, as people questioned Immelt's promises of double-digit growth. They also wondered how long it would be before GE would have to be split up, considering that at the rate of growth the management was promising, the company would reach revenues of $1 trillion by around 2020. In financial year 2002, GE's net earnings were $14.1 billion on revenues of $132 billion (refer to Exhibit 4 for GE's revenues and net profits in the early 2000s).

In an attempt to win investors over, GE redesigned its CEO compensation package in mid 2003. Under the new plan, Immelt was eligible to receive stock (performance share units) worth $7.5 million over a period of five years. Half of the performance share units would vest if GE's cash flow from operations rose at least 10 percent annually over the next five years. The other half would accrue to him if GE's stock met or exceeded the average performance of the S&P's 500 stock index[28] over the same period.

Immelt also modified the equity packages of other GE executives to link their stock options to the company's performance. "We believe that our pay should be completely transparent, that shareholders should know how we're paid. We have a philosophy on compensation that's based on performance," said Immelt.[29] He also said that while retention was an important issue in the granting of options for other GE executives, in his case, the only issue should be that of performance.

Immelt also tried to improve investor confidence by reshuffling GE's portfolio. Analysts said that he was trying to send across the message that GE was essentially a strong company and that there was no need for investors to be concerned about its business model. Immelt said that GE had acquired other companies, not simply to fuel expansion but also to improve the business portfolio. "I don't want us to be a company that does deals because we can. I want us to do the deals we need to do to improve strategically. If I didn't think this improved our business strategically for the long-term good of our shareholders, I wouldn't do it. We're not in the business of flipping assets. That's not our game," said Immelt.[30] By 2002, Immelt had started trying to beef up GE's portfolio by spinning off less-lucrative businesses and acquiring other strategically significant ones.

On October 8, 2003, GE announced the final terms of its acquisition of the French media giant Vivendi Universal's American assets in an equity deal valued at $14 billion. The combined company was expected to have $13 billion in 2003 revenues, with holdings that included film and TV studios, theme-park interests, and cable channels. Analysts were a little surprised by this acquisition, as GE had stayed away from the production business for years, despite owning the NBC television network. The company had long believed that NBC could survive without the backing of a studio and a content library. Therefore, analysts wondered whether Immelt had just been attracted by the bargain price of the deal.

On October 9, 2003, GE acquired Instrumentarium, a Finnish medical-equipment maker and immediately after that, on October 10, 2003, it purchased Amersham, a British life-sciences and medical-diagnostics company. The three deals together were valued at $25 billion. Analysts said that Immelt was trying to showcase a bold business transformation through these deals. However, they were skeptical about whether these deals would actually benefit the company or create more trouble for it.

By 2005, Immelt had sold less profitable GE businesses, including insurance, and had spent more than $60 billion to acquire businesses in new and fast-growing industries like renewable energy, cable and film entertainment, bioscience, and security. Slow-growth low-margin businesses such as lighting were also reduced to 10 percent of GE's portfolio from 33 percent in 2000 (refer to Exhibit 5 for Immelt's important acquisitions in the early 2000s).

Immelt also tried to increase GE's global orientation in the early 2000s. GE had always been a global company, but Immelt saw the potential to push it further. He invested hugely in setting up new research centers in Shanghai (China), Bangalore (India), and Munich (Germany) in 2004, and increased the company's R&D budget from $286 million in 2000 to $359 million in 2004. Immelt said that he wanted to create something like a "global brain trust" that the company could use to spur innovation, which explained the diverse locations of the facilities. Immelt also thought that globalizing research would allow GE to stay more in touch with customer needs. (GE predicted in 2004 that 60% of the company's growth in the next 10 years would come from developing countries campared to 20% in the 1990s).

By 2003–2004, Immelt had begun to put his stamp on GE's culture, and insiders said that they could see several changes in the company. For one thing, GE had always had a culture of promoting communications within the company. But under Immelt, the company had increased its external communications. Communicating with investors and third parties had become important in the early 2000s, due to uncertain external conditions. Immelt reportedly spent more than 70 percent of his time away from his office at GE's headquarters. He was either in the field meeting employees or he was meeting with investors.

Analysts said that GE's culture had softened under Immelt. The focus had shifted from performance and strictly quantifiable results, to more abstract aspects, such as customer satisfaction and value. Immelt also tied executive compensation to factors like the ability to boost sales, to come up with innovative ideas, and to generate customer satisfaction, rather that just the ability to meet performance targets.

In a departure from the company's traditional way of basing compensation on the bottom-line results, the new GE was focused on intangible factors that were more difficult to measure. Immelt thought that removing the emphasis from the bottom line would encourage employees to take risks and come up with innovative ideas. It was his aim to stretch GE's Six Sigma quality initiative into its industrial customers' processes to help them create more value for their customers.

GE however continued with the practice of firing the least effective 10 percent of its workforce every year. But analysts said that the way the firing was done seemed to be more subtle than in the Welch era, where it was done more publicly and with a view to let the entire organization know the reasons for the firing.

Another significant change within GE was the increased number of outsiders brought into the company at senior positions. Immelt believed that bringing in

Exhibit 5 Some of GE's Business Acquisitions Under Immelt

Industry	Acquisition
Media content	Universal Entertainment
Biosciences	Amersham
Security	Edward Systems
Water	Ionics and Osmonics
Renewable energy	Enron Wind

Source: 2005 Shuffling the Portfolio, *BusinessWeek*, March 28.

people from outside brought in new ideas, creative energy, and a new perspective on the company's policies. This practice contrasted with GE's traditional policy of promoting from within. Managers within GE were also being encouraged to "develop a passion" for and become experts in industries of their interest by spending a longer time at one job, rather than moving frequently between jobs. This mind-set was also different from the Welch era where managers were transferred between industries every few years. Under Welch, the focus had been on enhancing general management skills rather than industry expertise.

Immelt focused on establishing a greater level of diversity in GE's workforce. Traditionally GE had one of the lowest levels of workforce diversity among large companies in the United States. Welch, however, maintained that this was not due to the company's policies or work environment, but because of the nature of GE's businesses, which did not seem to attract women. This pattern was changing under Immelt. In the early 2000s, 50 percent of all senior executive hires and 54 percent of new corporate officers were women, minorities, or foreign employees. Immelt also created a separate diversity forum within the company and actively encouraged mentoring programs for women, minorities, and foreigners.

Within GE, Immelt was thought to be more people-oriented than Welch. Welch was an intimidating boss, but Immelt used a "friendly, regular-guy approach"[31] in dealing with employees. He was also not as demanding as Welch, and reportedly, employees found him more approachable than his predecessor. Describing Immelt's style of functioning, an article in *BusinessWeek* stated, "He prefers to tease where Welch would taunt. Immelt likes to cheer his people on rather than chew them out."[32]

Immelt was also responsible for shifting GE's focus from production to marketing. For a long time, GE had operated on the premise that winning products sold themselves. In contrast Immelt stressed that "the best managers are great marketers and not just great operators."[33] In 2002, Immelt appointed Beth Comstock as GE's chief marketing officer with the mandate of improving the company's marketing expertise.

Comstock said that it was not easy to get the employees of the production-oriented company to take to marketing. However, she put together a commercial leadership strategy that identified the best marketers within GE and gave them extensive training by sending them across the organization for two years. (Under Welch this type of training was done for audit staff, who played an important role in maintaining financial discipline in the company). GE also designed new marketing courses to train the company's marketing executives.

GE continued with its tradition of borrowing winning ideas from other companies and in November 2004, some GE marketing executives spent time at P&G, learning how the company examined and debated strategies and issues to arrive at marketing decisions. Employees also spent time at FedEx, which was known for its exceptional customer service, in the early 2000s.

Immelt set up a high-profile group known as the Commercial Council in 2002. It consisted of a handful of the top sales and marketing executives from GE's different units as well as unit heads from critical businesses such as Consumer Finance. The Commercial Council met every quarter to discuss growth strategies and ways to reach customers innovatively, as well as evaluate new ideas from the senior staff. According to GE insiders, these meetings were generally more "collegial and experimental" than other typical GE meetings. Meetings led by Immelt were also not as aggressive as those led by Welch.

Innovation and creativity were also promoted by Immelt. Immelt was worried that the uncertain economic scenario of the early 2000s would make GE employees risk-averse and hesitant to take bold decisions. Besides, GE had been criticized as being excessively dependent on acquisitions for its growth. To combat this image, he launched a program called Innovation Breakthrough in 2003. Employees were expected to come up with ideas to improve GE's existing products or for the development of new products through the Innovation Breakthrough program.

All business leaders were expected to submit at least three innovative project ideas per year that would then be reviewed and discussed by the Commercial Council within GE. For a project to qualify under the Innovation Breakthrough program, it had to take GE into a new line of business, a new geographic area, or a new customer base. Each project also had to have the potential to give GE incremental revenue of $100 million.

Since mid 2003, when the project was launched, GE invested more than $5 billion in 80 projects that ranged from creating microjet engines and cleaner coal to desalination. The company expected to have more than 200 projects under way by 2007 and estimated that the first lot of 80 projects would generate $25 billion in revenue. Analysts said that this move was aimed at proving that GE could grow internally and organically and not just through acquisitions.

GE also wanted to develop ways to spark idea generation. Executives were encouraged to hold "idea jams," where employees from different departments came together to brainstorm. GE Energy had also set up a "virtual idea box" where employees could post ideas on the Web, and then presented Excellerator awards for the development of ideas.

Exhibit 6 Ge's Business Reorganization in 2005

GE's 11 Core Businesses before 2005	
1	Healthcare
2	Transportation
3	Energy
4	Infrastructure
5	Commercial Finance
6	Consumer Finance
7	NBC
8	Advanced Materials
9	Consumer & Industrial
10	Equipment & Other
11	Insurance
GE's 6 Core Businesses after 2005	
1	Commercial Finance
2	Consumer Finance
3	Healthcare
4	Industrial
5	Infrastructure
6	NBC Universal

Source: Adapted from http://www.ge.com.

In early 2005, Immelt reorganized GE's businesses to make them more customer focused. Toward the end of Welch's tenure, GE was organized around 11 businesses based on product lines. This number was pared down to six in 2005, and the grouping was done based on the customers served. The reorganization was done to lower costs and eliminate redundancies, as well as to implement new systems of customer management. It was expected that as opposed to a product-based grouping, customer-based grouping made it easier for GE to mine and manage customer information better. "This change allows us to leverage our exceptionally deep leadership team to accelerate growth and improve productivity," said Immelt[34] (refer to Exhibit 6).

Under Immelt GE was also becoming "cleaner and greener." In 2005, GE announced that it would double its investment in ecoimagination projects to $1.5 billion by 2010. Ecoimagination projects related to the development and use of technologies that would eventually lead to cleaner and environmentally responsible products and processes at the company. Some of the ecoimagination projects at GE included producing a diesel and electric hybrid vehicle, developing cleaner coal-fired power plants and other products that would put less strain on the environment. Immelt's acquisition of Enron Wind (the only manufacturer of utility-scale wind turbines in the United States) in 2002 reflected the company's commitment to exploring alternative sources of energy.

Immelt announced in late 2005 that by 2010, all GE businesses would aim at reducing the emission of carbon dioxide—the main greenhouse gas[35] behind global warming—by a significant percentage. The company would focus on the by-products of energy-intensive businesses such as locomotives and plastics to achieve its environmental targets, but even non-energy-based businesses like GE Capital would have to take up environmentally responsible initiatives. The company had also started evaluating managers on their involvement in environmental responsibility.

Previously GE had never displayed any special consideration for the environment. The company had long been criticized for boosting coal and nuclear power and for dumping chemicals in the Hudson River near New York. Therefore, analysts were skeptical about the company's seriousness in this initiative and were inclined to dismiss it as "greenwash." However, Immelt seemed committed to this cause. GE's new environmental mantra was "green is green" (invoking the green color of currency in America), and the company was poised to make substantial investments in environmental projects.

Immelt also initiated the process of making governance changes at GE. GE had always had a reputation for good governance, and Immelt was trying to enhance it by bringing more outside directors to the board. The company had also adopted some accounting changes in an attempt to make its financials more transparent from 2002.

Making changes at GE was not easy for Immelt for several reasons. The most important was that he was a follow-up act to Welch, and Welch had already been established as one of the greatest business managers of all time. Therefore, making changes at GE, especially those that contradicted Welch's policies would not be easily accepted at the company.

Moreover, every step he took was being analyzed in the media in terms of what Welch would have done in the same situation. In addition, Immelt had to fight an uphill battle at GE to introduce concepts such as creativity, customer satisfaction, and value to employees who were steeped in the Six Sigma culture and for years had only understood quantifiable bottom-line results.

As of mid-2006, Immelt still had several challenges before him. He had to consolidate his position at and put his personal stamp on a company that had been molded to a great extent by a strong and charismatic predecessor. He also had to operate in a difficult economic environment and yet post double-digit growth every year, and he was having to prove time and again that GE had not lost its magic after Welch left.

Notes

1. 2002, The days of Welch and roses, *BusinessWeek Online,* April 29.
2. Ibid.
3. Succession planning to identify Welch's successor had started in 1994, and the final decision was announced in November 2000.
4. The Thomas-Houston Electric Company was founded in 1879 by Elihu Thomson and Edwin J. Houston. It was a competitor to EGEC until the merger of the two companies.
5. Over the years, Crotonville became a major corporate training center. It was also the birthplace of several management techniques, including SWOT analysis, management by objectives (MBO), and strategic planning.
6. Strategic business unit, or SBU, is understood as a business unit within the overall corporate identity, which is distinguishable from other business units because it serves a defined external market where management can conduct strategic planning in relation to products and markets.
7. At that time, raises were standardized at GE and the company did not differentiate between meritorious employees and nonperformers.
8. Noryl was a modified PPO (polyphenyleneoxide)/PS blend resin that offered optimized processing and enhanced productivity for applications of business equipment and communications, and electrical and electronic appliances.
9. The GE matrix, which was based on the BCG Matrix, was developed for GE by McKinsey and Co. The GE matrix cross-referenced market attractiveness and business position using three criteria for each: high, medium, and low. The market attractiveness considered variables relating to the market itself, including the rate of market growth, market size, potential barriers to entering the market, the number and size of competitors, the actual profit margins currently enjoyed, and the technological implications of involvement in the market. The business position criteria looked at the business's strengths and weaknesses in a variety of fields. These assessments included its position in relation to its competitors, and the business's ability to handle product research, development, and ultimate production (http://www.palgrave.com).
10. In reference to the neutron bomb that killed people but left buildings standing (see 2000, The CEO Trap, *BusinessWeek* http://www.businessweek.com December 11.)
11. 2001, Assessing Jack Welch, http://beginnersinvest.about.com, September 10.
12. 1998, How Jack Welch runs GE, *BusinessWeek,* June 8.
13. Motorola was a major manufacturer of mobile phones and communication systems in the early 2000s.
14. AlliedSignal was a major business conglomerate in the 1980s and 1990s, with interests in chemicals, dyes, and aerospace products. The company merged with Honeywell Inc., another technology and manufacturing conglomerate in 1999.
15. 1998, How Jack Welch runs GE, *BusinessWeek,* June 8.
16. Ibid.
17. AT&T's credit card division.
18. 1998, How Jack Welch runs GE, *BusinessWeek,* June 8.
19. 1998, How Jack Welch runs GE, *BusinessWeek,* June 8.
20. A system that allowed a company to have zero working capital by increasing inventory turnover rates.
21. This technique employed "out-of-the-box" thinking and cross-functional teams to remove obstacles to cost reduction.
22. QMI was a system of getting rapid feedback directly from the customer.
23. It was discovered in 1994 that a Kidder & Peabody trader named Joseph Jett had created about $350 million in phantom profits to increase his own bonuses.
24. United Technologies was one of the major manufacturers of building systems and aerospace products. It owned brands such as Carrier (air conditioners), Otis (lifts), Hamilton Sundstrand (engine controls, environmental systems, propellers, and other flight systems), etc.
25. Anthrax, also referred to as splenic fever, is an acute infectious disease caused by the bacteria bacillus anthracis and is highly lethal in some forms. It is therefore used as a weapon in biological warfare. Anthrax most commonly occurs in wild and domestic herbivores, but it can also occur in humans when they are exposed to infected animals, tissue from infected animals, or high concentrations of anthrax spores.
26. Enron Corporation was an energy company based in Houston, Texas. Prior to its bankruptcy in late 2001, Enron employed about 21,000 people and was one of the world's leading electricity, natural gas, pulp and paper, and communications companies, with claimed revenues of $101 billion in 2000. At the end of 2001, it was revealed that its prosperous financial condition was sustained mostly by institutionalized, systematic, and "creatively" planned accounting fraud. The company's European operations filed for bankruptcy on November 30, 2001, and it sought Chapter 11 protection in the United States two days later, on December 2.
27. Tyco was a major conglomerate with interests in electronic components, health care, fire safety, security, and fluid control. The company's CEO Dennis Kozlowski and CFO Mark Swartz were accused of theft of the company's funds in 2002. The case went on trial in 2004, and both men were convicted in 2005.
28. The Standard & Poor's 500 Index was one of the most watched indices of the financials among large firms in the United States.

29. 2004, On the record: Jeffrey Immelt, *The San Francisco Chronicle*, June 6.
30. 2003, Jeff Immelt: We know this world, *BusinessWeek Online*, http://www.businessweek.com, September 15.
31. 2002, The days of Welch and roses, *BusinessWeek*, April 29.
32. Ibid.
33. 2005, The Immelt Revolution, *BusinessWeek*, March 28.
34. 2005, GE begins reorganizing around the customer, http://customer.corante.com, June 23.
35. Greenhouse gases are those components in the atmosphere that contribute to the "greenhouse effect," or global warming. The main natural greenhouse gases are carbon dioxide, water vapor, and ozone.
36. The normal distribution is one of the most important distributions used in probability. It is useful for describing a variety of random processes. A normal distribution is fully described with just two parameters: its mean and standard deviation. The distribution is a continuous, bell-shaped distribution, which is symmetric about its mean and can take on values from negative infinity to positive infinity.

Case 12

The Home Depot

Dan Phillips, Bo Young Hwang, Sarah Sheets, Tristan Longstreth

Arizona State University

Introduction

The succession of CEOs, presidents, and board of directors provides a challenge for businesses as they reform, reposition, and restructure. Although these successions may provide a company with beneficial results, many experience hardship. Top company officials leave due to a variety of reasons, but a common reason is conflict with employees related to executive leadership style and the culture it creates.

Robert Nardelli, former CEO of Home Depot Inc., resigned in January 2007. Numerous factors led to Nardelli's resignation: Shareholders experienced dissatisfaction with the performance of Home Depot's stagnating stock prices; Nardelli's militaristic leadership style and centralized organizational structure affected the performance of employees resulting in excessive layoffs; and the expansion of retail stores became unmanageable. The once successful and highly valued Home Depot culture had changed, affecting Home Depot's sales and customer loyalty. Along with the change in Home Depot's business culture, it faced challenges associated with the dramatic boom and fall in the housing market. These problems affected Home Depot's employee morale, stockholders, and customers. CEO successor Frank Blake has much to address in order to reposition Home Depot as the industry giant it has been for 20 years.

History

Bernie Marcus and Arthur Blank cofounded Home Depot on June 29, 1978, after being fired from Handy Dan, a small chain of home improvement stores. Their vision was to offer "warehouse stores filled from floor to ceiling with a wide assortment of products at the lowest prices" along with superior customer service provided by a knowledgeable staff.[1] This vision became a reality after acquiring sufficient capital from a New York investment banker. They opened two Home Depot stores on June 22, 1979, in the company headquarters, Atlanta, Georgia. Home Depot grew rapidly in a short period of time and went public in 1981. In 1986 Home Depot broke the $1 billion mark in sales with 50 stores that expanded into eight markets.

Home Depot revolutionized the home improvement industry by offering a wide selection of merchandise, low prices, and superior customer service to both the professional contractor as well as the do-it-yourself patron. In-store inventory contains premium products imported from more than 40 countries, including 40,000–50,000 different types of building materials, home improvement supplies, and lawn and garden products. An additional 250,000 products are available upon special order. In addition, merchandise is localized throughout each store to match the area's specific market needs.

Today Home Depot is the largest home improvement retailer in the world.[2] The 2,100 stores located throughout the United States, Canada, China, and Mexico employ roughly 335,000 people. Home Depot also operates 34 EXPO design centers, 11 landscape supply stores, and two floor stores.[3] In addition, Home Depot has become one of the leading diversified wholesale distributors in the United States due to its former HD Supply division. HD Supply Centers caters to the professional contractor for home improvement and municipal infrastructures with nearly 1,000 locations in the United States and Canada.[4]

Marcus and Blank implemented a decentralized structure with an entrepreneurial style of management, which consisted of a laid-back organization known for

The authors would like to thank Professor Robert E. Hoskisson for his support under whose direction the case was developed. The authors do not intend to illustrate either effective or ineffective handling of a managerial situation. The case solely provides material for class discussion. This case was developed with contributions from Kevin Holmberg.

the independence of its store managers.[5] Over time the changes in leadership, structure, and management style diverged from what the originators intended.

Strategic Leaders

Robert L. Nardelli acted as president, CEO, and chairperson of the board from December 2000 until January of 2007. Nardelli received his BS in business from Western Illinois University and earned his MBA from University of Louisville. Nardelli joined General Electric in 1971 as an entry-level manufacturing engineer and by 1995 became president and CEO of GE Power Systems.

After leaving GE he was quickly hired as CEO of Home Depot despite the fact that he lacked any retail experience. From GE he brought a new management strategy based on Six Sigma to Home Depot. Using Six Sigma principles he centralized the management structure of the company by eliminating and consolidating division executives, he initiated processes and streamlined operations, such as the computerized automated inventory system, and centralized supply orders at the Atlanta headquarters. He took the focus off the retail stores, moving beyond the core U.S. big-box business to conquer new markets by building up its Home Depot Supply division, and expanded into China.[6] Under Nardelli, Home Depot's sales over a five-year period went from $45.7 in 2000 to $81.5 billion in 2005,[7] and stock prices stagnated during Nardelli's six-year reign at just over $40 per share.[8] The weak financial profits and his results-driven management style, which allegedly affected the cherished culture of the company, led to a backlash and push for his resignation in January 2007.

Frank Blake succeeded Nardelli as chair and CEO of Home Depot in January of 2007. He earned his bachelor's degree from Harvard College and a jurisprudence degree from Columbia Law School. Blake originally joined the company in 2002 as executive vice president of Business Development and Corporate Operations.[9] His responsibilities included real estate, store construction and maintenance, credit services, strategic business development, special orders and service improvement, call centers, and installation services business. Prior to this role, Blake was deputy secretary for the U.S. Department of Energy and also a former GE executive. Blake also has public sector experience, serving as general counsel for the U.S. Environmental Protection Agency, deputy counsel to Vice President George Bush, and as a law clerk to Justice Stevens of the U.S. Supreme Court.[10] As Home Depot's new leader, Blake faces significant challenges, especially when it comes to rising above competition.

Competition

Competition fuels businesses to be efficient in almost every way. Competition forces companies to control their costs, develop new products, and stay at the forefront of technology. Companies that provide similar services are required to differentiate from the rest of the pack. All of these facets of competition exist in the home improvement industry. Home Depot has more than 25 direct competitors including Lowe's, Menards, True Value, Ace Hardware, Do It Best, Sears, Target, and Wal-Mart.[11] Only a select few pose a true threat to Home Depot.

Lowe's

Lowe's is Home Depot's largest competitor and holds a significant market share. Founded in 1946, Lowe's grew from a small hardware store in North Carolina to the second largest home improvement wholesaler in the world. It currently operates 1,375 stores in 49 states and ranks 42 on the *Fortune* 500 list. Lowe's can attribute its success to a philosophy similar to Home Depot's: "Providing customers with the lowest priced and the highest quality home improvement products."[12] However, Lowe's distinguished itself from Home Depot by targeting the individual customer, especially women, as Home Depot began to focus on contractors. Lowe's will continue to differentiate from competitors by promoting and expanding through exclusive private labels or select brands. Premium kitchen cabinets and stone countertops are a few new product lines that Lowe's is implementing within their stores. Much like Home Depot, Lowe's is looking to expand by pursuing interest in installing services, special orders, and commercial sales.[13]

Menards

Menards is Home Depot's second biggest competitor.[14] Although most competitors construct their stores in a compact fashion in order to adhere to real estate constraints, Menard's is moving ahead with an opposing strategy. The midwestern home center chain has started to build two-story urban stores. "We might be No. 3 as far as store counts go, but we are a regional player and we are innovative," said Menards spokeswoman Dawn Sands. Customers navigate the two-story stores using escalators that accommodate both the customer and their shopping cart. The stores also brag a unique customer experience, including a baby grand piano that provides in-store music, new boutique departments, upscale merchandise, specialty departments, wider aisles, and lower, more convenient merchandise shelves.[15]

Home Depot's competitive position is not only affected by the strategies used by the top two competitors, but also by the relationships it maintains with suppliers.

Suppliers

Home Depot relies on 10,000 to 12,000 suppliers to keep its shelves stocked, creating a tremendous challenge in regard to the process and coordination of the logistics.[16] During the reign of CEO Robert Nardelli, Home Depot expanded at a rapid rate and failed to take the additional supply requirements into consideration,[17]and thus found its brand image in jeopardy when suppliers were unable to keep up with the increased production demands.

When Robert Nardelli became CEO, he inherited a disorganized system of suppliers that relied on archaic accounting practices, including individual product order forms and fax-only lines of communication.[18] Nardelli placed increased emphasis on renovating the Home Depot supplier networks. The first thing he did was to gradually implement the Home Depot Online Supplier Center and the Cognos 8 Scorecarding software. The Center "features continuously updated information on how to do business with Home Depot, including the corporate performance policy, updates, news, information on events and training and scorecards."[19] The Cognos 8 system gathers data from warehouse management sources, purchase orders, and contract terms, and condenses it. The data is then analyzed and each supplier is rated on various aspects of the transaction. All the information is available online via the supplier center, allowing suppliers to see what areas they should improve to become more efficient.[20]

Nardelli also held workshops for specific groups of Home Depot suppliers. For instance, Nardelli hosted meetings with Home Depot's top 15 strategic suppliers four times a year to discuss plans for new products and store promotions. The suppliers toured a Home Depot Store and gave Nardelli input on product placement.[21] Because Home Depot has such a wide variety of suppliers, including suppliers from many different countries, it offers overseas workshops to educate prospective suppliers. The latest workshop took place in Shanghai and was conducted by native speakers in an effort to educate vendors on "how to do business with Home Depot, and be a better supplier overall."[22]

Another area of innovation is Home Depot's inventory and warehousing procedure. Home Depot prefers to receive products directly from their suppliers, eliminating the need for distribution centers, which are popular with many other retail organizations.[23] This system has serious benefits and drawbacks. First, it allows Home Depot to leverage the space it has and display a multitude of products in a warehouse setting. This capability is beneficial because customers are able to see the products available and purchase them in the same visit. The major drawback to this system is that each store must have an extremely efficient and organized warehouse supply chain operation. If a store runs out of a particular item, the customer will have to wait until the supplier can produce more of that item, which can take more time than transporting an out-of-stock item from a distribution center to a local store.[24] Finally, Home Depot has utilized a system of "less than truck load" store deliveries, which allows its trucking partners to carry inventories to Home Depot stores along with products destined for other customers to save on transportation costs. But as Home Depot expands, it may switch to a dedicated trucking system with full truck loads servicing multiple stores in a specific region.[25] Home Depot has developed many innovations to help make transactions with suppliers more efficient. One of Home Depot's biggest challenges is ensuring good interactions with its customer base.

Customers

Although Home Depot was originally designed as a home improvement superstore that would cater to both individual consumers and building contractors, throughout its tumultuous history, Home Depot has changed its focus a number of times. During Nardelli's reign, cost cutting was a key focus and the individual customer was neglected in lieu of professional contractors who purchased materials in bulk amounts. Many long-time Home Depot customers have switched to competitors, mainly Lowe's, because of constant inefficiencies at Home Depot. One customer explained that he had to wait three months to get his kitchen remodeled due to errors on Home Depot's behalf and he will now "go out of [his] way to go to Lowe's."[26] This customer's experience is not unique and new CEO Frank Blake has acknowledged the magnitude of this issue. Home Depot has sold its contractors supply division, which will allow them to resume the focus on the individual customer.[27] Due to the wide range of customers it caters to, Home Depot will likely face significant competition from other firms selling substitute services that match the information provided by Home Depot in the do-it-yourself segment.

Substitute Information Services for Do-It-Yourself Customers

Most companies focus on differentiating their products and services in order to combat rivalry, but also obtain enough loyalty to dissuade customers from switching to a substitute product. Not many substitutes can realistically threaten the success of Home Depot's product sales because they offer such a wide variety of products and people will always need to build houses and desire to improve existing homes. However, Home Depot's services, such as installation, may be hampered by substitutes. Today numerous Internet sites offer "How to" information as well as structured plans for various types of home improvement projects. HGTV and other home improvement shows may also deter customers away from Home Depot's services. One way to fend off threats from rivalry and possible substitutes is for Home Depot to expand its operations internationally.

International Operations

Home Depot is the largest home improvement retailer in the world and employs 335,000 people. In light of the industry trends that are occurring, Home Depot is reaching out to new markets, which may give them additional sources of revenue as well international business experience. Stores are opening in Canada and Mexico. In Canada, Home Depot acquired Canadian hardware store Aikenhead Hardware, and has ambitions to take over its biggest Canadian competitor Rona Hardware.[28] The most recent stage of expansion includes 12 stores in China, called "The Home Way."[29] This foothold in Asia will allow them access to markets that were previously inaccessible.

The Chinese home improvement industry is a refreshing niche market with a lot of potential for new sales for Home Depot. In China, when a consumer purchases a home from a contractor, they purchase an unfinished shell. The house itself is little more than four walls and floor.[30] In order to make the house livable, Chinese consumers must pay contractors, including electricians, plumbers, and drywall experts, to renovate the house. Home Depot plans to provide Chinese consumers with the hardware and skills to do much of the renovation work themselves. In order to meet this goal Home Depot will need to train an army of knowledgeable salespeople who can provide assistance and workshops for consumers.[31] Home Depot will face a number of challenges as they expand into China. It must contend with the bureaucratic communist government that rules China. There are relatively few safeguards against nationalization, if the government decides to appropriate Home Depot assets or property. In addition the Chinese consumers may not have the desire to renovate their homes by themselves. Upper management must decide which method of entry would be most appropriate, and the most effective way to appeal to the average Chinese consumer. In addition, given the recent domestic housing recession, upper management must decide whether expansion into China is the most effective use of the firm's money. Because of the diverse ventures Home Depot is involved in, Nardelli and more recently Frank Blake adopted some basic strategies that can be applied in order to maintain the company's viability.

Strategies Used

As previously mentioned Home Depot historically used a decentralized organizational structure with an entrepreneurial management style, focusing on the retail stores. Store managers were given immense autonomy, and its stores were staffed with well-trained and knowledgeable employees who could offer advice and help customers find items they wanted quickly.[32] Home Depot used to place a huge emphasis on creating a customer-friendly atmosphere with clean aisles, organized shelves, and well-stocked inventory.

However, profit from the retail stores began to decrease as the home improvement retail industry matured and became saturated. Home Depot needed to find its next great idea that would sustain growth. Nardelli believed that the key to Home Depot's success was the acquisition and incorporation of existing business into Home Depot Supply, while simultaneously squeezing efficiencies out of its retail stores.[33]

Home Depot Retail

A critical part of Nardelli's strategy was to reshape Home Depot into a more centralized organization.[34] The centralization effort was evident in the management system that one journalist referred to as a "Command and Control Management system," with a goal to replace the old, sometimes random, management style with a strict one.[35] Management in corporate headquarters started to rank every employee on the basis of four performance metrics: financial, operational, customer, and people skills. Nardelli created an equation to measure effective performance. The equation is $VA = Q \times A \times E$: the value-added (VA) of an employee equals the quality (Q) of what the employee does, multiplied by its acceptance (A) in the company, times how well the employee executes (E) the task.[36]

Influenced by his military background, Nardelli often hired employees who had military experience. Of the 1,142 people who were hired into Home Depot's store leadership program, which consisted of a two-year training program for future store managers, 528 were junior military officers.[37] He also brought many militaristic ideas into managing Home Depot, which required his employees to carry out his "command." Home Depot began to measure everything from gross margin per labor-hour to the number of greets at its front doors to maintain better information, allowing the CEOs to improve control of the Home Depot operation.

However, this lead to many underperforming executives being routinely pushed out of their positions. Since 2001, 56 percent of job changes involved bringing new managers in from outside the company.[38] This hiring trend is quite different from the past, when managers ran Home Depot stores based on the knowledge built through the years of internal experience in Home Depot operations.

In an effort to drive down labor costs, many full-time employees were replaced by part-time employees. But this approach did more than just cut costs; it damaged employee morale, diminished the knowledgeable staff available to customers, and led to many complaints about poor customer service and understaffing. As one customer from San Fernando, California, stated:

The Home Depot at 12960 Foothill Boulevard, San Fernando, California 91342, has virtually no customer service. First I thought I couldn't find any employees to help me because I used to go after work at around 5:00 P.M. Then I tried going during my lunch hour, then during off-work week days. To my surprise, no matter what time I go, there are no present employees out on the floor. The one or two that I've seen are obtained by hassling the cashiers. Try getting help from the guy out in the garden department and he answers with "I don't know, I'm not an expert. They didn't train me." What kind of answer is this, what kind of store is this? The commercials on TV make it almost seem like a mom and pop candy store. You go in and you're by yourself. You need a refrigerator? Tough. There's nobody there to sell it to you. You need a chandelier? Tough—no one in this department to help you. What about the next department? Oh, he replies he knows nothing about the department next door. Customers beware: shop elsewhere.[39]

According to the University of Michigan's annual American Customer Satisfaction Index released on February 21, 2006, with a score of 67, down from 73 in 2004, Home Depot scored 11 points behind Lowe's. Claes Fornell, a professor at University of Michigan, stated that the drop in satisfaction was one reason why Home Depot's stock price has declined at the same time Lowe's has improved.[40]

The general appearance of Home Depot retail stores was becoming a drawback for customers. They often complained that Home Depot had become more like a "warehouse" that was unclean, unorganized, and far from the enjoyable shopping experience it had been in the past.[41] This neglect of the Home Depot's retail stores may have been the result of Nardelli shifting his focus toward new ventures, including Home Depot Supply.

Home Depot Supply

The building supply market during the early 1990s was a growing yet fragmented market segment worth $410 billion per year.[42] Nardelli saw an opportunity to enter this new market because there were few large competitors. To reduce the cannibalization of sales from its existing retail stores, he announced that Home Depot would cut retail store openings by nearly half over a five-year period.[43] Using the money saved from cutting retail store construction, Home Depot spent about $6 billion acquiring more than 25 wholesale suppliers to build up Home Depot Supply (HDS). HDS was a wholesale unit that sold pipes, custom kitchens, and building materials to contractors and municipalities.

Because Home Depot had acquired so many wholesalers, HDS became one of the leaders in the building supply industry. For example, in 2005 Home Depot purchased National Waterworks and entered the municipal water pipe market. Home Depot's biggest purchase was that of the $3.5 billion acquisition of Hughes Supply in 2006, which made Home Depot a leading distributor of electrical and plumbing supplies. HDS expected to have 1,500 supply houses with revenues of $25 billion annually by 2010.[44]

Due to the fragmentation of the building supply market, many contractors were associated with their regional suppliers based on long-standing relationships. Those regional suppliers offered a highly trained sales staff and specialized service, whereas HDS stores worked much like the standard warehouse format.[45] Home Depot was challenged to satisfy a new range of customers' needs, which were different from do-it-yourself customers. Therefore, HDS encouraged its sales employees by rewarding them, primarily in commissions, to win contracts. Furthermore, Home Depot retained most of the management of acquired suppliers, realizing the importance of cultural continuity. Nardelli insisted that top management, salespeople, and internal cultures of the acquired companies maintain their corporate names and colors on stores and delivery trucks.[46] He believed that these efforts would help them keep existing long-term relationships with contractors. HDS was expected to earn 20 percent of the company's overall sales.

As mentioned, when Blake took over as CEO he saw the need to refocus Home Depot's vision and again cater to the retail market. Therefore, in June 2007 Home Depot announced the sale of Home Depot Supply for $10 billion to a group of private equity firms (Brian Capital Partners, Carlyle Group, and Clayton, Dubilier, and Rice).[47] The proceeds from the sale will be used to implement necessary changes in Home Depot such as increased capital spending, upgrading merchandise, and hiring trained and qualified staff and sales associates.[48] The latter is especially important because many employees were beginning to feel dissatisfied with their positions, leading to a dangerously volatile corporate culture.

Corporate Culture

Home Depot's corporate culture has changed drastically as a result of Nardelli's leadership style. Due to Nardelli's military background, many of the changes he implemented were designed to create a more vertically oriented management structure. Originally each Home Depot store enjoyed a sense of autonomy, as each store director was able to set prices and promote products within that store to match the needs of the community in which it was located. Under Nardelli, each executive and store director was responsible for various financial targets, and if these targets were not met, they were immediately terminated. This expectation created a general atmosphere of fear and distrust. Throughout Nardelli's tenure as CEO, 97 percent of top executives were removed and replaced.

To further cut costs, Nardelli implemented a part-time workforce and eliminated many of the full-time employee positions. This trend caused a great deal of resentment from employees who had previously worked full time for Home Depot, because they could no longer receive medical and dental benefits. When the part-time workforce was combined with a management system that only focused on the bottom line, no time was left for taking care of the customer.

The advent of new technology had a big impact on corporate culture, and ultimately customer service. Nardelli believed that by implementing automated checkout lines, customers would be able to pay for their purchases quickly and save time. This innovation would also cut down on employee hours, and checkout personnel would no longer be used. However, this plan backfired when the automated checkout machines malfunctioned more often than they worked correctly, and the few employees who were not laid off as a result of the innovation experienced a significant amount of stress due to having to fix the checkout machines, and answer customer questions at the same time. This frustration was mirrored by customers who were unable to find sales associates when they had specific questions. In addition to significant corporate culture problems, Home Depot's financial statements were beginning to show signs of trouble for the home improvement giant.

Financial Issues

Due to the housing and home improvement boom, sales soared from $46 billion in 2000, the year Nardelli took over, to $81.5 billion in 2005, with an annual average growth rate of 12 percent.[49] The Home Depot's gross margins increased 3.5 percent from 2000 to 35.5 percent in 2005.[50]

For fiscal 2006, net sales were $90.8 billion with earnings of $5.8 billion, an 11.4 percent increase from fiscal 2005. Fiscal 2006 net sales in the retail segment were $79.0 billion, a 2.6 percent increase from 2005, which was driven by the opening of new stores. The Home Depot Supply segment contributed $12.1 billion, an increase of 161.6 percent from 2005. This increase was driven by solid organic growth and sales from acquired businesses.[51] Although Home Depot remains one of the world's largest home improvement retailers in the world, results for fiscal 2006 were disappointing, according to Frank Blake, current chair and CEO.[52] Housing slowdowns have hurt the financial goals for the retail segment of Home Depot. In the third quarter of 2006, same-store sales at Home Depot's 2,127 retail stores declined 5.1 percent.[53]

Economic and current market conditions caused a slowdown in the residential and housing market and an overall market share decline. Analysts do not expect an improvement until late 2007 or early 2008. The company's main focus for fiscal 2007 will be on the retail segment of their business, with total investments of $2.2 billion of capital spending and investments.[54] For Home Depot's income statement, balance sheet, statement of cash flows, and key ratios, see Exhibit 1. For a comparison of January 2006 and January 2007 consolidated statement of earnings, balance sheet, and segment information, see Exhibits 2, 3, and 4, on pages 160, 161, and 162, respectively.

Shareholders

Even though Nardelli was helping Home Depot achieve drastic structural changes, stock prices were affected by the lack of focus of this retail organization. Home Depot's shares were down 7 percent while archrival Lowe's stock prices had soared more than 200 percent since 2000. The poor stock performance led to anger among many of the shareholders.[55] (For a comparison of Home Depot's top competitors and their industry and market, see Exhibit 5, on page 162.)

Investment bankers are currently working on different ways to solve the share price problem such as returning $1.4 billion in cash to shareholders through dividends paid.[56] The company's dividend payout ratio is now approximately 24 percent.[57] In addition, during fiscal year 2006, Home Depot returned cash to shareholders by spending $6.7 billion to repurchase 174 million shares, or 19 percent of its outstanding shares. A stock chart is provided in Exhibit 6, on page 163, which illustrates share prices between March 27, 2006, and March 27, 2007.

Exhibit 1 Highlights of Key Financial Statements and Ratios for Home Depot

Income Statement (in US$ millions, except for per-share items)	01/28/07	01/29/06	01/30/05 Restated 01/29/06	02/01/04 Restated 01/29/06	02/02/03
Net Sales	90,837.00	81,511.00	73,094.00	64,816.00	58,247.00
Cost of Goods Sold	29,783.00	27,320.00	24,430.00	20,580.00	18,108.00
Income Before Tax	9,308.00	9,282.00	7,912.00	6,843.00	5,872.00
Net Income	5,761.00	5,838.00	5,001.00	4,304.00	3,664.00

Balance Sheet	01/28/07	01/29/06 Restated 01/28/07	01/30/05 Restated 01/29/06	02/01/04 Restated 01/30/05	02/02/03
Assets					
Total Current Assets	$18,000.00	$15,269.00	$14,273.00	$13,328.00	$11,917.00
Net PP&E	26,605.00	24,901.00	22,726.00	20,063.00	17,168.00
Total Assets	52,263.00	44,405.00	39,020.00	34,437.00	30,011.00
Liabilities and Shareholders' Equity					
Total Current Liabilities	$12,931.00	$12,706.00	$10,455.00	$ 9,554.00	$ 8,035.00
Long-Term Debt	11,643.00	2,672.00	2,148.00	856.00	1,321.00
Total Liabilities	27,233.00	17,496.00	14,862.00	12,030.00	10,209.00
Total Shareholders Equity	25,030.00	26,909.00	24,158.00	22,407.00	19,802.00
Total Liabilities & Shareholders Equity	52,263.00	44,405.00	39,020.00	34,437.00	30,011.00

Cash Flow Statement	01/29/06	01/30/05	02/01/04 Restated 01/30/05	02/02/03 Restated 01/30/05	02/03/02
Net Cash Flows from Operations	$ 6,484.00	$ 6,904.00	$ 6,545.00	$ 4,802.00	$ 5,963.00
Net Cash Flows from Investing	(4,586.00)	(4,479.00)	(4,171.00)	(2,601.00)	(3,466.00)
Net Cash Flows from Financing	(1,612.00)	(3,055.00)	(1,931.00)	(2,165.00)	(173.00)

Key Ratios	As of 03/26/07
Price/Earnings (TTM)	$13.64
Annual Dividend	.90
Annual Yield %	2.36
Quick Ratio (MRQ)	.40
Current Ratio (MRQ)	1.39
Return on Equity (TTM)	16.22
Return on Assets (TTM)	11.92
Return on Investment (TTM)	16.22

Data provided by Marketguide. Shareholder.com, the producer of this site, and The Home Depot, Inc. do not guarantee the accuracy of the information provided on this page, and will not be held liable for consequential damages arising from the use of this information.

Source: Home Depot, 2007, http://ir.homedepot.com/summary_financials.cfm.

Exhibit 2 Statement of Earnings for Home Depot

THE HOME DEPOT, INC. AND SUBSIDIARIES
CONSOLIDATED STATEMENTS OF EARNINGS
FOR THE THREE MONTHS AND YEARS ENDED JANUARY 28, 2007 AND JANUARY 29, 2006

(Unaudited)
(Amounts in Millions Except Per Share Data and as Otherwise Noted)

	Three Months Ended		% Increase (Decrease)	Years Ended		% Increase (Decrease)
	1-28-07	1-29-06		1-28-07	1-29-06	
NET SALES	$20,265	$19,489	4.0 %	$90,837	$81,511	11.4 %
Cost of Sales	13,627	12,896	5.7	61,054	54,191	12.7
GROSS PROFIT	6,638	6,593	0.7	29,783	27,320	9.0
Operating Expenses:						
Selling, General and Administrative	4,594	4,132	11.2	18,348	16,485	11.3
Depreciation and Amortization	442	413	7.0	1,762	1,472	19.7
Total Operating Expenses	5,036	4,545	10.8	20,110	17,957	12.0
OPERATING INCOME	1,602	2,048	(21.8)	9,673	9,363	3.3
Interest Income (Expense):						
Interest and Investment Income	4	8	(50.0)	27	62	(56.5)
Interest Expense	(127)	(35)	262.9	(392)	(143)	174.1
Interest, net	(123)	(27)	355.6	(365)	(81)	350.6
EARNINGS BEFORE PROVISION FOR INCOME TAXES	1,479	2,021	(26.8)	9,308	9,282	0.3
Provision for Income Taxes	554	736	(24.7)	3,547	3,444	3.0
NET EARNINGS	$ 925	$ 1,285	(28.0)%	$ 5,761	$ 5,838	(1.3)%
Weighted Average Common Shares	1,993	2,119	(5.9)%	2,054	2,138	(3.9)%
BASIC EARNINGS PER SHARE	$0.46	$0.61	(24.6)%	$2.80	$2.73	2.6%
Diluted Weighted Average Common Shares	2,004	2,128	(5.8)%	2,062	2,147	(4.0)%
DILUTED EARNINGS PER SHARE	$0.46	$0.60	(23.3)%	$2.79	$2.72	2.6%

SELECTED HIGHLIGHTS

	Three Months Ended		% Increase (Decrease)	Years Ended		% Increase (Decrease)
	1-28-07	1-29-06		1-28-07	1-29-06	
Number of Customer Transactions (1)	304	308	(1.3)%	1,330	1,330	– %
Average Ticket (1)	$56.27	$57.20	(1.6)	$58.90	$57.98	1.6
Weighted Average Weekly Sales per Operating Store (000's) (1)	$617	$676	(8.7)	$723	$763	(5.2)
Square Footage at End of Period (1)	224	215	4.2	224	215	4.2
Capital Expenditures	$1,032	$1,028	0.4	$3,542	$3,881	(8.7)
Depreciation and Amortization (2)	$476	$445	7.0%	$1,886	$1,579	19.4%

(1) Includes retail segment only.
(2) Includes depreciation of distribution centers and tool rental equipment included in Cost of Sales and amortization of deferred financing costs included in Interest Expense.
Source: Home Depot, 2007, http://www.homedepot.com.

Exhibit 3 Consolidated Balance Sheets for Home Depot

THE HOME DEPOT, INC. AND SUBSIDIARIES
CONSOLIDATED BALANCE SHEETS
AS OF JANUARY 28, 2007 AND JANUARY 29, 2006
(Amounts in Millions)

	1-28-07 (Unaudited)	1-29-06 (Audited)
ASSETS		
Cash and Short-Term Investments	$ 614	$ 807
Receivables, net	3,223	2,396
Merchandise Inventories	12,822	11,401
Other Current Assets	1,341	665
Total Current Assets	18,000	15,269
Property and Equipment, net	26,605	24,901
Goodwill	6,314	3,286
Other Assets	1,344	949
TOTAL ASSETS	$52,263	$44,405
LIABILITIES AND STOCKHOLDERS' EQUITY		
Short-Term Debt	$ –	$ 900
Accounts Payable	7,356	6,032
Accrued Salaries and Related Expenses	1,295	1,068
Current Installments of Long-Term Debt	18	513
Other Current Liabilities	4,262	4,193
Total Current Liabilities	12,931	12,706
Long-Term Debt	11,643	2,672
Other Long-Term Liabilities	2,659	2,118
Total Liabilities	27,233	17,496
Total Stockholders' Equity	25,030	26,909
TOTAL LIABILITIES AND STOCKHOLDERS' EQUITY	$52,263	$44,405

Source: Home Depot, 2007, http://www.homedepot.com.

What Should Happen to Improve Home Depot?

Home Depot has been plagued by many problems in its recent history. Robert Nardelli's strategic approach of focusing on suppliers and improving efficiency demoralized much of the human capital in its retail business, and as a result seemingly reduced the effectiveness of Home Depot's cherished organizational culture. The approach left employees afraid of their own executives, which forced them to focus on maintaining their current positions through hyperefficiency and in effect to fall short in customer service. This bottom-line thinking had drastic implications for Home Depot's customer base as more customers left Home Depot to shop at other stores such as Lowe's and Wal-Mart to meet their home improvement needs. In addition, a cyclical market and international expansion are issues that will need to be addressed. Frank Blake as the new CEO faces the monumental task of making the home improvement giant profitable again and restructuring to repair the damaged aspects of the corporation. With Blake in command, Home Depot has a good chance of leveraging its core competencies in the retail market and becoming an excellent corporation for customers and shareholders. Shareholders and employees alike anxiously await the future to see what lies in store for Home Depot.

Exhibit 4 Segment Financial Information for Home Depot

THE HOME DEPOT, INC. AND SUBSIDIARIES
SEGMENT INFORMATION
FOR THE YEARS ENDED JANUARY 28, 2007, AND JANUARY 29, 2006
(Unaudited)
(amounts in $ millions)

Year Ended January 28, 2007

	HD Retail (a)	HD Supply	Eliminations/ Other (b)	Consolidated
Net Sales	$79,027	$12,070	$(260)	$90,837
Operating Income	9,024	800	(151)	9,673
Depreciation and Amortization	1,679	197	10	1,886
Total Assets	42,094	10,021	148	52,263
Capital Expenditures	3,321	221		3,542
Payments for Businesses Acquired, net	305	3,963	–	4,268

Year Ended January 29, 2006

	HD Retail (a)	HD Supply	Eliminations/ Other (b)	Consolidated
Net Sales	$77,022	$4,614	$(125)	$81,511
Operating Income	9,058	319	(14)	9,363
Depreciation and Amortization	1,510	63	6	1,579
Total Assets	39,827	4,517	61	44,405
Capital Expenditures	3,777	104	–	3,881
Payments for Businesses Acquired, net	190	2,356	–	2,546

(a) Includes all retail stores, Home Depot Direct and retail installation services.

(b) Includes elimination of intersegment sales and unallocated corporate overhead. Operating Income for the year ended January 28, 2007, includes $129 million of cost associated with executive severance and separation agreements.

Source: Home Depot, 2007, http://www.homedepot.com.

Exhibit 5 Industry Statistics and Comparisons

	Home Depot	Lowe's	Menard	True Value
Annual Sales	$81,511	$43,243	$6,500	$2,043
Employees	345,000	185,000	35,000	2,800
Market Cap ($ millions)	$77,488	$48,852.8	0	0

Comparison of Home Depot to Industry and Stock Market

Valuation	Company	Industry[1]	Stock Market[2]
Price/Sales Ratio	0.83	0.83	2.22
Price/Earnings Ratio	12.51	12.51	18.98
Price/Book Ratio	2.70	2.93	2.16
Price/Cash Flow Ratio	12.02	12.02	13.44

[1]**Industry:** Building Materials, Hardware, Garden Supply, and Mobile Home Dealers

[2]**Market:** Public companies trading on the NYSE, AMEX, and NASDAQ

Source: © 2007, Hoover's, Inc., All Rights Reserved, http://www.hoovers.com/home-depot/—ID__11470,ticker__—/free-co-fin-factsheet.xhtml.

Exhibit 6 Home Depot Stock Chart

Source: Home Depot, Inc. (HD), http://moneycentral.msn.com/stock_quote?Symbol=HD.

Notes

1. 2007, Home Depot, http://corporate.homedepot.com/wps/portal, March 28.
2. Ibid.
3. Ibid.
4. Ibid.
5. R. Farzad, D. Foust, B. Grow, E. Javers, E. Thornton, & R. Zegel, 2007, Out at Home Depot, *BusinessWeek*, http://www.businessweek.com, January 15.
6. Ibid
7. 2007, Home Depot, http://ir.homedepot.com/releaseDetail.cfm?ReleaseID=194738&ShSect=E, July 3.
8. Ibid.
9. 2007, Home Depot, http://corporate.homedepot.com/wps/portal, March 28.
10. Ibid.
11. 2007, http://www.hoovers.com, April 1.
12. 2007, Lowe's , http://www.Lowe's.com, April 1.
13. D. Howell, 2005, Lowe's hammers home growth objective: National in a year, http://findarticles.com/p/articles/mi_m0FNP/is_6_44/ai_n13726491.
14. 2007, HD: Competitors for Home Depot, *Yahoo! Finance*, July 10.
15. Ibid.
16. R. Bowman, 2006, Home Depot turns its attention to supplier performance management, *Global Logistics & Supply Chain Strategies*, http://www.glscs.com/archives/06.06.casestudy.htm?adcode=5, June.
17. Ibid.
18. Ibid.
19. Ibid.
20. Ibid.
21. Ibid.
22. Ibid.
23. R. Bowman, 2001, Global supply chain partnerships, *Global Logistics & Supply Chain Strategies*, http://www.glscs.com/archives/7.02.homedepot.htm?adcode=5, July.
24. Ibid.
25. Ibid.
26. B. Grow & S. McMillan, 2006, Home Depot: Last among shoppers, *BusinessWeek Online*, http://www.businessweek.com, June 19.
27. H. Weber, 2007, Home Depot undecided on supply business, *BusinessWeek Online*, http://www.businessweek.com, March 22.
28. 2007, Home Depot, http://en.wikipedia.org/wiki/Home_depot, accessed on April 17.
29. Ibid.
30. B. Grow & F. Balfour, 2006, Home Depot: One foot in China, *BusinessWeek Online*, http://www.businessweek.com, May 1.
31. Ibid.
32. D. Brady & B. Grow, 2006, Renovating Home Depot, *BusinessWeek*, http://www.businessweek.com, March 6, 50–56.
33. Ibid.
34. Ibid.
35. Ibid.
36. R. Farzad, D. Foust, B. Grow, E. Javers, E. Thornton, & R. Zegel, 2007, Out at Home Depot.
37. D. Brady & B. Grow, Renovating Home Depot.
38. Ibid.
39. 2004, http://www.complaints.com/directory/2004/june/14/15.htm.
40. D. Brady & B. Grow, Renovating Home Depot.
41. H. Weber, 2006, Home Depot needs makeover, *Washington Post*, http://www.washingtonpost.com, January 6.
42. 2006, Home Depot will buy building supply chain, *Winston-Salem Journal*, http://www.journalnow.com/servlet/Satellite?pagename=WSJ%2FMGArticle%2FWSJ_BasicArticle&c=MGArticle&cid=1128769238504&path=!business&s=1037645507703%20, January 11.
43. C. Terhune, 2006, Home Depot knocks on contractors' doors, *Wall Street Journal*, August 7.
44. P. Bond, 2006, Commercial wholesale division doubles Home Depot's supply business, *The Atlanta Journal-Constitution*, August 6.
45. C. Terhune, 2007, Home Depot knocks on contractors' doors, *Wall Street Journal Online*, http://online.wsj.com/article/SB115491714152328447.html, July 13.
46. Ibid.
47. M. Flaherty & K. Jacobs, 2007, Bids for Home Depot Supply due Friday, *BNET Today*, http://www.bnet.com/2407-13071_23-88489.html, July 5.
48. Ibid.
49. D. Brady & B. Grow, Renovating Home Depot.
50. Ibid.
51. Home Depot, 2007, The Home Depot announces fourth quarter and fiscal 2006 results, http://ir.homedepot.com, February 20.
52. Home Depot, 2007, The Home Depot announces fourth quarter dividend, http://ir.homedepot.com, February 22.
53. R. Farzad, D. Foust, B. Grow, E. Javers, E. Thornton, & R. Zegel, 2007, Out at Home Depot.
54. Home Depot, 2007, The Home Depot presents 2007 key priorities and financial outlook, http://ir.homedepot.com,February 28.
55. D. Brady & B. Grow, Renovating Home Depot.
56. Home Depot, 2007, The Home Depot announces fourth quarter dividend, http://irhomedepot.com, February 22.
57. Ibid.

Case 13

China's Home Improvement Market: Should Home Depot Enter or Will it Have a Late-Mover (Dis)advantage?

R. Muthu Kumar, Nagendra Chowdary

ICFAI University

China, the fastest-growing economy in the world, is witnessing rapid growth in the private housing market after its introduction of housing reforms in 1998. As the Chinese people's income and purchasing power increases, their property investment is also on the rise. In 2005, real estate investment accounted for 8.65 percent of China's GDP and it is expected to rise to 9.3 percent in 2006.[1] As a result, the total value of property under construction in 2005 was RMB 5.1 trillion ($637.42 billion), contributing to 28 percent of China's GDP.[2] Consequently, China's home improvement market also projected great potential for growth. Many foreign home improvement retailers such as B&Q and IKEA have established their strong presence along with the domestic home improvement players.

"The home improvement market on the mainland is the most promising in the world: $50 billion in sales in 2005 and growing at 12% a year. Homeownership has skyrocketed, from near zero two decades ago, when there was virtually no private property, to 70% of all housing today," *BusinessWeek* reported.[3] However, China's home improvement market is not that easy to navigate although the potential is highly tempting.

U.S.-based Home Depot has not yet started its operations in China and its "China Strategy" is in progress. Some think it missed the bus by not being an early entrant and therefore will suffer from late mover disadvantage. Others think the delay will help shorten its learning curve and it will rise rapidly.

China's Economy and Real Estate

China is the second-largest economy in the world (see Exhibit 1) when measured by Purchasing Power Parity, with a GDP (PPP) of $9.412 trillion in 2005. When measured in USD-exchange rate terms, it is the fourth largest in 2005 (Exhibit 1) with $2.25 trillion. It is the world's fastest-growing major economy with a population of 1.3 billion (see Exhibit 2). Its per capita GDP was $1,703 in 2005 and varied for each region in China (see Exhibit 3, on page 167).

Economic Growth

China's economic evolution happened over a period of four generations (see Exhibit 4, on page 167). To speed up the industrialization process, the central government invested heavily in the 1960s and 1970s. A large share of the country's economic output was controlled by the government, which set production goals, controlled prices, and allocated resources. As a result, by 1978 nearly three-fourths of industrial production was manufactured by state-owned enterprises based on centrally planned output targets. The central government's major goal was to make China's economy self-sufficient. Foreign trade was restricted to obtain only those goods that could not be manufactured in China. Only countries that maintained diplomatic relations with China could participate in foreign trade. Though China's real GDP grew at an average annual rate of 5.3 percent from 1960 to 1978, the economy was almost inactive due to the huge population base and lack of competition. In addition, the economy was inefficient because of the few profit incentives for enterprises and workers. Price and production controls also caused widespread distortions in China's economy.[4]

Since 1978, the government had been devising strategies to shift from a centrally planned economy to a more market-oriented economy. China's economic development had occurred in two phases. The first phase began in 1979,

Exhibit 1 World Economies GDP Rankings

List of Countries by GDP (PPP)			List of Countries by GDP (Nominal)			Economy of China: 2005 Statistics	
Rank	Country	GDP (in $ billion)	Rank	Country	GDP (in $ billion)		
1	United States	12277.583	1	United States	12485.725	GDP (Nominal) Ranking	4
2	**China**	**9412.361**	2	Japan	4571.314	GDP (PPP) Ranking	2
3	Japan	3910.728	3	Germany	2797.343	GDP (Nominal)	$2.22 trillion
4	India	3633.441	**4**	**China**	**2224.811**	GDP (PPP)	$9.412 trillion
5	Germany	2521.699	5	United Kingdom	2201.473	GDP per capita	$1,703
6	United Kingdom	1832.792	6	France	2105.864	GDP per capita (PPP)	$6,200
7	France	1830.11	7	Italy	1766.16	GDP growth rate	9.90%
8	Italy	1668.151	8	Canada	1130.208		
9	Brazil	1576.728	9	Spain	1126.565		
10	Russia	1575.561	10	Korea	793.07		

Source: Compiled from "International Monetary Fund, World Economic Outlook Database," http://www.imf.org/external/pubs/ft/weo/2006/01/data/dbcoutm.cfm? April 2006.

Exhibit 2 Population of China (2000–2004)

	2000	2001	2002	2003	2004
Male	654.4	656.7	661.1	665.6	669.8
Female	613.1	619.6	623.4	626.7	630.1
Total (million)	**1,267.4**	**1,276.3**	**1,284.5**	**1,292.3**	**1,299.9**
% change, year on year	0.8	0.7	0.6	0.6	0.6
Urban (million)	459.1	480.6	502.1	532.8	542.8
% of total	36.2	37.7	39.1	40.5	41.7
Rural (million)	808.4	795.6	782.4	768.5	757.1
% of total	63.8	62.3	60.9	59.5	58.2

Source: "Country Profile 2006," http://www.eiu.com.

when the then Chairman Deng Xiaoping launched a series of reforms, including decollectivization of agriculture and a return to household farming.

In the 1980s, China tried to combine central planning with market-oriented reforms to increase productivity, living standards, and technological quality without exacerbating inflation, unemployment, and budget deficits. The country pursued agricultural reforms, dismantling the commune system and introducing household farming that authorized peasants with greater decision-making powers in agricultural activities. The government also encouraged non-agricultural activities, such as setting up of village enterprises in rural areas, promoting more self-management of state-owned enterprises, and increasing competition in the marketplace.

These reforms led to average annual rates of growth of 10 percent in agricultural and industrial output. Rural per capita real income doubled. Industry posted major gains especially in coastal areas, where foreign investment helped drive output of both domestic and export goods. However, beginning in 1985, agricultural output witnessed a steady decline due to subsidy cuts and rising costs of inputs.

From the 1990s, during the second phase of China's growth, as the country further opened up, many foreign companies began entering China. China's economy boomed in the early 1990s. During 1993, output and prices were accelerating, and economic expansion was fueled by the introduction of more than 2,000 special economic zones (SEZs) and the influx of foreign capital that the SEZs facilitated. But the economy slowed down in the late 1990s, influenced in part by the Asian Financial Crisis of 1998–1999. Economic growth fell from 13.6 percent in 1992 to 7.1 percent in 1999 (see Exhibit 5, on page 168). From 1995 to 1999 inflation dropped sharply, reflecting the tighter monetary policy of central banks and stronger measures to control food prices.

However, the average annual growth rate of China's GDP through 2001 had been 8.9 percent since its economic

Exhibit 3 China GDP per Person by Province, 2005

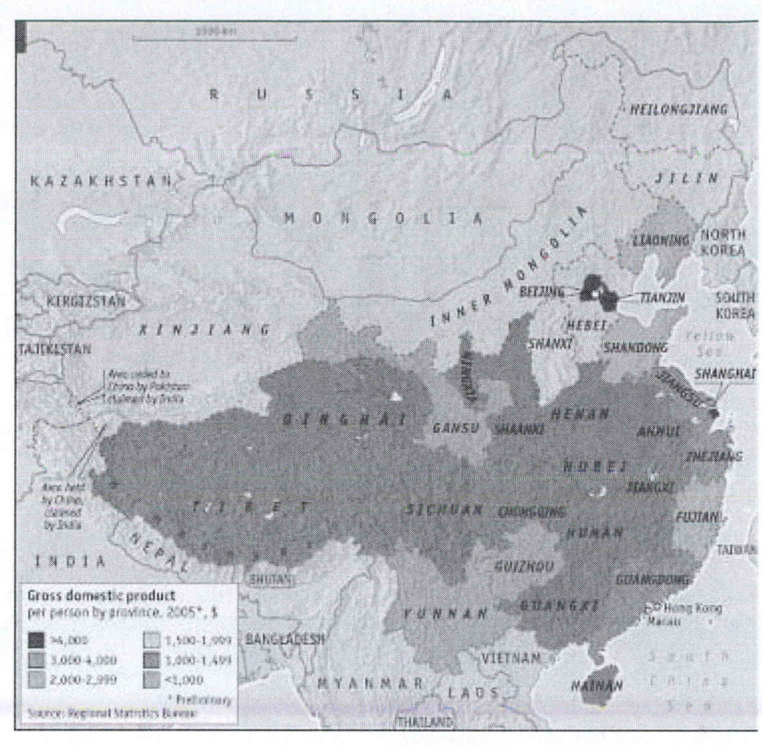

Source: "Coming out," http://www.economist.com/surveys/displaystory.cfm?story_id=5623226, March 23, 2006.

Exhibit 4 Four Generations of China's Economic Growth

Mao Era, 1949–1976

After the Communist victory in 1949, China had a strong central government for the first time since the fall of the Qing dynasty in 1911. But a succession of political campaigns, including the Great Leap Forward and the Cultural Revolution, brought famine and upheaval. Agriculture was collectivized and industry nationalized. Economic growth suffered. China largely cut itself off from the world, and relations with the United States were hostile until President Richard Nixon's 1972 visit.

Deng Era, 1978–1990s

Deng Xiaoping launched his famous economic reforms in 1978, which led to the flourishing of private enterprise in the 1980s. U.S.-China ties blossomed following the normalization of relations in 1979 and amid mutual distrust of the Soviet Union. Killings of pro-democracy Tiananmen protesters in 1989 tarnished Deng's legacy, bruised ties with the United States, and slowed reform. But Deng's 1992 call for faster reforms reignited economic growth.

Jiang Era, 1990s–2002

Catapulted from relative obscurity, Jiang consolidated his power as Deng's influence waned in the years before his death in 1997. Jiang jettisoned Marxist ideology and fostered the shift to a market-oriented economy. He expanded social freedoms for the urban elite and curbed military clout. His attempts to make the state sector more competitive and clean up the financial sector were less successful. In 2002, he oversaw China's entry into the World Trade Organization.

Fourth Generation, 2003–

Lacking revolutionary experience, this generation is the best-educated to date. Hu Jintao may be president, but no one leader will dominate, and consensus will be the rule. On the economic front, the leadership will likely focus on reforming agriculture, state-owned enterprises, and the financial sector. There is disagreement between those who favor maintaining an authoritarian approach and those who insist economic reform must be accompanied by limited democracy.

Source: Roberts Dexter and Clifford Mark L., "China's Power Shift," http://www.businessweek.com/magazine/content/02_08/b3771018.htm, February 25, 2002.

Exhibit 5 China's GDP Percentage

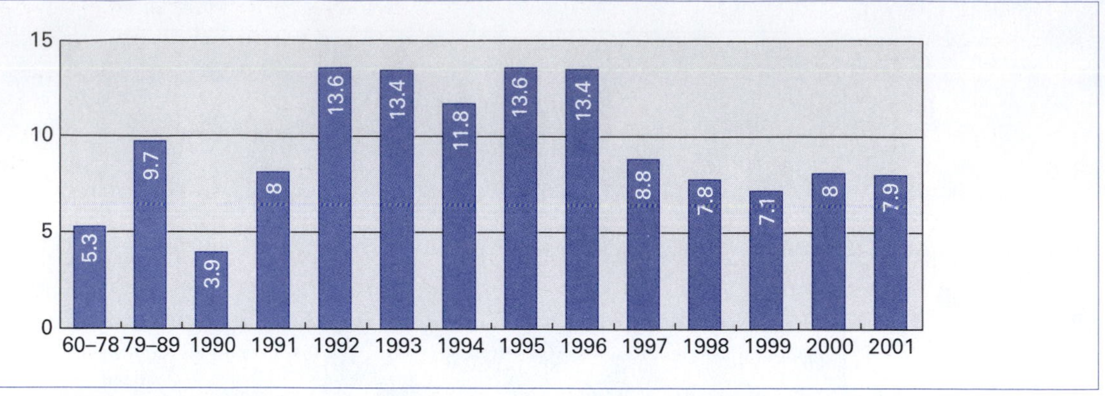

Source: Ye Xiannian, "China Real Estate Market—Economic Development," http://www.china-window.com/china_market/china_real_estate/china-real-estate-market-2.shtml, August 20, 2004.

Exhibit 6 China's GDP and the Percentage Share of GDP in Total GDP for the Three Areas (1978–2001)

		Eastern Area		Central Area		Western Area	
	National GDP (million yuan)	GDP (million yuan)	%	GDP (million yuan)	%	GDP (million yuan)	%
1978	346,354	181,832	52.5	106,466	30.7	58,056	16.8
1979	394,275	203,873	51.7	123,687	31.4	66,715	16.9
1980	439,596	229,585	52.2	136,908	31.1	73,103	16.6
1981	479,347	250,961	52.4	151,041	31.5	77,345	16.1
1982	533,108	279,868	52.5	166,131	31.2	87,109	16.3
1983	595,085	311,019	52.0	189,495	31.7	97,571	16.3
1984	712,537	373,412	52.4	223,875	31.4	115,250	16.2
1985	862,066	455,246	52.8	267,538	31.0	139,282	16.2
1986	965,648	511,314	53.0	300,087	31.1	154,247	16.0
1987	1,144,177	612,845	53.6	352,365	30.8	178,967	15.6
1988	1,445,266	786,501	54.4	434,060	30.0	224,705	15.5
1989	1,635,691	895,790	54.8	489,251	29.9	250,650	15.3
1990	1,833,023	989,966	54.0	547,920	29.9	295,137	16.1
1991	2,110,312	1,164,293	55.2	605,130	28.7	340,889	16.2
1992	2,584,738	1,459,328	56.5	725,345	28.1	400,065	15.5
1993	3,422,001	1,981,049	57.9	931,780	27.2	509,172	14.9
1994	4,521,683	2,652,547	58.7	1,212,823	26.8	656,313	14.5
1995	5,763,278	3,361,540	58.3	1,586,764	27.5	814,974	14.1
1996	6,730,552	3,970,377	59.0	1,916,757	28.5	843,418	12.5
1997	7,547,520	4,445,350	58.9	2,164,300	28.7	937,870	12.4
1998	8,106,540	4,807,090	59.3	2,287,150	28.2	1,012,300	12.5
1999	8,619,170	5,156,430	59.8	2,397,450	27.8	1,065,290	12.4
2000	9,527,990	5,752,720	60.4	2,625,020	27.6	1,150,250	12.1
2001	10,501,650	6,362,436	60.6	2,867,045	27.3	1,272,169	12.1

Source: Zhang Wei, "Can the Strategy of Western Development Narrow Down China's Regional Disparity," *Asia Economic Paper*, 2005, 3.

reforms. The pace of GDP growth in different regions was uneven due to variation in their incomes. Based on geographical location and government regulations, China can be divided into three areas—eastern coastal, central and western. The average growth rate of GDP in these areas during 1978–2001 were 10.2 percent, 9.08 percent, and 8.19 percent, respectively. The GDP share of eastern area in the total national GDP increased from 52 percent to 60 percent, while the other two areas' share decreased (see Exhibit 6).

Between 1978 and 2001, the ratio of GDP per capita in the eastern area to the average GDP per capita nationwide increased from 1.28 to 1.42, while for the other areas it decreased (see Exhibit 7).

In addition, economic inequalities between rural and urban regions were high in China. From 1994, a steep rise in unemployment had turned many rural farmers into absolute economic losers. Meanwhile, the inflow of foreign direct investment and the rise of industrial joint ventures had increased the urban-rural disparity. China's levels of inequality surpassed that of Eastern European transition economies, Western European industrialized nations, and other Asian developing nations such as India, Pakistan, and Indonesia. Since the inception of reforms in 1978, the disparities had witnessed a cyclical pattern (Appendixes I(a) and I(b)) that was attributed to urban-biased industrial development strategy over agricultural development. Since the reforms, the politically powerful urban population had pressured the government for fast income growth. As a result, the government followed an urban bias in order to preserve regime stability and political legitimacy.

The people's response to such urban-based policies has been rural social unrest and mass migration to cities in

Exhibit 7 China's GDP per Capita and the Ratio of GDP per Capita to National GDP per Capita for the Three Areas, 1978–2001

		Eastern Area		Central Area		Western Area	
	National GDP per Capita (yuan)	GDP per Capita (yuan)	R*	GDP per Capita (yuan)	R*	GDP per Capita (yuan)	R*
1978	361.4	462.2	1.28	311.0	0.86	260.7	0.72
1979	406.0	511.3	1.26	356.1	0.88	296.3	0.73
1980	447.4	569.0	1.27	389.2	0.87	321.5	0.72
1981	481.1	612.6	1.27	423.8	0.88	335.8	0.70
1982	527.1	672.4	1.28	459.3	0.87	373.1	0.71
1983	585.0	739.0	1.26	517.9	0.89	414.1	0.71
1984	689.6	877.4	1.27	604.8	0.88	485.1	0.70
1985	824.9	1,058.0	1.28	714.2	0.87	580.1	0.70
1986	911.3	1,172.0	1.29	790.2	0.87	633.1	0.69
1987	1,063.5	1,383.3	1.30	913.9	0.86	723.8	0.68
1988	1,322.7	1,750.1	1.32	1,107.2	0.84	894.4	0.68
1989	1,474.8	1,965.8	1.33	1,227.4	0.83	983.8	0.67
1990	1,611.0	2,104.0	1.31	1,345.7	0.84	1,134.6	0.70
1991	1,835.2	2,451.8	1.34	1,468.4	0.80	1,296.5	0.71
1992	2,225.2	3,042.4	1.37	1,741.7	0.78	1,507.3	0.68
1993	2,918.3	4,093.2	1.40	2,215.2	0.76	1,899.9	0.65
1994	3,819.3	5,436.9	1.42	2,854.0	0.75	2,421.3	0.63
1995	4,816.3	6,812.0	1.41	3,698.7	0.77	2,972.9	0.62
1996	5,548.9	7,946.8	1.43	4,421.2	0.80	3,014.5	0.54
1997	6,327.6	8,821.9	1.39	4,952.2	0.78	3,723.8	0.59
1998	6,743.0	9,474.2	1.41	5,194.2	0.77	3,977.6	0.59
1999	7,114.8	10,089.5	1.42	5,406.8	0.76	4,145.7	0.58
2000	7,737.7	10,728.3	1.39	5,974.1	0.77	4,497.4	0.58
2001	8,490.6	12,070.6	1.42	6,400.9	0.75	4,858.4	0.57

*R is the ratio of the GDP per capita for a given area to the national GDP per capita.

Source: Zhang Wei, "Can the Strategy of Western Development Narrow Down China's Regional Disparity," *Asia Economic Paper*, 2005, 4.

search of jobs. Many other countries including the United States had faced similar dilemmas of human displacement in the course of their development. The significant urban-rural income disparity led to massive rural-to-urban migration. Numbers of migrants peaked during the planting and harvesting seasons, desperate for jobs.

As China joined the WTO in 2001, the import quotas, subsidies, and tariffs that had traditionally protected Chinese agriculture disappeared. Some experts commented that entry into WTO would further exacerbate the issues of unemployment and inequality. But the Chinese government hoped that the WTO membership would induce more foreign investment and much-needed technology that would sustain long-term growth and would reduce the income disparity and unemployment rates. GDP growth accelerated again in early 2000s, reaching 9.3 percent in 2003, 9.4 percent in 2004, and 9.8 percent in 2005 (see Exhibits 8 (a) and 8 (b)).

In 2005, China's GDP grew by 9.8 percent. China's economy is expected to grow further with an increase in trade and the expected huge investment for the 2008 Olympics. Industry observers said that high GDP growth is coming at the expense of a gaping chasm between the rich and the poor.[5] Joe O'Mara, partner in-charge of KPMG's North America's China practice said, "It's one of the fastest-growing economies with 1.3 billion people. There is a growing middle class—over the last 20 years, per capita income has ballooned more than 700 percent."[6]

Real Estate

After the founding of People's Republic of China in 1949, the first Chairman Mao Zedong (Mao) seized land from private landowners (killing thousands of them in the process) and redistributed it to peasants.[7] To facilitate the mobilization of agricultural resources, improve the efficiency of farming, and increase government access to agricultural products in the 1950s, private land ownership was eliminated. Mao took the land away from them and put it under the "collective" ownership of communes. Peasants had become property-less members of "People's Communes."[8] Private ownership of housing in the urban areas was nearly extinguished.

The communes were dismantled in the early 1980s, a few years after Mao's death. Peasants were allocated land for farming, but ownership remained collective. Under Deng Xiaoping, agricultural production soared for the first time as peasants were allocated (but not given full ownership of) plots of land to farm independently, and marked the start of the economic transformation in the rural areas.

Since the 1990s, leases of 30 years had been granted for these tiny plots, but the peasants were not allowed to use the land as collateral for loans or to sell it. They could rent it out, but this arrangement often involved paying a fee to the village administration.

So whereas trade in land and property had become an important engine of growth in urban China (where residential leases run for 70 years and others for 40 or 50), farmers had been far removed from the effects of this boom. When land was seized, peasants were compensated for its agricultural value, which averaged about one-tenth of its market value. Out of that village administration took a cut, and so the amount received by the peasants was far less. However, in the cities, the privatization of housing since the late 1990s had created a middle class that was utilizing its property as collateral to borrow. Trading in property had become a huge source of urban wealth.

The government was alarmed that creating a free market in rural land would prompt peasants to sell their holdings to pay their debts. As a result a flood of landless farmers fled to cities that had no social security infrastructure to deal with the influx. In order for rural land reform to work, fiscal transfers from the center to the provinces required fairer reforms. This required considerable political

Exhibit 8 (a) China's Gross Domestic Product (at market prices), 2000–2004

	2000	2001	2002	2003	2004
Total (US$ bn)					
At current prices	1,080	1,159	1,304	1,471	1,720
Total (Rmb bn)					
At current prices	8,940	9,593	10,790	12,173	14,239
At constant (1990) prices	4,857	5,221	5,639	6,164	6,744
% change, year on year	8.0	7.5	8.0	9.3	9.4
Per Head (Rmb)					
At current prices	7,054	7,517	8,400	9,420	10,954
At constant (1990) prices	3,832	4,091	4,390	4,770	5,188
% change, year on year	7.2	6.8	7.3	8.7	8.8

Source: "Country Profile 2006," http://www.eiu.com.

Exhibit 8 (b) China's GDP (% increase on a year earlier), 1990–2005

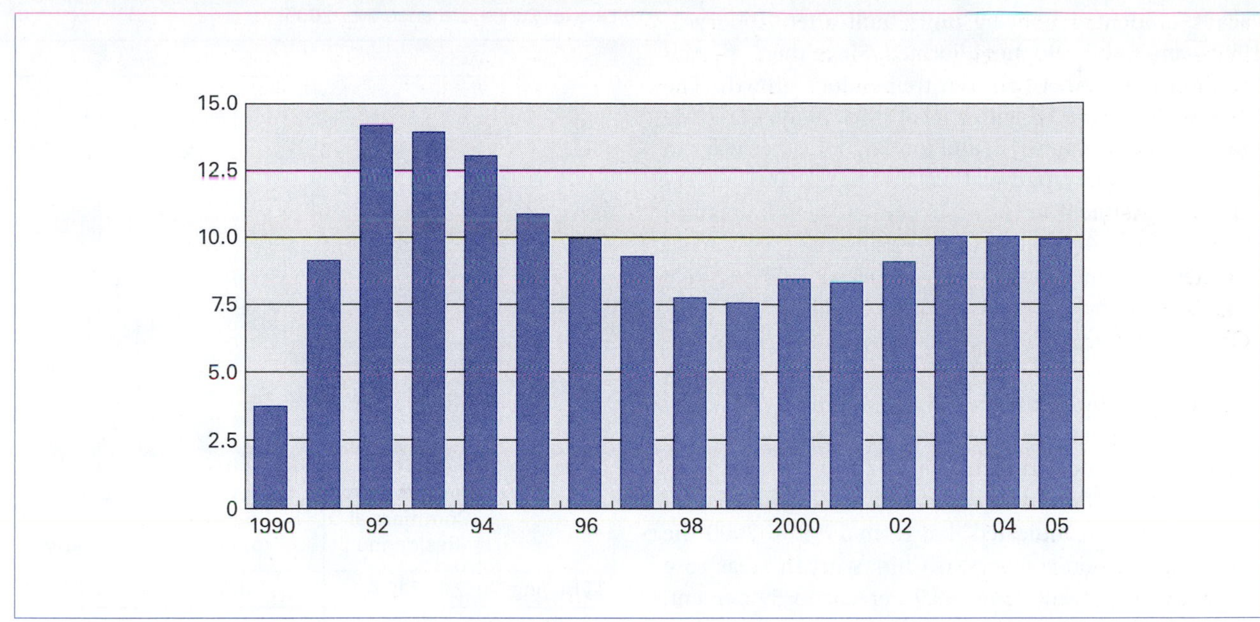

Source: "Coming out," http://www.economist.com/surveys/displaystory.cfm?story_id=5623226, March 23, 2006.

will because richer provinces would be reluctant to lose their privileges. However, in 1998, the government ordered written land-use contracts to be issued to peasants. A law introduced in 2003 restricted the right of collectives to reassign land within villages and provided a legal basis for transfer of land between peasants for farming.[9]

The leasing of land to households in the early 1980s began as an initiative that gradually gained official support. Under the 1982 Constitution, urban land in China is owned by the state and the collectives own the rural land. Since the local and central governments administer the rural collectives, it can be construed that all land ownership is under the control of the state. However, the Constitution's Amendment Act of 1988 to Article 10 adopted on April 12, 1988, states that a land use right may be transferred in accordance to law. Accordingly, a land use right was accorded with a sort of land ownership, thus making land use right likely to be privatized. Individuals, including foreigners, were allowed to hold long-term leases for land use. They were eligible to own buildings, apartments, and other structures on land, as well as own personal property.[10]

In the 1980s, almost all urban housing was owned by the state. Most of the people in China's urban centers had patronized the welfare housing system in which the government provided nearly free housing to urban residents. All employees from government agencies, academic and public institutions, and state-owned companies, received housing facilities from the government or their work units. In March 1998, Chinese Premier Zhu Rongji introduced a package of reforms that included a series of housing reforms intended to stimulate the domestic economy. He declared that subsidized housing traditionally available to Chinese workers would be phased out and that workers would be encouraged to buy their own homes or pay rent closer to real market prices. The reforms intended for workers to utilize their savings, along with the one-time housing subsidies they received, to purchase their own houses. *The Economist* observed, "In one of the most dramatically successful economic reforms of the past quarter century in China, most housing is now privately owned. This has fostered the growth of a middle class that wants guarantees that its new assets are safe from the party's whims. Property owners are electing their own landlord committees—independent of the party—to protect their rights. A new breed of lawyers, not party stooges as most once were, is emerging to defend those whose properties are threatened by the state. Property owners want a clean environment around their homes. Green activism, which hardly existed in China a decade ago, is spurring the development of a civil society."[11]

In the 1990s, with the emergence of better public housing, improved incomes, and raised expectations of the community at large, the housing market had grown beyond the provision of shelter to the quest to provide pleasant homes tailored to the community needs.

The Chinese government began to divest state housing and create a class of homeowners, primarily in the larger cities but gradually across the country. With the proposed development of a secondary housing market in the future, eventually it is envisaged that the Chinese housing market will come to resemble that of mature private property markets.

In August 1999, the government announced that all vacant residential housing units built after January 1, 1999, were to be sold, not allocated. Since then, the private housing market has seen tremendous growth. The Chinese people, faced with a local stock market offering low returns and high-risk and looking for other ways to invest their money, poured their money into property.

The investment in China's real estate development in 1999 was RMB 401 billion ($48.43 billion), up 10 percent from 1998. From January to November of 2000, the total investment in the real estate sector reached RMB 374.4 billion ($45 billion). In 2000, commercial housing construction had increased by 17.9 percent, finished construction area increased by 22.3 percent, sales volume increased by 38.8 percent, and housing purchase increased by 44.5 percent over the same period in 1999.[12]

A study by the *Sinomonitor* and the British Market Research Bureau indicated that from 1999 to 2000 the percentage of homeowners in China's urban areas rose nearly by 10 percent, from 49.9 percent to 59 percent. The study also commented that the housing reform had boosted home purchase and construction in China.[13]

China's state banks also started lending to home buyers. From 1998 to 2003, mortgage and consumer credit liabilities rose from virtually zero to 11.6 percent of GDP.

As many middle-class families started investing in property, the real estate prices started increasing. Some believed that in some cities it was rising too fast. The government announced that it would reduce the prices in favor of construction of more affordable housing for relatively low-income earners. The government had ordered in 2005 its city leaders to contain the rising housing prices. The main target of this order was Shanghai, which had the largest and most expensive housing market in China. This order resulted in the price reduction in the range of 15 to 20 percent on average.

Consequently, the local Shanghai property speculators started moving to other cities such as Beijing and Chongqing in the west. "The problem is that China has built up this huge pile of wealth and there is nowhere else for it to go, other than into property," said Sam Crispin, a Shanghai-based property consultant.[14]

The National Bureau of Statistics says that new house prices in Beijing have gone up by 7.6 percent in the first quarter of 2006 (see Exhibit 9). Some economists argue that China faces a risky property bubble. While urban property prices are rising fast, so are incomes, and hence property is generally affordable.

Exhibit 9 China Property Price Increase by City, First Quarter 2006 (% change over 2005)

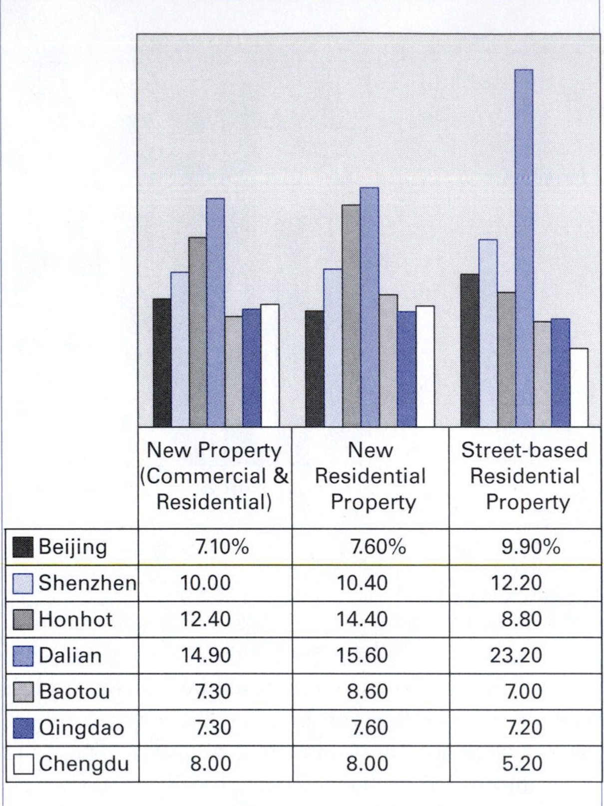

	New Property (Commercial & Residential)	New Residential Property	Street-based Residential Property
Beijing	7.10%	7.60%	9.90%
Shenzhen	10.00	10.40	12.20
Honhot	12.40	14.40	8.80
Dalian	14.90	15.60	23.20
Baotou	7.30	8.60	7.00
Qingdao	7.30	7.60	7.20
Chengdu	8.00	8.00	5.20

Source: Compiled from Browne Andrew, "China reins in real-estate sector," *Wall Street Journal,* May 19–21, 2006, 3.

China's Home Improvement Market

Since the mid-1990s, the home improvement market had grown rapidly, as housing reform encouraged home ownership in China. In 1998, the Chinese government made changes in its home ownership policy by getting state companies out of the business of providing housing facilities to their workers. Instead, these companies had to extend financial assistance to the employees for housing purposes, which for many raised their incomes by half. The employee could buy the work-unit flat he was already living in at a heavy discount.[15] It encouraged people to buy homes, offering low-cost mortgages or bargain prices on older apartments. Coupled with rising urban incomes, the private housing market boom in the late 1990s in Beijing, Shanghai, and other cities ushered in a new revolution in the Chinese housing sector.

New apartments were built, largely for private buyers. Private buyers bought 88 percent of the homes, compared with about 50 percent before 1995. In Shanghai, China's most sophisticated city, 10 percent of households owned their own homes in 1997, while the figure was about 25 percent in 2000.[16] However, Chinese construction industry operates quite differently.

Newly constructed homes in China do not have bathrooms, kitchens, and even interior walls. These features do not come with the new house. The Chinese contractors do not do any finishing work; they just hand over

Exhibit 10 (a) China's Home Improvement Market: Percentage Breakdown by Sector, 1996–2000

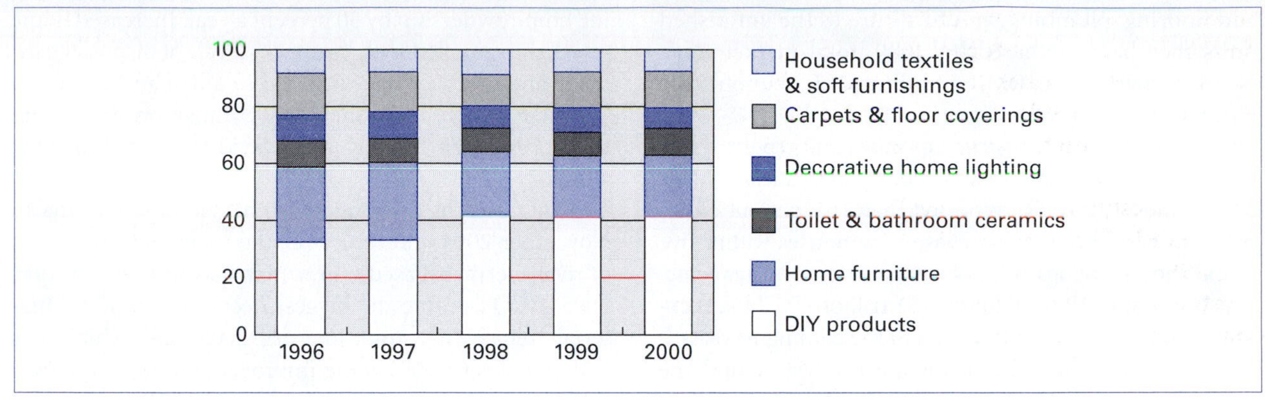

Source: "Doing it for themselves," *The Economist Intelligence Unit (Business China)*, 27(21), September 24, 2001, 9.

concrete shells. Chinese homeowners have to fix up these shells themselves. They have to install everything with the help of locally hired workers. The home improvement stores operating in China undertake to provide the necessary workforce. As a result, home purchases generated significant sales of appliances and other home improvement items. Many foreign retailers such as IKEA (1998) and B&Q[17] (1999) entered China.

China has proven to be a huge market for foreign home improvement players for more than one reason. In China, retailing is overspecialized; one store sells door handles, another paint, and yet another paintbrushes. Decorating takes loads of energy, requiring the homeowners to make trips to scores of stores, and hunt for a reliable contractor. Foreign stores profit from this activity, providing end-to-end "home solutions" under one roof with a do-it-yourself (DIY) model. B&Q can fit out an entire house, including furniture, and guarantee all the work. Another key advantage that foreign chains have is trust reposed in them by the Chinese consumers. "Chinese shoppers are used to being sold shoddy goods backed by dodgy guarantees," observed *The Economist.*[18] Chinese homeowners trust international retailers when they promise "no fakes" and money-back guarantees. B&Q even takes Chinese customers to workshops to reassure them about quality.

As a result, the homeowners began focusing on decorating and even handling home-decoration projects themselves. The sales of DIY products were on the rise compared to other home improvement products (Exhibits 10 (a) and 10 (b)). The DIY sector has become the major area of growth in the market, due to increasing demand for basic tools for household repair and decorating, as well as decorative products, such as paint, wallpaper, and tiles.

Statistics from the Ministry of Construction indicated that the business volume of interior renovation and decoration registered a 50 percent year-on-year rise in 1998 to more than RMB 75 billion. More than 60 percent

Exhibit 10 (b) China's Home Improvement Market: Growth of DIY Products, 1994–2000

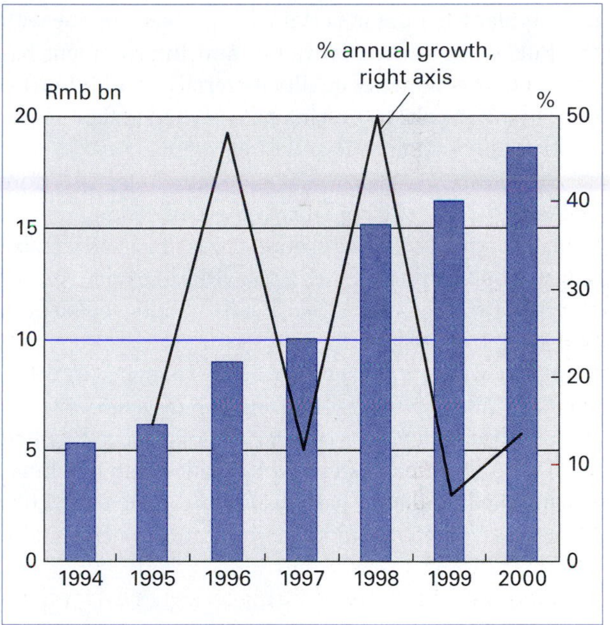

Source: "Doing it for themselves," *The Economist Intelligence Unit (Business China)*, 27(21), September 24, 2001, 9.

of urban households had spruced up their houses, with the average cost reaching RMB 20,000 per household. In 1998, Beijing residents spent more than RMB 2 billion on housing improvements.[19] It was reported that only 70 percent of the market demand was supplied in 1999.[20]

Based on a national development plan on housing construction, China will build at least 200 million square meters of residential housing annually by 2010. The plan is aimed to help 4.5 million residents to have spacious living space.[21]

In a survey, *McKinsey* found that nearly three-quarters of the respondents upgraded their furniture and home appliances when they moved into a new apartment.[22] New homeowners dug into their savings to add flooring, plumbing, and furniture to the unfinished units they had purchased. In 2000, total market value of home market was RMB 43 billion ($5.2 billion) (see Exhibit 11).[23]

In 2004, *China Construction magazine* reported that about 59 percent of the urban residents in China own their own homes. It was also reported that 21.9 percent of the residents would like to purchase new houses within five years. Family savings were the main source of financing, which was at RMB 6700 billion ($1 trillion).[24] China is expected to build 70 million houses in the coming 10 years.[25]

Home ownership has been the catalyst behind the home improvements market and has encouraged consumers to engage in home improvement/decorating activities. Industry analysts said, "As living standards improve in China and the government opens up the property market, interior decoration, design, and DIY are becoming popular pastimes in certain key markets. In line with the interest in home decoration and improvement has come a desire for better quality materials."[26] Additionally, this growth in private housing has resulted in fierce competition among domestic and foreign retailers.

Sweden-based IKEA, which opened its first store in Shanghai in 1998, opened outlets in Beijing and in the southern city of Guangzhou a year later. IKEA also plans to open a total of 10 stores within 2010, including expansion to the country's west with an outlet being built in the city of Chengdu.[27]

B&Q, which opened a store in Shanghai in 1999, later expanded to Beijing and increased its stores to 14. Its sales have doubled each year since it opened its first store in China. B&Q estimates that one-tenth of China's 400 million households have disposable income of $1,000 or more a year to spend on home improvements and it is increasing rapidly. Government deregulation is boosting home ownership by 30 percent a year. Increased home ownership coupled with "western" levels of disposable income and lifestyles have ushered in a demand for decor. "Chinese people have the money, intention and desire to improve their homes," said David Wei, head of B&Q China.[28]

B&Q bought five outlets from PriceSmart China in November 2004 and took over the mainland operations of rival, German-based OBI, which had 13 stores in April 2005. B&Q became the biggest decorative building materials retailer in China in April 2005 (see Exhibit 12). It dominates China's home improvement market. B&Q's sales rose by nearly 48 percent to 313 million pounds ($547 million) in 2005.[29] As of early 2006, the company had 49 stores in eight Chinese cities, including Shenzhen. B&Q plans to have 75 stores in 30 Chinese cities by the end of 2008.[30] Wei said, "In the past five years, we have enjoyed average double-digit like-for-like growth and we continue to see double-digit as a trend and our forecast for our next five years. The company's market share has risen sharply, from 0.8 percent at the beginning of 2005, as B&Q has opened new stores and sales have increased at existing ones. Getting statistics in China is really difficult, but whatever figures you quote as the national market, we will probably be at 2 to 3 percent."[31] He wants to double B&Q's store count in China by 2010.

Local competitors include Home Mart, controlled by retail conglomerate Friendship Co., with about 20 outlets, and Orient Home, a part of Orient Group Inc. Foreign competition is also heating up. France's Leroy Merlin opened its first China store in Beijing in 2004 and said that it would have 20 outlets across the country by 2010. German franchiser OBI (owned by Tengelmann Warenhandelsgesellschaft) also operates four stores in China.

Exhibit 11 Growth of Total Home Improvement Market of China, 1994–2005

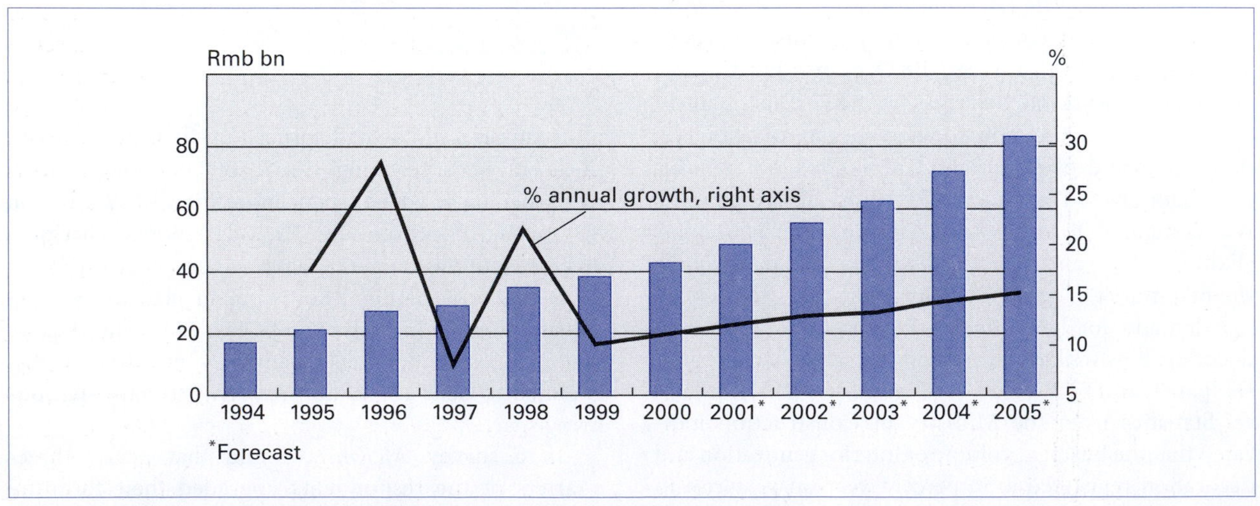

Source: "Doing it for themselves," *The Economist Intelligence Unit (Business China)*, 27(21), September 24, 2001, 9.

Exhibit 12 China Home Improvement Market: The Major Players

Hammer Down

Competition is building in China's do-it-yourself retail market

COMPANY	DESCRIPTION	NO. OF STORES	2005 SALES
B&Q	British-owned retailer dominates the big coastal cities	49	$542 million
ORIENT HOME	Beijing-based chain is possible takeover target for Home Depot	30	$350 million*
HOMEMART	State-owned Shanghai chain has good locations but indifferent service	27	$300 million*
HOMEWAY	Tianjin-based retailer benefited from training cooperation with Home Depot	11	$215 million
HOME DEPOT	Has two global sourcing centers in China but no stores—yet	0	0

*Estimate Data: Business Week, companies

Source: Frederik Balfour and Brain Grow, "One Foot In China," http://www.businessweek.com/magazine/content/06_18/b3982068.htm, May 1, 2006.

"The growth has been very strong between IKEA, B&Q, even local brands like Orient Home. It's very competitive. Over 100 cities in China have more than 1 million people. If even a small percentage of these people are able to purchase home furnishings, it would be really promising," said Anna Kalifa, head of research in Beijing for consulting firm Jones Lang LaSalle.[32]

In China, housing construction is growing by 33 percent a year. In 2006, Chinese banks relaxed controls on loans to purchase houses. This would result in the growth of the home improvement market estimated at $50 billion annually.[33] It is projected that the China's home improvement market will have growth rate of 10 to 20 percent a year.[34] Wei said that it is highly fragmented industry dotted with mom-and-pop outfits, niche stores that stock one product type, and a few budding domestic one-stop shops.

After witnessing the growth of the home improvement market in China and B&Q's success, Atlanta-based Home Depot, the world's biggest DIY group, also planned to set up shops in China.[35] In June 2005, *Reuters* announced that Home Depot was seeking to buy a stake in a Chinese peer Orient Group Inc. for up to $500 million to win a foothold in the country's fast-growing home improvement market. An agreement would mark the U.S. group's entry into the Chinese home improvement market. However, it already has an indirect interest in China through its links with the Homeway chain. In 2004, Home Depot opened a business-development office in China and named Bill E. Patterson for the newly created position of president, The Home Depot Asia. Home Depot runs two procurement centers in China. Home Depot announced plans in mid-2004 to start opening retail stores in China, but has yet to set up shop.

Should Home Depot Enter or Will It Have a Late-Mover (Dis)advantage?

Amid many speculations about the Home Depot's foray into China, the company remained tight-lipped. Home Depot's China head said, "China is an incredibly exciting opportunity. We're going to make the prudent decision. We're going to make sure we have the right business model."[36] For Home Depot's CEO Robert Nardelli, China is a top priority and he said, "A successful strategy there would offset the challenge of sustaining string sales growth back home and could even boost the stock."[37] He added, "China's economy is over $1 trillion. It has GDP growth of 7% to 8%. No one has dominance there. It's a unique opportunity to get a footprint, to really be part of the expansiveness and the growth. Sixty percent of the world concrete is being consumed in China today. Surveys say that Chinese consumers are looking for Westernized products and brands."[38]

However, there are many challenges in China's home improvement market. Some of them concern Chinese consumer behavior while others have more to do with the market (competition) dynamics. Unless addressed with a clear strategic intent (as opposed to short-term), the potential virtue can become mere wishful thinking, not converting into a reality.

The big challenge facing Home Depot and its rivals in China is that most customers are not doing home improvement themselves. "Chinese DIY is still really BIY—buy it yourself,"[39] admits Wei. He added, "You need time for DIY. There aren't many public holidays or paid leave. And you need the incentive to do it. Labor is so cheap in China there's no incentive to save money by doing your own work."[40] Since the government policy is to build homes that are more finished, the foreign players have to convert DIY into more of a hobby and the Chinese into a nation of home improvers, like the Americans and British. Yet, for many middle-class Chinese, it is not befitting to build a cabinet or fit a shelf by themselves. Thanks to abundant cheap labor, they've never had to do it themselves, nor do they have the skills. "Many Chinese don't know how to wire a plug or rise to the challenge of scumble painting,"[41] observed *The Economist*. B&Q, for instance, conducts training sessions for customers, showing them how to use a drill and even teaching children the mysteries and the fun of DIY. However, to utilize the potential, B&Q has initiated CIY (create-it-yourself) that helps customers to be involved in the process of creation. B&Q staffers help customers design a floor plan and choose materials and then perform all the installation work. In Beijing and Shanghai, B&Q started to build a DIY culture starting with a DIY kids club, where on the weekends people who do not have DIY skills could come and learn some basic skills. It is provided free of cost to attract kids and parents to the stores. Also, Chinese shoppers like to handle the merchandise before buying. However, products were stacked high on shelves. They still believe that foreign retailers display the most expensive products. They are intimidated by the exorbitant rates.

Another challenge for foreign home improvement players in China is managing their supply chain. Efficient suppliers are the key to success in a low-margin industry like retailing. Getting goods into stores in China is costly and expensive. B&Q's gross margins in China are half of those of its international division. *The Economist* observed, "China's huge size and enormous regional variations mean retailers struggle to establish a national infrastructure, let alone a national brand."[42] It is almost like operations in different countries. In humid summers, laminated wood cannot survive in Shenzhen. During a winter in Beijing, aquariums freeze. (Chinese believe fish bring good luck.) The biggest retailers, therefore, "remain in thrall to regional manufacturers—and their middlemen—which raises costs."[43] For 15 of B&Q's China stores, it has 1,800 vendors, while its 350 British stores have only 600 vendors. Moreover, these middlemen enter into deals clandestinely. Even on the shop floor, vendor representatives regularly offer customers "special" prices. "This is a state-controlled economy. Price fixing is endemic. Retailers are at the bottom of the food chain in China. They have far less power than manufacturers. It is the opposite of the rest of the world,"[44] said Steve Gilman, head of B&Q international.

Another concern for foreign home improvement retailers is regarding the treatment meted out to them in China in sales tax imposition and allocation of land. Foreign retailers face discrimination. Foreign home improvement retailers are forced to pay much more sales tax than the domestic counterparts. Using *Guanxi* (connections), the tiny stores avoid paying sales tax. They are often offered the poorest sites to carry out their business operations. For instance, B&Q had to build its new Shenzhen store under a residential tower block. Low-cost labor does not translate into quality labor either, forcing the foreign home improvement retailers to employ more workers to meet the greater service levels expected and continue to win the customers' trust.

Home Depot is studying the industry environment, competitors, and searching for suitable locations. According to the company, China has few large-format home improvement stores, and the country is largely served by small outdoor markets and shopping malls. Patterson said, "About 70 percent of home improvement spending in China is for completion of interior space in new homes. We see that as a solid growth opportunity given The Home Depot's strength in merchandise and services geared to finishing out a home."[45] However, experts say that due to the urban-rural divide and income disparity, requirements for houses are quite different due to different regions and culture. Housing consumption witnesses strong regional and multilevel characteristics.[46]

Home Depot's major rivals such as B&Q and IKEA were early entrants to the Chinese home improvement market. It has helped them gain better traction in many areas, such as government connections for getting approvals for zoning and licensing. Wei said, "Also, we have had the opportunity to recruit the best people and train them. New entrants may nick a few people, but it won't damage our management team and forces. And we understand product mix. Building relationships with suppliers and getting the pricing and supply chain right take time."[47]

In the United States, Home Depot has benefited from high labor prices for skilled labor, which encourages Americans to improve their own homes. But in China labor is low-cost and plentiful, and is often the single cost-effective element in home improvement. For this reason, some analysts say Home Depot's largest customers might not be homeowners, but interior designers and construction contractors.[48] If Home Depot decides to enter China, it has to train its employees to do installations also.

Home Depot faces stiff competition from foreign players such as B&Q and IKEA and domestic players including Homemart, Homeway, and Orient Home. Homeway, which had a brief alliance with Home Depot in the mid-1990s, adopted much of the Home Depot model, including the orange work aprons. These retail chains spent many years cultivating relationship with local suppliers and are already located in prime retail locations in the big cities. B&Q has already learned many lessons about operating in China. B&Q attracts consumers with stylish brands and more fashionable products, with an improved decorative-lighting section. Homeowners in China started switching from small local retailers to B&Q and other warehouse chains to buy flooring, cabinets, and curtain rods.

In China, due to increasing urbanization, most customers of home improvement chains are urban residents and the stores had to be located in urban centers. Locating in urban centers will require new strategies for its stores (in the United States, its stores are mostly in the suburbs). Home Depot needs to meet the unique demands of these urban customers and a multitude of challenges related to dealing with large urban markets. Analysts say, "It will be good if companies such as Home Depot learn from their experiences in China's urban markets. In Connecticut, as well as in many other parts of the United States, large retailers tend to overlook or avoid the large urban market due to what they perceive as potential problems. Perhaps companies that have

Appendix I (a) Per Capita Consumption of Rural and Urban Residents of China, 1952–1997 (Units: nominal yuan per year; Ratio: rural = 1)

Year	National Average	Rural Residents	Urban Residents	Ratio (Nominal)	Ratio (Real)
1952	76	62	149	2.4	
1953	87	69	181	2.6	
1954	89	70	183	2.6	
1955	94	76	188	2.5	
1956	99	78	197	2.5	
1957	102	79	205	2.6	
1958	105	83	195	2.4	
1959	96	65	206	3.2	
1960	102	68	214	3.2	
1961	114	82	225	2.8	
1962	117	88	226	2.6	
1963	116	89	222	2.5	
1964	120	95	234	2.5	
1965	125	100	237	2.4	
1966	132	106	244	2.3	
1967	136	110	251	2.3	
1968	132	106	250	2.4	
1969	134	108	255	2.4	
1970	140	114	260	2.3	
1971	142	116	267	2.3	
1972	147	116	295	2.6	
1973	155	123	306	2.5	
1974	155	123	313	2.6	
1975	158	124	324	2.6	
1976	161	125	340	2.7	
1977	165	124	360	2.9	
1978	175	132	383	2.9	2.9
1979	197	152	406	2.7	2.6
1980	227	173	468	2.7	2.5
1981	249	194	487	2.5	2.3
1982	267	212	500	2.4	2.1
1983	289	234	531	2.3	2.0
1984	329	266	599	2.3	2.0
1985	406	324	747	2.3	1.9
1986	451	353	850	2.4	2.0
1987	513	393	997	2.5	2.0
1988	643	480	1288	2.7	2.1
1989	700	518	1404	2.7	2.2
1990	803	571	1686	3.0	2.4
1991	896	621	1925	3.1	2.5
1992	1070	718	2356	3.3	2.5
1993	1331	855	3027	3.5	2.7
1994	1781	1138	3979	3.5	2.6
1995	2311	1479	5044	3.4	2.6
1996	2677	1756	5620	3.2	2.4
1997	2936	1930	6048	3.1	2.3

Source: Yang Dennis Tao and Fang Cai, "The Political Economy of China's Rural-Urban Divide," http://scid.stanford.edu/pdf/credpr62.pdf, August 2000.

Appendix I(b) Real Per Capita Total Income for Rural and Urban Residents of China, 1978–1997
(Units: nominal yuan per year; Ratio: rural = 1)

Year	Urban per Capita Income	Rural per Capita Income	Ratio of Urban to Rural Income
1978	454	134	3.4
1979	523	160	3.3
1980	560	190	3.0
1981	567	219	2.6
1982	597	261	2.3
1983	620	296	2.1
1984	690	330	2.1
1985	692	358	1.9
1986	784	360	2.2
1987	801	369	2.2
1988	783	370	2.1
1989	778	343	2.3
1990	855	374	2.3
1991	916	378	2.4
1992	989	399	2.5
1993	1073	413	2.6
1994	1133	443	2.6
1995	1179	487	2.4
1996	1217	551	2.2
1997	1252	584	2.1

Source: Yang Dennis Tao and Fang Cai, "The Political Economy of China's Rural-Urban Divide," http://scid.stanford.edu/pdf/credpr62.pdf, August 2000.

learned strategies in China will be able to bring back some of lessons and be more willing to invest in the potentially lucrative inner city markets."[49]

About the foray of Home Depot into China, *BusinessWeek* says, "Is Home Depot blowing it? Or is it biding its time for the right reasons? The China home improvement market is a lot tricker to navigate than those hot growth numbers would indicate. For starters, it barely resembles the do-it-yourself market back in America, where Home Depot workers dispense advice, then send customers back home to lay their own tiles and install some track lighting."[50]

As Home Depot executives try to gauge the risks and rewards in China, they do not want to get off on the wrong foot either. Home Depot's foreign forays have yielded mixed results. Although it was successful in Canada and Mexico, it had to close its stores in Chile and Argentina in 2001.

Goldman Sachs analyst Matthew Fassler said that Home Depot's reported interest in the Chinese home improvement market was "consistent" with Home Depot's goals and Wall Street expectations. He added, "We believe that an alliance . . . or minority investment with option for increased ownership would enable Home Depot to participate in China's economic development without the difficulties associated with navigating its political and cultural challenges alone."[51] Keith Davis, analyst at investment managers Farr Miller Washington, said, "It's going to take a long time to see any effects to the bottom line from an expansion into China, but in the more near term it will hopefully alleviate some concerns about opportunities for growth going forward."[52] Tian Guanyong, CEO of CGen Media,[53] said, "Home Depot had better make up its mind about China before it's too late."[54]

However, some analysts are skeptical whether Home Depot will suffer from any late-mover disadvantage and whether the early movers will enable Home Depot to compete more effectively and efficiently against them. *BusinessWeek* says, "It's likely that Home Depot will try some mix of building its own stores and buying share in China through an acquisition. Yet the longer it waits, the tougher it will be to break in. Securing the best locations requires good government connections. Getting to know the market and forging relationships with local suppliers can take years."[55]

Notes

1. A. Browne, 2006, China reins in real-estate sector, *Wall Street Journal,* May 19–21, 3.
2. Ibid.
3. F. Balfour & B. Grow, 2006, One foot in China, http://www.businessweek.com/magazine/content/06_18/b3982068.htm, May 1.
4. Ye Xiannian, 2004, China real estate market—Economic development, http://www.china-window.com/china_market/china_real_estate/china-real-estate-market—2.shtml, August 20.
5. 2004, Market for luxury brands booms in Shanghai, http://www.chinadaily.com.cn/english/doc/2004-03/13/content_314462.htm, March 13.
6. 2004, Chinese consumer markets: Exploding demand, worries, http://www.kpmginsiders.com/display_analysis.asp?cs_id=107803, July 2.
7. A peasant is a farm worker who does not own the land he farms, but pays part of the crops he grows to the owner of the land as rent. Peasants cannot ever prosper, because, if they work hard and grow a surplus, the landowner will inevitably raise the amount of the crop to be paid in "rent."
8. People's communes, in the People's Republic of China, were formerly the highest of three administrative levels in rural areas in the period from 1958 to 1982–85, when they were replaced by townships. Communes, the largest collective units, were divided in turn into production brigades and production teams. The communes had governmental, political, and economic functions.
9. 2006, Fat of the land, http://www.economist.com/surveys/displaystory.cfm?story_id=5623357, March 23.
10. China real estate market—Economic development, op.cit.
11. 2006, How to make China even richer, http://www.economist.com/opinion/displaystory.cfm?story_id=5660833, March 23.
12. Ye Xiannian, 2004, China real estate market—Housing reforms, http://www.china-window.com/china_market/china_real_estate/china-real-estate-market-4.shtml, August 12.
13. China real estate market—Housing reforms, op.cit.
14. R. McGregor, 2006, Beijing confronts calls for ceiling on spiralling property prices, http://www.ft.com, May 19.
15. 2000, Housing's great leap forward, http://www.economist.com, September 28.
16. Ibid.
17. It is a subsidiary of Europe-based Kingfisher plc, the largest home improvement retailer in Britain. It is the world's third-largest home improvement chain, with more than 650 stores in 10 countries in Europe and Asia.
18. 2003, Doing up the Middle Kingdom, http://www.economist.com, October 9.
19. 1999, Home improvement boom in China, http://www.hartford-hwp.com/archives/55/279.html, June 11.
20. Ibid.
21. Ibid.
22. K. P. Lane & I. St-Maurice, 2006, The Chinese consumer: To spend or to save? *The McKinsey Quarterly,* 1, 1, 6–8.
23. 2001, Doing it for themselves, *The Economist Intelligence Unit (Business China),* 27(21), September 24, 9.
24. China real estate market—Economic development, op.cit.
25. 2004, China's real estate industry in a boom, http://www.china-window.com/china_market/china_real_estate/chinas-real-estate-indust.shtml, March 24.
26. 2001, Home improvement in China: A market analysis, http://www.the-infoshop.com/study/ae8399_home_china.html, August.
27. J. McDonald, 2006, IKEA happily feeds China's hungry home-improvement market, http://the.honoluluadvertiser.com/article/2006/Apr/11/bz/FP604110318.html, April 11.
28. Doing up the Middle Kingdom, op.cit.
29. 2006, B&Q expects more double-digit growth, http://en.ce.cn/Business/Enterprise/200603/21/t20060321_6435244.shtml, March 21.
30. Doing up the Middle Kingdom, op.cit.
31. B&Q expects more double-digit growth, op.cit.
32. IKEA happily feeds China's hungry home-improvement market, op. cit.
33. J. Beystehner, 2005, Asia's ideas market, http://www.pressroom.ups.com/execforum/op-eds/op-ed/0,1399,52,00.html, June 1.
34. IKEA happily feeds China's hungry home-improvement market, op. cit.
35. Home Depot, which was started in the late 1970s, has grown from a single-store operation in Atlanta to a network that now boasts more than 1,700 stores with a revenue of $60 billion in 2004.
36. One foot in China, op. cit.
37. Ibid.
38. M. A. Schwarz, 2004, Fixer-uppers spruce up profit at Home Depot, http://www.usatoday.com/money/companies/management/2004-07-05-insana-nardelli_x.htm, July 7.
39. Doing up the Middle Kingdom, op. cit.
40. F. Balfour, 2006, B&Q Stores: Renovating China's attitudes, http://www.businessweek.com/globalbiz/content/apr2006/gb20060425_120572.htm?campaign_id=search, April 25.
41. Doing up the Middle Kingdom, op. cit.
42. Ibid.
43. Ibid.
44. Ibid.
45. Home Depot to establish China business operation, http://www.buildingonline.com/news/viewnews.pl?id=320306/10/2004.
46. China's real estate industry in a boom, op. cit.
47. 2006, B&Q stores: Renovating China's attitudes, http://www.businessweek.com/globalbiz/content/apr2006/gb20060425_120572.htm?campaign_id=search, April 25.
48. P. Denlinger, 2004, Home depot plans China strategy, http://www.china-ready.com/news/June2004/HomeDepotPlansChinaStrategy060804.htm, June 8.
49. Y. Zhang, 2003, Learning to pay more attention to urban consumers: What home improvement companies could learn in China, www.cerc.com/pdfs/home_improve.pdf.
50. One foot in China, op. cit.
51. 2006, Home Depot mum on China chain, http://www.foxnews.com/story/0,2933,184699,00.html, February 13.
52. 2004, U.S. DIY store in China expansion, http://news.bbc.co.uk/2/hi/business/3785871.stm, June 8.
53. A company that installs flat-panel screens that play ads in retail outlets.
54. One foot in China, op. cit.
55. Ibid.

Case 14

Huawei: Cisco's Chinese Challenger

Phoebe Ho, Ali F. Farhoomand

The University of Hong Kong

Users are looking for a challenger [to Cisco] and value for money. Huawei has got the channel strategy and the pricing is right.[1]

Immaculately trimmed green lawns, basketball courts, swimming pools, ergonomically designed office spaces set in a casual yet high-tech atmosphere—images frequently associated with technology parks in Silicon Valley—were found on the outskirts of Shenzhen, China, where Huawei Technologies housed its corporate headquarters. The 1.8-square-kilometer property signified the state of exponential growth the company had gone through since its inauguration in 1988.

Huawei (pronounced Hua-way) was incorporated in 1988 as a private enterprise manufacturing telecommunications equipment for local Chinese companies at a fraction of the price of its international rivals. By 2002, the company overtook Shanghai Bell, an Alcatel joint venture, to become the dominant supplier of digital switches and routers in China. It then entered the low-end international markets, supplying routers that were 40 percent cheaper than its competitors. The company had developed a full product portfolio consisting of wireless and fixed-line networking equipment, handsets, optical communications platforms, data networking, products for virtual private networks (VPNs), and Internet protocol (IP) telephony. It boasted an annual revenue of US$6.7 billion in 2005, of which 60 percent came from international sales.[2] With 55 branch offices worldwide, eight regional headquarters, world-scale research institutes in strategic locations, and a host of customer support and training centers, the company came to be known as the Cisco of China.

In early 2006, Huawei Technologies was among the ranks of China's "National Champions," along with Haier, Lenovo TCL, and the Wanxiang Group, poised to compete with global leaders in the international marketplace.[3] As concluded by an industry analyst, Huawei's threat came not from low-cost manufacturing, but from low-cost engineering.[4] With an inexpensive and highly qualified research and development (R&D) workforce, the company was able to deliver customized, innovative solutions to global enterprises looking to reduce their capital expenditures. Could Huawei climb up the technology value chain, replicating its success in low-end telecom networking in high-technology products and services? Could it build a global brand? If so, how profound was this threat to established global leaders in the telecom equipment sector? Were there any lessons for other Chinese companies in their respective paths to globalization?

The Global Telecom Equipment Industry

The global telecom equipment industry had gone through a series of changes within the past few decades. In the 1960s and 1970s, network equipment suppliers were few and were categorized by the types of products they specialized in, primarily through in-house development. Manufacturing was largely decentralized as suppliers operated independent subsidiaries to serve different countries and regional markets around the world. With the introduction of digital technology in the 1980s, product lines proliferated and country-specific operations were integrated into single, global organizations. Manufacturing tended to become more centralized to increase production volumes and decrease unit costs. By the 1990s, the pace of technological advances, commercialization of the Internet, and privatization of telecom service providers worldwide had created an unprecedented level of competition in the industry. Telecom equipment suppliers took on the role of broad-based system integrators, building extensive product lines through third-party contracts, original equipment manufacturers (OEMs) and other partnership arrangements.[5] Service providers used acquisition-based strategies to keep pace with consumer demand and drove the market for global networking products to US$50 billion by the end of 2000, up from US$15 billion in 1995.[6]

The dotcom bubble burst in 2001 and devastated the overheated telecom industry on a global scale. Service providers had difficulty accessing capital and the industry as a whole suffered from overcapacity. Global networking suppliers had to scale back and reposition themselves in light of the market slowdown. However, technological advances in the Internet boom had persisted up to 2006, and the technology choices and service requirements of service providers such as AT&T, AOL, and PCCW were more diverse than ever (see Exhibit 1 for the worldwide equipment capital expenditures by segment). Telecom equipment suppliers could be broadly divided into five subsectors and global players tended to align themselves with two or more of these subsectors: optical transmission systems, switch systems, access systems, data communications, and mobile communications (see Table 1).

Exhibit 1 Worldwide Equipment CAPEX Spending by Segment, 2004

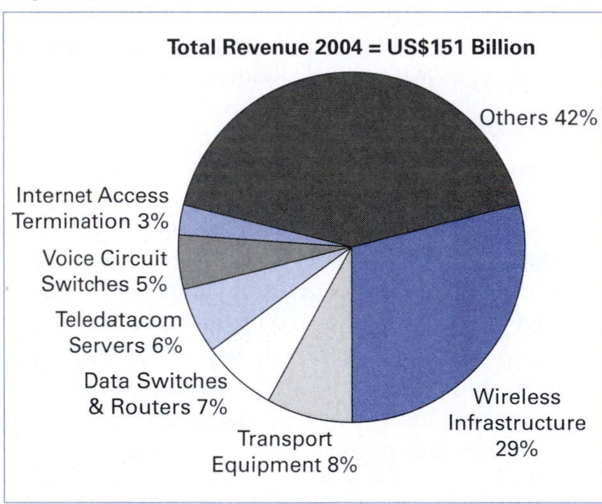

Source: 2005, In-Stat, June.

Table 1 Leading Firms in the Global Telecom Equipment Industry, 2001[7]

Subsectors	Leading Firms
Optical Transmission Systems	Alcatel, Lucent, Nortel
Switch Systems	3Com, Cisco
Access Systems	DSL: Alcatel, Siemens, Lucent Cable Modem: Motorola, Toshiba, Ambit
Data Communications	Routers: Cisco, Juniper Networks Ethernet Switches: Cisco, Nortel, Enterasys
Mobile Communications	Ericsson, Motorola, Nokia, Lucent

China's Telecom Equipment Industry

In the 1980s, China's telecom industry achieved substantial double-digit growth, and by the end of 2002, China surpassed the United States to become the largest telecom market in the world. Overall, China's telecom industry recorded US$112 billion in business transactions in 2004, with an annual growth rate of 34.9 percent, 3.7 times China's GDP growth rate of 9.5 percent.[8] Phone subscriptions had increased to 390 million mobile phone users and 348 million fixed-line users by October 2005.[9] Telecom service providers were shifting their focus from infrastructure development to network improvement and value-added service offerings. According to the Gartner research group, China's telecom equipment market would continue to grow at a compound annual rate of 10.9 percent between 2004 and 2008, from US$30 billion to US$45 billion.[10]

As the market grew, most of the leading global telecom equipment firms started operations in China in the 1980s and 1990s. Due to ownership restrictions, most foreign firms entered the market by setting up joint ventures with local Chinese companies, usually involving equity investments. They leveraged their Chinese partners' local market knowledge and distribution networks in order to reduce investment risk.[11] Among the leading multinationals in China (Motorola, Siemens, Nokia, Alcatel, Lucent Technologies, and Ericsson), Cisco was a latecomer. Cisco first entered the Chinese market in 1994, but it was not until 1998 that the company intensely focused its attention on China[12] (see Cisco's story in the next section). High-end networking products were the traditional strongholds of foreign players, with the market divided between North American, European, and Japanese vendors. American companies accounted for 75 percent of the telecom equipment market in China in 2001, within which Cisco accounted for 62 percent and 26 percent of the routers and switching markets respectively.[13]

Even though the entry of these multinational telecom enterprises had facilitated the building of China's telecom infrastructure, they had also contributed to the growth of domestic manufacturers in China. Domestic firms had progressed from being far behind foreign companies in every subsector of the industry in the 1980s, to catching up in the switch market in the middle 1990s, to capturing the access market in the late 1990s, and finally to becoming competitive in the optical transmission, data communications, and mobile technology in the new millennium. Domestic Chinese vendors started to emerge, most notably the four companies, Huawei, ZTE, DTT, and GDT, collectively known as "Great China."[14] According to the CRC-Pinnacle market research firm, domestic Chinese equipment manufacturers occupied a

Table 2 Telecom Equipment Market Share by Leading Vendors in China, 2005[15]

Company Name	Market Share (%)
Huawei*	13.5
ZTE*	12
Ericsson	12
Alcatel Shanghai Bell	7
Motorola	6.9
Nokia	6.2
UTStarcom*	6.1
Siemens	5.3
Lucent	4.7
Nortel	4
Cisco	4
Others	18.3
Total	100%

*Denotes domestic Chinese companies.

combined 32 percent of the Chinese market by 2005, of which Huawei Technologies became the market leader with 13.5 percent market share (see Table 2).

The Cisco Story[16]

Cisco started as a one-product company in 1984 when two Stanford computer scientists, Len Bosack and Sandy Lerner, a married couple, built a multi-protocol router for networking between different types of computers. The couple ran the business out of their living room and sold to networking-intensive customers such as Hewlett-Packard, the U.S. Defense Department, and American universities. By 1987, the company had outgrown its capacity and, after a period of legal battles with Stanford University, managed to secure a sizable venture capital from Silicon Valley for its large-scale expansion.

The phenomenal growth of the Internet in the 1990s precipitated the building of the Cisco empire. As communication networks grew in complexity and size, Cisco expanded from a one-product router company into a comprehensive, service-based leader in the networking business. John Chambers, Cisco's president and CEO since 1995, recognized that the company could not rely on its own R&D departments to prevail as a leader in multiple product categories. He began to take on a series of acquisitions to broaden the company's service and product portfolios. The acquisitions consisted primarily of small companies developing leading technologies in different areas within the networking industry. To move into new market segments, Cisco formed extensive strategic alliances, frequently with equity investments, with companies in the networking value chain. Chambers used these acquisitions and strategic alliances as a way to accommodate the rapid market shifts in the exploding IT sector. By the end of the 1990s, Cisco had become a virtual manufacturer of networking products, running a network of outsourced operations.

As the Internet expanded its footprint across the globe, Cisco also began to develop its global presence. Cisco opened its first offices outside of the United States in 1991, in Britain and France initially, then Canada, Japan, Belgium, Mexico, and Hong Kong. Cisco entered these markets as foreign governments invested in their public Internet infrastructures, domestic telecom markets were liberalized, and commercial investments in the sector increased. To meet global demand for its products, Cisco made alliances with local original equipment manufacturers (OEMs) and distributors, but maintained a centralized management structure by region. The Netherlands, for example, was chosen as Cisco's regional headquarters to manage its European, African, and Middle Eastern markets.

Cisco entered China in 1994 with the opening of its first office in Beijing. Its original intention was simply to establish a presence and sell its equipment in China. In 1998, the company began to intensely focus its attention on China and announced a capital expenditure of $100 million over two years to expand its business in China. Cisco's strategy in China was to focus on recruiting and training employees to service the high-end markets of telecom service providers and enterprise markets. Instead of forming joint ventures with local partners (like most of its international competitors did in China), Cisco opened its own subsidiary in China, Cisco Networking Technology Co. Ltd, to promote education, demonstration, and development of network technology. It provided its market-leading switches and routers to all the major telecom service providers in China, including China Telecom, China Unicom, and China Mobile. Cisco also embarked on a number of education initiatives to develop favorable relations with Chinese authorities and to cultivate new areas of business within China. The Cisco Network Academy was one such initiative where 157 university-based, technical schools offered free network technology education to more than 7,000 students. On the business solution side, Cisco established its Internet Business Solutions Group to help top business leaders transform their own businesses into e-businesses, enhancing their business operations using supply chain management, customer care, or workforce optimization. Recognizing the large, low-cost, and skilled labor force in China, Cisco made further commitments to invest in a new R&D center in Shanghai. The facility would employ more than 100 people after its launch in 2005. Chambers's plans for the research facility were to allow Cisco access to technology and local talent so as to buy into the local Chinese market.

In all these endeavors, Cisco insisted on maintaining its leadership position in cutting-edge technology and single-system images (SSI) throughout the world. Most of its applications, and its Web site, were hosted in the United States. The company's entire data center was constantly replicated between San Jose, California and Raleigh, North Carolina. Global standards and consistencies were maintained such that applications were designed from a structural point of view and local content was dumped into a standardized functional design.

Cisco was by far the largest telecom networking company in the world, with 35,000 employees and an annual revenue of US$22 billion in 2003–2004. Its broadened service and product portfolio meant that it was not competing head-on with Huawei; rather they were competing in the data communications subsector. Cisco's leadership position in the telecommunications equipment sector was, however, not entirely insurmountable. Chinese competitors were using their aggressive pricing strategies to expand into the international markets, and were rapidly using their low-cost advantage to move up the value chain. Both Huawei and ZTE were expected to make further inroads into international markets in the next few years, competing head-to-head with the established Western players for the same global accounts. In Chambers's own words, "China will provide even stiffer competition over the next decade. . . . Half of our top 12 competitors will be Chinese vendors."[17]

Huawei: The Home-Grown Chinese Multinational

Huawei, meaning "China achievement," was considered the model home-grown multinational company in China. Founded in 1988, Huawei Technologies was almost single-handedly created by Ren Zhengfei, a former People's Liberation Army officer and telecom engineer. Since the outset, Zhengfei's vision was to build innovation capability into the company. Contrary to the country's policy of "exchanging market for technology,"[18] Zhengfei believed that joint venturing with foreign companies would not enable the Chinese to obtain foreign technologies, and they might end up losing the domestic market to foreign players. He stated his goals as:

. . . to develop the national industry, not to set up joint ventures with foreign companies, to closely follow global cutting-edge technology, and to insist on self-development, to gain domestic market share, and to explore the international market and compete against international rivals.[19]

R&D Powerhouse

In accordance with these goals, Huawei focused its resources on building itself into an R&D powerhouse. In the early years, the company started with 500 R&D staff and only 200 production staff. By the end of 2005, of its 24,000 employees, 48 percent were engaged in R&D. Huawei had a policy of investing no less than 10 percent of its total annual revenue in R&D (compared to 15 percent in leading foreign technology companies). Yet it was still able to establish the early winning formula for the company as its development leapfrogged into the Global Systems for Mobile Communications (GSM), obtaining almost 90 percent of the Chinese domestic market in mobile network equipment by 2002. Because of the low labor cost in China, Huawei's focused R&D strategy became a significant competitive advantage over its international competitors.

Another major foresight was its early and heavy investment in the third-generation (3G) mobile communications technology. Huawei started its own R&D in Code-Division Multiple Access (CDMA) in 1995. In the next few years, it invested more than US$370 million[20] in wide-band CDMA (WCDMA) technologies with a dedicated R&D staff of 3,500 scattered through its research centers in China and overseas. In 2006, Huawei had a 21-story research center at its corporate headquarters in Shenzhen; six other research laboratories in Beijing, Shanghai, Nanjing, Huangzhou, Xi'an, and Chengdu; a software development center in Bangalore (India) with 1,500 engineers working on-site; and research facilities in Moscow (Russia), Stockholm (Sweden), and the Silicon Valley in California (see Exhibit 2 for Huawei's R&D Institutes).

Also noteworthy was the education level of the company's employees. Huawei frequently boasted about having the most educated workforce in all of mainland China. Among its 24,000 employees, more than 85 percent had a bachelors or higher degree, and about 60 percent had a master's or PhD. As a result of its generous R&D spending and high-caliber labor pool, Huawei held an impressive record of patent ownership. By the end of 2004, its patent applications had totaled more than 8,000, of which 800 were applied for in more than 20 countries and territories, including the United States and Europe. In 2004 alone, its patent applications reached 2,000, on par with its international rivals in the telecom equipment sector.

In addition to internal development, Huawei had actively undertaken joint R&D laboratories with foreign companies, including Texas Instruments, Motorola, IBM, Intel, Sun Microsystems, and Microsoft, focusing on various telecom technologies. To Huawei, these joint development efforts were used as a complementary approach to enhancing its innovation capabilities. As one of Huawei's senior R&D officers pointed out:

Huawei does not view R&D cooperation with foreign companies as an effective mechanism to gain technological competitiveness. There is no reason for foreign firms to transfer their most advanced core technologies to a

Exhibit 2 Huawei's R&D Institutes

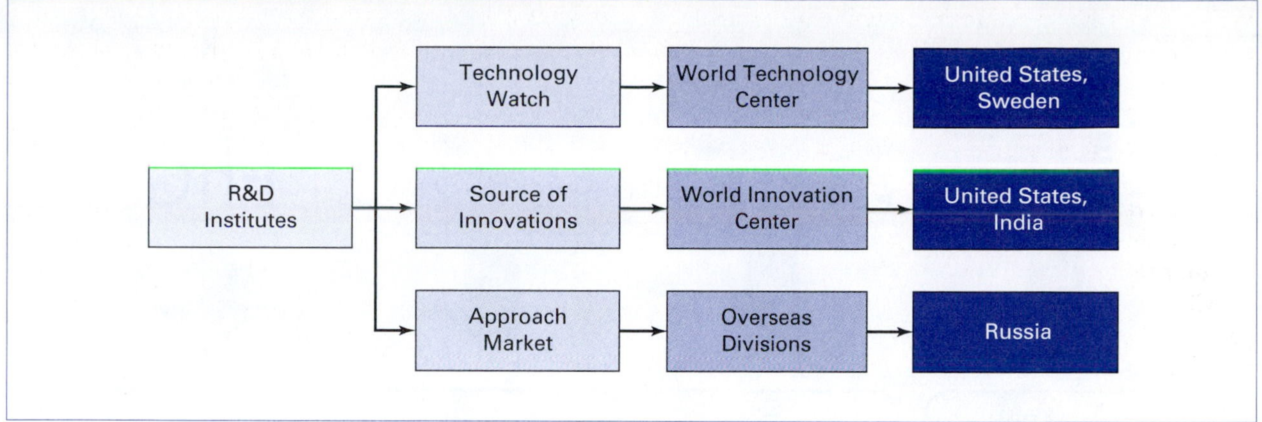

Source: J. Chen, 2005, Towards Indigenous Innovation: Pathways for Chinese Firms, Workshop of Technology Innovation and Economic Development, Zhejiang University, China, May 25–27.

Chinese partner over whom they do not have management control.[21]

The Military-Styled Wolf-Pack Enterprise

Ren Zhengfei's history with the Chinese military was a topic of much interest (and concern) in the Western world. Zhengfei's connection to the army had undoubtedly created a guanxi (relationship) network few other competitors could match. In fact, in its early years the company had relied on big contract orders from the military to secure a foothold in the telecom network market. The company visitors' book contained such influential names as Jiang Zemin, Zhu Rongji, Li Peng, Hu Jintao, Wen Jiabao, and other central military dignitaries. The company received financial support from the state-owned Chinese Development Bank in the form of a US$10 billion facility for Huawei's international expansions over five years, and an additional US$600 million from the official Export-Import Bank of China. Zhengfei was reluctant to speak of his relationship with Beijing, but did give credit to the favorable industry policies his company benefited from:

Huawei was somewhat naïve to choose telecom-equipment as its business domain in the beginning. Huawei was not prepared for such intensified competition when the company was just established. The rivals were internationally renowned companies with assets valued at tens of billions of dollars. If there had been no government policy to protect [nationally owned companies], Huawei would no longer exist.[22]

Ren Zhengfei's military background had also instilled a unique corporate culture within Huawei. He was known to frequently extol patriotism and cite Mao Zedong's thoughts in speeches and internal publications. All new employees were put through intensive military-style training for a few months. Zhengfei urged his employees to learn from the behavior of wolves, who had a keen sense of smell, were aggressive, and, most importantly, hunted in packs. In Zhengfei's own words, "An enterprise needs to develop a pack of wolves. Huawei's marketing arm has to focus on organizational aggressiveness."[23]

Exhibit 3 2004 Average Annual Wage of Staff and Workers by Sector and Region, 2004

Region	IT and Computer Service and Software Sector
Beijing	57,412 RMB
Tianjin	38,257
Liaoning	36,976
Heilongjiang	28,554
Shanghai	58,874
Jiangsu	36,754
Zhejiang	47,690
Hubei	19,451
Guangdong	45,624
Chongqing	30,607
Yunnan	21,855
Shaanxi	30,085
Xinjiang	24,032

Source: 2005, *Chinese Statistics Year Book.*

Over time, the company developed a national recruitment system with exceptionally high pay by Chinese standards (see Exhibit 3). According to a Huawei ex-employee, the lowest monthly salary in 2000 for a bachelors degree holder was US$500.[24] With housing and other benefits, an employee's first-year compensation could total as much as US$12,500.[25] To replicate a Western model of corporate management, the company had engaged a team of foreign experts to adopt international best practices in the areas

Exhibit 4 Huawei's Corporate Management Systems

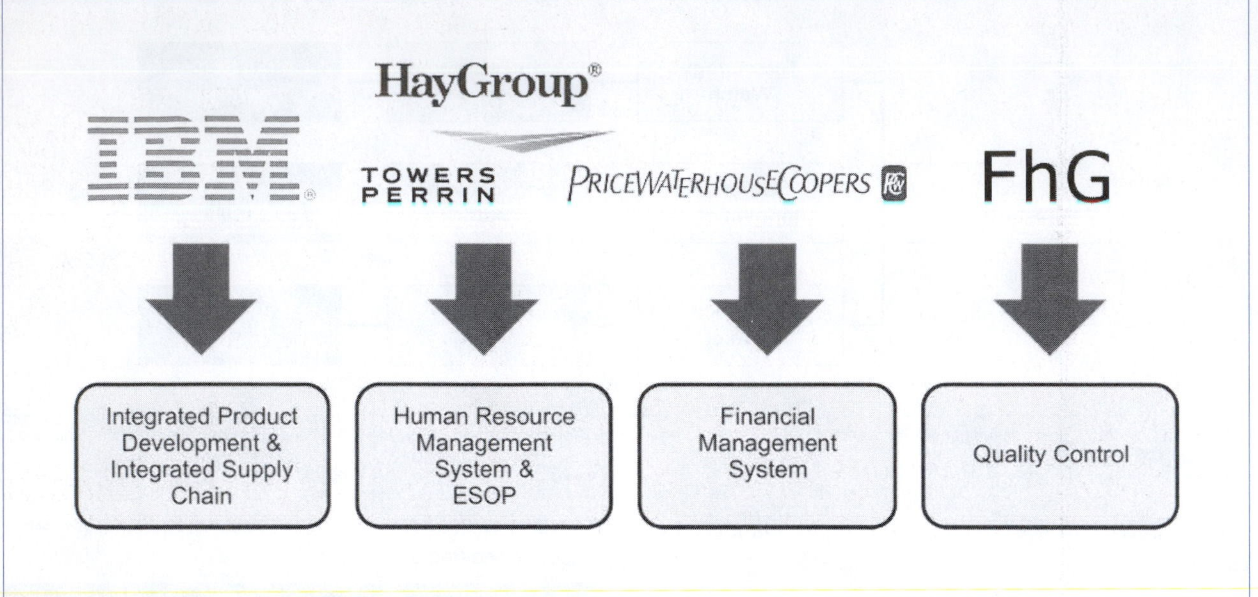

Source: J. Chen, 2005, Towards Indigenous Innovation: Pathways for Chinese Firms, Workshop of Technology Innovation and Economic Development, Zhejiang University, China, May 25–27.

of product development, supply chain integration, human resources management, financial management, and quality control (see Exhibit 4). Among these foreign consulting firms, IBM had been the most involved in reengineering Huawei's business processes and supply chains. For a while, 70 IBM consultants were working at the Huawei headquarters alongside Huawei employees and manufacturing facilities worldwide.

A Strong and Integrated Chinese Network

Huawei was undisputedly the largest Chinese telecom equipment manufacturer, with an annual revenue of US$6.7 billion in 2005, and a net profit of US$470 million. Market capitalization was estimated to be up to US$10 billion. In China, Huawei's major customers included all the big names such as China Telecom, China Mobile, China Netcom, and China Unicom. Huawei's networks in China served more than 400 million people communicating across the country,[26] occupied 25 percent market share in the mobile networks, and supplied 80 percent of all short messaging services from China Mobile.[27] The company had been selected as one of the major equipment suppliers for China Telecom's ChinaNet Next Carrying Network, or CN2, the core network for the country's next-generation business and consumer services, paving the way for China Telecom's entry into the 3G mobile market. In addition to the inexpensive R&D labor pool in China, the company had the advantage of integrating its marketing people into its core R&D team. The needs of service providers and telephone companies could thus be communicated through the marketers to the R&D headquarters in a timely and responsive manner.

Huawei's products could be divided into the following categories (see Exhibit 5 and 6):

- Wireless network
- Fixed-line network
- Optical network
- Data communications network
- Value-added services
- Handsets and terminals (with a full series of switches and routers)

Despite the original desire to not form a joint venture with foreign firms, it became necessary to form such a relationship in order to remain a leader in the industry. In November 2003, Huawei entered a joint venture with 3Com in China and Japan, called Huawei-3Com, in which Huawei held a 51 percent stake. The joint venture was aimed at selling to corporate customers, Cisco's stronghold. Products manufactured by the joint venture were sold under the individual Huawei and 3Com brands throughout the world, except in China and Japan where the joint Huawei-3Com brand was used. In February 2006, 3Com increased its stake in the equity joint venture to 51 percent. The joint venture had captured about 35 percent of the Chinese corporate market and was expected to overtake Cisco to be the largest network equipment provider in China.

Exhibit 5 Huawei's Products Lines

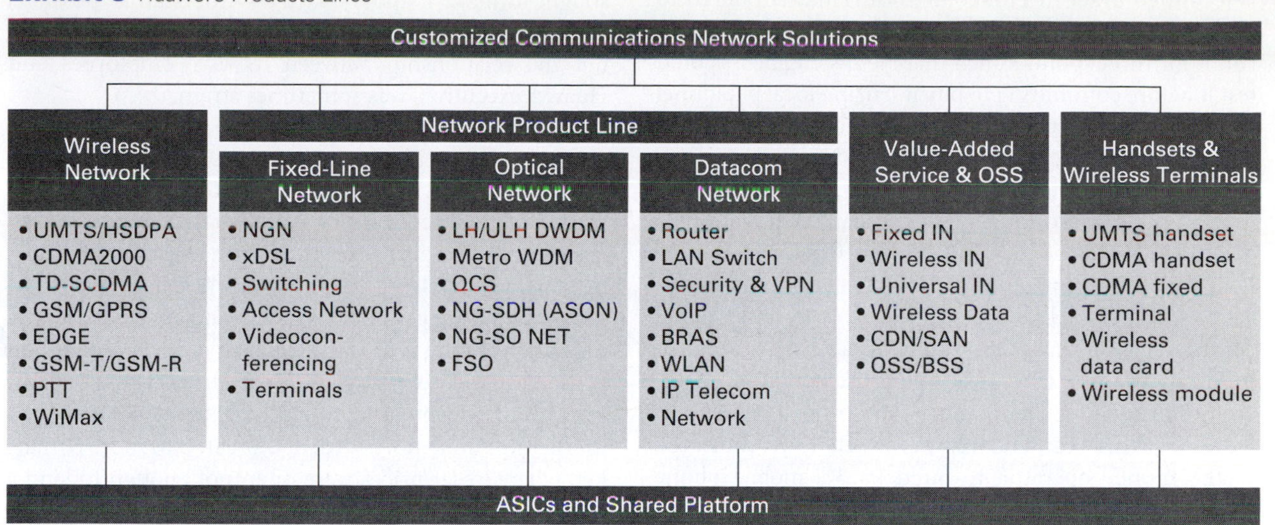

Source: J. Chen, 2005, Towards Indigenous Innovation: Pathways for Chinese Firms, Workshop of Technology Innovation and Economic Development, Zhejiang University, China, May 25–27.

EXHIBIT 6 Huawei's Sales by Technology

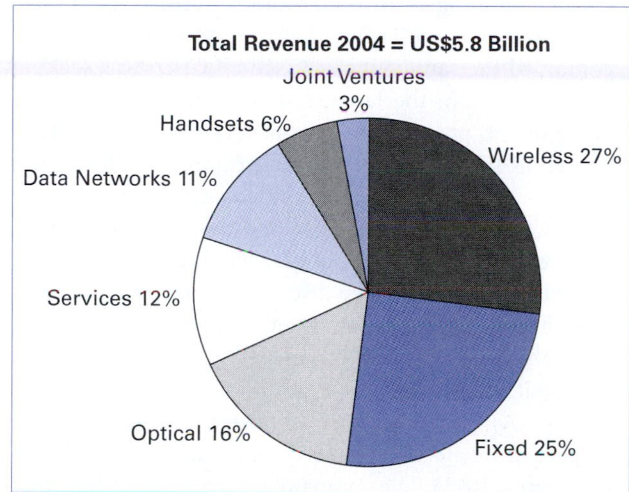

Source: EuroLAN.

As part of the joint venture arrangement, 3Com contributed US$160 million in cash, assets related to its operations in China and Japan, and licences to certain intellectual property. Moreover, the main reason Huawei entered into the joint venture with 3Com was that it wanted to leverage the latter's strong brand to increase profitability. Already a strong OEM with efficient production facilities, good R&D capabilities, and an extensive worldwide distribution network, what Huawei needed was a global name, because building a brand like 3Com's would be expensive and take a long time.

Path to Globalization

One dominant player [Cisco] has two-thirds of the market—the opportunity is there to become number two. With more than 65 percent of the market looking at one vendor, we believe some of that remaining 35 percent are unhappy and some of that 65 percent are very unhappy. We expect to be clearly number two.

—D. RICHARDSON

CHANNEL OPERATIONS CONSULTANT, HUAWEI UK

Huawei began considering international expansion in 1996 when it was looking for diverse sources of growth beyond the Chinese market. To avoid head-to-head competition with its international rivals such as Cisco and 3Com, the company made its initial overseas move in the markets of developing countries. Huawei made its first significant international sale to a Russian telecom service provider in 2000, which was quickly followed by Advanced Info Service, Thailand's largest mobile service provider, and Tele Norte Leste Participacoes, Brazil's fixed-line carrier.

The years between 1999 and 2001 were our breakthrough years. We would go to any country where we saw a market for telecom equipment. We invited as many prospective buyers as possible to come to our corporate headquarters, meet our people and see our products. We also went to all kinds of trade shows and exhibitions to show ourselves to the international customer base.

—WILLIAM XU

PRESIDENT OF HUAWEI'S EUROPEAN REGION[28]

As a newcomer battling against the perception that Chinese products were cheap and unreliable, Huawei had to use aggressive tactics to win contracts. In addition to unbeatable pricing (typically 30 percent lower than those of established suppliers), Huawei went out of its way to offer powerful incentives. To win the Neuf

Telecom contract in France in 2001, Huawei offered to build part of the customer's network free of charge and to run it for three months such that Neuf's engineers could test it before committing to buy it. Hiring local personnel was also part of Huawei's strategy to tailor technologies and services to customer's specific needs.

Major contracts won in recent years included the network upgrade contract with Etissalat, the telecommunications carrier of the United Arab Emirates, making UAE the first Arab country with 3G wireless communications. In 2004, Huawei became one of the first global communications suppliers to set up a CDMA network in Europe when it completed the construction of a project in Portugal for Denmark-based Radiometer A/S. In December that year, Huawei was selected by Telfort, the Dutch mobile operator, to build its 3G mobile phone network, signifying the company's first win in Europe's intensely competitive 3G market, and its arrival in the big league of telecom equipment suppliers. In late 2005, Huawei was selected as one of the four preferred suppliers to British Telecom's US$19 billion, five-year-long 21st Century Network upgrade project, along with the U.S.-based Ciena Corporations and Lucent Technologies, and Germany's Siemens AG. It had also signed a global framework agreement with the Vodafone Group to supply mobile phone networks to any Vodafone company worldwide. In all these countries, Huawei had taken business from global giants in the rank of Siemens and Alcatel. In 2004, of the 19 licences awarded around the world for 3G wireless networks, Huawei was involved in building 14 of them.

Struggles in the United States

Compared to Huawei's footprint in the European and other overseas markets, Huawei's presence in the United States was more limited. When it opened its first office in 2001 in Plano, Texas, the company made every effort to blend into the local culture. It shared the building with law offices, realtors, and the regional office of the lingerie company Victoria's Secret. A Texas state flag and an American receptionist welcomed visitors on the ground-floor lobby. Shortly after the U.S. launch, Huawei executives realized that Americans had difficulty pronouncing the company's name and came up with a working name, Futurewei. The new name, however, was never consistently adopted or promoted effectively. Magazines would still advertise Huawei, while trade shows, brochures, and other materials would feature Futurewei. Even though Americans had an easier time pronouncing the new name, they were confused by two different names belonging to the same company. In addition, the Chinese employees had a difficult time adapting to the Texas accent and other aspects of the local culture. The company sought to make its public face as American as possible, and hired local telecom talent in the area to that effect, but the relationship between its U.S. employees and Huawei executives was sometimes strained.

Contrary to its success in winning deals in developing countries, Huawei had run into snags in making deals in the United States. In a mature market where phone companies and their equipment suppliers had long-term ties, customers looked for exceptional leading-edge technology and a compelling reason to switch. One telecom service provider suggested that they would consider Huawei only after putting it through exhaustive trials, a common procedure for sourcing from an unknown company. Huawei management admitted that it was not prepared for the time and effort needed to break into the U.S. market, where lower prices were often not enough to land a deal.

Six months after setting up its subsidiary in the United States, Huawei was sued by Cisco for having allegedly infringed a number of Cisco's patents and copyrights by copying Cisco's user interface, user manuals, and source code for running its low-end routers. According to Cisco, the copying was so "lavish" that Huawei's router software contained the same bugs as Cisco's.[29] Cisco was seeking stiff penalties in the lawsuit, including the discontinuation of the production of Huawei's Quidway routers, as well as impoundment and destruction of all Huawei routers and manuals in the United States. At the same time, Cisco launched a "cease and desist" order against Huawei's UK distributor, Spot Distribution. Analysts observed that Huawei's steep discounting of Cisco products in its home turf, the U.S. market, had prompted the lawsuit, which was Cisco's first intellectual property lawsuit despite its huge intellectual portfolio.

Huawei initially denied the allegations, asserting its respect of intellectual property rights and its own focus on original R&D. The company then acknowledged that it had inadvertently obtained a small amount of Cisco's source code and used it in its own products. After Huawei agreed to withdraw its Quidway routers and other related products from sale in the United States, Cisco finally dropped the lawsuit in July 2004. In the midst of the legal proceedings, numerous sales contracts that Huawei was trying to close were killed. When the allegations were finally cleared, the company stumbled again. In June 2004, a Huawei employee was caught taking pictures of the insides of some high-tech equipment from Fujitsu in a Chicago trade show. Huawei later explained that it never used those photos and that it was the employee's first time in the United States.

After these blunders, Huawei landed the first contract with a U.S. wireless carrier in February 2004. It subsequently secured several other contracts with small wireless carriers in the United States. Huawei had serious intensions for the U.S. market, but results were yet to be seen. As Albert Lin, Huawei's head of R&D for North America, explained, "We need to present ourselves better. We also have to make it clear that we are not just testing the waters in the United States."[30]

3G and Huawei's Future

The industry was of the opinion that Huawei's success as a global company eventually hinged on its performance at home.[31] China, with its huge and rapidly growing telecom market, would be the ultimate battleground for the world's telecom infrastructure suppliers. Core to the battle was the much-anticipated launch of 3G mobile phone services in early 2006. According to an estimate by China's Institute of Telecommunications Science and Technology, China's 3G users would reach 200 million by 2010, with associated revenue in the range of US$124 billion.[32] Confirmation of the 3G technology standards and the issue of licences were the two imminent issues for all players in China's much-coveted telecom market.

China was conducting standardized on-site testing on all three internationally recognized 3G technologies: the Chinese home-grown TD-SCDMA standard, the European-origined WCDMA standard, and the American CDMA2000 standard. Huawei had made heavy investments in WCDMA since 1995, formed a 3G research joint venture with Japan's NEC and Matsushita in 2003, and had deliberately entered the mobile handset market in early 2004 to prepare itself for the 3G market down the road. Concurrently, Huawei had formed a joint venture with Siemens, called TD-Tech, to test TD-SCDMA handsets and network gears. Huawei had been investing one-third of its R&D spending in 3G technologies for the past two years. To Huawei and other telecom players in China, the stakes were enormous as the launch of 3G services was expected to push the company onward to its next wave of growth and expansion.

Conclusion

It's like the global automotive industry in the 1970s and 1980s when the Japanese started to penetrate Europe and the United States with lower-cost products and then started to work their way up.

—K. DEUTSCH

VICE PRESIDENT, A. T. KEARNEY[33]

Incumbent Western firms should be very scared of Huawei. Its reputation as a low-cost vendor is only the visible part of the iceberg.

—J. DOINEAU

OVUM IT CONSULTANTS[34]

The low price is not the only reason that our customers choose us. Equipment reliability, service quality, and the company's association with long-term development are elements of its success.

—JOHNSON HU

VICEPRESIDENT, CORPORATE BRANDING AND COMMUNICATIONS, HUAWEI TECHNOLOGIES[35]

To distance itself from its low-cost image, Huawei launched its first global image-building campaign in mid-2004. To emphasise the reliability of its telecommunication networks, one print media boasted that Huawei's networks were able to withstand Siberian winters and Saharan summers.[36] In early 2005, a survey report of 100 telecom operators worldwide ranked Huawei eighth among wireline-equipment suppliers, up from eighteenth the previous year. In addition, Huawei ranked fourth in service and support. The report called Huawei's ascendancy "astounding" as it surpassed several incumbent vendors in perceived market leadership.[37] Huawei's threat to the international telecom equipment suppliers was not to be overlooked (see Exhibit 7 for select financial performance of Huawei and its global competitors).

However, the battle could only become more intense. Huawei's track record was disappointing in the United States, just short of solid distribution networks to break into the lucrative enterprise markets; the network of choice in the developed countries was still Cisco. Huawei and other Chinese peers would have a difficult time matching the brand recognition and level of service provided by Cisco and other U.S. counterparts. Network security was another major concern expressed by service providers and enterprise customers. As stated by Cisco's CEO John Chambers, "Networks would have to be capable of responding to intrusions and viruses before human operators become aware of them. And security will be the most effective and efficient if a common strategy extends through all of a corporation's wired and mobile networks." During two years' time, Cisco acquired over 14 companies involved in network security and aspired to be "not just a vendor, but a trusted business advisor."[38]

In Asia, according to research firm IDC, Cisco's share of the Asian market (excluding Japan) in routers and LAN switches was still going strong at 62 percent versus Huawei's 6.2 percent.[39] In mobile handsets, Chinese suppliers were losing ground to their foreign counterparts; market shares of the Chinese companies of the local market fell from 50 percent in 2004 to 38 percent in the first six months of 2005. Foreign suppliers were also dominating the mobile switching infrastructure market.

Huawei was a privately owned global company. The industry speculated that the company could raise up to US$1.5 billion in an initial public offering on the back of its strong growth and high penetration in international

Exhibit 7 Select Performance of Huawei and Its Global Competitors

Huawei			
Calendar year	**2004**	**2003**	**2002**
Net sales (billions of $)	5.6	3.8	2.7
Net profit (billions of $)	0.47	0.38	0.11
Number of employees	22,000		
Cisco Systems			
Fiscal year through	**July 2004**	**July 2003**	**July 2002**
Net sales (billions of $)	22.0	18.9	18.9
Net income (billions of $)	4.4	3.6	1.9
Number of employees	35,000		
3Com			
Fiscal year through	**May 2004**	**May 2003**	**May 2002**
Net sales (billions of $)	0.699	0.933	1.259
Net income (loss) (billions of $)	(0.349)	(0.284)	(0.596)
Alcatel			
Calendar year	**2003**	**2002**	**2001**
Net sales (billions of $)	9.4	12.4	19.1
Net income (loss) (billions of $)	(1.5)	(3.6)	(3.7)
Juniper Networks			
Calendar year	**2003**	**2002**	**2001**
Total sales (billions of $)	0.701	0.547	0.887
Net income (loss) (billions of $)	0.039	(0.120)	(0.013)
Motorola			
Calendar year	**2003**	**2002**	**2001**
Net sales (billions of $)	27.1	27.3	30.0
Net profit (loss) (billions of $)	0.9	(2.5)	(3.9)
Nokia			
Calendar year	**2003**	**2002**	**2001**
Net sales (billions of $)	22.1	22.6	23.5
Net profit (billions of $)	2.7	2.5	1.7

Note: For Nokia and Alcatel, Euros were converted into U.S. dollars at the rate of €1.33 = US$1, as per the U.S. Federal Reserve Bank exchange rate on December 21, 2004.

Source: D. Normile, 2005, Chinese Telecom Companies Come Calling, *Electronic Business*, 31(2): 38–43.

telecommunications markets. Huawei stated that it had no intention to go public before 2008 because it had no urgent need for funds. The vice president of Huawei, however, expressed that the company was preparing to save more capital to look for good opportunities for overseas mergers and acquisitions in order to enhance its technical strength. The company's position was that it would seek acquisitions overseas to compete with its international rivals such as Nokia, Motorola, Alcatel, and NEC. Buying 3Com was always a possibility as the U.S. company continued to stumble in its global sales.

The general feeling was that Chinese vendors were mostly using Western engineering and not inventing much of their own. As with earlier technology migration from the United States to the Far East in the consumer electronics and personal computer businesses, Asian manufacturers were turning complex and high-profit products into standard commodities. Some had observed that Huawei's products appeared to be derived from those of other companies, either through patent-mining or reverse engineering. To become a serious global contender, Huawei would have to move beyond low-cost versions of Western gear. Its low-cost strategy seemed increasingly untenable because its reliance on local service partners in foreign markets would ultimately raise its cost of running the business. At the same time, foreign companies were increasing their manufacturing base and R&D facilities in China and would soon become equally competitive in terms of pricing.

Last but not least, Huawei's connection to the Chinese army continued to cast a shadow around Huawei's image for some overseas customers. A number of U.S. distributors remained skeptical about the potential military influence the company was subject to and were wary of any implication to international business relationships. Zhengfei's military background and the company's recent sales to Iraq had created suspicion in the eyes of the Western world. In 2005, Huawei lost its bid to acquire British telecom equipment provider Marconi to the world giant Ericsson largely because of Huawei's baffling connection with the Chinese military. Although the company was trying to improve its corporate image and increase transparency, questions of trust and reputation could undermine its efforts to win contracts with governments and international enterprises in the long run. Facing so many thorny challenges, Huawei's management had to draft a sustainable global strategy.

Notes

1. C. Walton, 2005, Huawei moves in on Cisco, MicroScope, September 5.
2. R. McGregor, 2005, Huawei reaches foreign sales milestone, *Financial Times,* London, November 30.
3. M. Zeng & P. Williamson, 2003, The hidden dragons, *Harvard Business Review,* October.
4. D. Normille, 2005, Chinese telecom companies come calling, *Electronic Business,* 31(2): 38–42.
5. K. Nissen, 2005, New world telecom: A survival guide for global equipment suppliers, *Business Communications Review,* September.
6. F.W. McFarlan, G. Chen, & D. Kiron, 2001, Cisco China, Harvard Business School Case, Harvard Business School.
7. P. Fan, 2004, Catching up through developing innovation capability: Evidence from China's telecom-equipment industry, Department of Urban Studies and Planning, MIT, November 11.
8. Annual Report, China's post and telecommunications industry 2005, Ministry of Information Industry, China.
9. 2005, China to have over 440 Million mobile phone users by end of next year, http://www.today.com.
10. A. Harney, 2005, The challenger from China: Why Huawei is making the telecoms world take notice, *Financial Times,* London, January 11.
11. A. Farhoomand, Z. Tao, Y. Jiang, & T. X. Liu, 2005, China's telecommunications industry in 2004, Asia case research center case, University of Hong Kong.
12. F. W, McFarlan, G. Chen, & D. Kiron, 2001, op. cit.
13. Ibid.
14. When the first characters of the four companies were arranged in reverse order (Ju-Great Dragon, Da-DTT, Zhong-ZTT, Hua-Huawei), the phrase "Great China" was created.
15. 2006, China's telecommunications market 2005, CRC-Pinnacle Consulting Co. Ltd., http://www.buyusainfo.net/docs/x_8130085.pdf November 13.
16. Information in this section was extracted from the following Harvard Business School cases: F. W., McFarlan, G. Chen, & D. Kiron, 2001, Cisco China, Harvard Business School Case; and G. Jones, & D. Kiron, 2005, Cisco goes to China: Routing an emerging economy, Harvard Business School Case.
17. G. Long, 2005, Power Shift, Telecom Asia, March.
18. China's "exchanging market for technology" policy encouraged foreign companies with the desired technological expertise to develop business in China, on the condition that they would share certain technical knowledge with their Chinese counterparts.
19. P. Fan, 2004, Catching up through developing innovation capability: Evidence from China's telecom-equipment industry, Department of Urban Studies and Planning, MIT, November 11.
20. US$1 = RMB 8.07 on December 29, 2005.
21. A. Smith-Gillespie, 2001, Building China's high-tech telecom equipment industry: A study of strategies in technology acquisition for competitive advantage, Masters Thesis, MIT.
22. P. Fan, 2004, Catching up through developing innovation capability: Evidence from China's telecom-equipment industry, Department of Urban Studies and Planning, MIT, November 11.
23. R. Tang, 2004, Hungry like a wolf, *The Standard,* September 24.
24. US$1 = RMB 8.07 on December 29, 2005.
25. R. Tang, Hungry like a wolf.
26. Refers to networks built with Huawei equipment in China, as noted by J. Hu, the company's vice president, corporate branding and communications.
27. J. Chen, 2005, Giant rises in the east, *National Post,* June 10.
28. C. Wu, 2004, Huawei reveals its difficult journey to globalization, http://tech.sina.com.cn/it/t/2004-08-06/0751399261/shtml.
29. 2003, A New Global technology player, *Exchange,* March 14.
30. C. Rhoads & R. Buckman, 2005, Trial and error: A Chinese telecom powerhouse stumbles on road to the U.S., *Wall Street Journal,* July 28.
31. A. Harney, 2005, The challenger from China: Why Huawei is making the telecoms world take notice, *Financial Times,* London, January 11.
32. A. Farhoomand, Z. Tao, Y. Jiang, & T. X. Liu, 2005, China's telecommunications industry in 2004, Asia case research centre case, University of Hong Kong.
33. 2003, A new global technology player, *Exchange,* March 14.
34. 2005, Business: See Huawei run, *The Economist,* March 5.
35. J. Chen, 2005, Giant rises in the east, *National Post,* June 10.
36. R. Flannery, 2004, An air of mystery, *Forbes* Online, http://www.forbes.com/business/global/2004/1129/030.html.
37. 2005, Business: See Huawei run, *The Economist,* March 5.
38. D. Normile, 2005, Chinese telecom companies come calling, *Electronic Business,* 31(2): 38–43.
39. 2005, Business: See Huawei run, *The Economist,* March 5.

Case 15

ING DIRECT: Rebel in the Banking Industry

Dr. Kurt Verweire
Dr. Lutgart A. A. Van den Berghe

Vlerick Leuven Gent Management School

ING DIRECT USA is built on the foundation of being unconventional. We aren't like other banks. We've not only developed a unique business model, but the way we look at the business is different than how our competitors look at it. Our purpose is to be a servant of the average person. Rather than getting people to spend more—which is what most banks do—our approach is to get Americans to save more—to return to the values of thrift, self-reliance, and building a nest egg.

ING DIRECT was born in an age of broken promises. The last thing America needed was another bank, but that didn't mean America didn't need us. ING DIRECT's mission is to make it easy to save by offering the same great values to all Americans.

—**ARKADI KUHLMANN**
PRESIDENT AND CEO, ING DIRECT
(UNITED STATES AND CANADA)

Many organizations have tried to enter the banking industry with innovative business models. But incumbents have always been able to defend their markets successfully. Today, ING DIRECT is changing the odds. Arkadi Kuhlmann, founder of ING DIRECT, is clear about his goals: "There's no such thing as an industry that can't be reenergized!"

Customers welcomed the company with open arms. In just five years, ING DIRECT has become the largest Internet-based bank—passing E*TRADE Bank—in the United States, and one of the 30 largest banks of any sort in the country. The company adds an astonishing 100,000 customers and $1 billion in deposits every month, and in 2005 (its fifth year of operations) generated a profit of $360 million. And above all, 90 percent of the ING DIRECT customers believe it provides a much better service than the competitors.

Profile of the ING Group

ING DIRECT is one of the six business lines of ING Group, a major international financial services group. ING Group is active in more than 50 countries and is often cited as the example of an integrated financial services provider, offering a wide array of insurance, banking, and asset management services to a broad customer base: individuals, families, small businesses, large corporations, and institutions and governments.

ING Group is a financial conglomerate founded in 1991 by the merger between Nationale-Nederlanden, the Netherlands' largest insurance company, and NMB Postbank Group, one of the largest banking groups in the Netherlands. NMB Postbank Group itself was the result of a merger between the very entrepreneurial NMB Banking Group and the Postbank. Postbank had been split off from the Dutch Post Office and was privatized. Many people within ING believe that Postbank has been the true inspiration for ING DIRECT.

The merger between Nationale-Nederlanden and NMB Postbank Group created the first bancassurer in the Netherlands. Since 1991, ING has developed from a Dutch financial institution with some international businesses to a multinational with Dutch roots. It acquired banks and insurance companies in the United Kingdom (Barings Bank, 1995), Belgium (Bank Brussels Lambert, 1998), Germany (BHF-Bank, 1999), United States (Equitable of Iowa, 1997; ReliaStar, 2000; Aetna Financial Services, 2000), Canada (Wellington, 1995; Canadian Group Underwriters, 1998; Allianz of Canada, 2004), and other countries. Some of these financial institutions were sold later, such as parts of Barings and BHF-Bank. As such, ING Group has become one of the 15 largest financial institutions worldwide and top-10 in Europe

Exhibit 1 20 Largest Financial Institutions Worldwide

Source: http://www.bloomberg.com

(in market capitalization). Exhibit 1 provides an overview of the 20 largest financial institutions, measured by market capitalization.

ING also used greenfields to grow the business. Greenfields were set up in the emerging markets, where ING leveraged the bancassurance concept it continued to refine in its home markets. ING Group also set up other initiatives to fuel the group's revenue and profit growth. It created a new international retail/direct banking division, which was composed of a team of Postbank's best marketing and IT people. Hans Verkoren, CEO of Postbank, became the head of this new division. This new venture was to explore to what extent Postbank's strategy could be expanded outside its Dutch home market. Postbank operated in a "branchless" manner for many years, offering simple checking accounts, savings, mortgages, consumer loans, and investment products.

This new division operated autonomously from the rest of the company. The parent company gave the new organization the necessary freedom to experiment. After detailed marketing research, the team introduced to Canada ING's first foreign direct banking experiment in 1996.

ING chose Canada because it had no presence there, and the market was dominated by a small number of players. ING agreed it was important for this new experiment to survive or fail on its own. It created optimal conditions for success by providing it with adequate financial means and a brand new management team, lead by Arkadi Kuhlmann.

A Growing Success Story in the Banking Industry

Arkadi Kuhlmann, a Harley-riding painter and poet, was a professor of International Finance and Investment Banking at the American Graduate School of International Management (Thunderbird) in Phoenix, Arizona. He also served as president of North American Trust, CEO of Deak International Incorporated, and held various executive positions at the Royal Bank of Canada. When Hans Verkoren asked him in 1996 whether he was interested to start up a new foreign bank in Canada, he accepted the challenge.

Arkadi had noticed that few foreign banks had successfully entered the North American banking industry and had built a sustainable competitive position in that market. But he realized that those incumbents were not invincible.

Traditional banks are stuck. They have high fixed costs and use technology in an inefficient way. They have rigid distribution systems. And they charge too high prices. The customer always loses. When we came in, we said: "How can we do something different?" We looked at other industries and copied some ideas from successful players in the retail and airline industry. It is true that we actually haven't defined something new. In the context of Southwest Airlines or Wal-Mart, there are similarities. For decades, Southwest Airlines has defied the industry's standard approaches to economics and customer service, and has achieved good results. And we are on our way to do the same in the banking industry. Most companies, especially in our industry, are truly boring. If you do things the way everybody else does, why do you think you're going to be any better?

ING DIRECT differentiates itself from traditional banks in many ways. But in essence, its differentiation lies in being direct.

Our biggest advantage in standing out in the financial service market from all other players is that we are direct. Anyway we can emphasize that we are direct, thereby cutting out the middleman, is a way of saving money. So being a retail business, being simple, focused and direct adds up to good value. This is a retail trend that consumers know and one we should emphasize in everything we do.

ING DIRECT is a direct-to-the-customer operation, an Internet-based savings bank, although customers can also bank by mail or telephone.

The bank operates no branches, no ATMs, just a couple of cafés in big cities where it sells coffee and mountain bikes in addition to savings accounts, a few certificates of deposit, home mortgages, home equity lines, and a handful of mutual funds.[1] The bank does not offer traditional paper-based checking accounts—that costs too much. For these accounts, ING DIRECT points customers back to their local bank. ING DIRECT charges no fees and maintains no minimum deposits for savings accounts and a limited number of product offerings.

What started as a small successful experiment in Canada in 1997 has become one of the success stories in today's financial services industry. ING DIRECT launched operations in Spain and Australia in 1999. One year later, it entered France and the United States.

Since then, ING DIRECT has entered Italy, the United Kingdom, and Germany, and it has plans to set up operations in Japan. ING DIRECT globally ended the first quarter of 2006 with €194 billion in deposits and €15,7 million customers (see Exhibit 2). In 2005, ING DIRECT's profits constituted 7 percent of ING's total profits. Exhibit 3 shows ING DIRECT's global profit progression from its creation to 2005.

Exhibit 2 ING DIRECT's Clients and Funds Base

	2005 Profit (in € millions)	Deposits (in € millions)	Customers
Canada	69.4	12,579	1,360,588
Spain	51.0	13,726	1,341,759
Australia	73.8	10,757	1,282,459
France	23.9	11,389	555,922
USA	162.9	39,031	3,785,927
Italy	29.0	13,426	699,603
Germany	242.1	57,654	5,488,865
UK	(27.7)	33,704	1,038,650
Austria	(15.6)	2,475	210,808
Total ING DIRECT	612.3	194,741	15,764,581

Source: ING DIRECT, http://www.ingdirect.com

Exhibit 3 ING DIRECT's Global Profit Progression (in € millions)

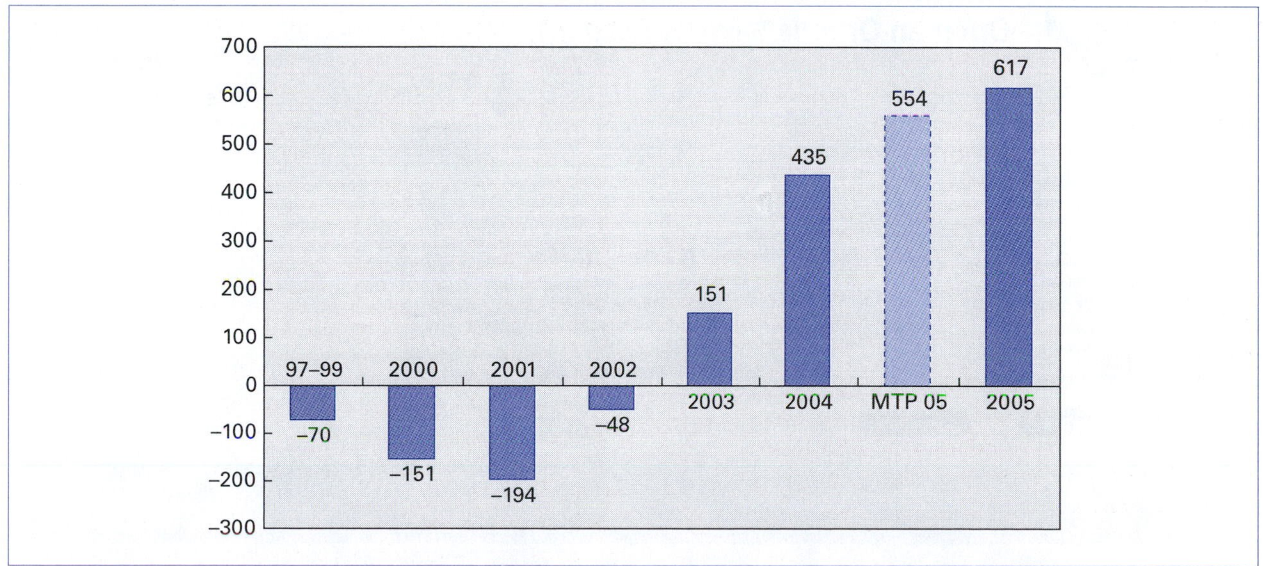

Source: ING DIRECT, http://www.ingdirect.com.

Reenergizing the U.S. Retail Banking Industry

ING DIRECT has attracted a lot of attention in the United States for several reasons. Despite the wide acceptance of the Internet in American households, online banks have not been particularly successful. Nevertheless, ING DIRECT has experienced a meteoric growth since its launch in September 2000. What is more, the venture broke-even after only two years.

More striking is the way that ING DIRECT positions itself in the U.S. banking industry. Arkadi Kuhlmann rejects the characterization of ING DIRECT as an Internet bank, even though the Web is its primary customer channel.

We're actually a pure savings bank, focusing on residential mortgages and savings accounts. You can't get any more old-fashioned than that.

In all of its communication, ING DIRECT points out that it is a federally chartered bank and that its savings are FDIC insured in order to guarantee credibility with its customers.[2] But that is where the comparison with typical retail banks stops. In fact, there is nothing typical about ING DIRECT.

ING DIRECT's Product Offering and Value Proposition

In a typical bank, first and foremost, the focus is on payments services. Once you get the payment services—such as checking, face-to-face teller services, and ATMs (automatic teller machines)—you're "owned" by the bank. But Arkadi Kuhlmann's strategy is different. The last thing he wants is to hold the traditional demand deposit accounts (i.e., checking account). These accounts typically have a large number of transactions per month and require a physical branch and a great deal of internal labor to process them. All this activity is too costly. Rather ING DIRECT wants to be "your other bank," offering a simple, high-return savings account, called the Orange Savings Account—ING's theme colour is orange. Customers are encouraged to shift money back and forth between their ING DIRECT savings account and their checking accounts with their existing bank. The account generates one of the highest rates in the market; sometimes the rate is four times higher than the industry average (see Exhibit 4). ING DIRECT sells its products with the simple slogan: "Great rates, no fees, no minimums."

ING DIRECT also offers a limited number of mutual funds. And the bulk of the assets of the bank consists of

Exhibit 4 "Great Rates, No Fees, No Minimums"

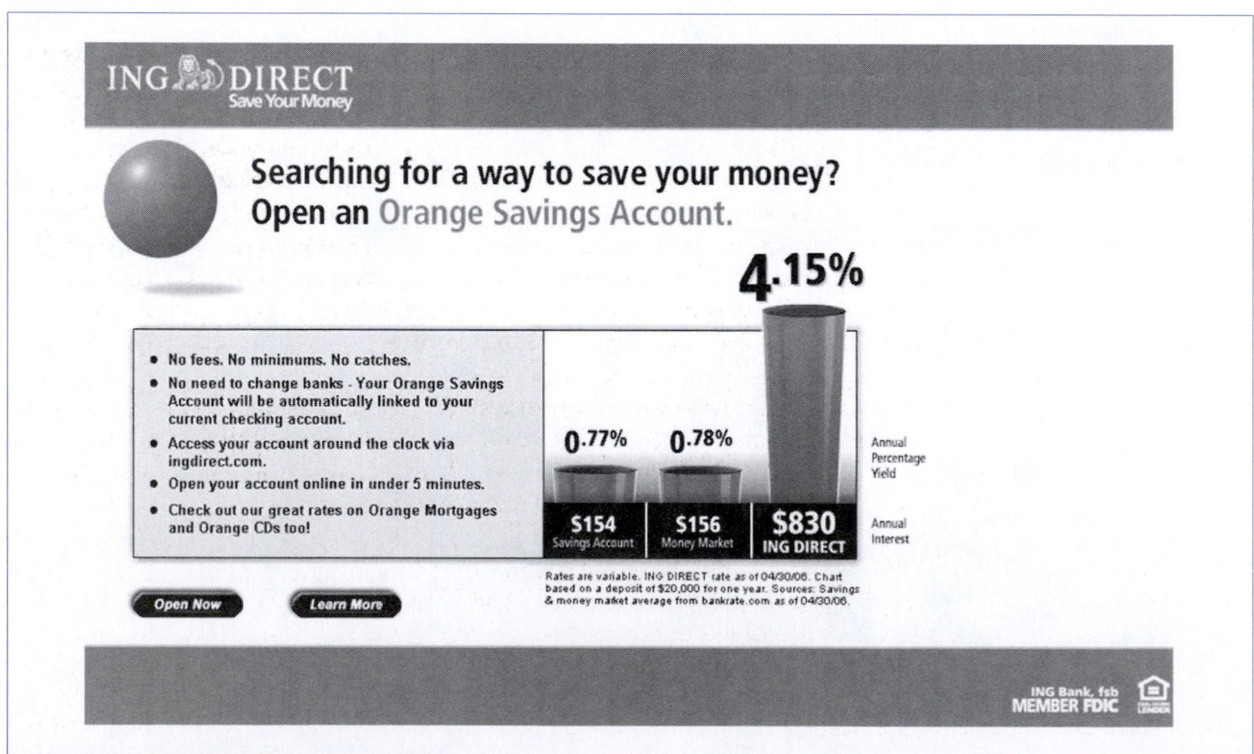

Source: ING DIRECT Web site, May 2006, http://www.ingdirect.com.

simple residential mortgages and a small percentage of home equity lines of credit and customer loans. Nearly 90 percent of the loan portfolio consists of mortgages. All products have low fees and few requirements.

But what's so unique about high rates? Arkadi Kuhlmann comments:

Nothing . . . . What is unique is that we offer consistently great rates and at the same time a high quality service. The key to deliver high quality service is simplicity: no tricks, no catches. Customers must immediately understand ING DIRECT products. Educating people about financial products is very expensive.

Although some banking professionals consider mortgages a difficult product to standardize and to sell via the Internet, Arkadi Kuhlmann disagrees:

You can turn mortgages into simple products too. But it requires that you reengineer the product and the processes behind it. And to some extent, you need to reengineer the customer as well.

And that strategy did not only attract many new customers, but also allowed the company to retain most of them.

Savings accounts can be set up in five minutes online. Mortgages take seven minutes to close (with all customer documentation available), as is demonstrated in Exhibit 5. The company tries to avoid customer contact over the phone. The Web site plays a crucial role in informing customers how to deal with the bank. ING DIRECT makes opening a savings account and transferring money extremely simple and straightforward. On the Web site, it posts: "It's that simple to earn more!" For the people who prefer human contact, ING DIRECT's U.S. operations have more than 500 call center associates in three

Exhibit 5 Online Banking: It's as Easy as . . .

Source: Picture taken at ING DIRECT Café (New York), May 2006.

call centers. Those associates are trained to provide fast response and prompt service to the customers. The company strives to get 80 percent of the calls answered in 20 seconds. As a matter of fact, employees have their bonuses tied to achieving this goal. In order to reach that goal, employees receive extensive training—about 20 days for five products (which is a lot compared to traditional banks). Overall, the brand strategy of ING DIRECT is best described by the acronym GRASP, "Great deals, Responsive, Accessible, Simple and easy, and Passionate."

The Target Customers

The first order of business for ING DIRECT is to introduce products that make it easy and financially rewarding for customers to save more. But part of the strategy is choosing the products it won't offer and the customers it won't serve. Unlike its traditional competitors, the company is not interested in rich Americans (unless they do what it wants them to do). "We want to *serve* the average American" as long as he/she behaves in the way ING DIRECT wants. In 2004, the company "fired" more than 3,500 customers who didn't play by the bank rules. Those customers relied too much on the call centers, or asked for too many exceptions from the standard operating procedures.

People should not come and explain their financial problems. We sell products and commodities, not solutions.

Communicating the Message

So far ING DIRECT USA has managed to communicate well the message about its rules and target customers. In five years, the bank has attracted more than 3.5 million customers. This growth can partially be explained by the huge efforts the company undertook to build the ING DIRECT brand: One third of its budget is allocated to marketing programs. Many customers are attracted by the combination of rates and a hip brand. ING DIRECT's marketing campaigns project a differentiated brand and "unbank-ness." They have a simple, clear message, and feature the bright colour orange, capturing customers' attention by communicating in a humorous, "anti-establishment" tone. Exhibit 6 presents some outdoor advertising ING DIRECT used in 2006. Some of those campaigns were locally adapted to the target markets (see Exhibit 7). (Exhibit 8 presents some marketing campaigns of ING DIRECT in other countries.) The purpose of the guerrilla marketing tactics is clear, according to Arkadi Kuhlmann:

People are sleeping. You have to shock people a little bit to get them to think differently about how they manage their money. So we wake them up with one of our marketing campaigns. They switch their money and go back to sleep.

Exhibit 6 Outdoor Advertising from ING DIRECT USA

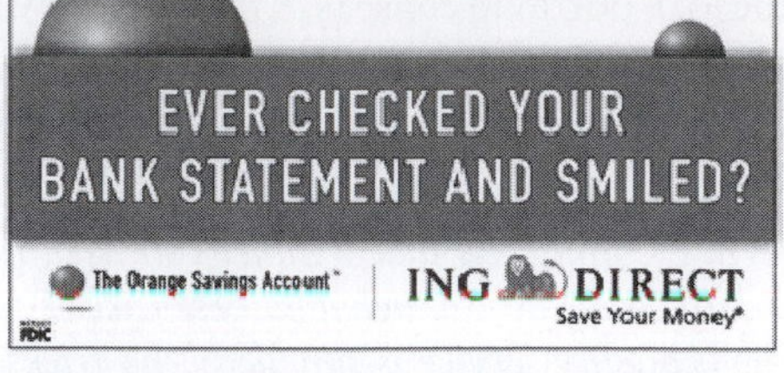

Source: ING DIRECT, http://www.ing.com.

Exhibit 7 Local Marketing Campaigns, ING DIRECT USA

Washington D.C.

New York

Phoenix & Philadelphia

Source: ING DIRECT, http://www.ing.com.

Exhibit 8 Marketing Campaigns, ING DIRECT in Countries Outside of the United States

Source: ING DIRECT, http://www.ing.com.

ING DIRECT does not restrict itself to the more traditional marketing campaigns. The bank continuously organizes innovative promotion campaigns to attract new customers. The company's "Save your money at the movies" campaign attracted many spectators and publicity in the press. In Baltimore and Washington, D.C., ING DIRECT surprised more than 8,000 people with a free movie at two participating Regal Cinemas. In a similar way, it offered free gas in Baltimore to 1,000 drivers at three selected Shell stations, and asked them to put that money into an Orange Savings Account. By the end of the three-hour promotion campaign cars lined up for more than three kilometres. ING Direct also let commuters ride the Boston "T" lines for free one morning, while ING representatives danced around in orange Paul Revere costumes. Those kinds of events certainly do wake people up.

Another uncommon feature of the marketing strategy is ING DIRECT's cafés. The cafés, each located in a big city of the targeted countries—such as New York, Washington, Philadelphia, Los Angeles—are not substitutes for branches. Rather they introduce the customers to the ING DIRECT brand. When ING DIRECT started its marketing and operations in Canada, early prospects were somewhat suspicious about the new brand. So they began visiting the company's call center in Toronto to check out the new bank to verify its physical existence. The employees from ING DIRECT Canada

Exhibit 9 Pictures of ING DIRECT Cafés in New York, Los Angeles, Philadelphia, and Wilmington

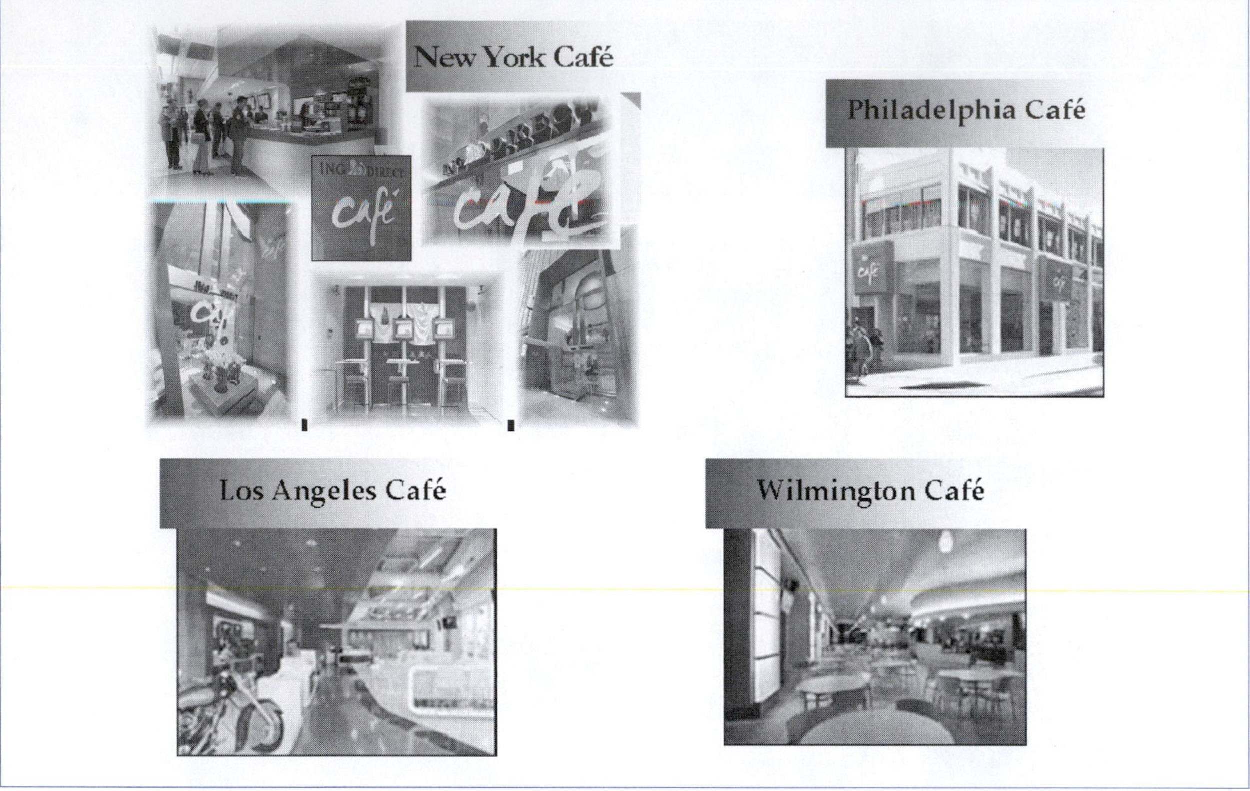

Source: ING DIRECT, http://www.ing.com.

offered those prospectors a cup of coffee in the coffee corner of the call center. That is how the idea emerged. It took Arkadi Kuhlmann some time to convince the managers at ING in Amsterdam to set up "coffee shops,"[3] but now the cafés are a typical element of ING DIRECT's marketing strategy. Pictures of the ING DIRECT cafés are shown in Exhibit 9.

The cafés sustain ING DIRECT's atypical bank image, and they offer the customers a place to go to speak with an ING DIRECT café member, each a trained banker, and experience the simplicity the brand denotes. While serving coffee, the café staff members—called sales associates—can discuss financial products or help check information on one of the online terminals located on the premises. Consistent with the brand, the coffee is much less expensive than similar coffee at Starbucks, and Internet usage at the cafés is free.

We believe saving money should be as simple as getting a cup of coffee. So we invite you to come in and experience just how refreshing it is to sip a latte, surf the Internet for free, and talk to us about how we can help Save Your Money.

Managing a Rebellious Organization

Obviously, the cafés have helped to build the brand. But it requires more than a handful of cafés to achieve the revenue and profit figures ING DIRECT has achieved so far. Behind that rebellious image is a well-oiled machine, designed to deal with high-volume, low-margin commodity products. Exhibit 10 shows the key components of the company's strategy execution. Although significant attention is paid to understand demand and increase revenues, the execution challenge also involves cost control and efficiency improvement. Even though most retail banks in the United States operate at a margin spread of 250 basis points (2.50 percentage points), ING DIRECT operates on a spread of 175 basis points. ING DIRECT is able to operate at lower costs by managing both the "front and back" offices.

Managing the Front and Back Office

A big part of its lower cost structure stems from the things that it doesn't offer, and where it doesn't have to invest. The company does not invest in an ATM network

Exhibit 10 Strategy Execution at ING DIRECT

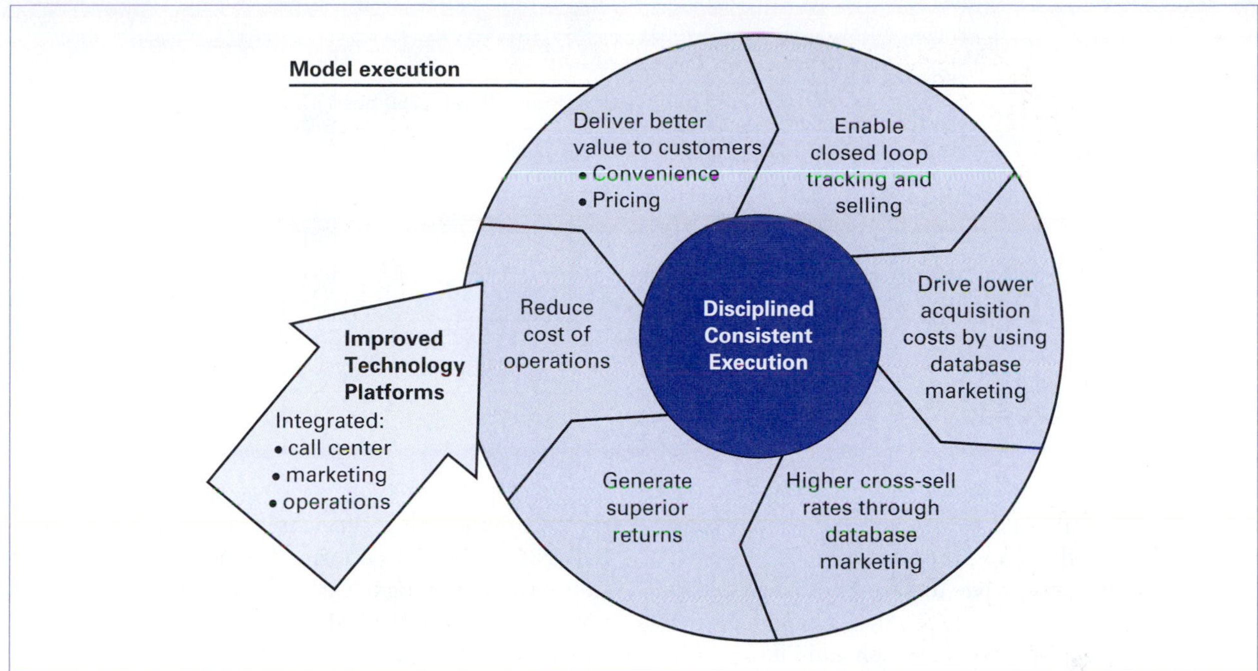

Source: ING Group, http://www.ing.com.

or in traditional branches. It encourages customers to open accounts online or by using an interactive voice response (IVR) system. Online servicing of accounts and mortgage applications cuts down on costs. The company's acquisition costs are estimated to be lower than $100. According to Jim Kelly, chief marketing officer for ING DIRECT: "It is not unusual for a bank to have customer acquisition costs of about $300–400."[4] Similarly, maintenance costs are kept low as well. Says Arkadi Kuhlmann:

If you don't have any activity in a month, we're not sending you a statement. Savings account customers who insist on a paper statement should go back to Chase.

The company also communicates to its customers that a high number of calls to the call center will lead to higher fees or lower interest rates. So customers should understand why ING DIRECT discourages telephone calls to (expensive) operators at the call center. To further discourage the use of these operators, customers who call frequently are put at the end of the operator's queue.

All of these aspects require that ING DIRECT manages its processes in a rigorous way. Processes are documented, and a large number of guidelines and procedures exist for the core processes within the organization. The company is constantly looking to simplify financial products and financial transactions, and uses tools such as Lean Six Sigma to achieve the efficiency of the manufacturing industry. In 2004, ING DIRECT Canada won a Canadian Information Productivity Award of Excellence for its Mortgage Application Processing Solution (MAPS). This solution enabled ING DIRECT to simplify the process of obtaining a mortgage dramatically. And this new solution is also leveraged in the other ING DIRECT entities.

The sharing of best practices and materials is common within the ING DIRECT business units. For example, ING DIRECT shares marketing campaigns across all of the countries in which it has operations and reuses marketing concepts and graphic designs.

Information Technology

ING DIRECT benefited from the absence of "legacy" information technology systems. ING DIRECT started from scratch, which helped the company significantly to operate with a higher performing IT architecture at a lower cost. The challenge was to develop a flexible IT architecture providing brand uniformity across borders, but allowing for adaptation to local banking regulations.

ING DIRECT buys the IT hardware centrally, exploiting its buying power, and then makes it available to the various country organizations. For software, the company's strategy is to "re-use (from sister companies) before buy, and buy before build." This approach saves an enormous amount of money, and at the same time helps to insure a high level of service and ease in accommodating growing numbers of accounts. A central IT Group develops and maintains the IT policies and standards

Exhibit 11 Evolution of ING DIRECT's Operational Cost Base to Assets (excluding marketing)

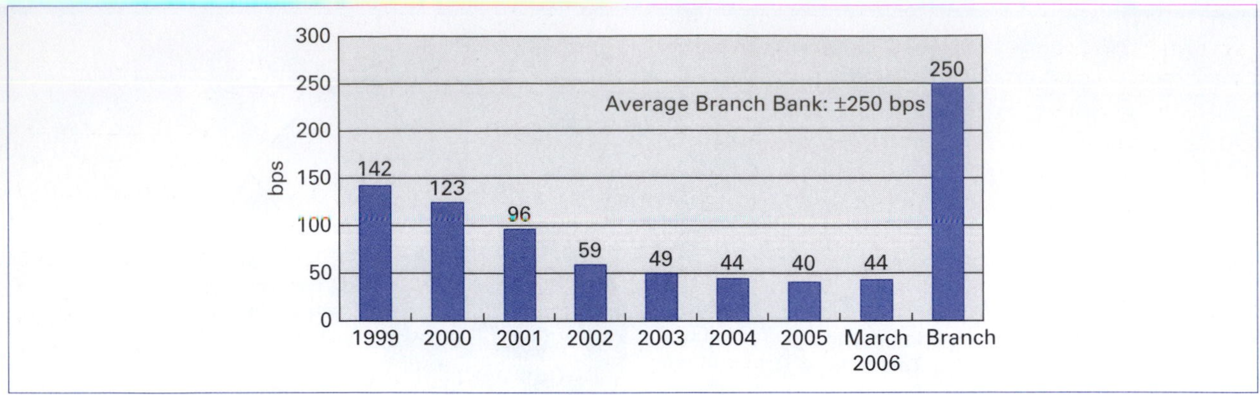

Source: ING Group, http://www.ing.com.

across the company, and works with the various countries to update and improve the systems.

ING DIRECT also strives to have its different departments in close contact with each other. The process flow is specified for the whole organization and takes into account all processes from the various departments simultaneously. Streamlining processes is a key element in ING DIRECT's business architecture, and business process orientation is a necessary element, says Arkadi Kuhlmann.

We put our marketing and IT departments in one area. If your core competencies are marketing and IT, you really have to do both of them together.

Product Development

Product development is also done in close coordination with marketing and IT. To develop and introduce a new product, a country unit would first develop a business plan that includes forecasts of demand and marketing expenditures. The plan also evaluates the operational, financial, and legal risks associated with the launch of the product. And it specifies clearly what IT and operational requirements are necessary to support the product. The hurdles for a new product are high. Brunon Bartkiewicz (former manager at ING DIRECT, now heading ING's banking operations in Poland) explains:[5]

Every new product reduces our simplicity, increases our risk and defocuses our people. A person who is working on marketing seven products cannot know all the details, all the figures, all the logic that a person focused on one product does. In the end, the whole game is efficiency: efficiency in marketing, in operations, and in systems.

Performance Measurement

Another important element of ING DIRECT's business model is the obsession for measuring how customers react to marketing campaigns and online advertising. But ING DIRECT's performance measurement doesn't stop at the marketing department. The company's operations centers compete against each other for recognition and monthly bonuses based on their ability to meet sales and service goals. Everybody in ING DIRECT measures and is measured. Some performance measures are posted daily on an intranet site, accessible to everyone within the company. The performance measures are continuously analyzed and are the input for action plans, allowing new product and process initiatives.

All operational performance measures have a direct impact on the company's five high-level targets. These targets are: (1) total profit, (2) nonmarketing expenses/ending assets, (3) net-retail funds entrusted (on balance sheet) growth, (4) net mortgage growth, and (5) call-center service level. Efficiency and cost effectiveness are monitored carefully. Exhibit 11 presents the evolution of the operational costs of ING DIRECT (all countries) from 1999 to March 2006. There we can see that the expense-to-assets ratio (excluding marketing expenses) for ING DIRECT (all countries) decreased from 96 basis points in 2001 to 40 basis points in 2006. An average branch bank has an expense-to-asset ratio of about 250 basis points. In a similar way, total assets per employee for ING DIRECT are $48 million, whereas traditional branch-based banks have an average of $5–$6 million per employee.

Those figures are impressive. But equally impressive is how ING DIRECT has "structured" its measurement processes. ING DIRECT used Microsoft Excel spreadsheets to create annual reports summarizing the company's performance until the company's fast growth necessitated a more structured approach toward measuring company performance. In 2004, the company hired a consultant who helped it set up a performance measurement system, generating enterprise-wide, relevant management information that steers the company's future growth. The powerful reporting and analysis tools help identify further cost-saving opportunities and gain in-depth visibility into the key performance metrics. In addition, the performance measurement system allows ING DIRECT to measure the effectiveness of marketing campaigns, to track market and risk exposure, and to gain a better understanding of its new and existing customer base. Arkadi Kuhlmann agrees that ING DIRECT has been getting more efficient with customer acquisition and with lowering customer acquisition costs due to the introduction of the new performance measurement system.

Leadership, People, and Culture

What really sets ING DIRECT apart from its competitors is its people. You can't be a rebel if you have all traditional bankers in your organization. That is why ING DIRECT tries to hire people who do not come from the big banks. Only for functions such as risk management, treasury, or asset-liability management does the bank hire employees with a banking background. Of course, ING DIRECT can benefit from ING's expertise in these technical matters. CEO Arkadi Kuhlmann himself is an experienced banker with a deep knowledge of all core functions within the bank. But he profiles himself as the outsider—even the bad guy—of the industry: "When the rest of the banking industry decides to zig, I zag," he says. And he ensures that the entire organization zags with him.

Arkadi Kuhlmann truly is a visionary and inspiring leader. You won't hear Arkadi talk a lot about financial metrics. Arkadi Kuhlmann is out for a more inspiring mission and vision.

We are leading the Americans back to saving. One way or another, most financial companies are telling you to spend more. That's not what we want.

In all communication, the focus is on saving. And that's why credit cards and traditional checking accounts don't fit in the product portfolio.

Above all, it is the way that Arkadi conveys the message that makes him an inspiring leader: "You can't do meaningful things without passion and a powerful idea about what you're trying to do," he argues. In the United States, he has about 1,300 people who help him on his crusade. What is striking is that the employees of ING DIRECT are as determined as the CEO himself.

But then ING DIRECT spends a lot of time and effort to ensure that it hires people willing to do things differently from the industry, and inspires them with the same set of values that it uses to connect with its customers. The company hires people with the right attitude, who can easily be trained and introduced to a competitive selling culture. But above all, people are selected based on whether their personal values fit with the values of ING DIRECT. Rick Perles, head of human resources at ING DIRECT, comments:

Everyone, no matter what level, starts in the new hire program. The new hire program used to be three days but we have expanded it to five, which is a big investment in our people and not something most companies do. All new hires take customer calls. During those first days, they'll hear a lot about culture and what ING stands for. Some people don't subscribe to it, but they realize it even before the five days are up.

The Maiden Voyage refers to the next 90 days, where we spend another week or two facilitating technical training with our sales associates. During those first 90 days, there are things the new hire has to do before coming back for the second part of new hire training. These activities include volunteering in the community, working in one of our Cafés, and reading The Alchemist *by Paulo Coelho.*[6]

Values and culture are not idle concepts within ING DIRECT. Arkadi Kuhlmann is aware that the most differentiating aspect of the whole company is situated in what is called the "Orange Code." The Orange Code specifies in 13 statements what ING DIRECT is all about and what it stands for. The Orange Code brings the vision to life and provides employees with common goals. For example, one of those statements is "We will be for everyone." In the company, this vision is made concrete by removing all titles and offices. Everybody is in the bonus program, and the metrics are the same for everybody.

The reward strategy is also particular. Employees can earn substantial bonuses, based on how they perform relative to some well-specified financial, customer, and operational targets. Bonuses can be up to half of the fixed salary. Interestingly enough, the employees' fixed salary is also higher than the industry average. Although a cost leader, the company prides itself on paying at the 75th percentile or higher. Maybe that's why in a recent employee survey, 99 percent of the employees were proud to say that they are part of ING DIRECT. The survey indicated however that the employees' positive attitude is based on other facets than the reward policy. In particular, the employees consider ING DIRECT an attractive employer for the strength of its business model, and its "nonbanking" culture. ING DIRECT is a flat organization with few management layers. And employees can provide input in the many action plans that the organization sets up. Arkadi Kuhlmann describes it as follows: "I make sure that managers tell the employees *what* to do, but not *how* to do things. This is the starting point for real empowerment."

The growth of the company and the support of the ING Group is another driving force for the employees to help fulfill ING DIRECT's ambitious goals.

The Orange Code also ensures that the employees don't become too complacent. One of the statements reads as follows: "We aren't conquerors. We are pioneers. We are not here to destroy. We are here to create!"

Challenges

The market has been created and ING DIRECT has developed an attractive position within that market. But the easy success of the online savings bank has attracted other newcomers. MetLife launched an Internet bank in late 2002 and has been heavily promoting high interest rates. And in 2006, HSBC's Internet Bank stepped in with higher rates than those of ING DIRECT. Other banks are soon to follow.

Arkadi Kuhlmann acknowledges that he will have to cope with more challenging competitors in the future. At the same time, the success of ING DIRECT has also created even higher expectations on the financial potential of its business model. A key question for the management team will be how the company can sustain its growth. What products should the company introduce? And which markets should it enter?

The company carefully analyzes what other ING DIRECT products customers will desire. In line with the general philosophy of the company, such an offer will only be made with the customers' consent. But only a small number of customers have opted into the permission marketing program. Should the company more aggressively try to cross-sell?

ING DIRECT also has to manage internal challenges. One of these challenges is how to cope with the growth the company has experienced. More customers mean increased pressure on the systems and processes. In the banking industry, size quite often implies *dis*economies of scale. Furthermore, will the company find employees who embrace its unique culture? Managing a unique culture is easier if the company is small. But it gets more challenging as the company grows.

One of the internal challenges also relates to the relationship that ING DIRECT has with its parent organization, ING Group. ING Group, known as the integrated financial services group, actively stimulates synergies between its banking, insurance, and investment entities across different countries. But Arkadi Kuhlmann has always been able to limit ING DIRECT's participation in the Mandated Synergies program to what he calls the "low hanging fruit." ING DIRECT will help to exploit the benefits of cooperation with sister companies, but not at all costs. How long will ING DIRECT's management benefit from that exceptional status? And what will be the implications if ING DIRECT becomes more integrated and incorporated within the traditional ING businesses.

One of those synergies is to integrate brand development. ING DIRECT positions itself as the rebel in the banking industry, but at the same time it wears the brand of one of the most respected, traditional financial institutions, ING. The more that ING DIRECT contributes to ING's profit increases, the greater the dilemma.

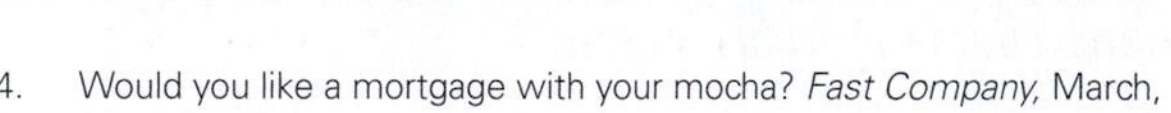

Notes

1. ING DIRECT has opened cafés in Toronto, Vancouver, Sydney, Barcelona, Madrid, New York, Philadelphia, Los Angeles, Wilmington, and a couple of other cities.
2. The Federal Deposit Insurance Corporation (FDIC) is a governance institution that insures deposits in thrift institutions and commercial banks.
3. Coffee shops have a different connotation in the Netherlands than in the United States.
4. Would you like a mortgage with your mocha? *Fast Company,* March, 68, 110.
5. ING DIRECT: Your other bank, IMD Case, IMD-3-1343, 7.
6. 2005, Interview with Rick Perles by Irene Monley, *Delaware Society for Human Resource Management,* October, 2(4).

Case 16

JetBlue Airways: Challenges Ahead

Theodore Bosley, Christopher Calton, Jeffrey Deakins, Tomoko Nakajima, Sally Orford, Robin Pohl, Robin Chapman

Arizona State University

Introduction

We're going to bring humanity back to air travel.
—DAVID NEELEMAN
FOUNDER AND CHAIRPERSON

David Neeleman, JetBlue's founder and chairperson, sought to "bring the humanity back to air travel."[1] Since launching operations in February 2000, JetBlue distinguished itself from its competitors by providing superior customer service at low fares. The JetBlue experience included brand new airplanes, leather seats, and personal satellite TV service. The firm experienced rapid early growth. In a period when most U.S. airlines struggled in the aftermath of the September 11, 2001, terrorist attacks, JetBlue reported 18 consecutive quarterly profits.

Then in 2005, JetBlue announced its first net loss of $20 million. The disappointing results were attributed to spiraling fuel prices, aggressive competition, and increasing operating costs. Global events such as war, political turmoil, and natural disasters contributed to the rise in fuel prices. The average price for a barrel of oil in 2003 was $30, by the summer of 2005 prices had climbed above $60 per barrel. The legacy airlines were becoming more competitive after exiting bankruptcy and streamlining their operations to benefit from economies of scale.[2] Analysts speculated that JetBlue was experiencing growth pains:, their maintenance costs on aging planes were increasing, employees were becoming more senior, and new profitable routes were harder to obtain.[3] The company continued to lose money in 2006. While major competitors, such as AMR, the parent company for American Airlines, and Continental, reported higher than expected returns, JetBlue announced a narrow third-quarter loss of $500,000. Following its third-quarter loss, JetBlue announced plans to slow down growth by delaying deliveries of some aircraft, selling others, and eliminating some cross-country flights.[4] Despite these actions, in a recent interview Neeleman insisted, "We're still a growth airline."[5] It remains to be seen how JetBlue will continue to grow in the face of increasing strategic challenges.

History

Founding History of Jet Blue

David Neeleman founded JetBlue Airways Corporation in 1999, after raising $130 million in investment capital. Building on his past experiences, Neeleman hired talented executives, such as David Barger, previous vice president of the Newark, New Jersey, hub for Continental, and John Owen, previous vice president of Operations Planning and Analysis for Southwest.[6] JetBlue chose John F. Kennedy International Airport in New York as its hub and initially obtained 75 takeoff and landing slots.

Neeleman's vision was to provide "high-end customer service at low-end prices."[7] Although JetBlue imitated competitor Southwest Airlines with a single seat class, it did so with Airbus A-320 narrow-body jets instead of Boeing 737s. The A-320 provided wider cabins and wider seats for JetBlue passengers with more room for carry-on baggage.[8] JetBlue implemented innovative IT programs such as an Internet booking system that allowed customers to make reservations online or with a touch-tone phone, and a paperless cockpit to allow pilots to prepare for flight more quickly, helping planes to stay on schedule.[9] JetBlue also provided complementary, unlimited snacks and beverages, preassigned seating, and a selection of first-run movies available from Fox InFlight on flights longer than two hours. For further differentiation, JetBlue installed 36 channels of free DIRECTV programming.

The authors would like to thank Professor Robert E. Hoskisson for his support under whose direction the case was developed. The authors do not intend to illustrate either effective or ineffective handling of a managerial situation. The case solely provides material for class discussion.

Early in 2000, the first JetBlue flights departed from New York to Fort Lauderdale, with a fleet of two planes. JetBlue gradually increased its destinations during the year to include 12 additional airports in California, Florida, New York, Utah, and Vermont. By December, Neeleman announced the landmark of JetBlue's millionth customer and reported $100 million in revenues.

Rapid Growth in 2000–2004

The September 11, 2001, terrorist attacks on America resulted in a widespread fear of air travel, negatively impacting most of the airline industry. While other airlines announced millions in lost revenue following 9/11, JetBlue made a profit and within eight weeks expanded its network to include six more destinations and resumed IT spending to further improve services offered.[10] In February 2002, JetBlue won the 2002 Air Transport World "Market Development Award" for its successful first two years of service, and also was named "Best Overall Airline" by *Onboard Service* magazine.[11] On April 11, 2002, JetBlue announced its initial public offering (IPO) of 5.86 million shares of common stock at a price of $27 per share.[12] JetBlue grew steadily between 2003 and 2004, with annual operating revenues growing from $998.4 million in 2003, to $1.27 billion in 2004. Exhibits 1 through 3 show JetBlue's financial statements for the years 2001 to 2005.

Slowed Growth in 2005–2007

In November 2005 JetBlue decided to add nine new Embraer E190s to its fleet. JetBlue ordered the aircraft with a 100-seat configuration, bigger television screens than the Airbus A-320, and 100 channels from XM Satellite Radio. Also, in late 2005, JetBlue decided to fund $80 million of an airport expansion project at John F. Kennedy Airport, which had a total budget of $875 million. The expansion would allow for more than double the number of flights at JetBlue's hub airport within three years.[13]

However, JetBlue's quarterly financial report started to show growth saturation. Quarterly growth records of operating revenue in 2005 were 29.5 percent, 34.5 percent,

Exhibit 1 Consolidated Statement of Income

JetBlue Airways Corporation
(in $ millions, year ended December 31)

	2006	2005	2004	2003	2002
Operating Revenues					
Passenger	$ 2223	$ 1620	$ 1220	$ 965	$ 615
Other	140	81	45	33	20
Total Operating Revenues	2363	1701	1265	998	635
Operating Expenses					
Salaries, wages, and benefits	553	428	337	267	162
Aircraft fuel	752	488	255	147	76
Landing fees and other rents	158	112	92	70	44
Depreciation and amortization	151	115	77	51	43
Aircraft rent	103	74	70	60	41
Sales and marketing	104	81	63	54	27
Maintenance materials and repairs	87	64	45	23	9
Other operating expenses	328	291	215	159	127
Total Operating Expenses	2236	1653	1154	831	530
Operating Income	$ 127	$ 48	$ 111	$ 167	$ 105
Other Income (Expenses)					
Interest expense	(173)	(107)	(53)	(29)	(21)
Capitalized interest	27	16	9	5	5
Interest income and other	28	19	8	8	5
government compensation				23	
Total other income (expense)	(118)	(72)	(36)	7	(10)
Income (Loss) before income taxes	9	(24)	75	174	95
Income tax expense (benefit)	10	(4)	29	71	40
Net Income (Loss)	$ (1)	$ (20)	$ 46	$ 103	$ 55

Source: JetBlue Airways Corporation 2006 Annual Report.

Exhibit 2 Consolidated Balance Sheet

JetBlue Airways Corporation
(in $ millions, except share data)

	December 31				
	2006	2005	2004	2003	2002
Assets					
Cash and short-term Investments	$ 699	$ 484	$ 450	$ 607.31	$ 257.85
Total receivables, net	77	94	37	16.72	11.93
Total inventory	27	21	10	8.3	4.84
Prepaid expenses	124	36	17	13.42	5.59
Other current assets, total	0	0	0	0	2.85
Total Current Assets	$ 927	$ 635	$ 514	$ 645.74	$ 283.06
Property/Plant/Equip, total	$ 3438	$ 2978	$ 2130	$ 1421	$ 997
Goodwill, net	0	0	0	0	0
Intangibles, net	32	43	54	62	68
Long-term investments	0	0	0	0	0
Note receivable long-term	0	0	0	0	0
Other long-term assets, total	446	236	99	57	30
Other assets, total	0	0	0	0	0
Total Assets	$ 4843	$ 3892	$ 2797	$ 2186	$ 1379

	December 31				
	2006	2005	2004	2003	2002
Liabilities and Shareholders' Equity					
Accounts payable	$ 136	$ 99	$ 71	$ 53	$ 46
Payable/Accrued	0	0	0	0	0
Accrued expenses	164	111	94	85	54
Notes payable/Short-term debt	39	64	44	30	22
Current port. of LT debt/capital	175	158	105	67	51
Leases					
Other current liabilities, total	340	243	174	135	98
Total Current Liabilities	$ 854	$ 676	$ 488	$ 370	$ 270
Long-term debt and leases	$ 2626	$ 2103	$ 1396	$ 1012	$ 640
Deferred income tax	136	116	121	99	39
Minority interest	0	0	0	0	0
Other liabilities, total	275	86	38	34	17
Total Liabilities	$ 3891	$ 2981	$ 2043	$ 1515	$ 964
Redeemable preferred stock	$ 0	$ 0	$ 0	$ 0	$ 0
Preferred stock-non	0	0	0	0	0
Common stock	2	2	1	1	1
Additional paid-in capital	813	764	581	552	407
Retained earnings	144	145	165	120	16
Other equity, total	(7)	0	7	(2)	(9)
Total Equity	952	911	754	671	415
Total Liabilities & Shareholders' Equity	$ 4843	$ 3892	$ 2797	$ 2186	$1,379

Source: JetBlue Airways Corporation 2006 Annual Report.

Exhibit 3 Consolidated Statement of Cash Flows

JetBlue Airways Corporation
(in $ millions)

	December 31				
	2006	**2005**	**2004**	**2003**	**2002**
Cash Flows from Operating Activities					
Net Income	$ (1)	$ (20)	$ 46	$ 103	$ 55
Operating Activities					
Deferred income taxes	10	(4)	29	69	40
Depreciation	136	101	67	45	25
Amortization	18	16	11	7	2
Stock-based compensation	21	9	2	2	
Changes in certain operating assets and liabilities					
Increase in receivables	(12)	(28)	(20)	(4)	7
Increase in inventories	(28)	(20)	(6)	(11)	(4)
Increase in air traffic liabilities	97	69	39	37	46
Increase in accounts payable and other accrued liabilities	33	54	21	38	35
Other, Net	0	(7)	10	1	11
Net Cash Provided by Operating Activities	274	170	199	287	216
Cash Flows from Investing Activities					
Capital expenditures	(996)	(941)	(617)	(573)	(544)
Predelivery deposits for flight equipment	(106)	(183)	(180)	(160)	(109)
Purchase of held-to-maturity investment	(23)	(5)	(19)	(26)	(11)
Proceeds from maturities of held-to-maturity investment	15	18	25	9	2
Purchase of available-for-sale securities	(1002)	(79)	76	(235)	(80)
Increase in restricted cash and other assets	(16)	(86)	(5)	(2)	(1)
Net Cash Used in Investing Activities	$ (1307)	$ (1276)	$ (720)	$ (987)	$ (744)
Cash Flows from Financing Activities					
Proceeds from:					
Issuance of common stock	28	178	20	136	174
Issuance of long-term debt	855	872	499	446	416
Aircraft sale and leaseback transactions	406	152		265	0.3
Short-term borrowings	45	68	44	33	150
Repayment of long-term debt	(390)	(117)	(77)	(57)	27
Repayment of short-term debt	(71)	(47)	(30)	(25)	(71)
Other, Net	–15	(13)	(19)	(9)	(34)
Net Cash Provided by Financing Activities	$ 1037	$ 1093	$ 437	$ 789	$ (5)
Increase in Cash and Cash Equivalents	$ 4	$ (13)	$ (84)	$ 89	$ 129
Cash and cash equivalent at beginning of period	$ 6	$ 19	$ 103	$ 14	$ 117
Cash and cash equivalent at end of period	$ 10	$ 6	$ 19	$ 103	$ 247

Source: JetBlue Airways Corporation 2006 Annual Report.

40.2 percent, and –5.2 percent, respectively. JetBlue announced a fourth quarter net loss of $42.4 million, representing a loss per share of $0.25. It was JetBlue's first quarterly net loss.[14]

In 2006, the firm announced unstable earnings, and reported a loss of $32 million, a profit of $14 million, and a loss of $0.5 million in the first three quarters, respectively.[15] Even though JetBlue served 47 destinations with up to 470 daily flights, it decided to reduce its rate of growth over the next three years by delaying the delivery of additional planes.[16] Data for destination and service commenced are listed in Exhibit 4. Effort to slow the growth rate was intended to preserve cash, enabling JetBlue to remain stable among competitors.

The first quarter of 2007 did not get off to a great start for JetBlue. Bad weather in February resulted in many

Exhibit 4 JetBlue's Destinations

Destination	Service Commenced
New York, New York	February 2000
Fort Lauderdale, Florida	February 2000
Buffalo, New York	February 2000
Tampa, Florida	March 2000
Orland, Florida	June 2000
Ontario, California	July 2000
Oakland, California	August 2000
Rochester, New York	August 2000
Burlington, Vermont	September 2000
West Palm Beach, Florida	October 2000
Salt Lake City, Utah	November 2000
Fort Myers, Florida	November 2000
Seattle, Washington	May 2001
Syracuse, New York	May 2001
Denver, Colorado	May 2001
New Orleans, Louisiana	July 2001
Long Beach, California	August 2001
Washington, D.C. (Dulles Airport)	November 2001
San Juan, Puerto Rico	May 2002
Las Vegas, Nevada	November 2002
San Diego, California	June 2003
Boston, Massachusetts	January 2004
Sacramento, California	March 2004
Aguadilla, Puerto Rico	May 2004
Santiago, Dominican Republic	June 2004
San Jose, California	June 2004
New York, New York (LGA Airport)	September 2004
Phoenix, Arizona	October 2004
Nassau, The Bahamas	November 2004
Burbank, California	May 2005
Portland, Oregon	May 2005
Ponce, Puerto Rico	June 2005
Newark, New Jersey	October 2005
Austin, Texas	January 2006
Richmond, Virginia	March 2006
Hamilton, Bermuda	May 2006
Sarasota-Bradenton, Florida	September 2006
Cancun, Mexico	November 2006
Island of Aruba	November 2006
Chicago, Illinois	January 2007
White Plains, New York	March 2007
San Francisco, California	May 2007

Source: JetBlue Airways Corporation Form 10-K, Fiscal year ending December 31, 2006.

cancelled flights and stranded passengers. The climax of the crisis occurred when nine airplanes full of angry passengers sat on the tarmac for six hours, because JetBlue leaders had expected the weather to clear and did not cancel flights. CEO David Neeleman received bad press for his management of the situation. Neeleman responded by humbly admitting "that his company's management was not strong enough. [It] was the result of a shoestring communications system that left pilots and flight attendants in the dark, and an undersize reservation system."[17] Rapid efforts were made to regain its brand image such that a JetBlue Customer Bill of Rights was created, a customer advisory council was formed, plans were made to cross-train crew members, and new communication strategies were put in place.[18] In addition JetBlue waived change fees and fare differences to assist customers who may be affected by additional storms throughout the winter of 2007. Despite his sincere efforts to bounce back from this predicament, Neeleman eventually had to step down as CEO in order to appease shareholders. David Barger, former COO succeeded Neeleman as CEO and needed to establish a strong position against JetBlue rivals.

Competitive Environment

In 1978, the Airline Deregulation Act eliminated government control over fares and routes, opening up the industry to increased competition. The airline industry is now highly competitive, consisting of 43 mainline carriers and 79 regional airlines. The U.S. Department of Transportation (DOT) classifies airlines into three categories based on annual revenue: major (revenue more than $1 billion), national (revenue between $100 million to $1 billion), and regional/commuter (revenue less than $100 million).[19] With annual revenue of $1.7 billion, JetBlue is one of the smaller major carriers and competes primarily on point-to-point routes. Its major competitors are low-cost carrier Southwest Airlines and traditional carriers, AMR Corp, United Airlines, US Airways, Continental Airlines, and Delta Air.[20]

Southwest is JetBlue's most obvious competitor, but the traditional airlines are becoming more aggressive in the low-fare market. Following recent bankruptcies, legacy airlines are emerging with clean balance sheets and lower cost structures. As the major airlines become more competitive and expand their domestic businesses, the low-cost airlines struggle to find new markets.[21]

Competition also comes from the regional carriers, which typically partner with the major airlines to share routes, risk, and costs. For example, Mesa partners with United Airlines and operates as United Express, with Delta Airlines as Delta Express, and with US Air as US Air Express. In exchange for an agreed proportion of revenue, Mesa operates flights on select local routes, while its partners handle reservations and marketing. In recent years, the regional airlines fared better than most, growing twice as fast as the national carriers.[22] However, as the competitive environment toughens, many of the large airlines are renegotiating the agreements, and in some cases—such as Atlantic Coast, a former partner of United Airlines—regional airlines are deciding to operate independently.[23]

The major airlines also form alliances—with each other and international carriers—to share marketing and scheduling capabilities. American Airlines partners with British Airways, Quantas, and various European airlines to form the One World Alliance, which serves 135 countries and operates a shared frequent flyer program. The Star Alliance, spearheaded by United Airlines, with Lufthansa, Scandinavian Air System, All Nippon Airways, and Air Canada, serves 157 countries.[24] Such alliances increase the market power of their members, and research has shown they increase passenger volume by an average of 9.4 percent.[25] Although the benefit is more significant for global carriers seeking to expand their network abroad, researchers observed an average improvement in number of tickets booked by 7.4 percent on short-haul flights.

Although JetBlue does not currently participate in any alliances, it has had discussions about forming one with international airlines in an effort to leverage its power at the hub in JFK. JetBlue does not want to enter a traditional agreement with other airlines, because many of these agreements include increased overhead costs. JetBlue is hoping to create an agreement that will increase traffic without increasing costs.[26]

Fare pricing is an important competitive factor within the industry. For many years excess capacity posed a significant problem, causing airlines to either leave planes on the ground or fly planes with empty seats. In order to avoid this dilemma, carriers try to increase market share by discounting tickets. Even the legacy airlines slash fares in order to compete on low-cost routes. Although low-cost airlines, like JetBlue, still offer the greatest number of discounted fares, some of the cheapest tickets are now available from traditional airlines, such as American, Delta, and United.[27]

Rumors of consolidation in the industry could change the competitive landscape. US Airways made a hostile bid for bankrupt Delta Airlines in fourth quarter 2006, but withdrew its offer in January 2007 due to the inability to reach financial agreement with Delta creditors.[28] The merger would have created the largest airline in a fragmented industry and would likely have triggered further consolidations.[29] Even though a wave of consolidation may create a more efficient airline industry with fewer major players, consolidations affect ticket prices, usually leading to higher ticket prices, and complicate the flight paths offered by airlines. Therefore, consolidations affect all competitors within the industry.

Key Competitors

Southwest Airlines

Southwest is the leading low-fare, no-frills, U.S. carrier. The company was founded in 1967 as a Texas-based airline to serve Dallas, Houston, and San Antonio. The airline now flies to more than 63 cities across the United States. In 2006, Southwest reported a $499 million profit and net sales of $9.86 billion.[30] Exhibit 5 compares key financial data for the major airlines. In 2005, America West's CEO, Douglas Parker, described Southwest as follows: "They really were at one point the scrawny kid who was lifting weights in his basement. Now they come out and they're bigger than anybody else and stronger than anybody else."[31]

Southwest's strategy emphasizes low costs; the firm was the first to sell tickets online and to introduce unassigned seating. It operates a single aircraft fleet of 481 Boeing 737s. The company is also lauded for its unique and friendly culture and its high level of customer service.[32] However, evidence now indicates a shift in its strategy—from serving underserved routes, to competing in major markets such as Denver and Philadelphia. Southwest is now the largest U.S. airline in terms of number of passengers (Exhibit 6), and in order to continue to grow, Southwest is competing against United in its Denver hub, and US Airways, on routes out of Philadelphia.[33]

Exhibit 5 U.S. Major Airlines' Select Financials for Year Ended 2006 (in $millions)

	JetBlue	UAL	SWA	Delta	Continental	US Airways	AMR Corp.
Total revenues	$2,363	$ 19,340	$ 9,086	$ 17,171	$13,128	$11,557	$ 22,563
Cost of revenues	1,653	14,114	6,311	14,430	11,007	9,049	17,659
Gross profit	570	5,226	2,573	1,694	1,453	1,814	4,904
Profit as % of revenue	24%	27%	28%	10%	11%	16%	22%
Operating income (loss)	127	23,381	934	(6,148)	468	558	1,060
Net income (loss)	$ (1)	$ 22,386	$ 499	$ (6,203)	$ 343	$ 304	$ 231
Total assets	$4,843	25,369	$13,460	$ 19,622	$11,308	$ 7,576	$ 29,145
Current assets	927	6,273	2,601	5,385	4,129	3,354	6,902
Total liabilities	$3,891	$ 23,221	$ 7,011	$ 33,215	$10,961	$ 6,606	$ 29,751
Current liabilities	854	7,945	2,887	5,769	3,955	2,712	8,505
Total owner equity	$ 952	$ 2,148	$ 6,449	$ (13,593)	$ 347	$ 970	$ (606)

Source: 2007, MSN Money Central, http://moneycentral.msn.com/investor/research/welcome.asp, July 24.

Exhibit 6 Top 10 U.S. Airlines, Ranked by August 2006 Domestic Scheduled Enplanements

Passenger numbers in millions

August 2006 Rank	Carrier	August 2006 Enplanements	August 2005 Rank	August 2005 Enplanements
1	Southwest	8.7	1	8.1
2	American	6.5	3	6.8
3	Delta	5.4	2	7.0
4	United	5.1	4	5.0
5	Northwest	4.1	5	4.2
6	Continental	3.1	7	2.9
7	US Airways	2.6	6	3.1
8	America West	1.8	8	1.9
9	AirTran	1.8	9	1.5
10	JetBlue	1.7	13	1.3

Note: Percentage changes based on numbers prior to rounding.

Source: Bureau of Transportation Statistics, T-100 Domestic Market.

AMR Corp.

As the world's largest airline, American Airlines (AMR's main subsidiary) offers flights to 150 destinations throughout North America, Latin America, the Caribbean, Europe, and Asia. It has had its share of success and failures; two of its planes were hijacked during the September 11, 2001, terrorist attacks and the firm barely avoided bankruptcy in 2003.[34] In 2006, AMR Corp. reported net earnings of $231 million, an improvement over its net loss of $861 million in 2005 and other significant losses in preceding years.[35] In order to return to profitability, the firm streamlined costs and expanded its routes in Asia.

United Airlines

United also lost two planes on September 11, 2001, and after several years of financial difficulties, UAL eventually filed for Chapter 11 bankruptcy in 2002.[36] UAL emerged from bankruptcy as a more competitive firm. In February 2004, United launched its own low-cost off-shoot, Ted. The firm is now looking for new ways to expand and improve profitability. Global expansion is central to UAL's strategy; in July 2006, the firm announced plans to expand its Asia/Pacific routes.[37] Recent rumors report that UAL hired Goldman Sachs to assess possible merger options.[38]

US Airways

US Airways Group is the product of a merger between US Airways and America West. CEO Parker believes this acquisition strategy is successful; when comparing the firm's post-bankruptcy performance to United, he stated, "The big difference is we were able to generate synergies that United was not able to."[39] Shareholders experienced a 45 percent increase in stock price during the first full year after the merger.[40]

Delta Air

With an 11.8% domestic market share, Delta places third among traditional airline icons.[41] Delta is strongly focused on international expansion, adding 50 new international routes in 2005–2006. Delta now serves over 450 destinations in 95 countries. Delta filed for bankruptcy and was a target acquisition by US Airways just before it emerged from bankruptcy in April 2007.

Continental Airlines

Continental targets the business traveler by serving diverse U.S. and international routes.[42] Continental has a strong balance sheet, having recently retired $100 million in debt.[43] In the third quarter of 2006, Continental followed in the path of the other legacy airlines by reporting stronger than expected results. The positive results were attributed to greatly increased number of passengers, especially on Continental's regional and Latin American routes.[44]

As well as domestic competitors, the international airline market conditions are a factor that JetBlue must consider.

International Market Conditions

The demand for international travel has increased significantly over the past decade (see Exhibit 7). The international travel growth rate is more than double the domestic travel growth rate in the United States.[45] Travel to Southeast Asia and China increases every year by about 7.3 percent and 8.0 percent. Looking forward, the number of transatlantic plane tickets purchased is expected to grow by 4.6 percent annually. Global business transactions have contributed, as well as more discretionary income for consumers, and lower airfare resulting from greater efficiencies in international travel.

The international market is attractive to many airlines because they can include fuel surcharges in the ticket price and recover some of the costs associated with higher-priced fuel.

However, the airline industry is monitored more scrupulously by the government than any other industry conducting business internationally. The government has many regulations on when, where, and how airlines can fly, how much they can charge, and how they can market international travel.[46] Many lobbyist firms and politicians in the United States have been fighting for deregulation and less restrictions on international air travel so that the United States might be more of a force in the international market. The European airline industry, more specifically AirFrance/KLM, has taken the lead in revenues for international aviation.[47]

Not only is it important for JetBlue to consider its competitive environment, but it is also important to understand the companies/industries that supply the provisions necessary to remain competitive.

Key Suppliers

Fuel

Fuel is usually the second-highest expense for an airline next to labor.[48] Therefore, fuel price increases are a major contributor to rising operating costs in the airline industry. A Merrill Lynch analyst indicated that for every $1 increase in price for a barrel of fuel, the airline industry experiences a $450 million loss in pretax profits.[49] According to the FAA, jet fuel costs rose by 20.1 percent in 2004, 40.5 percent in 2005, and 30.4 percent in 2006.[50] In 2006, fuel costs became JetBlue's largest operating expense at 33.65 percent.[51] The FAA forecasts fuel costs will remain high for the next several years. Neeleman seriously considers fuel costs and is investigating alternative sources of energy, such as liquid coal. Because the

Exhibit 7 U.S. Commercial Air Carriers Total U.S. Passenger Traffic

	Revenue Passenger Enplanements (millions)			Revenue Passenger Miles (billions)		
Fiscal Year	**Domestic**	**International**	**System**	**Domestic**	**International**	**System**
Historical*						
2000	641.2	56.4	697.6	512.8	181.8	694.6
2001	626.8	56.7	683.4	508.1	183.3	691.4
2002	574.5	51.2	625.8	473.0	158.2	631.3
2003	587.8	54.2	642.0	492.7	155.9	648.6
2004	628.5	61.4	689.9	540.2	177.4	717.7
2005	661	86.2	747.2	573.7	221.5	795.1
Forecast						
2006	660.9	89.7	750.6	577.6	232.5	810.1
2007	693.3	75.8	769.1	603.3	221.5	824.7
2008	713.8	79.8	793.6	624.6	234.5	859.0
2009	735.7	84.0	819.7	647.7	247.9	895.6
2010	758.9	88.3	847.2	671.9	262.1	934.1
2011	782.6	92.9	875.5	697.6	276.9	974.5
2012	807.7	97.6	905.2	724.5	291.9	1,016.4
2013	833.4	102.3	935.7	752.6	307.4	1,059.9
2014	860.5	107.2	967.7	782.2	323.5	1,105.7
2015	888.4	112.3	1,000.7	813.3	340.2	1,153.5
2016	917.7	117.6	1,035.3	846.1	357.5	1,203.6
2017	848.4	123.1	1,071.6	880.6	375.2	1,255.8
Average Annual Growth 2005–2017	2.9%	5.0%	3.1%	3.6%	5.5%	4.1%

Source: Forms 41 and 298-C, U.S. Department of Transportation.

United States has an abundant supply of coal, Neeleman is urging his customers to support a new bill to fund additional coal-to-liquid plants.[52]

Airlines engage in fuel hedging in order to manage unpredictable costs. However, the jet fuel commodities market is illiquid, and it is especially difficult for the large airlines to hedge sufficient quantities of fuel.[53] JetBlue is increasing its efforts to systematically hedge against future fuel needs. JetBlue also seeks more efficient fuel usage through the planes purchased and improved flight planning.[54]

Aircraft Manufacturers

The aircraft industry is dominated by two companies, Airbus and Boeing. Due to the weak economy following September 11, 2001, their orders for new commercial planes fell sharply. However, as commercial business improved, the large manufacturers profited from the buoyant space and defense markets. Embraer, the number four aircraft manufacturer, has seen lackluster commercial sales, but is benefiting from increased sales in the military sector.

Typically, the low-cost airlines operate few aircraft types, reducing their maintenance, scheduling, and training costs. JetBlue currently owns two airplane models, and its growth plans include the addition of 96 Airbus A-320s and 92 Embraer E190s.[55] Cost efficiencies would be lost if JetBlue switched suppliers, exposing the firm to any problems related to either of its aircraft suppliers. But currently more pressing for JetBlue are the challenges associated with the airline industry.

General Environment

A number of new trends are emerging in air travel. After September 11, 2001, the industry saw a drop in the number of corporate travelers, but five years later this trend appeared to be reversing. According to a survey by the National Business Travel Association, 65 percent of businesses expect employees to take more flights in 2007, and 75 percent predict an increase in the amount of business travel.[56]

Another factor in the environment of air travel is the characteristics of the airport and FAA density regulations. JetBlue experiences general performance setbacks by operating in high traffic areas such as the northeastern United States, and the airport congestion hampers performance statistics.[57] The FAA regulates airport slot (a slot is a time frame allotted for takeoff and landing)[58] allocations with the intent to ease congestion problems and enhance airport capacity. For example, recent measures at New York La Guardia airport include growth limitations, regulations encouraging use of larger aircraft, and a proposal for 10-year slot reallocation.[59]

Natural disasters and annual weather patterns also affect the performance statistics for air travel. Florida is quite popular during the winter months and the western states during summer months. Air travel is also affected by winter weather in the Northeast and tropical storms along the Atlantic and Gulf coasts.[60]

In the airline industry, more than 60 percent of employees are unionized.[61] Although JetBlue is nonunionized, it can be affected by the industry environment. In June 2006, the International Association of Machinists and Aerospace Workers campaigned to represent JetBlue's ramp service workers. The bid was unsuccessful; however JetBlue's management commented, "We can expect ongoing attempts by unions to organize groups of JetBlue crewmembers."[62]

As can be expected from the general environment, JetBlue is exposed to the widespread attraction of media coverage and negative press. One recent major incident appearing in headlines is the mechanical failure of Flight 292 landing in Los Angeles.[63] On September 21, 2005, JetBlue Flight 292 left Burbank, California, bound for JFK in New York City. Soon after takeoff, the pilot acknowledged problems with the landing gear. The decision was made to have an emergency landing at Los Angeles International Airport and after circling Orange County for three hours, to burn off fuel, Flight 292 landed safely. None of the 139 passengers or six crew members was injured during the landing. Upon landing it became certain that the nose gear had rotated 90 degrees and was locked in the down position[64] (see Exhibit 8). Although the outcome was ultimately favorable, had Flight 292 crashed or lives been lost, JetBlue's image would have suffered drastically. The perceived safety of air travel is important for all airlines.

Airlines also face a heightened sense of consumer information privacy. In 2002, JetBlue offered extensive passenger data to a data mining company, Torch, who in conjunction with the U.S. Army, tested a customer profiling system to identify high risk passengers that might threaten military installations.[65] According to the District Court, Eastern New York, Memorandum & Order 04-MD-1587, JetBlue was responsible for the release of "each passenger's name, address, gender, home ownership or rental status, economic status, social security number, occupation, and the number of adults and children in the passenger's family as well as the number of vehicles owned or leased."[66] With increased online purchases, all airlines are publicly pressured to protect passengers' identity.

Exhibit 8 JetBlue Airbus A-320 Flight 292 with Its Nose Landing Gear Jammed

Source: JetScott, 2005, http://www.aerospaceweb.org/question/planes/q0245a.shtml, October 2.

JetBlue must make a conscious effort to rise above all of the setbacks associated with the general environment and ensure that all actions are in alignment with its corporate and business strategies.

JetBlue Strategies

Because many of the other airlines play a significant role in the low-cost carrier segment within the airline industry, JetBlue competes by differentiation. The goal is to achieve an image of far superior customer service.

Superior Customer Service

JetBlue delivers this service by offering additional preflight and on-board conveniences that other low-cost carriers do not provide as a whole package. Before traveling, customers benefit from JetBlue's simple-to-use reservation system, ticketless travel, and preassigned seating. The cabin features leather seats and an additional two inches of leg room than most carriers. As previously mentioned, on board JetBlue passengers receive free DIRECTV service, and its Embraer E190 planes have XM Satellite Radio.[67] To improve the customer experience, JetBlue added healthier snacks and, as of November 2006, offers a 100 percent transfat-free selection. All snacks are complementary and unlimited.

All passengers on "shut eye" flights receive a comfort kit from Bliss, which includes earplugs, lip balm, an eye mask, and hand lotion. Crewmembers wake customers with the smell of Dunkin' Donuts coffee and offer a hot towel service.[68]

It is valuable to customers to have their flight depart as planned. To provide customers with confidence, JetBlue focuses on its completion rate, even at the expense of its on-time rate. At the end of third quarter 2006, JetBlue had a 99.6 percent completion rate. In addition, customers want to be confident that they will have their bags at the end of the flight. At 2006 year-end, JetBlue was ranked number 1 out of the 15 busiest airlines in regard to the least number of lost or mishandled bags.[69]

A critical factor in achieving superior service is employee moral. As Neeleman has stated, the crewmembers are the "real secret weapon."[70] His philosophy is that if crew members are treated well, they will in turn treat the customers well.

Culture

Currently, David Neeleman, chairperson, and Dave Barger, CEO, are hands-on people who like to interact with employees and customers. Each week members of top management fly with 8 to 12 crew members and almost always attend new hire training to teach new crewmembers about JetBlue's brand, how the company makes money, and how crewmembers contribute to the bottom line. Whenever they fly, they help the crew clean the plane after the flight to ensure a quick turnaround time. In addition they have informal meetings with crewmembers to learn about issues and problems as crewmembers see them.[71] This management style continues to attract motivated new hires; JetBlue has a reputation as a great place to work, company profit sharing, high productivity of planes and people, and rapid advancements. In 2004 alone, JetBlue hired 1,700–1,800 people.[72]

The combined effort to provide exceptional service and instill a valued-employee culture will fulfill Neeleman's hope that JetBlue can "keep our folks fresh and keep our customers coming back."[73]

However, as proven by Delta's Song and the installation of leather seats in its planes, the "superior service" attributes can be imitated by competitors. What has also allowed JetBlue to remain one step ahead in its competitive environment is cost management.

Cost Management

JetBlue's cost-saving initiative includes electronic ticketing, paperless cockpits, and online check-in.[74] In order to achieve paperless cockpits, JetBlue supplied pilots and first officers with laptops to retrieve electronic flight manuals and make preflight load and balance calculations.[75] In the year following implementation of paperless cockpits, the company saved approximately 4,800 hours of labor.[76] One of JetBlue's more original strategies to cut costs is its telephone reservation system. Reservation agents work from their homes in Salt Lake City, using personal computers equipped with VoIP technology. VoIP stands for Voice over Internet Protocol and utilizes the Internet to make free phone calls.[77] This system gives JetBlue flexibility to handle varying call volumes without needing a costly call center.[78]

JetBlue also uses technology to manage its marketing costs. JetBlue employs Omniture software to increase efficiency of Internet searches, decreasing associated search conversion costs by 94 percent.[79] By using animation in its television ads with its advertising agency, JetBlue produced eight ads for the standard price of one.[80]

Another value-adding initiative is BlueTurn, the name for JetBlue's ground operations. In an effort to improve the overall on-time performance statistics, BlueTurn allows crewmembers to minimize ground time and decrease the turnaround time for aircraft.[81]

JetBlue operates two aircraft types and a single travel class. This simplicity reduces training, maintenance, and operating costs relative to competitors that operate multiple aircraft types.

These cost-cutting strategies follow the standard low-cost, low-fare business model, without sacrificing the ultimate strategy of providing superior customer service with happy employees.

In order to best market its services, JetBlue has carefully considered its marketing approach.

Marketing Strategy

Neeleman believes that marketing is best accomplished by word of mouth; therefore top management aims to make sure that customers are treated well and employees feel valued.[82] Yet, they have made concerted efforts to market in other ways. To establish a media campaign, JetBlue hired J. Walter Thompson (JWT) as its advertising agency.[83] To create a fresh identity, JWT found candid statements by customers on JetBlue service. Online sources were consulted such as Craigslist and Epinions. The statements, written as short stories, were used to create eight different animated ads as testimonials to JetBlue's customer service. Other forms of direct marketing were used such as leather benches and snack bins in serviced airports. JetBlue also created comical postcards and distributed to customers to mail back their comments.[84]

In order to record customers' opinions on JetBlue service, an interactive video installation called the "JetBlue Story Booth" was set up in Rockefeller Center, and is traveling around the country to other cities served by JetBlue.[85] In the one-week New York exhibit, an estimated 20,000 people participated in the installation.[86] A vehicle called Blue Betty was created to simulate an airplane cabin and showcase in-flight amenities. As it traveled to various events across the country, visitors could enter a contest (or lottery) for ticket giveaways. JetBlue also used direct marketing to target college students with a public relations team called CrewBlue. This group used unconventional methods of posters, flyers, and chalk art to educate students about various aspects of the airline's services. Other marketing efforts include "Blue Days," where students were encouraged to wear blue and were rewarded with airline tickets through drawings. A 2005 survey indicated this marketing campaign was successful and increased JetBlue awareness by 41 percent.[87]

In addition to marketing initiatives, JetBlue on a consistent basis updates its business strategy to increase growth and revenue.

Current Strategies

In the first quarter of 2006, due to operating losses, JetBlue executives announced a turnaround plan called "Return to Profitability." Items included in this initiative were revisions to fare structures, corrections to flight capacity, and reprioritizing of flight segments (short, medium, and long haul).[88]

The growth rate has been slowed. The company expects to grow between 14 and 17 percent over the next year versus the 18 to 20 percent originally forecasted.[89]

JetBlue plans to fuel this growth by adding a number of flights on existing routes, connecting new city pairs among the destinations already served, and entering new markets usually served by higher-cost, higher-fare airlines. To determine which cities JetBlue should include in its flight pattern, executives study information made available from the Department of Transportation, which outlines the historical number of passengers, capacity, and average fares over time in all city-pair markets within North America.[90] This information along with JetBlue's historical data allows them to predict how a market will react to the introduction of JetBlue's service and lower prices.

JetBlue expects to use the new Embraer fleet to create demand in many midsized markets that could benefit from its point-to-point service.[91]

In addition, as mentioned previously, JetBlue is in the midst of some discussions about creating a partnership to enter the international market. Due to the limited type of aircraft in JetBlue's fleet, an alliance is the only way for JetBlue to capitalize on the international market opportunities, because its aircraft are not large enough to fly overseas.

The firm is also optimistic that recent moves to expand distribution channels will increase revenue. In August of 2006, the company signed a five-year agreement with Sabre Holdings and Galileo International. This arrangement will allow more than 52,000 travel agencies to purchase tickets for JetBlue travelers with a single connection. These deals are an attempt to reach a broader customer base, especially business travelers.[92]

Moreover, JetBlue is constantly striving to introduce new methods of providing superior customer service. As of March 2007 the first 11 rows in the cabin feature four inches of legroom between each row rather than the previous two inches.[93] To augment its flight services, JetBlue has established complementary products and services.

Associated Products and Services

In addition to air travel, JetBlue sells combined flight and hotel packages, which it terms "JetBlue Getaways." When JetBlue Getaways launched in November 2005, Tim Claydon, vice president of Sales and Marketing, commented, "By working with the hotels directly, rather than through an intermediary, we are able to offer our customers only the finest properties at great prices. Using the latest technology to combine the lowest JetBlue airfare with the best hotel or resort rate, we are able to offer our customers a new level of value with vacations beginning and ending on JetBlue Airways—something not available on any other online travel site."[94]

An American Express card was issued in 2005 called the "JetBlue Card," which earns TrueBlue points for members.[95] Customers earn TrueBlue points when purchasing flights, movie tickets, sporting event tickets, and gym memberships. When a customer amasses 100 TrueBlue points (equivalent to approximately five medium-length round trips), the customer earns a free round-trip valid for one year. In 2006, award travel accounted for only 2 percent of JetBlue's total revenue passenger miles.[96]

In order to sustain its business and corporate strategies, JetBlue monitors its financial situation regularly.

Financial Condition

JetBlue's current financial situation is highlighted by its short-term liquidity, long-term stability, and company profitability. Stockholder profitability signals whether JetBlue is meeting its stockholders' expectations.[97]

Short-Term Liquidity

JetBlue's balance sheet over the past five years is shown in Exhibit 2. JetBlue has struggled with financial performance since 2005. The growth of current liabilities from 2003 to 2006 is significant, compared to the growth of current assets. However, the payables turnover ratio has been increasing, which indicates that JetBlue has been able to pay its suppliers at a faster rate even though it has not been as efficient in collecting receivables as in years past. (Liquidity ratios are shown in Exhibit 9 and turnover ratios are shown in Exhibit 10.)

Long-Term Stability

Long-term financial stability will be an issue as JetBlue toils to consistently turn a profit. JetBlue has maintained

Exhibit 9 Liquidity Ratios

	2006	2005	2004	2003	2002
Current ratio	1.1	0.94	1.05	1.75	1.05
Quick ratio	1.05	0.91	1.03	1.72	1.03

Source: JetBlue Airways Corporation 2006 Annual Report.

Exhibit 10 Receivables and Payables

Receivables	2006	2005	2004	2003	2002
Receivable turnover	30.6	26	47.1	69.7	38.8
Days to collect	11.9	14.1	7.8	5.2	9.4
Payables	**2006**	**2005**	**2004**	**2003**	**2002**
Payable turnover	16.4	13.8	12.9	11.5	9.5
Days to pay		26.4	28.3	31.7	38.5

Source: JetBlue Airways Corporation 2006 Annual Report.

Exhibit 11 Stability Ratios

	2006	2005	2004	2003	2002
Debt/Asset ratio	0.8	0.8	0.7	0.7	0.7
Asset/Equity ratio	5.1	4	3.5	3.3	3.5
Debt/Equity (financial leverage)	4.1	3.3	2.7	2.3	2.3
Interest coverage ratio	0.7	0.7	2.7	8.4	7.1

Source: JetBlue Airways Corporation 2006 Annual Report.

Exhibit 12 Fuel Expenses

	2006	2005	2004	2003	2002
Operating revenue	$2363	$1701	$1265	$998	$635
Aircraft fuel	752	488	255	147	76
Aircraft fuel %	31	29	20	15	12
Other Costs % Revenue					
Salaries and benefits %	23	25	27	27	26
Aircraft rent %	4	4	6	6	6
Sales and Marketing %	4	5	5	5	7
Maintenance %	4	4	4	2	1

Source: JetBlue Airways Corporation 2006 Annual Report.

a fairly consistent debt-to-asset mix as most of the cash received from issuances has been invested in capital assets. The majority of JetBlue's issuances are floating rate bonds, exposing the firm to increases in the Federal Reserve's prime rate.[98] JetBlue's first quarter 2007 assets/equity ratio stood at 5.4 compared to the industry average of 3.[99] (See Exhibits 3 and 11 for details.)

Company Profitability

JetBlue's gross margins continued to decline in recent years, which can be mainly attributed to increasing fuel charges as shown in Exhibit 12. Salaries, landing fees, and other expenses remain fairly stable as a percent of revenues (most have actually decreased, see Exhibit 1). For 2006, gross margins remained 23 percent (see Exhibit 13). As stated earlier, interest expense has a negative effect on profitability.

Exhibit 13 Profitability

	2006	2005	2004	2003	2002
Gross margins	20%	27%	33%	40%	45%
Operating margins	5.4%	3%	9%	17%	17%
Net profit margins	0.4%	−1%	4%	10%	9%
Return on equity	0.97%	−2%	6%	19%	19%
Return on assets	2%	2%	3%	6%	6%

Source: JetBlue Airways Corporation 2006 Annual Report; 2007; http://www.finance.yahoo.com.

Stockholder Profitability

In July 2007, the stock was trading at $11.01 versus $14.90[100] at the end of April 2002. In addition to the lackluster stock movement, JetBlue has never paid dividends, so the overall return for the past four years is 5.5 percent. According to moneycentral.com and Yahoo! Finance, the average analyst recommendation is "Hold" for JetBlue. The declining return on equity and inconsistency of net income appears to be having negative implications for JetBlue.

Strategic Challenges

JetBlue faces many challenges as it continues to operate in the highly competitive airline industry. The main challenges are maintaining JetBlue's culture as it grows, dealing with the surfacing complexities of two fleet types, managing maintenance expenses as airplanes and engines begin to age, and dealing with an increasingly senior labor pool. Although fuel prices are a concern, they affect the industry in the same way, and airlines have opportunities to mitigate these risks. Southwest hedged its fuel position more effectively than other airlines, but these hedges will expire and everyone will have a more level playing field when it comes to fuel prices.[101]

Maintaining the JetBlue culture will be difficult to do as the airline grows. The explosive increase in employees may hinder the ability to sustain high utilization and maintain a positive work environment. The time that top management has to interact with individual crewmembers will decrease. Neeleman stated that he would no longer be able to respond to every crewmember's e-mail.[102] This change will hinder a popular cultural component because the chairperson and CEO may no longer be seen as accessible.[103]

Multiple Aircraft Types

JetBlue will have a challenge as it continues to integrate two different types of aircraft. The firm suffered a setback when it incorporated the Embraer E190 into its fleet. JetBlue wanted to fly the new planes 14 hours a day, similar to its A-320s. However, the airplane characteristics were different from the Airbus.[104] Both pilots and mechanics needed additional time and training to understand the new plane. These factors caused flight delays and cancellations throughout the JetBlue system.[105] JetBlue had to reevaluate its plans.

Another issue associated with two types of aircraft is that JetBlue must staff two groups of pilots and flight attendants. The different aircraft require unique training and integration procedures. JetBlue will need separate inventories, training programs, and facilities to accommodate two fleet types.[106] In addition, the pay scales are different, which requires additional support from corporate employees.

Increased Maintenance Expenses

Maintenance expense will be a significant concern for JetBlue in coming years. As with a new car, new airplanes rarely need maintenance and when they do, they are covered under warranty. In 2004, JetBlue experienced a 94 percent increase in maintenance costs.[107] The increase in maintenance costs was not as significant in 2005 and 2006 at 36 percent and 42 percent, respectively (see Exhibit 1); however, as the large fleet of new planes comes due for heavy maintenance at the same time, JetBlue will experience a significant increase in maintenance costs.

Airplane operators have A, C, and D levels of scheduled maintenance and inspection intervals. A-checks occur every 400–500 hours and are similar to an oil change on a vehicle. C- and D-checks are more extensive, more expensive, and longer. The C-check schedule is every 18 months/6,000 hours/3,000 cycles.[108] Additionally, the fourth C-check consists of more inspections, and takes 10 days, compared to just 4 days for regular C-checks.[109] Furthermore, JetBlue decided to outsource maintenance to Air Canada Technical Services in Winnipeg, and Aeroman in El Salvador. Because these operations are not co-located with any of its scheduled service, JetBlue has to spend additional money ferrying planes and paying employees to work in these facilities. JetBlue spends "seven figures" each year in ferrying planes and as much as $700 per day extra for people to monitor the quality of work.[110] As JetBlue's planes enter more extensive service, the amount of time to ferry airplanes and actual maintenance will increase.

Engine expense is another huge maintenance cost for JetBlue. In July 2005, JetBlue signed a 10-year service agreement with a German company, MTU. It covers all scheduled and unscheduled repair for all A-320 engines.[111] At year-end 2006, JetBlue had more than 90 A-320 aircraft, and with two engines per plane and a healthy spares inventory, JetBlue has a significant number of engines to maintain (including its 23 E190 airplanes and engines).[112] Typical charges for a comparable engine overhaul range from $1 million to $1.5 million per heavy visit.

In addition to engines and airframes, airplane operators have additional equipment they must maintain and arrange for contract maintenance support. They have auxiliary power units, landing gear systems, environmental systems, avionics, and flight controls.

As the number of aircraft increases, the cost to maintain will increase. JetBlue may lose economies of scale because multiple aircraft types require multiple repair facilities, and they will have to employ and house multiple sets of inventory and people.

Increased Payroll Expenses

Payroll costs will multiply at JetBlue as the company ages. During 2006 salaries, wages, and benefits increased 29 percent, or $125 million, due primarily to an increased workforce (refer to Exhibit 1).[113] According to the Bureau of Transportation (see Exhibit 14), JetBlue experienced a 212 percent staff growth and ranks third among low-cost carriers for total number of employees in the United States.

Currently, all of the crewmembers are near the bottom of the pay scales, and JetBlue enjoys a relatively low-cost labor pool. However, as these people attain seniority with the company their pay level will increase.[114] Not only will salaried employees get annual pay raises, but crewmembers are paid for each hour flown, according to type of aircraft and depending on the number of years with the company (see Exhibit 15). A more senior staff means the company will start paying higher wages.

Because JetBlue desires to remain nonunionized, it will have to pay its employees well to ensure they do not become disgruntled and demand representation. Unions have not gained a foothold in JetBlue, but the Air Lines Pilot Association has JetBlue as a target. In addition to pilots, flight attendants, mechanics, ground crews, and gate agents will also receive pressure from other national unions for representation. If by chance the employees of JetBlue succumb to union pressure, union negotiators will then push for increased wages and other amenities—such as hotel requirements, time off, minimum number of flight hours per month, and so on—resulting in higher costs.

Exhibit 14 Low-Cost Carrier Full-Time Equivalent Employees, August 2002–2006

(Numbers in thousands)

Rank		2002	2003*	2004*	2005*	2006	Percent Change 2002–2006
1	Southwest	34	33	31	31	32	–4.5
2	America West	12	11	11	12	13	7.0
3	JetBlue	3	5	6	8	10	212.4
4	AirTran	5	5	6	6	7	56.9
5	Frontier	3	3	4	4	5	70.6
6	ATA	7	7	7	4	3	–61.5
7	Spirit	2	2	2	2	2	–14.4
8	Independence	N/A	4	4	3	N/A	N/A
	Total****	65	71	72	71	71	9.3

*Employment numbers in 2003, 2004, and 2005 for Independence Air, which changed its business model from a regional to low-cost carrier in mid-2004, are included with low-cost carriers. The carrier did not meet the standard for filing in previous years. The airline discontinued flights on January 5, 2006.

N/A = Not applicable because carriers did not meet the standard for filing.

Source: Bureau of Transportation Statistics.

Exhibit 15 Pay Scale Table

2004 Year	A-320 Captain	EMB190 Captain	A-320 FO	EMB190 FO
12	$126	$89	$76	$53
11	$126	$87	$76	$52
10	$126	$85	$76	$51
9	$125	$84	$75	$50
8	$124	$82	$74	$49
7	$123	$80	$74	$48
6	$122	$79	$73	$47
5	$121	$77	$72	$46
4	$118	$76	$67	$44
3	$116	$74	$61	$42
2	$113	$72	$56	$40
1	$110	$71	$51	$37

Note: Guarantee of 70 hrs/month; above 70 hours paid at 150%.

Source: 2006, Will fly for food, http://www.willflyforfood.cc/Payscales/PayScales.htm.

JetBlue's Challenge in Coming Years

David Neeleman started an airline based on previous experience and an entrepreneurial spirit. He knew what people wanted and how much they would pay for it. JetBlue attracted high-quality employees because of the unique culture that stressed customer service and differentiated offerings. Allowing at-home reservations agents, paperless cockpits, and crewmembers' easy access to executives has created an environment with which people want to associate. In addition, by purchasing brand new Airbus airplanes and having a junior staff, JetBlue has minimized labor and maintenance costs, both major operating expenses, for several years. As growth slows in the domestic market, its aircraft begin to age, and the workforce becomes more senior, the number of challenges will increase. Barger and Neeleman are faced with persistent questions about how to continue to grow the airline profitably. Does JetBlue attack Southwest, United, Delta, American, or Continental strongholds in the Midwest and/or smaller airports? Does it form an alliance in order to expand into international markets such as Europe and Asia? To minimize expenses related to airplanes, should JetBlue return to one airplane type? Finally, while unions are prevalent at every other airline, how can JetBlue maintain an environment where employees remain committed, dedicated, and satisfied?

Notes

1. 2002, JetBlue Airways Corporation, *International Directory of Company Histories,* Vol. 44. St. James Press. 2006, Reproduced in Business and Company Resource Center. Farmington Hills, Mich.: Gale Group.
2. M. Trottman & S. Carey, 2006, Legacy Airlines may outfly discount rivals, *Wall Street Journal,* October 30, C1.
3. T. Fredrickson, 2006, Middle-aged JetBlue finds it's harder to fly; Ballooning fuel costs, intense competition turn it into a loser, *Crain's New York Business,* February 13, 22(7):4.

4. J. Bernstein, 2006, JetBlue posts quarterly loss, *Newsday*, October 25.
5. J. H. Dobrzynski, 2006, We're still a growth airline, *Wall Street Journal*, November 4, A6.
6. JetBlue Airways Corporation, http://galenet.galegroup.com.ezproxy1.lib.asu.edu/servlet/BCRC.
7. S. Overby, 2002, JetBlue skies ahead, *CIO Magazine*, http://www.cio.com, July 1.
8. 2006, Airbus, http://www.airbus.com/en/aircraftfamilies/a320/a320/.
9. S. Overby, JetBlue skies ahead.
10. Ibid.
11. 2002, JetBlue announces second quarter 2002 earnings—Low-fare carrier achieves record operating margin of 18.6%, JetBlue Airways Corporation press release, July 25.
12. 2002, JetBlue announces initial public offering of its common stock, JetBlue Airways Corporation press release, April 11.
13. 2005, JetBlue's New Terminal 5 will more than double airline's JFK capacity within three years, JetBlue Airways Corporation press release, December 7.
14. 2006, Fourth quarter of 2005, JetBlue Airways Corporation press release, February 1.
15. 2006, Third quarter of 2006, JetBlue Airways Corporation press release, October 24.
16. Ibid.
17. J. Bailey, 2007, JetBlue's C.E.O. is mortified after fliers are stranded, *New York Times*, http://www.nytimes.com, February 19; T. Keenan, 2007, JetBlue damage control, http://www.foxnews.com, February 27.
18. 2007, JetBlue announces the JetBlue Customer Bill of Rights, JetBlue Airways Corporation press release, February 20.
19. 2006, Air transportation, scheduled, *Encyclopedia of American Industries*, online ed., Thomson Gale.
20. 2006, Hoover's Company Records, JetBlue Airways Corporation, October 31.
21. R. M. Schneiderman, 2006, Legacy carriers fly back into favor, *Forbes*, http://www.forbes.com, October 20.
22. 2006, Air transportation, scheduled.
23. J. Schoen, 2006, Airline woes spark industry dogfight, http://www.msnbc.com, July 31.
24. 2006, Star Alliance, http://www.staralliance.com/en/travellers/index.html.
25. K. Iatrou & N. Skourias, 2005, An attempt to measure the traffic impact of airline alliances, *Journal of Air Transportation*, 10(3): 73–99.
26. C. Jones, 2006, JetBlue seeks international partnerships, *Deseret News*, Salt Lake City, March 16.
27. D. Rosato, 2006, How to score a cheap airline ticket, *CNNMoney*, http://www.cnnmoney.com, October 27.
28. 2007, US Airways withdraws offer for Delta Air Lines, press release, http://www.usairways.com, January 31.
29. C. Palmeri, D. Frost, & L. Woellert, 2006, Doug Parker wants to fly Delta, *BusinessWeek*, http://www.businessweek.com, November 16.
30. 2006, Southwest Airlines Co. Annual Report.
31. W. Zellner, 2005, Southwest: Dressed to kill . . . competitors, *BusinessWeek*, February 21.
32. R. E. Hoskisson, M. A. Hitt, & R. D. Ireland, 2003, *Competing for Advantage*, Mason, OH: South-Western, 24.
33. D. Reed, 2006, At 35, Southwest's strategy gets more complicated, *USA Today, July* 11.
34. 2006, Hoover's Company Reports: In-depth records, AMR Corporation, November 28.
35. 2006, AMR Corp Annual Report.
36. 2006, Hoover's Company Reports: In-depth records, UAL Corporation, November 28.
37. Ibid.
38. R. M. Schneiderman, 2006, Report: UAL looking to merge, *Forbes*, December 1.
39. C. Palmeri, D. Frost, & L. Woellert, 2006, Doug Parker wants to fly Delta.
40. 2006, USAirways Group, Inc. Annual Report.
41. 2006, Airline Domestic Market Share: September 2005–August 2006, *Bureau of Transportation Statistics—The Intermodal Transportation Database*, http://www.transtats.bts.gov/, December 6.
42. 2006, Hoover's Company Reports: In-depth records, Continental Airlines Inc., November 28.
43. R. Fozard, 2006, Continental's surprising ascent, *BusinessWeek*, July 31.
44. R. M. Schneiderman, 2006, Continental packs 'em in, *Forbes*, October 19.
45. 2006, Congressional testimony, *Congressional Quarterly, Inc.*, February 8.
46. Ibid.
47. Ibid.
48. E. Roston, 2005, Hedging their costs: Whether oil prices go up or down, smart airline companies are covered, *Time*, July 27.
49. 2005, Oil prices will prune revenue gains but Southwest, JetBlue look good, *Airline Business Report*, July 4, 23(12).
50. 2007, FAA aerospace forecast fiscal years 2007–2020, http://www.faa.gov/data_statistics/.
51. 2006, JetBlue Airways Corporation Form 10-K, Fiscal year ending December 31, 21.
52. C. Jones, 2006, JetBlue founder pushes for alternative fuel, http://www.timesdispatch.com, November 15.
53. K. Johnson, 2005, Fuel hedging gets tricky, *Wall Street Journal*, May 19.
54. 2005, JetBlue Airways Corporation Form 10-K, Fiscal year ending December 31, 4.
55. Ibid, 9.
56. 2006, *Wall Street Journal* (Eastern edition), November 22.
57. 2005, JetBlue Airways Corporation Form 10-K, Fiscal year ending December 31, 2.
58. 2000, http://www.house.gov/transportation/aviation/hearing/12-05-00/12-05-00memo.html.
59. D. Bond, 2006, The FAA's demand-management plans for LaGuardia call for bigger aircraft, market-based slot turnover, *Aviation Week & Space Technology*, September 4.
60. 2005, JetBlue Airways Corporation Form 10-K, Fiscal year ending December 31, 69.
61. S. Overby, 2002, JetBlue skies ahead.
62. S. Lott, 2006, IAM fails in first attempt to organize JetBlue ramp staff, *Aviation Daily*, July 20.
63. 2006, Significant safety events since 2000 for JetBlue Airlines, AirSafe.com, LLC, http://www.airsafe.com, May 6.
64. J. Scott, 2005, http://www.aerospaceweb.org/question/planes/q0245a.shtml, October 2.
65. R. Singal, 2003, Army admits using JetBlue data, Wired News, http://www.wired.com, September 23.
66. 2002, United States District Court Eastern District of New York, Memorandum & Order, JetBlue Airways Corp: Privacy Litigation: 04-MD-1587 (CBA), http://www.epic.org/privacy/airtravel/jetblue/decision_0705.pdf.
67. 2005, JetBlue Airways Corporation Form 10-K, Fiscal year ending December 31, 2.
68. 2006, JetBlue Announces 6.6 Percent Operating Margin for Third Quarter 2006, JetBlue Airways Corporation press release, October 24.
69. J. Miner, 2006, http://luxuryresorttravel.suite101.com/article/cfm./jetblue_airways_pros_and_cons, November 13.
70. S. Salter, 2004, And now the hard part, *Fast Company*, http://www.fastcompany.com, May, 82: 67.
71. Ibid.
72. Ibid.
73. B. Harrell, 2005, http://www.yaleeconomicreview.com/issues/fall2005/davidneeleman.
74. 2005, JetBlue Airways Corporation Form 10-K, Fiscal year ending December 31, 3.
75. S. Overby, JetBlue skies ahead.
76. Ibid.
77. R. Valdes, How VoIP works, http://electronics.howstuffworks.com/ip-telephony.htm.
78. S. Salter, 2004, Calling JetBlue, *Fast Company*, http://www.fastcompany.com, May, 82.
79. 2005, JetBlue soars with Omniture Research Center, Omniture, Inc., http://www.omniture.com, December 2.
80. D. Sacks, 2006, Rehab: An advertising love story, *Fast Company*, http://www.fastcompany.com, June, 106.
81. Ibid.
82. B. Harrell, http://www.yaleeconomicreview.com/issues/fall2005/davidneeleman.
83. 2005, JetBlue Airways Corporation Form 10-K, Fiscal year ending December 31, 3.

84. D. Sacks, Rehab: An advertising love story.
85. 2006, XS Lighting & sound lights JetBlue interactive kiosks, *Prism Business Media,* http://www.livedesignonline.com, June 7.
86. K. Prentice, Your client's ad, taking it to the streets, *Media Life Magazine,* Http://www.medialifemagazine.com, May 15.
87. Ibid.
88. 2005, JetBlue announces first quarter results, JetBlue Airways Corporation press release, April 1.
89. 2006, JetBlue announces 6.6 percent operating margin for third quarter, JetBlue Airways Corporation press release, October 24.
90. 2005, JetBlue Airways Corporation Form 10-K, Fiscal year ending December 31, 10.
91. Ibid.
92. R. M. Schneiderman, 2006, JetBlue courts Corporate America, *Forbes,* August 11.
93. D. Neeleman, 2006, http://www.jetblue.com/about/ourcompany/flightlog, December 14.
94. 2005, Introducing JetBlue getaways, JetBlue Airways Corporation press release, November 3.
95. 2005, JetBlue Airways Corporation Form 10-K, Fiscal year ending December 31, 1.
96. 2006, JetBlue Airways Corporation Form 10-K, Fiscal year ending December 31, 19.
97. Financial Accounting Module 3.
98. 2005, JetBlue Airways Corporation Form 10-K, Fiscal year ending December 31, 17.
99. 2006, Industry data from www.moneycentral.msn.com.
100. 2006, Yahoo! Finance, http://finance.yahoo.com/q/hp?s=JBLU&a=03&b=18&c=2001&d=10&e=30&f=2006&g=m.
101. K. Prentice, 2006, After backing away, some airlines turning to fuel hedging again, Associated Press State & Local Wire, September 4.
102. S. Salter, On the runway, *Fast Company,* http://www.fastcompany.com, May (82).
103. S. Salter, And now the hard part, 67.
104. D. Reed, 2006, Loss shifts JetBlue's focus to climbing back into black, http://www.usatoday.com, Feb 22.
105. Ibid.
106. M. Bobelian, 2003, JetBlue lands expansion plans, *Forbes,* http://www.forbes.com, June 10.
107. T. Reed, 2006, TheStreet.com, http://www.thestreet.com/stocks/transportation/10260392.html, January 6.
108. 2006, *Aircraft Technology, Engineering & Maintenance,* October/November, 99.
109. 2005, McGraw-Hill Companies *Overhaul & Maintenance,* Magazine for MRO Management, October 2.
110. Ibid, 5.
111. 2006, JetBlue Airways Corporation, Form 10-Q, October 24.
112. *Aircraft Technology Engineering & Maintenance,* 101.
113. 2006, JetBlue Airways Corporation Form 10-K, Fiscal year ending December 31, 41.
114. T. Reed, http://www.thestreet.com.

Case 17

Corporate Governance at Knight Transportation, Inc.

R. S. Chithra Gopal, T. R. Venkatesh

ICFAI Business School

Knight Transportation, Inc. (KTI), a U.S.-based trucking company started in 1989, had been rated by *Forbes* as "one of the best small companies" in the United States, consecutively for 10 years (1995–2004), mainly for its "up operating quarters."[1] In October 2004, KTI was ranked 66 in the *Forbes* list of 200 best small companies in the United States. KTI was also setting standards in corporate governance, by adopting written charters in compliance with the Sarbanes-Oxley Act for public companies (Appendix I). The charters were adopted in March 2005. In June 2005, the Institutional Shareholder Services (ISS) rated KTI's Corporate Governance Quotient better than 15.6 percent of S&P 600[2] companies and 37.2 percent of transportation companies (see Exhibit 1).

KTI's common stocks were initially listed on the Nasdaq National Market (NASDAQ)[3]. As per the rules promulgated by the National Association of Securities Dealers, Inc. (the NASD), the company started implementing the corporate governance guidelines, but the compliance cost (especially section 404 of Sarbanes-Oxley Act)[4] for small public companies in NASDAQ was found to be disproportionate to its benefits.

Based upon a survey of our companies, as a percent of revenue, smaller issuers appear to have spent approximately 11 times more than larger companies on 404 compliance.

—**Edward S. Knight,**
Executive Vice President and General Counsel, NASDAQ[5]

KTI opted to transfer[6] its common stocks from NASDAQ to the New York Stock Exchange (NYSE), the world's largest market worth US$20 trillion that secured the best prices 89 percent of the time in the listed stocks in 2004. The stocks were accepted for listing (under the symbol KNX) in December 2004[7] and the trading on these shares commenced by December 30, 2004. But the listing standards of NYSE called for stricter norms for selection of independent directors, voting requirements for their election, and limiting executive compensation packages. It was also mandatory for the chief executives and financial officers to personally check the accounting details before filing them for public scrutiny. With strict corporate governance standards, KTI's management was expecting to realize higher returns for its shareholders in the long run.

Background Note

KTI, headquartered in Phoenix, Arizona, was started by Kevin Knight, his brother Keith Knight, and his cousins Randy and Gary, with a total of 80 years of experience in the trucking industry. The business activities included transporting commodities such as consumer goods, packaged foodstuffs, paper products, beverage containers, refrigerated goods, and so on for shippers throughout the United States, and selling trucks and trailers. In just two years after inception, the company posted annual revenues of US$13 million. By 1993, KTI had 200 trucks in business.

In 1994, KTI became a public company (initial stock price was US$8/share). In 1996, two new terminals were started in Katy, Texas, and Indianapolis, Indiana, with a total of 500 tractors. In 1997, Knight Management Services, a consultancy firm was started. In 1999, KTI acquired the Action Express of Corsicana, Texas, and also opened two more terminals in Charlotte, North Carolina, and Salt Lake City, Utah. KTI operated 1,200 trucks and the yearly revenue rose to US$150 million. KTI also invested in Concentrek Logistics, which offered supply chain consulting. During 2001–2002, additional terminals in Kansas City, Missouri; Portland, Oregon; and Memphis, Tennessee, were opened. By 2002, KTI was listed in S&P SmallCap 600.

This case was written by R. S. Chithra Gopal, under the direction of T. R. Venkatesh, ICFAI Business School, Bangalore. It is intended to be used as the basis for class discussion rather than to illustrate either effective or ineffective handling of a management situation. The case was compiled from published sources.

Appendix I Summary of Sarbanes-Oxley Act of 2002

The act was passed by the U.S. Congress to safeguard the investors in corporations from financial losses due to mismanagement. A Public Company Accounting Oversight Board (Board) was created as a nonprofit organization to oversee the implementation of the act. Some of the important sections covered in the act included the following:

- The Board should consist of five financially literate members (people who could understand financial statements), each serving for a term of five years. Two of the Board members should be certified public accountants. While serving on the Board, the members were not allowed to claim any payments (other than retirement payments) from a public accounting firm.
- The public accounting firm (hired by the company) should register with the Board.
- The SEC should conduct regular inspections of the registered public accounting firms.
- The Board could initiate disciplinary proceedings whenever violations were noticed. The disciplinary hearings were made public by the Board only with the consent of concerned parties.
- The SEC had the authority to initiate actions against the Board for possible violations of the act.
- The accounting firm had to report to the audit committees all the accounting practices used and the possible outcomes of disclosures.
- The CEO, CFO, controller, and the chief accounting officer should not have been employed by the audit firm hired by the company during the one-year period preceding the audit. This requirement was to curb any conflicts in interests.
- Each member of the audit committee should be a member of the board of directors or else an independent ("Independent" was defined as not receiving, other than for service on the board, any consulting, advisory, or other compensatory fee from the issuer, and as not being an affiliated person of the issuer, or any subsidiary thereof). At least one member in the AC should be a financial expert.
- The AC should oversee the appointment and compensation paid to the accounting firms, and internal control measures.
- The CEO and the CFO should personally certify the financial disclosures.
- No company personnel should interfere with the process of auditing.
- If the SEC rules against any noncompliance, federal courts were authorized to "grant any equitable relief that may be appropriate or necessary for the benefit of investors."
- Each financial statement was to be prepared according to GAAP rules.
- Personal loans to executives were prohibited.
- Disclosures should be made on a rapid and current basis.
- The SEC was authorized to freeze any sort of extraordinary payment to any director, officer, partner, controlling person, agent, or employee of a company during an investigation of possible violations of securities laws.
- The SEC could prohibit a person from serving as an officer or director of a public company if the person had committed securities fraud.

Source: http://www.aicpa.org/info/sarbanes_oxley_summary.htm.

Exhibit 1 Corporate Governance Quotient (CGQ®)

The ISS was a global leader in providing corporate governance services to institutional investors. From 2002, ISS started gathering firm-specific corporate governance data from public disclosure documents, press releases, corporate Web sites, and proxy statements. A corporate governance rating system covering 7,500 companies worldwide was developed to measure the strengths, deficiencies and risks of a company's corporate governance practices and board of directors. A total of 61 variables were considered, which were categorized under eight areas: (1) board of directors, (2) audit, (3) charter and bylaw provisions, (4) anti-takeover provisions, (5) executive and director compensation, (6) progressive practices, (7) ownership, and (8) director education.

Two CGQ ratings were generated for each company: (1) **CGQ index score** that was relative to its market index (CGQ index score compared to relevant market indices like S&P 500, Mid-Cap 400, Small-Cap 600, Russell 3000, ISS Small-Cap, S&P/TSX), and (2) **CGQ industry score** that was relative to its industry group (peer group).

Source: http://finance.yahoo.com/q/pr?s=knx, http://help.yahoo.com/help/us/fin/research/research-57.html.

As of December 31, 2004, the company operated 7,126 trailers and 2,574 tractors, from 18 regional dry van operations centers and one temperature controlled subsidiary in Phoenix. The revenue registered a compounded annual growth rate of 19 percent, from US$207.4 million in 2000 to US$411.7 million in 2004. The net income recorded a 28 percent compounded annual growth rate, from US$17.7 million in 2000 to US$47.9 million in 2004.

In compliance with the corporate governance standards, KTI opted for more transparency in its financial dealings by the timely filing of all relevant details with the Securities and Exchange Commission (SEC)[8] on Forms 10-K,[9] 10-Q,[10] 8-K,[11] and 14-A.[12]

The Board of Directors

As per the NYSE listing standards, the Board was expected to have a majority of independent directors. The main criterion of independence was the complete absence of any form of material relationship with KTI (nonemployee) as decided annually by the Board. A member of the board of directors (BoD) could not serve in more than four corporate boards, besides KTI's. Likewise, the chief executive officer (CEO) couldn't serve in more than two other corporate boards, in addition to KTI's BoD.

KTI's BoD was to consist of 7–11 members, each serving for a term of three years. As of 2005, the BoD consisted of 9 members. A director's tenure was limited to 20 years. Thus every 3 years, if nominated by the BoD, they could stand for reelection by the shareholders. The term for a director elected to fill a vacancy expired in one year. In each annual shareholder meeting, one-third of the BoDs were elected. The retirement age of a director was also fixed at 82 years. In the case of director succession, the BoD recommended suitable candidates for election by the shareholders.

The directors were expected to work according to the Code of Ethical Conduct of KTI, which laid out firm commitment to corporate governance issues. From 2005, as per NYSE rules, the independent directors were to meet at least once a year to promote interaction without involving the management personnel who worked for KTI. Such meetings were referred to as executive sessions. In 2004, two executive sessions were held as per NASD rules.

The BoD was free to contact any of the company officials, external legal representatives, and advisors. The shareholders were also free to send written communications to board members at any time. If they wished to contact the members personally, the company secretary (Timothy M. Kohl, as of 2005) always provided the contact information on demand. The BoD also decided the amount of compensation to be paid to the independent directors and the mode of payment. The employees of KTI and shareholders owning more than 10 percent of KTI shares, who served on the board, didn't get any additional pay for undertaking the board duties. The board also played an active role in evaluating the qualifications of potential successors for all the key posts (chairperson of the BoD, CEO, president, chief financial officer (CFO), etc.), besides suggesting a comprehensive training program for them.

In 2004, the BoD, consisting of 10 members, met six times. The attendance of each director on an average in all the board meetings and committee meetings was 75 percent. They were all present in the annual shareholders' meeting. On May 26, 2005, pursuant to the annual meeting of the shareholders, the membership in different committees was decided by the BoD. Donald A. Bliss, G. D. Madden, Michael Garnreiter, Mark Scudder, and Kathryn L. Munro were appointed as independent directors (Appendix II).

Board's Responsibilities and Functions

The BoD was responsible for the overall management of KTI. The key decisions were always made by the BoD, taking into consideration the best interests of the company and the shareholders (see Exhibit 2).

The BoD fixed employee compensation plans, the amount of cash dividends for the shareholders, and the frequency of payment of cash dividends after taking into consideration the financial condition, cash requirements,[13] tax requirements, and corporate law requirements pertaining to KTI's business activities.

As of March 31, 2005, KTI had one stock-based[14] compensation plan for the employees. The plan was first established by the BoD in 1994 as an incentive to retain its executives, directors, and key employees and also to align their interests with the shareholder returns. In order to comply with section 409A of the Internal Revenue Code of the American Job Creation Act of 2004,[15] the BoD decided that the exercise price[16] of the stock on the date granting should be at least equal to the fair market value[17] of the stock. This amendment to the original plan became effective March 15, 2005.

The valuation method was based on the guidelines prescribed by the Accounting Principles Board. KTI used the intrinsic-value-based method of accounting (as laid out in the Statement of Financial Accounting Standards (SFAS) No. 123), in which the compensation expense was recorded on the date of grant only if the current market price of the stock exceeded the exercise price. If the exercise price was equal to the market price on the date the stocks were granted, then the compensation expense was not reflected in the net income. Once the valuation was over, for disclosure, KTI followed the requirements set forth by the amendment SFAS No. 148.[18]

KTI went for a stock-split[19] (3:2) on July 20, 2004. On April 18, 2005, a cash dividend of US$0.02 per share (common stock) was paid to all the shareholders as of March 31, 2005. As per BoD's decision, quarterly dividends were paid to shareholders. All these transactions were reflected in the earnings per share and were duly accounted for in the financial statements.

Financial Disclosures

The original report of Form 8-K, was filed by KTI on April 7, 2005. All the subsequent decisions were reported

Appendix II Profile of Independent Directors

- Donald A. Bliss—Director in KTI since 1995, Age 72 years.

  Until his retirement in December 1994, Mr. Bliss was the vice president and chief executive officer of U.S. West Communications, a U.S. West company. Mr. Bliss also was a director of the Western and Southern Life Insurance Company, Continental General Insurance Company, and the Biltmore Bank of Arizona. Mr. Bliss served as Chairman of the Western Region Advisory Board of AON Risk Services of Arizona, Inc., from October 2001 to February 2005.
- G. D. Madden—Director in KTI since 1997, Age 65 years.

  Since 1996, Mr. Madden had been president of Madden Partners, a consulting firm he founded, which specialized in transportation technology and strategic issues. Prior to founding Madden Partners, he was president and chief executive officer of Innovative Computing Corporation, a subsidiary of Westinghouse Electric Corporation. Mr. Madden founded Innovative Computing Corporation (ICC), a privately held company, which grew to be the largest supplier of fully integrated management information systems to the trucking industry. Mr. Madden sold ICC to Westinghouse in 1990 and continued to serve as its president and chief executive officer until 1996.
- Michael Garnreiter—Director in KTI since 2003, Age 53 years.

  Since April 2002, Mr. Garnreiter had served as the executive vice president, treasurer, and chief financial officer of Main Street Restaurant Group, Inc., a publicly held restaurant operating company. Prior to joining Main Street, Mr. Garnreiter served as a general partner of Arthur Andersen LLP. Mr. Garnreiter began his career with Arthur Andersen in 1974 after graduating with a bachelor of science degree in accounting from California State University at Long Beach. In 1986, he became the managing partner of Arthur Andersen's Tucson, Arizona, office. Mr. Garnreiter was a certified public accountant in California and Arizona.
- Mark Scudder—Director in KTI since 1999. Age 42 years.

  Mr. Scudder was the principal of Scudder Law Firm, P.C., L.L.O., in Lincoln, Nebraska, and had been involved in the private practice of law since 1988. Mr. Scudder was also a member of the board of directors of Covenant Transport, Inc., a publicly held, long-haul trucking company, and Genesee & Wyoming Inc., a publicly held, international, short-line railroad.
- Kathryn L. Munro—Director in KTI since 2005, Age 56 years.

  Kathryn L. Munro was appointed to the board of directors in April 2005. She was the principal of BridgeWest, LLC, a private equity investment company specializing in wireless technology companies. Ms. Munro was the chairperson of BridgeWest from February 1999 until July 2003. From 1996 to 1998, Ms. Munro served as chief executive officer of Bank of America's Southwest Banking Group, and was president of Bank of America, Arizona, from 1994 to 1996. Ms. Munro had served on the boards of directors of Flow International Corporation, a Seattle-based manufacturer of industrial tools, since 1996; Pinnacle West Capital Corporation, the holding company of Arizona Public Service and Pinnacle West Energy, since 2000; and Capitol Bancorp Limited, a Michigan-based multi-bank holding company, since 2002.

Source: http://www.sec.gov/Archives/edgar/data/929452/000100888605000104/proxy2005.htm.

Exhibit 2 Specific Functions of the BoD

- Selecting, evaluating, and compensating CEO, and overseeing CEO succession planning
- Providing counsel on and oversight of the selection, evaluation, retention, and compensation of qualified senior executives
- Reviewing, approving, and monitoring important financial and business strategies and corporate actions
- Advising management on significant issues facing the company
- Nominating qualified directors for service on the board
- Ensuring processes are in place for maintaining effective corporate governance practices

Source: http://www.knighttrans.com/shareholders/corpgov/govguide.cfm.

as amendments to the original report. As per the rules of the SEC, the financial statements followed the Generally Accepted Accounting Principles (GAAP[20]) in the United States. The consolidated financial statements[21] were submitted in Form 10-K by December 31 of every year, whereas the quarterly reports were submitted in Form 10-Q.

The different operating terminals of KTI offered the same services (short- to medium-haul truckload carriers[22]) catering to almost similar customers and hence registered similar financial performance indicators, including average revenue per mile and operating ratio. As per the guidance in SFAS No.131—disclosures about segments of an enterprise and related information—the consolidated report was prepared.

The disclosures (Form 10-Q) of KTI's balance sheet by March 31, 2005, showed US$38.7 million in cash and cash equivalents, no long-term debt, and a shareholders' equity of US$303.9 million. KTI maintained a line

Exhibit 3 Members of Board Committees, May 26, 2005

Name	Audit Committee	Nominating and Corporate Governance Committee	Compensation Committee	Executive Committee
Donald A. Bliss	X	X		X
G. D. Madden	X	X	X	
Michael Garnreiter	X	X		
Mark Scudder			X	X
Kevin P. Knight				X
Gary J. Knight				X
Kathryn L. Munro		X	X	

Source: http://www.sec.gov/Archives/edgar/data/929452/000100888605000104/proxy2005.htm.

of credit[23] (issued but unused) amounting to US$9.8 million for liquidity purposes as of March 31, 2005. Unlike other trucking companies, KTI held no tractors under operating leases in 2005.[24]

KTI was also expected to disclose information on market risk as per the new regulations, which was compiled using sensitivity analysis.[25] As of March 31, 2005, with no outstanding borrowings, the management opined that increases in short-term interest rates would not affect the company's financial condition. Because the operations depended on diesel fuel, any significant increase in fuel price, which could not be offset by fuel surcharge passed on to customers,[26] was bound to affect the financial condition. As part of risk management, in February 2002, KTI entered into a hedging contract with the New York Mercantile Exchange (NYMX), to deal with fluctuations in the price of heating oil. This contract was in connection with bulk purchases of diesel fuel needed by KTI in the future. As per the contract, if the price of heating oil on NYMX happened to fall below US$0.58, KTI would pay the difference between US$0.58 and the index price for 750,000 gallons per month for the remaining months of 2005. This arrangement was entered at fair value[27] in the financial statements.

The regulation also called for disclosure of all material information to the certifying officers of financial reports and the BoD, as part of disclosure controls. Subsequently, the CEO and CFO had certified the effectiveness of procedures adopted in KTI. The timely availability of required information helped the company to file the reports within the time periods specified in SEC rules. The form 10-Q (first quarter of 2005) of KTI was duly certified by Kevin P. Knight and David A. Jackson (CEO and CFO, respectively).

Board Committees

The board had constituted different committees including Audit Committee (AC), Nominating and Corporate Governance Committee (NCGC), Compensation Committee (CC), and Executive Committee (EC). The Board reserved the right to remove any of the members from the committees if his/her work was found unsatisfactory. Information regarding the changes in the principal officers was reported as an amendment in Form 8-K/A, filed by the CFO on June 2, 2005 (see Exhibit 3).

The Audit Committee

The AC was mainly intended to assist the BoD by supervising the integrity of KTI's financial statements, assessing the expertise and independence of the accounting firm hired by KTI, and examining the general compliance with the financial regulations. The AC was initially appointed in June 1994, by the BoD, to work as per a written charter. This charter was later amended to comply with the SEC rules (1999), the Sarbanes-Oxley Act of 2002 (enacted on July 30, 2002), and other NASDAQ listing requirements. To comply with the NYSE listing standards, the charter was restated effective March 2, 2005. As per the charter, the AC was to function as a liaison between the external auditors and the company management. The AC was to have an "audit committee financial expert" as a member, with prior experience as a public accountant/auditor/principal financial officer/comptroller/principal accounting officer. Each member of the AC was independent according to NYSE, and the rules under the Exchange Act (amended version of the Securities Exchange Act of 1934). In 2004, the AC met four times. The audited financial statements were finally approved by the AC and recommended for inclusion in the annual report on Form 10-K.

The Nominating and Corporate Governance Committee

The NC was established in February 2003 for the purpose of making recommendations to the BoD regarding potential candidates for director posts. The shareholders were also able to put forth nominees for consideration by the NC. Based on their recommendations, the BoD finally arrived at the nominations. The final selection depended on the result of voting in the annual shareholder meeting. In November 2004, NC was reconstituted as the NCGC with members Donald A. Bliss, Michael Garnreiter, and G. D. Madden. The functions involved selecting and recommending nominees to the board, implementing succession plans, reviewing the corporate governance guidelines, and conducting training and evaluation programs for the directors. All the members of the NCGC were independent as per NYSE rules. NCGC also worked in accordance with a written charter, adopted in March 2005. Each member could serve for one year and the NCGC was to meet at least twice a year.

The NCGC recommended to the BoD any modification in the corporate governance guidelines pertaining to the tenure and the succession of the directors. The screening and evaluation of the director candidates were also done by the NCGC. Among the factors considered were business skills, past reputation, response to interests of shareholders, and so on. In the case of independent directors, the NCGC rated the independence by assessing whether the potential candidate served as a partner, shareholder, or officer, or in any other similar post in a company that had a business or financial relationship with the KTI. For the newly elected directors, the NCGC conducted an orientation program involving the senior officials, covering the management issues in KTI. The executive sessions of the independent directors were to be presided over by the chair of the NC and CGC.

They were also expected to serve as contact persons for the independent directors. The NC and the CGC came up with an annual report on succession planning as well. This report was prepared in consultation with the chairperson of the board and CEO. The NC and CGC also implemented a self-evaluation report for the BoD members every year to assess their compliance level with the corporate governance guidelines and weaknesses, if any, that could be rectified.

The Compensation Committee

In accordance with the NYSE corporate governance rules, the charter for the CC was laid out on March 2, 2005. The CC reviewed the compensation details of the directors and recommended the same to the BoD. A detailed survey of the payment guidelines in other public companies and affiliations of independent directors with other organizations or consultancies was undertaken every year by the CC before making the recommendation.

The CC had at least two independent directors. Each member served for a period of one year. The main purpose of the CC was to review and recommend the compensation for the CEO and other executive officers in KTI. The company's stock option plan and incentives for executives were also reviewed annually.

The report on executive compensation was duly filed in the proxy statement sent to the shareholders prior to every annual meeting or in the annual report on Form 10-K.

The Executive Committee

The EC was initially set up in November 2000. The main purpose was to act on behalf of the BoD when it was not in session. As of 2005, the members included Kevin P. Knight, Gary J. Knight, Donald A. Bliss, and Mark Scudder.

Board Compensation

As of June 2, 2005, the CC of the BoD approved an annual base salary of US$290,000 for Timothy M. Kohl (president), and an annual base salary of US$100,000 for David A. Jackson (CFO). The base salaries and compensation packages[28] for other executives (Kevin P. Knight, CEO, Keith T. Knight, executive vice president, and Gary J. Knight, vice chairman) were also decided. All the deals upon finalization and approval by the CC were reported on Form 8-K, duly signed by the CFO (see Exhibit 4).

The compensation packages for independent directors included the following,

- Annual retainer of US$9,000
- US$750 for meetings of BoD; US$500 for meetings of the AC and NCGC; US$450 for meetings of CC and other meetings of the BoD
- For chairpersons of the board committees, an additional annual retainer of US$2,500 was to be paid
- An annual grant of nonqualified stock options numbering 1,000 shares[29] to each of the independent directors

The independent directors had the freedom to accept shares (common stock) instead of cash compensation. The stocks were issued on February 15 and August 15 of each year at a market price prevailing on the trading day prior to the day of issue.

Future Outlook

In December 2004, a research study[30] on corporate governance and firm performance came out with a broad summary measure of corporate governance, namely Gov-Score. Six performance measures under three categories: operating performance (return on equity, profit margin, and sales growth), valuation, and shareholder payout (dividend yield and share repurchases) were used by the researchers to arrive at Gov-Score,[31] which ranged from 13 to 38 (average value was 22.5) for 2,327 individual firms. KTI posted a score of 21. KTI seemed to be in the right path with the implementation of written charters at all levels of corporate management (see Exhibit 5).

To oversee the future growth, strict guidelines were enforced in the area of succession planning. The selection procedures ensured that well-qualified potential

Exhibit 4 Summary of Executive Compensation

		Annual Compensation			Long-Term Compensation: Awards		Long-Term Compensation: Payouts	
Name and Principal Position	**Year**	**Salary**	**Bonus**	**Other Annual Compensation**	**Restricted Stock Award(s)**	**Securities Underlying Options/ SARs (#)**	**LTIP Payouts**	**All Other Compensation**
Kevin P. Knight, Chairman and Chief Executive Officer	2004	$383,846	$191,820	—	—	45,000	—	$10,925
	2003	308,249	78,000	—	—	—	—	625
	2002	265,000	—	—	—	—	—	1,785
Gary J. Knight, Vice Chairman	2004	272,789	56,875	—	—	15,000	—	6,025
	2003	279,422	58,000	—	—	—	—	625
	2002	265,000	—	—	—	—	—	2,365
Keith T. Knight, Executive Vice President	2004	283,654	72,500	—	—	15,000	—	4,625
	2003	273,647	56,000	—	—	—	—	625
	2002	265,000	—	—	—	—	—	1,965
Timothy M. Kohl, President and Secretary	2004	222,692	80,850	—	—	15,000	—	1,210
	2003	187,320	50,000	—	—	15,000	—	1,210
	2003	140,310	25,000	—	—	18,750	—	1,462

Source: http://www.knighttrans.com/shareholders/annualreports/KnightAnnualReport2003.pdf.

Exhibit 5 Stock Performance Graph

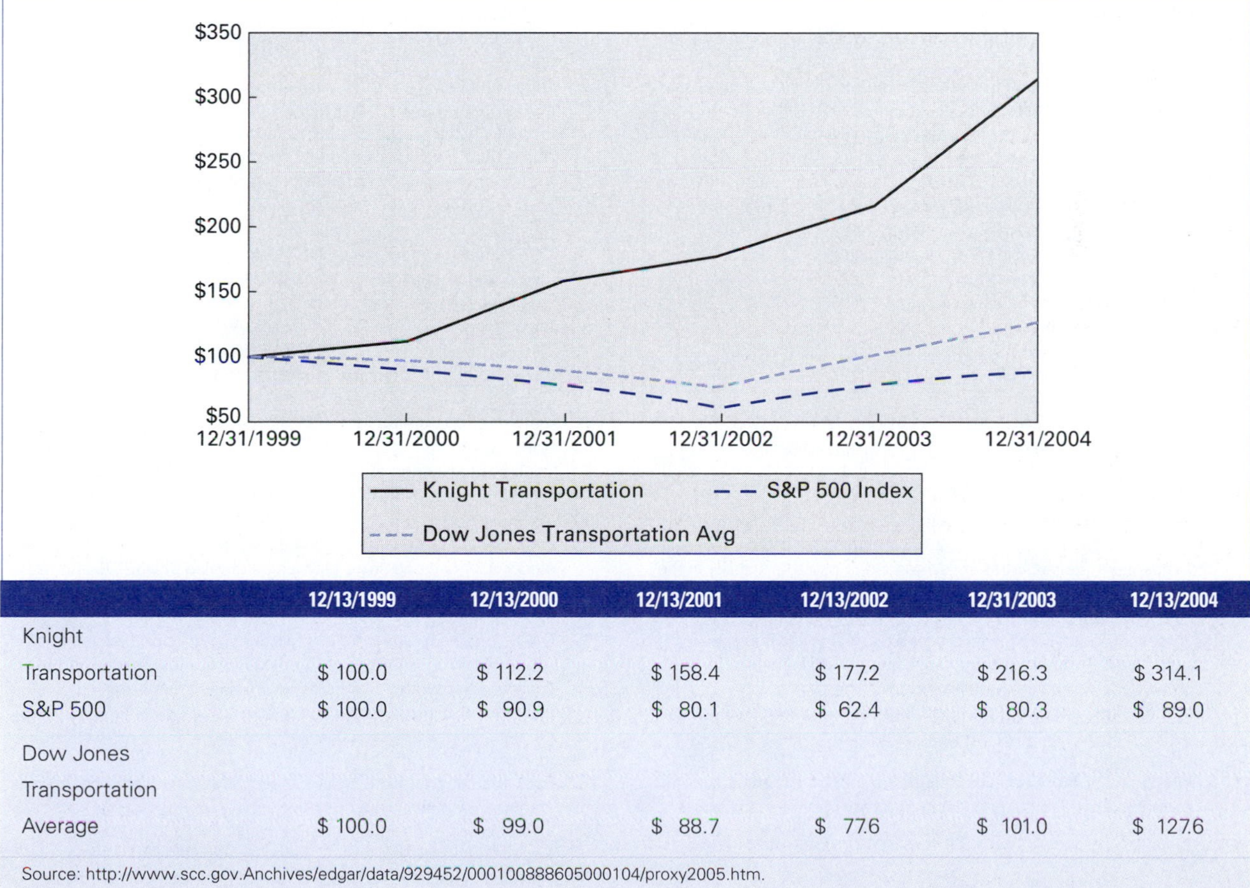

	12/13/1999	12/13/2000	12/13/2001	12/13/2002	12/31/2003	12/13/2004
Knight Transportation	$ 100.0	$ 112.2	$ 158.4	$ 177.2	$ 216.3	$ 314.1
S&P 500	$ 100.0	$ 90.9	$ 80.1	$ 62.4	$ 80.3	$ 89.0
Dow Jones Transportation Average	$ 100.0	$ 99.0	$ 88.7	$ 77.6	$ 101.0	$ 127.6

Source: http://www.scc.gov.Anchives/edgar/data/929452/000100888605000104/proxy2005.htm.

candidates were facing the annual shareholder meeting to get elected. An annual report on management succession was also presented to the BoD by the NCGC. This report was updated regularly by the BoD to maintain a list of potential long-term successors for the key posts of CEO, president, CFO, and other members of the senior management.

Mandatory personal assurances by the top executives on the fairness of financial statements were considered as a potential challenge in the area of compliance. But KTI, with the help of outside agencies in internal auditing, was conducting training programs for BoD, board committees, senior managers, and corporate counsel to keep them abreast of potential wrongdoings that might give rise to scandals.

We're very hard workers; we're very committed to the industry and very committed to our people. We've tried to build a business that creates value for all of our stakeholders. We've been good at building the business.

—KEVIN P. KNIGHT,
CHAIRMAN AND CEO, KTI[32]

Notes

1. Operating expenses were worked out as a percentage of revenue. Fuel surcharge, which was collected from customers, was not accounted for while calculating operating expenses and revenue. In the trucking industry, where most of the companies were working at operating ratios as high as 100s, KTI was posting a low value of 80s.
2. The S&P SmallCap 600 Index was one of the U.S. market indices, consisting of 600 small-cap stocks. A small-cap company generally registered a market capitalization in the range of US$300 million to US$2 billion. The index was introduced in 1994 and as of 2005, its total holdings ranged from US$60 million to more than US$3 billion, with the average company boasting a market cap of about US$750 million.
3. At Nasdaq National Market, KTI shares were traded under the symbol KNGT.
4. This section pertained to the internal controls. The smaller companies were spending more as compensation to qualified finance staff when compared to the benefits they were getting from remaining listed in NASDAQ. The public companies had to engage firms other than their outside auditors to provide services such as financial information systems design and implementation, appraisal or valuation services, internal audit services, and human resource services.
5 2005, NASDAQ Executive Vice President and General Counsel Edward S. Knight applauds focus on smaller public companies, http://news.corporate.findlaw.com/prnewswire/20050617/17jun20051153.html, June 17.
6. In 2004, out of the 152 new companies that joined the NYSE, 16 were transfers from NASDAQ.
7. CNF Inc. (the parent company of Con-Way Transportation) and SIRVA Inc. (the parent company of Allied and North American relocation companies) were the only trucking companies besides KTI listed in NYSE.
8. SEC was established by the U.S. Congress in 1934 to restore the confidence of investors in capital markets, which was shaken badly by the Stock Market Crash of 1929. The primary function of SEC was to implement the securities laws intended to promote stability in the market.
9. The audited report contained details of sales by product group, officer compensation, status of legal proceedings if any, and management's assessment of future risks and prospects to help investors to compare the company's performance over the years.
10. This unaudited document provided details of financial results for the quarter. It also included information on any stock-split or acquisition undertaken in the company.
11. Reports on specific events that happened in the company.
12. The form referred to the proxy statement sent to the shareholders to inform them in advance of all details relevant to the agenda of the annual meeting.
13. The variable costs included fuel expenses and driver-related expenses (wages, benefits, training, and recruitment, and independent contractor costs). Maintenance costs, tire expenses, and total cost of insurance and claims had both fixed and variable components (varying with the miles traveled and fixed with respect to fleet efficiency, fleet age, and safety). Acquisition of long-term assets such as equipments, terminal facilities, and compensation for non-driver personnel were the main components in fixed cost.
14. The annual shareholders' meeting on May 26, 2005, authorized an increase in the number of shares in common stock from 1,500,000 to 4,000,000.
15. The act provided for tax benefits for the domestic manufacturers in the United States.
16. Exercise price referred to the price at which an option purchaser bought or sold the underlying security.
17. The fair market value of a stock referred to the price at which trading took place between a willing seller and a willing buyer, both having a reasonable knowledge of relevant facts.
18. Under the fair-value-based method, compensation cost was measured at the grant date based on the value of the award and was recognized over the service period (vesting period). Under the intrinsic-value-based method, compensation cost was the excess, if any, of the quoted market price of the stock at grant date or other measurement date over the amount an employee should pay to acquire the stock. The Statement of Financial Accounting Standards (SFAS) No. 123, Accounting for stock-based compensation, as amended by SFAS No. 148, Accounting for stock-based compensation—transition and disclosure, established accounting and disclosure requirements using a fair-value-based method of accounting for stock-based employee compensation plans. As allowed by SFAS No. 123, KTI elected to apply the intrinsic-value-based method of accounting, and followed the disclosure requirements of SFAS No. 123.
19. In a stock split, the number of shares in a company is increased without any increase in the number of shareholders. Therefore, if a stockholder had one share with a market value of US$100 after the stock split of 2:1, he would own 2 shares, each worth US$50. This exercise made the shares more marketable.
20. GAAP referred to statements of accounting principles issued by the AICPA (American Institute of Certified Public Accountants) and FASB (Financial Accounting Standards Board). GAAP facilitated interyear and interjurisdiction comparison of financial statements.
21. All material intercompany balances and transactions were excluded to avoid duplication.
22. Each operating terminal on an average catered to customers in cities within a 560-miles radius.
23. Line of credit referred to a preestablished loan authorization with a specified borrowing limit extended by a lending institution to an individual or business based on creditworthiness. It allowed the

borrowers to obtain a number of loans without reapplying each time as long as the credit limit was not exceeded.

24. In 2004, it was operating 285 tractors on lease. Lease amount paid was also mentioned in the income statement.
25. This analysis helped to see the changes in outcomes in response to changes in assumptions.
26. KTI generally passed on to customers 80 to 90 percent of increases in fuel prices by way of fuel surcharge. In the quarter that ended March 31, 2005, fuel expense accounted for 16.4 percent of total operating expenses (excluding the fuel surcharge amount) compared to 16.9 percent for the same quarter in 2004.
27. The particular hedge was treated as a firm commitment. Hence, it was referred to as fair value hedge. Once the hedge proved ineffective to safeguard the real changes in cash flows for KTI, the hedge accounting would be discontinued. For May 2005 contracts, the price of heating oil was US$1.46 (as of April 15, 2005).
28. Compensation packages referred to the incentive bonus program for fiscal 2005.
29. The exercise price was equal to the fair market price of the stock on the date of granting. In this type of stock option, which had become popular, the employee should report income upon exercising the stock. The advantage was that the difference between the sale price and the purchase price was treated as income for tax purposes.
30. The study was done by Lawrence D. Brown (Professor of Accountancy, Georgia State University) and Marcus L. Caylor (PhD student, Georgia State University).
31 Gov-Score summed up 51 corporate governance factors where each factor was coded 1 (0) if it did (not) represent minimally acceptable governance. The higher the score, the better was the firm's performance in corporate governance. The data were supplied by ISS.
32. D. Lockridge, 2005, Kevin Knight, http://www.heavydutytrucking.com/2005/01/120a0501.asp, January.

Additional Readings and Reference

1. 2005, Amended and restated charter of the Audit Committee of the Board of Directors of Knight Transportation, Inc, http://www.knighttrans.com/shareholders/corpgov/charterofauditcom.cfm, March 2.
2. 2005, Amended and restated charter of the Compensation Committee, http://www.knighttrans.com/shareholders/corpgov/charterofcompcom.cfm, March 2.
3. A. Herringshaw, J. Pober, & P. Roberts, Student investment fund—spring 2005, http://64.233.179.104/search?q=cache:sEU0__LJNdkJ:price.ou.edu/sif/sif_body/data/Executive_summary.doc+%22Knight+Transportatio-n%22%2Bcomposition+of+the+board&hl=en.
4. 2005, Charter of the nominating and corporate governance committee of the board of directors, http://www.knighttrans.com/shareholders/corpgov/charterofnominate.cfm, March 2.
5. 2005, Corporate governance guidelines, http://www.knighttrans.com/shareholders/corpgov/govguide.cfm, March 2.
6. Corporate governance quotient, http://finance.yahoo.com/q/pr?s=knx; http://help.yahoo.com/help/us/fin/research/research-57.html.
7. D. A. Nadler, 2004, Building better boards, http://harvardbusinessonline.hbsp.harvard.edu/ b02/en/common/item_detail.jhtml?id=R0405G, May 1.
8. L. Deborah, 2005, Kevin Knight, http://www.heavydutytrucking.com/2005/01/120a0501.asp, January.
9. 2003, Final rule text Section 303A.08-Shareholder approval of equity compensation plans, http://www.nyse.com/pdfs/finalruletext303A.pdf, June 30.
10. 2005, Form 8-K for Knight Transportation Inc, http://biz.yahoo.com/e/050407/knx8-k.html, April 7.
11. Form 8-K June 8th 2005, http://www.sec.gov/cgi-bin/browseedgar?action=getcompany&CIK=0000929452&owner=exclude.
12. 2005, Frequently asked questions on equity compensation plans, http://www.nyse.com/pdfs/equitycompfaqs.pdf, January 11.
13. GovernanceMetrics international-first rating, http://www.gmiratings.com/(1nf40l45rnx4zsefl0od4yjw)/QuickSearch.aspx?Ticker=K NX&CoName=.
14. 2005, Knight Form 10-Q first quarter 2005, http://www.sec.gov/Archives/edgar/data/929452/000100888605000121/form10q.htm#toc, May 6.
15. 2004, Knight to be listed on NYSE, http://www.landlinemag.com/todays_news/Daily/2004/Dec04/122004.htm, December 20.
16. Knight Transportation, Inc.—Audit committee-complaint review procedure, http://www.knighttrans.com/shareholders/corpgov/ComplaintReviewProc.cfm.
17. 2003, Knight Transportation, Inc.—Code of ethical conduct, http://www.knighttrans.com/shareholders/corpgov/COdeEthicalConduct.cfm, July 1.
18. 2004, Knight Transportation to be listed on NYSE, http://www.bizjournals.com/phoenix/stories/2004/12/13/daily54.html?GP=OTCMJ1752087487, December 17.
19. L. D. Brown & M. L. Caylor, 2003, Corporate governance and firm performance, http://papers.ssrn.com/sol3/papers.cfm?abstract_id=586423, February 1.
20. LexisNexis, 2005, Knight Transportation now listed on NYSE, http://www.newratings.com/analyst_news/article_865581.html, June 9.
21. LexisNexis, 2005, Project: corporate counsel (compliance readiness) Part II; Corporate governance does not end with Sarbanes-Oxley, http://www.newratings.com/analyst_news/article_876013.html, June 16.
22. 2005, NASDAQ Executive Vice President and General Counsel Edward S. Knight applauds focus on smaller public companies, http://news.corporate.findlaw.com/prnewswire/20050617/17jun20051153.html, June 17.
23. 2004, NYSE listed company manual Section 303A—Corporate governance listing standards—Frequently asked questions, http://www.nyse.com/pdfs/section303Afaqs.pdf, February 13.
24. 2005, NYSE market quality benefits-issuers and investors, the exchange, http://www.nyse.com/pdfs/02-05_newsletter_full.pdf, 12(2).
25. 2003, Policy governing responsibilities of financial managers and senior officers, http://www.knighttrans.com/shareholders/corpgov/FinancialManagers.cfm, July 1.
26. 2004, Section 303A-Corporate Governance rules, http://www.nyse.com/pdfs/section303A_final_rules.pdf, November 3.
27. 2003, Standards relating to listed company audit committees, http://www.sec.gov/rules/final/33-8220.htm, April 10.

Web Sites

http://cpaclass.com/gaap/gaap-us-01a.htm
http://finance.yahoo.com/q/pr?s=knx
http://www.aicpa.org/info/sarbanes_oxley_summary.htm
http://www.fasb.org/st/summary/stsum123.shtml
http://www.knighttrans.com/shareholders/
http://www.newratings.com/analyst_news/search.asp?search=corporate+governance
http://www.sec.gov/Archives/edgar/data/929452/000100888605000104/proxy2005.htm

Case 18

Lufthansa: Going Global, but How to Manage Complexity?

Simon Tywuschik, Ulrich Steger

International Institute for Management Development

In the glamorous, but financially not so glorious, airline industry, Lufthansa is one of the three companies worldwide whose debt is rated as investment-grade. For most of the other companies, if they are not already in bankruptcy procedures or being bailed out by the government, the financial situation is simply a nightmare. Since World War II the industry has never earned its cost of capital over the business cycle. Especially after the deregulation (beginning in 1978 in the United States), which increasingly replaced the government-organized IATA cartel,[1] the situation got worse. By 2005, the cumulative losses of airlines since 2001 amounted to about US$40.7 billion.[2] As mergers are still legally prevented across many country borders, the airlines' response to globalization was to form alliances (refer to Exhibit 1 for an overview).

Lufthansa is the leading, probably pivotal, member of the largest alliance, the Star Alliance. If globalization means increasing complexity (refer to Exhibits 2 and 3 for the characteristics of globalization and how it relates to complexity), alliances are even more complex to manage than individual companies because they lack the hierarchical conflict resolution mechanisms that individual companies can employ.

But despite their pride in mastering the turmoil of the past, some nagging questions remain for Lufthansa's management as the globalization of the airline industry moves full speed ahead.

- Is the current strategy sufficient to maintain Lufthansa's position as one of the few profitable airline companies, given the uncertainties and dynamics in the highly competitive but cyclical market?
- Has Lufthansa done enough to reduce complexity in the right places and to survive the competition, especially against the background of customer satisfaction and high value added?
- Are all employees in the corporation embraced culturally?
- Is Lufthansa prepared for the sustainability challenges—in particular global warming—which create new uncertainties?

Exhibit 1 Key Facts for the Main Airline Alliances

Key Features	Star Alliance	One World	Sky Team
Year of formation	1997	1999	2000
Members	18	8	10
Passengers (in millions)	425	258	373
Destinations	842	605	728
Fleet Size	2800	2161	2151
Market Share (Rev.)	28.4%	15.8%	23.9%
Headquarters	Frankfurt (Ger)	Vancouver (Can)	None
Organization type	Formalized organization	Governing Board	Committee

Sources: Web sites of the alliances, 2006; PATA, 2006. www.staralliance.com; www.oneworld.com; www.skyteam.com.

Exhibit 2 The Six Features of Globalization

Feature	Explanation
(1) Eroding Borders	Never before in history have so many boundaries in the social, political, and economic realm been weakened or abolished. However, boundaries fulfill two core functions: First, they contain effects (inside a certain entity); and second, they define the difference between "us" and others (identify creation). As a consequence of the erosion of boundaries, complexity increases (see also Exhibit 3).
(2) Mobility	The erosion of boundaries facilitates greater mobility of goods, capital, knowledge/technology, and people.
(3) Heterarchy	Organizations across all industries are not structured hierarchically (top down), but rather heterarchically (i.e., changing dependencies and interdependent influencing channels are common). Due to the interdependency between different organizational layers, the process of power exertion has become more costly.
(4) Erosion of Legitimacy	Because it is almost impossible to clearly identify one-way cause-and-effect relationships within complex systems, responsibilities (institutional as well as personal) are difficult to establish. This process leads to the erosion of legitimacy within many organizations, in particular of democratically elected governments. Although they can no longer provide for the welfare of nation states, they remain the only addressee of the voter, which therefore leads to disenchantment with politics.
(5) Variety of Options	In complex systems no foreseeable and stable structures are evident (from a person's choice of profession to a global player's determination of corporate strategy), but the number of options can (on a personal and institutional level) also lead to information overload and failure (anxiety).
(6) Asymmetry between Past and Future	Asymmetry between past and future: The future is not a smooth continuation of the past; rather abrupt breaks are characteristic of development of the economic, social, and political spheres.

Exhibit 3 Complexity and Consequences for Corporations

	Situation	Challenge	Approach
Definition and Key Concepts	In systems theory, complexity is defined by the number of different potential states of a system that depend on certain complexity drivers (see below for drivers).	Ashby's Law of Variety suggests that organizations can handle high external complexity only by a similar internal complexity. The internal implementation of such complexity would create problems particularly for multi-business line corporations. Hence, these corporations look for drivers that *decrease* complexity (see below).	The more open and globally spread out a system is, the greater the velocity of change. The main challenge of corporations is to manage complexity. A global company must be characterized by certain features in order to manage complexity and survive competition (see below).
Key Drivers and Features	• Difference and diversity of values, aims, interests, cultures, and types of behaviors. • Interdependence that provides for greater interaction. • Ambiguity of situations and of information in its meaning. • Fast flux: Through eroding borders, the number of actors and interdependencies increases. The different interests and information uncertainty increase the number and intensity of actions that influence a system. It means that adjustment processes occur continuously, which again cause interventions.	• A common business culture and values and one clearly formulated and focused business strategy should help to establish one clear direction. • Standardized processes decrease variations (and hence complexity) in the course of business and create more transparency. • Focus on certain activities (such as "core" competencies). • Decentralization of decision power reduces the need for coordination (and hence of interaction) and early warning systems allow for more time to adjust.	• Activities in several world regions provide for a certain homogeneity of demand on the one hand and advantages for corporations on the other hand, among others economies of scale. • One global strategy for the fulfillment of common aims. • Employees of different ethical and professional backgrounds. • Standardized norms and processes.

Surviving the Changes in the Airline Industry

In 1992 Lufthansa—similar to other airlines—was close to bankruptcy, as the first Iraq war reduced international air traffic. It became obvious that the massive European and global expansion strategy that Lufthansa had been pursuing since the early 1980s was not economically viable (refer to Exhibits 4 and 5 for an overview of passenger sales and growth rate).

The fixed costs were too high for a cyclical business. On the other hand, strong reasons supported the belief that the "network effect" and economies of scale were leading to a global airline industry, dominated by a handful of key players (similar to the car industry).

However, the deregulation process had not gone far enough to allow for major mergers (in the United States, foreigners can own only 25 percent of an airline; in the EU non-European ownership is limited to 49 percent; in most of Asia any acquisition of a major airline might not be illegal, but it is practically impossible). But deregulation and the erosion of the IATA cartel went far enough to allow for scores of new competitors. No-frills low-cost airlines spread from the United States to Europe and

Exhibit 4 Lufthansa's Passenger Transportation Turnover by Region, 1980, 1990, and 2000

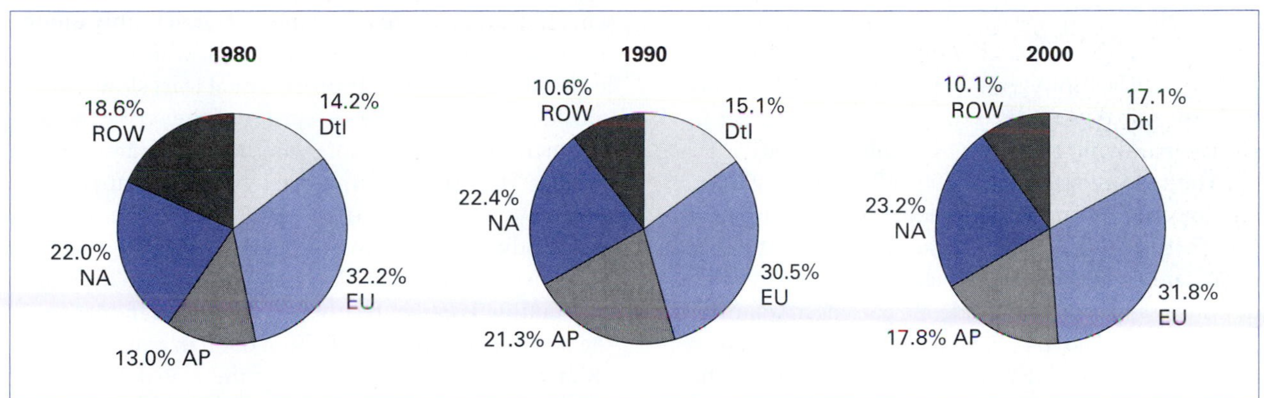

Note: Data for 1980 and 1990 also include cargo and mail services. Data for 2000 excludes CityLine.

Abbreviations: NA = North America; AP = Asia Pacific; ROW = Rest of the World; EU = Europe; Dtl = Germany

Sources: Lufthansa's annual reports; author's calculations.

Exhibit 5 Lufthansa's Annual Turnover Growth Rate in Passenger Transportation, 1981–2005

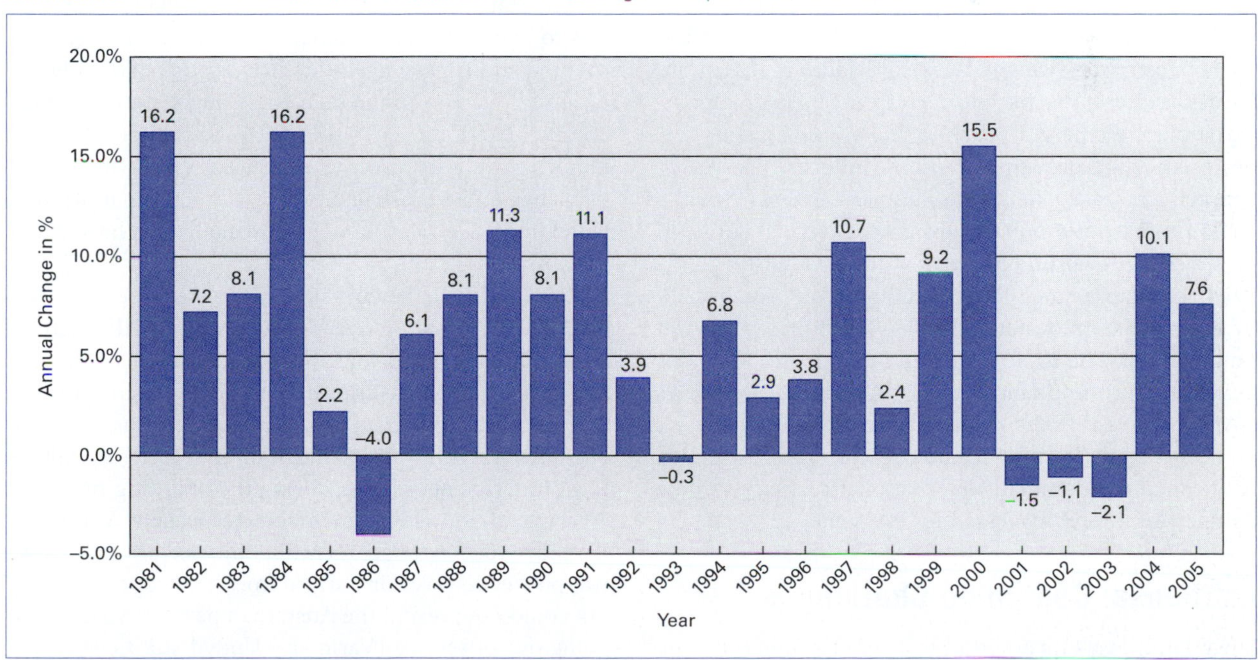

Note: From 1995, only passenger revenue is considered (excludes mail and cargo). Figures represent net sales.

Sources: Lufthansa's annual reports from 1981 to 2005; author's calculations.

then Asia, nurtured by the abundance of used aircraft and leasing opportunities (e.g., easyJet was started with less than £5 million). Unlike the "flag carriers," with their hubs, they offered point-to-point connections on high traffic density routes. Also business class passengers were targeted with new offerings (such as Virgin Airlines). Overcapacity and persisting government subsidies (especially in southern Europe, Asia, and Latin America) combined to create permanent price pressure: From the early 1990s, a minimum of 3 percent reduction in costs was needed every year, which was likely to continue.

Economic and political developments did not have a positive effect on the airline industry either. After recovering from the effects of the first Iraq war, air traffic was once again slowed down by the Asian financial crisis—starting in 1997—followed by similar events in Russia and Latin America. However, everything the airline industry had experienced so far was dwarfed when terrorists used airplanes as flying bombs on September 11, 2001.

The succeeding "War on Terror"—especially the second Iraq war—along with spreading tensions through the Middle East and the SARS scare delivered a three-year nightmare for the industry, which was in a cyclical business downturn anyway: Worldwide air passenger volumes fell by 3.3 percent and 2.4 percent in 2001 and 2003, respectively, and remained flat in 2002.[3] Lufthansa's traffic turnover even decreased between 2001 and 2003 by 4.6 percent.[4] Then, once passenger demand began to recover, oil prices escalated dramatically in 2005–2006. Currently, fuel costs are the second-highest cost category per seat kilometer, accounting for 26 percent of operating costs in Europe airlines (labor costs account for approximately 30 percent).[5]

Add in the issue above and the traffic jams and queues at major airports—which makes high-speed trains a more attractive alternative for journeys up to 500 kilometers—and a picture emerges. As such, the airline industry appears as a "high-growth–low-profit" industry. Everybody expects air traffic to grow—despite a highly volatile environment—but nobody expects a similar surge in profits. Because airline companies are now mostly privatized (Lufthansa since 1996, with about 40 percent held by diverse foreign owners), they have to fight for survival on their own. The bankruptcies of Swissair and Varig, for example, and the financial difficulties of Japan Airlines (JAL) indicate that the former flag carriers cannot bank on governments coming to their rescue. The fate of Pan Am—once the dominant international carrier and now defunct—is a sobering lesson for everyone.

Lufthansa: Continued Challenges

Since Lufthansa's turnaround in 1992–1993, in only one year have no new cost-cutting initiatives been launched, implemented, or (after 2001) even accelerated. In fact, a certain management routine on how to implement and control such cost-cutting initiatives has even been established. Compared to 1992, the cost base has been reduced by approximately 40 percent, despite rising wages, security and airport fees and the roller coaster of fuel prices.

Lufthansa needed to ensure cash flow (especially after 2001), and it needed to reduce costs (e.g., by hiring foreign crew members). Lufthansa transformed fixed costs into variable costs (by outsourcing), and rationalized every step in the value chain, especially via electronic processes which is very tricky when it comes to interfacing with the customer.

The "art" of the endeavor was to push the cost-cutting through, without losing consensus with the employees—who, like everywhere in the industry, are highly unionized[6]—and the strong work-councils, who had several levers to derail the whole process or at least slow it down considerably. With one exception of the strike in early summer 2001 by the pilots who have a separate union and felt "disrespected," the magic worked. But employers always face the risk of a "burn out" syndrome, when everybody asks: Will this ever stop?

However, sometimes Lufthansa executives think that cost-cutting is easier, relatively speaking, than managing the Star Alliance (refer to Exhibit 6 for an overview of its 18 members), now the biggest of the global airline alliances, with 28.4 percent market share and 842 destinations in 152 countries.[7] Many think of Lufthansa as the leader and integrator, because the biggest member, United Airlines, was preoccupied for more than three years with emerging from Chapter 11 bankruptcy procedures in the United States.[8] From the beginning, Lufthansa's strategy was to drive the Star Alliance from the revenue side by keeping more passengers in the network. This idea of "seamless" travel is implemented through "code-sharing," coordinated flight schedules, common lounges, baggage handling, and so forth, leading to a higher utilization of planes and infrastructure (lower cost per unit), and sometimes also to economies of scale in purchasing and sales.

A constant balancing act is necessary between the alliance members' independence (including the right to leave) and the need for common processes, especially in IT, and quality insurance. Another constant point of debate centers on the needs and expectations of global customers. Are they the same or do they differ by culture (e.g., in terms of greeting during the boarding process)? A crisis of individual members (especially Varig and United) could endanger the whole alliance, and Lufthansa was pushed to save Air Canada from bankruptcy in 1999, but could not prevent the Australian partner Anselt from going out of service (Varig and United still flew during the bankruptcy process and received only technical aid from Lufthansa). In any case, Lufthansa management

Exhibit 6 Global Airline Alliances and Their Members

STAR ALLIANCE THE AIRLINE NETWORK FOR EARTH	oneworld	SKYTEAM
1. Air Canada 2. Air New Zealand 3. ANA 4. Asiana Airlines 5. Austrian Airlines 6. bmi 7. LOT Polish Airlines 8. Lufthansa 9. SAS Scandinavian Airlines 10. Singapore Airlines 11. South African Airways 12. Spanair 13. SWISS 14. TAP Air Portugal 15. Thai Airways International 16. United 17. US Airways 18. Varig	1. AerLingus 2. American Airlines 3. British Airways 4. Cathy Pacific 5. Finnair 6. Iberia 7. LAN 8. Qantas	1. Aeroflot 2. Aeromexico 3. Air France/ KLM 4. Alitalia 5. Continental 6. Czech Airlines 7. Delta 8. Korean Air 9. Northwest
Market Share: 28.4%	**Market Share: 15.8%**	**Market Share: 23.9%**

Note: The membership structure of the alliances and market share undergo continuous changes.

Sources: Web sites of alliances, 2006; PATA, 2006. www.stralliance.com; www.oneworld.com; www.skyteam.com.

tries to avoid too much involvement in the affairs (and risks) of the other airline members and creates the perception that Lufthansa is seeking a role as a dominant force (e.g., looking for shareholdings in other airlines), a factor that contributed considerably to the downfall of SWISS in 2001. However, when its new incarnation, SWISS, was "up for grabs" in 2005, Lufthansa violated this principle and acquired the airline to prevent it falling into the hands of arch rival British Airways and the OneWorld Alliance. And more acquisitions may be in the cards: Lufthansa maintains 10 percent of its own shares (the legal maximum) for the purpose of a "reserve."

For Lufthansa—trained in the art of consensus more than others—it seems to be easier to accept only an 80 percent workable solution, if everybody is behind it and has bought into the compromise. Nevertheless, it was a learning process over several years; many compromises ran counter to a Lufthansa culture that takes pride in engineering excellence and maintaining standards, not only in back-office processes like IT, but also with customer interfaces (e.g., Lufthansa thought that the electronic check-in should be completed in half the time than the other alliance members found acceptable for their customers). Sometimes alliance initiatives run counter to the interests of Lufthansa divisions: The idea of creating a common Star Alliance IT infrastructure would rob the IT systems' divisions of most of their customers.

Despite the time-consuming negotiation and consensus-building processes in the Star Alliance management superstructure (refer to Exhibit 7) and despite the higher transaction costs, Lufthansa executives remained strong supporters of the alliance. The reason is quite simple: Because no alternatives (mostly M&As) are (legally) available, alliances are the only way to operate in a global network without increasing one's own investments in an economically unsustainable way (a lesson learned the hard way). It is estimated that for Lufthansa the net operating profit increase through the Star Alliance is about €500 million per year, which roughly corresponds to the profits for 2005. Hence, in the overall profitability equation for flag carriers, the regional business seems to fulfill a marketing activity for international routes rather than being a profit source of its own.

Exhibit 7 Organizational Structure of Star Alliance

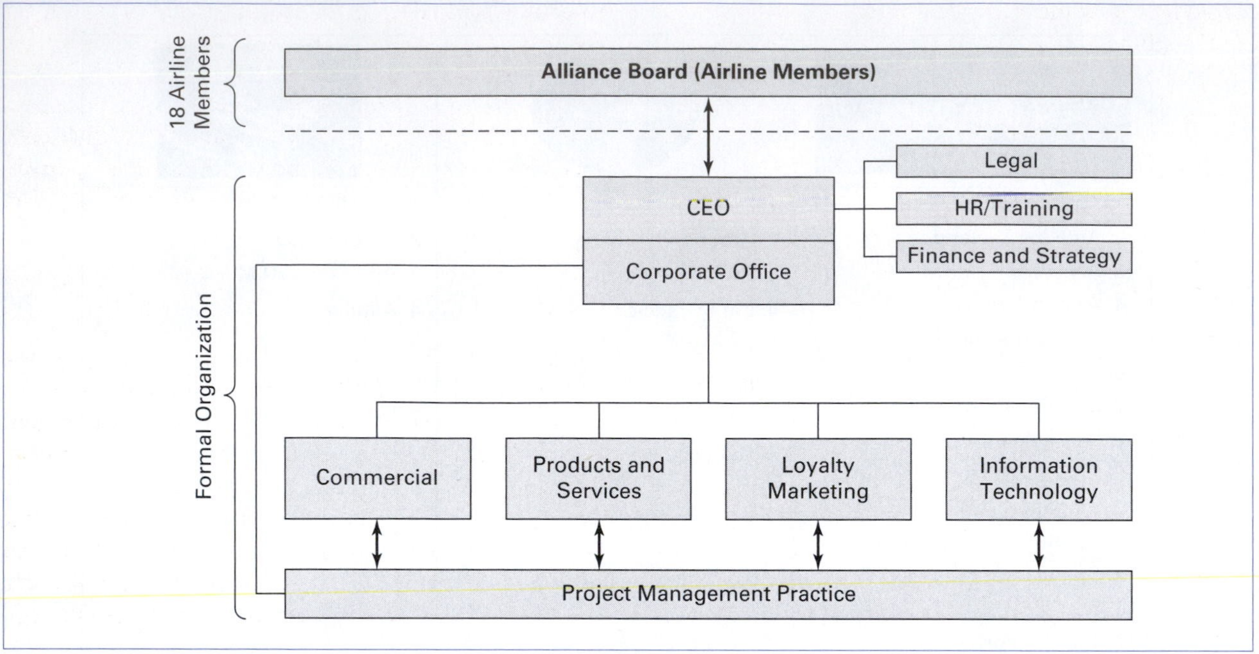

Source: Star Alliance, 2005. http://www.staralliance.com.

Exhibit 8 Structure of Lufthansa Holding and Lufthansa Regional

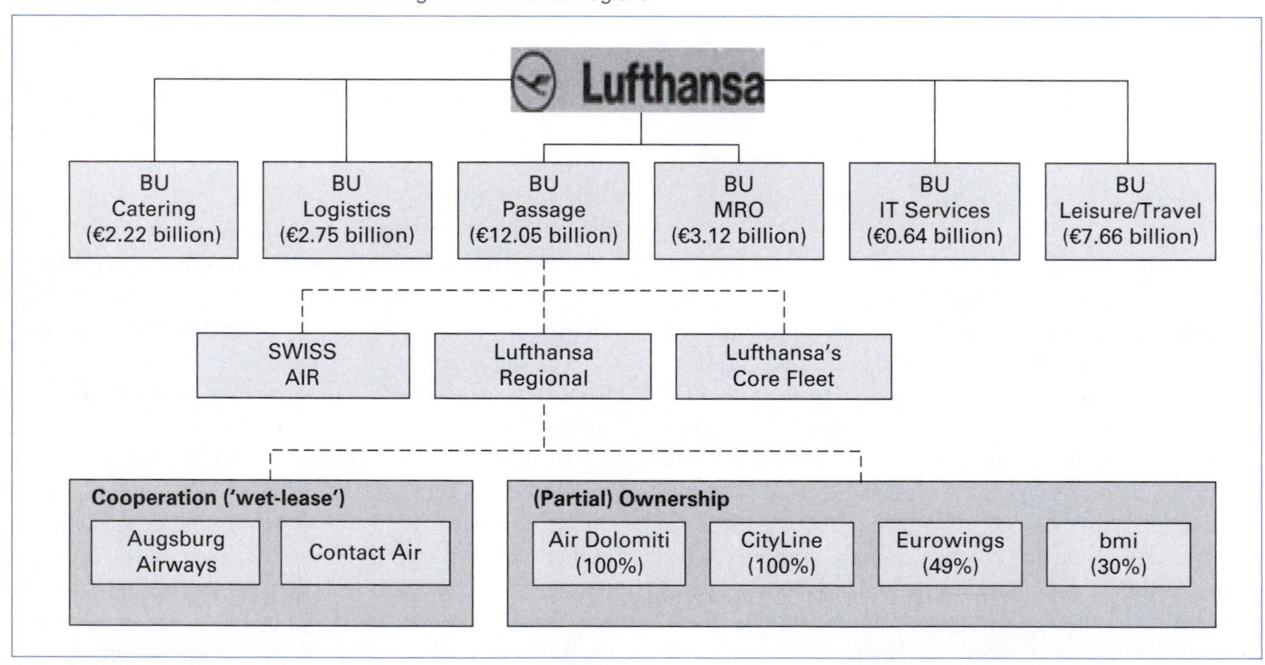

Note: Revenue figures refer to 2005.

Source: Company information, 2006. http://www.lufthansa.com.

Although the Star Alliance is great for intercontinental and business travel, it does not provide an answer to the onslaught of the low-cost carriers. Alongside some second-tier partnerships outside the Star Alliance, Lufthansa created "Lufthansa Regional" (refer to Exhibit 8 for the organizational structure), which carries out approximately 50 percent of the company's German and European flights. Within Lufthansa Regional, Eurowings and CityLine (partially) belong to the Lufthansa Group.[9] However, the planes from the other partners are operated via "wetleasing," whereby Lufthansa leases the aircraft complete with crew and maintenance contracts. In this case the planes are integrated into Lufthansa's scheduling and the company carries the risk of the revenue side only.

Operating in a high-price competitive market, Lufthansa Regional needs a lower-cost structure than Lufthansa's core fleet. The cost savings at Lufthansa Regional come partly from the slightly lower wages, the smaller planes adjusted to the traffic density, a reduced service level, an operating base in second-tier airports, and point-to-point-service so that the time in the air is greater than for "network" airplanes. On the revenue side, Lufthansa gains through the "feeder function" to intercontinental flights (otherwise passengers might go via other big hubs) and the density of the connections: Only a few attractive routes can be developed by low-cost carriers without facing competition from the outset directly with Lufthansa (and its ability to cut prices when needed, a source of continuous controversy with the antitrust authorities).

However, as compelling as the business logic for Lufthansa Regional may appear to financial and industry analysts, the "two-class society" is a cause of friction and ongoing tension among the employees, as well as sometimes irritating to customers because of the different service standards, which are not matched in price differences. Another ongoing debate concerns in which category the newly acquired SwissAir belongs. Is it a low-cost provider or an equal partner in the Star Alliance? Often SWISS deliberately competes in its marketing efforts with the no-frill sector; on other occasions it refers to its tradition as a premium airline.

Can Organization Provide Stability?

Since 1996 Lufthansa has been organized as a holding with six business lines (refer to Exhibit 9 for a brief description), dissolving the once "integrated" corporation. Although "Passage" is dominant, with approximately two-thirds of the turnover, each division is fully responsible for its own financial results and any interactions with other group companies occur on market price terms. However, as in every decentralized organization, the holding company needs to unite its businesses under one "strategy

Exhibit 9 Evolution of the Organizational Structure of Lufthansa

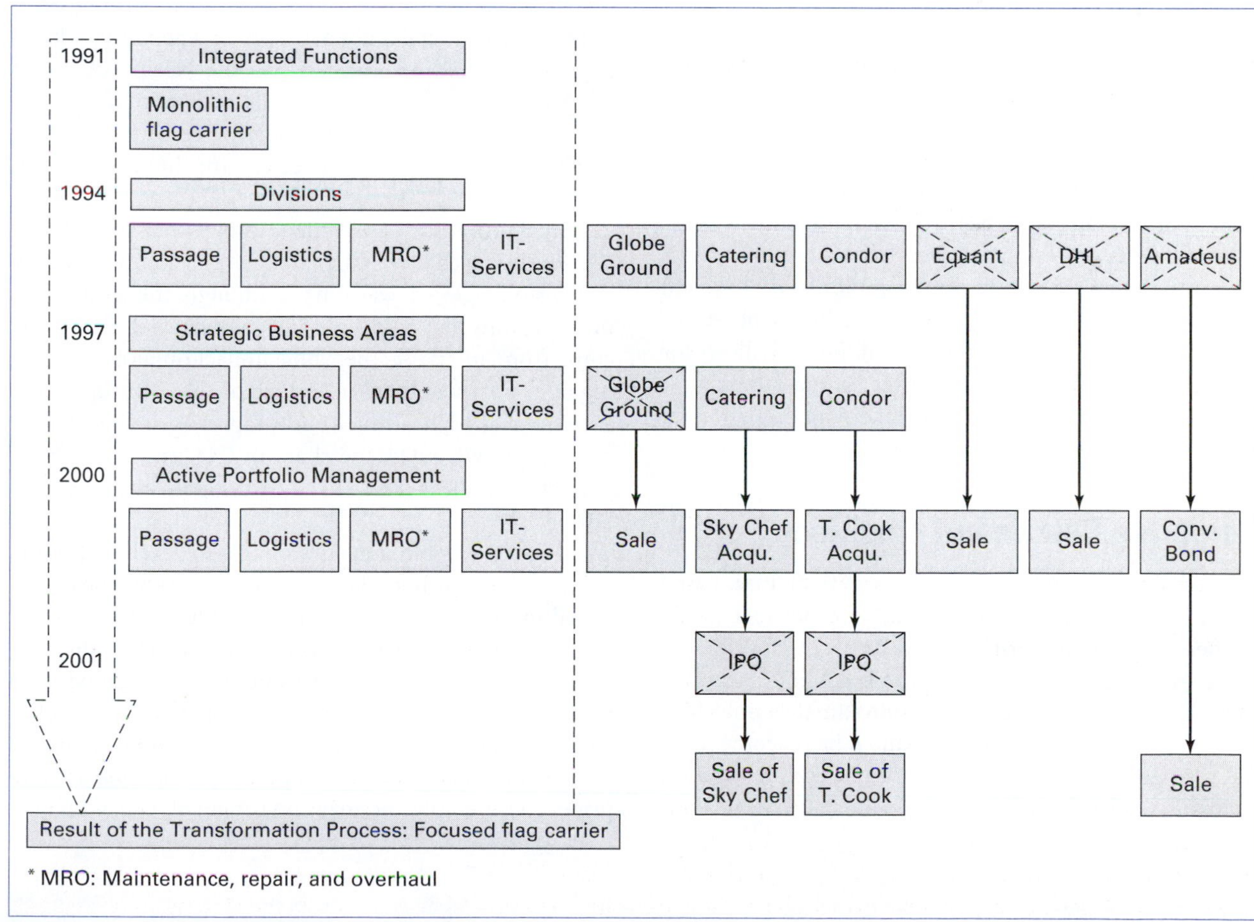

Sources: Company information; author's illustration, 2006.

roof," avoiding "silos" and any duplication of functions. These goals might have been the drivers at Lufthansa for a more focused corporate strategy, the sale of Ground Globe (airport ground service) and several financial divestments (e.g., the shareholding in the reservation system Amadeus). Then, just at the very end of 2006, Lufthansa sold its 50 percent stake in Thomas Cook, the tourism company into which Lufthansa integrated its charter airline Condor, for €800 million to KarstadtQuelle.[10] And finally, even more might be for sale with LSG Sky Chefs (catering) when its turnaround is finalized (some parts of LSG Sky Chefs have been sold).

The permanent attempt to remove intermediaries is representative of the focus not only on cost cutting but also on streamlining the business model. In 2005 Lufthansa abolished any discount on its tickets for independent travel agencies (they now have to charge their customers for issuing tickets) and promotes direct booking via the Web or call centers or controlled distribution channels (e.g., LH City Centers, a franchise travel agency chain with 540 offices in 49 countries as of 2006).

Above All: Maintaining Financial Discipline

Every business cycle challenges the precious investment-grade rating that Lufthansa enjoys. In the crisis from 2001 to 2004, the gearing increased from 36 percent in 2000 to 85.4 percent in 2005, despite an increase in shareholder capital.[11] As a result, financial operating goals are dominant and Lufthansa has learned to focus its cost cutting on the cash flow impact. Depreciation of airplanes is higher than British Airways for example (12 vs. 20 years) to ensure a rapid capital recovery and reduce debt service as quickly as possible. Leasing part of the fleet allows for quicker adjustment of capacity (after 2001 approximately 20 percent of plane capacity was taken out of operation; now it is building up again).

Corporate Culture in Transition

Lufthansa was once known for its strong culture, based on pride in being a "Lufthanseat," the positive image of the company in Germany and its reputation for engineering excellence, underpinned by ongoing training and educational activities. Now approximately one-third of the workforce is non-German, and it has become more fragmented in its interests, perceptions, communication channels, and expectations. The pilots' strike in 2001, which put the pilots in confrontation with the ground personnel (who suffered the brunt of passenger anger), was not only about money. It was also about the pilots' feeling that they were no longer sufficiently appreciated, a lack of integration into the "normal" flow of communication and consensus building.

Management has tried to improve the situation; ongoing "town hall" meetings with members of the management board and the CEO are held, as well as an extensive written communication flow about the development of the company. Such initiatives are state-of-the-art in the industry today and Lufthansa has included them in the "leadership values" for its employees. As a result, every employee has individual targets and managers of all levels are evaluated on an annual basis (in a dialogue with his/her boss).

Continuous education and training is also high on the agenda, not only for employees but also for management. Among German-based companies, Lufthansa pioneered a "corporate university" in 1998. The "Lufthansa School of Business" is recognized worldwide as one of the best in the industry.

To increase employees' identification with the company and to help passengers "feel valued" (despite the high fuel consumption), Lufthansa is embarking on a wide range of social and environmental activities—from supporting children in need (via the "Help Alliance") to protecting endangered animals and recycling or introducing fuel efficiency initiatives (see http://konzern.lufthansa.com/en/html/ueber_uns/balance/index.html).

But Lufthansa management knows that past efforts are now being challenged by an issue of a completely new dimension—global warming. Although the airline industry claims that only 3 percent of global CO_2 emissions come from air traffic, the whole impact on global warming is approximately twice that factor (e.g., through NOx emissions at high altitude) and rapidly growing. Given current growth rates, the share of CO_2 emissions from air traffic might increase to approximately 20 percent by 2020.

Unlike many other energy sources in developed countries, fuel for airlines is not taxed—a point constantly raised in public criticism. So far the industry has avoided taxation because it would require some sort of international agreement, but the pressure is rapidly growing to price the "externalities" of air transport into travel costs. The industry is considering a kind of emission trading to avoid taxation, but even this approach would increase fuel prices considerably and may end the era of "cheap flights."

Notes

1. As of 2006, IATA (International Air Transport Association) represents 261 airlines comprising 94 percent of international scheduled air traffic.
2. IATA, 2006. The figure represents the sum of the net profits between 2001 and 2005 for all IATA member companies. These are (in US$ billion): –13.0 (2001), –11.3 (2002), –7.6 (2003), –5.6 (2004), –3.2 (2005). The estimated value for 2006 is US$ –1.7 billion.
3. Datamonitor, Airline Report, 2005; IATA Air Transport Statistics, 2001, 2002, and 2003.
4. Lufthansa's annual reports between 2000 and 2003. These figures represent the total passage revenue (including cargo and mail), which dropped from €12.55 billion for the year 2000 to €11.66 billion for the year 2003.
5. IATA, 2005, 2006. In the United States and Asia, the share of labor costs in operating costs is 38 percent and 20 percent, respectively.
6. Furthermore, in Lufthansa's case the chairman of the (Civil) Service and Transportation Union is the deputy chairman of the supervisory board due to the co-determination law.
7. Star Alliance; PATA, November 2006. PATA data are calculated on the basis of IACO data.
8. The formal bankruptcy procedure began on December 9, 2002, and closed on February 1, 2006.
9. The low-cost airline Germanwings is a 100% subsidiary of Eurowings.
10. Before this deal, KarstadtQuelle held the other 50% of Thomas Cook. Further, the deal that was announced in December 2006 makes Lufthansa a minority stakeholder in Condor.
11. Gearing is calculated as the ratio of a company's long-term funds with fixed interest to its total capital. A high gearing is generally considered speculative.

Case 19

Microsoft's Diversification Strategy

Ali F. Farhoomand, Samuel Tsang

University of Hong Kong

Since the early 2000s, a string of bad news had seriously undermined the future growth of Microsoft. The delay in rolling out the new version of the Windows operating system ("OS") announced in June 2005 further reinforced the prevailing impression that the software giant was in strategic disarray. In late 2005, Bill Gates finally announced a long-awaited corporate strategy to revamp the software giant. By formally recognizing the emerging business opportunities introduced by the new Internet era (Web 2.0),[1] Microsoft began to reinvent itself. It restructured key business units, streamlined decision-making processes, and realigned itself to become more nimble in producing software. The restructuring initiative was undertaken in tandem with the company's new diversification strategy of moving beyond the personal computer (PC) software business and into other devices such as mobile phones, television setup boxes, and game consoles.

In November 2005, Microsoft launched Xbox 360, its latest game console. It was an extraordinary event, not because of the glamorous business executives and journalists attending the event, the cool festival mood soaking Mojave Desert, or the graphic technologies dazzling the giant consoles surrounding the conference room. Rather, the air was filled with a mix of trepidation and excitement about the viability of the company's new strategy of moving beyond Windows-based PCs. Everybody in the room wondered whether Microsoft could regain its past glory by wading into new territories. What opportunities and challenges, they thought, awaited it in markets where it did not have proprietary advantage? What specific strategies would it adopt to capitalize on these opportunities and counter the challenges? How best could Microsoft execute its diversification strategy?

Brief History of Microsoft

In 1975, Bill Gates founded Microsoft in Albuquerque, New Mexico, after dropping out of Harvard. He partnered with Paul Allen to sell a version of BASIC, a programming language that the duo had written for Altair (the first commercial microcomputer) when Gates was still at Harvard. In 1979, Microsoft relocated to Seattle and began to develop software that helped users write their own programs. In 1980, IBM selected Microsoft to develop the operating system for its PCs. Subsequently, Microsoft bought QDOS, or "quick and dirty operating system," for US$50,000 from a Seattle programmer, and renamed it the Microsoft Disk Operating System (MS-DOS).

In 1983, Allen developed Hodgkin's disease and left the start-up. In the mid-1980s, Microsoft introduced Windows, a graphics-based version of MS-DOS that borrowed features from its rival Apple's Macintosh system. In 1986, Microsoft went public and Gates became the industry's first billionaire. In 1993, Microsoft introduced Windows NT to compete with UNIX, a popular operating system on minicomputers.

As Microsoft continued to dominate the desktop software market and expanded aggressively into other industry sectors, the U.S. Justice Department filed antitrust charges in 1998 against the software company, claiming that Microsoft had stifled Internet browser competition and limited consumer choice. The courts initially ruled in 2000 that Microsoft be split up into two companies. Subsequently, a tentative settlement was reached between the company and the U.S. Justice Department. The settlement left Microsoft intact, but imposed restrictions on the licensing policies for its operating systems. More specifically, Microsoft agreed to uniformly license its operating systems and allowed computer manufacturers to include rivals' software with Windows. In addition, Microsoft also reached settlement agreements with major players (e.g., Netscape, Sun Microsystems, and IBM) in the market owing to the antitrust investigation. While Microsoft was settling the majority of its antitrust issues, an ongoing investigation was pending by the European Union (EU). In March 2004, the EU fined Microsoft and ordered it to offer European computer manufacturers a stripped down version of Windows by taking out its media player software. Microsoft announced plans to appeal the decision.[2]

With the growing importance of the networked economy, Microsoft was initially reluctant to adopt the Internet. Not until 1995 did it found Microsoft Network (MSN), a Web portal that offered a wide range of services. Like many other established IT companies, Microsoft experienced its toughest economic downturn due to the burst of the dot.com bubble. Although Microsoft recovered, its near-monopoly on PC operating systems and basic office software had been challenged by a string of start-ups. These new competitors were able to churn out popular programs such as e-mail, desktop search engines, and instant messaging over the Internet much faster than Microsoft. Such sluggishness in new product development was caused by Microsoft's inefficient approach. In particular, its flagship product, Windows, had been developed as a massive program that was stitched together into one gigantic computer program. The code base of Windows had become complex, and extremely difficult to build and test. And in fact, the next generation of Windows (namely Vista) was two years behind its original schedule when it was rolled out in 2006. It would also mark the longest interval between two versions of Windows.[3]

In view of antitrust regulation in the United States and European Union, and increasing competition in the desktop software market, Microsoft was determined to move beyond the PC software industry. Its strategy was to extend its software products into Web-based services for businesses and consumers. By transforming itself from a traditional software provider to a broader technology services and media company, Microsoft aimed to position its operating systems, software, and services as a de facto standard for accessing, communicating, and doing business over the Internet.

Exhibit 1 Aggregate Capital Expenditure of U.S. Companies on IT (US$ billion)

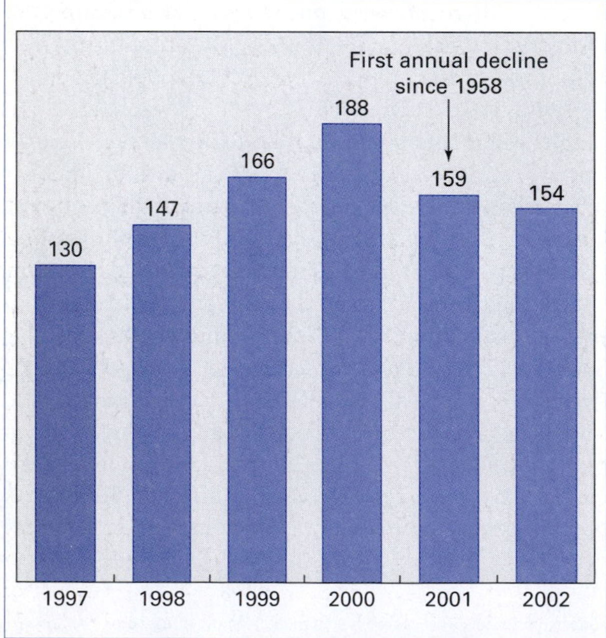

Source: K. B. Davis, A. S. Rath, & B. L. Scanlon, 2004, How IT spending is changing, *McKinsey Quarterly*.

Development Factors in the Emerging IT Industry

According to a study conducted by McKinsey & Co. in 2004 on IT spending trends, chief information officers (CIOs) from the *Fortune* 500 companies would spend money differently after the burst of the dot.com bubble. Although IT spending had increased since 2003 after three years of decline (see Exhibit 1), customers would expect to get more out of their technology investments. Companies had been more concerned about the value of IT and enforced stringent rules and guidelines for IT spending. For instance, procurement departments became more involved in the IT purchasing process, and in particular, for the commodity products such as PCs and desktop software. Many had applied formal bidding mechanisms that required vendors to go through a competitive process in finalizing the complex deals. In addition, chief executive officers (CEOs) became more demanding of the return on investment (ROI) on new technology spending. As a result, CIOs were required to develop stronger business cases to support their investments, and tie the overall performance of IT to their personal performance measures. Subsequently, the growth of overall IT spending was expected to be more modest (amount 4 percent to 6 percent) from 2003 onwards. This would be far below the double-digit figures of the heydays in the 1990s.[4]

The IT industry was considered to be in the midst of an eight-year period of "technology digestion." Hence, senior managers had become reluctant to make major technology investments. Forrester Research Inc., a technology and market research firm, explained "technology digestion" as follows: Investment in IT had continued to increase since 1956. In the United States, the ratio of IT investment to gross domestic product (GDP)

Exhibit 2 Stages of Technology Innovation and Digestion

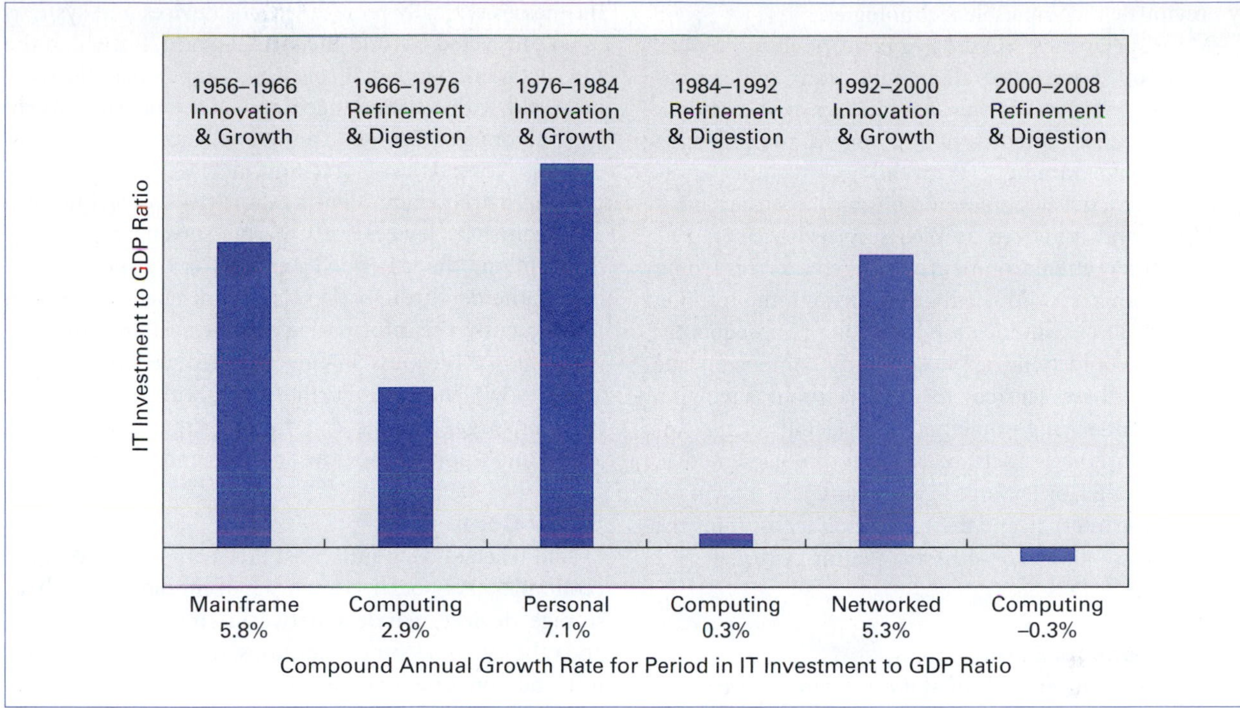

Source: Adapted from A. Bartels, 2004, IT spending outlook: 2004 to 2008 and beyond, Forrester Research Inc., Cambridge, MA.

increased from 1 percent in the mid-twentieth century to more than 4 percent at the beginning of the twenty-first century. However, such growth was not always constant. In fact, it was characterised by periods (8–10 years) of fast growth followed by equally long periods of slow or negative growth. Based on previous historical data, three growth periods were identified in the IT industry corresponding to the introduction of the new technologies (see Exhibit 2). The first period was the introduction of mainframe computing between the mid-1950s and mid-1960s. The second period was the introduction of personal computing from the mid-1970s to the mid-1980s. The third period was the introduction of network computing between the early 1990s and the early 2000s. In these periods, companies often invested in new technologies on faith and without strong links to ROI measurements. Subsequently, companies went many years before fully exploiting the technologies. During these digestion periods, companies often focused on changing the relevant business processes as well as the corresponding organizational structures, often leading to lower spending on new technologies. These spending lags were also noted by researchers from MIT's Center for eBusiness. Based on large-scale statistical results, they cited that companies often implemented new technologies years ahead of time before they could get value from them. This delay in value realization was particularly true in terms of infrastructural investments.[5]

Toward the Next Big Thing

Although the IT industry looked rather gloomy in 2006, analysts predicted, based on previous cycles, that the industry would take off again in 2007 or 2008. In particular, a number of emerging factors would drive the next growth cycle for the technology industry.[6] Some foresaw that software spending would reach US$325 billion by 2008, and the growth rate of the market was expected to be in the range of 3 percent to 7 percent annually.[7]

Service-Oriented Architecture and Web Services

Customers frequently looked for ways to modify and upgrade their enterprise applications to meet their changing business needs. However, many of them found that their IT infrastructure was unable to keep up with such rapid changes. In particular, their IT infrastructure was often confined to specific technologies, often proprietary, that were used by the functional applications. The IT department's infrastructural support was too limited to support the changes in business processes across the enterprises. To address such issues, companies began redesigning their IT infrastructures around business processes rather than functional applications. By leveraging the concept of service-oriented architecture (SOA), companies were able to capture business processes and represent them in a common digital form, (i.e., Web services). In this way, organizations could eliminate those silos of functional applications across business processes that were created by previously incompatible technologies.

More specifically, SOA was a conceptual framework that developed and integrated applications and emphasized code reuse and business modeling. It was also an evolution of distributed computing based on the loosely coupled design paradigm. With this architecture (i.e., its specification), developers would be able to package business logic and functions as Web services that could be used in different environments. All Web services would then be connected with each other through the Internet (the common communication backbone). Subsequently, developers could build applications by composing one or more of these services together without having to know the underlying implementation details of the services. For instance, a service could be implemented in Microsoft's .NET or in Sun Microsystems' Java, the lingua franca on the Internet, and the applications consuming the same service could be on different platforms (e.g., legacy mainframes or PCs).[8]

Applications as Services

Most Web sites were full of static information; executable functions (e.g., buy, search, and cancel) were rarely evoked to execute tasks that were not on the individual PCs but which were, rather, on the servers of the host Web sites. As new Web services technologies continued to take hold, players were able to develop and centrally maintain a variety of executable programs, or applications as services, which could be downloaded to the individual PCs and could then be used to carry out tasks locally. For instance, the search, desktop, toolbar, and map programs created by Google were prime examples of such executable programs. These programs would not only improve the productivity of desktop computing, but also bridge the divide between desktop computing and the Internet. Moreover, as many of these programs were available for free to customers (in the case of Google, these programs were funded by advertising and syndication), they would spread extremely fast on the Internet. Sooner or later, companies would have to incorporate these executables into their existing systems to stay relevant to their customers. In addition, because these free programs were as powerful as the paid desktop programs but far more flexible to use and cost effective, they would not only replace static Web pages on the Internet, but also standard desktop software, mostly created by Microsoft. Besides desktop applications, many had foreseen that enterprise applications such as enterprise resource planning (ERP), supply chain management (SCM), and customer relationship management (CRM) software would be increasingly developed and distributed under the application-as-services model, and perhaps enterprise applications would one day be given away freely.

Extended Internet

Businesses typically require various devices and systems to be connected beyond the virtual world, for which the Internet was extended. It connects computers in the digital world with various machines in the physical world (e.g., automobile and electronic appliances with built-in wireless connections, tracking devices with embedded radio frequency identification (RFID) technology, and biometric devices with remote sensing capability). In addition, the extended Internet can collect richer data gathered through these network-enabled devices. Subsequently, the information analyses will improve and the value of business intelligence deduced from these analyses will increase. Furthermore, with the extended Internet, organizations can tighten control over their assets, and improve the flow of goods and customers.

Social Computing

IT had reached deep into most households in developed economies. As social computing technologies such as storage devices, wireless networks, instant messaging, and others had become ubiquitous, having a tremendous influence on how people access the relevant information sources. In the case of the United States, broadband Internet access was expected to grow from 0.6 million households in 1998 to more than 63 million households in 2008.[9] Some analysts expected that home computer networks would connect PCs and other devices in more than 40 million households by 2008. Such an explosion in home computer networks would foster a convergence of IT with television and cable broadcast, entertainment, consumer electronics, and gaming industries. Social computing technologies would empower individuals through many activities such as searching, downloading, streaming, consumer-to-consumer commerce, blogging, podcasting, and instant messaging, and would change individual behaviors in communications, marketing, media, and commerce.

Microsoft's Strategic Repositioning

As the desktop software market matured, Microsoft continued to diversify and hoped to make headway into the non-PC markets. The company expanded its product lines into enterprise software, consumer products, and services markets. Facing fierce competition on all fronts, Microsoft was driven to reinvent itself. In September 2005, Microsoft announced a major restructuring exercise, which reorganized the company into three business units. The new diversification strategy was to group products and services that had high synergies, streamline decision making, and further realign the company to become nimbler in producing software. The first unit was the Platform Products and Services Division, which oversaw the Windows Client, Server and Tools, and MSN groups and aimed to leverage MSN's success in the development of Windows-based products. The second unit was the Business Division, which oversaw the Information Worker (Microsoft Office-related products) and Microsoft Business Solutions (enterprise application software products) groups. The third group was the Entertainment and Devices Division, which oversaw the Home and Entertainment group (Xbox videogame) and the Mobile and Embedded Devices group, and aimed to compete with players such as Apple and Sony. Ray Ozzie, the highly regarded guru from Groove Networks, would assist the three units in adopting a network-based development approach.[10]

Platform Products and Services Division

Microsoft had ventured into the services market through MSN in order to generate new revenue. MSN was a Web portal that offered a wide range of online services including: news, information search (which was once based on Google's technology before Microsoft developed its own search capability), e-mail (Hotmail was acquired by Microsoft in 1997), instant messaging, online shopping and games, chat rooms, and message boards. In addition, MSN also operated various fee-based services including a dial-up Internet service, MSN TV (interactive television based on WebTV Networks, a company purchased by Microsoft in 1997), Hotmail Plus (upgraded e-mail service), Radio Plus (commercial-free online music radio), MSN Music (online music business), and an online travel service that was offered in partnership with Expedia.

Based on its success in MSN, Microsoft had hoped to leverage its experience to transform its Windows-based platform products into Web-based services for consumers and enterprises. In late 2004, in view of this strategic move, Microsoft adopted the modular or Lego-like development approach that was adopted by MSN and favored by Google and other players. By first developing a core for Windows, the engineers of Microsoft could gradually add new features to the program. Through this new approach, Microsoft could more easily plug in and pull out new features without disrupting the entire Windows program. Moreover, Microsoft also leveraged MSN to generate revenue through traditional advertising on its Web site, and also sold text-based advertisements to compete with Google's AdWords and AdSense, and Yahoo! Search Marketing.

In 2005, the company acquired Groove Networks (founded by Lotus Notes developer Ray Ozzie), a collaboration software maker; Sybari Software, an antivirus security provider; and FrontBridge Technologies, an e-mail security developer. These technologies were critical to Microsoft's existing platform product lines. Subsequently, Microsoft extended its Windows operating system as an online service (namely Windows Live). In addition, to complement its platform products and Internet services, Microsoft further strengthened itself in the Web services technology market by leveraging its .NET technology, which was originally developed to compete with the Java technology created by Sun Microsystems. Moreover, Microsoft had developed a number of essential tools that would help customers build the key elements in SOA platforms, and develop specific Web service-based modules and solutions.

Business Division

Traditionally, the Office application family within the Information Worker Group had been the second most money-generating division for Microsoft. However, in view of the pressing threats from Google and other players that provided similar software as free online services, Microsoft announced that it would provide its Office application product family as an online service, namely, Office Live. Although it was basically a repackaging of existing products, and they were not yet available as free software like the e-mail program provided by Google, the action demonstrated the seriousness of the matter in Microsoft's eyes.

In the enterprise software market, Microsoft deliberately chose not to compete with leading enterprise applications providers such as SAP and Oracle for large multinational companies. Instead, the software giant aggressively pursued opportunities with small and midsized enterprises. In 2001, after acquiring Great Plains Software, a long-time partner and a specialist in accounting applications for small and midsized businesses, for US$1.1 billion, Microsoft Business Solutions was formed. The new division combined the expertise of Great Plains with its existing small business software operations, including the bCentral small business services unit. The division grew substantially in 2002, when Microsoft acquired Navision, a Denmark-based enterprise software maker for about US$1.5 billion. Microsoft Business Solutions offered a wide range of software applications including accounting, customer relationship management, supply chain management, analytics and reporting, e-commerce, business portals and online business services, human resources, manufacturing and retail management, field services management, and project management.

Entertainment and Devices Division

In terms of the consumer market, one of Microsoft's most important moves was its entry into the video gaming business in 2001. Since the first launch of the video game console, Xbox, the software giant had sold 22 million units worldwide. According to Forrester Researcher

Inc., a technology and market research firm, this move put Microsoft in the distant second place behind Sony's Playstation 2 (92 million units sold) and slightly ahead of Nintendo's GameCube (19 million units sold). The gaming business was cyclical. Generally, every five to six years, a new generation of game consoles would be created. With the new Xbox 360, Microsoft was determined to capture the top spot in the latest cycle of the gaming business, and to challenge Sony's dominant position. First, the software giant's Xbox 360 was launched several months ahead of its rivals' products: Sony's Playstation 3 was expected to appear in the market in spring 2006; and Nintendo's Revolution would be launched in late 2006. Some believed that the success of Sony's Playstation 2 had been partly due to its advantage in reaching the market earlier than its rivals. Hence, Microsoft copied this marketing trick by becoming the first game console in the new business cycle. Second, learning from the flop of the original Xbox in Japan, this time Microsoft worked closely with the producers of the Japanese games in the hope of neutralizing the traditional advantages of its two main rivals. Third, Microsoft abandoned its previous approach of using off-the-shelf parts provided by Intel and Nvidia. Although efficient, that approach lacked the flexibility that Microsoft's rivals enjoyed in reducing the consoles' costs and increasing the profit margins during their lifetime. For instance, Sony had gradually reduced the number of chips required by its Playstation 2 without sacrificing its performance. So Microsoft adopted a new design for Xbox 360, hoping to achieve a new degree of flexibility that could help integrate various components and profitability in the future. In addition to producing and selling game consoles, Microsoft's Xbox Live had been a leader of online gaming. The system provided classic arcade games, game trailers, and upgrade packs that were downloadable.

In addition to gaming, Microsoft ventured into the mobile communications market. For years, the software giant was denied entry into the market by mobile handset manufacturers. In fact, these manufacturers even deliberately formed a consortium (called Symbian) to prevent Microsoft from developing smartphone software. In order to address this disadvantage, Microsoft went to the mobile operators. During this time, many mobile operators, particularly in Europe, started to leverage original design manufacturers (ODM), mostly in Taiwan, to produce handsets that would bear their own brand names in order to create market differentiators. Microsoft spotted this opportunity and persuaded the operators and handset manufacturers to develop phones based on its Windows Mobile operating system. In 2002, Orange launched the first Windows-based smartphone developed by High Tech Computer Corporation (HTC), a leading ODM in Taiwan. Other operators followed suit, particularly owing to the large volume of data-driven, revenue-generating smartphones. In 2003, Motorola left Symbian and licensed the Windows Mobile software for some of its smartphones. Others would be based on Symbian software and Linux (the open-source operating system). In addition to the opportunity of partnering with the ODMs and operators, the convergence of mobile phone and handheld computers had played to Microsoft's strengths. In late 2005, Palm (Microsoft's rival in handheld devices) decided to adopt the Windows Mobile software and replace its Palm OS with its Treo smartphone. This move further signaled Microsoft's success in penetrating the mobile and handheld market segments. Although Microsoft had made huge progress in the mobile industry, it remained an outsider in many respects. Nonetheless, as mobile phones had become evermore like handheld PCs, particularly with the success of inexpensive PDA phones, Microsoft would have the opportunity to further establish itself in the market.

The cable television market was one in which Microsoft had struggled for many years. In particular, Microsoft had been deliberately kept out of the market by cable operators' refusal to adopt its software in their cable boxes. Cable operators were concerned that once Microsoft entered the market it would repeat its monopolistic practices of the PC business in the cable industry. In view of this situation, Microsoft had formed strategic partnerships, hoping to improve its position in the cable market. For instance, the software giant formed a partnership with NBC Universal Cable to provide MSNBC Interactive News and MSNBC Cable services. In 1999 Microsoft agreed to invest US$5 billion for a minority stake in AT&T as part of that company's move to acquire cable operator MediaOne. The overall results from these moves, though, were less than satisfactory. Microsoft saw a new opportunity, however, as telecom operators began to compete with cable operators by offering television service on top of their broadband data service. Television services delivered on the broadband networks was based on a technology called Internet protocol TV (IPTV), which could also support various kinds of interactivity such as video-on-demand services. Although the technology held great potential, telecom operators were reluctant to invest and build the entire system by themselves. Seeing this particular issue, Microsoft partnered with Alcatel, a French telecom technology provider, for it to provide the required hardware. In this way, Microsoft established itself as a leading IPTV technology provider. Through this arrangement, a number of leading telecom operators, including Deutche Telekom, SBC (acquired AT&T and BellSouth), Bell Canada, British Telecom (BT), and Telecom Italia, adopted Microsoft's software for their IPTV services.

Key Competitors

With the arrival of the new Internet era (Web 2.0) and the ongoing convergence of IT, telecommunications, and media, many players were eyeing the same markets. Hence, Microsoft was expected to face many more competitors as it moved beyond the PC business. The following section highlights Microsoft's key competitors (for performance details, see Exhibit 3).

Red Hat

Red Hat dominated the market for Linux, the open-source computer operating system, and the main rival to Microsoft's Windows-based products. Besides Enterprise Linux OS, Red Hat also provided other products such as database, content, collaboration management applications, and software development tools. The company also offered various services such as consulting, custom software development, support, and training.

Red Hat compiled and distributed the significantly improved version of Linux, first through CD-ROMs and later through the Internet. Because Linux itself was free, Red Hat's revenue came from manuals, technical support, and other value-added services that were challenged by the software's ever-changing source code. Until 1997, Linux and Red Hat's package was only known to a small group of programmers who were looking for an alternative to Microsoft's Windows. Only after Intel, Netscape, Compaq, IBM, Novell, Oracle, and SAP made investments in the company in the subsequent two years did Red Hat become famous. Subsequently, the company went public in 2000.

In 2001, Red Hat expanded its software products and included database applications and an e-commerce software suite designed for midsized businesses. In late 2003, Red Hat acquired Sistina Software of Minneapolis, a supplier of data storage infrastructure software for Linux operating systems. Sistina was founded in 1997 and had about 20 employees. Red Hat paid about US$31 million in stock to acquire Sistina. SAP Ventures, the venture capital arm of SAP, had invested in Sistina earlier in 2003. With Linux's popularity on the rise, Red Hat turned its focus to corporate customers. In particular, the company decided to end its routine maintenance of the Red Hat Linux line

Exhibit 3 Microsoft's Income Statement, 2003–2005 (US$ million)

Income Statement	June 2005	June 2004	June 2003
Revenue	$39,788	$36,835	$32,187
Cost of Goods Sold	5,345	5,530	4,247
Gross Profit	34,443	31,305	27,940
Gross Profit Margin	86.60%	85.00%	86.80%
SG&A Expense	19,027	21,085	13,284
Depreciation & Amortization	855	1,186	1,439
Operating Income	14,561	9,034	13,217
Operating Margin	36.60%	24.50%	41.10%
Nonoperating Income	2,067	3,162	1,509
Nonoperating Expenses	0	0	0
Income Before Taxes	16,628	12,196	14,726
Income Taxes	4,374	4,028	4,733
Net Income After Taxes	12,254	8,168	9,993
Continuing Operations	12,254	8,168	9,993
Discontinued Operations	0	0	0
Total Operations	12,254	8,168	9,993
Total Net Income	12,254	8,168	9,993
Net Profit Margin	30.80%	22.20%	31.00%
Diluted EPS from Continuing Operations ($)	1.12	0.75	0.92
Diluted EPS from Discontinued Operations ($)	0	0	0
Diluted EPS from Total Operations ($)	1.12	0.75	0.92
Diluted EPS from Total Net Income ($)	1.12	0.75	0.92
Dividends per Share	3.40	0.16	0.08

Source: Adapted from J. Lower, 2006, Microsoft Corporation, *Hoover's Company Information*, Austin, TX: Hoover's Inc.

in 2004 in order to focus on enhancing and supporting its Enterprise Linux products. Red Hat established the Fedora Project, an open-source software effort relying on the work of volunteer programmers, for support of its original Linux distribution. In 2005, Red Hat began to focus on the government sector and to establish a dedicated unit to look after that business (see Exhibit 4).

Google

Google had been revered as the most successful online search engine company in the world. The company operated one of the most popular search engines by offering search results from more than 8 billion Web pages. It was also about to become one of the most innovative software makers that stood to change the face of the software industry. Throughout the years, Google had rolled out a series of powerful programs (e.g., Toolbar, Desktop Search, Gmail, and Froogle—a comparison shopping service) that aimed to seamlessly bridge customers' desktops and the Internet. Many customers downloaded these free software products and used them extensively in their homes and offices. Moreover, Google changed the funding model for product development by using the income earned from its advertisements and syndication to cover the costs of developing these innovative products. With the success of this subsidizing approach, some predicted that the software industry would one day be funded by advertising; whether it was for the consumer's desktop or for enterprise application software such as sales automation or supply chain software.

Since its beginning in 1998, Google upheld its unique company philosophy by first releasing new products and then perfecting them on the fly. It developed business plans based on the feedback it gathered from customers. Google went public in 2004 and successfully raised US$1.6 billion in a highly anticipated initial public offering (IPO). Besides developing innovative products and making them available for free in the market, Google had invested effort in digitizing books and other materials collected in the various university and public libraries, including those at Stanford, Harvard, and Oxford, as well works in the New York Public Library collection.

Although Google seemed to be ahead of the pack, it had been competing fiercely with Yahoo! and MSN in the search-driven advertising sector. Both these rivals launched their own search technology and targeted

Exhibit 4 Red Hat's Income Statement, 2003–2005 (US$ million)

Income Statement	Feb. 2005	Feb. 2004	Feb. 2003
Revenue	$196.50	$126.10	$90.90
Cost of Goods Sold	25.60	27.80	26.00
Gross Profit	170.90	98.30	64.90
Gross Profit Margin	87.00%	78.00%	71.40%
SG&A Expense	130.10	87.90	74.10
Depreciation & Amortization	13.90	7.30	6.50
Operating Income	26.90	3.10	–15.70
Operating Margin	13.70%	2.50%	—
Nonoperating Income	24.40	10.80	10.80
Nonoperating Expenses	6.40	0	0
Income Before Taxes	44.90	13.90	–6.40
Income Taxes	–0.50	0	0
Net Income After Taxes	45.40	13.90	–6.40
Continuing Operations	45.40	14	–6.30
Discontinued Operations	0	0	0
Total Operations	45.40	14	–6.30
Total Net Income	45.40	14	–6.60
Net Profit Margin	23.10%	11.10%	—
Diluted EPS from Continuing Operations ($)	0.24	0.08	–0.04
Diluted EPS from Discontinued Operations ($)	0	0	0
Diluted EPS from Total Operations ($)	0.24	0.08	–0.04
Diluted EPS from Total Net Income ($)	0.24	0.08	–0.04
Dividends per Share	0	0	0

Source: Adapted from J. Lower, 2006, Red Hat, Inc., *Hoover's Company Information,* Austin, TX: Hoover's Inc.

advertising programs. To further capture market share, Google continued to launch additional online services. Following its acquisition of Picasa in 2004, Google made the photo-sharing software freely available. Subsequently, the search company acquired Keyhole in the same year and released a free version of that company's 3-D satellite imaging software as the latest component of its localized content offerings. In 2005, Google introduced an instant messaging client, Google Talk. It also acquired Urchin Software, a maker of Web analytics tools.

Besides creating its own desktop programs, Google released data on its online information services, such as Google Maps, to encourage "mashing" (combining data and capabilities of various Web sites to produce hybrid sites). This prime example shows how Google leveraged open standards propagated by the Internet in generating innovations outside its four walls. In addition, the building of the mash-up sites let Google tap into the creativity of software developers around the globe, and further its advertising channels[11] (see Exhibit 5).

Yahoo!

As a pioneer in Internet search and navigation, Yahoo! had been one of the best-known online brands. It was the largest Web portal and the second most popular Internet search engine after Google. The company drew more than 345 million people to its sites (published in 15 languages in 20 countries) with a mix of news, entertainment, and a range of online services.

Afer the dot.com crash and the recession thereafter, Yahoo! had diversified its revenue streams with a mix of paid content and services. Besides offering registered users free personalized Web pages, e-mail, and message boards, Yahoo! earned revenue from sales of advertisements and subscriptions for premium paid services such as online gaming and music downloading. Moreover, Yahoo! provided fee-based online marketing and other commercial services. For instance, Yahoo! sold search results and targeted advertising through Yahoo! Search Marketing, and job listing services through Yahoo! HotJobs. In addition, it offered Web hosting and

Exhibit 5 Google's Income Statement, 2003–2005 (US$ million)

Income Statement	Dec. 2005	Dec. 2004	Dec. 2003
Revenue	$6,138.60	$3,189.20	$1,465.90
Cost of Goods Sold	2,277.70	1,309.20	570.80
Gross Profit	3,860.90	1,880.00	895.10
Gross Profit Margin	62.90%	58.90%	61.10%
SG&A Expense	1,459.80	890.30	497.60
Depreciation & Amortization	293.80	148.50	55
Operating Income	2,107.30	841.20	342.50
Operating Margin	34.30%	26.40%	23.40%
Nonoperating Income	124.40	10	4.20
Nonoperating Expenses	0	0	0
Income Before Taxes	2,141.70	650.20	346.70
Income Taxes	676.30	251.10	241.00
Net Income After Taxes	1,465.40	399.10	105.70
Continuing Operations	1,465.40	399.10	105.60
Discontinued Operations	0	0	0
Total Operations	1,465.40	399.10	105.60
Total Net Income	1,465.40	399.10	105.60
Net Profit Margin	23.90%	12.50%	7.20%
Diluted EPS from Continuing Operations ($)	5.02	1.46	0.41
Diluted EPS from Discontinued Operations ($)	0	0	0
Diluted EPS from Total Operations ($)	5.02	1.46	0.41
Diluted EPS from Total Net Income ($)	5.02	1.46	0.41
Dividends per Share	0	0	0

Source: Adapted from J. Bramhall, 2006, Google Inc., *Hoover's Company Information*, Austin, TX: Hoover's Inc.

merchant services to small businesses. Besides online services, Yahoo! provided branded Internet access through partnerships with telecommunications companies, including SBC Communications and Verizon i n the United States; BT Group in the United Kingdom; and Rogers Communications in Canada.

As online advertising continued to grow, Yahoo! faced challenges from Google and Microsoft's MSN. In particular, Google had significantly captured the search market by building a range of free Web services to attract customers. Although it lagged far behind both Yahoo! and Google, MSN had launched its own search-driven advertising program. In response to the threats, Yahoo! lured the former head of programming at ABC television, Lloyd Braun, to create original content and to form content partnerships with major studios. In addition, Yahoo! had improved its search technology by acquiring Inktomi in 2003. In the same year, its purchase of Overture, an online marketing firm, had given Yahoo! a significant boost in advertising revenue. The company continued to strengthen its Web services portfolio through acquisitions. For instance, Yahoo! purchased Flickr, a photo sharing Web site; Dialpad Communications, an Internet telephony business; and Musicmatch, an online music downloading service to compete with Apple Computer's iTunes service and Napster.

Yahoo! expanded its international presence, which accounts for about a quarter of its revenue. In particular, the company acquired Kelkoo (a European comparison shopping service) and Yisou.com (a Chinese search site). In mid-2005, Yahoo! acquired a 40 percent stake in Alibaba.com, the leading e-commerce company in China, for US$1billion. Under the new partnership, Alibaba.com would take over operations of Yahoo! China. In addition, the company also announced plans to buy out the remaining shares of Yahoo! Europe and Yahoo! Korea from its partner SoftBank[12] (see Exhibit 6).

Exhibit 6 Yahoo!'s Income Statement, 2003–2005 (US$ million)

Income Statement	Dec. 2005	Dec. 2004	Dec. 2003
Revenue	$5,257.70	$3,574.50	$1,625.10
Cost of Goods Sold	1,808.30	1,133.20	252.8
Gross Profit	3,449.40	2,441.30	1,372.30
Gross Profit Margin	65.60%	68.30%	84.40%
SG&A Expense	1,944.50	1,441.70	917
Depreciation & Amortization	397.10	311.00	159.70
Operating Income	1,107.80	688.60	295.60
Operating Margin	21.10%	19.30%	18.20%
Nonoperating Income	1,226.10	591.40	95.20
Nonoperating Expenses	0	0	0
Income Before Taxes	2,671.90	1,280.00	390.80
Income Taxes	767.80	438.00	147.00
Net Income After Taxes	1,904.10	842.00	243.80
Continuing Operations	1,896.20	839.60	237.90
Discontinued Operations	0	0	0
Total Operations	1,896.20	839.60	237.90
Total Net Income	1,896.20	839.60	237.90
Net Profit Margin	36.10%	23.50%	14.60%
Diluted EPS from Continuing Operations ($)	1.28	0.58	0.19
Diluted EPS from Discontinued Operations ($)	0	0	0
Diluted EPS from Total Operations ($)	1.28	0.58	0.19
Diluted EPS from Total Net Income ($)	1.28	0.58	0.19
Dividends per Share	0	0	0

Source: Adapted from J. Bramhall, 2006, Yahoo! Inc., *Hoover's Company Information*, Austin, TX: Hoover's Inc.

Oracle

In 2003, Oracle launched a hostile takeover bid for PeopleSoft, which had just disclosed its own plans to acquire a mid-market rival, JD Edwards. Initially, the board of PeopleSoft rejected the offer of US$5.1 billion in cash: They considered the bid inadequate and were troubled by associated antitrust issues. After many rounds of negotiations and offers, Oracle finally reached an agreement to acquire PeopleSoft for US$10.3 billion in December 2004. Subsequently, Oracle cut the newly combined workforce by 9 percent. Although the layoff mostly affected PeopleSoft's employees, Oracle retained the majority of PeopleSoft's development and support teams.

In 2004, Oracle continued to pursue its acquisition-driven growth in order to strengthen its presence in the market. When SAP announced its plan to acquire Retek, a retail software developer, for about US$500 million, Oracle immediately acquired 10 percent of Retek and offered to buy the remaining shares. After a short bidding battle, Oracle purchased Retek for $670 million and formed a new business unit called Oracle Retail Global. In addition, Oracle acquired Oblix, a software developer for identity management; TimesTen, a software developer for data management; and ProfitLogic, a software developer for retail inventory management. In September 2005, nine months after acquiring PeopleSoft, Oracle announced its purchase of Siebel Systems Inc., the leading CRM software maker in the world, for US$5.8 billion. The deal was expected to close in early 2006.

In order to solidify its position in the enterprise software market after its strategic acquisitions, Oracle announced Project Fusion in early 2005. This new strategic initiative aimed to create a comprehensive platform of its next-generation enterprise technologies, applications, and services. The move sought to unite Oracle's full range of software products (from enterprise applications to database software) with the best functionality from the product lines of PeopleSoft, JD Edwards, Retek, Siebel, and other newly acquired companies through the Web services technologies. Through this strategic initiative, Oracle emphasized that it would create the most integrated and complete enterprise solution in the market to operate business processes for its customers. Oracle also promised to ensure continuity of the existing Siebel, PeopleSoft, and JD Edwards' product lines; provide customers options of staying with their existing technology platforms created by rivals (e.g., IBM's DB2 database management products, BEA's middleware products); offer customers more flexibility in creating their own upgrade schedules; and reduce the total cost of ownership of the enterprise software.[13]

Besides building the most comprehensive development and integration platform for large customers, Oracle continued to equip itself to be a provider of enterprise-software-as-a-service by hosting and running the enterprise applications at Oracle's premise. The service catered to small and medium-sized customers that did not have the resources or capabilities to deal with the complexities and costs of an on-site implementation of their enterprise application software[14] (see Exhibit 7).

SAP

In 2001, SAP conducted one of the most daring corporate campaigns in its 33-year-history—it opened up its proprietary software through its new technology, NetWeaver. SAP was determined to counter the increasingly heterogeneous nature of the computing environment by providing free access to its software. After putting in more than US$1 billion in research and development, SAP introduced NetWeaver—an open platform that allows applications to be developed and accessed as Web services. This new technology was designed to link up various applications (packaged as Web services) running on different systems, from legacy mainframes to Internet-enabled devices to enterprise applications. By leveraging NetWeaver, SAP was able to break up its software products into open and modular pieces. Customers were then able to pick and choose the specific SAP Web services modules that met their needs. Moreover, customers could add in modules developed by other companies as long as these products met the specification of the NetWeaver framework. As a result of SAP's move, customers could speed up the creation and modification of their own applications, improve the overall fit of the applications, and eventually reduce the associated development costs that it would normally have incurred.

Because the software products were broken up into smaller chunks, SAP changed the delivery mode of features and functions for its products. Rather than making customers wait for massive releases to take place periodically (minor releases can take months and major releases can take years), the Web services approach allows improvements of the software products to be made immediately. SAP found that with this new engineering approach, it solicited tremendous customer support. In 2003, SAP released the early version of NetWeaver as free bundled software, which was aimed at bridging SAP and non-SAP software programs by reducing the need for building customized links. The full version of the software launched in 2007. Since mid-2005, more than 1,300 customers had tested NetWeaver and some of them were highly satisfied with it and would welcome the opportunity to refer it to future buyers.

By leveraging a universally accepted platform, thousands of individual developers were able to develop specialized modules that would serve highly targeted industry segments, which were traditionally too fragmented to be

Exhibit 7 Oracle's Income Statement, 2003–2005 (US$ million)

Income Statement	May 2005	May 2004	May 2003
Revenue	$11,799	$10,156	$9,475
Cost of Goods Sold	2,445	2,083	2,015
Gross Profit	9,354	8,073	7,460
Gross Profit Margin	79.30%	79.50%	78.70%
SG&A Expense	4,552	3,975	3,693
Depreciation & Amortization	425	234	327
Operating Income	4,377	3,864	3,440
Operating Margin	37.10%	38.00%	36.30%
Nonoperating Income	164	102	1
Nonoperating Expenses	135	21	16
Income Before Taxes	4,051	3,945	3,425
Income Taxes	1,165	1,264	1,118
Net Income After Taxes	2,886	2,681	2,307
Continuing Operations	2,886	2,681	2,307
Discontinued Operations	0	0	0
Total Operations	2,886	2,681	2,307
Total Net Income	2,886	2,681	2,307
Net Profit Margin	24.50%	26.40%	24.30%
Diluted EPS from Continuing Operations ($)	0.55	0.5	0.43
Diluted EPS from Discontinued Operations ($)	0	0	0
Diluted EPS from Total Operations ($)	0.55	0.5	0.43
Diluted EPS from Total Net Income ($)	0.55	0.5	0.43
Dividends per Share	0	0	0

Source: Adapted from J. Lower, 2006, Oracle Corporation, *Hoover's Company Information,* Austin, TX: Hoover's Inc.

addressed by using the old one-size-fits-all approach. This factor was particularly important for SAP in capturing the millions of new small and midsized enterprise customers around the world. So, to realize this strategy based on NetWeaver, SAP fostered a new ecosystem. In the past, SAP mainly relied on its internal programmers (mostly residing in Walldorf, Germany) to develop its products. With the new NetWeaver platform, the software company needed to change from being an industry introvert that focused on its supreme engineering capabilities to an extrovert that attracted tens of thousands of individual developers in joining the virtual development network (see Exhibit 8).

IBM

Because software was a key component of its new corporate strategy, On Demand Strategy, IBM acquired a number of companies to strengthen its software capability. As a leader in the software industry, IBM Software Group offered a wide range of products, particularly in the areas of database management, systems management, and application integration and development. The division was also a leader in collaboration and communication applications through its Lotus product line. In addition, the division's Tivoli product lines were well established in the storage and security software markets. The global strength of IBM's massive hardware and services businesses continued to sustain the growth of its software products, which accounted for 17 percent of IBM's total sales.

In order to streamline its diverse product lines, IBM Software Group consolidated its disparate software products into five major subgroups: information management software (DB2); collaboration software (Lotus); systems development software (Rational); systems management software (Tivoli); and application server and integration software (WebSphere).

WebSphere, in particular, was the centerpiece of IBM's software development and integration strategies, and was the answer to their rivals' competitive products, including SAP's NetWeaver. WebSphere was a platform for building a basic but robust Web services environment.

Exhibit 8 SAP's Income Statement, 2003–2005 (US$ million)

Income Statement	Dec. 2005	Dec. 2004	Dec. 2003
Revenue	$10,074.50	$10,179.10	$8,831.30
Cost of Goods Sold	3,212.40	3,221.40	2,913.70
Gross Profit	6,862.10	6,957.70	5,917.60
Gross Profit Margin	68.10%	68.40%	67.00%
SG&A Expense	3,870.10	3,942.00	3,479.30
Depreciation & Amortization	240.90	284.00	270.90
Operating Income	2,751.10	2,731.70	2,167.40
Operating Margin	27.30%	26.80%	24.50%
Nonoperating Income	9.70	96.40	71.20
Nonoperating Expenses	4.60	11.00	5.00
Income Before Taxes	2,741.30	2,807.60	2,233.60
Income Taxes	967	1,025.80	870.80
Net Income After Taxes	1,774.30	1,781.80	1,362.80
Continuing Operations	1,771.00	1,775.20	1,354.10
Discontinued Operations	0	0	0
Total Operations	1,771.00	1,775.20	1,354.10
Total Net Income	1,771.00	1,775.20	1,354.10
Net Profit Margin	17.60%	17.40%	15.30%
Diluted EPS from Continuing Operations ($)	1.43	1.42	1.09
Diluted EPS from Discontinued Operations ($)	0	0	0
Diluted EPS from Total Operations ($)	1.43	1.42	1.09
Diluted EPS from Total Net Income ($)	1.43	1.42	1.09
Dividends per Share	0.28	0	0.13

Source: Adapted from J. Lower, 2006, SAP Aktiengesellschaft, *Hoover's Company Information,* Austin, TX: Hoover's Inc.

Although Microsoft and others offered similar products, WebSphere contained most of the basic components and tools required, and a number of extensions that helped customers: integrate systems and applications with Web services applications; present data on various devices; deploy applications; secure and manage Web services application environments.

To further strengthen its WebSphere product line, IBM made a number of strategic acquisitions in 2005. They included Gluecode Software (an open-source application server developer), PureEdge Solutions (an electronic forms developer), and Ascential Software (a leading provider of data integration software for US$1.1 billion)[15] (see Exhibit 9).

Apple

Since the success of its digital music player iPod in 2002, Apple Computer has become a consumer electronics powerhouse rather than a computer vendor. After its initial launch, Apple provided regular updates to its iPod line, including color displays with video playing capability and flash memory-based models. In 2003, Apple launched its iTunes Music Store in the United States, an online music service. The site included songs from the five largest record labels in the world, allowing users to download songs for 99 cents, thereby further boosting sales of iPods. Subsequently the company created international versions of iTunes that served Canada, and European and Asian countries. Given the popularity of the online music service, Apple, Motorola, and Cingular Wireless launched the first iTunes-enabled mobile phone in the world in late 2005. Besides its vastly popular iPod products and iTunes services, Apple's desktop and laptop computers, including iMac, iBook, Power Mac and PowerBook, continued to capture small but significant shares of the consumer, education, and high-end design and publishing professional markets. Additionally, Apple offered servers (Xserve), wireless networking equipment (Airport), publishing and multimedia software, and database software through its FileMaker subsidiary.

Exhibit 9 IBM's Income Statement, 2003–2005 (US$ million)

Income Statement	Dec. 2005	Dec. 2004	Dec. 2003
Revenue	$91,134	$96,293	$89,131
Cost of Goods Sold	49,414	55,346	51,412
Gross Profit	41,720	40,947	37,719
Gross Profit Margin	45.80%	42.50%	42.30%
SG&A Expense	27,156	25,057	22,929
Depreciation & Amortization	5,188	4,915	4,701
Operating Income	9,376	10,975	10,089
Operating Margin	10.30%	11.40%	11.30%
Nonoperating Income	3,070	1,192	930
Nonoperating Expenses	220	139	145
Income Before Taxes	12,226	12,028	10,874
Income Taxes	4,232	3,580	3,261
Net Income After Taxes	7,994	8,448	7,613
Continuing Operations	7,994	8,448	7,613
Discontinued Operations	–24	–18	–30
Total Operations	7,970	8,430	7,583
Total Net Income	7,934	8,430	7,583
Net Profit Margin	8.70%	8.80%	8.50%
Diluted EPS from Continuing Operations ($)	4.91	4.94	4.34
Diluted EPS from Discontinued Operations ($)	–0.01	–0.01	–0.02
Diluted EPS from Total Operations ($)	4.9	4.93	4.32
Diluted EPS from Total Net Income ($)	4.88	4.93	4.32
Dividends per Share	0.78	0.7	0.63

Source: Adapted from J. Lower, 2006, International Business Machines Corporation, *Hoover's Company Information,* Austin, TX: Hoover's Inc.

Although it was no longer the top seller in the PC market, which had been dominated by Microsoft Windows software and Intel processors, Apple continued to attract and maintain a group of loyalists who were fond of the Macintosh's aesthetic sense and its user-friendliness. Moreover, this group of customers was willing to pay premium prices and tolerate any potential interoperability issues with Windows (which had largely been addressed through the years). In addition to its proprietary operating system, the basis of its unique interface and design, another differentiator for Apple's machines was its use of IBM's PowerPC processors. Nonetheless, in 2005, Apple decided to use Intel chips for its PC products starting in 2006, with complete transition by the end of 2007.

Although computer companies were increasingly interested in selling their machines only through the online channel, Apple made a significant effort to appeal to consumers via hundreds of retail stores in the United States, Canada, Japan, and the United Kingdom. In 2005, Apple generated 17 percent of its sales through its retail channel. In order to counter the sluggishness in the global PC sales, Apple cut prices on many of its products and continued to roll out unique offerings. For instance, Apple introduced Mac mini, its cheapest machine with a base price of US$499. Additionally, the company increasingly looked to software development to drive sales. Many of the company's multimedia applications such as iTunes, iMovie, and iPhoto were available for free, but the company charged for bundled versions of its software.

With its massive marketing campaign that urged Windows users to switch to Macs, Apple further complicated its relationship with Microsoft. Although it was an alternative to Microsoft's Windows operating system, Apple's relative size and market share had not been a real threat to the software giant. In fact, both Microsoft and Apple had long maintained a working relationship; the Mac-compatible version of Microsoft's popular Office suite was a key software title for Apple, and Apple had scored crossover hits with Windows-friendly editions of iPod and iTunes. Soon after Apple released its Safari Web

Exhibit 10 Apple's Income Statement, 2003–2005 (US$ million)

Income Statement	Sept. 2005	Sept. 2004	Sept. 2003
Revenue	$13,931	$8,279	$6,207
Cost of Goods Sold	9,709	5,870	4,386
Gross Profit	4,222	2,409	1,821
Gross Profit Margin	30.30%	29.10%	29.30%
SG&A Expense	2,393	1,910	1,683
Depreciation & Amortization	179	150	113
Operating Income	1,650	349	25
Operating Margin	11.80%	4.20%	0.40%
Nonoperating Income	165	57	93
Nonoperating Expenses	0	0	0
Income Before Taxes	1,815	383	92
Income Taxes	480	107	24
Net Income After Taxes	1,335	276	68
Continuing Operations	1,335	276	68
Discontinued Operations	0	0	0
Total Operations	1,335	276	68
Total Net Income	1,335	276	69
Net Profit Margin	9.60%	3.30%	1.10%
Diluted EPS from Continuing Operations ($)	1.56	0.36	0.1
Diluted EPS from Discontinued Operations ($)	0	0	0
Diluted EPS from Total Operations ($)	1.56	0.36	0.1
Diluted EPS from Total Net Income ($)	1.56	0.36	0.1
Dividends per Share	0	0	0

Source: Adapted from J. Lower, 2006, Apple Computer, Inc., *Hoover's Company Information*, Austin, TX: Hoover's Inc.

browser, however, Microsoft announced it would cease development of the Mac version of its Internet Explorer (see Exhibit 10).

Sony

Sony's PlayStation 2 had captured 70 percent of the game console market, whereas Nintendo's GameCube and Microsoft's Xbox had only about 15 percent each. Sony was one of the leading consumer electronics companies (e.g., digital cameras, Walkman stereos), and PC and semiconductor companies in the world. These products accounted for more than 60 percent of its sales. Sony's entertainment assets included recorded music and video (Epic and Columbia), motion pictures (Sony Pictures Entertainment, Sony Pictures Classics), DVDs (Sony Pictures Home Entertainment), and TV programming (Columbia TriStar). Sony had also partnered with Ericsson to develop and sell mobile phones. Moreover, Sony also owned an 8 percent stake in music club Columbia House.

Although the PlayStation product lines had dominated the video game market, its sales of other electronics (DVD recorders, TVs, and computers) and music products had dropped. Weak consumer demand, price wars, and increased competition from Apple Computer's iPod had undermined sales of Sony's CD and mini-disk Walkman, and TV products. These challenges, as well as costs incurred in streamlining operations, had significantly decreased its market value. To rectify the situation, Sony began to emphasise high-definition products for consumers and broadcasters, integrated mobile video, music, and gaming products, and semiconductors (aimed at achieving performance improvements of products, by reducing the total number of chips required by PlayStation).

In 2005, Sony brought in Sir Howard Stringer to replace Nobuyuki Idei as chair and CEO, the first non-Japanese chief of the company. Prior to this post, Stringer was the head of the company's U.S. and electronics divisions. Since taking over the top post, Stringer announced

Project Nippon, a corporate restructuring plan aimed at revamping the electronics business and fostering better collaboration between the company's divisions. Stringer also announced that he planned to implement a concrete research and development scheme with greater emphasis on consumer demands and to reestablish Sony's leading presence in Japan.

The new reorganization plan was to continue Sony's "Transformation 60," the restructuring exercise started in 2004 that aimed to reduce the company's headcount by 20,000, combine operating divisions, and shift component sourcing to low-cost markets such as China. Stringer's new plan aimed to cut 10,000 jobs, shut down 11 manufacturing plants, and reduce the company's electronics product lines by 20 percent. Moreover, Stringer had abolished Sony's "Network Companies" structure in favor of five product-focused business groups (i.e., TV, video, digital imaging, audio, and VAIO). In addition, Sony had streamlined its operations from R&D to distribution and marketing. The two new product development groups and two business units would focus on semiconductors and electronic components. The company spun off Sony Communication Network, the subsidiary that operated So-Net Internet service (which had nearly 3 million subscribers) in an IPO in December 2005.

Sony's PlayStation 3 was released in the spring of 2006, several months after Microsoft's Xbox 360. Similar to Xbox 360, PlayStation 3 was designed to be a multimedia entertainment hub. Its computing power allows users to play video games, chat online, listen to music, and view high-quality animations similar to those projected by the cinematic digital projector. The machine is also backward-compatible with games designed for previous PlayStations. In addition to the video game console, Sony's PSP (PlayStation Portable), a Walkman-like device with DVD-quality video was launched in Japan in late 2004. The marketing hype surrounding the device's U.S. launch led to long lines at Sony stores when it was released in early 2005. The PSP generated US$150 million in sales for Sony the first week it hit the stores. Lastly, PSX, an electronics and game technology, was released in Japan in late 2003 and in the United States in 2005. It also rolled out a "portable broadband TV" in 2004—the device plays television shows and videos and allows users to connect to the Internet.

To compete with its competitors, Sony was expected to invest US$1.67 billion to build a leading semiconductor plant in Japan. The company hoped that in 2006 it would be able to sell home servers for broadband and high-definition TV systems powered by its new Cell computer chip, jointly developed with IBM and Toshiba. This powerful chip would also power the new PlayStation 3. Sony also joined Matsushita and Samsung, plus a few other companies, to jointly develop the Blu-Ray Disc. The alliance, formed in 2004, aimed to establish the new DVD format for optical storage media. In late 2004, Disney agreed to use the Blu-ray format. Games designed for PlayStation 3 would be the first mass utilization of the Blu-ray format. In May 2004 the company launched Sony Connect (formerly known as Net Music Download), an online music service available to users of Sony's electronics and mobile devices. The service would eventually expand to include video downloads. This site was managed by a newly formed subsidiary of Sony Corporation of America. At the same time, Sony launched VAIO Pocket, a portable music player designed to compete with Apple's iPod. VAIO Pocket debuted in the United States in late 2004. Sony also introduced a similar product, Network Walkman—its first Walkman with a hard drive. In October 2004, the company launched a music download system in Japan dubbed MusicDrop. The system utilized Microsoft's Windows Media Player.

In the entertainment industry, Sony merged its music division with BMG and formed Sony BMG Music Entertainment. The company also led a consortium of companies, including Comcast (a cable company) and a number of investment firms, to acquire the movie studio MGM in early 2005. Such a move allowed Sony to license and distribute MGM's sizable film library. In addition, the deal enabled Sony to participate in film co-productions, cable channels, and video demand services that would likely generate additional revenue for the company through Comcast-Sony Networks, a joint venue between the cable and the electronics and media companies (see Exhibit 11).

Looking Ahead

By pursuing its diversification strategy, Microsoft continued to move beyond its comfort zone, the highly monopolized desktop and server software industry. Hence, one of the major challenges Microsoft would face was many new competitors in new segments.

As Microsoft's Windows-based products continued to hold the near-monopoly in the operating system market, the only product that could challenge Microsoft's dominant position would be Linux, the operating system created in the public domain and distributed by players such as Red Hat. Besides the Windows-based products, the MSN services were another critical component in its diversification strategy. The key competitors, Google and Yahoo!, had adopted the application-as-services model coupled with a new advertising-driven funding approach, which enabled them to develop open-source and free software products for the general public.

Exhibit 11 Sony's Income Statement, 2003–2005 (US$ million)

Income Statement	Mar. 2005	Mar. 2004	Mar. 2003
Revenue	$66,912	$72,081	$63,264
Cost of Goods Sold	40,673	42,175	40,672
Gross Profit	26,239	29,906	22,592
Gross Profit Margin	39.20%	41.50%	35.70%
SG&A Expense	18,856	22,152	15,402
Depreciation & Amortization	6,057	6,462	5,621
Operating Income	1,326	1,292	1,569
Operating Margin	2.00%	1.80%	2.50%
Nonoperating Income	644	377	379
Nonoperating Expenses	230	268	231
Income Before Taxes	1,740	1,401	1,717
Income Taxes	150	507	684
Net Income After Taxes	1,590	894	1,033
Continuing Operations	1,575	871	978
Discontinued Operations	0	0	0
Total Operations	1,575	871	978
Total Net Income	1,531	851	978
Net Profit Margin	2.30%	1.20%	1.50%
Diluted EPS from Continuing Operations ($)	1.52	0.89	1
Diluted EPS from Discontinued Operations ($)	0	0	0
Diluted EPS from Total Operations ($)	1.52	0.89	1
Diluted EPS from Total Net Income ($)	1.48	0.87	1
Dividends per Share	0.23	0.21	0.2

Source: Adapted from M. Drapes, 2006, Sony Corporation, *Hoover's Company Information*, Austin, TX: Hoover's Inc.

Bill Gates knows how to compete with anyone who charges money for products . . . but his head explodes whenever he has to go up against anyone who gives away products for free.

—George Colony

chairman and CEO, Forrester Research[16]

In addition, with the growth of online service businesses, Microsoft, Google, and Yahoo! had been fighting fiercely to become the primary gateway to the Internet or the leading Web portal. These players had provided Internet users a range of services from search to e-mail and discussion blogs to news. In particular, Google and Yahoo! had formed partnerships with various telecommunication or cable service providers in order to position their respective portals as the default entrance to the Internet. Google had struck a deal with Comcast, the largest cable provider in the United States and a partner of Sony's. Yahoo! had been working with SBC (AT&T) and Verizon, the top three telecommunication operators in the United States. Furthermore, Google had tied the knot with AOL by acquiring 5 percent of the shares of the troubled online service pioneer owned by Time Warner. Although it was considered one of the smallest portals in the market, AOL was rich in content (thanks to its media parent) and still owned a sizable subscription base (through its dial-up access) in the U.S. market. Hence, such a partnership with AOL would help Google enrich its content and be on par with Yahoo! With these new arrangements, MSN was put in a highly unfavorable position against its competitors in the portal business.[17]

With the major mergers and acquisitions orchestrated by Oracle in 2004 and 2005 (the purchase of PeopleSoft and Siebel in particular), it seemed that the consolidation in the enterprise application segment would come to an end, because not many large players would be left in the market. SAP, Oracle, and IBM had emerged as dominant players in this segment. Traditionally, Oracle and SAP had been fierce rivals while Microsoft, IBM, and SAP were partners. For instance, SAP and Microsoft had been in partnership to jointly develop a product that would link Microsoft Office Applications to SAP products. IBM had been a SAP partner in implementation, middleware, and database software. As these software vendors began to develop their own unique SOA and Web services platforms, friction was expected to arise: As competition became fierce, long-term partnerships would likely be jeopardized.[18]

In the entertainment and consumer markets, with the Xbox game console and the ventures in mobiles and IPTV, Microsoft would be competing with players such as Apple and Sony. These players were much more consumer-oriented and media savvy than Microsoft. On one hand, Apple's iMac and iPod products, and iTunes services were designed to cater to the high-end media-centric consumers. On the other hand, although it had been in strategic disarray, particularly in the consumer electronics segment, Sony's video games and entertainment business remained one of the strongest in the industry.

With its new diversification strategy, Microsoft had entered various new markets in which it had no proprietary advantages. Facing many new challenges in such a fast-changing competitive landscape, Microsoft could not conquer these markets alone. It had to significantly leverage existing and new partnerships, particularly with established players in the newly targeted industries. Microsoft needed to constantly monitor the dynamic changes in the relevant ecosystems, and adjust its alliance strategies to capture opportunities in these markets.

1. With a range of Internet-enabled innovations introduced to the market, many had come to believe a new era of the Internet (Web 2.0) had arrived.
2. J. Lower, 2005, Microsoft Corporation, *Hoover's Company Information,* Austin TX: Hoover's Inc.
3. R. Guth, 2005, Microsoft Sets Big Restructuring Plan, *Wall Street Journal,* September 21; R. Guth, 2005, Microsoft Changes How it Builds Software, *Wall Street Journal (Europe),* September 27.
4. K.B. Davis, A.S. Rath, & B.L. Scanlon, 2004, How IT Spending is changing, *McKinsey Quarterly,* 2004 Special Edition; IT Spending growth to slow, *Red Herring,* August 1, 2005; D. Nystedt, IDC Lowers 2005 Global IT Spending growth forecasts, *Computerworld,* May 4, 2005; A. Bartels, 2004, IT spending outlook: 2004 to 2008 and beyond, Forrester Research Inc., Cambridge, MA.
5. E. Brynjolfsson and L. Hitt, 1998, Beyond the productivity paradox, center for e-business, Massachusetts Institute of Technology, Cambridge, MA.
6. C. Mines, 2005, The seeds of the next big thing, Forrester Research Inc., Cambridge, MA; G. Colony, 2005, My view: The Google future, Forrester Research Inc., Cambridge, MA.
7. Davis, Rath, and Scanlon, 2004, op. cit.; Bartels, 2004, op. cit.; Business's digital black cloud, *The Economist,* July 16, 2005; Software: Expect the giants to stay sluggish, *BusinessWeek,* January 10, 2005.
8. R. Heffner, 2005, Digital business architecture: Harnessing IT for business flexibility, Forrester Research Inc., Cambridge, MA.
9. Mines, 2005, op. cit.
10. R. Guth, 2005, Microsoft sets big restructuring plan, *Wall Street Journal,* September 21; R. Guth, 2005, Microsoft changes how it builds software, *Wall Street Journal Europe,* September 27; Spot the dinosaur, *The Economist,* April 1, 2006.
11. 2005, Mashing the Web, *The Economist,* September 17; G. Colony, My view: The Google future, forrester research inc., Cambridge, MA; J. Bramhall, 2005, Google Inc., *Hoover's Company Information,* Austin TX: Hoover's Inc.
12. J. Bramhall, 2005 Yahoo! Inc., *Hoover's Company Information,* Austin TX: Hoover's Inc.
13. J. Lower, 2005, Oracle Corporation, *Hoover's Company Information,* Austin TX: Hoover's Inc.; Reinhardt, 2005, op. cit.; J. Mirani and A. Ozzimo, 2005, Oracle applications: Committed to your success, Oracle's white paper, Redwood: Oracle Corporation.
14. B. Perez, 2005, Oracle unveils on-demand future, *South China Morning Post,* September 27.
15. J. Lower, 2005, International Business Machine Corporation, *Hoover's Company Information,* Austin, TX: Hoover's Inc.
16. *The Economist,* 2006, op. cit.
17. 2005, The battle of the portals, *The Economist,* October 20; S. Hansell and R. Siklos, 2005, Time Warner to sell 5% AOL stake to Google for $1 billion, *New York Times,* December 17.
18. Heng, 2005, op. cit.; A. Reinhardt, 2005, SAP: A sea change in software, *BusinessWeek,* July 11: J. Evers, and J. Blau, 2005, Microsoft and SAP to link Office with ERP, *Computerworld,* April 26.

Case 20

Nestlé: Sustaining Growth in Mature Markets

Dr. Sebastian Raisch, Flora Ferlic

University of St. Gallen

When Peter Brabeck-Letmathe took over as CEO of Nestlé in June 1997, he inherited a company that enjoyed the leading position in the global food industry. His predecessor Helmut Maucher, the CEO between 1982 and 1997, had divested the firm's unattractive activities, while establishing its position in higher-margin segments such as pet food and water. Maucher had transformed Nestlé from a manufacturer with a strong European base focused on milk and coffee, into a truly diversified global food company. During his 16-year reign, sales had more than doubled, profits had tripled, and the total return to shareholders was an excellent 17 percent annually.[1] (See Appendices 1 and 2.)

Despite Nestlé's success, one fundamental challenge would have to be dealt with in the coming years: revitalizing the group's organic growth in a maturing market. Maucher had heavily relied on acquisitions to develop Nestlé. He had invested more than CHF33.1 billion in a string of takeovers, including those of Carnation in 1985, Buitoni and Rowntree in 1988, and Perrier in 1992.[2] This expansion strategy had helped the firm reduce its dependence on coffee sales, while gaining sufficient scale and market reach in its new business segments. By 1997, however, the limits of the external growth strategy had been reached with Nestlé ranked first in nearly all the product segments in which it operated.[3] Brabeck was well aware of the need for strategic reorientation:

Our first priority is to achieve real internal growth. Internal growth reflects the company's performance and competitiveness better, even more so than acquiring another company's turnover. Acquisitive growth requires three people: a manager, a lawyer, and a banker. You need to activate 250,000 people for organic growth—the entire organization. However, it is a far more sustainable path to growth.[4]

One of Brabeck's first actions as CEO was to move Nestlé's goal of 4 percent real internal growth to the top of the company's strategic agenda.[5] Compared to an average market growth of just 2 percent in the mature global food industry, this goal was rather challenging.[6] To reach this target, Nestlé had to grow at twice its competitors' rate.

Nestlé first achieved its 4 percent internal growth target in 2000 and consistently repeated this performance in the subsequent years. Since 2000, the company has significantly outperformed the food sector and realized higher organic growth than any of its major competitors.[7] Nestlé's success can be related to Brabeck's unique campaign for profitable growth. In this case study, we return to the initial situation in 1997 and retrace the company's development over the following decade. The objective is to outline Brabeck's most important strategic and organizational initiatives that enabled the company to achieve a rate of profitable internal growth that was far above its competitors.

Nestlé in 1997

In 1997, Brabeck took control of one of the oldest and most truly global companies in the food industry, with international activities dating back to its beginnings in 1866. Over the previous 130 years, Nestlé had acquired profound knowledge of markets all over the world, and enjoyed great success in adapting its products to local tastes. The company operated factories in 77 countries and sold its products on all six continents. Offering thousands of local products, Nestlé is often referred to as a role model company that thinks globally but acts locally.

In 1996, the year before Brabeck took control, Nestlé had generated sales of CHF 60 billion and a net income of CHF 3.4 billion.[8] At the time, its product portfolio comprised 19 categories from coffee, milk, and confectionary to pet foods, clinical nutrition, and mineral water. The company was either the market leader or held a strong second position in most of its product segments. Businesses in which Nestlé had failed to reach a dominant position had largely been divested under Maucher's reign. Its core food and beverage businesses contributed to more than 95 percent of the company's 1996 sales. Its top five product categories (coffee, milk products, confectionary, ophthalmics, and dehydrated cooking aids) accounted for 60 percent of group sales and more than 75 percent of operating profits.[9]

Despite Nestlé's leading position, Brabeck was faced with considerable challenges that stood in the way of his objective of 4 percent real internal growth. The most important of these challenges was that the company generated more than 70 percent of its sales in mature markets with a limited potential for organic growth.[10] The leading countries in terms of market size, such as the United States, Russia, and Japan, were also the ones yielding the lowest growth rates. Besides the challenging market conditions, Nestlé was increasingly facing fierce competition as many food-producing rivals had achieved significant improvements in their operating efficiency. Although the number of truly global competitors was limited—the most notable being Kraft, Masterfoods, and Unilever—Nestlé was also facing strong competition at the national and regional level.[11]

The growing competitive pressure was exacerbated by Nestlé's relatively weak profitability, whose root causes could be traced to Nestlé's various acquisitions. Although strategically important, the acquisitions had required massive investments and their integration had negatively affected operational efficiency. The EBIT margin in the core business was roughly 12 percent, but the acquired businesses' margin had sunk to 6 percent.[12] Furthermore, Nestlé's portfolio included several low-margin product segments that negatively affected profitability. In 1997, the company ranked eighth among the world's top 12 packaged food companies in terms of returns on capital. Its net margin was only half that of its major rival Unilever.[13]

Earning the Right to Grow

Brabeck had to identify new growth opportunities to realize his goal of 4 percent internal growth. Organic growth in mature markets could only be reached by strengthening Nestlé's innovative capacity. This approach required significant investments in the group's R&D and marketing capabilities. Because Nestlé has always been a model of rock-solid accounting, Brabeck intended to generate the massive cash flows required for a large-scale growth offensive by improving the company's capital efficiency. His strategy was to force the businesses to become more efficient by cutting back on their investment budgets: "The investment budget is declining. Our efforts must switch to maximizing existing assets, maximizing capacity utilization and maximizing distribution logistics."[14] Paradoxically, the first task on the road toward achieving the internal growth target was thus to strengthen the company's operational efficiency. Lars Olofsson, the former head of Nestlé Europe, explains: "The real objective is to generate growth. To reach this objective, however, costs have to be reduced so that we can have more resources that can be used to strengthen the brands, spur innovation and thus allow us to remain competitive."[15]

Initially, Brabeck launched a manufacturing efficiency program called MH97. The objective was to reduce raw material costs and to optimize production processes. Between 1997 and 2002, 165 factories were closed, which generated savings in excess of CHF 4 billion.[16] MH97 was followed by a program called Target 2004+ that focused on improving operating performance by creating a regional manufacturing network. The project relied strongly on benchmarking and best practice transfer. By refocusing on a small number of high-performing factories, the program generated savings of more than CHF 3 billion between 2002 and 2004.[17] Target 2004+ was succeeded by a program called Operation Excellence 2007 that redeploys many of the prior projects' concepts. This program's key objectives are to improve supply chain productivity, optimize planning, eliminate overheads, and reduce product complexity.

In addition to the manufacturing-related efficiency programs, Nestlé initiated the FitNes initiative to drive efficiency in the group's administrative processes. FitNes was launched in 2002, and it is predicted to incur savings in excess of CHF 1 billion.[18] Wolfgang Reichenberger, former CFO of Nestlé, comments on FitNes: "It's an area that the group has not addressed in the past, it's uncharted territory, and it's fascinating."[19]

The most important business transformation initiative in Nestlé's 140-year history is, however, the Global Business Excellence (GLOBE) initiative, launched in 2000. Although it covers a broad range of strategic objectives, the program is also designed to improve operational efficiency by integrating the company's businesses on a global scale. The project's major objectives are to establish best practices in business processes, to align data standards, and to install common information systems. Due to Nestlé's highly decentralized structure and its large number of acquisitions, it runs multiple versions of accounting, planning, and inventory software. Sharing information between markets and operating units is thus difficult. The project's impacts range from the way raw materials are bought, to production, marketing, and sales. "We're now transitioning to become a genuinely global food company, to behave as one," says the former CFO

Reichenberger. He describes the program's main benefits as follows: "When GLOBE has been introduced in the most relevant markets, all inter-market systems will communicate much better with each other than they do now. Through these aligned systems we should achieve substantial improvements over the years to come."[20] By the end of 2005, GLOBE had been rolled out to 30 percent of the businesses.[21] It is projected that GLOBE will enable total savings of CHF 3 billion.[22]

Besides these programs directed toward increasing Nestlé's operational performance, Brabeck also worked on reducing marketing expenditures by better exploiting the synergies between brands. Brand strategies were centralized as far as possible to drive synergies and increase control. The most important strategic initiative was to allocate as many of the company's 127,000 products as possible to six strategic brands: Nestlé, Buitoni, Maggi, Nescafé, Nestea, and Purina. By 2005, more than 70 percent of the company's portfolio belonged to one of these six brands.[23] These strategic brands deliver higher margins, occupy more shelf space, and help retailers generate top-line growth. Nescafé, for example, has a brand value of nearly CHF 15 billion, a name recognition of almost 100 percent in the world's leading markets, and margins of about 18 percent.[24] The remaining local brands have been complemented with the Nestlé logo, a bird's nest with a parent bird and two hatchlings, to strengthen product identity and to communicate product characteristics such as quality, taste, and safety.[25] (See Appendices 3, 4, and 5.)

The efficiency initiatives' combined outcome has been impressive. Nestlé's net margin rose from 5.7 percent in 1997 to 8.7 percent in 2005. The various cost initiatives incurred total savings of CHF 12 billion. Net income soared from CHF 4 billion in 1997 to CHF 8 billion in 2005, while the free cash flow nearly doubled.[26]

The Nutrition and Wellness Initiative

Nestlé's efficiency improvements were the basis for further strong investments in internal growth. Brabeck's primary task shifted toward generating new sources of growth for the company's future expansion. "It was clear that with tomato paste, oil, and dry pasta, we were not going to create value in the long term," Brabeck said, referring to the low-growth products that Nestle had largely divested in the past decade, "We had to identify areas from which new growth could come."[27]

Early on, Brabeck sensed that the growing demand for wellness and nutritional products could provide an excellent opportunity for sustained growth in Nestlé's mature markets. "Brabeck was on a nutrition kick long before it was fashionable," says John McMillan, analyst at Prudential.[28] One of Brabeck's first official acts as CEO was the creation of a dedicated unit engaged in nutrition related to performance, infants, and diet. The rationale behind the new unit was to develop an innovative product segment with a strong potential for future growth and considerably higher margins than traditional products in the food industry. Building on this first initiative, Brabeck announced his vision of transforming Nestlé from a food company into a food, nutrition, health, and wellness company in 2000. An entire package of measures, which included strategic initiatives and organizational changes, was implemented to integrate nutritional thinking into the group as a whole. In pursuit of a strong internal growth potential, Brabeck aimed at two main strategic goals. The first objective was to develop nutrition and wellness as a value-added feature in the mainstream food and beverage business. The second objective was to reinforce the company's leading position regarding specialized nutritional products. The creation of two dedicated business units, the Corporate Wellness Unit and the Nestlé Nutrition Unit, reflected these twin objectives.

The creation of the Corporate Wellness Unit was directed at fulfilling the first strategic objective, namely spreading Nestlé's nutrition and wellness orientation throughout the group and across all product categories. Matt Hall, head of the strategic unit "Generating Demand," describes the strategy: "Nestlé remains within its traditional products and categories, but starts leveraging these products. We increase their value by adding health and nutritional elements."[29] Aspects of health, wellness, and nutrition are incorporated into a vast array of product categories, ranging from ice cream, frozen foods, and confectionaries to pet food. The elements added to the existing products promote digestive health, improve the immune system and skin's defenses, positively affect weight management as well as physical and mental performance, and contribute to healthy aging. To date, Nestlé has modified more than 700 products by adding nutritional functionalities.[30] An example of such a nutritional value added is Prebio, a supplement that promotes intestinal health and is added to infant nutritional products. Other examples are Calci-N, which promotes bone health, and ActiCol, which lowers plasma cholesterol. The company refers to these add-ins as "branded active benefits" (BABs). The first products enriched with BABs were introduced as long ago as 1998.

The Nestlé Nutrition unit is focused on the core nutrition business. The Nutrition unit provides products for those consumers whose primary purchasing motivation is the products' nutritional value, while taste is simply a value added. The product portfolio encompasses infant formulas, hospital nutrition, baby cereals, and sports nutrition. These products operate in a medical environment and require strong scientific support and long-term research and development. Nestlé devotes about one-fifth of its overall R&D budget to nutrition research. Three-quarters of the current projects at the central Nestlé Research Center (NRC) in Lausanne focus on health and well-being.[31]

Besides these two dedicated units, Nestlé established a number of ventures for growth into new areas related to wellness and nutrition. In cooperation with L'Oreal, one of the world's largest beauty and cosmetics companies, Nestlé moved into the area of nutricosmetics. Under the brand name Inneov, a joint venture by Nestlé and L'Oreal, a range of products has been developed that combines Nestlé's knowledge of nutrition with L'Oreal's expertise in beauty products. The products are aimed at improving the quality of skin, hair, and nails by supplying nutrients that are essential to their care. Inneov quickly gained a leading position in this high-growth segment. By 2005, Inneov had already achieved an 11 percent market share in Europe.[32]

Nestlé's nutrition business contributed significantly to the company's success. Sales generated by products with added nutritional benefits grew from CHF 200 million in 1998 to CHF 3 billion in 2005. Furthermore, these products' profit margins are twice as high as those of traditional food products, and thus contribute strongly to Nestlé's margin improvements.[33]

Strengthening Innovation

Nestlé is considered the innovation leader in the global food and nutrition sector. The driving force behind the innovation is the company's extensive research and development (R&D) network. More than 3,500 scientists work on improving existing products and creating tomorrow's nourishments.[34] Strengthening the company's R&D success was a key objective in Brabeck's quest for internal growth. Three strategic measures contributed to this objective.

First, Brabeck set the company's R&D activities a challenging target: one-fifth of the entire product portfolio has to be innovated or renovated every year. *Innovation* refers to moving the group into promising new product segments, whereas *renovation* relates to improvements to existing products, such as changes in the packaging, shape, taste, or quality. The distinction is an important one for Nestlé, as explained by Herbert Oberhaensli, Head of Economics and International Relations, "You always need to renovate your existing offer in order to keep the products alive. However, renovation and innovation do not contradict each other. Improving our products is a process of many small steps and a few big leaps. We have to do both if we want to be successful."[35] Especially in mature markets where Nestlé generates the bulk of its sales, the continuous upgrading of existing products is an important source of internal growth. As Brabeck puts it, "There are no 'mature markets,' only mature managers."[36] Two-thirds of the company's R&D activities are dedicated to renovating existing products, while the remaining third is reserved for more radical product innovations.[37] (See Appendix 6.)

Second, a strong budgetary increase as well as improvement in its operating efficiency enabled the R&D to achieve these challenging targets. Nestlé's R&D expenditures nearly doubled, increasing from CHF 770 million in 1997 to CHF 1.5 billion in 2005.[38] At the same time, the R&D efficiency increased through improvements on the operational level. Rupert Gasser, who was in charge of Nestlé's R&D activities when Brabeck took over, said, "We eliminated a number of R&D units that were dealing with issues with resources that were below a critical minimum required to do an efficient job. We then redeployed their resources to established centers that had all the technical and scientific know-how needed to support the renovation and innovation process in a given business area."[39]

Third, a number of organizational changes were made to improve the R&D's connection with the markets in which Nestlé operates. The most relevant of these organizational measures were the creation of Product Technology Centers, Local Application Centers, and Clusters.

The Product Technology Centers' (PTC) objective is to transform research concepts provided by Nestlé's fundamental research centers into consumer products. These centers are closely linked to the company's strategic business units and are located in key consumer markets. The PTCs allow ground-breaking innovations to be transformed into marketable products more swiftly. Currently, there are nine PTCs located in France, Germany, Great Britain, Switzerland, and the United States.[40]

Local Application Centers work inside the most relevant regional markets and are concerned with adapting global products to local tastes and requirements. Local tastes in respect of culinary products, such as prepared dishes, cereals, or confectionary, vary widely. For a global company like Nestlé, market success depends heavily on the ability to adapt its products to local needs. Apart from adaptations in taste, color, and shape, the form and/or packaging of products are also frequently changed. There are, for example, more than 100 local variations of Nescafé offered around the world. As Jean-Daniel Luthi, senior vice president and group controller, explains, "You have to know the consumer in different places of the world; you need the capabilities to make your products in one place and sell them many thousands of kilometers away."[41]

Clusters are cross-divisional project structures designed to improve the communication and knowledge sharing between the R&D and the rest of the company. Clusters unite researchers with the heads of business and regional units that face similar market environments. The objective is to jointly launch R&D initiatives with respect to new product development. Cooperation in clusters results in synergies, shared investments, and faster product roll-outs. Products developed within these clusters are either implemented as global solutions, or as "cluster solutions" in the participating regions. If necessary, the company's local application centers adapt the provided solutions to the specific market requirements.[42]

Nestlé's seven strategic business units are the driving forces behind the clusters and, more generally, behind product development and consumer-oriented renovation and innovation. Contrary to geographical zones that are operationally responsible for their businesses, and have clearly set annual profit targets, strategic business units are free from such short-term targets and thus free to fully concentrate on sustainable long-term development. They develop global business strategies for their respective categories in which they describe how the product segments should evolve over the next three to five years, what innovations are required, and how much of the portfolio should be renovated. In close cooperation with the markets and R&D, the strategic business units lead Nestlé's innovation process and ensure cooperation and communication between the company's disparate units.[43]

External Growth as a Platform for Organic Growth

Despite his dedication to internal growth, Brabeck did not entirely turn away from acquisitions, but used external growth as a means to spur and enable Nestlé's internal growth. Luis Cantarell, executive vice president of Nestlé Europe, clarifies: "You cannot establish a company on external growth; however, you can use external growth to support internal growth."[44] Similarly, Brabeck understands acquisitions as first and foremost a platform for further organic growth: "The emphasis is clearly on organic growth, with acquisitions being used to accelerate it."[45]

One motivation behind Brabeck's acquisitions was to gain a critical mass in terms of market share in businesses in which scale is vital for success. As in many other industries, size provides considerable economies of scale in the food industry. Brabeck had always asserted that he wanted Nestlé to be the market leader, or at least hold a strong second position in all product categories. Although the company had indeed reached a critical mass with the majority of its businesses, some segments still had a poor geographical reach. Consequently, the acquisition of Dreyer's, for example, helped Nestlé to become market leader in the U.S. ice cream business.[46] The Ralston Purina acquisition in 2002 made the company the global leader in pet care. Most recently, the acquisition of Jenny Craig, a weight management company, reinforced Nestlé Nutrition's presence in the United States, the world's largest nutrition and weight management market.[47]

Besides the objective of reaching a critical mass in terms of market share, Brabeck used external growth to gain expert knowledge for further expansion into new product segments. Nestlé introduced two venture funds to gain access to new expertise, thus giving the research and development additional impetus. The company founded the Life Ventures fund (capitalized with CHF 235 million) in 2002, and the Nestlé Growth Fund (of CHF 790 million) in 2005. Both funds use acquisitions, as well as minority investments, licensing, and joint ventures to give Nestlé access to new technology and know-how. They both invest on a global scale and focus on long-term capital growth.[48]

The rationale behind the creation of the Life Ventures fund was to accelerate Nestlé's innovation process. By investing in start-ups in the area of nutrition and food science, Nestlé gains access to leading-edge know-how and may incorporate these ideas into its own R&D network. In 2003, for example, the fund invested in eight businesses in the fields of naturally derived bioactives, phytonutraceuticals, and health care nutrition.[49]

The Nestlé Growth Fund invests in companies on the verge of entering the market with their products. "This fund will contribute significantly to fostering and accelerating the group's expansion into health, wellness and nutrition, as it will be investing in companies with products or processes in the final testing stage or about to enter the market. The idea is to accelerate Nestlé's strategic repositioning as a health, nutrition and wellness company," said Francois-Xavier Perroud, a group spokesperson.[50] The idea is to grow these companies until they are large enough to integrate their products into Nestlé's mainstream business.

It should be noted that Nestlé is one of the most successful companies regarding the effective integration of acquisitions. Its secret recipe is its patience. There are, for instance, no rules whatsoever limiting the amount of time invested in integrating an acquired company. This slowness provides ample time to identify synergies and select the most appropriate integration approach. Additionally, great importance is accorded to retaining as many of the acquired company's employees as possible. Besides patience and the willingness to accept the acquired company's distinct culture, Nestlé's readiness to promote managers from the acquired company to its head office is regarded as a main success factor.[51] The CEO of Rowntree, a company that Nestlé bought in 1988, was, for example, appointed to its head office and became the general manager of its chocolate and confectionary business. As Tom Coley, head of Nestlé's dairy SBU, puts it: "You obtain additional sales and, what is a lot more important, you obtain additional competencies if you acquire a business."[52]

Besides acquisitions, divestitures played an important role in aligning the group's product portfolio to the objective of sustainable organic growth. Between 1997 and 2005, Brabeck divested numerous activities that either yielded low margins, or offered only limited growth opportunities. The divestitures were related to canned foods, cheese and meat, and parts of the frozen food and the confectionary businesses. In addition, Brabeck moved Nestlé from commodity food processes, such as raw material conversion, toward the consumer and added-value areas of the food industry's value chain by divesting manufacturing assets and processes. The proceeds of these divestures were reinvested in acquisitions and product development in areas promising higher growth and returns.[53] (See Appendices 7 and 8.)

Nestlé Today

Currently, Nestlé commands a product portfolio comprising food for every eating occasion, for every age, and for every evolutionary stage within a country. In 2005, the group posted sales of CHF 91 billion and record profits of CHF 8 billion.[54] Under Brabeck's tenure, the 140-year-old food giant has been revitalized and well-prepared for future challenges. Brabeck will hand over the company's reins in 2008. His successor faces the task of maintaining the successful company's momentum. Further efforts will be required to boost the health and nutrition sales in the face of tough competition. Relentless renovation and innovation are essential to retaining and improving the firm's position. (See Appendix 9.) In the words of Luis Cantarell, executive vice president of Nestlé Europe,

I think that the main challenge is a question of ambition. It is about people not accepting that our job is done. I think it is also a question of mind-set. We need to make sure that Nestlé's people are thinking about how we could be delivering better growth, because growth is the basis of everything we do.[55]

Notes

1. For more detailed information about Nestlé's development under its former CEO Helmut Maucher, please refer to E. Ashcroft and R. A. Goldberg, 1996, *Nestlé and the Twenty-First Century*, Harvard Business School Cases.
2. W. Hall, 1997, Maucher steps aside at Nestlé, *Financial Times*, May 7.
3. G. von Pilar, 1996, Nestlé erwartet Nachfragebelebung. *Lebensmittel Zeitung*, November 22.
4. Personal interview with Peter Brabeck (November 19, 2004; Vevey, Switzerland). For related quotes, please also see Brabeck's interview with S. Wetlaufer, 2001, The business case against revolution, *Harvard Business Review* 79: 112–119.
5. Real internal growth equals sales growth less impact from acquisitions, divestitures, price changes, and foreign currency exchange rates. At Nestlé, real internal growth of 4% equals an organic growth of roughly 6%.
6. For more details about the food industry's specific characteristics, please refer to M. O'Bornick, 2004, *The top 10 global leaders in food*, Business Insights Ltd.
7. Transcript of a presentation on *Strategic Demand Generation* held by Ed Marra at the Nestlé Investor Seminar 2005.
8. Nestlé Annual Report, 1996.
9. K. Mahon and A. Smith, 1998, *Nestlé'* Schroders Broker Report.
10. E. Ashcroft and R. A. Goldberg, 1996; op. cit.
11. M. O'Bornick, 2004; op. cit.
12. K. Mahon and A. Smith, 1998; op. cit.
13. Data taken from the *Thomson One Banker* database.
14. K. Mahon and A. Smith, 1998; op. cit.
15. G. von Pilar, 2004, Effizienz ist Treibstoff für Dynamik. *Lebensmittel Zeitung*, October 29.
16. N. A., 2004, Nestlé's future, *The Economist*, August 7.
17. http://www.ir.nestle.com.
18. Ibid.
19. B. McLannahan, 2003, Nestlé's crunch, *CFOEurope.com*, February.
20. B. McLannahan, 2003; op. cit.
21. W. Ackerman, A. Smith, S. Peterson, and J. Stent, 2006, *Nestlé SA*, Citigroup Broker Report.
22. N. A., 2002, Financing the future at Nestlé, *Corporate Finance*, November 1.
23. Personal interview with Matt Hall (September 21, 2005; Vevey, Switzerland).
24. R. A. Goldberg and H. F. Hogan, 2002, *Nestlé S.A.*, Harvard Business School Cases.
25. Personal interview with Luis Cantarell (January 16, 2006; Vevey, Switzerland).
26. We calculated these figures based on data published in Nestlé's annual reports.
27. D. Ball, 2004, With food sales flat, Nestle stakes future on healthier fare, *Wall Street Journal*, March 18.
28. J. Caplan, 2005, Nutritious Nestle, *Time Magazine*, April 11.
29. Personal interview with Matt Hall (September 21, 2005; Vevey, Switzerland).
30. M. Kowalsky and E. Nolmans, 2005, Peter Brabeck: Der Prophet des Wachstums, *Bilanz*, March.
31. D. Ball, 2004; op. cit.

32. Nestlé Annual Report, 2005.
33. W. Ackerman et al, 2006; op. cit.
34. N. A., 2002, Forschung ist die Grundlage des Erfolges, *Die Presse,* May 13.
35. Personal interview with Herbert Oberhaensli (October 12, 2005; Vevey, Switzerland).
36. Personal interview with Peter Brabeck (November 19, 2004; Vevey, Switzerland).
37. Personal interview with Matt Hall (September 21, 2005; Vevey, Switzerland).
38. Data taken from the *Thomson One Banker* database.
39. R. A. Goldberg and H. F. Hogan, 2002; op. cit.
40. Personal interview with Herbert Oberhaensli (September 12, 2006; Vevey, Switzerland).
41. Personal interview with Jean-Daniel Luthi (September 21, 2005; Vevey, Switzerland).
42. Personal interview with Tom Coley (October 17, 2005; Vevey, Switzerland).
43. Personal interview with Tom Coley (October 17, 2005; Vevey, Switzerland).
44. Personal interview with Luis Cantarell (January 16, 2006; Vevey, Switzerland).
45. M. Gelnar, 2006, Nestle will continue to look for acquisitions, *Dow Jones International News,* April 6.
46. N. A., 2003, Nestlé: Behörde gegen Fusion mit Dreyer's, *Lebensmittel Zeitung,* März 5.
47. Datamonitor Company Profiles, 2004, *Nestle S.A.—SWOT Analysis,* Datamonitor PLC.
48. Nestlé Annual Reports (2003; 2005).
49. Personal interview with Luis Cantarell (January 16, 2006; Vevey, Switzerland).
50. T. Wright, 2005, Nestle surprises with new finance chief and a fund, *International Herald Tribune,* September 27.
51. A. J. Parsons, 1996, Nestlé: The visions of local managers, *McKinsey Quarterly,* February.
52. Personal interview with Tom Coley (October 17, 2005; Vevey, Switzerland).
53. R. A. Goldberg and H. F. Hogan, 2002; op. cit.
54. Nestlé Annual Report, 2005.
55. Personal interview with Luis Cantarell (January 16, 2006; Vevey, Switzerland).

Appendix 1 Nestlé's Sales and Net Income Development

Total Sales 1997–2005 (in CHF millions)

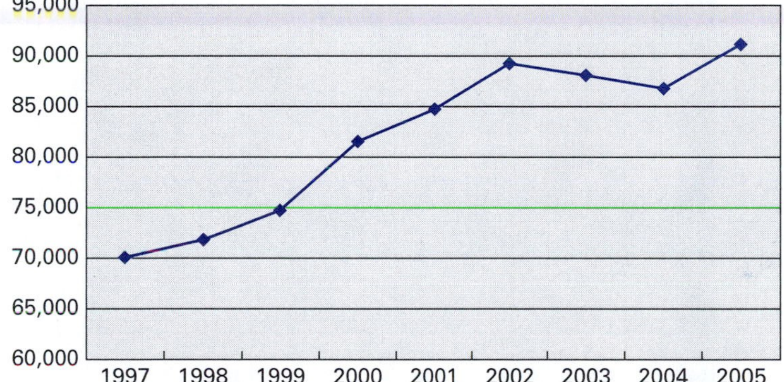

Source: Worldscope.

Net Income 1997–2005 (in CHF millions)

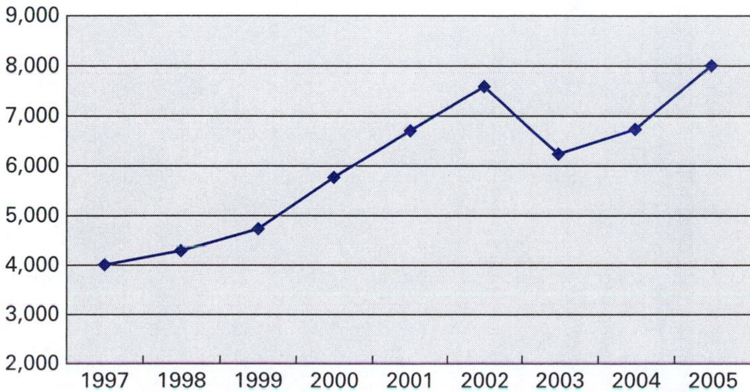

Source: Worldscope.

Appendix 2 Nestlé Financial Information, 1997–2005

In CHF millions	1997	1998	1999	2000	2001	2002	2003	2004	2005	CAGR
Sales	69,998	71,747	74,660	81,422	84,698	89,160	87,979	86,769	91,075	3.34%
Total Operating Expenses	62,758	64,423	66,344	71,924	75,622	80,530	79,108	78,082	79,706	3.03%
Costs of Goods Sold	33,127	33,354	33,223	35,205	35,025	35,790	34,920	33,362	35,218	0.77%
Research and Development Expenses	777	807	893	1,038	1,162	1,208	1,205	1,413	1,499	8.56%
EBIT	7,245	7,787	8,331	9,701	9,647	10,778	9,214	8,769	11,055	5.42%
Net Income	4,005	4,291	4,724	5,763	6,681	7,564	6,213	6,717	7,995	9.03%
Total Assets	53,727	54,401	56,646	62,955	91,868	85,833	88,163	85,648	101,700	8.30%
Current Assets	25,586	26,562	27,080	30,662	39,008	35,342	36,233	35,285	41,765	6.32%
Total Liabilities	28,396	30,805	31,568	32,442	57,639	50,201	50,340	45,372	50,265	7.40%
Current Liabilities	20,985	22,591	22,182	23,174	41,492	33,737	30,365	29,117	35,818	6.91%
Cash Flow	6,999	7,201	7,797	9,093	9,906	11,733	10,447	11,100	10,723	5.48%
ROE	16.41%	18.64%	19.32%	19.27%	19.85%	21.72%	16.85%	17.13%	16.04%	—
ROA	9.89%	10.03%	10.47%	11.76%	11.97%	9.25%	8.16%	8.43%	10.24%	—
Number of Personnel	225,808	231,881	230,929	224,541	229,765	254,199	253,000	247,000	250,000	1.28%

Source: Worldscope.

Appendix 3 Nestlé's Sales per Region and Product Segment, 2005

Nestlé Sales per Region, 2005

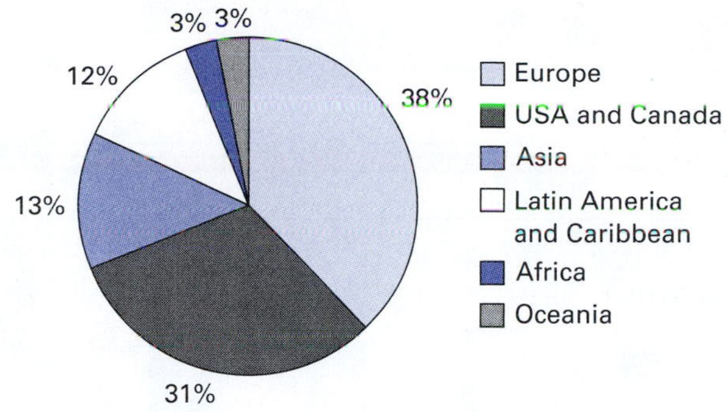

3%
3%
12%
38%
13%
31%
Europe
USA and Canada
Asia
Latin America and Caribbean
Africa
Oceania

Source: Worldscope.

Nestlé Sales per Product Segment, 2005

6%
1%
26%
12%
12%
18%
25%
Beverages
Milk Products, Nutrition, and Ice Cream
Prepared Dishes and Cooking Aids
Chocolate, Confectionary, and Biscuits
Pet Care
Pharmaceutical and Cosmetic Joint Ventures
Others

Source: Worldscope.

Appendix 4 Nestlé EBITA Margins per Region and Product Segment, 2005

Nestlé EBITA Margin per Region, 2005

EBITA Margins 2005
18%
16%
14%
12%
10%
8%
6%
4%
2%
0%
Europe
Americas
Asia, Oceania, and Africa

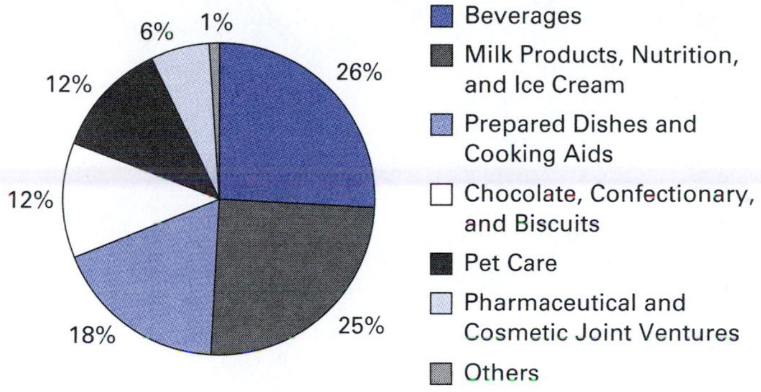

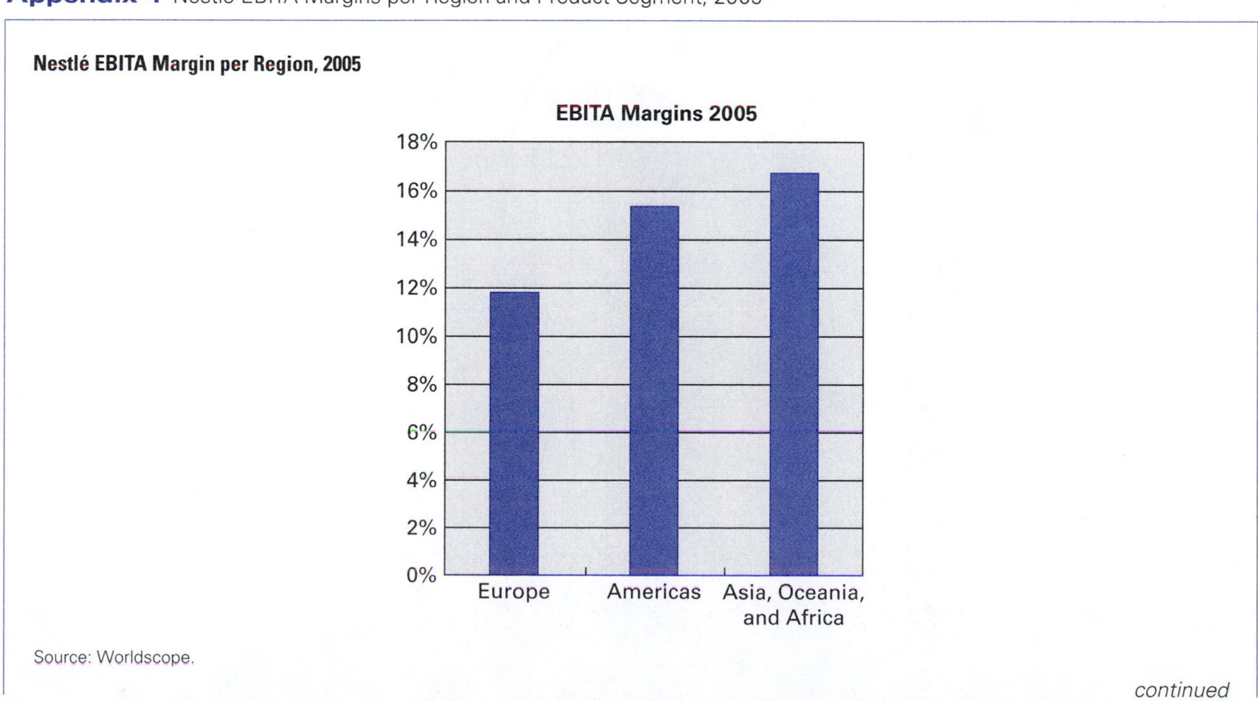

Source: Worldscope.

continued

Nestlé EBTIA Margin per Product Segment, 2005

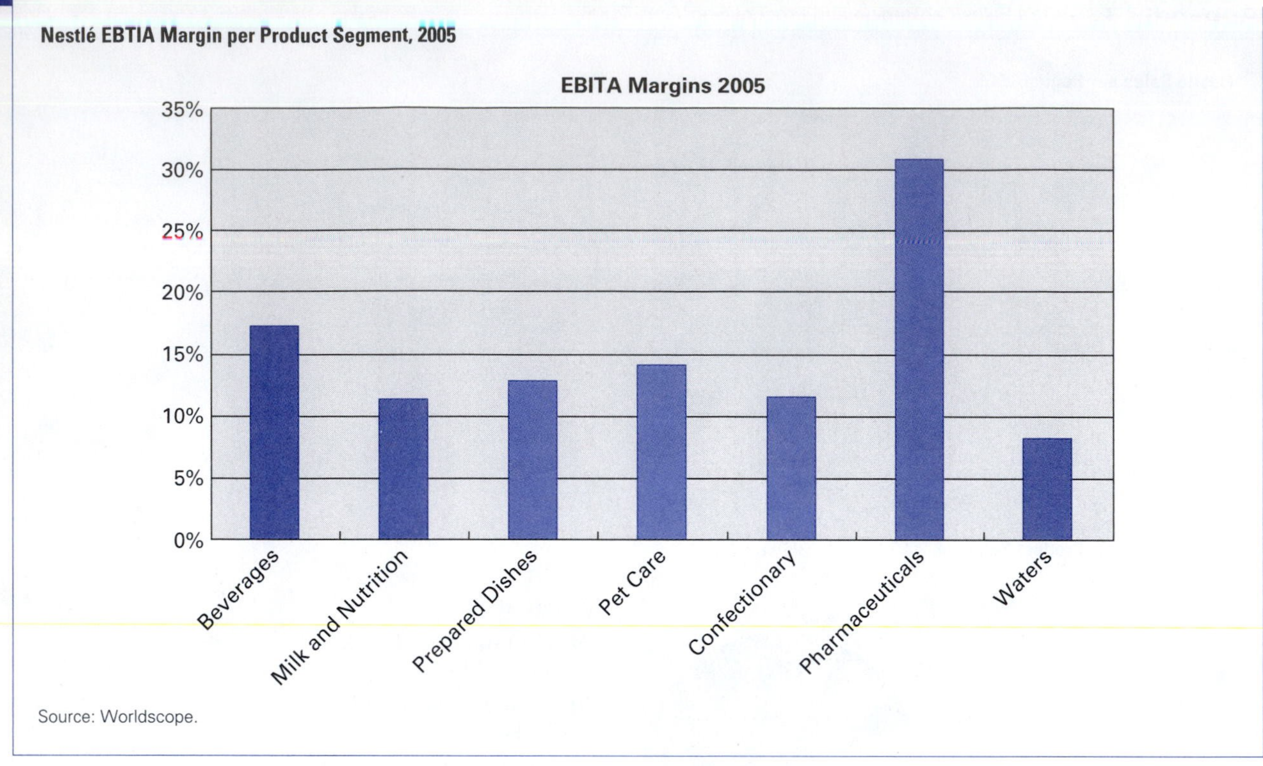

Source: Worldscope.

Appendix 5 Nestlé's Corporate Sign and the Six Strategic Brands

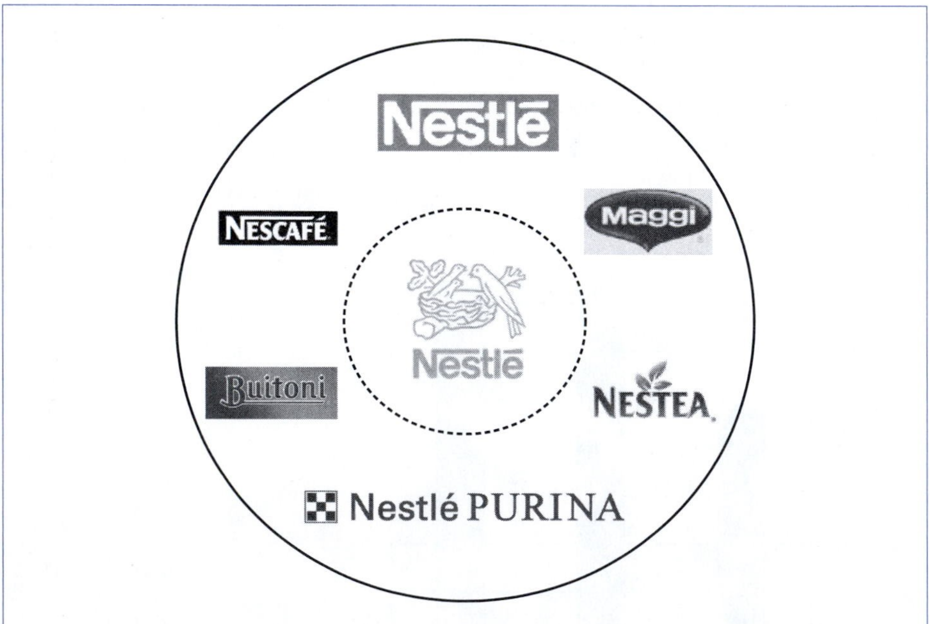

Appendix 6 Nestlé's Worldwide Research and Development Network

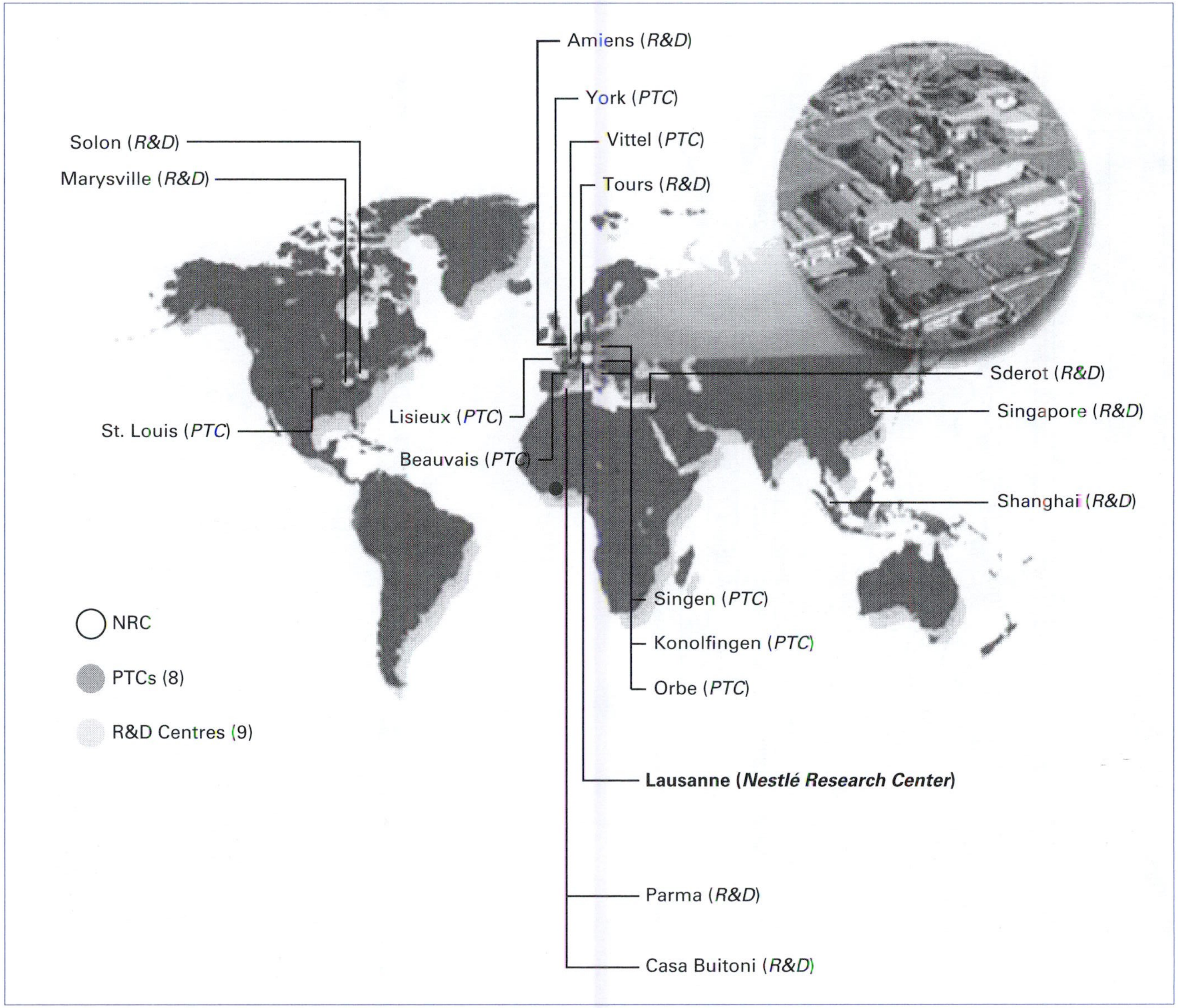

Source: http://www.ir.nestle.com/News_Events/Presentations/Group_Presentations/Group_General/.

Appendix 7 Total Shareholder Return (TSR) Development in Health, Wellness, and Food & Beverages Markets, 1995–2005

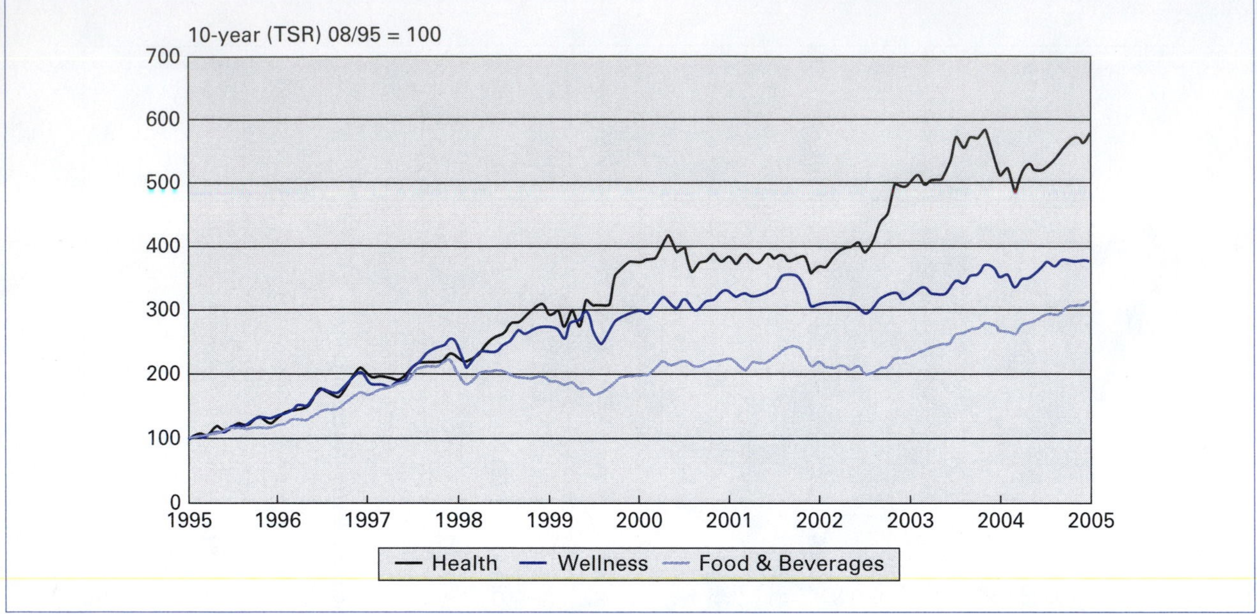

Source: http://www.ir.nestle.com/News_Events/Presentations/Group_Presentations/Group_General/.

Appendix 8 Total Shareholder Return of Nestlé and Its Main Competitors

Food	1 Year	3 Years	5 Years	10 Years
Hershey	1%	73%	88%	306%
Nestlé	**35**	**44**	**15**	**267**
Danone	32	46	20	248
Procter & Gamble	7	43	64	235
Unilever	22	10	0	190
Cadbury Schweppes	16	56	37	177
General Mills	2	13	26	127
Heinz	–11	13	–6	57
Campbell	2	36	–2	31
Coca Cola	3	–2	–27	26
Kraft	–19	–22	N/A	N/A

Source: http://www.ir.nestle.com/News_Events/Presentations/Group_Presentations/Group_General/.

Appendix 9 Timeline of Nestlé's Major Strategic and Organizational Changes on the Road to Sustaining Growth in Mature Markets

1997	1998	2000	2002	2004	2005
Announcement of 4% RIG target		Brabeck beats target of 4% RIG			
Launch of first manufacturing efficiency program *MH97*		Launch of GLOBE initiative	Foundation of Life Ventures Fund		Creation of clusters to spur innovation
Creation of a dedicated unit engaged in performance, infant, and clinical nutrition	Introduction of first products enriched with BABs	Announcement of transforming Nestlé into a food, nutrition, health, and wellness company	Launch of efficiency programs Target 2004+ and FitNes	Foundation of Nestlé Nutrition and the Corporate Wellness Unit	Foundation of Nestlé Growth Fund

Case 21

Netflix

Amy Falter, Scott Thompson

Arizona State University

Netflix is one of the most recognizable online movie rental services in the world. Since the company's launch in 1998, its business model has revolutionized the movie rental business and the way U.S. viewers rent and watch movies. Netflix's service has captured approximately 6.7 million subscribers and offers a video library of more than 90,000 movies, television, and other entertainment videos on DVD.[1] The majority of Netflix subscribers pay about $18 per month and are allowed to keep up to three movies at a time.[2] Although Netflix was the first company to tap this new market of online movie rental, they would not be the last trying to capitalize on its potential.

In August 2004, Blockbuster countered Netflix's entry into the movie rental business with a strategic response by introducing Blockbuster Online, its own online rental service.[3] Blockbuster Online offered the same services as Netflix, putting the two companies in direct competition with each other for the first time. In late 2006, Blockbuster revamped the online rental service and renamed it "Blockbuster Online Total Access."[4] This new Blockbuster service gives the customer the option of either returning the video through the mail or dropping it off at a local Blockbuster store.[5] It does however, encourage customers to return videos rented online to the store by offering a voucher for a new in-store rental.[6] As Blockbuster boasts, "With this kind of access, you'll never have to wait to have a new movie to watch!"[7] The only caveat with the new in-store rental is that normal due dates and late fees typical of brick-and-mortar video rental stores are enforced.[8] Without any physical stores, Netflix executives now face the difficult challenge of finding a legitimate and value-adding way to compete with Blockbuster.

Netflix also faces the development of video streaming and downloads on PCs as well as mobile devices. "Computers, portable MP3 video players, and telephones are now options for watching downloaded TV shows and movies, especially among younger audiences."[9] Companies such as Amazon, Apple, and YouTube have all been looking at ventures in this market.[10] To stay atop the online rental market, Netflix must decide how to adjust its current business model in order to grow and adapt to the market's dynamic environment.

To better understand these salient strategic challenges, the following topics will be touched upon: Netflix's history, current strategic leaders, the competitive environment, supplier relationships, Netflix's current strategies and functional operations, and recent financial outcomes.

Brief History

Reed Hastings founded and incorporated Netflix in August 1997 as a more conventional rental service, with online offerings.[11] It was not until April 1998 that Netflix opened its Internet store for DVD rentals and then offered a subscription service in September 1999.[12] Netflix's rapid growth can be attributed to its early strategic relationships with leading DVD hardware and home theater equipment manufacturers (Sony, Toshiba, RCA /Thomson Consumer Electronics, Pioneer, and Panasonic) and marketing tactics (promotional techniques) to build brand recognition and acceptance among the growing DVD-rental consumer base.[13] In December 1999, Netflix announced the elimination of due dates and late fees, helping it to quickly become a popular rental service, as it also did not charge shipping and handling fees and per-title rental fees.[14] On May 22, 2002, Netflix made an initial public offering (IPO) of 5.5 million shares of common stock at $15 per share.[15]

Due to the overwhelming acceptance of and demand for Netflix services, it became necessary for Netflix to

The authors would like to thank Professor Robert E. Hoskisson for his support under whose direction the case was developed. The authors do not intend to illustrate either effective or ineffective handling of a managerial situation. The case solely provides material for class discussion. This case was developed with contributions from: Garret Lumley, Evan Mallonee, & Terri Phillips.

Exhibit 1 Monthly Plans

Movie Rentals	Cost
1 at-a-time (2 per month)	$ 4.99 per month
1 at-a-time (unlimited)	$ 9.99 per month
2 at-a-time (unlimited)	$14.99 per month
3 at-a-time (unlimited)	$17.99 per month
4 at-a-time (unlimited)	$23.99 per month
5 at-a-time (unlimited)	$29.99 per month
6 at-a-time (unlimited)	$35.99 per month
7 at-a-time (unlimited)	$41.99 per month
8 at-a-time (unlimited)	$47.99 per month

Source: http://www.netflix.com/MediaCenter.

build new distribution and shipping centers every year. In the 2003 fiscal year, Netflix recorded its first profitable year with record revenues of $272.2 million, up 78 percent from the 2002 fiscal year with earnings of $152.8 million.[16] As Netflix grew, it developed tailored service packages based on consumers' desired number of rentals per month (see Exhibit 1). In 2005, the number of subscribers grew to a record high of 4.2 million, 60 percent over the previous year.[17] Both 2005 and 2006 were also solid growth years, leaving CEO Reed Hastings optimistic about future growth and earnings potential: "Our accomplishments during the year [2006]—strong subscriber growth, continued improvement in the customer experience, and increased profitability—together with the recent launch of the first generation of our online video option, leave us better positioned than ever to achieve our long-term objective of being the movie rental leader."[18] In February 2007, Netflix celebrated the delivery of its one-billionth DVD by giving the recipient a free lifetime Netflix membership.[19]

Netflix recently offered new features to its subscribers. In January 2007, Netflix launched "Watch Now."[20] This feature allows subscribers not only to rent online and continue to receive DVDs through mail, but also watch more than 1,000 movies and television shows via their PCs.[21] Netflix hopes to eventually bring this type of technology to any device with access to the Internet.[22] Another new endeavor Netflix has launched is Red Envelope Entertainment; this new division "looks to leverage its proprietary technology to offer subscribers unique and original content to which they wouldn't otherwise have access."[23] The unique and original content includes independent films such as those found at the Sundance and Toronto Film festivals.[24]

At year end 2006 Netflix employed 1,300 full-time and 646 temporary employees at the corporate headquarters in Los Gatos, California, and in its shipping centers across the nation.[25] Many of Netflix's senior officers have been with the company for a majority of the company's lifespan. The current strategic decision makers of Netflix are six key individuals from the C-suite.

Netflix Strategic Leaders

Founder, CEO, and Chairperson. Reed Hastings has served as chairman since the company's inception.[26] Hastings studied mathematics at Bowdoin College in Brunswick, Maine, and was awarded the Smyth Prize in 1981 by the math department and received his BA in 1983.[27] To round out his education, Hastings went to Stanford University and received a master's degree in computer science.[28] A former Netflix director, Bob Pisano, said of Hastings "[he is] an engineer, is analytical and very charismatic . . . that's a rare combination."[29]

Hastings created the vision for Netflix and is in perpetual motion to evolve and sustain his business based on critical factors developed by other members of his management team.

Neil Hunt, Chief Product Officer. Neil Hunt created and manages the Netflix site. He has served in this capacity since 1999.[30] His job and decisions are of critical importance, because his output is the portal customers ultimately interact with via the company. Hunt's focus is "Customization and personalization [ensuring] every Netflix member [receives] a unique experience every time they visit the site. This includes the movies they see on each page, the recommendations they receive on movies, and the critical account management tools they use, such as their dynamic queue to order movies."[31] Mr. Hunt is a noteworthy scientist who has the leadership skills to inspire teams to be innovative, and create powerful software that is user-friendly.

Ted Sarandos, Chief Content Officer. Since 2000, Mr. Sarandos's role is to manage and cultivate relationships with studios, networks, film makers, and producers to gain access to films and distribution channels.[32] His most critical role is making sure customers' needs are satisfied through the current video selection and by staying abreast of new trends within the entertainment industry.

Leslie Kilgore, Chief Marketing Officer. Because Netflix is an online entity, Ms. Kilgore's responsibility is to find the most effective and cost-efficient methods to acquire new subscribers through various marketing approaches.[33] Her success is demonstrated in that "more than 90 percent of trial members convert to paying subscribers and more than 90 percent of those tell family and friends about the service."[34]

Barry McCarthy, Chief Financial Officer. Since 1999 Mr. McCarthy has overseen the financial and legal affairs for Netflix. Barry has vast experience in his field, including work with Credit Suisse First Boston. He has helped Netflix become a billion dollar revenue company within 7 years.[35]

Patty McCord, Chief Talent Officer. Ms. McCord has been with Netflix since 1998 and helps the company attract and retain high-talent employees. Having 16 years of human resources experience with high-tech companies, she plays a large role in establishing a culture in which employees are devoted to superior customer service. "She is adamant about keeping a lean organization in which openness, approachability, and honesty are valued above all else."[36]

The strategic leaders have directed Netflix to target three distinct customer segments: those who like the convenience of free home delivery, the movie buffs who want access to the widest selection of, say, French New Wave or Bollywood films, and the bargain hunters who want to watch 10 or more movies for 18 dollars a month. The challenge is to keep all segments happy at the same time.[37]

Netflix hopes that catering to the needs and desires of its different customer segments will help it remain a key player in this rapidly developing and competitive industry.

Competitive Environment

Until recently, Blockbuster Inc. dominated the movie rental industry, with few threatening competitors and drawing annual revenues of more than $3 billion.[38] Netflix challenged the traditional brick-and-mortar video rental chains. With the continual advent of new technology and widespread Internet adoption and usage, the Netflix business model appealed to many consumers, especially those who were frustrated with Blockbuster's late fees. With Netflix's entire business model focused on providing unique online rental, free delivery to households, no due dates or late fees, and movie recommendations to all its subscribers, Netflix appeared to have found a niche market.[39]

As a result of the short product life cycles in the technological sector, continual improvements in products, and lower costs in technology, it has become more common for consumers around the globe to own their own movie viewing devices and access the Internet from home. Thus, the online movie rental market base is expected to grow continuously. In 2005, the online movie rental industry had more than 6 million subscribers in the United States and Europe, and by the end of 2006 that number rose to more than 8 million subscribers.[40]

Emerging Competitors

Progress in technology is changing the competitive dynamics. The main impetus challenging movie rental companies is video on demand (VOD). Video on demand is gaining more attention and popularity, especially among cable/satellite companies, television networks, and dot-com companies. In contrast to buying or renting a video, VOD allows the user to download the entire movie to a computer or stream the video, where the movie is viewed in realtime.[41]

Downloadable movies are in an embryonic stage, with early adopters experimenting with the service, but are not yet widely utilized among Internet users.[42] A potential current pitfall of this product is that neither downloaded nor streaming videos come in high definition yet, and this could be a deal buster for many consumers who have recently bought into the high definition craze.[43] However, most of the key online rental industry players have sought relationships with video on demand providers to maintain a competitive advantage.

New entrants are crafting technology devices specifically designed to support these new services. One major player will be Apple; movies and television shows can be viewed on Apple TV, iPods, and Macs. Smartphones will also begin to offer the downloadable movie and television show service, acting as portable TVs.[44] The downloadable Amazon Unbox allows consumers to access DVD-quality movies and television shows for rent or purchase.[45] Wal-Mart joined the fight for market share by creating its own downloading movie business in February 2007.[46] Wal-Mart has gained the interest of studios such as 20th Century Fox, Lions Gate, Disney, MGM, MTV Networks, Paramount Pictures, Universal Studios, Sony Pictures Entertainment, and Warner Bros.[47] Wal-Mart currently offers approximately 3,000 titles for download purchase ranging in price from $14.88 to $19.88.[48]

Netflix is in its infancy stage of introducing streaming videos and television shows offered to current subscribers.[49] This new addition of streaming service was built upon the Microsoft infrastructure.[50] Over time, the company hopes to make Netflix's service available on other software combinations, portable devices, and televisions screens.[51] Netflix has also partnered with video recorder maker TiVo to allow TiVo customers access to DVDs on Netflix's Web site.[52] CEO Reed Hastings has stated, "We want to be ready when video on demand happens. That's why the company is [called] Netflix and not DVD-by-mail."[53]

Even though Blockbuster has been Netflix's strongest competitor, other companies are strengthening their competitive position to challenge these two giants and gain market share. These competitors seem to believe they can differentiate their service and product offerings in order to challenge Netflix in an entirely new dimension.

Key Competitors

Blockbuster Inc.

Blockbuster is the world's largest video and video disk retail chain today, with approximately 9,040 company-owned or franchised brick-and-mortar stores located in more than 25 countries (about 60 percent located within the United States).[54] Each year, Blockbuster rents more than a billion videos, DVDs, and video games through its retail outlets.[55] Blockbuster became a video giant through its foresight, acquisition strategy, and prime store locations.

History. In 1982, David P. Cook determined that "most [video] stores were relatively modest family operations that carried a small selection of former big hit movies."[56] Cook wanted to create a nationwide movie rental company chain with a vast selection of videos.[57] The biggest selling point to enter this industry was that he could use his computer skills to create an innovative computing system for inventory control and checkout; therefore, it would decrease manual labor costs and help eliminate high costs associated with theft.[58] Cook used the proceeds from the sale of his computer data services company to open a flashy video rental store that maintained the video catalog via computer bar code systems. He named his new company Blockbuster Entertainment, with the first store opening in Dallas, Texas, in 1985.[59]

Growth Strategy. Initially, Blockbuster's growth strategy included franchising and selling the Blockbuster name and proprietary computer system.[60] After being in existence for only one year, Blockbuster altered its strategy to horizontal acquisitions to spur rapid growth. Blockbuster desired to be the first-mover in the superstore video rental chain.[61] "Blockbuster's management continued to maintain that since the video 'superstore' concept was open for anyone to copy, it needed to grab market share as fast as possible in order to exploit its ground-breaking concept."[62]

Although Blockbuster rapidly expanded nationally and experienced astronomical growth (company earnings in 1988, 1989, and 1990 were 114%, 93%, and 48% respectively), the rental industry was beginning to reach maturity.[63] Blockbuster began to offer video game equipment and games for rental and purchase.[64] In addition, Blockbuster continued to expand globally with market entries in the United Kingdom, Japan, Australia, Europe, and Latin America.[65]

To further diversify its business portfolio, Blockbuster purchased Music Plus and Sound Warehouse, a music retail chain, from Shamrock Holdings in 1992, for $185 million and created Blockbuster Music.[66] Within the past 15 years, Blockbuster has entered into many agreements with movie production companies, communication companies, and other entertainment companies, many of which proved beneficial; but some relationships had to be severed, such as Blockbuster Music (1998), so as to not drain Blockbuster of all its financial resources.

Revenue Sharing Program. The current CEO, John Antioco, took the reins in the summer of 1997 with Blockbuster in a world of mess.[67] Not only was its stock 50 percent below its value from the previous year, but suppliers were not delivering newly released movies on time, and there was not enough qualified staff to allow for effective store operations.[68]

Antioco turned the company on its head. He scaled back on expansion and eliminated the nonrental operations (i.e., selling retail merchandise in Blockbuster stores).[69] He also implemented a revenue sharing program with major Hollywood movie studios. "Now instead of paying $65 for new tapes, Blockbuster paid $4 and turned over 30 to 40 percent of the rental income to the studio."[70] This arrangement allowed Blockbuster to stock more videos on its shelves with a lower cost structure. In 2007 Antioco announced his resignation as chairperson and CEO due to various disagreements with Blockbuster's board about salary.[71] The succeeding CEO James Keyes confronts the challenge of holding market share in a volatile industry.

Challenge to Netflix. As noted previously, in response to the success and popularity of Netflix, Blockbuster launched its Blockbuster Online service in 2004 "where members can rent unlimited DVDs online and have them delivered via mail for a monthly fee."[72] This service has evolved into its current state called Blockbuster Total Access, where DVDs are still ordered online and delivered to households, but now customers can return the DVDs for a free in-store rental.[73] Blockbuster also developed a subscription service called Blockbuster Movie Pass where customers can have 2 or 3 movies out at a time without any late fees.[74]

Most recently, Blockbuster and Weinstein Co. entered into an agreement where Weinstein Co.—an independent American film studio—will sell its titles such as *Sicko, Miss Potter,* and *Hannibal Rising* exclusively to Blockbuster outlets for a three-year period in exchange for the aforementioned revenue sharing program.[75] This strategic action will prohibit Netflix access to any of the titles produced by this studio. Netflix has pursued its own agreements with independent film producers, so it remains to be seen whether these relationships will prove beneficial for each company.

Also, Blockbuster recently acquired Movielink LLC, an online movie downloading company owned by major Hollywood studios, such as MGM, Paramount Pictures, Sony Pictures Entertainment, Universal Studios, and Warner Brothers.[76] In this agreement, Blockbuster will have long-term deals for content with the major film studios, which will significantly enlarge its current video library used by both the brick-and-mortar stores and online subscribers.[77] Blockbuster has also sought out a video download partner so its customers will have three ways to attain movies—in-store, mail order, or download. "While Blockbuster trailed behind in the online DVD rental business after entering it in 2004—five years after Netflix—it's not taking a wait-and-see attitude toward movie downloads."[78]

Movie Gallery, Inc.

Movie Gallery is the second-largest North American video rental retail chain, with more than 4,700 stores located in all 50 states, Canada, and Mexico.[79] Its growth strategy is internal growth and pursuing selective complementary acquisitions. "By focusing on rural and secondary markets, [Movie Gallery] is able to compete very effectively against the independently owned stores and small regional chains in these areas."[80] Movie Gallery's acquisition of Hollywood Entertainment in 2005 made the company stronger and more competitive with Blockbuster by challenging Blockbuster on its strength—owning stores in prime locations.

By acquiring Hollywood Entertainment, Movie Gallery inherited 74 automated movie vending machine kiosks similar to ATMs, which "provide around the clock availability of movies" for rent.[81] Because of the minimal overhead and fixed costs associated with the kiosks Movie Gallery intends to expand its fleet with a rollout of an additional 200 units through 2007.[82]

Joe Malugen, chairperson, president, and CEO of Movie Gallery, stated "While we firmly believe that our retail brick-and-mortar stores will remain the foundation of our business, over the past three years we have been diligently pursuing alternative delivery platforms to further complement our base business."[83] As such, in March 2007 Movie Gallery purchased MovieBeam, a movies-on-demand service, which was created and funded by Walt Disney Co., Cisco Systems, and Intel Capital.[84] Movies are "beamed" into consumer homes using MovieBeam's patented over-the-air data-casting technology to the set-top box.[85] Currently, this technology is limited to television set use only, but Movie Gallery plans to expand these services to video on demand capability over the Internet.[86]

Hastings Entertainment. Hastings Entertainment operates in approximately 20 midwestern and western states, focusing on small to medium-sized towns with underserved markets (towns with populations of 33,000 to 105,000).[87] This multimedia retailer "combines the sale of new and used CDs, books, videos, and video games, as well as boutique merchandise, with the rental of videos and video games in a superstore format."[88] Sales and rentals of videos and games account for the primary revenue stream (35 percent) with music sales pulling in the second highest amount (25 percent).[89] According to Hoover's Inc., "As is the case throughout most of the rental industry, Hastings video rental sales continue to drop in the face of mail-order rental houses like Netflix and video on demand services from cable companies."[90] Although Blockbuster, Movie Gallery, and Hastings Entertainment are the "Big Three" competitors for Netflix, other movie delivery methods exist and capture some of the market share.

Other Competitors

While movie rentals are the most common method for viewing newly released films or older pictures, other channels are available. These channels include movie retail stores (e.g., Best Buy, Wal-Mart, and Amazon.com); subscription entertainment services (e.g., Showtime and HBO); Internet movie providers (e.g., iTunes, Amazon.com, Movielink, CinemaNow.com, and Vongo); Internet companies (e.g., Yahoo! and Google); and cable and direct broadcast satellite providers.[91]

To remain a key player in the industry it is just as important for Netflix to consider the movie content providers as it is the competitors.

Content Providers

Netflix has exercised great effort in establishing strong relationships with a number of entertainment film providers. They have sought to ensure that the relationships are mutually beneficial. Netflix obtains content from the studios through either revenue sharing agreements or direct purchase. The revenue sharing program provides Netflix with a tremendous cost savings, and in return provides the studios a percentage of Netflix's subscription revenues for a defined period of time. This agreement also allows the studios an additional distribution outlet for new releases, television shows, and so on. Once the defined period for the revenue sharing has ended for a particular movie title, Netflix will destroy the title, purchase the title, or return it to the studio.

Netflix contracts movies offered through its instant-viewing feature with studios and other content providers on a fixed fee or per-view basis. The general arrangement is the same, but the specific terms are often unique to each provider.[92]

Netflix orders movies in two different formats: HD DVD and Blu-Ray[93] through content providers such as Hollywood Film studios, 20th Century Fox, Walt Disney Studios, Columbia Pictures, Lions Gate Films, New Line Cinema, Paramount Pictures, Universal Pictures, Warner Bros. Pictures, and other independent film studios.[94]

The online rental industry has enjoyed large growth and success up to this point largely due to the distribution rules established by studios. Currently, DVDs are available for movie rental and retail sales three to six months before the movies are available on pay-per-view and VOD, nine months before satellite and cable, and two to three years before basic cable and syndicated networks. The studios have discussed either eliminating the distribution windows or shortening them, which would adversely affect Netflix.[95]

Netflix has been able to establish a relationship with content providers and differentiate itself among competitors through its strategic approach.

Netflix's Strategies and Functional Operations

Netflix is focused on continuous improvement and metrics to add value to the business and the customers' experience.[96] All these goals culminate into one overlying company strategic goal—to maintain a low-cost structure. Dillon states,

The Company's fulfillment costs are about half what Blockbuster's are, which enables profitability at a lower price. Every penny counts in a high-volume business. As we keep lowering our cost, we're able to lower our price. It's a very elastic market; so, the lower the price, the more our market grows.[97]

As mentioned previously, the company developed strategic alliances with sources in the film and television sectors.[98] These arrangements provided a significant cost savings, which freed up funds to use for other projects and investments, such as the continued investment and development of its proprietary software for inventory management, logistics, and shipping.[99]

Netflix has also carefully managed its payroll expenses to keep in line with the low-cost structure. "When the company first started in 1999, Netflix had 75,000 customers and was using 100 employees to package software for customer support."[100] Netflix cut that number roughly in half with just 45 current employees serving more than 6 million subscribers.[101] This dramatic cut in staffing is driven by an essentially self-service Web site and home-grown support software that enables representatives to handle higher volumes.[102] Tom Dillon, COO explains,

We firmly believe in building IT from scratch; this is a custom business. . . . If you want to get it done exactly the way you want, build it yourself. . . . IT is not a strategic weapon in most companies. But in our company, IT is the business. We live and breathe [the idea] that the way you get more competitive, lower your costs, and provide better service is through continuous improvement of the information technology.[103]

Netflix transcended the norms for IT use and will continue to rely on its information technology capabilities and resources. It has built a strong, reliable Web platform that is compatible with all kinds of portals and browsers in order to sustain a large number of users and maintain a positive "brand experience."[104]

Netflix is a company that competes on its strong foundation of mathematical, statistical, and data management expertise and uses these strengths to further distinguish itself from other competitors.[105] It uses analytics in two different ways. Internally created, algorithmically driven software makes movie recommendations for customers through a system called Cinematch.[106] This capability essentially led to the creation of personalized Web sites for each customer who visits Netflix and gives a customized interaction with every individual.[107] Netflix also uses a process called *throttling.* With this process, the company balances the frequent-use and infrequent-use distribution shipping requests of its customers.[108] Infrequent-use customers are given higher priority in shipping than frequent-use customers.[109] Some customers became disgruntled when they learned that Netflix uses the throttling process. Netflix's senior leaders did not seemed concerned about the complaints as shown in a statement by CEO Reed Hastings, "Few customers have complained about this 'fairness algorithm.' We have unbelievably high customer satisfaction ratings." In January, 1995 Netflix changed its "terms of use" to read "In determining priority for shipping and inventory allocation, we give priority to those members who receive the fewest DVDs through our service."[110]

Netflix's services provide value for its large customer base. The value provided has led Netflix to be almost four times larger than Blockbuster's in regard to subscribers for the online service, and to maintain this position, Netflix is continually reinvesting its money into marketing.[111]

Marketing Approaches

Marketing has been a key advantage for Netflix. Early on it established an agreement with Best Buy in that Best Buy set up a cobranded version of the online DVD rental service on its five online Web sites and instituted a joint-marketing program in the 1,800-plus retail stores. In return, Netflix directs its customers interested in buying DVDs to Best Buy's Web sites.[112] It has a

Exhibit 2 Advertising Expenditures

As of	Blockbuster	Netflix
December 2006	$154,300,000	$225,524,000
December 2005	252,700,000	144,562,000
December 2004	257,400,000	100,534,000
December 2003	179,400,000	49,949,000

Sources: http://www.marketwatch.com; Netflix SEC10-K 2003, Netflix SEC10-K 2004, Netflix SEC10-K 2005, and Netflix SEC10-K 2006.

Exhibit 3 Historic Stock Price and P/E Ratios

	2006	2005	2004	2003	2002
High Price	33.12	30.25	39.77	30.50	9.10
Low Price	18.12	8.91	9.25	5.93	2.42
Year-End Price	25.86	27.06	12.33	27.35	5.51
High P/E	46.61	47.16	119.18	294.52	−12.25
Low P/E	25.50	13.89	27.72	57.21	−3.26
Year-End P/E	36.39	42.19	36.95	264.05	−7.41

Source: http://stocks.us.reuters.com/stocks/performance.asp?symbol=NFLX.O&WTmodLOC=L2-LeftNav-18-Performace.

similar agreement with Wal-Mart; both companies have promoted one another since 2005 when Wal-Mart exited the online movie market.[113]

Other marketing efforts include online advertisements such as banner ads, paid search listings, pop-up advertisements, and text on popular Web portals—Yahoo!, MSN, and AOL.[114] Netflix was ranked as being the number two company to spend the most money on online advertisements.[115] Most online retailers face budget restrictions on advertising expenditures, as did Netflix in the beginning, and therefore are selective in the channels of advertising,[116] but as Netflix's subscriber base has grown, so has its advertising budget and expenditures (see Exhibit 2).

Netflix also targets a broad demographic in its advertising plan by running ads on the mainstream networks—ABC, NBC, FOX, and CBS, as well as radio advertisements.[117] Direct mail, print advertising, and promotions in certain consumer package goods are used as well in their marketing strategy.[118]

For online video rental, Netflix pioneered the use of database marketing to develop a personalized relationship with consumers. The database, possible because of Netflix's strengths in IT, allowed Netflix to understand individual customers, aggregate and predict behaviors, and then send customized e-mails informing customers of what new movies are available. Netflix has a strong culture of analytics and a test-and-learn approach to its business.[119] Metrics tracked include Web site users, advertising testing, data mining, subscriber satisfaction, segment research, and marketing material effectiveness.[120] Often, the effectiveness of its marketing endeavors can be assessed by reviewing the company's financials.

Financial Results

Stock Related Issues

Netflix's stock price has been highly volatile since its IPO on May 22, 2002. After adjusting for the eventual 2-for-1 stock split on February 12, 2004, its first year stock was valued anywhere between $2.42 and $9.10.[121] In the following three years, the stock price fluctuated even more until it started showing signs of stabilization in 2006 (see Exhibit 3). The earnings per share (EPS) for Netflix has been constantly on the rise (see Exhibit 4). Estimates for 2007 and 2008 suggest that this trend will continue at a reasonable rate, which can also be seen in Exhibit 4.

Also important to note is Netflix's P/E ratios. Netflix's 2006 P/E ratio of 32.88 (2007) is showing a trend toward becoming more in line with the rest of the industry, which has a current P/E ratio of 29.17.[122] This high P/E ratio indicates that the market views Netflix as having a higher potential for future earning compared to others in the video rental industry. Netflix's P/E ratio has moved from an extremely high number in 2003 to its more stable current P/E ratio. Historic P/E ratios can be found in Exhibit 3.[123]

Company Liquidity

The current ratios for 2002–2006 can be found in Exhibit 6. Netflix has consistently had a high current ratio, always above 1.75.[124] As of December 2006, its current ratio was 2.20, while the rest of the industry had a less favorable ratio of .59.[125] At 2006 year end, the cash ratio was 2.09 and the debt ratio was .319. With all these ratios considered, Netflix seems to be in a favorable position. (See Exhibit 5 for balance sheet information.)

Company Profitability

Netflix has continued to increase revenues since its IPO at a significant rate.[126] The net profit margin has remained in the 4 to 6 range for the past three years and appears to be the most stable profitability ratio. This value is significantly lower than the industry's net profit margin at 14.80.[127] Return on assets, return on stockholders' equity, operating profit margin, and net profit margin have all been computed and listed in Exhibit 7.

Competitor and Industry Financial Ratios

See Exhibit 8 for a list comparing Netflix to its main competitors—Blockbuster, Hastings Entertainment, and Movie Gallery—and to other industry averages.

Exhibit 4 Income Statement

Income Statement (in US$ thousands, except per share data)							
	2002	2003	2004	2005	2006	2007 (est.)	2008E
Revenues	$150,818	$270,410	$500,611	$682,213	$996,660	$1,295,550	$1,595,890
Cost of revenues							
Subscription	77,044	147,736	273,401	393,788	532,621		
Fulfillment expenses	20,421	32,623	58,311	71,987	94,364		
Total cost of revenues	$ 97,465	$180,359	$331,712	$465,775	$626,985		
Gross profit	53,353	90,051	168,899	216,438	369,675		
Operating expenses							
Technology and development	$ 17,632	$ 21,863	$ 29,467	$ 35,388	$ 48,379		
Marketing	37,423	51,535	100,534	144,562	225,524		w
General and administrative	9,867	13,390	22,104	35,486	36,155		
Gain on disposal of DVDs	(896)	(1,209)	(2,560)	(1,987)	(4,797)		
Total operating expenses	$ 64,026	$ 85,579	$149,545	213,449	$305,261		
Operating income (loss)	$(10,673)	$ 4,472	$ 19,354	$ 2,989	$ 64,414		
Other income (expense)							
Interest and other income	1,697	$ 2,457	$ 2,592	$ 5,753	$ 15,904		
Interest and other expense	(11,972)	(417)	(170)	(407)	–		
Income (loss) before income taxes	$(20,948)	$ 6,512	$ 21,776	$ 8,335	$ 80,318		
Provisions for (benefit from) income taxes	–	–	181	(33,692)	31,236		
Net income (loss)	$(20,948)	$ 6,512	$ 21,595	$ 42,027	$ 49,082		
Net income (loss) per share:							
Basic	$ (0.74)	$ 0.14	$ 0.42	$ 0.79	$ 0.78	$ 0.79	$ 1.04
Diluted	$ (0.74)	$ 0.10	$ 0.33	$ 0.64	$ 0.71		
Weighted average shares outstanding							
Basic	$ 28,204	$ 47,786	$ 51,988	$ 53,528	$ 62,577		
Diluted	$ 28,204	$ 62,884	$ 64,713	$ 65,518	$ 69,075		
Year-end price per share	$ 5.51	$ 27.35	$ 12.33	$ 27.06	$ 25.86		
Price/earnings ratios	(7.45)	273.50	37.36	42.28	36.42	29.83	$ 21.79

Sources: Netflix SEC10-K 2002, Netflix SEC10-K 2003, Netflix SEC10-K 2004, Netflix SEC10-K 2005, and Netflix SEC10-K 2006; http://stocks.us.reuters.com/stocks/estimates.asp?symbol=NFLX.

Exhibit 5 Balance Sheet

Balance Sheet (in US$ thousands, except share and per share data)	2002	2003	2004	2005	2006
Assets					
Current assets					
Cash and cash equivalents	$59,814	$89,894	$174,461	$212,256	$400,430
Short-term investments	43,796	45,297	–	7,848	4,742
Prepaid expenses	2,753	2,231	2,741	5,252	9,456
Prepaid revenue sharing expenses	303	905	4,695	13,666	3,155
Other current asses	409	619	5,449	4,669	10,635
Total current assets	107,075	138,946	187,346	243,691	428,418
DVD library, net	9,972	22,238	42,158	57,032	104,908
Intangible assets	6,094	2,948	961	457	969
Property and equipment, net	5,620	9,772	18,728	40,213	55,503
Deposits	1,690	1,272	1,600	1,249	1,316
Deferred tax assets	–	–	–	21,239	15,600
Other assets	79	836	1,000	800	2,065
Total assets	$130,530	$176,012	$251,793	$364,681	$608,779
Liabilities and Stockholders' Equity					
Current liabilities					
Accounts payable	$20,350	$32,654	$ 49,775	$ 63,491	$93,864
Accrued expenses	9,102	11,625	13,131	25,563	29,905
Deferred revenue	9,743	18,324	31,936	48,533	69,678
Current portion of capital lease obligations	1,231	416	68	–	–
Total current liabilities	40,426	63,019	94,910	137,587	193,447
Deferred rent	288	241	600	842	1,121
Capital lease obligations, less current portion	460	44	68	–	–
Total liabilities	$41,174	$63,019	$95,510	$138,429	194,568
Commitments and contingencies					
Stockholders' equity	45	51	53	55	69
Additional paid-in capital	260,044	270,836	292,843	315,868	454,731
Deferred stock-based compensation	(11,702)	(5,482)	(4,693)	–	–
Accumulated other comprehensive income (loss)	774	596	(222)	–	–
Accumulated deficit	(159,805)	(153,293)	(131,698)	(89,671)	(40,589)
Total stockholders' equity	$89,356	$112,708	$156,283	$226,252	$414,211
Total liabilities and stockholders' equity	$130,530	$176,012	$251,793	$364,681	$608,779

Sources: Netflix SEC10-K 2002, Netflix SEC10-K 2003, Netflix SEC10-K 2004, Netflix SEC10-K 2005, and Netflix SEC10-K 2006.

Netflix experienced some financial setbacks in the first quarter of 2007, most of which can be attributed to its key strategic challenges.

Key Strategic Challenges

Netflix faces a rapidly developing competitive environment with new technological innovations affecting product and service offerings among the various movie rental businesses, whether it be a brick-and-mortar store, click-and-mortar store, or online business. However, perhaps the main challenge Netflix will encounter is trying to figure out how to adjust its business model to the new technological pressures while staying true to the company's strengths and providing value to its subscribers.

Churn

Churn is the cancellation of a subscription service. Churn can be triggered by a number of factors: insufficient use of the service does not justify the expense; delivery is

Exhibit 6 Liquidity Ratio

	2002	2003	2004	2005	2006
Current ratio	2.65	2.20	1.97	1.77	2.20

Sources: Netflix SEC10-K 2002, Netflix SEC10-K 2003, Netflix SEC10-K 2004, Netflix SEC10-K 2005, and Netflix SEC10-K 2006.

Exhibit 7 Profitability Ratios

	2002	2003	2004	2005	2006
Return on assets (%)	−19.56	3.70	11.53	11.52	8.06
Return on stockholders' equity	−23.44	5.78	13.93	18.58	11.85
Operating profit	−13.89	2.41	4.35	1.22	8.06
Net profit margin	−13.89	2.41	4.31	6.16	4.92

Sources: Netflix SEC10-K 2002, Netflix SEC10-K 2003, Netflix SEC10-K 2004, Netflix SEC10-K 2005, and Netflix SEC10-K 2006.

Exhibit 8 Comparative Performance of Netflix and Key Competitors

	Blockbuster BBI	Hastings Entertainment HAST	Movie Gallery MOVI.O	Netflix NFLX	Industry Median
Profitability					
Gross profit margin	54.68%	67.62%	60.19%	37.09%	48.94%
Pre-tax profit margin	−0.15%	1.51%	−0.95%	8.06%	16.47%
Net profit margin	1.23%	0.59%	−1.01%	4.93%	14.82%
Return on equity	10.54%	5.22%	–	15.33%	11.84%
Return on assets	2.15%	1.26%	−2.03%	10.08%	6.37%
Valuation					
Price/Sales ratio	0.22	0.12	0.06	1.60	2.82
Price/Earnings ratio	21.43	13.99	–	32.92	18.97
Price/Book ratio	2.06	0.69	–	3.84	3.80
Operations					
Inventory turnover	7.57	3.28	7.30	–	27.08
Asset turnover	1.75	2.13	2.00	2.05	0.52
Financial					
Current ratio	1.12	1.63	0.89	2.22	0.63
Quick ratio	0.88	0.16	0.37	2.22	0.48
Total debt/Equity ratio	1.33	0.42	–	0.00	0.68

Sources: http://stocks.us.reuters.com/stocks/ratios.asp?symbol=NFLX.O&WTmodLOC=L2-LeftNav-16-Ratios; http://stocks.us.reuters.com/stocks/ratios.asp?symbol=BBI.N; http://stocks.us.reuters.com/stocks/ratios.asp?symbol=MOVI.OQ; http://www.investor.reuters.wallst.com/stocks/Ratios.asp?rpc=66&ticker=HAST.O.

too long; poor service; or competitive services provide better added value and/or experience to the consumer. These factors are critical to any online movie rental business, but especially for Netflix because its entire business model is based on attracting and maintaining subscribers (see Exhibits 9 and 10).

Some of the company's key competitors have more brand name recognition, experience, and financial resources to provide value to the customer. This makes it difficult for Netflix to compete at its existing price level or at lower price level structures in the future. Netflix needs to offer services that compete effectively.

Managing Growth

Finally, Netflix must have the ability and foresight to manage extensive growth to maintain its current service

Exhibit 9 Potential Growth for Netflix

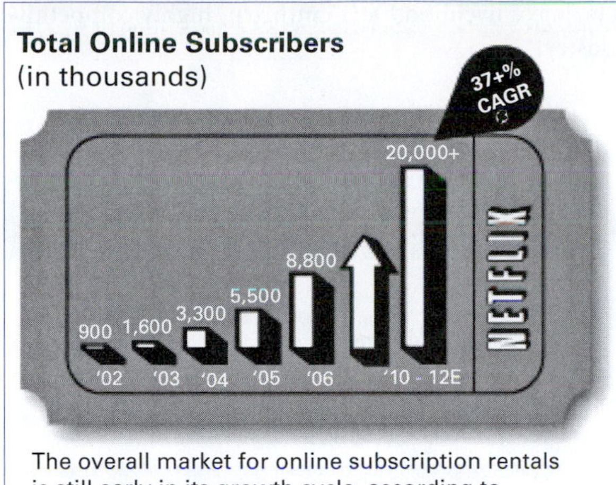

The overall market for online subscription rentals is still early in its growth cycle, according to estimates from Adams Media Research and internal Netflix estimates.

Exhibit 11 Subscriber Growth

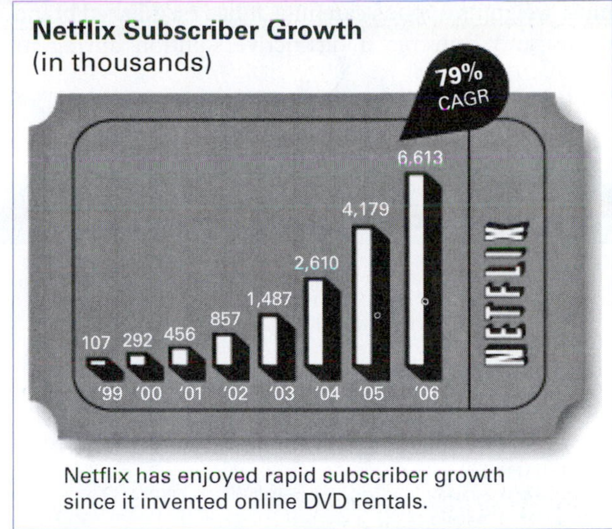

Netflix has enjoyed rapid subscriber growth since it invented online DVD rentals.

Exhibit 10 Subscriber Churn

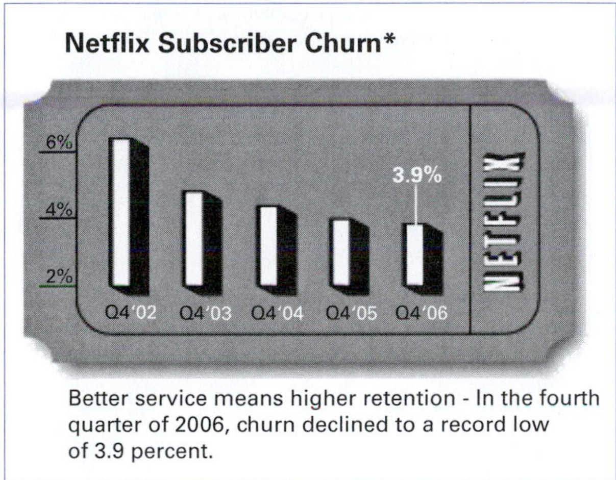

Better service means higher retention - In the fourth quarter of 2006, churn declined to a record low of 3.9 percent.

Exhibit 12 Netflix Distribution Network

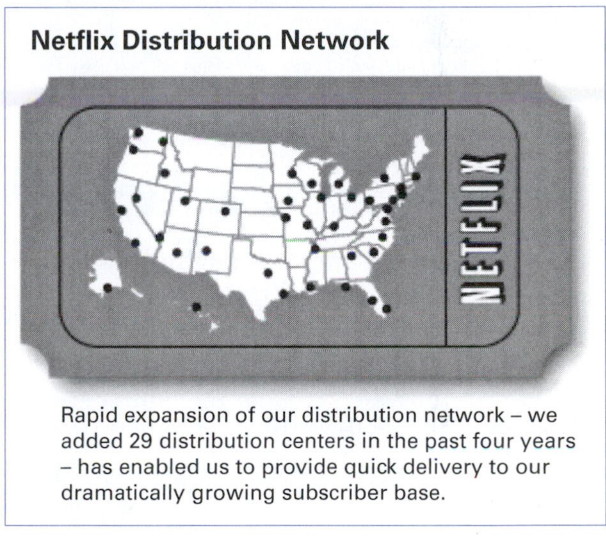

Rapid expansion of our distribution network – we added 29 distribution centers in the past four years – has enabled us to provide quick delivery to our dramatically growing subscriber base.

level. Since the company's launch in 1998, Netflix has seen phenomenal growth and profitability (see Exhibit 11). As the company grows, it must add additional distribution centers to its already existing infrastructure (see Exhibit 12). However, if the company does not properly prepare for a continual increase in clientele Netflix's managerial operations and financial resources could be spread too thin, which translates into orders not being met and customer satisfaction levels decreasing.

The Central Question

Reed Hastings started Netflix on the premonition that users would buy into his business concept of online movie rental without the hassle of late fees and due dates while choosing a movie from the confines of their home. With Hastings's vision and charisma, along with his strong supporting cast of IT, marketing, and entertainment industry experts, Netflix set in motion a new wave of how consumers viewed the movie rental business. Netflix was the primary proponent of change in the movie rental business. Now, the key concern is how to cope with industry and technological trends that are evolving. Should Netflix transition from an online movie rental business to solely VOD or streaming services? Or can Netflix maintain its stronghold position with its current business model while making slight improvements to keep current with VOD and other new technologies? Should Netflix's strategic leaders and decision makers consider a merger or a joint venture with another company in order to offer a unique basket of services to consumers? Netflix must weigh its options carefully. It has established brand equity and delivered a distinctive solution during its short history. Now Netflix must realize how it can sustain its business livelihood in a cutthroat, highly competitive industry.

Notes

1. 2006, Netflix Inc. Annual Report.
2. M. Helft, 2007, Netflix to deliver movies to the PC, *New York Times*, http://www.nytimes.com/2007/01/16/technology/16netflix.html?ex=1326603600&en=71618d2092f5b372&ei=5088&partner=rssnyt&emc=rss, January.
3. 2007, Hoover's Company Reports—Full Overview, Netflix, February 8.
4. 2007, Hoover's Company Reports—Full Overview, Blockbuster Inc., February 10.
5. 2007, Blockbuster Total Access—How It Works, http://www.blockbuster.com.
6. Ibid.
7. Ibid.
8. Ibid.
9. 2007, Netflix, Blockbuster competes for supremacy with new DVD services, *Pittsburgh Post Gazette*, January 30.
10. Hoover's company reports.
11. 2007, About Us, http://www.netflix.com, March.
12. 2007, First online DVD rental stores open, http://www.netflix.com/mediacenter, March.
13. 2007, Netflix's aggressive growth plan, http://www.netflix.com/mediacenter, March.
14. 2007, Netflix.com transforms DVD business eliminating late fees and due dates from movie rentals, http://www.netflix.com/mediacenter, March.
15. 2007, Netflix announces IPO, http://www.netflix.com/mediacenter, March.
16. 2004, Netflix announces Q4 revenue growth of 80% year over year and a 2-for-1 stock split, Netflix financial release, http://www.netflix.com, January 21.
17. 2006, Netflix announces Q4 2005 financial results, Netflix press release, http://www.netflix.com, January 24.
18. 2007, Netflix announces Q4 2006 financial results, Netflix press release, http:// www.netflix.com, January 24.
19. 2007, One billion and counting, http://www.netflix.com/mediacenter, March.
20. 2007, Netflix offers subscribers option of instantly watching movies on their PCs, http://www.netflix.com/mediacenter, March.
21. Ibid.
22. 2007, Netflix press release, http://www.netflix.com/MediaCenter, March 27.
23. 2007, http://www.netflix.com/mediacenter.
24. 2007, Netflix Hoover's Full Overview, http://premium.hoovers.com.
25. 2006 Netflix Inc. Annual Report.
26. 2007, Netflix board of director's committee composition, http://ir.netflix.com/committees.cfm.
27. J. Hopkins, 2006, Charismatic founder keeps Netflix adapting, *USA Today*, http://www.usatoday.com/money/companies/management/2006-04-23-exec-ceo-profile-netflix_x.htm, April 23.
28. Ibid.
29. Ibid.
30. 2007, Management, http://www.netflix.com/mediacenter.
31. Ibid.
32. Ibid.
33. Ibid.
34. Ibid.
35. Ibid.
36. Ibid.
37. P. Sauer, 2005, How I did it: Reed Hastings, Netflix, http://www.inc.com/magazine, December.
38. T. H. Davenport & J. G. Harris, 2007, Competing on analytics: The new science of winning, *The Nature of Analytical Competition*, http://harvardbusinessonline, 3.
39. Ibid., 4.
40. M. Kirdahy, 2007, Blockbuster takes on Netflix, *Forbes*, http://www.forbes.com, January 3.
41. 2007, Video on Demand (VOD): About Broadband Movies, Downloads and More, Broadbandinfo.com, http://www.broadbandinfo.com/got-high-speed/video-on-demand/default.html.
42. 2006, What's next for Netflix? *Financial Times*,http://www.ftpress.com/articles/article.asp?p=671844&rl=1, November 2.
43. 2007, The big picture, Hoovers.com, *Pittsburgh Tribune Review*, January 28.
44. Ibid.
45. 2007, Amazon.com, Amazon Unbox, http://www.amazon.com/gp/video/help/faq.html/ref=atv_dp_faq_dscvr/103-7381394-1357468#discover.
46. P. Gogoi, 2007, Wal-Mart enters the movie download wars, *BusinessWeek*, http://www.businessweek.com, February 6.
47. Ibid.
48. Ibid.
49. Ibid.
50. Ibid.
51. Ibid.
52. T. Krazit, 2004, Netflix, TiVo team up on broadband movie delivery, *PC World*, http://www.pcworld.com, September 30.
53. P. Sauer, How I did it: Reed Hastings, Netflix.
54. 2007, Blockbuster Inc., Netflix Full Overview, http://premium.hoovers.com, February 10.
55. Ibid.
56. Ibid.
57. Ibid.
58. Ibid.
59. Ibid .
60. 2000, Blockbuster Inc., Funding Universe—Company History, *International Directory of Company Histories*,http://www.fundinguniverse.com/company-histories/Blockbuster-Inc-Company-History.html.
61. Ibid.
62. Ibid.
63. Ibid.
64. Ibid.
65. Ibid.
66. Ibid.
67. Ibid.
68. Ibid.
69. Ibid.
70. Ibid.
71. 2007, Blockbuster CEO Antioco to leave company, *Yahoo! Finance*, http://www.finance.yahoo.com, March 23.
72. 2007, Blockbuster, Inc. Full Overview, Hoovers, http://premium.hoovers.com, February 10.
73. Ibid.
74. Ibid.
75. S. Ault, 2006, Blockbuster, Weinsteins sign exclusive deal, http://www.videobusiness.com.
76. M. Halkias, 2007, Blockbuster may buy downloading firm, *The Dallas Morning News*, March 1.
77. Ibid.

78. Ibid.
79. 2007, About Movie Gallery, Moviegallery.com, http://www.moviegallery.com, March 18.
80. Ibid.
81. 2007, Movie Gallery to introduce online video rental service and extend automated video vending machine program, *Movie Gallery* press release, http://phx.corporate-ir.net/phoenix.zhtml?c=85959&p=irol-newsArticle&ID=975465&highlight=, March 25.
82. 2007, Movie Gallery to launch online service, http://www.businessweek.com, March 19; R.C. Lim, 2007, Movie Gallery mayhem, *Motley Fool Stock Advisor*, www.fool.com/investing, July 24.
83. Ibid.
84. P. Sweeting & C. Spielvogel, 2007, Movie Gallery acquires MovieBeam, www.videobusiness.com, March 7; 2007, Movie Gallery News Release, http://www.moviegallery.com, March 7.
85. Ibid.
86. Ibid.
87. 2007, Hastings Entertainment, Hoovers.com, http://premium.hoovers.com/subscribe/co/overview.xhtml?ID=ffffctthjfcxryycrk, February 10.
88. 2007, About Hastings, Gohastings.com,http://www.gohastings.com/Investor/AboutHastings.stm, February 10.
89. 2007, Netflix Full Overview, http://premium.hoovers.com, February 10.
90. Ibid.
91. 2006, Netflix Inc. Annual Report.
92. Ibid.
93. Ibid.
94. 2007, Motion Picture access, major film studios in the U.S., http://ncam.wgbh.org/mopix/studios.html.
95. 2006, Netflix Inc. Annual Report.
96. Ibid.
97. Ibid.
98. Ibid.
99. Ibid.
100. Ibid.
101. Ibid.
102. Ibid.
103. Ibid.
104. M. Levy, 2002, Netflix analyzed via the value framework, http://www.valueframeworkinstitute.org/May2002/feature.article.htm, May.
105. T. H. Davenport & J. G. Harris, 2007, Competing on analytics.
106. Ibid.
107. Ibid.
108. Ibid.
109. Ibid.
110. 2006, Frequent Netflix renters sent to the back of the line, *Associated Press*, http://www.msnbc.msn.com/id/11262292/, February 10.
111. P. Sauer, 2005, How I did it: Reed Hastings, Netflix.
112. 2001, Best Buy and Netflix offer co-branded online DVD movie rental service, *Retailer Merchandiser*, http://www.allbusiness.com/retail, September 11.
113. P. Sauer, How I did it: Reed Hastings, Netflix.
114. 2006, Netflix Inc. Annual Report.
115. L. Punch, 2007, Advertising to the masses, http://www.internetretailer.com, January.
116. Ibid.
117. Ibid.
118. 2006 Netflix Inc. Annual Report.
119. Ibid.
120. Ibid.
121. 2007, Historical prices for Netflix Inc., *Yahoo! Finance*, http://finance.yahoo.com/q/hp?s=NFLX&a=00&b=5&c=2002&d=03&e=17&f=2007&g=m.
122. 2007, Summary for Netflix Inc., *Yahoo! Finance*,http://finance.yahoo.com/q?s=nflx&x=0&y=0.
123. 2007, Netflix Inc. performance, http://stocks.us.reuters.com/stocks/performance.asp?symbol=NFLX.O&WTmodLOC=L2-LeftNav-18-Performace.
124. 2006, Netflix Inc. Annual Report.
125. 2007, Netflix Inc. ratios, http://stocks.us.reuters.com/stocks/ratios.asp?symbol=NFLX.O&WTmodLOC=L2-LeftNav-16-Ratios.
126. 2006, Netflix Inc. Annual Report.
127. Ibid.

Case 22

An Entrepreneur Seeks the Holy Grail of Retailing

Lauranne Buchanan

Thunderbird, The Garvin School of International Management

For an entrepreneur, Wal-Mart *is* the Holy Grail of retailers. With 5,300 outlets worldwide and 138 million customers per week,[1] a run in Wal-Mart can transform a niche product into a household name.

But landing a spot on Wal-Mart's shelves isn't easy. First, consider the competition—more than 10,000 suppliers vie for the opportunity to present to a Wal-Mart buyer each year. Then comes the interview: a mere 30 minutes to convince a seasoned—and skeptical—buyer for the world's most powerful retailer to give the product a chance. Finally, during the test period is the opportunity to prove that an unknown and underfunded product can hold its own against the biggest brand names in the industry.

If the process isn't discouraging, the statistics should be: Only 2 percent of vendors will be given a trial run; of those, only three quarters will make it past the test period. Even then, they won't move to permanent locations without proven sales figures.[2] Nonetheless, entrepreneurs everywhere dream of having the chance to supply Wal-Mart. On a rainy day in Bentonville last November, Colin Roche and Bobby Ronsse, the creators of PenAgain, had that chance.

The PenAgain is an ergonomically designed, writing instrument with a unique, wishbone shape. The idea for the pen came to Colin Roche while he was in Saturday detention at Palo Alto High School in 1987. "I was always that guy that was daydreaming of building something, making something," says Mr. Roche.[3] He attended California Polytechnic State University, San Luis Obispo, where he and a fraternity brother, Bobby Ronsse, ran a pet-sitting business employing other students. The two went different ways after college. But after the dot-com bubble burst, Mr. Roche returned to his idea. He phoned Mr. Ronsse, a mechanical engineer, and said he wanted to talk about the "pen, again"—hence the brand name. The two joined forces, putting in $5,000 each to form Pacific Writing Instruments. By December 2001, they had filed a patent approval, launched a Web site (www.penagain.com), and set up production in the Bay area.

PenAgain's design allows the writer to slip the index finger through the wishbone to guide the pen, while resting the shaft of the pen comfortably on the hand. "It makes writing fun," says Mr. Roche, who has suffered from writer's cramp since childhood. "It uses the natural weight of your hand and eliminates the need to grip tightly or push down hard."[4] In addition, the design lessens wrist strain—attractive benefits to aging Baby Boomers as they face the prospect of carpal-tunnel syndrome and arthritis. Despite the growing need for an easier-to-use pen, established competitors in the $4.8 billion writing instruments category have shown little imagination in addressing the problem. BIC and PaperMate, for example, have tinkered with the pen's length and width and the cushion grips at the tip, but they haven't altered the basic stick design of the pen.

Roche and Ronsse were therefore understandably nervous and excited as they arrived to present to the Wal-Mart buyer—an opportunity for which they had paid $10,000. But almost before they sat down, the buyer dismissed the product with, "I've seen this design before and passed."[5]

Come Prepared

But the two entrepreneurs were prepared for the buyer's skepticism. Before approaching Wal-Mart they had spent four years developing a track record with other retailers, building a broad product mix, and expanding their production capability.

To develop a market for their product, the entrepreneurs began by pounding the pavement, approaching smaller retailers such as Edwards Luggage in San Francisco. Fred Ebert, the owner, later commented that the pen "was gimmicky, but it looked good." He took a chance on the newfangled pen and placed an order. Today, he sells about 700 pens a year at $12.95, making PenAgain his top-selling brand.

The two entrepreneurs also attended trade shows, once staying up all night to glue 300 pen samples in their hotel since the manufacturer hadn't heat-welded the pieces in time. These shows provided contacts with more buyers and distributors. But their big break came from their most unconventional channel—doctors' offices. The pen's unique design provides a natural benefit to those who suffer from arthritis and Parkinson's, and what better place to reach these people than through their doctor. So the team made a concerted effort to contact as many doctors as they could, many of whom started using the pen themselves and recommending it to their patients. As important as the sales were, the channel provided the entrepreneurs with something even more valuable: testimonials for the product and additional exposure. Scott Koerner, senior vice president of merchandising for Office Depot, saw the PenAgain in his optometrist's office and noticed on a return visit, that it had sold out. "We sell to a lot of small business, and this doctor happened to be a small business and that caught my attention," Mr. Koerner said.[6] That was enough for Office Depot to place an order for all 1,049 of its stores.

To maintain interest in the product, Roche and Ronsse knew they needed to be more than a one-product shop. So they began expanding the product line to include other writing instruments and tools. Over time, they introduced a pencil, highlighter, white-board marker, and children's pens, then a hobby knife—all based on the wishbone design. In addition, they expanded each product line with a wide array of colors and textures.

Sales grew. By 2004, PenAgain had $2 million in revenues across a wide range of retailers, including 5,000 independent stationery and office-supply stores, 200 Staples in Canada, and other chain outlets such as Fred Meyer and Hobby Lobby. In addition, the company picked up orders of 1.2 million units in Europe from promotional-products companies. And Internet sales have also been steady—providing revenues of approximately $5,000 each month. Among office supply products sold on Amazon.com, PenAgain has been the number one or two seller.[7]

But to break into the big league, the entrepreneurs knew they needed a lower price point and high-volume manufacturing capabilities—which meant moving production overseas. With funds from four outside investors, they went to China in search of manufacturers. Having located the right partners, they invested in having multiple molds produced, costing $10,000 each (roughly half of what they would pay in the United States). The additional molds meant that when a big order came in, PenAgain could ramp up quickly. "It allows us to push hard on expanding the distribution channels without fear of being unable to deliver," Mr. Roche says.[8] It also helped them reduce the price to $3.99 on one model—which would be critical to winning over Wal-Mart.

The Order

To the Wal-Mart buyer's outright dismissal of the product, Mr. Roche responded: "The difference is that we are building a brand. Rather than going to you first, we've got a base of independent retailers and distributors worldwide who have already picked us up."[9] He kept talking, showing her the testimonials, media write-ups, and product extensions. And she continued to take notes.

Their patience in approaching the super-retailer would make a difference: Before Wal-Mart takes on a new product, it wants to know that product will sell. "We like companies to have a sales history and to be sold somewhere else first, even if it's just a downtown boutique," says Excell La Fayette Jr., Wal-Mart's director of supplier development. Furthermore, Wal-Mart doesn't like to account for more than 30 percent of a supplier's total business.

Finally, the buyer closed her notebook and said, "OK, we will give you a trial period." The parameters of the trial: 500 stores would carry the product for six weeks, with the expectation that PenAgain would sell 85 percent of the product.[10] If they were unable to meet the goal, they would be out.

Even though many would consider this trial a win, the seasoned entrepreneurs knew the game had just begun.

The Trial

42 days. 500 stores. 85% product sell-through. Succeed, and one day PenAgain might be a household name like BIC. Fail, and the 34-year-old entrepreneurs would be blowing the biggest break of their five-year-old product.

From the time the buyer says "OK" to approval as an official Wal-Mart vendor takes some eight to ten months. Much of this time is spent completing the intensive paperwork. Until approval is granted, there are no guarantees. Even so, the entrepreneur cannot afford to wait to start production; upon receiving approval, they will have a narrow window in which to deliver product to the store. To ensure that they could meet Wal-Mart's deadlines, production had to be ramped up in advance.

By the time the PenAgain team received the official document on April 12, 2005, they had produced some 53,000 pens—the 48,000 Wal-Mart ordered, plus 5,000 as backup.

Every detail must be considered when working for Wal-Mart. Orders have to conform to Wal-Mart's rigid packaging and shipping requirements, or they won't be accepted. Packaging has to be printed with shipping labels that include purchase-order numbers and distribution-center details. And because the order of PenAgain was hurried out of China, all of this information had to be added to the boxes after they got to the United States. Store displays are just as critical. Any detail—from the thickness of the cardboard used in display cartons to the red stripe around the outside that says "stationery"—can delay getting the product on the floor. "We didn't sleep during that three weeks," said Mr. Roche.[11] Their sleepless nights paid off—the pens were delivered to and accepted by Wal-Mart's distribution center on time.

The mistake many hopeful vendors make, at this point, is to assume that being in Wal-Mart means the product will sell itself—or that Wal-Mart will sell it. Neither of which is true. "A lot of times, what will hurt suppliers more than anything is that they may not monitor the product very well. . . . They are busy still trying to sell the [Wal-Mart] buyer on that item. You've sold them. Now, just make sure that the information is out there, and drive customers to the product," says Mr. La Fayette of Wal-Mart. The PenAgain partners couldn't afford traditional advertising, so they reached out virally to anyone they felt would support the brand—from their national fraternity headquarters to the doctors, patients, and medical organizations who had already shown interest in the product.

Even more important, the entrepreneurs monitored store sales. And in doing so, they quickly learned that delivering the product didn't mean that it would get to the shelf right away or that it would get to the assigned spot. Some pens sat in stockrooms; others were placed near pet food or potato chips rather than on the assigned end-of-aisle displays. "The lesson is, 'Oh my God, there are these big companies with heavy back-end systems that can track everything. But if human beings are involved, problems are going to happen,'" says Mr. Roche.[12] They hired a third-party merchant service organization to send reps into stores to check out display placement and consumer traffic. They themselves visited 50 stores to check on displays. Without this type of monitoring, they wouldn't have known that by the end of the first month pens hadn't even shown up in 38 of the 500 test stores.[13]

Tracking sales every day from every store via Wal-Mart's Retail Link software system allowed Mr. Ronsse to demonstrate PenAgain's performance. He sorted sales data using Microsoft Excel to pinpoint exactly where the pen was selling and where it wasn't. "In some places, we were selling per day what we should do in a week," said Mr. Ronsse.[14] According to Wal-Mart's Mr. La Fayette, leaving this type of monitoring to Wal-Mart is another common mistake made by rookie suppliers. "When you have a buyer with 10 to 20 different categories, they cannot monitor everyone's pieces, and they depend on the supplier to inform them of what is going on."[15]

Again, the extra effort paid off for the entrepreneurs. By making sure the Wal-Mart buyer was aware of the most accurate sales figures when evaluating the results of the test market, the team won a limited reorder from the mass merchant—even though its 75 percent sell-through rate fell short of the target.

Balancing the Mix

Price—or more precisely, Wal-Mart's price—is a concern for other retailers. Wal-Mart sells the PenAgain for $3.76, compared to an almost identical version selling for $6.49 on Amazon and $12 elsewhere. By slashing the price for Wal-Mart, the PenAgain team risked angering their bread-and-butter base of 5,000 retailers, many of them being small stationery shops.

To appease this group, PenAgain founders created exclusive offerings for small stores, including an ergonomic sample set for $15 to $20 and a brushed metal pen for $20 to $30. Their smaller retailers welcome the effort: Fred Ebert, owner of Edwards Luggage, Inc., sells the same model as Wal-Mart at a higher price. He says Wal-Mart "worries" him and at some point, he will probably stop ordering PenAgain until it comes out with a higher-end model. "I don't want to be way out of line on pricing anything because it sends a bad message," he explained.[16]

In addition, PenAgain founders are assembling an advisory group of independent store owners to case the small retailers' concerns. One of the group's first assignments is to give the company feedback on the merchandisers. "If a Staples or a Wal-Mart sells a less-expensive product and then the manufacturer comes out with a nicer version, that can really build up the sales," says Bob Norins, store manager for Arthur Brown International Pen Shop in Manhattan.

The added exposure from Wal-Mart could double sales for PenAgain to $4 million to $5 million this year. But the loyalty of small retailers cannot be taken for granted. "That's our goal: to try and prove that we will live in both worlds," explains Mr. Roche.[17]

Notes

1. G. Bounds, 2005, The long road to Wal-Mart: What does it take for entrepreneurs to break into the nation's largest retailer? *Wall Street Journal*, Septemer 19, R1.
2. G. Bounds, 2005, One month to make it, *Wall Street Journal*, May 30, B1.
3. L. Thomas, 2004, Handy tool, http://www.sfgate.com, June 30.
4. Ibid.
5. Bounds, The long road to Wal-Mart.
6. Bounds, One month to make it.
7. Bounds, The long road to Wal-Mart.
8. Ibid.
9. Ibid.
10. Ibid.
11. Bounds, One month to make it.
12. G. Bounds, 2006, Pen maker's trial by Wal-Mart, Part III, *Wall Street Journal*, July 18, B1.
13. Ibid.
14. Ibid.
15. Bounds, One month to make it.
16. Ibid.
17. Ibid.

Case 23

PSA Peugeot Citroën: Strategic Alliances for Competitive Advantage?

Sachin Govind, S. Sam George

ICFAI Center for Management Research

I don't want to boast, but I can say that we are probably the champions in the sphere of the joint projects.[1]

—JEAN-MARTIN FOLZ,
PRESIDENT, BOARD OF DIRECTORS, PSA PEUGEOT CITROËN, IN 2003

Introduction

In February 2005, PSA Peugeot Citroën (PSA) entered into an agreement with Mitsubishi Motor Corp.,[2] the ailing Japanese car maker. According to the terms of the deal, Mitsubishi agreed to supply 30,000 units of a new sports utility vehicle (SUV) every year to PSA, which would then be sold under the Peugeot and Citroën marques. The deal enabled Mitsubishi to utilize its idle production capacity, and PSA to fill a major gap in its product range.

The deal with Mitsubishi was typical of PSA's strategy of entering into alliances with other major automobile makers. Over the years, PSA has entered into long-term relationships with Renault S.A,[3] Fiat Auto SpA,[4] Ford Motor Co.,[5] Toyota Motor Corp.,[6] and BMW AG.[7] Such alliances have helped PSA share costs, risks, and investment. At the same time, PSA was also pursuing R&D independently to sharpen its competitive edge.

In January 2006, PSA announced that its profits for the year 2005 would be less than previously estimated. This profit warning—the second in three months—reflected the poor sales performance of the company's cars in Europe. The competition in the automobile market in Europe remained intense, which contributed to lower margins. PSA launched several new models in 2005. Even so, worldwide sales of Peugeot branded cars in 2005 fell by 1.5 percent. However, Citroën car sales were 3.5 percent higher in the same period.

The Peugeot arm of PSA expected to sell 2 million cars in 2006. The company hoped to sell, by the end of 2007, half a million units of its new model, the 207, a compact car launched in January 2006.

Background Note

About Peugeot

The history of PSA dates back to the nineteenth century. In 1810, Jean-Frederic Peugeot, together with his brother Jean-Pierre Peugeot, transformed their textile mill in Alsace, France, into a foundry. The brothers invented a new process of making sprung steel. Using this new technology, they started making saws, watch springs, and other products. In 1858, Peugeot adopted the now familiar lion logo as its symbol (refer to Exhibit 1 A for

Exhibit 1 Company Logos

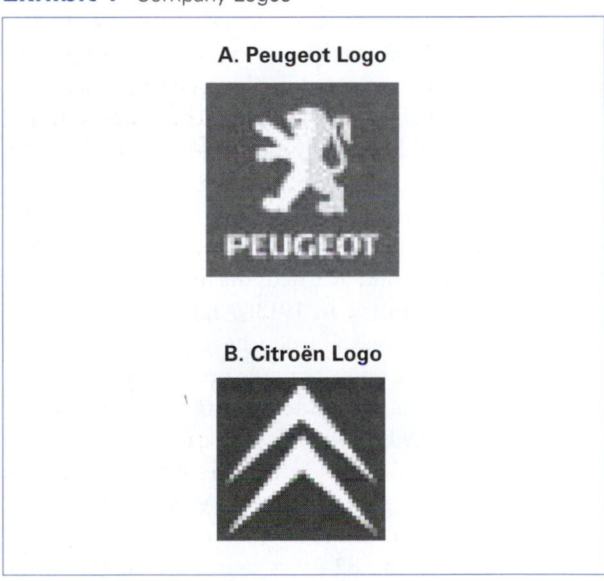

Source: http://www,psa-peugeot-citroen.com.

the logo). In the 1880s, Peugeot was managed by Armand Peugeot, Jean-Pierre's grandson. In 1885, Peugeot started producing bicycles. In 1889, Peugeot unveiled its first automobile—a steam-powered three-wheeler. However, almost immediately, the steam engine was dropped in favor of the petrol engine patented by Gottlieb Daimler. The first "customer" car was delivered in 1891. In 1892, Peugeot made 29 cars and by 1899, production had increased to 300 cars a year.

Peugeot established a presence in several rallies and competitions in the 1890s. The first appearance of a Peugeot in a race was in the 1894 Paris-Rouen Trial (which is widely considered the world's first motor race). Peugeot tasted its first success in the 1895 Paris-Bordeaux-Paris race.

In 1896, Peugeot started making its own engines. The same year, Societe Anonyme des Automobiles Peugeot, a separate automobile company, was set up by Peugeot. In 1900, the company's first small car christened Bebe was launched. In 1902, the company opened a new factory in Lille. Soon, the factory started making motorbikes as well. With the success of its products, yet another factory was opened in 1910 in Sochaux. All this time, the company's cars continued to do well at motor races.

After World War I, the company began to concentrate on making diesel-powered cars. In 1922, Peugeot Quadrilette, a diesel car, replaced the Bebe. The Quadrilette was a huge success. In subsequent years, Peugeot acquired several companies including the Bellanger Car Company in Neuilly, and De Dion Bouton factory in Puteaux. In 1929, Peugeot launched the 201 model. The 1930s saw the launch of the 202 and 402 models, which went on to become bestsellers.

No new model launches occurred during World War II. In 1947, the 203 model was launched. During this period were made new acquisitions such as Chenard-Walcker and Hotchkiss. In 1955, the company launched the 403, which sold 1.2 million units in a decade.

About Citroën

In 1912, André Citroën paid a visit to Ford's plant in the United States and learned the operational details of mass producing cars. In 1913, André established the Société des Engrenages Citroën headquartered at Quai de Grenelle in Paris. Soon he made preparations to transform an armaments plant into an automobile factory. In 1919, the company launched its first car, the Type A, the first mass-produced model in Europe. Around this time, the chevron[8] shape of its gear teeth was adopted as the company logo (refer to Exhibit 1 B for the logo). In 1921, a second model—the B2—was launched, replacing the Type A. In 1922, a Citroën achieved the unique distinction of being the first car to cross the Sahara desert.

In 1924, a new company, Société Anonyme André Citroën, was created. The same year, sales subsidiaries were opened at Brussels, Cologne, Milan, Amsterdam, and other important cities in Europe. In 1924–1925, Citroën became popular for a motor expedition referred to as the black cruise.[9] In 1927, the C4 was launched. In 1931–1932, Citroën organized yet another motor expedition called the yellow cruise.[10] In 1934, the company launched the 7A, which incorporated several innovative features including front wheel drive, torsion bar suspension, aerodynamic body, hydraulic brakes, and so on. However, during this period the company faced financial problems. In 1934–1935, Michelin, the French tire maker, acquired a major stake in Citroën and started a restructuring exercise that included layoffs. Michelin was able to wipe off Citroën's debts and improve its efficiency. In 1935, André passed away.

During World War II, the Citroën factory was bombed, which led to a drastic fall in production. However, the company soon rebuilt the plant. In 1948, the 2CV van was launched. In 1953, the company entered into an agreement with Panhard, an armored vehicle maker, to partially merge the two companies' sales networks. In 1958, the company set up a new plant at Vigo, Spain, to manufacture its 2CV vans. In 1965, Citroën acquired Panhard. In 1967, the company acquired a majority stake in Berliet, another automobile company. In 1968, a parent company—Citroën SA, which owned Citroën, Panhard, and Berliet—was formed. In 1974, Peugeot acquired a 38.2 percent stake in Citroën SA.

PSA Peugeot Citroën

In May 1976, Peugeot took complete control of Citroën SA, and PSA Peugeot Citroën was formed. PSA, the holding company, was the full owner of both the companies (Automobiles Peugeot S.A and Automobiles Citroën S.A). In the same year, the 10 millionth Peugeot car rolled out of the factory premises (refer to Exhibit 2 for new model launches during 1977–2005). In 1977, Société Mécanique Automobile de l'Est (SMAE) was established to manufacture gear boxes and engines. In the same year, SAMM, an aeronautics component manufacturer, was also acquired by the group. In 1978, the European arm of Chrysler[11] (Chrysler France, Chrysler UK, and Chrysler Spain) was acquired by PSA. PSA sold the models of the former Chrysler's European subsidiaries, including Simca[12] and Sunbeam[13] under the Talbot marque. In 1980, Peugeot and Talbot merged and a single dealership for both marques was established. The marketing for both product ranges was handled by Peugeot.

In 1982, Citroën shifted its headquarters to Neuilly, France. In the same year, a new plant to manufacture gear boxes was inaugurated at Valenciennes. In 1986, the Talbot models were discontinued. In 1990, Peugeot celebrated its 100th year as an automaker. In 1991, Peugeot

Exhibit 2 New Model Launches, 1977–2005

Year	Models	Year	Models	Year	Models
1977	Peugeot 305	1986	205 convertible, 309 GTI, Citroën AX	1998	206, Partner Electric, Xsara Coupe, Xsara Estate, Berlingo Electric
1978	Citroën Visa, Simca Horizon	1987	405	1999	206 S16
1979	505, 604 turbo diesel	1989	605, Citroën XM	2000	Xsara Picasso, 607, 206 CC
1980	305 Station Wagon, 505 turbo, Talbot Solara	1991	106, Citroën ZX	2001	307, C5
1981	Peugeot J5, Samba, Tagora, Visa II, C25	1993	306, Citroën Xantia	2002	206 SW, 307 SW, 307 Estate, 807, C3, C8
1982	Citroën BX, 505	1994	806, 306 Convertible, Citroën Synergie, Relay	2003	307 CC, Citroën C2, C3 Pluriel
1983	205	1995	406, 106 electric, Peugeot Expert, Citroën Xantia Activa, AX Electric, Jumpy	2004	407
1984	205 GTI	1996	Citron Saxo, Berlingo, Saxo Electric, Peugeot Partner, 406 Estate	2005	107, C1, 1007, 407 Coupe
1985	309, BX Estate	1997	306 Estate, 406 Coupe, Xantia LPG, Berlingo Multispace, Xsara		

Source: http://www.psa-peugeot-citroen.com.

established its subsidiary, Peugeot do Brasil. In 1992, the group entered China and Egypt through partnership agreements.

In 1994, Citroën celebrated its 75th anniversary. In 1998, the group unveiled its new high-pressure direct injection (HDi) engine, which was incorporated in all its models. In 2001, the group received ISO 14001 certification for several of its facilities. In the same year, the group entered into an agreement with two French technology research institutions—Scientific Research Center (CNRS) and Atomic Energy Commission (CEA)—for joint research on fuel cells. In 2005, the group sold Panhard.

In 2005, PSA worldwide sales reached 3,389,900 units, with sales of the Peugeot marque totaling 1,995,450 units and the Citroën marque another 1,394,450 (refer Exhibit 3 for region-wide sales of PSA). As of 2006, the group was selling more than 22 models (refer to Exhibit 4 for a list of models of Peugeot and Citroën as of 2006).

Forging Alliances

PSA could be considered the pioneer of strategic alliances in the automobile industry. Its first alliance with Renault started in 1966. Over the years, the company benefited considerably from its strategic alliances with several automobile and auto component companies. Subsequently,

Exhibit 3 Regional Sales* for PSA, 2005

Region	Sales (in units)
France	777,000
Other Western European countries	1,583,400
Central Europe and Turkey	209,700
Africa	83,600
The Americas	194,500
Asia-Pacific	511,900
Other	29,800
TOTAL	**3,389,900**

*Sales include passenger cars and light commercial vehicles.

Source: http://www.psa-peugeot-citroen.com.

Exhibit 4 List of Models, February 2006

Peugeot	107, 206, 206cc, 207, 307, 307cc, 407, 607, 807, 1007, Partner Combi
Citroën	C1, C2, C3, C3 Pluriel, C4, C5, C6, C8, Berlingo, Xsara Picasso

Source: http://www.peugeot.com and www.citroen.com.

Exhibit 5 Some Strategic Alliances in the Automobile Industry

No	Companies	Year	Remarks
1	Fiat Auto and Tata Motors	2006	Tata Motors was to manage distribution and after-sales service for Fiat in India. Fiat, in turn, would provide access for Tata Motors to world markets.
2	Fiat Auto and Suzuki	2005	Fiat Motors and Suzuki co-developed an SUV. Suzuki was to use Fiat's 1.9 l diesel engines for its version of the SUV.
3	Nissan and Mitsubishi Motors	2000	Integration of forklift business of both companies—from product development to marketing.
4	Fiat Auto and General Motors	2000	Share engines as well as platforms and pool purchase and finance operations in Europe and Latin America.
5	Toyota and General Motors	1999	Joint research on fuel cell technology, joint operation of auto manufacturing plant in California.
6	Suzuki and General Motors	1987	Joint establishment and management of a company in Ingersoll, Canada. The objective of the alliance for Suzuki was to gain entry into the North American market, while GM attempted to gain insights into Japanese manufacturing methods and management.

Compiled from various sources.

other automobile companies took the cue from PSA and entered into alliances and partnerships with their competitors (refer to Exhibit 5 for alliances in the auto industry).

PSA and Renault S.A

PSA and Renault had a series of agreements that involved several joint industrial and technological projects. As noted above, Peugeot and Renault first collaborated in 1966 when the two companies entered into a cooperation agreement for the joint production of mechanical subassemblies. In 1969, the two companies further strengthened their partnership by establishing a joint venture—La Française de Mécanique (LFM)—to produce long-series components and engines that were to be used in Peugeot and Renault cars. The 50:50 joint venture was located in Douvrin, in northern France. In the same year a limited company called Société de Transmissions Automatiques (STA), owned 80 percent by Renault and 20 percent by Peugeot, was founded. STA was established primarily to produce automatic transmissions for Renault and rear-axle assemblies for Peugeot. The STA plant was located in Ruitz in northern France.

In 1971, Peugeot, Renault, and Volvo[14] came together to design a V6 engine.[15] The three automobile makers formed an equally owned company called Peugeot Renault Volvo (PRV). The engines were manufactured by LFM and by 1974, they were being used in the Peugeot 504 and 604, and the Renault 30. However, in 1989, Volvo pulled out from PRV. As a result, Peugeot and Renault became 50 percent partners in the company.

In 1992, PSA entered into a fresh technological and industrial agreement with Renault to develop a new series of automatic transmissions. Meanwhile, LFM continued to develop improved versions of the V6 engines. In 1996, LFM introduced the new V6 ES 9 engine for mid-range and high-end Renault cars, the Peugeot 406, and the Citroën Xantia and XM models. Again in 1997, the self-acting automatic transmission—BVA—was jointly developed by PSA and Renault, with each company bearing FRF 2.8 billion as development costs. The transmission was manufactured at the STA plant in Ruitz and Peugeot's plant in Valenciennes.

In 2000, PSA and Renault launched an improved three-liter version of the V6 ES 9 engine. The new engine was installed in mid-range and high-end Renault, Peugeot, and Citroën cars and multipurpose vehicles. The LFM plant manufactured about 27,000 V6 ES 9 engines in 2000.

Fiat Auto SpA

PSA's strategic relationship with Fiat started in 1978 when the two companies signed their first cooperation agreement to design and manufacture a light commercial vehicle. A joint venture, Société Européenne de Véhicules Légers (Sevel SpA), owned 50 percent by Fiat, 25 percent by Automobiles Peugeot, and 25 percent by Automobiles Citroën, was established for this purpose. The production of the vehicles (Fiat Ducato, Peugeot J5, and Citroën C25) began at Val di Sangro facility, near Pescara, Italy, in 1981. In 1988, the scope of the joint venture with Fiat was expanded to include the design and production of multipurpose vehicles (MPVs).

In 1993, the Val di Sangro plant started the production of the Peugeot Boxer, and the Citroën Dispatch, both light commercial vehicles. The plant continued to manufacture Fiat Ducatos as well. In 1994, a new plant at Sevelnord, Valenciennes, France, began operations for the production of the Peugeot 806, the Citroën Synergie, and the Fiat Ulysses and Lancia Z (Zeta). The agreement between PSA and Fiat required the partners to manage the plants located in their country of origin (i.e., the Val di Sangro plant was managed by Fiat and the Sevelnord plant was managed by PSA). PSA and Fiat owned 50 percent in each plant and shared the production capacity equally. In 1995, the Sevelnord plant started production of the Peugeot Expert, the Citroën Relay, and the Fiat Scudo light commercial vehicles.

In 2002, PSA declared that its collaboration with Fiat in the development of light commercial vehicles would be extended through 2017 making it one of the most enduring alliances in the automobile industry. PSA and Fiat signed a major framework agreement that outlined various aspects of the collaboration. PSA and Fiat were to invest around €1.7 billion to manufacture two lines of light commercial vehicles.

In 2005, Tofas, a Turkey-based automobile manufacturer, entered into an agreement with PSA and Fiat, making it a three-way collaboration. The agreement involved the development and production of small, entry-level light commercial vehicles. The new models were to expand the product ranges of Peugeot, Citroën, and Fiat. They were to be manufactured at Tofas's plant in Bursa, Turkey, and were to be launched in 2008.

As of 2005, the PSA-Fiat partnership had jointly produced, since 1978, a total of 3.3 million light commercial vehicles and 400,000 multipurpose vehicles.

Ford Motor Co.

PSA's cooperation with Ford began in September 1998. The two automakers announced a large-scale agreement to jointly develop four families of small diesel engines incorporating the latest technologies, including Common Rail Direct injection (CRDi).[16] The initial announcement put the development time for the new engines at two and a half years. In 1999, the initial agreement was expanded to include an extended range of small aluminum direct injection diesel engines for cars and light commercial vehicles. The new agreement also included technological upgrades of a midsized second generation engine and a range of V-diesel engines for the luxury vehicles of both companies. PSA and Ford shared the total cost of the project equally. The partnership with Ford developed in four phases.

In 2001, in the first phase, PSA and Ford unveiled the first direct injection diesel engine developed under the cooperation agreements, which replaced the TUD[17] range of engines. The 1,398 cc engines were sold as HDi 1.4 by PSA and Duratorq TDCi 1.4 by Ford. The engines were mounted on the Peugeot 206 and 307, the Citroën C2 and C3, and the Ford Fiesta and Fusion. Both companies identified 23 applications for the new engine family. The production of the engines at the Douvrin plant saw high productivity levels with daily production reaching 6,000 engines. As part of the first phase, a new 1.6-liter (1,590 cc) common rail diesel engine was also launched.

In early 2003, PSA and Ford introduced a 2-liter CRDi diesel engine (1,988 cc) developed in the second phase of their cooperative venture. These engines were manufactured at PSA's Trémery plant. The high-performance and low-noise engines were reportedly more fuel-efficient and cleaner than those available in the market. The aggregate investment for the development of the engines came to nearly €1 billion.

The first two phases of the cooperation were carried out under the leadership of PSA; the third and fourth phases were led by Ford. In June 2003, as part of the third phase, a new 2.7-liter V6 24-valve engine was unveiled. Production of the engine began in the following months. The engine was first mounted on the Jaguar S-Type. Subsequently, it was used in the Peugeot 607, the Land Rover Discovery, the Range Rover Sport, the Jaguar XJ, the Peugeot 407 Coupe, and the Citroën C6.

In October 2005, under the fourth phase of their cooperation, PSA and Ford started the production of a new series of 2.2-liter CRDi diesel engines for light and medium commercial vehicles. In addition, they introduced a new 2.2-liter HDi/TDCi diesel engine that was eventually mounted on several Peugeot, Citroën, and Ford upper /medium and executive passenger car platforms. The engines were produced at the Trémery plant. The HDi/TDCi engine showcased the companies' ability to work together in developing high-performance diesel engines (see Table 1).

Table 1 A Comparison of Different Manufacturers' Diesel Engines

Manufacturer	Engine	Max. Power (PS)	Max. Torque (Nm)	Vehicles
PSA/Ford	2.7-L V6	207@4000 rpm	440@1900 rpm	Jaguar S-Type, Peugeot 607
Isuzu	3.0-L V6	180@4000 rpm	370@1900 rpm	Saab: 9; Renault: Vel Satis; Opel: Vectra & Signum
Volkswagen	2.5-L V6	180@6200 rpm	370@1500 rpm	Audi A6
DaimlerChrysler	3.2-L I6	204@4200 rpm	500@1800 rpm	Mercedes E- and S-class

Source: http://www.autoreport.com.

In all, PSA and Ford jointly produced four families of CRDi diesel engines, namely 1.4-liter/1.6-liter engines, a second-generation 2-liter engine, a 2.7-liter V6 engine, and a new family of engines for light commercial vehicles. The cooperation made PSA-Ford the world's leading diesel engine manufacturer. By 2005, they were jointly manufacturing more than 9,000 engines a day.

Toyota Motor Corp.

In July 2001, PSA and Toyota signed a cooperation agreement in Brussels, Belgium, to establish a joint venture company. Toyota Peugeot Citroën Automobile (TPCA) Czech was established for the joint development and production of small cars designed mainly for the European market. The companies also announced that the small cars developed by the joint venture would be priced below the entry-level cars of the two partners, which meant that the factory for the production of these cars had to be established in a low-cost country and meet stringent requirements. After an extensive search, Kolin in the Czech Republic was identified as the location for the plant. The plant started production of Toyota, Peugeot, and Citroën branded cars in 2005. The capacity of the plant was 300,000 vehicles per year, with 100,000 cars for each of the brands—Peugeot, Citroën, and Toyota.

Toyota was in charge of development and production, while PSA was responsible for purchasing and logistics. The total investment, primarily for R&D and industrial expenditure, of about €1.5 billion, was shared between the two automakers.

BMW AG

In 2002, PSA entered into a cooperation agreement with BMW to jointly develop and produce an all-new family of small 4-cylinder petrol engines incorporating the latest technologies. In June 2005, PSA and BMW presented the industrial plan for production of the engines. The engines were later used in Peugeot and Citroën cars and by Mini[18] (wholly owned by BMW). While the main engine was manufactured solely at PSA's Douvrin plant in Northern France, the engine assembly was done at Douvrin for PSA and Hams Hall in the United Kingdom for the Mini. PSA and BMW implemented a coordinated process to enable complete transparency between the two engine plants in order to deal effectively with any quality issues. PSA's Charleville and Mulhouse Metallurgy Division plants were assimilated into the industrial plan as suppliers of raw castings.

The design and development of the engine was done largely by BMW. PSA provided the logistics support for production of the engines. A complete production module was brought on line in late 2005 at the Francaise de Mecanique plant in Douvrin. The module was based on the development of a highly integrated, independent production unit that could easily be replicated on other sites. The plant was designed to produce 2,500 units a day. The first module, with an investment of €330 million, produced an engine every 26 seconds. At its maximum production capacity, overall annual production was expected to reach 1 million units. At full capacity, the module employed 1,120 employees, working in four shifts.

The cooperation resulted in a number of innovations.[19] The engines set new standards in performance, driving comfort, fuel economy, and CO_2 emissions.

Mitsubishi Motor Corporation

In February 2005, PSA and Mitsubishi announced a cooperation agreement for a new SUV, with 30,000 vehicles to be produced every year in Japan and to be sold under the Peugeot and Citroën marques. The SUV model, which was expected to roll out by 2007, was to be styled differently for the Peugeot and the Citroën versions. However, the two versions were to be equipped with the latest HDi diesel engines. Initially, the SUVs were to be marketed only in Europe. However, the two companies were expected to enter other markets in the future.

The Rationale Behind the Alliances

In the 1990s and 2000s, intense competition in the auto industry led to a wave of consolidation. Several auto companies bought stakes in their competitors. For example, DaimlerChrysler bought a 37 percent stake in Mitsubishi, Ford bought a 33 percent stake in Mazda, GM held a 20 percent stake in Fiat Auto, and Renault acquired a 44 percent stake in Nissan. PSA did not make any effort to buy or acquire stakes in other auto companies. "We can definitely get by on our own,"[20] Folz said. PSA, however, concentrated on entering into strategic alliances to counter the challenges posed by its competitors. A major advantage of such strategic alliances over a merger or acquisition was that PSA did not have to look for massive debt financing and experience years of inefficiencies due to duplications in manufacturing. PSA entered joint ventures mostly with strong players: Ford, Renault, Toyota, and BMW. And the purpose of these alliances was to share costs and investments and create synergies.

PSA believed that an important factor for success was the ability to bring out a variety of models with minimum costs. Folz said, "The key to succeeding in this car market is to rapidly produce cars as varied and attractive as possible and to do that at a competitive cost."[21] PSA's alliances with Toyota and Fiat helped it to expand its product range. At the same time, by sharing the costs and risks, it was able to provide more choice to its customers with minimum investment.

PSA's strategic alliances were also meant to achieve economies of scale, which in turn helped lower per unit costs and risks. The company brought out several models of cars based on a single platform using its superior styling and design skills to differentiate the models. Folz said, "The key to survival in the car industry today is not to produce three, four, or five million cars. The real challenge is one's ability to produce a maximum number of cars on a limited number of platforms. That's what we're trying to do."[22] The alliances with Toyota for small cars and with Fiat for light commercial vehicles served to create new platforms, which would be used to launch several future models.

PSA's alliances with Renault, Ford, and BMW helped it develop engines with the latest technology, something that it might have found it difficult to manage alone. The alliances were successful in creating synergies between PSA and its partners. Owing to its alliances with the major players, PSA managed to remain at the forefront of engine technology.

The shared costs and risks helped PSA not only to price its cars competitively but also enjoy higher margins. Even though Volkswagen, the market leader and PSA's rival in the European market, had a profit margin of less than 1 percent[23] in 2004, PSA enjoyed a margin as high as 4 percent in the same period.

Apart from sharing costs, risks, and investments, strategic alliances also helped PSA to acquire and develop new technologies. In the joint venture with Toyota, though the production was controlled by Toyota, 10 managers from PSA were stationed at the plant, providing them with the opportunity to learn about the world-renowned production system followed by Toyota. This experience was expected to improve the production system at PSA in the future.

PSA also seemed to be reaping unexpected rewards from its joint ventures. A case in point was again its joint venture with Toyota for the Peugeot 107, Citroën C1, and Toyota Ayga city cars. Toyota was known the world over for the superior quality and dependability of its cars. The high quality was the direct result of the famed Toyota Production System (TPS). On the other hand, PSA cars didn't figure very high on dependability, as evidenced by their poor customer satisfaction scores and low resale values. (See Table 2 for the 2005 J.D. Power and Associates' customer satisfaction index.) Analysts however expected the 107 and C1 cars to have higher resale values owing to Toyota's involvement in their production.

Table 2 2005 J.D. Power & Associates Customer Satisfaction Index

Rank	Brand	Score
1	Lexus	84.8
4	Toyota	83.5
	Industry Average	78.6
26	Citroën	76.6
30	Peugeot	74.6

Source: http://www.motor.org.uk.

The success of any alliance depends to a large degree on the partners having similar goals and common interests (refer Exhibit 6 for a short note on making alliances work). In the case of PSA's joint ventures, the alliances were as beneficial to the other partner as to PSA. For example, the former president of Toyota Motor Europe, Shuhei Toyoda, who was part of the negotiations with PSA, said, "We needed a partner to get the right volume for costs."[24] And the volumes were achieved by entering into a joint venture with PSA.

Exhibit 6 Making Alliances Work

The success of an alliance depends on three main factors: partner selection, alliance structure, and the way in which the alliance is managed.

Partner Selection: The choice of partner can make or break the alliance. In other words, the strength and success of the alliance depends to a large extent on the partner's characteristics. A good partner helps an organization achieve its strategic goals, which could be to share costs, risks, and investment concerning new product development or to gain access to technology. Additionally, a good partner would have similar expectations for the alliance. And finally, a good partner would not exploit the alliance unfairly.

Alliance Structure: The structure of the alliance also has a bearing on the success and duration of the alliance. Issues such as percentage of ownership, mix of financing, technology, and machinery to be contributed by each partner figure prominently. The alliance should be designed in such a way that it is difficult to transfer technology that was not part of the agreement. Contractual safeguards should be included in the alliance to guard against risk of opportunism by a partner.

Managing the Alliance: The management of the alliance should be based on mutual trust. Such trust can be achieved by building interpersonal relationships between the managers/workforce of the partners. A major determinant of success of an alliance is the ability of partners to learn from each other. In most cases, learning takes place at the lower levels of the organizations. Therefore, the lower-level employees must be informed about the partner's strengths and weaknesses and taught the importance of learning particular skills from the partner so as to improve the competitiveness of the organization.

Source: Adapted from *Introduction to Business Strategy*, ICMR.

Going It Alone

PSA was well aware that in an increasingly competitive market, it could sell more only if its vehicles were superior, distinct and offered unique advantages. Therefore, in spite of its many alliances, PSA was investing in excess of €2 billion in exclusive research & development facilities and projects. Pascal Henault, vice president (Innovation and Quality) said, "Innovation is a way to differentiate our cars in terms of concepts, styling and features that deliver perceptible customer benefits at affordable cost."[25] At its R&D centers at Belchamp La Garenne-Colombes and Velizy, hundreds of engineers and scientists were working toward new and innovative solutions, with the result that PSA filed more than 300 patents every year. In October 2004, PSA unveiled a new design center named Automobile Design Network near Paris to give a further thrust to its research initiatives.

PSA's research and development efforts were based on a "Research and Innovation Plan" that was an integrated and comprehensive system of research projects covering every area of automobile development. For example, PSA engaged scientists to improve the ergonomics, architecture, production process, and other aspects of its vehicles.

At a strategic level, PSA adopted a product policy wherein it focused its research efforts particularly on three critical areas: safety, fuel economy, and comfort. To improve the safety of its vehicles, the company conducted research on driver-support, anti-skid, and emergency braking systems. It was also working on energy-absorbing deformable mechanical structures. Fuel economy was another area on which the company focused its research efforts. Diesel and petrol engines with improved mileage, fuel cell technology, and hydrogen storage systems[26] were some of the research projects in which PSA was engaged. Driver-vehicle interface ergonomics was another area of focused research for PSA. The objective was to enhance driving pleasure and comfort.

Challenges

Volkswagen was the undisputed leader (in terms of the number of cars sold) in the European car market in 2005. Even though PSA continued to retain its second position in Europe, the gap with Volkswagen was widening. Volkswagen managed to increase its market share from 18.6 percent in 2004 to 19.3 percent in 2005, while PSA's share fell from 13.8 percent to 13.5 percent. Though Toyota was a distant eighth in the rankings, it had improved its sales in a shrinking market.[27] Moving toward its goal of capturing 15 percent of the world automobile market by 2010, Toyota was intensifying its efforts in Europe—an important market for the carmaker.

PSA's strength was in compact cars, which were hugely popular in most countries in Europe, its traditional market. However, the Japanese players (especially Toyota and Honda) were increasingly targeting the same segment. Even DaimlerChrysler and BMW were expanding their product ranges to include small cars.

PSA received a mere 15 percent of its revenues from outside Western Europe. In other markets where PSA had a presence, the company was not doing too well. In China, GM and Volkswagen were ruling the roost.[28] PSA's market share in China was stuck at about 5 percent over several years. And in India the company was not even present. However, its sales in Russia and Brazil were picking up (refer to Exhibit 7 for PSA's international presence).

Though PSA collaborated with its competitors, it was also sometimes critical of them. For example, PSA criticized some technologies introduced by Toyota. PSA was of the opinion that the Prius gasoline-electric hybrid car introduced by Toyota in the early 2000s was high-priced. The high price resulted in low sales, which it felt didn't do much to help the environment. "When you are not satisfying the mass market you are simply not doing

Exhibit 7 PSA's Worldwide Production Sites

Country	Production Site	Output (2004)
Brazil	Rio de Janeiro	50,000
Argentina	Buenos Aires	70,000
United Kingdom	Ryton	180,000
France	Rennes	292,000
	Sevelnord	162,300
	Mulhouse	379,100
	Sochaux	430,000
	Poissy	302,400
	Aulnay	418,380
Portugal	Mangualde	53,450
Spain	Madrid	138,100
	Vigo	458,550
Italy	Val di Sangro	183,195
China	Wuhan	141,000#
Iran^	Tehran	293,000
Morocco^	Casablanca	8,000
Indonesia^	Jakarta	500
Turkey^	Bursa	n.a
Nigeria^	Kaduna	n.a
Egypt^	Cairo	n.a
Czech Republic	Kolin	105,000+
Slovakia*	Trnava	n.a

Notes: ^ = assembly plant; * = will start operations in 2006; # = 2005 figure; n.a = not available.

Source: http://www.psa-peugeot-citroen.com.

the job," said Marc Boquet, a spokesman for PSA. "At PSA we produce advanced technology for everyone."[29]

Though PSA was considered a champion of alliances, analysts felt that competition from its partners in the future might affect its relationship with them. However, other analysts felt that the purpose of alliances was to lower costs and risks, and PSA was certainly reaping these benefits. Carlos Ghosn, chief executive for Renault talking about his company's alliances once said, "It [entering into alliances] doesn't mean that people will be complacent of each other. We're still competitors, and competing heavily. But at the same time we are business people. That means when an agreement makes sense it has to be done."[30]

In October 2005, PSA announced that its operating profits for the year 2005 would be less than 4 percent of sales (PSA traditionally enjoyed operating profits of close to 4.4 percent of sales). In January 2006, the company announced a second profit warning that put the operating profits at 3.4 percent of sales (refer to Exhibit 8 for PSA's financials). PSA saw its sales in the European market slide by 2.7 percent in 2005 (refer to Exhibit 9 for PSA's worldwide sales and production).

Exhibit 8 Financial Data of PSA Peugeot Citroën Consolidated Sales and Revenue (in millions)

	2004	2005
Automobile Division	45,239	45,071
Banque PSA Finance (car finance company)	1,601	1,656
Gefco (transportation and supply chain management company)	2,894	3,000
Faurecia (automotive equipment company)	10,719	10,978
Other Businesses	899	709
Intersegment Eliminations	(5,247)	(5,147)
Total	56,105	56,267
Consolidated Financial Highlights	**2004**	**2005**
Operating margin	2,481	1,940
Profit before tax and share in net earnings of companies at equity	2,439	1,530
Consolidated profit	1,680	990
Profit attributable to equity holders of the parent	1,646	1,029
Financial Position	**2004**	**2005**
Working capital	4,561	4,133
Gross capital expenditure	2,804	2,873
Equity	13,703	14,406
Net financial position of the manufacturing and sales companies	1,347	381
Number of employees	207,600	208,500

Source: http://www.psa-peugeot-citroen.com.

Exhibit 9 Worldwide Sales and Production of PSA

	2004	2005
Worldwide unit sales	3,375,300	3,389,900
Worldwide production	3,405,100	3,375,500

Source: http://www.psa-peugeot-citroen.com.

Exhibit 10 Europe Automobile Market Shares, 2005

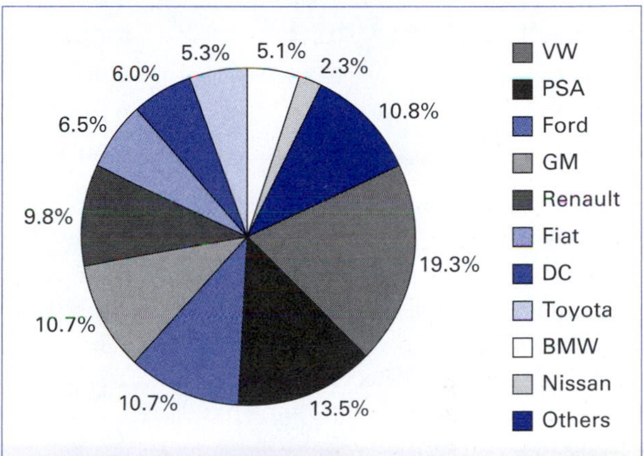

Compiled from various sources, and based on volume.

Exhibit 11 World Automobile Market, 2005

Region	Sales In 2005 (in million units)	Growth (% over previous year)
United States	7.60	1.4
Canada	0.84	3
Europe	15.22	–0.7
China	2.85	26.5

Source: Compiled from various sources.

Note: In 2005, the worldwide automobile market grew by 3.2 percent to 68.2 million passenger cars and light commercial vehicles. However, there was a marked difference in sales growth rates among different regions of the world. Owing to sluggish economic growth in several countries, the European automobile market shrank by about 3 percent. In the Central and East European market, after peaking in early 2004, a sharp decline occurred in 2005. Registrations in Poland slid 23.5 percent, and sales in Hungary slipped by 4.2 percent. The U.S. market showed growth with annual sales reaching 16.9 million units. The Canadian market grew by 3 percent to reach 1.58 million units. In Asia, the market expanded by 6.4 percent. The Latin American market rebounded with Brazil registering a healthy 9.5 percent. Argentina recorded a growth rate of 35.2 percent.

The 2005 full-year report, which was released in February 2006, showed a 37 percent drop in net profits compared to 2004. Intense competition (refer to Exhibit 10 for estimated market shares in 2005, and Exhibits 11 and 12 for general information on the world automobile market), a gloomy European economy, rising prices of gasoline, and an unfavorable product range were cited as reasons.

Exhibit 12 Estimated European Passenger Vehicle Sales by Company

Manufacturer	2005 Sales (in million units)	2004 Sales (in million units)
Volkswagen	2.944	2.853
PSA	2.061	2.122
Ford	1.628	1.686
GM	1.625	1.637
Renault	1.487	1.569
Fiat	0.988	1.129
DaimlerChrysler	0.914	0.922
Toyota	0.818	0.787
BMW	0.779	0.710
Nissan	0.357	0.381
Hyundai	0.317	0.313
Honda	0.259	0.236
Kia	0.242	0.173
Suzuki	0.234	0.204
Mazda	0.233	0.255
Mitsubishi	0.133	0.123
Others	0.195	0.225
Total	**15.222**	**15.332**

Compiled from various sources.

Exhibit 13 The Peugeot 207

Source: http://www.peugeot.com.

Outlook

The Peugeot 207 (refer to Exhibit 13 for a photograph of the Peugeot 207) was unveiled in early 2006, and was a successor to Peugeot 206—the company's most popular car ever. In 2005, PSA launched several models including the Peugeot 407 (saloon), the 407 coupe, the 1007 (a small car with electric sliding doors), the 107, the Citroën C1 city car, and the Citroën C6 luxury limousine.

In January 2006, PSA launched a new fuel cell called Genepac. Genepac was considered a major step in fuel cell technology because it could power a car for a distance of up to 500 kilometers, which was much more than all other fuel cells available in the market. However, it suffered from most other drawbacks that made fuel cells unviable. The 80 KW cell was the size of a large suitcase which made it difficult to use in ordinary passenger cars. Moreover, the cost of manufacturing the cells was too high. PSA was conscious of the problems but felt that the technology had potential. Folz stated in a news conference, "This technology is still at its early stages but offers a real answer for the future."[31] The company promised that it would try and halve the price of the cells by 2010. It would also make efforts to make the cell more compact.

PSA's explicitly stated policy of cooperation and collaboration with independent auto companies was seen by the company as the best way to counter the challenges posed by globalization and its larger competitors. At the same time, the company was making sure that it secured competitive advantages by going solo on several vital research projects. This dual strategy demonstrated obvious advantages. At one level, PSA reaped benefits such as higher margins, lower development costs and less time to market new models. In Folz's words, "These 'win-win' agreements allow us to share development and production costs without renouncing our independence, and to pool skills and expertise. They also generate the economies of scale we need to be competitive, by speeding our development and increasing production capacity. In addition, such cooperations offer many opportunities to learn about each other's culture and processes."[32] At another level, the strategy allowed PSA maintain its lead in technology and thus enhance its competitiveness.

Notes

1. 2003, Different brands, common strategy, http://www.zr.ru, April.
2. Mitsubishi Motor Co. launched its first passenger cars in 1917. Until 1970, the company was part of Mitsubishi Heavy Industries (MHI), which was founded by Tsukomo Shokai in 1870. In the 2000s, Germany-based DaimlerChrysler acquired a 37 percent share in the company.
3. Renault, the French automobile maker, was founded by Louis Renault in 1898. As of September 2005, the Renault group revenues touched €30.8 billion (nine-month period).
4. FIAT or Fabbrica Italiana Automobili Torino, the Italian automaker, was founded in July 1899 by a group of investors. In the 2000s,

the company faced a severe financial crisis with losses touching $1.2 billion, which necessitated a major restructuring exercise.

5. Ford was founded in 1903 by Henry Ford and a group of investors. In 2004, the company reported a loss of $155 million in its automotive business.
6. Toyota, the Japanese automaker, was established in 1937. The company has grown to become the second largest auto manufacturer in the world with net income crossing ¥1,171 billion in 2004–2005.
7. BMW or Bayerische Motoren Werke was founded in 1913 as Rapp Motoren Werke by an engineer Karl Friedrich Rapp. In 1917, the name was changed to BMW. The company caters to the premium segment and in 2004, its net profit had reached £2.2 billion.
8. The general shape of the "V" character, or a triangular shape pointing upwards/downwards, is referred as chevron.
9. The black cruise, described as "a great route to a great isle," was a 28,000-kilometer trip undertaken by Georges-Marie Haardt and his team. The expedition, which started at Colomb-Bechar in Algeria, passed through Niger, Chad, Oubangui-Chari (Central African Republic), and the Belgian Congo (Democratic Republic of Congo). At Kampala, the team split into four groups and reached Tananarive in Madagascar, each taking a different route (Mombasa, Dar-es-salam, Mozambique, and the Cape).
10. The yellow cruise was meant to open up the old "Silk Route" (an ancient trade route that connected China, Persia, Arabia, and Europe) to cars. The 30,000-kilometer trip started in Beirut, Lebanon, and passed through the Pamir region (Central Asia). Another group, which started in Tien Tsin (Tianjin, China), joined the Pamir group at Aksu (Xinjiang Uygur, China) and together proceeded to Peking (Beijing).
11. Chrysler Motor Corporation was established in 1925 by Walter P. Chrysler. The company merged with Daimler Benz in 1998 to form DaimlerChrysler. In 2004, DaimlerChrysler's revenues exceeded US$ 192 billion.
12. Societe Industrielle de Mecanique et Carrosserie Automobile or SIMCA was founded by Henri Pigozzi in Nanterre, France, in 1934. Initially, the company produced FIAT models under a license agreement. Subsequently, with the success of its Aronde models, the company's dependence on FIAT decreased. In the 1950s, the company acquired automobile companies such as Unic, Automobiles Talbot, and the French arm of Ford. In 1963, Chrysler bought a majority stake in Simca.
13. Sunbeam Motorcar Company Ltd. was established in 1905 by John Marston. In 1920, it merged with Darracq, a French automobile company. Darracq had earlier acquired Clement-Talbot Ltd, a London-based automobile company. STD Motors Ltd (where STD stood for Sunbeam-Talbot-Darracq) was created as the holding company. In 1935, due to financial problems, Clement-Talbot Ltd was sold to the Rootes Group. Soon, Rootes also purchased Sunbeam. In 1967, Chrysler took complete control of the Rootes Group.
14. Until 1998, Volvo Cars was part of AG Volvo. AG Volvo was founded in August 1926 in Gothenburg, Sweden. Volvo Cars was acquired by Ford in 1998.
15. V6 engine is a V engine with six cylinders. A V engine is a common configuration for an internal combustion engine wherein the pistons are aligned so that they appear to be in a V when viewed along the line of the crankshaft. (Source: http://www.wikipedia.org.)
16. CRDi is a modern variant of direct fuel injection system for diesel engines. It features a high-pressure (1000+bar) fuel rail feeding individual solenoid valves as opposed to mechanical valves.
17. The PSA TU engines were a family of small four cylinder engines used in Peugeot and Citroen cars. The first TU engine was introduced in 1987. They came in petrol and diesel variants. The diesel variant was referred as TUD.
18. Mini is a wholly owned subsidiary of BMW since 2001. It manufactures the MINI, a small car, which is a retro redesign of the classic Mini—a car made by British Motor Corporation from 1959 to 2000.
19. The innovations that came out of the alliance included the lost foam process for cylinder heads, pressurized aluminium casings with cast-iron jackets inserted into the casting, steel crankshafts with unmachined counterweights, connecting rods forged using the double impression method, and so on.
20. Radu Boghici, 1999, France's Peugeot on look-out for joint ventures, http://www.vectorbd.com, April 15.
21. C. Tierney, 2000, Can Peugeot go it alone? http://www.businessweek.com, April 17.
22. R. Boghici, 1999, France's Peugeot on look-out for joint ventures, http://www.vectorbd.com, April 15.
23. 2005, Volkswagen brakes for epic change, http://www.businessweek.com, July 25.
24. 2005, Revved up for battle, http://www.businessweek.com, January 10.
25. Strategy, 2004 Annual Report, http://www.psa-peugeot-citroen.com.
26. As part of its research on fuel cell technology, PSA designed two demonstrators powered by fuel cells—the TaxiPAC and H_2O. The TaxiPAC system uses hydrogen stored on board the vehicle. This system requires further refinement, and PSA was conducting research on making the hydrogen storage system safer and more efficient.
27. According to ACEA, the total light vehicle registrations in Europe (26 countries) in 2004 were 1.11 million. In 2005, the registrations dropped to 1.07 million.
28. In the first half of 2005, with 10.9 percent and 9.25 percent market shares, GM and Volkswagen (through their joint ventures) were the market leaders (in terms of sales) in the Chinese automobile industry.
29. J. Kanter, 2005, Toyota leads Asia drive in Europe, http://www.iht.com, July 23.
30. J. Madslien 2002, French car maker takes on the world, http://www.bbc.co.uk, October 9.
31. 2006, PSA Peugeot Citroën unveils small fuel cell, http://www.fuelcelltoday.com, January 10.
32. 2005, Citroën: Strength through cooperation, http://www.citroen.com, July 11.

Additional Readings and Reference

1. 2006, PSA Peugeot Citroen to sell diesel hybrids in 2010, http://www.planetark.com, February 1.
2. 2006, PSA Peugeot Citroen "cautiously optimistic" about 2006, http://www.just-auto.com, January 18.
3. 2006, Peugeot launches new 207 small car line, http://www.greencarcongress.com, January 12.
4. J. Marsden, 2006, Poor car sales lead PSA to cut outlook, http://www.icbirmingham.co.uk, January 12.
5. 2006, PSA Peugeot Citroen unveils small fuel cell, http://www.fuelcelltoday.com, January 10.
6. J. Kanter, 2005, Toyota leads Asia drive in Europe, http://www.iht.com, July 23.
7. 2005, Ford and PSA Peugeot Citroen strengthen diesel cooperation, http://www.media.ford.com, October 5.
8. 2005, Peugeot deal boosts Mitsubishi, http://www.bbc.co.uk, February 4.
9. 2005, Revved up for battle, http://www.businessweek.com, January 10.
10. D. Huq, 2004, Toyota and PSA Peugeot Citroën unveil jointly developed cars, http://www.jcnnetwork.com, December 2.
11. 2003, Different brands, common strategy.
12. 2002, BMW and PSA form joint engine project, http://www.all4engineers.com, October 18.
13. J. Madslien, 2002, French car maker takes on the world, http://www.bbc.co.uk, October 9.
14. 2002, PSA Peugeot Citroën and Toyota announce the name of new joint-venture company, http://www.toyota.com, January 10.

15. 2000, PSA Peugeot Citroen and Ford Motor Company announce cooperation in telematics in Europe, http://www.ford.com, September 27.
16. C. Tierney, 2007, Can Peugeot go it alone? http://www.businessweek.com, April 17.
17. 1999, PSA aims to form joint venture with Japan's Koyo Seiko, http://www.bloomberg.com, November 25.
18. 1999, J.-M. Lamy, Renault, Puegeot-Citroën, Michelin: Three flagships of the French motor industry, April.
19. 1998, PSA launches mega depot joint venture, http://www.worldcargonews.com, July.
20. Mergers, takeovers and product differentiation, http://www.bized.ac.uk.
21. Engines: Peugeot (PSA Peugeot Citroën), http://www.grandprix.com.
22. http://www.psa-peugeot-citroen.com.
23. http://www.all4engineers.com.
24. http://www.media.ford.com.

Case 24

Sun Microsystems

Scott Jacobs, Prescott C. Ensign

The University of Western Ontario

Press Release

The fourth quarter ended June 30, 2005. On July 26, 2005, Sun Microsystems unveiled fiscal year (FY) 2005 results: Q4 revenues were US$2.98 billion (2004 Q4 revenues were US$3.11 billion, but had included income of US$1.6 billion from a legal settlement with Microsoft); for the full fiscal year 2005, Sun Microsystems reported revenues of US$11.07 billion (FY2004 revenues were US$11.19 billion).

Sun Microsystems' chief financial officer (CFO), Steve McGowan, commented, "We achieved impressive operational improvements in fiscal 2005 . . . our 16th consecutive year of generating positive cash flow from operations." Sun Microsystems employees, investors, and analysts recognized that Bill Gates had helped out last year. But what explained this year? Perhaps Sun was righting itself?

"Putting our cash to work, we've expanded our product portfolio and announced plans to acquire companies that deepen and broaden our systems strategy. We've maintained our R&D commitment and delivered crown jewels like Solaris 10 to the market," said Scott McNealy, chair and chief executive officer (CEO) of Sun Microsystems. "Big-time progress in FY05. The company is now in a position to take advantage of the investments we have made over the past few years and we believe there is more to come in FY06."

McNealy continued, "Our demand indicators for Q4 were positive. We have great partners, lots of cash, and a strong team across the board. FY05 was a year of stabilized revenue and earnings. Our opportunity for FY06 is sustained growth and profitability."

"Profitability?" was the incredulous reaction of many who had followed Sun's struggle.

A Strategic Crisis

At the beginning of 2004, Sun Microsystems found itself at a serious inflection point (see Exhibits 1, 2, and 3, on pages 306, 307, and 308, respectively). It had lost money in eight of the last 10 quarters. As its market share slipped, again, this time from 12.1 percent in 2002 to 10.3 percent in 2003, Sun announced its largest product offering update in company history. The products were intended to stop the bleeding that had caused the company's share price to plummet to only one-tenth of its high value in 2000, a decline that in 2003 raised speculation of a takeover. Scott McNealy, cofounder CEO & chair of the board of directors originally named the company Stanford Unified Networks in 1982.

Since developing the vision that had endured throughout the company's history, "The Network is the Computer," McNealy had come under great scrutiny as many industry analysts relentlessly questioned Sun's business-level strategy. Specifically, many doubted the effectiveness and competitiveness of the products that the company offered during its recent decline in profitability.

On December 8, 2004, Scott McNealy delivered a keynote address at an industry show in San Francisco, California. He relayed some statistics about Sun's Java platform: 579 million Java-enabled phones by the end of the year, almost 1 billion Java smart cards, and nearly 900 companies were now contributing to Java. He spoke of how the world had envisioned the computer 50 years prior and remarked, "It's hard to imagine where we'll be 50 years from now." Some in the audience members were scratching their heads wondering where Sun was headed in the near future.

Exhibit 1 Sun Microsystems Income Statement (US$ millions)

	1996	1997	1998	1999	2000	2001	2002	2003	2004	2005
Revenue	**$7,094.8**	**$8,598.4**	**$9,790.8**	**$11,726.3**	**$15,721.0**	**$18,250.0**	**$12,496.0**	**$11,434.0**	**$11,185.0**	**$11,070.0**
COGS	3,972.0	4,320.5	4,693.3	5,648.4	7,549.0	10,041.0	7,580.0	6,492.0	6,669.0	6,481.0
Gross Profit	**3,122.7**	**4,277.9**	**5,097.5**	**6,077.9**	**8,172.0**	**8,209.0**	**4,916.0**	**4,942.0**	**4,516.0**	**4,589.0**
Operating Expenses										
Selling, General, and Administrative	1,732.7	2,402.4	2,777.3	3,173.0	4,137.0	4,544.0	3,812.0	3,329.0	3,317.0	2,919.0
Research and Development	657.1	826.0	1,190.2	1,383.2	1,642.0	2,093.0	1,835.0	1,841.0	1,996.0	1,785.0
Other	57.9	23.0	—	—	—	261.0	517.0	2,496.0	393.0	262.0
Operating Income	**675.0**	**1,026.5**	**1,130.1**	**1,521.8**	**2,393.0**	**1,311.0**	**(1,248.0)**	**(2,724.0)**	**(1,190.0)**	**(377.0)**
Other Income and Expenses										
Net Interest Income and Other	33.9	94.7	46.1	83.9	378.0	273.0	200.0	71.0	1,627.0	193.0
Earnings Before Taxes	**708.9**	**1,121.2**	**1,176.2**	**1,605.7**	**2,771.0**	**1,584.0**	**(1,048.0)**	**(2,653.0)**	**437.0**	**(184.0)**
Income Taxes	232.5	358.8	413.3	574.4	917.0	603.0	(461.0)	776.0	825.0	(77.0)
Earnings After Taxes	**476.4**	**762.4**	**762.9**	**1,031.3**	**1,854.0**	**981.0**	**(587.0)**	**(3,429.0)**	**(388.0)**	**(107.0)**
Accounting Changes						(54.0)				
Net Income	**476.4**	**762.4**	**762.9**	**1,031.3**	**1,854.0**	**927.0**	**(587.0)**	**(3,429.0)**	**(388.0)**	**(107.0)**
Diluted EPS Continuing Ops	0.2	0.3	0.2	0.3	0.6	0.3	(0.2)	(1.1)	(0.1)	(0.0)
Diluted EPS	0.2	0.3	0.2	0.3	0.6	0.3	(0.2)	(1.1)	(0.1)	(0.0)
Shares	3,147.0	3,111.0	3,154.0	3,256.0	3,378.0	3,417.0	3,242.0	3,190.0	3,277.0	3,368.0

Source: Company files.

Boom to Bust

In 1997, Thailand could no longer back its currency, the baht. High levels of debt and years of trade deficits had resulted in a spectacular crash in the value of the baht. The ensuing economic crisis engulfed most of Asia and spread throughout the entire world, slowing down economies from east to west. Most importantly for Sun, the crisis adversely impacted Japan, its largest single source of foreign revenue, at 9 percent.

The global economic collapse continued in January of 1999 when Brazil's currency, the real, was devalued. The devaluation dashed any immediate growth plans and delayed future growth there indefinitely. Brazil had been one of the countries on which Sun had been counting to lead information technology (IT) spending in South America.

The Brazilian and Asian financial crises provided compelling evidence that, even though Sun's diverse portfolio appeared to protect it from individual blips in economic stability, its product sales were highly sensitive to macroeconomic conditions. In 1998, the company reported that more than 45 percent of its revenues were generated outside of the United States. By 2003, Sun's reliance on foreign revenue had increased to more than 50 percent, and the economic crises had unfolded into a worldwide economic slowdown—with some analysts using the label "recession."

However, economic conditions alone did not lead to Sun's fall from profitability. Rather, the economic macro environment was a catalyst for change toward affordable enterprise computing. In addition, technological advancements led to performance improvements in the x86 platform.[1] Making use of these advances and using various sources of leverage to lower cost structures, many firms were able to offer products similar to Sun's, but at a fraction of the price.

Sun's expensive high-margin products lagged in demand while the company continued to present its same value proposition. To compound the adverse effect of developments in the x86 hardware space, Sun was also feeling competitive pressure from an inexpensive, and very controversial x86-based software product named Linux. This singular platform would change Sun's competitive environment drastically. Open source software on inexpensive standard hardware began to unravel Sun's offering: a product that bundled software, hardware, and service.

Exhibit 2 Sun Microsystems Cash Flows (US$ millions)

	1996	1997	1998	1999	2000	2001	2002	2003	2004	2005
Cash from Operating Activities										
Net Income	$476.4	$762.4	$762.9	$1,031.3	$1,854.0	$927.0	$(587.0)	$(3,429.0)	$(388.0)	$(107.0)
Depreciation/Amortization	284.1	341.7	439.9	627.0	776.0	1,229.0	1,092.0	918.0	730.0	671.0
Deferred Taxes	—	—	—	—	—	—	(673.0)	706.0	620.0	(315.0)
Other	(72.2)	0.9	323.7	858.6	1,124.0	(67.0)	1,048.0	2,842.0	1,264.0	120.0
Cash from Operations	**688.3**	**1,105.1**	**1,526.5**	**2,516.9**	**3,754.0**	**2,089.0**	**880.0**	**1,037.0**	**2,226.0**	**369.0**
Cash from Investing Activities										
Capital Expenditures	(295.6)	(554.0)	(830.1)	(738.7)	(982.0)	(1,292.0)	(559.0)	(373.0)	(249.0)	(257.0)
Purchase of Business	—	(23.0)	(244.0)	(130.3)	(89.0)	(18.0)	(49.0)	(30.0)	(201.0)	(95.0)
Other	170.9	33.3	(94.8)	(1,227.1)	(3,154.0)	(244.0)	647.0	(125.0)	(1,861.0)	(73.0)
Cash from Investing	**(124.7)**	**(543.7)**	**(1,169.0)**	**(2,096.1)**	**(4,225.0)**	**(1,554.0)**	**39.0**	**(528.0)**	**(2,311.0)**	**(425.0)**
Cash from Financing Activities										
Net Issuance of Stock	(467.5)	(374.8)	(190.8)	(242.7)	(285.0)	(899.0)	(354.0)	(317.0)	239.0	218.0
Net Issuance of Debt	—	—	—	—	1,500.0	—	(13.0)	(201.0)	(28.0)	(252.0)
Dividends	—	—	—	—	—	—	—	—	—	—
Other	18.9	(55.3)	(4.6)	88.7	4.0	(13.0)	—	—	—	—
Cash from Financing	**(448.6)**	**(430.1)**	**(195.5)**	**(154.0)**	**1,219.0**	**(912.0)**	**(367.0)**	**(518.0)**	**211.0**	**(34.0)**
Currency Adjustments	—	—	—	—	—	—	—	—	—	—
Change in Cash	115.0	131.3	162.1	266.7	748.0	(377.0)	552.0	(9.0)	126.0	(90.0)
Free Cash Flow										
Cash from Operations	688.3	1,105.1	1,526.5	2,516.9	3,754.0	2,089.0	880.0	1,037.0	2,226.0	369.0
Capital Expenditures	(295.6)	(554.0)	(830.1)	(738.7)	(982.0)	(1,292.0)	(559.0)	(373.0)	(249.0)	(257.0)
Free Cash Flow	**392.7**	**551.1**	**696.4**	**1,778.2**	**2,772.0**	**797.0**	**321.0**	**664.0**	**1,977.0**	**112.0**

Source: Company files.

Billion-Dollar Bets

In 2000, shares of Sun Microsystems hovered near US$60 per share. About that same time, Scott McNealy, CEO, put Masood Jabbar in charge of managing Sun's worldwide sales. McNealy was counting on Jabbar to formulate the right plan and strategy to capitalize on Sun's momentum and reputation for innovation. McNealy needed Jabbar to grow the business and build shareholder wealth.

In response, Jabbar developed a strategy that focused on five countries that were each potential billion-dollar-a-year markets for Sun's server business. They were Brazil, Spain, China, India, and Italy. Shareholders were optimistic about Sun's potential for growth.

Although shareholders responded positively to Sun's future, managers of the U.S. business at Sun's Palo Alto, California, headquarters were getting tense. It seemed as though a meeting could not take place without attention being diverted from the U.S. business toward conversations about foreign interest rates, political regimes, and foreign legal language. U.S. business managers simply could not have discussions on policy and strategy without some "foreign distractions." Many of the U.S. managers involved began to feel that those managers representing Mexico, South America, and Canada were muddying the waters with talk about fluctuating currency exchange rates and political instability. In fact, those territories accounted for less than a few percent of Sun's business at the time. The United States had nearly always accounted for roughly half of Sun's multibillion-dollar annual sales.

However, Jabbar's "billion-dollar bets" required that these emerging areas get attention in order to shift the distribution of sales. And yet, international managers felt they were getting little cooperation and support to expand business in their emerging markets. Jabbar also knew that under the current structure, U.S. managers could not focus on their own strategy and planning, which meant that a considerable portion of Sun's revenue could be threatened. The current organizational structure was just not working. Something at Sun had to change.

Jabbar approached Bob MacRitchie, who was managing the South American, Mexican, and Canadian lines of business under the umbrella of the U.S. organizational

Exhibit 3 Sun Microsystems Balance Sheet (US$ millions)

	1996	1997	1998	1999	2000	2001	2002	2003	2004	2005
Assets										
Cash and Equivalent	$528.9	$660.2	$822.3	$1,089.0	$1,849.0	$1,472.0	$2,024.0	$2,015.0	$2,141.0	$2,051.0
Short-Term Investments	460.7	452.6	476.2	1,576.1	626.0	387.0	861.0	1,047.0	1,460.0	1,345.0
Account Receivable	1,206.6	1,666.5	1,845.8	2,286.9	2,690.0	2,955.0	2,745.0	2,381.0	2,339.0	2,231.0
Inventory	460.9	438.0	346.5	307.9	557.0	1,049.0	591.0	416.0	464.0	431.0
Other Current Assets	376.6	511.2	656.8	856.5	1,155.0	2,071.0	1,556.0	920.0	899.0	1,133.0
Total Current Assets	**3,033.7**	**3,728.5**	**4,147.5**	**6,116.4**	**6,877.0**	**7,934.0**	**7,777.0**	**6,779.0**	**7,303.0**	**7,191.0**
Net Property, Plant, and Equipment	533.9	799.9	1,300.6	1,608.9	2,095.0	2,697.0	2,453.0	2,267.0	1,996.0	1,769.0
Intangibles						2,041.0	2,286.0	417.0	533.0	554.0
Other Long-Term Assets	233.3	168.9	262.9	695.1	5,180.0	5,509.0	4,006.0	3,522.0	4,671.0	4,676.0
Total Assets	**3,800.9**	**4,697.3**	**5,711.1**	**8,420.4**	**14,152.0**	**18,181.0**	**16,522.0**	**12,985.0**	**14,503.0**	**14,190.0**
Liabilities and Stockholders' Equity										
Accounts Payable	325.1	468.9	495.6	753.8	924.0	1,050.0	1,044.0	903.0	1,057.0	1,167.0
Short-Term Debt	87.6	100.9	47.2	1.7	7.0	3.0	205.0	—	257.0	—
Taxes Payable	134.9	118.6	188.6	402.8	422.0	90.0				
Accrued Liabilities	801.6	963.0	1,126.5	1,646.6	2,117.0	1,862.0	1,739.0	1,506.0	1,930.0	1,727.0
Other Short-Term Liabilities	140.2	197.6	265.0	422.1	1,289.0	2,141.0	2,069.0	1,720.0	1,869.0	1,872.0
Total Current Liabilities	**1,489.3**	**1,849.0**	**2,122.9**	**3,227.0**	**4,759.0**	**5,146.0**	**5,057.0**	**4,129.0**	**5,113.0**	**4,766.0**
Long-Term Debt	60.2	106.3			1,720.0	1,705.0	1,449.0	1,531.0	1,175.0	1,123.0
Other Long-Term Liabilities			74.6	381.6	364.0	744.0	215.0	834.0	1,777.0	1,627.0
Total Liabilities	**1,549.4**	**1,955.3**	**2,197.4**	**3,608.6**	**6,843.0**	**7,595.0**	**6,721.0**	**6,494.0**	**8,065.0**	**7,516.0**
Total Equity	**2,251.5**	**2,741.9**	**3,513.6**	**4,811.8**	**7,309.0**	**10,586.0**	**9,801.0**	**6,491.0**	**6,438.0**	**6,674.0**
Total Liabilities and Equity	**3,800.9**	**4,697.3**	**5,711.1**	**8,420.4**	**14,152.0**	**18,181.0**	**16,522.0**	**12,985.0**	**14,503.0**	**14,190.0**

Source: Company files.

division. The infrastructure was already in place. What remained was an official transition that emphasized Sun's commitment to pursuing its billion-dollar bets.

However, the transition itself was not easy. The same U.S. business managers who previously decried the waste of precious resources on those underperforming emerging markets felt a sense of loss they had not anticipated—a loss of power. "Egos were involved here," Jabbar explained. "It was hard to get those guys to give up the control."

Apart from being a functional decision, it was symbolic of the attention and commitment Sun would give to these emerging areas. Sun's strategy was to develop these billion-dollar bets in the midst of a booming economy that increasingly demanded enterprise computing products. Sun did not have to chase customers. The sales, it seemed, were coming to them. However, neither Sun nor any other company could contend with the competitive pressure created by the volatile nature of the new global economy.

Attack of the Giant Penguin—Linux

John Gantz, International Data Corporation's (IDC) chief research officer predicted that "Linux [would] eat Unix,"[2] in 2003. The irony was subtle—the Linux mascot was an innocuous penguin. Linux, an operating system named after its creator Linus Torvalds, took the enterprise computing industry by storm. Its open source, community approach to application creation was not only revolutionary in theory, but in practice as well.

Linux is open source, inexpensive, and scalable. Adoption of Linux products spread rapidly, especially internationally. In fact, countries outside the United States found Linux to be a viable alternative to Microsoft's Windows operating system, which many critics felt was unsecure and not readily scalable. In 2003, Brazil's government urged its federal agencies to adopt Linux in an effort to cut costs. Brazil represented no small piece of the pie; it imported more than US$1 billion more in software than it exported in 2001. Brazil was not alone.

China, Japan, and South Korea also switched to Linux to get IT spending under control.

Sun had resisted Linux for a long time because Sun designed its own operating system, Solaris. In addition, Sun's past success was due in large part to its strategy of integrating proprietary software (Solaris), hardware, and its own SPARC Unix microprocessor.[3] By developing not only its own microprocessors, but also its own operating system, the company could have complete control of the integration of the system hardware and software. This strategy ensured optimization and control over the entire design process. In effect, Sun created a lot of value for its customers through this integration. However, Sun's strategic focus on its operating system, Solaris, and its SPARC microprocessors prevented it from seeing the threat that Linux presented. Eventually, an x86 or Unix server running Linux offered customers a close substitute to Sun's products.

In February 2002, after years of denial, Sun Microsystems could no longer fend off the waves of criticism—it gave in to Linux. To demonstrate its commitment to Linux, Scott McNealy gave his keynote speech (in a penguin suit) at a Sun trade show to announce the company's new Linux products. Typically, Sun attacked other platforms by suggesting that they were not as reliable or did not offer the features of its own Unix servers. However, with the advent of Linux, users found a new, reliable, inexpensive choice to expensive Sun products.

The problem was serious. If Sun refused to offer Linux products, it would be cutting itself out of a considerable portion of the server market. Linux was dominating the inexpensive x86 server space. Yet, if Sun were to produce its own x86 products, it would have to purchase microprocessors from a third party for a new line of x86 hardware. Because essentially only one company was developing highly respected enterprise-level x86 microprocessors, Sun had few choices. Entering the x86 market would mean teaming up with a tried and true competitor—Intel.

For Sun, doing business with Intel would not only mean accepting the rise of Linux, but also the commoditization of enterprise computing, at least at the low end. Moreover, Sun's value proposition became increasingly diminished as the company lost control of the integration process. By using Intel chips, Sun would no longer offer value to customers through engineering and innovation as it had previously, but rather via an assembly of outsourced components. Although similar to some of Sun's competitors, that value proposition was a substantial departure from its original model. To counteract this change, Sun developed its own middleware, the Java Enterprise System, that would operate in Unix or Linux and offered a unique pricing model that made scalable enterprise computing more affordable.

In 2003, the People's Republic of China and Sun announced a deal. The arrangement was for 500,000 to 1 million copies per year of Sun's Java Enterprise System. Most industry observers believed the blockbuster result of this deal would not be the revenue, but rather the market share. Indeed the revenue would likely not be significant and would even take quite a while to capture, given the extended time frame of the agreement. With Java Enterprise System, Sun was trying to inject value into its offerings through research and development, one of Sun's competitive advantages.

Continuing to partner with Intel, however, remained a strategic disadvantage. After years of competition, joining forces and integrating development initiatives with Intel seemed unrealistic. Sun's future in the x86 space continued to look uncertain until November 2003, when Sun announced a newly formed strategic alliance with an emerging x86 microprocessor developer—AMD.

A New Entrant, Old Competitors, and Big Threats

In 2003, Advanced Micro Devices, also known as AMD, agreed to collaborate with Sun in a new strategic venture. By providing its x86-based Opteron chips for use in Sun's low-end servers, AMD stood to combat years of dominance by its rival Intel. AMD's new Opteron technology took its x86 technology to 64 bits,[4] a feat Intel had yet to master. In doing so, AMD became an industry leader. Along with that status came new friends. Sun was not the only firm to form an alliance with AMD—HP and IBM both struck similar deals, although seemingly less integrated than Sun's alliance.

Intel leveraged its technology, manufacturing capabilities, and market share in the PC space to produce chips able to compete in the enterprise computing domain, at least in the low-end segment. And it certainly did not suffer from diminishing relations with Sun. Dell capitalized in the low-end space by selling a large volume of servers running Linux on Intel. Finding operating efficiencies allowed Dell, the fourth largest server maker behind Sun, to turn the low-end server market into a battlefield by steadily dropping prices.[5]

Sun attempted to compete on the basis of price, but found it difficult to outprice companies such as Dell and even IBM, who reduced costs through sources of leverage, such as unit volume and consulting services, respectively. As a result, Sun was losing the low-end battle against Dell, IBM, and HP, and there continued to be little demand in the high-end for its expensive Unix servers. As if this situation were not bad enough, another competitor was posing a significant threat to Sun.

Japan's Fujitsu, ranked as the fifth largest server maker, licensed Sun's proprietary UltraSPARC chip designs to power its own SPARC64 chips found in its line of Unix servers. Fujitsu had great success in taking Sun's SPARC chips and turning them into more powerful SPARC64 Fujitsu chips—and winning Sun customers in the process. Fujitsu was much quicker to market than Sun, which was reliant on Texas Instruments to churn out its chips. The situation presented a difficult decision for Sun. Should it discontinue its relationship with Fujitsu or get in even tighter with the Japanese giant?

Sun Microsystems desperately needed the revenue from the licensing agreement, so it was extremely reluctant to cease the licensing contracts. To complicate matters further, Fujitsu was not only licensing Sun's chipset designs, it was also a leading reseller of Sun products. Fujitsu was more than a manufacturer; it served also as a reseller or channel partner. In fact, Fujitsu's role was significant. Sales to Fujitsu accounted for a large portion of Sun sales in Japan, Sun's leading foreign market in revenue terms.

Rumors surfaced in 2003 about a possible alliance or even merger with the Japanese firm. However, for Sun, forming a tighter alliance with Fujitsu might cause more problems than it would address. For instance, if Sun were to begin using the SPARC64 chips, it might mean spurning its long-standing chipproducing partner, Texas Instruments. Given a large installed base, such bridges were not to be burned hastily. Moreover, despite the fact that Sun and Fujitsu used the same instruction set for the microprocessors, Sun and Fujitsu products could not be used together without some reprogramming. Adopting the SPARC64 chips would mean massive reconstruction of its current products and the products it had in the pipeline, which suggested that Fujitsu would remain a competitor in the future.

Executive Exodus

A month-long executive exodus culminated with the chief operating officer (COO) and president Ed Zander resigning. He and four other high-level officers—all with at least 15 years each at Sun—departed effective July 1, 2002. The naysayers on Wall Street were having a field day: "The Captain goes down with the ship." McNealy was going to do it alone; he named no successor for the president and COO's position. Sun also now had vacancies for the vice president, two executive VPs, and the CFO. On July 18, 2002, it was announced that Masood Jabbar would retire from Sun after 16 years of service. The stock was at a 52-week low, hovering at about US$7 per share.

And things did get worse, at least according to the stock market. The share price slowly but steadily, in the coming years, fell to a mark below US$3. It would be almost two years before a president and COO was named, when the 38-year-old Jonathan Schwartz received the nod from McNealy in April 2004. Schwartz had come to Sun in 1996 when it acquired Lighthouse Design, Ltd.—the firm for which Schwartz was then CEO.

All Bets Are Off

Growth in the server industry was not flat by any means. IDC expected tech spending would increase in 2005 and beyond, regaining some of its lost momentum from the bubble burst of 2000.

Scott McNealy's vision of everything and everyone connected to the network was probably not that far from the eventual truth (see Exhibit 4). Yet, Sun's ability to determine the long-term direction of computing was more refined than its value-added strategy.

Exhibit 4 Sun Microsystems' Strategic Direction

A singular vision—The Network Is the Computer—guides Sun in the development of technologies that power the world's most important markets. Sun's philosophy of sharing innovation and building communities is at the forefront of the next wave of computing: the Participation Age.

VISION: Everyone and everything connected to the network.

Eventually every man, woman, and child on the planet will be connected to the network. So will virtually everything with a digital or electrical heartbeat—from mobile phones to automobiles, thermostats to razor blades with RFID tags on them. The resulting network traffic will require highly scalable, reliable systems from Sun.

MISSION: Solve complex network computing problems for governments, enterprises, and service providers.

At Sun, we are tackling complexity through system design. Through virtualization and automation. Through open standards and platform-independent Java technologies. In fact, we are taking a holistic approach to network computing in which new systems, software, and services are all released on a regular, quarterly basis. All of it integrated and pretested to create what we call the Network Computer.

Source: 2006 http://www.sun.com, February 11.

Most of Sun's billion-dollar bets that were developed by Masood Jabbar failed to materialize. In fact, Sun Microsystems was now desperate, fighting for revenue each quarter. In retrospect, Sun might have put the cart before the horse. Instead of focusing on the evolution of its competitive environment, it was distracted by the economic euphoria that reigned in the late 1990s. McNealy admitted, "Looking back, we probably hired too many people and signed too many leases, but we had a very natural and understandable desire to fill all the orders we could."

The network was still the computer, but recent product offerings and industry conferences suggested Sun Microsystems and especially McNealy had succumbed to some inevitable truths about the competitive environment of the industry. One was that the x86 platform was not going away as McNealy had once envisioned. It became clear that Sun's future strategy would include x86- and Linux-based products, as well as more compelling and competitive high-end Unix servers.

To sell Sun products, McNealy was banking on a healthy return on research and development. He asserted, "Sun is doing things that Intel isn't doing or AMD isn't doing." Innovation, however, was costly. Sun's R&D budget had been about US$2 billion annually for the last few years, dwarfing its competitors. Innovation was a key component of Sun's current strategy, but the results were not yet readily quantifiable. Still, McNealy claimed, "[Over the decade,] we're going to spend $20 billion to $30 billion minimum on R&D." Clearly, Sun was intent on continuing to add value through innovation rather than being relegated to a game of economies of scale and efficiencies.

Charles Cooper, editor of CNETNEWS.com, remarked, "[Sun's] strategy—if you can call it that—has been to throw a lot of stuff against the wall and wait to see what sticks." It was still hard to tell what the firm and specifically Scott McNealy were learning from the devolution of Sun's business. The well-known CEO admitted to strategic missteps but quipped, "I try to make a mistake only once. If your strategy isn't controversial, you have zero chance of making money. You have to have a wildly different strategy and you have to be right. It's that second part that gets tricky." McNealy recognized, "There's lots more to do." Now was the time to do it.

Notes

1. x86 hardware stands for x86 central processing units (CPUs) developed by Intel. This CPU forms the base of PCs. History of the chip: 286, 386, 486, 586 (dubbed Pentium), Pentium Pro, Pentium II, Celeron, Pentium III, Pentium IV, etc. Other manufacturers, such as Advanced Micro Devices (AMD) and Cyrix, have used the same CPU machine code with their own architecture to create equivalent chips, but with a lower price-to-performance ratio.
2. Unix software is an abbreviation for UNiplexed Information and Computing System, originally spelled "Unics." It is an interactive time-sharing operating system developed at Bell Labs in 1969. In the 1990s, Unix was the most widely used, multi-use, general-purpose operating system in the world. Unix is presently offered by many manufacturers and is the subject of international standardization efforts.
3. SPARC is an abbreviation for Scalable Processor ARChitecture, designed by Sun Microsystems in 1985. SPARC is not a chip per se, but a specification. The first standard product based on SPARC was produced by Sun and Fujitsu in 1986. In 1989, Sun transferred ownership of the SPARC specifications to an independent, nonprofit organization, SPARC International.
4. 64 bit is a computer architecture term, which refers to the bandwidth of the arithmetic logic unit, registers high-speed memory locations in the CPU and data bus (connections between and within the CPU, memory, and peripherals).
5. HP was the server market leader, followed by IBM.

Case 25

Teleflex Canada: A Culture of Innovation

Andrew C. Inkpen

Thunderbird, The Garvin School of International Management

Teleflex Canada, a division of Teleflex Inc., manufactured a range of products, including marine hydraulic steering systems, trim components for marine propulsion, heating equipment for both the truck and bus industries, a range of proprietary fluid controls, and field cookstoves for the U.S. Army. Over the past 30 years, Teleflex Canada grew from sales of a few million dollars to more than $160 million in 2004. The company has a reputation as a world leader in the design and manufacture of hydraulic and thermal technology products. Within Teleflex Canada was a consensus that continual innovation in product design, manufacturing, and marketing was critical to the success of the organization.

In 2005, Teleflex Canada executives were faced with various questions: Would size inhibit the ability to innovate? Would increased corporate centralization at Teleflex Inc. impact Teleflex Canada's ability to respond quickly to new market opportunities? At the Teleflex Inc. corporate level, different questions were being asked: Could the culture of innovation in Teleflex Canada be transferred to other parts of the company? What was the appropriate level of corporate support and control necessary to foster innovation and high performance at Teleflex Canada and at other Teleflex business units?

Teleflex Inc.

Teleflex Inc., a diversified manufacturing company was headquartered in Limerick, Pennsylvania, just outside Philadelphia. The company had three principal business segments: Commercial, Medical, and Aerospace.

Commercial

The Commercial segment manufactured various products for automotive, marine, and industrial markets, including manual and automatic gearshift systems; transmission guide controls; mechanical and hydraulic steering systems; vehicle pedal systems; heavy-duty cables; hoisting and rigging equipment for oil drilling and other industrial markets; mobile auxiliary power units used for heating and climate control in heavy-duty trucks, industrial vehicles, and locomotives; and fluid management products for automobiles and pleasure boats.

Medical

The Medical segment manufactured health care supply and surgical devices including anesthesiology devices, sutures, ligation solutions, chest drainage systems, and high-quality surgical and orthopedic instruments.

Aerospace

The Aerospace segment manufactured products for the commercial and military aerospace, power generation, and industrial turbine machinery markets. Aerospace businesses provided repair products and services for flight and ground-based turbine engines; manufactured precision-machined components and cargo-handling systems; and provided advanced engine surface treatments.

Products in the Commercial segment were generally produced in higher unit volumes than that of the company's other two segments. In the fiscal year ended December 31, 2004, Teleflex's consolidated sales were $2.49 billion, with 48 percent coming from the Commercial segment, while Medical and Aerospace represented 30 percent and 22 percent, respectively. With approximately 21,000 employees and major operations in more than 70 locations worldwide, Teleflex Inc. operations were highly decentralized, with dozens of small profit centers and a corporate office consisting of a few senior executives and support staff. A few years ago, a major effort was begun to redefine Teleflex as a unified operating company that shared people, products, and processes across divisions and business units. The objective of the reorganization was to establish some common operational standards to improve productivity. Not surprisingly in a company where autonomy had always been the hallmark of business unit activity, increased efforts at standardization, consolidation, and sharing of resources were met with some managerial resistance at the business unit level.

Teleflex Canada

Teleflex Canada, based in Richmond, British Columbia, in the metropolitan Vancouver area, had been one of the best performing business units within Teleflex for several decades. Through internal development, licensing, and acquisition, its growth rate averaged 20 percent per year for 25 years. As previously noted, total sales in 2004 were about $160 million. Teleflex Canada designed and produced a variety of products utilizing hydraulic and thermal technologies.

Marine and Industrial Hydraulic Systems

Teleflex Canada was created in 1974 when Teleflex Inc. purchased part of Capilano Engineering, a small machine shop in Vancouver that was developing hydraulic steering systems for boats. At that time, another Teleflex unit was producing marine steering systems with mechanical cable steering. Teleflex management knew that as marine engines got larger and more powerful, mechanical steering would become obsolete because it could no longer provide the necessary comfort and safety.

Teleflex Canada's hydraulic steering systems—SeaStar, SeaStar Pro, and BayStar—were designed to enable more comfortable control of pleasure boats. These products fundamentally changed the marine steering industry. In 2004 Teleflex Canada sold more than 100,000 SeaStar systems, an increase of more than 30 percent over the previous year (retail prices for the higher-end products ranged $1,200–$1,500 per system, while lower-end systems were about $250). The company had an estimated 95 percent market share in North America and 50 percent share in markets outside the continent. Teleflex Canada's steering products were usually among the highest-priced products available in the marketplace.

The marine steering industry had two main market segments. One segment included stern drive engine companies such as Volvo Penta, which would purchase a private label steering system and integrate it with its own engine to provide a complete steering and controls package to boat builders. A second segment was the marine distribution and dealer network that sold Teleflex-branded products to boat companies and individual boat owners. Sales of marine products were split almost equally between original equipment manufacturers (OEMs) such as Volvo Penta and aftermarket dealers.

In addition to steering systems, Teleflex Canada also produced components for marine engine companies, including Bombardier and Volvo Penta. These products were referred to as industrial actuation systems.

Energy

Teleflex Canada was successful in applying its boat-based technology to the needs of other markets. In 1985 Teleflex Canada began licensing an engine governor technology for large diesel trucks. In 1990 an auxiliary heater business for large trucks and buses was purchased from Cummins, which led to the development of the ProHeat vehicle heater product line. The heater technology was adapted in 1997 to create cookstoves, called modern burner units (MBUs), for use in army field kitchens. A major contract was signed with the U.S. military for the production of MBUs. By 1999 Teleflex was producing 10,000 MBUs per year for military purposes.

Innovation, Technology, and Product Development

Teleflex Canada's innovation focused on product and market development that solved customers' problems or created new markets. Much of Teleflex Canada's success has come about because demand was identified for new products in niche markets that were ready for a change in technology. As explained by a Teleflex Canada executive:

Our fundamental belief is that we don't use any technology that is not proven. We call ourselves product developers. We will not develop any technology that cannot be robust and highly reliable with a low repair requirement. We take existing technology and tweak it to make a better. . . . We usually don't invent anything radically new (although sometimes new technology had to be invented to solve a customer's problem). We are a company that has been innovative in applications engineering. We focus on products we know we can sell because we are close to the market and know the customers. . . . Innovation at Teleflex Canada involves three questions:

1. *How do we exploit existing technology?*
2. *How do we develop reliable and robust products from that technology?*
3. *How do we penetrate and dominate some market niche with that product?*

For example, we are looking for new areas where we can use electro-hydraulic applications. There are other markets where this technology could work, such as dental chairs and hospital beds or suspension systems for lawn and garden equipment. These are markets that will pay a premium for a customer-built system using hydraulics.

SeaStar Development

When Teleflex Inc. acquired Capilano Engineering, the intent was to expand into new markets. At that time, the company was producing a heavy-duty commercial hydraulic steering system. In 1978 Teleflex Canada introduced Syten, the world's first low-cost hydraulic system for the mass pleasure boat market. Cost was a big factor because Syten competed against low-priced mechanical steering systems. Unfortunately, Syten's plastic parts deteriorated when used beyond their mechanical capability, leading to unsatisfied customers and a risk that Teleflex Canada would lose its position in hydraulic steering. At that time, Teleflex Canada had about 10 percent of the hydraulic steering market (the largest competitor had a share of about 80 percent).

Teleflex Canada developed a new hydraulic steering system called SeaStar, which was introduced in 1984. SeaStar became the leading product on the market. In 1989 the new SeaStar was introduced. The mandate for the development team was to develop a smaller size to expand the potential market, lower cost, and better performance. Using some patented technology (a floating spigot), the new SeaStar was 30 percent cheaper to produce, 18 percent more efficient, and sold at the same price as the older model. In 1993 SeaStar Pro was introduced and was successful in the bass boat market where performance was the primary purchase criterion. BayStar, introduced in 2002 for the lower-end market, was also successful (although it cannibalized sales of a mechanical steering system produced by another Teleflex division).

Again, a Teleflex Canada executive explains:

To regain our reputation in the marketplace, we had to come out with an overkill approach with the product. We developed a much more sophisticated and rugged all-metal system, which became SeaStar. This decision involved heated internal debates because the development costs were substantial. This required a lot of trust from Bim Black (Teleflex Inc. chairperson and former CEO). He was willing to take some risk in the investment. There were a lot of skeptics. But the hydraulics technology was well-proven and used in automotive systems. We were applying existing technology to a customized marketplace. From a technology perspective, the risk was not high. From a market point of view, we knew that our current line of cables (from another Teleflex Inc. business unit) was not going to satisfy customers as boat engines got bigger and more difficult to steer.

We have 35 patents but the technology was not earth-shattering. The marketplace wanted higher horsepower and more comfort, and we were able convince people to change to hydraulics. . . . Harold (Copping, Teleflex Canada president at the time) kept a nice fence between corporate and Teleflex Canada. And we were small enough to fall under the radar screen at corporate. For example, we were able to order some tooling without approval.

When the development of SeaStar was done, the marine industry was going through a downturn. Our competitors were laying off engineers and trying to survive. We kept our engineers developing products. When we came out of the downturn, we had new products that allowed us to grow.

There are two keys to the success of SeaStar over the years. One we always kept innovating. Our competitors would copy our designs and in about six months we would have a better product on the market. Since our products were 30–40 percent better than the competition we could keep our margins up. As time went on, the performance gap narrowed. But, because we built scale economies through our size and innovated in manufacturing, we have the lowest cost. So, we have the lowest cost and the best-performing product. Two, a lot of our success is through innovation on the shop floor to ensure that we had a cost-effective product. The corporation pushed us to use more advanced machine tools and to be more analytical. SeaStar involved innovation in technology, product development, marketing, and manufacturing processes that were developed at the shop floor level. The product designs were enhanced because of the manufacturing processes, some of which must be kept in-house because they are proprietary.

Also, having a good product is only part of the story. You also need to sell the product. To me, selling is like being a farmer. You go out and spread some seeds, water them daily, and eventually they come to fruition. I always fought corporate—they kept telling me to close the deal. I was very patient. I was very generous with our product. I would give away our product and let them try it. I am out there constantly talking with customers, looking at the competition.

Our competitors are getting better, but our market share makes it difficult for other companies to compete on cost. We continue to focus on being the best and never giving any customers an excuse to go looking elsewhere. . . . One day, all boats will steer as comfortably as cars. That has been my mission. To make that happen. I have never deviated from it.

Energy Product Development

ProHeat, an auxiliary power and climate control system for trucks and buses, was introduced in 1992.

To get into heaters we bought a product line from Cummins Engine. Cummins was not successful with the product so we bought the remaining inventory. This got our foot in the door, and it is much easier to start a business when you have something to sell. When we did the deal with Cummins, we had already concluded that the product [the truck heater] was not any good. We did the deal anyway because it got us into a new market that we thought we could serve better with new products.

We never actually produced any of the Cummins products, but we learned a lot about the market. There was a clear demand for a product that could be used to heat trucks and was more fuel-efficient than leaving the engine idling. We were able to figure out the type of product innovation that was necessary and spent about two years bringing the product to market. The first truck heater was ProHeat in 1992. Once we had some success in the Canadian market to we looked to the U.S. market. We needed a different product because of air conditioning. Teleflex usually doesn't like to start from scratch so we looked around for a possible acquisition. We bought a small company in Ontario that had a product that allowed us to get into the market.

We then took the truck heater to the transit bus market. We started talking to different city bus companies and were able to adapt our technology for the bus market. These were not huge leaps, and to us they seemed very obvious. We never say build it and they will come. We try to get the order first and then build the product. We start by selling concepts along with our credibility in the market.

The development of the truck heater, along with several other products, including a heater for tents used by the military, provided Teleflex Canada with a solid base of experience in combustion technology. This expertise led to the development of the military cookstove called the MBU. The MBU used the same combustion technology as the truck heater and could be used as a block heater, passenger heat source, barbeque, or oven.

The MBU project started with an inventor who had built a prototype stove. The inventor was able to convince the U.S. Army to put the project out for bid based on the specifications he had developed in his prototype. Harold Copping described how the military cookstove project got started:

We understood the military market. When we did our licensing deal for the tent heater, we had an understanding that we would not develop a cookstove. Eventually, we agreed to license the technology for the cookstove. I visited the military and made sure the funding was in place. I knew the U.S. Army liked the design, and I saw a huge opportunity for Teleflex. I saw this as a chance to back a winner and take a gamble. We put together a team of some of our best people to develop a working prototype. It was not a big risk because I knew that we had very good burner technology and I knew the Army liked the people and the design. We were in their good books because we had had great success with previous projects for them. We spent $500,000 and it worked out well. Our people improved the inventor's design and made it manufacturable and safer.

Another Teleflex executive added the following comments about product development:

To make these programs work, it started at the very top of Teleflex Inc. There were skunk works going on, but they were tolerated. When we were trying to diversify the business, Harold protected us from the operations mentality. For each of the key projects, we put a dedicated team together whose priority was not operations. For several programs we moved engineers out of the building to off-site locations. We wanted these engineers to worry about the development project, not the stuff that was in production. We wanted their full attention on the product development. There has to be a wall between development and existing operations. The next challenge is how to reintegrate the new business into operations and try to avoid the us-and-them attitude. Operations people like stability, and design engineers like change.

You need a focused team that says our mission is to capture this market. In other groups in Teleflex, there is not the same acceptance about product development teams that may take years to bring a product to market. They ask: how can you justify that over the next quarter?

Teleflex Canada Culture

Harold Copping describes some of the characteristics of the Teleflex Canada culture:

I joined the company two years after the acquisition [by Teleflex Inc.]. My strength was an ability to recognize the strengths of other people. I cared a lot about people enjoying their work and doing interesting jobs. We had one person who was a mechanical genius but very difficult to work with. He was a great source of innovation in improved manufacturing methods and quality. He had a very temperamental personality, and in the early days there were fisticuffs on the shop floor and all kinds of things that should not happen. I protected him because I recognized how much he could do. We had another engineer who was brilliant and could think out of the box. He was off the wall and I had to protect him on two occasions against his bosses. I believed something good was going to come out of this guy [he is still at Teleflex Canada].

Right from the beginning, there was a nucleus of very good people in Teleflex Canada in terms of inventive creativity and willingness to solve problems and make things happen. There was some adversity that forced us to work together, such as vast quantities of products being returned by customers [the first innovative hydraulic steering system]. This helped me understand who contributed to solutions and who didn't. It also allowed me to play on the theme that if we did not do this right, the corporation will take it away from us. This was our chance to show them that we could manufacture in Vancouver.

We had discipline but we also had freedoms. We allowed a pretty free rein on innovation, and at the same time were adding systems and standardization. I tried to build the organization around a spirit of independence and risk-taking with a passionate group of people. I wanted the organization to work around the innovative people even if they were eccentric and hard to work with. Enthusiasm and passion are variables that are not measurable. I maintain that one degree of passion is worth 10 degrees of efficiency. All of our customers could sense the enthusiasm. People really cared at Teleflex Canada.

We had a culture of admiration for people with innovative engineering talent. We were also strongly motivated never to be second-class. There were drivers in the marketplace that pushed us to excel, and there was a constant focus on continuous improvement.

You have to create an identity and differentiation that is different from the rest of the corporation. If you lose the identity, you become an employee. You don't have the nice feeling of being part of a cause and a culture that you understand. Therefore, there has to be some symbolism around the identity and also some competition with other divisions of Teleflex. We tried to identify threats so that people would be scared and there would never be complacency. We used threats to draw people together. Some of our greatest successes came about when there was a lot of adversity because of customer problems or breakdowns.

Other managers echoed Harold Copping's views:

Harold was able to maintain a chemistry between individuals who had to make it happen. That is easier when you are a small company. Harold surrounded himself with people who were passionate about what they believed in. If there was a common denominator, it was passion to be the best and the most successful. If you did not believe in this, you were gone. We were almost competing with each other but still working together as a team. The chemistry was as good as it could have been.

Everybody can question anyone about technical details. We have always had a culture that allows people to question everything. Everyone realizes that they are in a position where they could be questioned. We all have egos, but people have to check them at the door at Teleflex Canada. Harold knew that if you put people on too high a pedestal, it can cost you money. . . . Harold was the president, but he did not have his own parking space. People related to that. He did not try to be better than anyone.

We had some people who were unorthodox but were real technical geniuses. We also had some managers who were eternal optimists. If you have a negative attitude, it will kill entrepreneurial thinking.

Managerial commitment to Teleflex Canada was another key element in the company culture, as indicated by the following statement:

After the reorganization in May 2004, we realized there were a few businesses that were in serious trouble. The first company I was asked to visit was in Ontario. Within the first few hours of discussion, I discovered that the fundamental issue was the uncontrolled financial expense relative to a declining market. I was asked to run the company as general manager for the next 3 to 4 months. This was not the best time from a personal perspective: I was in the middle of building a new house (acting as general contractor) and had a number of personal issues involving the sale of my current house and dealing with the planned move of my family.

I spoke to my wife and family the next day, and we both agreed that the need for me to work in Ontario was greater than the need for me to continue as general contractor for the house. She rearranged her work schedule, and my parents stepped in to help get the kids to their various activities. On May 30, 2004, I took the red-eye from Vancouver and went straight into work on arrival in Toronto. For the next 8 months I flew out every Sunday night, spent long hours at work from Monday to Thursday, and flew back for the weekend. Even the weekend we moved into our new house, I flew back on Friday, moved into the house, and flew out on Sunday. I appreciated the opportunity Teleflex Canada had provided me over the past few years, and this was my way of showing them how dedicated I was to the company's success.

Teleflex Inc. and Teleflex Canada

Harold Copping described the relationship between Teleflex Canada and Teleflex Inc.:

I was running a remote subsidiary in a decentralized company. That was a huge advantage. From the very outset, I had a feeling of positive support from corporate and a feeling that I was controlling my own destiny. I tried to help the staff understand that it was really up to us, and I tried to create a culture where we controlled our own destiny.

The relationship was not "control by corporate." It was "help being available from corporate." We had people available from corporate to help teach us about quality and engineering. I always felt that I could choose to use the corporate resources that were available to me. If I could use local resources cost effectively, I did so. I pushed back when someone tried to force corporate resources on me. . . . Access to the corporation definitely played a role in our progress. [Chairperson] Bim [Black] fostered a climate of cross-pollination between divisional and general managers by holding interesting meetings, although as the company got bigger there were fewer meetings. These meetings were very good in helping us know where to go and who to call. I used to find an excuse to visit other Teleflex facilities.

There was enough interaction and influence from corporate to allow people to create successful business relationships [with other parts of Teleflex Inc.]. Since they were not forced by corporate, only the viable relationships occurred. If we could help each other, we did. The attitude was based on open markets. . . . There were many benefits to being part of a large corporation. It was a nice environment to be in. As we got bigger, we were increasingly under the microscope.

We did not know the term core competence at the time. By the early 1980s we began to think that we were not really limited to the marine market. We were small enough and far enough away from corporate that nobody really cared what we did. We could explore new opportunities without being unduly restrained. As long as we were making money and growing, we had a lot of latitude. Nobody restricted me—freedom was a big factor.

Pull-Through Strategy

Rather than designing products and then looking for channels through which to sell them, Teleflex Canada focused on end users. Executives described this strategy as a pull-through strategy:

Our strategy in the truck business is pull-through. The reason why the truck companies [OEM manufacturers] put our ProHeat product on the truck is because the customer [the truck fleet operators] wanted it. The same thing happens with SeaStar. The boat builders buy it from us but the customer [the boat buyer] demands it.

A pull-through strategy is pragmatic. I can call on OEMs all day long but if no end users are asking for the product, we won't sell anything. We still have to negotiate with OEMs, but they don't get to make the call. It is the fleet customer who says we want ProHeat. We are trying to keep our products from becoming commodities, where the OEMs only care about price. They never ask for better—they only ask for cheaper. A lot of companies are confused about who their customers really are. The OEM is not the customer; the OEM is the channel. The customer is the person who will actually use the products.

The SeaStar technology was developed for a market that was prepared to pay a premium for higher comfort. People have asked, "Why don't you leverage this technology into high volume sectors like automotive?" The problem with those markets is that the pricing pressures are intense and the volumes are much higher. We build about a half-million steering systems per year. Plus, we see automotive as more of a commodity market. Marine customers are using surplus funds to buy their products. Nobody has to own a boat. Boats are not a commodity, and we can demand a higher premium in the marine market. We have never entered another steering market.

We want to move boats closer to car steering comfort levels. Our next level of product innovation is to take comfort to a new level through power steering. We thought we would sell 2,000 power steering systems this year and it looks like we will sell 20,000. The boat builders initially resisted the shift to power steering. We gave the boat builders the new systems to try. Our philosophy is not to sell to the boat builders; we want them to buy it from us.

It does not matter what the technology is. The market will decide. Everybody is willing to pay a fair price for fair value. . . . We always try to be a few steps ahead of our customers. For example, we have an expensive power steering system for 60- to 100-foot luxury yachts. It is a very technical product and there are varying levels of expertise within the boat building companies. We believe that if we want to capture a bigger share of the market, we will have to simplify the technology and make it "bubba-proof." That is what we strive for: How do we make our product better and easier for our customers to use? Since our competitors are followers they cannot think like this.

The Future

As Teleflex Canada executives looked toward the future, they faced various issues, such as the degree of vertical integration, the relationship with Teleflex Inc., managing the size of the organization, and the future for new product development.

Vertical Integration

Teleflex Canada had always been vertically integrated. The consensus was that, in the future, the company would be less vertically integrated.

All our customers want us to be as cost-effective as possible. In the past we were incredibly vertically integrated. For example, when we started with ProHeat, we needed various parts, like a flame sensor, a compressor, a blower, and a water pump. Nobody built any of these parts to our specs, so we developed them ourselves from scratch. What are we doing developing a flame sensor? There are companies out there who should be able to do these things better than us. We spent a lot of money doing a lot of things, and we would have been better served if we had had the option to look outside. We developed some stuff that we had no business developing. As a generalization, we will buy technology rather than develop technology. We will develop new products. That is not the way we got here, but it is the way we need to go.

We have developed a strategic plan that involves core and noncore capabilities. We went through all our manufacturing processes and asked what is really core, from process and intellectual property points of view. We have to protect intellectual property. We identified about 80 percent of our manufacturing processes as noncore.

We are going to try to shift from a manufacturer to an integrator and a tester. We will only fabricate what is considered absolutely core for protecting our manufacturing and quality processes and our intellectual property. Everything else is up for grabs. If we cannot be competitive here, the work will go elsewhere. We are going through a rapid change. We want to focus on marketing, sales, product development and engineering, prototyping, final assembly, and testing. Fabrication and subassembly may go elsewhere. We want to be an OEM or a tier 1 player.

Not everyone was in complete agreement that the shift from manufacturer to integrator and tester was the basis for a unique strategy. According to one manager:

Every company in the world is trying to be an early adopter with low-cost manufacturing and outsourcing of noncore activities. That is not a strategy—that is good business practice. If you lose the ability to innovate on the production floor, you lose some of the ability to lower costs. That is my fear with off-shore production. Also, how are we going to protect key product designs and innovation when we spread work out to partners?

Relationships with Teleflex Inc.

Within all of Teleflex Inc., an ongoing debate argued the merits and drawbacks of centralization and unified operating processes. Within Teleflex Canada, this debate was particularly relevant given the history of the subsidiary (i.e., 3,000 miles from headquarters) and its successful innovations:

The bigger area of conflict from a corporate unified perspective involves market and product development, who owns it, and how do we keep the innovation happening. With more centralization going on, how do you make sure you don't kill the entrepreneurialism? Everybody knows that if you go completely centralized, you totally lose the innovation. What we have agreed on is that product development has to stay close to the market. There has to be some consolidation at a group level but not at a corporate level. We are creating centers of excellence such as hydraulics and power generation.

I understand the need for centralization. I also understand that the centralization pendulum usually swings too far. As far as the centralization of patent attorneys, this will take away from our ability to get prompt intellectual property. We will get it, but it will be slower. It is critical to understand your intellectual property before you spend too much time in development. Centralization of HR may also affect us. For example, corporate edicts about raises may make it hard to keep engineers, since Vancouver is such a hot tech area.

If you take away all of the divisional autonomy, you cripple the divisions. Before, purchases for $25,000 or less could be approved at the division. Now everything has to go to corporate. Unless you are yelling or screaming, it can be a two- or three-month process to get approval. Because of Sarbanes-Oxley, things have to be done in a specific way. Too many rules will take away someone's incentive to stick their neck out and try something different. The old environment is gone, but we will make it happen somehow.

Managing Size

Teleflex Canada had grown rapidly over the past three decades. Size brings its own variety of challenges, as the following comments demonstrate:

We went from $4.5 million when I started to $160 million today. Every time we made a big jump in revenue, there were benefits and downsides. Getting big can be a problem, which is one reason Harold split the company into three divisions—he saw that we were getting too big.

The problem with growth is that as you get bigger, it gets more difficult to manage and control. Then you get to a point where the corporation becomes huge and the latest flavor of the month comes in, like "go to China for your raw materials." Now the buzz word is "cut costs, cut costs." If all we focus on is cutting costs, we will stifle the entrepreneurialism and that is the beginning of the end. Once you stifle entrepreneurialism, passion, and creativity, you become like any other corporation. Margins will drop because you cannot be fast and innovative. You slowly start losing. We are on the edge.

As we get bigger we have to follow more processes, sign more forms; and by the time you get done, it is too late. It is not how big you are that makes you successful—it is how fast you are to market. In efforts to consolidate, we are risking our fast response time. When we were smaller, I could get things done in 24 hours. Now it takes forever.

We have always been known as a company that solved customer problems. We were very good at getting to the root cause of the problem. When a customer calls us, we take care of them. This got us a lot of respect and market share, and this was not the way our competitors did it. As we get bigger we may not be able to react quickly enough.

To keep our edge, we need to keep up with the technology, move fast, and make sure quality does not suffer as we experiment with offshore sourcing. Basically, we need to continue to deliver what we promise. Do not take cost-cutting to the point where it affects what you have promised your customers.

One way we are trying to deal with size is with the Virtual Development Center. We are leaving too many opportunities on the table. This Center will be a small group that acts as an interface between the customers and the divisions. The Center will have two main objectives: (1) to make sure the customers get proper focus from the people best qualified to deal with their problems; and (2) to make sure the development project goes to the appropriate division. . . . Our goal is to provide a customer with a conceptual design in 7 days and a prototype within 30 days. In a way, we are trying to break free of the shackles of size by responding quickly to customers. Once we have a customer, we will put the product into the appropriate division to develop it, make it manufacturable, optimize it, etc.

There is a limit to how big the firm can get and still be innovative and entrepreneurial. It is easier with smaller groups. Once an organization gets over 150 people, it should be subdivided. You need to strike the right balance between operational efficiency, serving the customer well, and maintaining a spirit of identity. . . . Balancing operational efficiency with subdividing the organization is more of a challenge because there are trade-offs. When people work together in subunits and depend on each other for overall success, politics is minimized. The challenges are to work with people and stay connected with people at every single level. If people believe that they succeed together and make things happen together, they will have some job security and will reap some rewards. It is much easier to excite people about a portion of the business rather than the whole business.

Forward Thinking: New Product Development and New Technologies

New product development was central to the success of Teleflex Canada and central to continued growth. Executives were generally confident that the organization would continue to develop and exploit existing technologies. Some comments about the marine area follow:

I don't see an issue with product development. The bigger challenge is dealing with new technologies. The risk is that our existing products get replaced by new technologies in which we have no expertise. Take steering systems. We know that hydraulics will go away eventually, and the market will demand more comfort at lower prices. The boat builders may integrate steering into their outboards. Most stern drive engine steering uses a cable with a power steering system.

We will have to reduce costs and develop more robust designs for larger outboard engines. There will be new technologies that replace hydraulic steering. Electro over hydraulic with programmable tension and torque levels is the next generation and will come out soon. The next shift will be to electromechanical actuation or steer-by-wire, which is disruptive technology. We believe we can bring this to market, and we had the foresight to realize that we were going to become an electronics company. Five years ago we engaged a local university professor—an expert in fault tolerant systems—to work with us privately on steer-by-wire. Corporate and other engineers did not know we were doing this. We scavenged the money where we could and eventually bought an equity stake in an offshoot company owned by the university and the professor. When corporate found out what we were doing, they saw that it made sense and gave us steer-by-wire responsibility for the corporation. We are going to be ready with a steer-by-wire product when the world is ready for the technology.

We are also trying to develop new products for boats. We know that we will lose market share when hydraulic steering goes away. We also know that the engine companies want to integrate steering with their engines. We need to be forward-looking and help our customers sell their products. We need to make sure we are the company that the engine manufacturer wants as the integrator. Our plan is to develop new business with Yamaha, Bombardier, and other engine companies.

Conclusion

Teleflex Canada provided a high margin contribution to the Teleflex corporation for many years. Would success breed complacency and stagnation? Or would Teleflex Canada continue to grow, innovate, and develop new products? According to one executive:

We can't get fat and lazy, because that will be the beginning of the end. We have to continue to solve our customers' problems and make their lives easier. As long as we do what we promise and don't get arrogant, we will be fine. If we start acting like an 800-pound gorilla, customers will find a way to deal with us. We need to work with our customers and make their lives easier. It is a fine line and you need to know where the line is. Most of our boat builders are entrepreneurs; there are no barriers to entry in the boat business. This helps keep the automotive mentality out of this industry.

Case 26

Tyco International: A Case of Corporate Malfeasance

Michael J. Merenda, Alison Volk, Allen Kaufman

MICHAEL J. MERENDA
UNIVERSITY OF NEW HAMPSHIRE

ALISON VOLK
UNIVERSITY OF WISCONSIN

ALLEN KAUFMAN
UNIVERSITY OF NEW HAMPSHIRE

On June 17, 2005, Tyco's former chief executive, Dennis Kozlowski, and its former chief financial officer, Mark Swartz, were convicted of grand larceny, conspiracy, and fraud. In September 2005 Kozlowski and Swartz received 8- to 25-year sentences at Mid-State Correctional Facility near Utica, New York. State Supreme Court Justice Michael Obus ordered Kozlowski and Swartz to pay a total of $134 million in restitution; in addition, Kozlowski was fined $70 million, Swartz $35 million. The sentences end a case that exposed the executives' extravagant lifestyle after they pilfered some $600 million from the company including a $2 million toga birthday party for Kozlowski's wife on a Mediterranean island and an $18 million Manhattan apartment with a $6,000 shower curtain.[1]

Kozlowski and Swartz were just two of the more celebrated corporate malfeasance cases decided in the first half of this decade. John Regas, former CEO of Adelphia Communications, was sentenced to 15 years (it would have been longer but he was 80 and in poor health at the time of his sentencing) and his son Timothy, its chief financial officer got 20 years. They were found quilty of stealing $100 million and hiding $2 billion in corporate debt, thus looting and defrauding shareholders. Other notable sentences were Andrew Fastow of Enron (10 years), Sam Wakal of ImClone Systems (7 years), Jamie Olis of Dynergy (24 years), and Bernie Ebbers of WorldCom (25 years). What is significant about these cases is the severity of the sentences. Traditionally, corporate malfeasance cases resulted in convictions that amounted to a mere slap on the hand. These individuals received longer prison terms that are similar to sentences received by hardened criminals. Hubris cost these executives dearly in terms of retribution payments, personal freedom, and integrity.

These instances of corporate malfeasance ushered in a new era in corporate governance. They dramatically changed the relationship between corporate executives and company boards of directors and their shareholders. Increasingly shareholders' are voting against the recommendations of managers, particularly on the method by which members of the boards of directors are elected and the basis for keeping their seats on the board. One particular hot issue being fought by radical shareholders is their ability to vote out the chairperson of the board's compensation committee at any firm they think overpays managers.[2]

It is also evident that Tyco's board of directors did not exercise its fiduciary duties to the shareholders. Questions arise as to where and why it failed and whether the directors receive prison sentences because of their irresponsible and unethical behaviors. Finally, people are reluctant to question success, and they tend to give those responsible for "successful undertakings" too much leeway. These factors, coupled with the ethical and moral values of Kozlowski and the voodoo accounting of Swartz, resulted in the outcomes described in this case.

This case traces the events and decisions that led to Kozlowski's and Swartz's demise at Tyco and their public disgrace in the court room. It looks at management actions that not only violate public trust, but undermine the fabric of a democratic society. It is clear in the case that the principal characters not only behaved unethically and were socially irresponsible, but also broke the law and misappropriated monies that should have been distributed to shareholders.

Three issues need to be addressed: (1) What things led to Tyco's present state? (2) What can be done in the organization to prevent these situations from arising in the future? and (3) What resources does Tyco's new management team have at its disposal to enhance the reputation of the firm and turn it around? See Exhibits 1, 4 (on page 330), and 5 (on page 331) for financial highlights and financial ratios and indicators.

Tyco: The Pendulum Swings

Arthur Rosenberg, Tyco's Founder

Tyco, Inc., began in 1960 as an investment and holding firm in Waltham, Massachusetts. At that time, Tyco had two principal holdings, Tyco Semiconductor and the Materials Research Laboratory, which conducted industrial research and development in solid-state sciences and energy conversion. When Tyco merged these two divisions in 1962, its major customer remained to be the U.S. government.[3] However, Arthur Rosenberg, Tyco's founder, saw commercial opportunities. Over the next two years, Tyco became an industrial products manufacturer, going public in 1964. Tyco grew steadily over the next few years, adding 16 companies by 1968. Five years later, Tyco generated $40 million in sales.

Joseph Gaziano: Growth through Acquisitions

In 1973, Joseph Gaziano, an engineer trained at MIT, took over for Rosenberg as president and CEO. Under his leadership, Tyco pursued a path of aggressive and often hostile acquisitions. He wanted to turn Tyco into a $1 billion company by 1985, using any means necessary.

Gaziano died of cancer in 1982. The company he left behind, however, was large and diverse. It had a net worth of $140 million and was bringing in more than $500 million in sales. The conglomerate housed manufacturers of products as varied as undersea fiber optic cables, fire sprinkler systems, polyethylene film, and packaging materials.

John Fort: Performance over Growth

John Fort, an aeronautical engineer who held degrees from Princeton and MIT, became Tyco's third CEO in 1982. As Tyco's new CEO, Fort decided to set a different tone. He veered away from the acquisition-centered growth strategy of his predecessor and immediately trimmed the tremendous debt that Gaziano had accumulated and focused instead on cutting costs wherever possible. Fort told investors, "The reason we were put on earth, was to increase earnings per share."[4] He was thrifty and unglamorous, preferring to gain Wall Street's respect through his own economic restraint. Under Fort's leadership, Tyco became a company without frills. When it came time to find a location for the company's headquarters, for example, Fort had builders clear land in Exeter, New Hampshire. The facility that they consequently constructed consisted of three unpretentious, low-rise office buildings, without even a cafeteria on site.[5] He drastically cut costs and discarded a number of businesses that were not directly related to Tyco's operations. He separated the company's

Exhibit 1 Tyco International: Historical Stock Price, 1990–2002

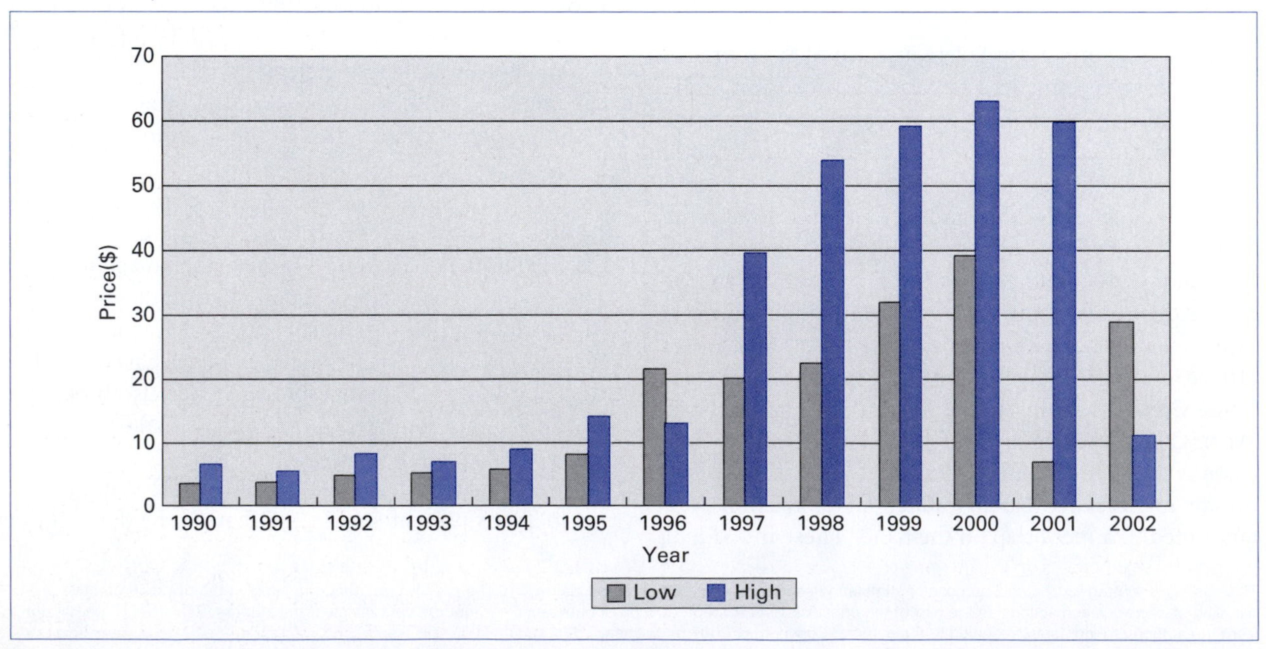

various businesses into three parts: Fire Protection, Electronics, and Packaging. This consolidation, however, did not signal an end to Tyco's acquisition strategy. Tyco simply became more selective about the companies that it pursued. Fort's main focus was on profits rather than growth. The stock price rose from $1.55 in January 1982 to $29.56 in July 1990. Sales grew to $3 billion in 1991. Fort retired in 1992 after serving 10 years as CEO. Dennis Kozlowski, Tyco's then chief operating officer, replaced him and further refined Tyco's art of acquisition.

Dennis Kozlowski: The Early Years

Kozlowski's Background

Dennis Kozlowski was the product of a working class family from Newark, New Jersey. His father was an investigator with Public Service Transport (which would later become New Jersey Transit) and his mother was a school crossing guard. He went to Seton Hall University in South Orange and majored in accounting. He lived at home to help save money and he worked at a variety of different jobs.

Kozlowski graduated from Seton Hall in 1968 and landed his first job as an auditor for SCM Corporation. In 1974, he was hired at Nashua Corporation, an office equipment manufacturer in New Hampshire, as the director of auditing. William Conway, Nashua's former CEO, described Kozlowski as "a smart young guy who could really help a business. Any problem that came up in the company—in administration, selling, manufacturing—he always had suggestions about how to fix it."[6]

Kozlowski stayed at Nashua for a year and was then approached by a headhunter to work at Tyco as the assistant comptroller and head of auditing. Shortly after he began, Gaziano purchased Grinnell Fire Protection from I.T.T. Kozlowski was promoted to vice president. At the time Grinnell was the largest of Tyco's divisions, but it was barely scraping by. In six months, Kozlowski cut costs and Grinnell showed $1 million in profit. Over the next seven years, Grinnell increased profits to $212 million. In 1983, Kozlowski became president of the division. In the next four years he managed to raise the division's profits to $700 million. His performance earned him an invitation to serve on Tyco's board in 1987, followed by a promotion to president and COO in 1989. In fact, Kozlowski engineered the acquisitions that generated the enormous revenue growth (from $1 billion in 1988 to $3 billion in 1991) under Fort's watch. Three years later, he took over the reigns from John Fort as CEO.

Kozlowski: The Great Conglomerator

I never started out with a game plan to be a $76 billion company. But I always envisioned one that had to grow every year in order to be successful.[7]

During Kozlowski's 10-year reign at Tyco, the same word kept popping up to describe him—*aggressive*. One Tyco board member said, "Dennis has only one gear—forward at 300 miles an hour. There is no reverse." He pursued acquisitions with a vigor that Tyco had not seen since the days of Gaziano. His style, however, was markedly different. He told the *Boston Globe* that he always followed two rules for acquisitions: Never do a hostile deal and immediately cut costs at the new facility.[8] He had learned from watching Gaziano that unfriendly takeovers often lead to failed business ventures. Kozlowski preferred that deals be made quickly and on good terms.

When Kozlowski took over as CEO, Tyco was a $1.3 billion (net revenue) company divided into four divisions: fire protection; valves, pipes and "flow control products"; electrical and electronic components; and packaging materials. Fire protection generated 53 percent of Tyco's revenues, flow control 23 percent, electronics 13 percent, and packaging 11 percent.[9] Even though Tyco operated in many industries, the majority of its divisions sold products to the construction industry, which accounted for 80 percent of Tyco's income.[10]

Changing the Product Mix

Kozlowski wanted to decrease Tyco's reliance on the construction business, which is infamously unpredictable, and transition into manufacturing products for more reliable consumers. This sentiment led the new CEO to suggest buying Kendall International in 1994, a producer of medical supplies, for $1 billion. Tyco's board balked, considering that Kendall had filed Chapter 11 two years earlier and their revenues were only increasing by 3 to 4 percent per year. Kozlowski, however, was determined to repair the company and the board agreed to the acquisition.

In the long run, Kozlowski's gamble paid off. After one year, the acquisition helped Tyco's earnings grow to $214 million. Kendall became the center of Tyco Healthcare, which, in turn, became a major producer of medical supplies, second in the country only to Johnson & Johnson.[11] By 1998, Tyco had six divisions: fire protection, flow control, disposable medical products, Simplex Technologies, packaging materials, and specialty products.

Between 1992 and 1998, Kozlowski perfected Tyco's acquisition strategy. In many respects, it resembled the conglomerate strategy developed during the 1960s and then abandoned by the 1980s. Originally, conglomerates assembled businesses in unrelated fields to counter business cycle movements. When one business was strained during the downside of a business cycle, another division would be performing well. This portfolio approach was to assure the corporate holding company a steady stream of cash. The central office functioned as a bank, using the firm's operating cash to weather economic storms, to acquire new cash-generating companies and to divest those firms that no longer fit the conglomerate portfolio. As long as cash streams steadily grew, the conglomerate's stock price rose, allowing the company's stock to be takeover currency.

Bring on the Hungry Young Talent

Tyco's central office functioned much like a conglomerate holding company, acquiring and divesting parts. However, Tyco did not seek out unrelated acquisitions to beat the business cycle. Instead, Kozlowski hunted after targets that fit into Tyco's broadly defined business divisions. Targets had to be the sort that investment bankers had favored for takeovers during the 1980s: "underperforming firms that were fat, dumb and happy."[12]

He would then replace highly paid executives with young, energetic middle managers, preferably ones who were "smart, poor and who wanted to be rich," which is how Kozlowski saw himself when he was younger. These ambitious individuals would strive for productive efficiency by closing facilities and dislocating workers. For example, in consolidating the firms that it acquired in 2001, Tyco closed approximately 300 plants and eliminated approximately 3,000 jobs.[13]

In this loosely held empire, the central office set stringent budgets and financial controls to oversee performance. By focusing on its financials, Tyco imitated the conglomerates that preceded it. But, to ensure that Tyco had syngery Kozlowski would annually ask investment bankers to map out a break-up strategy. If it beat Tyco's current value, then Kozlowski promised that he would undo the company.[14] Until 2002, Tyco outperformed break-up scenarios and Kozlowski did not have to make good on his promise.

In 1999, *BusinessWeek* reported that Kozlowski was scouting anywhere from 30 to 40 different business opportunities at a time. Tyco's biggest acquisitions during this period included Earth Technology Corporation (1995), builders and operators of wastewater and water treatment facilities; Carlisle (1996), makers of packaging materials and clothing hangers; and AMP (1999), manufacturer of electrical, electronic, and fiber-optic wireless devices.[15]

The merger with Bermuda-based ADT in 1997 was one of Tyco's most notable additions during this time period. The $5 billion plus deal added the world's largest producer of home security systems to Tyco's portfolio. The merger also allowed Kozlowski to transfer Tyco's headquarters from New Hampshire to Bermuda. The move saved Tyco $400 million in taxes in just one year.[16]

Under Kozlowski, Tyco had become larger and more diversified than ever, with subsidiaries that manufactured everything from medical syringes to undersea fiber-optic cables. Between 1997 and 2002, Tyco purchased more than 1,000 companies and spent $60 billion on acquisitions.[17] This growth enabled Tyco's stock to climb from just over $5 per share in 1992 to a high of $62 in 2001.[18] Between 1996 and 2001, revenues increased by 48.7 percent per year.[19] *BusinessWeek* named Tyco one of the 50 best companies in 1997.

Tyco's board members seemed to be relatively pleased with Kozlowski's performance. He was given a lot of freedom in running the company. In 1997 the board voted to allow the CEO to spend up to $50 million on an acquisition without getting their approval first. That number was increased to $100 million in 1999 and then $200 million in 2000. Tyco's steady stock climb allowed Kozlowski to borrow heavily to fund his purchasing spree. At its peak, Tyco's debt reached $28 billion, a figure that exceeded shareholder equity.

Management Incentives and Compensation

Running the Company

Kozlowski preferred Tyco to be a decentralized organization. The divisions acted almost entirely independent of one another. Managers from different operating segments rarely spoke to each other. Some thought that this kept Tyco from experiencing restraints on its growth potential. One top lieutenant said, "There is no limit to how big the company could get because of the way we manage it."[20] It seemed that Kozlowski had a deep disdain for bureaucratic hierarchies or managerial organization. He forbade memos and kept meetings short. He preferred communicating briefly with others, either over the phone or through e-mail. Kozlowski wanted his employees to be accountable for their own work and compensated or penalized accordingly.

Compensation Packages

To get the most out of his executives, Kozlowski liked the idea of a compensation package with a low base salary but weighted heavily with incentives. Tyco's managers would not get a bonus unless their division had achieved 15 percent of earnings for the year. If the division hit 15 percent, then the executives would receive compensation that would be, at a minimum, equal to their salary. If the division surpassed 15 percent, then "the sky was the limit."[21]

For senior executives, Tyco, like other large old-line companies, used stock options for incentive pay.

This preference arose from the Reform Tax Act of 1993, which disallowed firms to pay executive salaries that exceeded $1 million for tax purposes. During the 1992 presidential contest between George Bush and Bill Clinton, CEO pay became a contentious issue. Although wages for average workers remained stagnant during the Bush administration, CEO pay had increased steadily. Once in the White House, Clinton pursued tax policies designed to curb excess CEO salaries, hence the Tax Reform Act's deduction limit on executive salaries. The Tax Act, however, still allowed companies to continue to write off incentive-based pay. Congress believed that performance-based pay was compensation well deserved.

Stock Options and Other Incentives

Among the various sorts of incentive pay, corporate board compensation committees found stock options to be the most attractive. Although the federal government allowed these bonuses to be tax deductible, accounting rules did not require firms to report options as an expense. Thus, from a tax vantage point, options reduced the firm's tax burden. From an accounting standpoint, they were costless compensation. Shareholders were enamored by these plans for they allegedly aligned managers to shareholders' interests. Tyco's board did not differ from its *Fortune* 500 peers. Driven by tax and accounting incentives, Tyco's board loaded executive compensation packages with stock options. For example, in 2002, Kozlowski owned 3 million Tyco shares and held option on another 10 million.[22] Tyco's executives now had powerful incentives to push up shareholder value by any means possible. Tyco's compensation structure illustrates this change. In 1999, Kozlowski's first year as CEO and chairperson, he earned $1.2 million while Tyco's second highest executive received $950,000. By 2000, Kozlowski earned more than twice the second highest paid executive (CFO Mark Schwartz).

The Fame Game

In the late 1990s, Tyco's board brought in an image-consultant from New York City to help bolster Kozlowski and Tyco's reputation. Tyco modeled this campaign after GE's celebrity CEO, Jack Welch. As institutional investors came to dominate the stock market, money market managers increasingly relied on a CEO's reputation when evaluating investment opportunities. If a CEO had charisma, the markets reacted favorably. CEO charisma requires a publicity campaign that gives the CEO a larger-than-life appearance—a perception that is generally achieved with large offices, fancy suits, corporate jets, and expensive tastes.[23]

At Tyco, Kozlowski gave openly to charity, spoke at well-publicized events, and joined the boards of for- and not-for-profit organizations. Kozlowski's presence was felt especially in southern Maine and New Hampshire, where a number of local agencies benefited from his philanthropy. The Berwick Academy in South Berwick, Maine, was able to build a multimillion-dollar athletic center in 1997 after receiving a $1.7 million contribution from Tyco. The University of New Hampshire, Franklin Pierce College, St. Anselm's College, and the United Way of the Greater Seacoast also received a number of large donations from the company at the CEO's request. UNH in particular was able to set up a Tyco scholarship in the College of Engineering and Physical Science after the company presented a $5 million gift to the UNH Foundation Office. Kathy Gallant, owner of Blue Moon Market and Green Earth Cafè in Exeter, described Kozlowski as "the most engaging, generous human being."[24]

CEO/Senior Executive Entitlement

At the same time that he was giving openly to not-for-profit agencies, Kozlowski started buying lavish homes in New York and Boca Raton and filling them with exquisite furnishings and decorations. He used Tyco's cash to bankroll these investments. He also used Tyco's resources to benefit other members of his inner executive circle. These decisions seemed to make good business sense. For example, once Tyco decided to move corporate headquarters to New York, the Board's compensation committee approved Kozlowski's relocation expenses under the firm's New York City Corporate Headquarters Relocation Loan Program. It awarded relocated executives interest-free home loans, with some restrictions. In May 2000, Kozlowski received more than $7 million as a loan to relocate to 610 Park Avenue.

Kozlowski soon left this address and took up residence in a co-op at 950 Fifth Avenue that better suited Tyco's business needs than the Park Avenue address. Stephen Schwartz, a well-known investment banker and president of the prestigious Blackstone Group, owned the co-op, which had only seven units. Like other Fifth Avenue co-ops, Kozlowski had to gain the co-op board's approval. He interviewed with two co-op owners: Jonathan Tisch, CEO of Loews Hotels and member of the Tisch family, which controlled Loews Corporation; and Robert Hurst, a vice chairman at Goldman, Sachs, the investment banking firm with which Tyco had dealings. This move cost Tyco $16 million. Still, Kozlowski's name appeared on the title because the co-op prohibited corporate ownership.

TME Corporation and Tyco's Board of Directors

However, not every transaction that benefited Kozlowski or senior executives had board approval. Although Tyco under Kozlowski grew into a global company with more than 2,000 subsidiaries and 270,000 employees, corporate headquarters consisted of a staff of fewer than 400. These employees received their pay from another subsidiary, TME Management Corporation, which constituted Tyco's headquarters' company and employed about 40 senior executives.[25]

As a publicly traded corporation, Tyco's board of directors had final authority over the enterprise and its executives. To carry out its responsibilities, Tyco's board established a number of committees, including a board nominating and governance committee, an audit committee, and a compensation committee. Legally, TME Management answered to the board and its committees. Yet, as Tyco expanded rapidly and as Tyco's market value continued to grow, TME gained *de facto* discretionary powers in a variety of corporate functions. These divested responsibilities could easily be acquired because TME had separate treasury, tax, finance, investor relations, human resources, and internal audit units. Within TME, Kozlowski, as Tyco's CEO and board chair, exerted considerable influence. For example, TME's internal audit committee reported to him rather than directly to the board's audit committee. (See Exhibit 2 for a listing of Tyco's directors, officers, and key management.)

Exhibit 2 Tyco International Directors, Officers, and Key Management

Directors	Officers
L. Dennis Kozlowski Chairman of the Board and Chief Executive Officer	L. Dennis Kozlowski President Chief Executive Officer
Lord Ashcroft KCMG Chairman Carlisle Holdings Limited	Mark A. Belnick Executive Vice President Chief Corporate Council
Joshua M. Berman	Michael J. Jones Secretary
Richard S. Bodman Managing General Partner Venture Management Services Group	Mark H. Swartz Executive Vice President Chief Financial Officer
John F. Fort	**Business Segment Presidents**
Stephen W. Foss Chairman and Chief Executive Officer Foss Manufacturing Company, Inc.	Jerry R. Boggess President Tyco Fire and Security Systems
Wendy E. Lane Chairman Lane Holdings, Inc.	Albert R. Gamper, Jr. President Tyco Capital
James S. Pasman, Jr.	
W. Peter Slusser President Slusser Associates, Inc.	Jurgen W. Gamper President Tyco Electronics
Mark H. Swartz Executive Vice President and Chief Financial Officer	Richard J. Meelia President Tyco Healthcare
Frank E. Walsh, Jr. Chairman Sandy Hill Foundation	
Joseph W. Welch Chairman and Chief Executive Officer The Bachman Company	

Source: *Tyco International Annual Report 2002*, 90.

Mark Swartz and KELP

Tyco's chief financial officer, Mark Swartz also had considerable powers within TME. Appointed CFO in 1997, he joined Tyco's board in 2001. Within TME, Swartz controlled fund transfers, accounting entries, and those parts of human resources that oversaw various executive compensation, bonus, and loan programs.[26] Employees had few incentives to question Swartz's authority and powerful incentives to comply. For example, Patricia Prue, head of human resources, earned $15.1 million between 1999 and 2001.[27]

One policy—the Key Employee Loan Program (KELP)—became particularly useful for TME executives. Originally established in 1983, this program offered executives, who had been awarded stock as part of their compensation, loans to pay off state and federal taxes once the stock vested. Yet, Kozlowski used this program in 1997 and 1998 to borrow more than $18 million for personal properties in Connecticut, New Hampshire, Nantucket, and Boca Raton—monies that were never reported in the Director and Officer Questionnaire. Swartz, along with several other senior executives, benefited from this program as well. Control over the accounting books also allowed loan forgiveness. For example, in 1999, Kozlowski and Swartz were able to make accounting entries that reduced Kozlowski's KELP debt by $25 million and Swartz's by $12.5 million.

Kozlowski viewed this KELP financing of senior executives' homes and other private purchases as sound business decisions. Kozlowski reasoned that senior executives would have to sell off large amounts of their vested stock and stock options in order to buy large ticket items such as real estate and yachts. These sales would have surely spooked big investors, pushing down Tyco's stock value and hurting the average shareholder. Even though Kozlowski and other senior executives exercised KELP in dealings for which it was not designed, Kozlowski found these actions were true to KELP's spirit.[28]

The "Art" of the Deal

In 2001, Kozlowski used KELP to purchase artwork worth nearly $12 million for his New York City residence. Again, Kozlowski judged these purchases as Tyco investments. His well-provisioned Fifth Avenue co-op substituted as an office where he negotiated acquisition deals with investment bankers under the pretense of shared collector enthusiasm. Through this ruse, Kozlowski hid his acquisition deal-making from the business press. Conventional wisdom informed Kozlowski and other Tyco executives that had these negotiations become public, the news would have adversely affected Tyco's purchase price, as investors bid up target company stock.

Finally, without board approval, TME dispersed bonuses to select executives. For example, after Tyco's successful public offering of TyCom's shares and the lucrative divestment of ADT's (a Tyco subsidiary) automobile auction division, Tyco's top executives received handsome bonuses. In the TyCom issue, Tyco executives garnered $76.5 million, with $33 million going directly to Kozlowski. Tyco senior executives did not fare as well after the ADT divestiture. They earned $56 million in bonuses, with Kozlowski pocketing nearly half.

Although these sums may seem large, they were only a small portion of the profits that these transactions put into Tyco's coffer. The ADT division sold for more than $300 million over the price for which Tyco purchased it three years earlier. The TyCom issue yielded a one-time profit of $1.76 billion after executive bonuses were deducted. Surely such lucrative deals warranted rewards for the executives involved, even though TME did not report these bonuses to Tyco's board or to shareholders.[29] In fact, TME withheld or modified accounting figures reported to the board, all to sustain the steady rise of Tyco's stock price.

By all outward appearances, however, Kozlowski was running a tidy, reliable business, portraying a lot of the same no-frills qualities of his predecessor. He landed on the cover of *Barron's* in April 1999 under the heading: "Tyco's Titan: How Dennis Kozlowski Is Creating a Lean, Profitable Giant." The article reported that Tyco's offices were practically bare, claiming that Kozlowski clearly "hasn't forgotten where he came from."[30] *Time* magazine called the conglomerate "lean." *BusinessWeek* extended that description to "ultra-lean" and put Tyco high on their list of 50 top-performing companies.

The Beginning of the End: Denouement

David Tice

Despite the positive press, in October 1999, rumors began to circulate around Wall Street that Tyco's accounting practices might not be completely legitimate. David Tice, an analyst and mutual fund operator, wrote in his newsletter "Behind the Numbers" that Tyco was overstating its earnings and inflating its profits through unorthodox bookkeeping. He wrote, "Tyco's game plan is to buy bloated businesses, strip them of excess personnel and facilities, and treat the costs as nonrecurring in the company's income statement."[31] Even though the newsletter only reaches a couple hundred money managers, it garners a fair amount of respect. The newsletter has been credited with issuing warnings about Sunbeam, Mercury Finance, and Southland, long before anybody else predicted their failure.[32] A week after Tice issued his report, Tyco's stock dropped by 20 percent.[33]

At the same time, the *New York Times* reported that two of Tyco's acquisitions, U.S. Surgical (USSC) and AMP had taken big write-offs immediately before they were acquired. Before the USSC deal closed October 1, 1998, the company reported that it had earned $69 million in the nine months preceding its June 30, 1998 quarterly report. However, in an 8-K form filed with the SEC on December 10, 1998, Tyco recorded that USSC had lost $212 million dollars for the year ending September 30, 1998, and USSC had taken a $190 million write off just before Tyco closed the deal. Similar discrepancies occurred in the AMP acquisition. In its final 10-K report covering the fiscal year ending December 31, 1998, AMP reported a $376 million write-off from plant closures, plant consolidations, and employee discharges.[34] But Tyco did not divulge these write-offs to investors.[35] These write-offs enabled Tyco's profits to rise because it did have to depreciate charges. And Kozlowski made much of Tyco's gains from the acquisitions in a July press release, helping to push up Tyco stock.

Just after the release, Kozlowski, Swartz, and several other Tyco executives sold Tyco shares. Kozlowski sold more than 3 million shares for a tidy $160 million. A Tyco director, Michael Ashcroft, joined these executives in unloading 413,700 of Tyco shares for nearly $21 million. Kozlowski and Ashcroft sold their shares in range from $45.25 to $50.39 per share. On October 1, 1998, Tyco shares opened at $26.93.[36]

In December of 1999 the SEC began a "nonpublic informal inquiry" into Tyco's accounting practices. Tyco assured investors that nothing was wrong, but people began to grow wary of the company's operations. The stock price fell to $22.50, the lowest it had been in over a year.

Seven months later, in July 2000, the SEC relented that they had not uncovered anything illegal or suspicious about Tyco's activities. Although the company itself may have been reassured by the clean bill of health, Tice's allegations continued to worry investors. Tyco desperately needed to regain Wall Street's respect if it wanted to continue to grow.

By the end of 2001, Tyco's share price was roughly equivalent to what it had been at the beginning of the year. The stock seemed stable but dormant, which worried shareholders, particularly Tyco senior executive shareholders. Their fortunes rode on Tyco stock. In 2001, Kozlowski received stock grants priced at $50 per share. If he cashed in, taxes would surely eat up half of his returns. If the stock dropped down into the $20 dollar range he would have to take an after-tax loss. Moreover, Tyco's board had decided to put their interests in line with shareholders by taking their $75,000 annual fee in Tyco stock options. If it wasn't about the money, then, it was about Kozlowski's (and the board's) reputation. Tyco had been a growth star. Even in 2000 when the NASDAQ dropped by 17 percent, Tyco stock stayed the upward course.

Shifting the Business Model: Acquisition to Operating Company

Then, investment bankers from Goldman Sachs presented Kozlowski a scenario by which to increase Tyco's value. The bankers argued that Tyco's acquisition strategy for creating shareholder value had come to an end. Tyco was simply too large to gain significant growth from the sort of acquisitions in which the firm excelled. Having reached this limit, Tyco had to shift its business model from an acquisition to an operating model. To do so, Tyco had two options. It could either consolidate its holdings, converting its central office into a hands-on strategic unit. Or, the board could approve a company breakup. Goldman Sachs favored the spin-off strategy, arguing that shareholders could net up to $75 per share, more than a $20 increase of what the shares were selling. (Of course, Goldman Sachs stood to gain as well through $240 million in fees if the breakup went forward.) In January 2002, Kozlowski, after gaining board approval, announced the plan to separate Tyco into four publicly traded units, claiming that the parts were worth more than the whole.

Although the stock started to rally, it soon sloped under Enron's weight. Investors believed that such a drastic strategic change suggested deceitful accounting practices. Soon after, a number of claims began to surface concerning questionable activities on the part of Kozlowski and his CFO Mark Swartz. First, reports revealed that Kozlowski and Swartz had unloaded $500 million worth of their company shares since 1999. Additionally, Tyco admitted to making 700 acquisitions and spending close to $8 billion in the previous three years without alerting shareholders.[37] Finally, Kozlowski admitted publicly that he had approved paying Tyco director Frank Walsh a $20 million finder's fee for the eventual acquisition of CIT, a New York–based financial services firm.

When Josh Berman, a lawyer and Tyco director, was notified of the fee, he became outraged. He called the payment "a blatant conflict of interest" and demanded that Walsh return the money.[38] Walsh, a former chairperson of Wesley Capital, a prominent leveraged buyout firm, simply refused. After all, the acquisition was a $9 billion deal, rendering his fee immaterial. When the board met in January 2002, the directors unanimously voted for Walsh to reimburse Tyco. Walsh stood up and left the room.

Public Outcry

Public reaction to all of these events was heated. Tyco seemed to be in an uproar, and, in the wake of the Enron scandals, eyebrows began to rise. By February, Tyco's stock fell to $25, half of what it had been at the start of the year.[39] The stock price continued to fall throughout March and the beginning of April. The company's market value fell from $120 billion in December 2001 to $40 billion.[40] In an effort to calm the market's reaction, Kozlowski called off the break-up plan on April 25, hoping the public would read the announcement as a sign of Tyco's stability. Instead, the change of plans made Kozlowski seem erratic and unsure about the direction of the company.

On May 31, 2002, Kozlowski learned that he would be indicted for sales tax evasion. It became transparent that since August 2001 he had been buying art and shipping boxes to New Hampshire to avoid paying more than $1 million in sales tax. Apparently the boxes had been empty and the actual paintings were delivered directly to his Manhattan home.[41] When the Tyco directors learned about the legal proceedings they immediately called for Kozlowski's resignation.

The End of the Kozlowski Years

On June 3, 2002, Dennis Kozlowski stepped down from his role as CEO, and John Fort, a current director, took over as interim chair and CEO. He had held these positions for 10 years immediately proceeding Kozlowski's term. Tyco announced that the move was temporary and that same day they were planning to search for a replacement. In light of the questions surrounding Tyco's accounting procedures and the company's future, the resignation did not help investor confidence. That same morning, Tyco's stock fell 19 percent to $18. John Maack, a money manager at Crabbe Huson in Manhattan said, "This is just one more piece of uncertainty and the share price is telling you what shareholders think. What we needed here were signs of stability and that things were going to be OK. Not this."

On June 4, 2002, Dennis Kozlowski was led into a New York City courtroom, head hanging, shoulders slumped. It was a startling image and one that not many had seen before. This man was the CEO who had helped Tyco's stock climb to more than $63 per share. Over 10 years he built the company into a diversified, international presence (see Exhibit 3 for an overview of Tyco's divisions and products as of 2002). He had been lauded on the covers of *Barron's* and *Forbes*. He had watched as Tyco was named on *BusinessWeek's* list of 50 top-performing companies (see Appendix A). Brimming with self-confidence, he once seemed like the model of the modern American executive. Now, the CEO of this once thriving company was being indicted for tax evasion. His career was finished. The company he left behind was in disarray.

For Fort, this scandal must have proved particularly troubling. All the misreporting and executive compensation concealment had occurred while he was a board member. How could he and Tyco's other directors confidently say that they had acted as corporate fiduciaries? How could they tell investors that they had acted with a duty of care? Fort had little time to sort out these and other issues facing the company. In July 2002, Edward Breen took over as CEO. Prior to joining Tyco, Breen was president and chief operating officer of Motorola from January 2002 to July 2002; executive vice president and president of Motorola's Networks Sector from January 2001 to January 2002; executive vice president and president of Motorola's Broadband Communications Sector from January 2000 to January 2001.[42]

Breen's immediate task was to find ways to regain investor confidence, boost Tyco's image, and dissociate himself and Tyco's board from the lying, cheating, and stealing that suddenly seemed to be overtaking Tyco and corporate America. With Tyco's severe liquidity crisis many were wondering whether the conglomerate would even survive.[43] (See Exhibits 1, 4, and 5 for pertinent financial information.)

Exhibit 3 Tyco's Divisions and Products

Electronics: Worldwide supplier of active and passive electronic components. Products can be found in computers, telecommunications equipment, industrial machinery, aerospace and defense applications, automobiles, household appliances, and consumer electronics.

Engineered Products and Services: Consists of four global businesses: flow control, fire and building products, electrical and metal products, and infrastructure services. Valve and control products are used to transport, control, and sample liquids, powders, and gasses in oil and gas, chemical, petrochemical, power generation, waste and waste water, pharmaceutical, pulp and paper, food and beverage, commercial construction, and other industries.

Healthcare and Specialty Products: Worldwide manufacturer, distributor, and service provider of medical devices, including disposable medical supplies, monitoring equipment, medical instruments, and bulk analgesic pharmaceuticals and chemicals. Business segments include medical, surgical, respiratory, imaging, pharmaceutical, and retail products.

Plastics and Adhesives: Maker of products used in packaging, including polyethylene films, laminated and coated products, tapes, adhesives, plastic garment hangers, bags and sheeting, disposable dinnerware products, and tapes for industrial applications. This division was comprised of A&E products, Ludlow Coated Products, Tyco Plastics and Tyco Adhesives.

Fire and Security Services: Worldwide leader in fire protection and electronic security. It designs, manufactures, installs, and services electronic security systems, fire protection, detection and suppression systems, fire sprinklers, and extinguishers. It consists of more than 60 brands that are represented in more than 100 countries. It also makes electronic security systems and monitoring for consumers and business, including aviation, marine, transportation, and government security systems. Anti-theft systems for large and small retailers as well as video surveillance and life safety systems are also among its products.

Exhibit 4 Tyco International's Financial Highlights, 1998–2002

	Year Ended September 30,				
	2002	2001	2000	1999	1998
	(in millions, except per-share data)				
Consolidated Statements of Operations Data:					
Net revenues	$35,643.7	$34,036.6	$28,931.9	$22,496.5	$19,061.7
(Loss) income from continuing operations	(3,070.4)	4,401.5	4,519.9	1,067.7	1,168.6
Cumulative effect of accounting changes, net of tax	—	(683.4)	—	—	—
Net (loss) income	(9,411.7)	3,970.6	4,519.9	1,022.0	1,166.2
Basic (loss) earnings per common share:					
(Loss) income from continuing operations	(1.54)	2.44	2.68	0.65	0.74
Cumulative effect of accounting changes, net of tax	—	(0.38)	—	—	—
Net (loss) income	(4.73)	2.20	2.68	0.62	0.74
Diluted (loss) earnings per common share:					
(Loss) income from continuing operations	(1.54)	2.40	2.64	0.64	0.72
Cumulative effect of accounting changes, net of tax	—	(0.37)	—	—	—
Net (loss) income	(4.73)	2.17	2.64	0.61	0.72
Cash dividends per common share					
Consolidated Balance Sheet Data (End of Period):					
Total assets	$66,414.4	$71,022.6	$40,404.3	$32,344.3	$23,440.7
Long-term debt	16,486.8	19,596.0	9,461.8	9,109.4	5,424.7
Shareholders' equity	24,790.6	31,737.4	17,033.2	12,369.3	9,901.8

	Year Ended September 30, 1998	Nine Months Ended September 30, 1997	Year Ended December 31,		
			1996	1995	1994
	(in millions, except per-share amounts)				
Consolidated Statements of Operations Data:					
Net sales	$ 12,311.3	$ 7,588.2	$8,103.7	$6,915.6	$6,240.9
Operating income (loss)	1,923.7	(476.5)	(18.8)	649.6	653.6
Income (loss) before extraordinary items	1,177.1	(776.8)	(296.7)	267.5	304.8
Income (loss) before extraordinary items per common share:					
Basic	2.07	(1.50)	(.62)	.58	.65
Diluted	2.02	(1.50)	(.62)	.57	.63
Cash dividends per common share	.10				
Consolidated Balance Sheet Data:					
Total assets	$16,526.6	$10,447.0	$8,471.3	$7,357.8	$7,053.2
Long-term debt	4,652.6	2,480.6	1,878.4	1,760.7	1,755.3
Shareholders' equity	6,136.9	3,429.4	3,288.6	3,342.7	3,030.0

Source: 2007, Hoovers' 10-K report, January.

Exhibit 5 Tyco International's Financial Ratios and Indicators, 1997–2002

Profitability Ratios	9/30/2002	9/30/2001	9/30/2000	9/30/1999	9/30/1998[1]	9/30/1997[2]
Return on Equity (%)	–12.39	14.72	26.54	8.36	11.8	–22.65
Return on Assets (%)	–4.66	4.29	11.22	3.12	4.85	–7.44
Return on Investment	–47.83	17.67	74.4	22.79	34.93	–19.73
Gross Margin	0.035	0.042	0.038	0.036	0.033	0.033
EBITDA of Revenue (%)	1.82	24.66	18.92	9.5	16.25	–6.28
Operating Margin (%)	–4.43	17.04	18.92	9.5	10.22	–6.28
Pre-Tax Margin	–7.89	17.04	22.34	7.34	8.93	–7.77
Net Profit Margin (%)	–26.4	14.67	15.62	4.38	6.12	–11.01
Effective Tax Rate (%)	–9.17	23.86	29.79	37.56	31.37	–31.71
Liquidity Indicators						
Quick Ratio	0.62	1.23	0.62	0.82	0.82	0.61
Current Ratio	1.01	1.38	1.1	1.29	1.37	1.03
Working Capital/Total Assets	0	0.12	0.03	0.08	0.11	0.01
Debt Management						
Current Liabilities/Equity	0.79	1.06	0.69	0.74	0.71	1.16
Total Debt to Equity	0.67	1.2	0.56	0.74	0.55	0.72
Long Term Debt to Assets	0.25	0.35	0.23	0.28	0.23	0.24
Asset Management						
Revenues/Total Assets	0.54	0.33	0.72	0.68	0.79	0.73
Revenues/Working Capital	269.01	2.84	25.45	8.51	7.38	64.86
Interest Coverage	–1.61	—	8.65	4.02	6.53	–3.29

[1]As reported in the 1999 Annual Report; Certain prior year amounts have been reclassified to conform with current year presentation.

[2]For 9 months due to fiscal year end change.

Source: 2007, Mergent Online, January.

Notes

1. 2005, *Associated Press,* September 20.
2. 2006, The shareholders' revolt, *The Economist,* June 17, 71; 2005, A bad week to be bad, *The Economist,* June 23.
3. http://tycoint.com/tyco/history.asp.
4. A. Bianco, W. Symonds, & N. Byrnes with D. Polek, 2002, The rise and fall of Dennis Kozlowski. *BusinessWeek Online,* December 23.
5. J. B. Stewart, 2003, Spend! Spend! Spend! Where did Tyco's money go? *The New Yorker,* February 17.
6. Bianco, Symonds, & Byrnes, The rise and fall of Dennis Kozlowski.
7. S. Syre & C. Stein, 1999, The quiet giant: Tyco International takes unglamorous road to riches, *Boston Globe,* June 30.
8. Ibid.
9. Bianco, Symonds, & Byrnes, The rise and fall of Dennis Kozlowski.
10. Ibid.
11. Ibid.
12. J. Thottam, 2004, Can this man save Tyco? *Time,* February 9, 48.
13. 2001, Tyco planning 11,000 job cuts, *Financial Times,* August 14.
14. D. J. Collis & C. A. Montgomery, 1998, Creating corporate advantage, *Harvard Business Review,* May–June, 71–83.
15. http://tycoint.com/tyco/history.asp.
16. A. Berenson, 2002, Ex-Tyco chief, a big risk taker, now confronts the legal system, *New York Times,* June 10, C1.
17. Reuters, 2003, Ex-Tyco chief had broad acquisition authority, *New York Times,* October 15; R. M. Cook, 2004, Tyco decline leaves void in jobs, donations, *Daily Democrat,* March 28; S. Tully, 2004, Mr. Cleanup: Ed Breen has scrubbed the scandal out of Tyco. Now can he make it another GE? *Fortune,* http://www.fortune.com/fortune/ceo/articles/0,15114,735903,00.html, November 1.
18. http://timesonline.co.uk.
19. Bianco, Symonds, & Byrnes, The rise and fall of Dennis Kozlowski.
20. S. Finkelstein, 2003, Why smart executives fail: Seven habits of spectacularly unsuccessful people, *Business Strategy Review,* Winter.
21. W. C. Symonds, 2001, The most aggressive CEO, *BusinessWeek Online,* May 28.
22. J. B. Stewart, Spend! Spend! Spend! Where did Tyco's money go?
23. R. Khurana, 2002, The curse of the superstar CEO, *Harvard Business Review,* 80(9), September, 60.
24. R. M. Cook, 2004, Tyco decline leaves void in jobs, donations.
25. Supreme Court of the State of New York, The People of the State of New York against L. Dennis Kozlowski and Mark H. Swartz, Indictment No. 5259/02.
26. Ibid.
27. Mark Maremont, 2004, Kozlowski's defense strategy: Big spending was no secret, *Wall Street Journal,* February 9, 1.
28. J. B. Stewart, "Spend! Spend! Spend! Where did Tyco's money go?
29. Ibid.
30. J. Laing, 1999, Tyco's titan: How Dennis Kozlowski is creating a lean profitable giant, *Barron's,* April.

31. H. Weber, 2002, Decade of meteoric growth over for Tyco as company struggles to break itself apart, *Portsmouth Herald*, March 3.
32. http://www.thestreet.com/funds/funds/795362.html.
33. S. Woolley, 2000, The conglomerator wants a little respect, *Forbes*, October 16.
34. *Re Tyco International, Ltd., Securities Litigation*, U.S. District Court for the District of New Hampshire, 185 F. Supp. 2d 102, February 22, 2002.
35. F. Norris, 1999, Tyco shares plunge after company discloses SEC inquiry, *New York Times*, October 29.
36. *Re Tyco International, Ltd.*
37. J. Thottam, Can this man save Tyco?
38. J. B. Stewart, Spend! Spend! Spend! Where did Tyco's money go?
39. Ibid.
40. C. Ayres, 2002, The Tyco juggernaut grinds to a halt, http://www.timesonline.co.uk, June 5.
41. J. B. Stewart, Spend! Spend! Spend! Where did Tyco's money go?
42. A. Weinberg, 2002, Breen cleans Tyco's house, *Forbes Online*, August 2.
43. W. Symonds, 2004, Tyco: Lazarus with a ticker symbol, *BusinessWeek* Online, May 5.

Appendix A Tyco Timeline

1960	Arthur Rosenburg founds Tyco
1962	Becomes incorporated as Tyco Labs
1964	Goes public
1965	Makes first acquisition: Mule Battery Products
1968	Has acquired 16 companies by this time
1973	Joseph Gaziano becomes CEO
1974	Acquires Simplex Technology, undersea fiber optics telecommunications cable manufacturer
1975	Dennis Kozlowski starts at Tyco as assistant comptroller and head of auditing
1976	Acquires Grinnell Fire Protection Systems, fire sprinkler systems manufacturer
1979	Acquires Armin Plastics, polyethylene film products manufacturer
1981	Acquires Ludlow Corporation, packaging products manufacturer
1982	John Fort becomes CEO, organizes Tyco subsidiaries into 3 business segments: Fire Protection, Electronics, and Packaging
1983	Kozlowski becomes director of Fire Protection Division
1986	Acquires Grinnell Corporation
1987	Kozlowski joins Tyco board
1987	Acquires Allied Tube & Conduit, brings Tyco into Steel Tube Market
1989	Acquires Mueller Company, manufacturers of water and glass flow control products
1991	Acquires Wormald International Ltd., fire protections systems and products
1992	Kozlowski becomes CEO
1993	Company changes name to Tyco International
1995	Opens New York City office on Fifth Avenue
1997	Becomes incorporated in Bermuda by way of ADT Security Systems acquisition
1997	*BusinessWeek* names Tyco one of top 50 companies
1998	Acquires AMP Inc., biggest maker of electronic conductors
1999	New York District Attorney's office performs brief investigation to determine whether a Tyco director illegally sold his $2.5 million Florida home to the company's general counsel; investigations are inconclusive
Apr. 1999	Kozlowski is on the cover of *Barron's* "Tyco's Titan: How Dennis Kozlowski Is Creating a Lean, Profitable Giant"
Aug. 1999	Tyco pays $38.5 million in allegedly unauthorized bonuses to top executives
Oct. 1999	David Tice, analyst and money manager, newsletter "Behind the Numbers" accuses Tyco of inflating reported profits
Oct. 1999	*New York Times* article reports two of Tyco's acquisitions had taken big write-offs just before they were acquired; article accuses Tyco of not disclosing the write-offs to the SEC in November–December 1999; SEC begins "nonpublic informal inquiry"
July 2000	SEC ends investigations, reporting that Tyco's accounting practices look clean; Tice maintains his criticisms
Aug. 2000	Tyco pays $18 million for Fifth Avenue duplex for Kozlowski
Sept. 2000	Tyco pays $96 million in unauthorized bonuses to 50 employees
Oct. 2000	Kozlowski is on the cover of *Forbes*, "The Conglomerator Wants a Little Respect"
June 2001	Tyco buys CIT, a financial services firm, for $10 million
June 2001	Tyco pays for half of Kozlowski's wife's $2.1 million birthday party in Sardinia
Aug. 2001	Kozlowski begins buying art for his Manhattan apartment and having empty boxes shipped to New Hampshire
2001	Tyco cuts 11,000 jobs and closes/consolidates 300 plants in attempts to reduce costs
Jan. 2002	Kozlowski makes public plan to split Tyco up into four publicly traded units; met with strong resistance from shareholders

Jan. 2002	Investors learn of $20 million finder's fee paid to Tyco director Frank Walsh for acquisition of CIT without board's approval
Jan. 2002	Manhattan district attorney begins looking into tax evasion/money laundering scheme involving Kozlowski and Manhattan-based art dealer
April 2002	Kozlowski calls off Tyco break-up plan
June 2002	Kozlowski resigns
June 2002	Fort names interim CEO
July 2002	Edward Breen takes over as CEO (Prior to joining Tyco, Mr. Breen held executive positions with Motorola.)
June 2005	Kozlowski and Mark Swartz convicted of grand larceny, conspiracy and fraud
Sept. 2005	Kozlowski and Swartz received 8- to 25-year sentences at Mid-State Correctional Facility near Utica, New York, and ordered to pay a total of $134 million in restitution along with fines of $70 million for Kozlowski and $35 million for Swartz

Case 27

Vodafone: Out of Many, One[1]

Johannes Banzhaf, Ashok Som

ESSEC Business School

Abstract

In 2006, Vodafone Group PLC was the world's largest cell phone provider by revenue. Since 1999, Vodafone had invested US$270 billion (€225 billion) mostly in stock, building an empire spanning 26 countries. It controlled cell phone operations in 16 countries and had minority stakes in companies in 10 other countries. This case traces the history of Vodafone's growth and its capability to transform and adapt itself to the dramatically changing market environment in the dynamic telecommunication sector. The case analyzes Vodafone's growth through acquisitions and the subsequent integration of acquired units with a key focus on how it manages to coordinate its businesses on a global scale.

Arun Sarin reclined in his seat in a first-class compartment en route to London. The CEO of Vodafone, the world's largest mobile telephone operator, began reflecting on the events of the last few days, in particular Vodafone's decision to exit the Japanese market by selling Vodafone's stake in Japan Telecom to Tokyo-based Softbank in a deal valued at $15.4 billion, confirming that after the sale the company would return $10.5 billion to its shareholders. Vodafone had trailed behind NTT DoCoMo and KDDI since its entry into Japan in 2001, thanks to fickle consumers, the lack of a low-end tier in the segment, and the challenge of coordinating terminals and technologies across borders. The time had come to make a hard decision, and Sarin had made it.

It was not the first time he had been faced with such a decision. Two years earlier Vodafone had made headlines in the financial press with its failed attempt to take over the U.S. mobile operator, AT&T Wireless. After a long takeover battle, Vodafone's American rival Cingular Wireless had offered $41 billion in cash for AT&T Wireless.[2] At the time, Sarin had not been sure whether to regret the failed takeover. He could have easily financed a larger sum for the bid, but major shareholders had been explicit that anything beyond an offer of $38 billion would be detrimental to their interests.[3] Vodafone's offer had forced Cingular to increase its bid from $30 billion to $41 billion, meaning that it might take Cingular many years to digest the merger (refer to Exhibit 1 for share prices of Vodafone since 1989). More promising and cheaper ways to enhance its presence in the world's largest economy with a huge growth potential might also come Vodafone's way.

Sarin knew he could not afford to alienate Vodafone's shareholders by pursuing growth at all costs. However, Vodafone's current hold in the U.S. market (the noncontrolling stake in Verizon Wireless but the only one in the United States) was not comforting either. The relationship with the other main shareholder, Verizon, was quite strained, management had refused to adopt the single Vodafone brand, and had insisted on using the outdated American CDMA network standard instead of the group-wide GSM/UMTS standard.[4]

Being the CEO was definitely not an easy job, with so many things to consider and the shadow of his larger-than-life predecessor Sir Chris Gent looming over him. But these reasons were exactly why he was being paid £1.2 million a year as base salary.[5]

Company Overview: Vodafone Group Plc

In 2005, Vodafone was the leading mobile phone operator in the world. It had more than 150 million customers worldwide in 26 different countries.[6] Vodafone employed approximately 67,000 people around the world and had its headquarters in Newbury, England. Being listed on the stock exchanges of New York (ticker: VOD), London, and Frankfurt, it boasted a market capitalization

Exhibit 1 Vodafone Share Price Since 2001 (in pence)

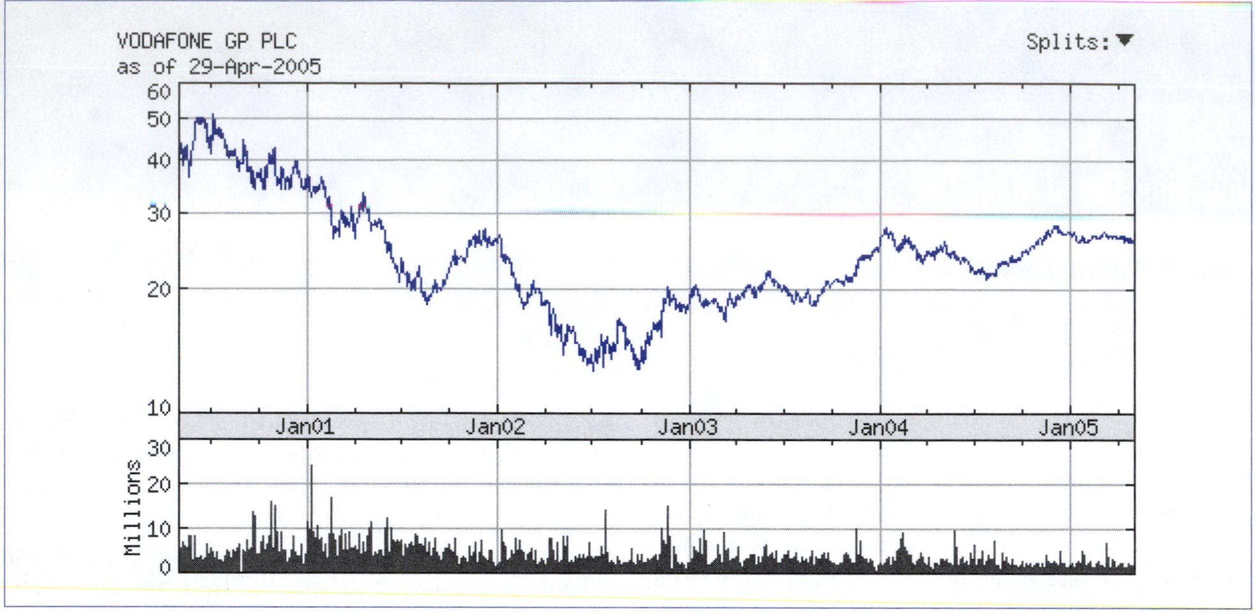

Source: http://finance.yahoo.com.

of US$165.7 billion[7] making it the eleventh most valuable company in the world. In FY2003 it suffered a loss of US$15.5 billion (on revenues of approximately US$48 billion). This figure was the result of large write-downs on the goodwill of acquired companies and huge amortization charges related to the acquisition of other mobile operators like Mannesmann D2. These charges amounted to US$18.8 billion.[8] In fact, if one excluded these extraordinary noncash charges, Vodafone was profitable, as indicated by its gross margins and its capacity to generate huge positive cash flows: The cash flow from operating activities (before capital expenditure and other outflows) amounted to £12.3 billion (approximately US$22.7 billion) in financial year 2004, while free cash flow exceeded an unbelievable £8 billion (US$15.7 billion—refer to Exhibit 2 for an overview of Vodafone Group's financials).[9] Vodafone had been consistently paying dividends and had recently announced a £3 billion share repurchase program.[10]

History of Vodafone[11]

The company was formed as Racal Telecom Limited in 1984 as a subsidiary of Racal Electronics Plc., a British electronics manufacturing company. It successfully bid for a private sector U.K. cellular license in 1982 and hosted the first-ever mobile phone call in the United Kingdom in 1985. The customer base stood at 19,000 on December 31, 1985.

In October 1988, Racal Telecom Ltd. went public by offering approximately 20 percent of the company's stock to the public. Three years later, it was fully de-merged from Racal Electronics and became an independent company, with a different name—Vodafone Group Plc—which was listed on the London and New York stock exchanges. Corporate legend has it that the "founders had the foresight to realize that people would do more than talk over their phones and so created a future-proof name that would embrace both VOice and DAta mobile communication: Vodafone."[12] Due to its early start, it managed the largest mobile network in the world by 1987.

In 1992, Vodafone pioneered again when it signed the world's first international "roaming" agreement with Telecom Finland, allowing Vodafone's customers to use their phone on a different network while still being billed in their home country. Four years later, Vodafone became the first operator in the United Kingdom to offer so-called prepaid packages that do not require the customers to sign a long-term contract.

Christopher Gent succeeded Sir Gerald Whent at the helm of the company on January 1, 1997. Gent was responsible for shifting Vodafone's growth strategy from organic to aggressive external, orchestrating its move toward globalization. In the same year, Vodafone's 100th roaming agreement was signed.

In early 1999, Vodafone signed up its 10 millionth customer, 5 million of them in the United Kingdom. Vodafone's growth reached the next level when it successfully merged with AirTouch Communications Inc. of the United States—a $61 billion deal. Vodafone renamed itself briefly into Vodafone AirTouch and more than doubled its customer base to 31 million customers worldwide (September 1999), having operations in

Exhibit 2 Vodafone Key Financials, 1995–2004

For the Financial Year Ended March 31	Turnover (in £m)	Profit (loss) for the Financial Year (after taxation, in £m)	Net Cash Inflow From Operating Activities (in £m)	Dividends per Share (pence)	Registered Proportionate Customers (in thousands)
1995	1,153	238	386	3.34p	2,073
1996	1,402	311	615	4.01p	3,035
1997	1,749	364	644	4.81p	4,016
1998	2,408	419	886	5.53p	5,844
1999	336	637	1,045	3.77p	10,445
2000	7,873	487	2,510	1.34p	39,139
2001	15,004	(9,763)	4,587	1.40p	82,997
2002	22,845	(16,155)	8,102	1.47p	101,136
2003	30,375*	(9,819)	11,142	1.70p	119,709
2004	33,559	(9,015)	12,317	2.03p	133,421

*See following chart for group turnover by geographic region.

Source: Company annual reports.

(in £ million)	2003	2002
Mobile Telecommunications		
Northern Europe	6,057	
Central Europe	4,775	
Southern Europe	8,051	
Americas	5	
Asia Pacific	8,364	
Middle East and Africa	290	
= **Total mobile operations**	**27,542**	**20,742**
Other Operations		
Europe	854	
Asia Pacific	1,979	
= **Total Group Turnover**	**30,375**	22,845

Note: "Other operations" mainly include the results of the group's interests in fixed line telecommunications businesses in Germany (Arcor), France (Cegetel), and Japan (Japan Telecom). The turnover figure for the Americas does not include the 45% stake in Verizon Wireless (U.S.).

Source: Adapted from company annual report, 2003.

24 countries across five continents.[13] In the late 1990s and the early new millenium, stock markets were steering toward a bubble, with "mobile" being the latest hype and insane sums being paid for mobile operators and the licenses to operate mobile networks. At the end of November 1999, the company had a market capitalization of approximately £90 billion. Vodafone's North American branch was integrated into a new entity branded Verizon Wireless together with Bell Atlantic's mobile business, with Vodafone retaining a 45 percent stake in the new venture. Verizon Wireless was the largest mobile phone operator in 2003 in a fragmented North American market (36 million customers, 24% market share as of September 30, 2003).[14]

In a move that sent shockwaves through corporate Germany in 1999, Vodafone launched a €100 billion takeover bid for Mannesmann in order to get hold of its D2 mobile phone business, the private market leader in Germany. A bitter struggle for Mannesmann's independence ensued, but finally the board of Mannesmann gave in and the deal was closed in 2000: €190 billion paid in stocks made it Germany's largest takeover ever.[15] The customer base was once again doubled and Vodafone found itself among the 10 largest companies in the world in terms of market capitalization. The mobile telephony boom reached its peak and former national providers (such as Deutsche Telekom, France Télécom, Telefonica) embarked on a buying binge that brought them on the verge of bankruptcy, when the bubble finally burst (Deutsche Telekom shares fell from more than €100 to €15).

The year 2001 saw a consolidation and restructuring within Vodafone, which reported 82.9 million customers for the financial year ending March 31, 2001. It grew at a somewhat slower pace than in previous years, about half of it generated by internal growth and the other half by acquisitions (e.g., acquiring Ireland's Eircell and increasing its stake in Spanish AirTel Movil to 91.7%). However, slower growth still meant that Vodafone had added approximately 20 million customers by the end of the year 2002. At that time, the company board announced that the Indian-born American Arun Sarin would take over the CEO position on July 30, 2003.

No large scale acquisitions took place in 2002 and 2003, but instead a host of smaller deals and partnership agreements were made. In February 2004, Vodafone's bid for AT&T Wireless in the United States failed against a higher offer by Cingular, clearly indicating that Vodafone had all but renounced its growth ambitions.

Growth at Vodafone

Traditionally growth at Vodafone was by acquisitions rather than organic. It had a track record in takeovers and their subsequent successful integration, Germany's Mannesmann being the most prominent example. Branded as "Vodafone Germany," Mannesmann was the group's most profitable venture (in terms of EBIT, which surpassed £2 billion in 2003) and its largest subsidiary. On the mobile telephony acquisition strategy, Alan Harper, Group Strategy and Business Integration Director, commented,

In the past 10 years there had been a sea of change in the evolution of the telecommunication industry. The rule in this industry has been "Hunt or Be Hunted." The strategy of the global players had been mobile-centric, multi-market strategies. Most of the companies like Hutchison, Mannesmann, Airtouch started much smaller, like a start-up, did not have any history as an operator and the parent company was usually a trading company. Vodafone acquired Mannesmann, Airtouch and the rest of the small players. FT acquired Orange. Docomo was restructured back into NTT.

Unlike many of its competitors, Vodafone used shares for its acquisitions. This practice might be one of the reasons why Vodafone emerged from the telecom crisis relatively early and could concentrate on growth again, while virtually all of its competitors were still occupied in trying to reduce their debt burden (Deutsche Telekom, France Télécom, MMO2, KPN, etc.).[16] However, Vodafone's shares had shown only lackluster performance in prior months, which meant that Vodafone increasingly had to use hard cash to increase its holdings in subsidiaries or for new acquisitions. Because Vodafone did not want to compromise its good credit ratings (by industry standards) under any circumstances, it slowed down on acquisitions and focused on internal growth for the preceding two years (refer to Exhibit 3 for Vodafone's strategic intent).

Vodafone had acquired other businesses along with the mobile phone business as in the case of Japan Telecom and Mannesmann, where it got ownership of fixed line operations. Vodafone had been always explicit in its concentration on its core business of mobile telecommunications. Usually it started looking for potential buyers for the other business. In the words of Alan Harper, Group Strategy and Business Integration Director,

We had been always mobile focused. In 1995, when I joined Vodafone, it was mobile focused. It has a turnover of £8 billion, it was the third largest mobile operator in the UK and had 80% business in the UK. Today, in 2005, we are still mobile focused, with a turnover of £100 billion, biggest in the world and only 10% in the UK.

Exhibit 3 Strategic Intent of Vodafone

The Company had maintained a strategy of focusing on global mobile telecommunications and providing network coverage to allow its customers to communicate using mobile products and services. The Company's strategy was increasingly focused on revenue growth and margin improvement from providing enhanced services to its customer base. This growth strategy had three principal components:

- to grow voice and data revenues through an increased marketing focus on our established high-quality customer base;
- to extend our operational leadership of the industry through maximizing the benefits of scale and scope, through the use of partner network agreements, by increasing equity interests in businesses where the Group had existing shareholdings and by promoting the Vodafone brand; and
- to extend service differentiation, investing in delivering Vodafone branded, easy to use, customer propositions for mobile voice and data.

Where appropriate, and if circumstances allow, the Company may also make further acquisitions or disposals of businesses.

Source: http://www.vodafone.com.

Vodafone balanced its investment options by taking its time to ensure a good investment and disinvestment option. For example, it sold Japan Telecom's fixed line operations in 2003 for ¥261.3 billion (£1.4 billion)[17] while it reinforced its long-term commitment to Japan in 2005 by making a further investment of up to £2.6 billion. Arun Sarin pointed out,

Our transactions in Japan will simplify the structure, confirm our commitment to the Japanese marketplace, and enable us to deliver on the changes needed to improve our position.

Arcor was not divested and was still part of Vodafone Germany as of 2005. Arcor might even serve as a strategic weapon to cannibalize on incumbent Deutsche Telekom's profitable fixed line business.[18]

Since mid-2001, Vodafone had entered into arrangements with other network operators in countries where it did not hold any equity stake. Under the terms of so-called Partner Network Agreements, Vodafone cooperated with its counterparts in the development and marketing of global services under dual brand logos. By 2003, Vodafone had extended its reach into 11 other countries, thus establishing a first foothold in these markets.[19] Such an agreement was a classic win-win situation: Vodafone not only gained new market insight with little risk, but at the same time was able to assess the quality of the partner in order to identify possible takeover targets, while the partner benefited from Vodafone's unique marketing and technological capabilities.

Vodafone's acquisition strategy always followed a similar pattern: First, the number one or two player within a national market was identified, while it carefully avoided acquiring the incumbent mobile operator that was linked to the state-owned telecom monopoly (like T-Mobile, which was the mobile division of Deutsche Telekom, or Orange, a business unit of France Télécom). It seems that Vodafone feared a bureaucratic inertia of these organizations, and would rather focus on more flexible, entrepreneurially minded challengers (with Mannesmann's D2 once again being a good example, or France's SFR) that would challenge the incumbents in different local markets. Referring to this strategy Alan Harper explained,

Our vision has been to leverage scale and scope benefits, reduce response time in the market, and ensure effective delivery to customers. This we have achieved by collecting or acquiring national (operational) companies and gave them a mission of a "challenger company" in each of the national markets. For example, Vodafone with SFR is a challenger to France Telecom in France, Vodafone UK is a challenger to British Telecom in the UK, and Vodafone Germany a challenger to Deutsch Telecom in Germany. Together with this challenger mind-set, we nurture and instill an entrepreneurial spirit inside Vodafone Group companies, and in this respect we do not behave as a traditional telephone company. Since we differ from being a traditional company, the cultural alignment of people working for Vodafone is a key issue in sustaining this challenger and entrepreneurial mind-set. To focus on this cultural alignment, we give autonomy to the local entity and reiterate that the local entity did not join a global company like IBM or HP. The local entity has to work in a matrix structure and keep alive the "challenger mind-set" on fixed line telephony and other incumbents, challenge the status quo every day, and evolve by being local entrepreneurs.

Branding, Identity, and Pricing

After a successful bid for a takeover target, Vodafone followed a diverse strategy in terms of branding, creating its identity and its own pricing models. Alan Harper explained,

We play different models of creating Vodafone's identity in the market. Which way we adapt depends on a number of factors and considerations, such as the strength of the local brand, the prevalent company culture and the general fit between Vodafone's processes and the acquired business' processes. But frankly, at the end of the day, it comes down to a question of management judgment. For example, in New Zealand when we acquired Bellsouth, we changed Bellsouth almost overnight to Vodafone New Zealand. Similarly in Portugal, we undertook an overnight integration of Telecel to Vodafone Portugal. Telecel transformed into Vodafone Portugal and became challenger to the traditional PTT. Whereas in Italy, when we acquired Omnitel, it took us 2.5 years to change Omnitel to Omnitel Vodafone. Onmitel colours were Green and White and we could not change it to Vodafone Red immediately. It was because Omnitel had a strong brand image, very well known and we had to be very cautious during the transition. The market would never have accepted it. The same was the case with DT in Germany.

The management judgment of fast or slow rebranding turned on the customer and organizational response of the acquired market and acquired company. Usually the national brand was kept alive for some time until the dust of the takeover battle had settled. Vodafone then carefully launched its phased rebranding campaign to bring the new subsidiary under the "Vodafone" umbrella. Usually, they added "Vodafone" to the original corporate brand. To better coordinate these branding efforts, Vodafone appointed David Haines, a former Coca-Cola manager, as global brand director.[20] Davin Haines explained,

For example "D2" became "D2 Vodafone." Within a year, Vodafone modified the logo to its typical red color and changed the order of company name, for example "D2 Vodafone" to "Vodafone D2." During the last phase, the original "national" name was eliminated completely and only the global brand and logo remained. This process could take more than two years and usually passed almost unnoticed by the customers, who got accustomed to the new logo due to the extensive branding campaigns, often in conjunction with the launch of a new global product (like Vodafone's Mobile Connect Card, enabling e-mailing and Internet access via a laptop and the mobile network) or service (e.g., Vodafone live! mobile Internet portal). Following this pattern, Vodafone Omnitel in Italy and J-Phone Vodafone in Japan became a single brand in May 2003 and October 2003, respectively.[21]

Vodafone launched its first truly global communications campaign in the beginning of August 2001 to reinforce its brand awareness and a global brand identity. Arun Sarin reiterated,

Throughout the past few years, Vodafone has done a terrific job of building brand awareness as we have moved toward a single global brand. Beyond brand awareness, we want people to understand that the Vodafone name represents great service, great value and great innovation. When our name becomes synonymous with these attributes we will achieve brand preference and expect to see our market share climb as a result.

Across all media, a homogenous corporate brand and identity was communicated including the slogan "How are you?" and introduced the inverted comma as logo. To keep in sync with Vodafone's global aspirations, the group selected two globally recognized brands: It sponsored the Manchester United Football Club and the Ferrari Formula 1 team to improve awareness and perception of the brand. In addition, it supported its brand by individual sponsorship contracts and other marketing communication programs at the local level. According to a Vodafone statement,

An audit of the first year of sponsorship of Scuderia Ferrari reveals that the sponsorship had outperformed all of the annual targets set internally by Vodafone and helped establish exceptional global brand awareness.[22]

Being number one or number two in most markets[23] it had entered, Vodafone never used "low prices" to attract new customers. Instead, it focused on creating and marketing new value-added services that enticed customers to sign up with Vodafone, even if it implied paying not the lowest rates available. According to Arun Sarin,

We have rededicated ourselves to delighting our customers because we believe this is the foundation for our continued success. We recognise that every customer interaction provides another opportunity to win loyalty and that's why we continue to raise standards on the quality of customer care in our call centres and our stores and the quality of our networks. Key to delighting our customers is our ability to deliver superior voice and data services according to differing customer needs.

Vodafone was not immune to the pricing policies of its competitors, which meant that it lowered its tariffs whenever the price differential became too great and the new subscriber market share dropped below a critical level. Given its size and healthy finances, it could usually weather price wars and simply waited until the aggressive player lost its thrust. Appendix I explores in some detail the role of fixed costs and their impact on pricing in the mobile telecommunication market.

Integrating to One Vodafone

Vodafone realized that real business integration extends far beyond having a single brand. Critics had pointed out that establishing a global brand and logo is among the easier tasks of managing a multinational corporation. Alan Harper stressed,

The careful re-branding policy not only targeted customers, but also tried to address the needs and concerns of the employees. The employees had to adjust to the fact that though they were "national challengers with an instilled entrepreneurial spirit," they were also part of the family of the global Vodafone Corporation based in Newbury, England. It was perceived that most employees were proud of having contributed to the success of challenging the incumbent operator and were reluctant to be incorporated into a larger corporation that they perceived as "distant."

After the heady days of Chris Gent and the acquisitions by the dozen, Arun Sarin had to find innovative ways to integrate "a disparate group of national operations" into one company. Arun Sarin recognized that winning over the hearts of the employees and achieving cultural alignment was perhaps the "biggest challenge of all." An analyst of Merrill Lynch praised Arun Sarin as "smart" and "strategically as good as it gets."[24] Sarin seemed to be a good fit for this extraordinary task ahead, as he was described as "an operating man rather than a dealmaker" and "the archetypal international executive."[25] The portrait of Sarin went on like this:

Born and brought up in India, but now an American citizen, Mr Sarin's background was an asset. There might seem to be a certain irony in putting an Indian-American in charge of the world's biggest mobile-phone operator, each of these countries had made a mess of introducing wireless telecoms. But Vodafone was a British company that aspired to be a true multinational. It had large operations in Germany, where it bought Mannesmann in 2000, in Italy and in Japan. To put another Brit into the top job might have bred resentment. [. . .] The son of a well-to-do Indian military officer, he went to a military boarding-school, but his mother encouraged him not to follow his father's career. Instead, he took an engineering degree at the Indian Institute of Technology, the country's equivalent of MIT. From there he went to the University of California at Berkeley on a scholarship, to earn a further degree in engineering and a MBA. He had lived in America ever since. The main remnants of his origins were an Indian wife (whom he met at Berkeley), a touch of an accent and a passion for cricket, which he shares with Sir Chris [Gent, his predecessor].[26]

Sarin, however, was not the only director on Vodafone's board with a distinct international background. As a result of Vodafone's past acquisitions and their pragmatic integration into the group, many skilled foreign (non-British) managers had been retained and had since joined the board, including two Germans, one Italian, one South African, and one Swede (see Exhibit 4(a) and (b)).

At the annual general meeting in July 2003, Sarin emphasized the need to benefit from economies of scale and scope. In June 2004, Arun Sarin redefined,

At Vodafone, everything we do furthers our desire to create mobile connections for individuals, businesses and communities. Our Vision is to be the world's mobile communications leader and we're delighted by the prospects for the future of our industry. Our commitment to this industry is underlined by our company values, which state that everything we do is driven by our passion for customers, our people, results and the world around us. . . . Operating in 26 markets (together with Partner Networks in a further 14 countries, with approximately 151.8 million registered customers, and approximately 398.5 million total venture customers) puts us in an enviable position to leverage our global scale and scope. . . . Another competitive advantage is our leadership position on cost and time to market. From network services to sales, and marketing to customer care and billing, we have many varied systems in use across the business. With strong co-operation between our various operating companies we can achieve further savings.

To coordinate, restructure, and integrate its various systems across 26 countries, Vodafone launched its "One Vodafone" initiative that aimed to boost annual pretax

Exhibit 4(a) Vodafone's Executive and Nonexecutive Directors

As of July 30, 2005, Vodafone had six executive directors and eight nonexecutive directors, including the chairperson, Lord MacLaurin.

- **Lord MacLaurin of Knebworth,** *Chairperson*
- **Paul Hazen,** *Deputy Chairperson and Senior Independent Director*
- **Arun Sarin,** *Chief Executive* (Indian-born and raised, graduated from the Indian Institute of Technology, but now American citizen. Former chief executive officer for the United States and Asia Pacific region until April 15, 2000, when he became a nonexecutive director. Former director of AirTouch from July 1995 and president and chief operating officer from February 1997 to June 1999. Appointed chief executive on 30 July 2003.)
- **Peter R. Bamford,** *Chief Marketing Officer*
- **Thomas Geitner,** *Chief Technology Officer*
- **Julian M. Horn-Smith,** *Group Chief Operating Officer*
- **Kenneth J. Hydon,** *Financial Director*
- **Sir John Bond**
- **Dr. Michael J. Boskin**
- **Professor Sir Alec Broers**
- **Dr. John Buchanan**
- **Penelope L. Hughes**
- **Sir David Scholey, CBE**
- **Professor Jürgen Schrempp**
- **Luc Vandevelde**

Exhibit 4(b) Vodafone's Executive and Nonexecutive Directors

- **Arun Sarin,** Chief Executive
- **Sir Julian Horn-Smith,** Deputy Chief Executive
- **Ken Hydon,** Financial Director
- **Peter Bamford,** Chief Marketing Officer
- **Thomas Geitner,** Chief Technology Officer
- **Jürgen von Kuczkowski,** Chief Executive Germany
- **Pietro Guindani,** Chief Executive Italy
- **Bill Morrow,** Chief Executive United Kingdom
- **Paul Donovan,** Regional Chief Executive
- **Brian Clark,** Chief Executive Asia Pacific and Group Human Resources Director Designate
- **Shiro Tsuda,** Chief Executive Japan
- **Alan Harper,** Group Strategy and Business Integration Director
- **Phil Williams,** Group Human Resources Director
- **Stephen Scott,** Group General Counsel and Company Secretary
- **Simon Lewis,** Group Corporate Affairs Director

Source: http://www.vodafone.com.

operating profit by £2.5 billion by FY2008.[27] Alan Harper explained in detail:

We are in a period when we are integrating our company. With acquisitions all over the world, one of our challenges is to integrate seamlessly not only technology (which by the way is more or less similar across the world) but people. And this is a key part of the Branding Evolution that we had witnessed. The challenge of this restructuring program is to balance the need of coordination and synergies while encouraging local initiatives.

The One Vodafone program is a business integration activity and we are in the process of "gradual integration of our business architecture." For example, we are running down a real-time billing system to an integrated system for 28mn customers. It is a very difficult task if one tries to understand the billing system of mobile telephones. Under the One Vodafone, there are currently 8 programs, Networks (design and supply procurement, coordination, and consolidation initiatives), IT (design, back office, billings, ERP/HR, operations—data centre processes), Service platforms, Roaming (mapping footprints), Customer (next practice services), Handset portfolio, MNC accounts, Retailing (one won't believe, we are the eighth largest retailer in the world taking together our stores that are owned or franchised). . . . We are trying to integrate national operating units across footprints and trying to leverage scale and scope while trying to retain the local autonomy and responsiveness of our challenger national units.

Alan Harper agreed that implementation of "One Vodafone" is a challenge. He explained,

To implement One Vodafone, we have undertaken a change in organizational structure of the Group [refer to Exhibit 5]. We still operate in a matrix format. What One Vodafone tries to achieve is to simplify the integration issues in terms of brand strength and integrating local culture and processes. We centralize all our marketing efforts, branding and product development. Technology is standardized. Network design (switching, radio) are coordinated. Best practices are benchmarked by Advance Services such as service platforms and portals (Vodafone Live!). Knowledge is shared via the HQ, HR, strategy, and Marketing departments, through lateral processes, including our governance processes. We keep and encourage local initiatives such as customer services, sales, network billing, and IT systems. We are trying to incorporate the best of all the cultures to the maximum extent possible and in this way we tried to transform Vodafone UK into a new Vodafone.

One Vodafone was clearly communicated across the company via the Internet, intranet, different training programs as well as a monthly employee magazine called "*Vodafone life!* The global magazine for all Vodafone people." The HR department prepared special "initiation" training programs to acquaint new employees to the Vodafone way, labeled the "Vodafone footstep," which included its vision and values (see Exhibit 6) and the "Ten Business Principles."[28] On translating the vision and values alongside changes in structure and systems, Vodafone witnessed revamping of people processes within the organization. Commenting on employees, Arun Sarin explained,

As the business expands and the environment around us evolves, it is crucial for us to develop, recruit and retain the

Exhibit 5 Board Changes and New Organizational Structure as of January 2005

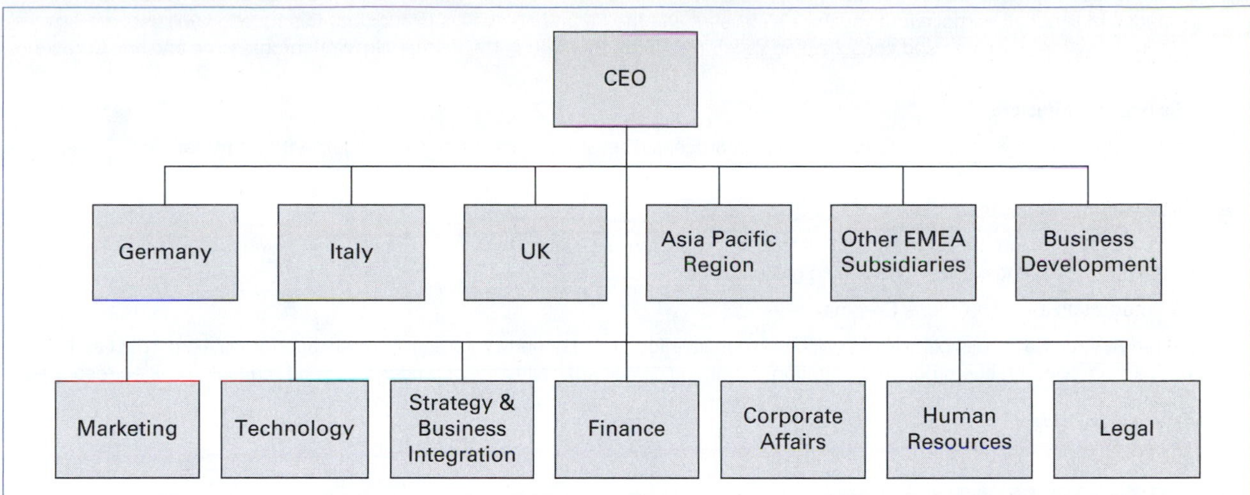

Vodafone Group Plc ("Vodafone") announces Board changes and a new organisational structure which will enable continued improvement in the delivery of the Group's strategic goals. This structure will become effective as of 1 January 2005.

The new organization is designed to:

- Focus more attention on customers in Vodafone's local markets;
- Enhance Vodafone's ability to deliver seamless services to corporations;
- Facilitate coordinated delivery of 3G across all markets;
- Function as an integrated company, delivering on One Vodafone; and
- Simplify decision-making, accountabilities and governance structures to speed up execution.

Vodafone will simplify its existing regional structure with major countries and business areas reporting to the Chief Executive. All first-line management functions in the Operating Companies will have a dual reporting line to the respective functions at Group level.

Arun Sarin, Chief Executive said: "We are creating an organisation that is better positioned to respond to the high expectations of our customers. Faster execution will enable us to extend our lead within the mobile industry and deliver the benefits to our customers, our employees and our shareholders."

Main Board Appointments

Sir Julian Horn-Smith will be appointed Deputy Chief Executive with effect from 1 January 2005. Vodafone separately announces that Andy Halford has been appointed Financial Director Designate. Andy will succeed Ken Hydon when he retires on 26 July 2005.

Operating Company Structure

Vodafone's operating company structure will be streamlined to ensure effective and fast decision making, enabling improved time to market across a number of business initiatives. Consequently, the following operating companies and business areas will report directly into the Chief Executive:

- European Affiliates (Belgium, France, Poland, Romania and Switzerland) and Non-European Affiliates (China, Fiji, Kenya, South Africa and United States), led by Sir Julian Horn-Smith;
- Germany, led by Jürgen von Kuczkowski;
- Italy, led by Pietro Guindani;
- United Kingdom, led by Bill Morrow;
- Other EMEA Subsidiaries (Albania, Egypt, Greece, Hungary, Ireland, Malta, Netherlands, Portugal, Spain and Sweden), led by Paul Donovan;
- Asia Pacific (Australia, Japan and New Zealand), led by Brian Clark who will also be appointed Group Human Resources Director Designate.

Vodafone's Group functions will be strengthened to support the delivery of seamless global propositions and Vodafone's continued integration. The following functions will also report directly to the Chief Executive:

- Marketing, led by Peter Bamford, the Chief Marketing Officer. This function will be reinforced by a newly created Multi National Corporate unit which will assume full accountability for serving Vodafone's global corporate customers. Group Marketing will also manage the global handset portfolio and procurement;
- Technology, led by Thomas Geitner, the Chief Technology Officer. In addition to standardized network design and global supply chain management, this function will introduce the concept of shared service operation for IT and service delivery;

continued

- Business Development, a new function led by Sir Julian Horn-Smith. Sir Julian will be responsible for driving Vodafone's product and services portfolio into Vodafone's affiliates and the Partner Networks. In addition, this function will assume responsibility for expanding and consolidating Vodafone's footprint through the Partner Network programme and any Corporate Finance activities.

New Governance Structure

Vodafone also announces changes to its governance process. The Group will have two management committees which will oversee the execution of the Main Board's strategy and policy.

- The Executive Committee

  Chaired by Arun Sarin, this committee will focus on the Group's strategy, financial structure and planning, succession planning, organizational development and group-wide policies.

- The Integration and Operations Committee

  Chaired by Arun Sarin, this committee will be responsible for setting operational plans, budgets and forecasts, product and service development, customer segmentation, managing delivery of multi-market propositions and managing shared resources.

Source: http://www.vodafone.com.

Exhibit 6 Vodafone's Vision and Values

We have one vision and a set of values that underpins everything we do. Both our vision and our values were shared throughout the global organization.

Our Vision

To be the world's mobile communications leader—enriching customers' lives, helping individuals, businesses and communities be more connected in a mobile world.

- Our customers use mobile communications to make their lives richer, more fulfilled, more connected. They will prefer Vodafone because the experience of using Vodafone will be the best they can find.
- We will lead in making the mobile the primary means of personal communications for every individual around the world.
- Through our leadership, our scale, our scope, and our partnerships, we will bring online mobile services to the world.

Our Values
Passion for customers

Our customers have chosen to trust us. In return, we must strive to anticipate and understand their needs and delight them with our service.

- We value our customers above everything else and aspire to make their lives richer, more fulfilled and more connected.
- We must always listen and respond to each of our customers.
- We will strive to delight our customers, anticipating their needs and delivering greater quality and more value, faster than anyone else.

Passion for our people

Outstanding people working together make Vodafone exceptionally successful.

- We seek to attract, develop, reward, and retain outstanding individuals.
- We believe in empowerment and personal accountability.
- We enjoy what we do.
- We believe in the power of our teams.

Passion for results

We are action-oriented and driven by a desire to be the best.

- We are committed to be the best in all we do.
- We all play our part in delivering results.
- We seek speed, flexibility, and efficiency in all we do.

Passion for the world around us

We will help people of the world to have fuller lives—both through the services we provide and through the impact we have on the world around us.

- We recognize the responsibilities that accompany the growth we have achieved.
- We will be a force for good in the world.
- A spirit of partnership and mutual respect is critical in all our activities.

Source: http://www.vodafone.com.

people that will lead us into this new world. We are working hard to make sure our employees have the right skills and knowledge to anticipate our customers' needs. We are identifying new ways to share the best of what we do on a global basis. We continue to reap the benefits of a motivated team with a strong customer service culture, which will help earn a reputation for Vodafone that is second to none.

The HR Department had set up a fast-track career path (the Global Leadership Programme, GLP) for high-potential managers, rotating them across business functions and countries and equipping them with crucial multicultural skills.

Despite the integration and standardization efforts, the corporate headquarters had to ensure a certain level of independence for individual country subsidiaries to take into account differing business models and customer expectations. For example, 48 percent of Vodafone's customers in Germany had a contract, while this kind of long-term commitment to an operator was almost unheard of in Italy (92 percent were prepaid customers).[29]

To orchestrate the move toward greater coordination as well as to identify and disseminate best practices, the group created two new central functions, Group Marketing (to drive revenue growth), and Group Technology and Business Integration (to drive cost and scale benefits).[30] Communicating Vodafone's new focus on integrating the bits and pieces resulting from past acquisitions was clearly a top management task. The Integration and Operations Committee was instituted, staffed with members of the executive board and chaired by Arun Sarin himself. This committee was responsible for "setting operational plans, budgets and forecasts, product and service development, customer segmentation, managing delivery of multi-market propositions and managing shared resources" across geographies.[31] Alan Harper, who had been heading the group strategy department at Vodafone since 2000, saw his job title changed to Group Strategy and Business Integration Director. Simultaneously, Vodafone restructured itself at the corporate level to include the two new functions, which directly reported to the group's COO, Julian Horn-Smith.

Thomas Geitner was appointed head of the new unit Group Technology & Business Integration as chief technology officer.

The purpose of Group Technology will be to lead the implementation of a standardized architecture for business processes, information technology and network systems. This will support the next generation of products and services and the critical role of introducing and operating 3G capacity.[32]

A key focus of the Group Technology activities were the management and control of group-wide projects in relation to the ongoing rollout of "third generation" (3G) networks, the enhancement of Vodafone live! and the development of the Group's business offerings. This work included the continued development of technical specifications, creation and management of global contracts with suppliers as well as testing of terminals.[33]

It was committed to provide underlying terminal and platform technologies on a global basis. Within the mobile phone industry, a shift of power away from handset makers (Nokia, Siemens, Ericsson, etc.) could be observed. Global operators such as Vodafone had increasingly succeeded in forcing the producers to offer specially designed and branded products: the thriving Vodafone live! multimedia service was launched on Sharp GX-10 handsets, exclusively manufactured and branded for Vodafone.[34] If this trend persisted, Vodafone would be the first to benefit from its huge purchasing power and could even force Nokia (which had an almost 40 percent world market share) to cater more toward Vodafone's needs.[35] Vodafone could also use its unrivalled clout when negotiating with network equipment suppliers (such as Alcatel, Nokia, Siemens, etc.) to squeeze their margins.

Peter Bamford was appointed chief marketing officer and head of the Group Marketing department, which was in charge of

"providing leadership and coordination across the full range of marketing and commercial activities including brand, product development, content management, partner networks and global accounts."[36]

For Vodafone, the question was how customers could derive a benefit from Vodafone's increasingly global reach, ultimately driving top-line growth. Alan Harper explains,

We are a technology and sales & distribution group focused on local companies winning market share against incumbents in respective countries. We do not develop technology but we are users of technology. Technology is developed by companies such as Nokia, Ericksson, Nortel. We buy their technology—and technology evolution in our sector is more or less standard, it evolves, grows without major differentiations and after a period of time it is standardized. Now the challenge is how best we can leverage using and integrating the technology across our companies. . . . With the evolution and growth of our company we are today more of a company that prides itself in the differentiation of services that we bring to our customers. We are still 100 percent sales driven but we are much more customer centric and customer service oriented and take pride in understanding customer needs as we graduate to offering our customers the next best service and focusing on customer delight (e.g., Amazon). We now execute much better and it is because of the reason of the shift in our competencies.

Vodafone started creating service offerings and product packages directly leveraging Vodafone's network and delivering tangible value to customers. For example, it created a tariff option that enabled customers to seamlessly roam the globe, on a special per minute rate, on the same network, without having to worry about high interconnection fees or differing technical standards. A new unit within Group Marketing was created to develop and market services specifically tailored to the needs of global coordination, such as seamless wireless access to corporate IT systems and special rates for international calls on the network. Such a global service offering could clearly serve as a differentiating factor to competitors that could not match Vodafone's global footprint.

Woes in the United States and France

There were still two nagging issues for Arun Sarin: Vodafone's 45 percent stake in Verizon Wireless and the unresolved issues about control in France's SFR, for which Vodafone had been at loggerheads with Vivendi for several years now. Vodafone was far from happy about these minority stakes, because it did not fit with its single-brand, "One Vodafone" strategy.

In the United States, Vodafone customers still could not use their cell phones on the Verizon Wireless network, because it operated under a different standard. It was indicated that this situation was likely to continue well into the era of 3G, because Verizon planned to adopt an incompatible standard.[37] Without a single technological platform and a uniform brand, Vodafone could extract little value from its American venture (except the cash dividend of $1 billion a year it received from it).[38] After the failed bid for AT&T Wireless, Vodafone had several options at its disposal, all of them with their own pros and cons.

Probably the most obvious option would be to take over Verizon (the parent company of Verizon Wireless) completely, including its fixed line business, in order to force them to adopt Vodafone standards. It was deemed likely that such a bid could escalate to a US$150 billion hostile takeover battle, a figure that might be too large even for juggernaut Vodafone.[39] Verizon's management clearly was not willing to cede the wireless operations to Vodafone, but dreamed of becoming the single owner of Verizon Wireless itself.

Alternatively, Vodafone could buy another operator outright. But regulatory constraints would require it to sell its stake in Verizon Wireless first, because it was prohibited from owning more than a 20 percent stake in two competing operators at once. Under the current agreement with Verizon, Vodafone held a put option, which allowed it to sell some of the shareholding each year at a fixed price to Verizon. If Vodafone decided to exercise this option, it had to do so by July 2006 in order to realize a maximum value of US$20 billion. Verizon could choose to pay Vodafone either in cash or stock, although Vodafone had a right on a minimum cash sum of US$7.5 billion.[40]

Some observers questioned the idea of selling Verizon and buying another operator, because Verizon Wireless was the most successful and profitable one—why swap "a minority stake in a very good operator for a controlling stake in a less good one?"[41]

In France, Vodafone was in an equally uncomfortable position. It shared ownership of Cegetel, the parent company of France's number two mobile phone business SFR (35 percent market share with 13.3 million customers), with Vivendi having the majority stake in the venture. On March 31, 2003, Vodafone's ownership interest in SFR was approximately 43.9 percent, comprising a direct holding of 20 percent in SFR and an indirect holding through its stake in Cegetel.[42] Commenting on Vodafone's struggle with Vivendi about SFR, an analyst at Global Equities SA joked: "We have a saying: small minority shareholdings for little idiots; big minority shareholdings for big idiots."[43]

Even though Vodafone managers had a certain say about the operations and strategy of SFR (SFR launched the co-branded multimedia services of Vodafone live!), Vivendi continued to refuse to sell SFR to Vodafone. Several talks between Sarin and Fourtou, the CEO of Vivendi, had not yielded any results, and Vivendi's true strategic intentions with SFR remained unclear.[44] The remaining 56 percent stake in SFR was valued at roughly £8 billion ($13 billion).[45] After Vivendi declined Vodafone's offer for SFR in 2002, Vodafone issued a statement claiming that it was "a long-term investor in Cegetel and SFR" and that it "looks forward to continuing its successful partnership with Vivendi."[46]

"*France is a very simple market for us,*" noted Alan Harper in April 2005. "*We know the market, we know the business model and we know the management of SFR, which takes part in routine Vodafone management meetings.*" Pugnaciously, he added, "*The natural home of SFR is Vodafone. We are a very patient company.*"

It remains to be seen whether Vivendi wants to keep its cash cow or if it was simply trying to push the price in this cat-and-mouse game.

Challenges Ahead

Arun Sarin knew that his job would not become uninteresting anytime soon, as many challenges lay ahead! Certainly, Vodafone was the largest player in the industry, but being active in 26 countries out of 200 in the world left a lot of room to grow. As he closed his eyes and thought of Vodafone's global footprint, instantly he was reminded that Vodafone was not present in Latin America and in many African countries. Then there was the Middle East. Vast untapped markets lay ahead with today's mobile penetration of about 1.7 billion, of which Vodafone has about 3.5 million. In five years it shall be 2.5 billion, only half of world's population! And there was his native country, India, where he invested US$1.5 billion to buy a 10 percent stake in Bharti Tele-Ventures, the largest mobile operator in the country. Countries of Eastern Europe, many of which had recently entered the European Union (EU), should definitely become Vodafone's home turf: Vodafone had just announced that it would be willing to invest up to US$18 billion on acquisitions in Russia and other Eastern European countries.[47] The 2005 acquisition of the mobile operators MobiFon (Romania) and Oskar (Czech Republic) was certainly just the first step in enlarging Vodafone's footprint.[48] Not to mention China. The sheer size of the market was awe-inspiring. Vodafone's strategic partner, China Mobile, alone had more than 150 million customers, but Vodafone only had a minuscule 3.27 percent stake in the company.[49] For Vodafone, according to Alan Harper, this stake served as a:

strategic foothold in a very important market with a relatively small scale investment. China Mobile is the fastest growing mobile company in the world today, connecting about 2–3 million customers a month. It has 70% of the Chinese market share. Vodafone clearly understands that China Mobile can never become Vodafone China. That is a reality due to investment options and quasi-political situation of Chinese mobile telephony market. Knowing all this we still invested in China mobile because we feel that we learn everyday from China Mobile and our intention is to have regular knowledge flow between Vodafone and China Mobile. This is because our strategy is to make the technology standardized so that the learning between us is much faster. . . . Our investment in China mobile is through China Mobile HK. We have a clear exit strategy with liquid assets, if our investment does not do well in the future. If it does well, we might think of increasing our foothold but not to a sizeable extent. We are happy to have a foothold in one of the largest and fastest growing markets of the world, with our investment we have an insider position, we have a position of influence with the operator, with the Chinese government, we have seat on the board, we have regular dialogue and our interest is to make China use the same technology as ours so that we can benefit from the scale and scope.

At the same, significant business risks lurked in all markets and Arun Sarin was well aware of them. In 2006, the merger of AT&T with Bellsouth Corp. put pressure on Verizon Wireless to buy off Vodafone and force it to exit the U.S. market. The introduction of 3G, which had a very promising start in Germany with good sales of mobile connect cards, might shift the focus of the whole industry away from networks to content. Revenue from voice traffic was flat or even declining due to competing technologies such as Internet calling that was fundamentally changing the telecom industry. Sarin knew that most of the growth would have to come from new data services. Competitors had also begun to get their feet on the ground again, with rumors about a merger between MMO2's German operations (O2 Germany) and KPN's E-Plus.

Nokia had just presented its first WiFi-powered phone that did not need the traditional mobile network but a wireless LAN hotspot. If this technology should ever become popular, it would undermine Vodafone's current business model and could turn billions of fixed assets into worthless electronic scrap.[50]

At the beginning of 2006, Arun Sarin made some tough decisions. He faced up to slowing growth in his core market by unveiling an impairment charge of £23 billion to £28 billion ($40 billion to $49 billion) and exited the Japanese market by selling its stake to Tokyo-based Softbank in a deal valued at $15.4 billion and confirmed that after the sale it would return $10.5 billion to its shareholders. Vodafone had trailed behind NTT DoCoMo and KDDI since its entry in 2001 in Japan, due to fickle consumers, the lack of a low-end tier in the segment, and the challenge of coordinating terminals and technologies across borders. He managed to tighten his grip on the company and put down a boardroom revolt that had questioned his leadership. He not only won a public expression of support from Lord Ian MacLaurin, the company's board chair, but he also forced out Sir Christopher Gent, the honorary life president and former chief executive.

Arun Sarin thought Vodafone could have the best of two worlds. Now was the time to combine Vodafone's superior skills in acquiring companies with best-of-breed business integration and operational capabilities. He could ensure Vodafone's exceptional profitability for many years to come by keeping Vodafone a wireless company to the core and also use innovations such as broadband wireless technology known as WiMAX, to offer new services. It was now up to him to shape Vodafone's future.

Appendix I
The Economics of the Mobile Phone Market: The Role of Fixed Costs

The mobile phone market was characterized by extremely high fixed costs. The setting up of a nationwide network could require significant investments running into billions of euros.[51] Usually, an operator did not have the choice to offer network coverage limited to metropolitan areas (which would dramatically reduce the scale of initial investment required), either because of regulations prohibiting such a selective offer, or simply because national coverage was a key success factor for literally "mobile" customers.

In some countries, the licenses to operate using a certain bandwidth cost as much as €8 billion (the record price each operator in Germany paid for its UMTS license to the government), adding huge financing charges to the already existing fixed costs.[52] However, once capacity is installed, the cost of an additional customer using the network is virtually zero, and every euro of revenue adds to the companies' bottom line. An installed and running network provides a foundation for reaching very high operating margins. Vodafone, for example, estimates that once the initial investments had been made, less than 10 percent of revenues were needed to maintain the network.[53] Even the marketing campaigns benefited from the economies of scale: The larger an operator's customer base, the lower its per-user cost of such advertising efforts.

Much of the costs described here were not only fixed, but also sunk, further aggravating the problem of price pressure. The investment into network could hardly be sold to anybody else (because of differing technological standards) and hence the initial cost was "sunk." Companies realized that they could not undo their decision to invest, because the infrastructure was already there. Therefore, it is rational for companies to act as if their initial investment was zero.

The existence of high fixed costs explained the periodic price wars that had driven prices down ever since mobile telecommunications started. Some operators had begun offering free calls or flat rates during the weekend (when capacity utilization was at the lowest). Usually, it was the smaller operators and the new market entrants who offered lower prices to reach as quickly as possible a critical mass. In Germany, one of the largest markets for mobile telephony with more than 60 million customers and a high population density, the threshold for an acceptable return on investment was estimated to be about 20 percent of the total market share, which had neither been attained by O2 (a subsidiary of MMO2) nor by E-Plus (KPN).

The economics of the market necessitated no more than three or four operators in a country (refer to Exhibit 7). In Germany, Mobilcom and Quam never reached the critical size and had to exit the market in 2003 and 2002, respectively, writing off their individual investments of €8 billion each in 3G licenses.[54]

Growth for a mobile phone company had so far mainly come from increased penetration, which stood at about 80 percent (e.g., Germany: 74%) in most mature markets. With new customers becoming increasingly rare (refer to Exhibit 8 for customers by country of Vodafone), operators were constantly searching for new sources of revenues and had introduced text messaging and other basic value-added services, such as downloadable ringtones and logos.[55] The standard measure in the industry to gauge the quality of the customer base was the average revenue per user (ARPU).[56]

Exhibit 7 Customers by Country, June 30, 2003

Country	Customers
United Kingdom	13,313
Ireland	1,765
Germany	23,261
Hungary	952
Netherlands	3,312
Sweden	1,331
Italy	15,044
Albania	364
Greece	2,373
Malta	126
Portugal	3,129
Spain	9,184
United States	15,332
Japan	10,035
Australia	2,593
New Zealand	1,349
Egypt	1,609
Others	17,614
Group Total	122,686

Source: Adapted from Interim Report November 2003.

As the new 3G networks (third generation, enabling high-speed data transmission) go online, available capacity will take another quantum leap with unpredictable consequences for pricing. There seems to be promising opportunities to concentrate on the huge market for fixed line telephony. Not surprisingly, there was a clear relation between the per minute price of a call and the average amount of cell phone usage. Conversely, there was no relation between the ARPU and the average price per minute charged, which indicated that customers substituted their fixed line minutes with cell phone minutes whenever a price drop occurred. In other words, the increased quantity usually compensated the operator for the lower revenue per minute (refer to Exhibit 9).

Another key performance indicator that had attracted management attention in recent years was the

Exhibit 8 Vodafone's Subsidiaries, Partners, and Investments around the Globe

Country	Service Name	Ownership (%)	Subsidiary (S), Associate (A), or Partner (P)	Proportionate Customers (1000s)	Number of Competitors
Europe					
Albania	Vodafone Albania	83.0	S	472 (31 Dec 2003)	1
Austria	A1	n/a	P	n/a	n/a
Belgium	Proximus	25.0	A	1,067 (31 Mar 2003)	2
Croatia	VIP	n/a	P	n/a	n/a
Cyprus	Cytamobile	n/a	P	n/a	n/a
Denmark	TDC Mobil	n/a	P	n/a	n/a
Estonia	Radiolinja	n/a	P	n/a	n/a
Finland	Radiolinja	n/a	P	n/a	n/a
France	SFR	43.9	A	5,931 (30 Jun 2003)	2
Germany	Vodafone Germany	100.0	S	24,668 (31 Dec 2003)	3
Greece	Vodafone Greece	98.2	S	2,373 (30 Jun 2003)	2
Hungary	Vodafone Hungary	87.9	S	1,170 (31 Dec 2003)	2
Iceland	Og Vodafone	n/a	P	n/a	n/a
Ireland	Vodafone Ireland	100	S	1,871 (31 Dec 2003)	2
Italy	Vodafone Italy	76.8	S	15,852 (31 Dec 2003)	3
Lithuania	Bite GSM	n/a	P	n/a	n/a
Luxembourg	LUXGSM	n/a	P	n/a	n/a
Malta	Vodafone Malta	100.0	S	162 (31 Dec 2003)	1
Netherlands	Vodafone Netherlands	99.8	S	3,400 (31 Dec 2003)	4
Poland	Plus GSM	19. Jun	A	949 (31 Mar 2003)	2
Portugal	Vodafone Portugal	100.0	S	3,332 (31 Dec 2003)	2
Romania	Connex	20. Jan	A	537 (31 Mar 2003)	3
Slovenia	Si.mobil	n/a	P	n/a	n/a
Spain	Vodafone Spain	100.0	S	9,685 (31 Dec 2003)	2
Sweden	Vodafone Sweden	99.1	S	1,409 (31 Dec 2003)	3
Switzerland	Swisscom Mobile	25.0	A	3,635 (31 Mar 2003)	3
United Kingdom	Vodafone Group	n/a	n/a	n/a	n/a
United Kingdom	Vodafone UK	100.0	S	13,947 (31 Dec 2003)	4
Americas					
United States	Verizon Wireless	44.3	A	16,638 (31 Dec 2003)	Various
Africa and Middle East					
Bahrain	MTC-Vodafone Bahrain	n/a	P	n/a	n/a
Egypt	Vodafone Egypt	67.0	S	1,838 (31 Dec 2003)	1
Kenya	Safaricom	35.0	A	303 (31 Mar 2003)	1
Kuwait	MTC-Vodafone	n/a	P	n/a	n/a
South Africa	Vodacom	35.0	A	2,756 (31 Mar 2003)	2
Asia Pacific					
Australia	Vodafone Australia	100.0	S	2,676 (31 Dec 2003)	4
China	China Mobile (Hong Kong) Ltd	3.3	Investment	4,048 (31 Mar 2003)	2
Fiji	Vodafone Fiji	49.0	A	44 (31 Mar 2003)	None
Japan	Vodafone K.K. (Japan)	69.7	S	10,268 (31 Dec 2003)	3
New Zealand	Vodafone New Zealand	100.0	S	1,527 (31 Dec 2003)	1
Singapore	M1	n/a	P	n/a	n/a

Source: Adapted from http://www.vodafone.com.

Exhibit 9 Relationships between Per-Minute Prices and ARPU in European Countries

Relation between Cost per Minute and ARPU in European Countries

ARPU (€)/month vs. Price/Minute (€)

$y = -8{,}2539x + 35{,}017$

$R^2 = 0{,}0064$

Relation between Price per Minute and Cell Phone Usage (in minutes) in Europe

Average Usage per Month and User (minutes) vs. Price/Minute (€)

$R^2 = 0{,}5217$

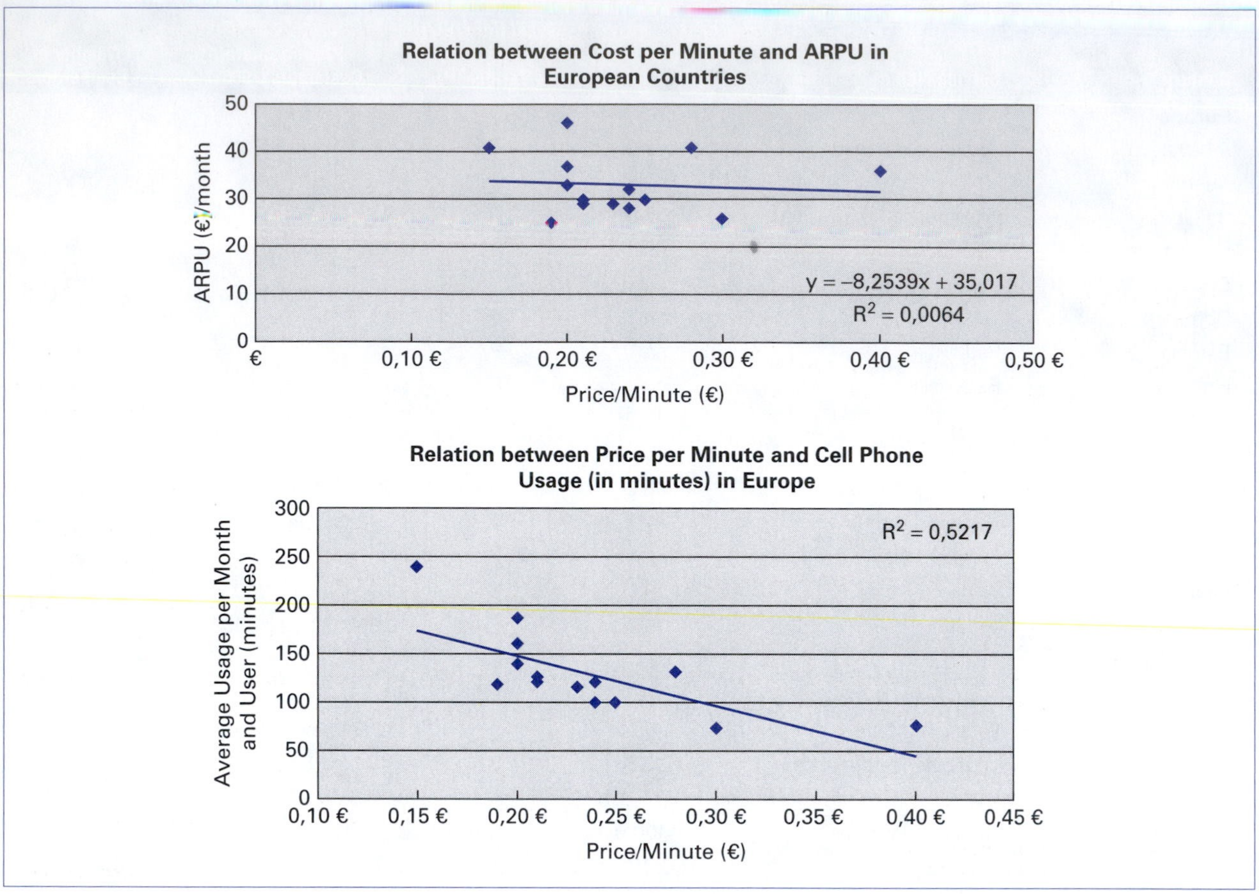

Note: Countries included in this sample are Belgium, Germany, Netherlands, Spain, Greece, Austria, Sweden, Italy, Denmark, France, Ireland, United Kingdom, Portugal, and Finland.

Source: Author's analysis based on data by Merrill Lynch, Diamond Cluster; published in the *Frankfurter Allgemeine Zeitung,* Octobre 27, 2003, 21.

so-called "churn rate," a percentage of the customer base being lost to competitors each year. In competitive markets with high handset subsidies, churn rates of operators could be anywhere between 19 percent (Germany) and 30 percent (UK).[57] In other words, on average after three to five years, an operator had churned its entire customer base! These churn rates carried high costs for the operators, because they had to spend heavily mainly on marketing and handset subsidies to attract new customers and to retain the old ones. Customer acquisition costs easily exceeded €100 per new customer or made up to 12.4 percent of service revenue (figure for Vodafone Germany).[58] If an operator added low-value customers (i.e., those with a low monthly ARPU), it could take many months until the operator could break even on a customer.

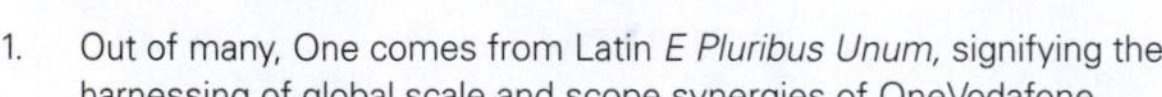

Notes

1. Out of many, One comes from Latin *E Pluribus Unum,* signifying the harnessing of global scale and scope synergies of OneVodafone.
2. The scenario described herein was fictional. However, all data relating to the AT&T Wireless deal was factual. *Financial Times Deutschland,* February 17, 2004, http://www.ftd.de
3. *Financial Times Deutschland,* February 12, 2004, http://www.ftd.de
4. *Financial Times Deutschland,* February 17, 2004, http://www.ftd.de
5. Equal to Christopher Gent's compensation as reported in the Company Annual Report 2003. This figure does not include stock options and performance-based pay.
6. Source: Corporate website http://www.vodafone.com/, data current as of December 31, 2003.
7. Source: Yahoo! Finance, http://finance.yahoo.com, March 13, 2004.
8. Annual Report 2003, available at http://www.vodafone.com.
9. Interim Results for the Six Months to 30 September 2003, published November 18, 2003; available at http://www.vodafone.com.
10. Company Annual Report 2004.
11. Source: This historic overview follows information provided at http://www.vodafone.com/, accessed on March 5, 2004.
12. http://www.vodafone.com.

13. Reportedly, Sir Gent closed the deal with AirTouch via his cell phone from Australia, where he was watching a game of cricket. *The Independent* (London), January 17, 1999: "Vodafone's boss realises longheld ambition with the acquisition of AirTouch."
14. *Financial Times Deutschland*, February 17, 2004, http://www.ftd.de
15. A chronology of the takeover battle was provided at http://www.managermagazin.de/unternehmen/artikel/ 0,2828,242161-2,00.html.
16. A New Voice at Vodafone, *The Economist;* August 2, 2003, Vol. 368.
17. Interim Results for the Six Months to 30 September 2003, published November 18, 2003; available at http://www.vodafone.com
18. Vodafone Starts Wireline Attack, First in Germany, *Dow Jones International* News; March 10, 2005.
19. Ibid.
20. Keeping pole position, *Total Telecom Magazine*, August 2003.
21. Ibid.
22. www.vodafone.com.
23. With Australia and Japan being notable exceptions.
24. Quoted in "Vodafone dominance tipped to keep rolling," *Utility Week*, January 31, 2003.
25. A new Voice at Vodafone, *The Economist*; August 2, 2003, Vol. 368.
26. Ibid.
27. Presentation to analysts and investors on September 27, 2004, available at http://www.vodafone.com.
28. http://www.vodafone.de and http://www.vodafone.com.
29. Ibid, p. 8.
30. Press release on June 23, 2003, available at http://www.vodafone.com.
31. http://www.vodafone.com.
32. Ibid.
33. Interim Results for the Six Months to 30 September 2003, p. 16.
34. According to the "Key Performance Indicators" for the quarter ended December 31, 2003; released on January 28, 2004; available at www.vodafone.com, Vodafone live! had over 4.5 million customers in 15 countries as of November 13, 2003.
35. Keeping pole position, *Total Telecom Magazine*, August 2003.
36. Ibid.
37. A new Voice at Vodafone, *The Economist;* August 2, 2003, Vol. 368.
38. Where Does Vodafone Turn Now? *Business Week Online*; February 18, 2004. Keeping pole position, *Total Telecom Magazine*, August 2003, quotes £564 million as cash dividend in financial year 2002/2003, equivalent to 11% of Vodafone's free cash flow. This arrangement expires in April 2005.
39. Where Does Vodafone Turn Now? *Business Week Online*; February 18, 2004
40. Keeping pole position, *Total Telecom Magazine*, August 2003.
41. Bob House of Adventis, a consultancy, quoted in: Vodafone's dilemma, *The Economist*, Feb 12, 2004.
42. Annual Report 2003.
43. Laurent Balcon quoted in: Keeping pole position, *Total Telecom Magazine*, August 2003.
44. Clear as mud: Vodafone versus Vivendi, *The Economist*; December 7, 2002.
45. *Euromoney*, Nov 2003, Vol. 34 Issue 415.
46. Clear as mud: Vodafone versus Vivendi, *The Economist*; December 7, 2002.
47. www.Vwd.de Vereinigte Wirtschaftsdienste GmbH, February 26, 2004.
48. According to a Vodafone press release on March 15, 2005, the Group paid approximately US$3.5bn in cash for the transaction and thus could add 6.7 m customers.
49. Annual Report 2004, p. 8.
50. Nokia takes leap into Wi-Fi Phones, *Wall Street Journal Europe*, February 23, 2004.
51. Vodafone for example had £24.1 bn as gross fixed assets in its balance sheet, 83% of which were accounted for by network infrastructure. Annual Report 2003, p. 90.
52. Vodafone prescht im Rennen um UMTS-Einführung vor, Handelsblatt, February 13/14, 2004.
53. Annual Report 2003, p. 94.
54. Vodafone prescht im Rennen um UMTS-Einführung vor, Handelsblatt, February 13/14, 2004.
55. In some instances, these new services already generate up to 20% of revenues. Ibid.
56. For example, Vodafone's ARPU in the UK was £297 and 312€ in Germany for the year, according to the Interim Results for the Six Months Ended September 30, 2003; available at http://www.vodafone.com.
57. Data for Vodafone, which can be considered as representative for the industry. Ibid.
58. Ibid.

Case 28

Wal-Mart Stores, Inc. (WMT)

Francine Barley, David Bragg, Misty Dawson, Hammad Shah, Brian Sillanpaa, Nathan Sleeper

Arizona State University

Lee Scott ignored his fear of public speaking as he prepared to step in front of 20,000 people at the Bud Walton Arena in Fayetteville, Arkansas, on June 1, 2007.[1] For his seventh year as Wal-Mart CEO, Scott addressed his company's shareholders at its annual meeting.

Outside the building, the local "Against the Wal" protesters were back for the fourth year in a row, clutching a list of seven demands: "living wage," "affordable health care," "end discrimination," "zero tolerance on child labor," "respect communities," "respect the environment," and "stop union busting."[2]

Inside the arena, shareholders had their own concerns, with declining share prices and 11 shareholder proposals—all opposed by the company.[3] Since Scott became CEO in 2000, Wal-Mart's stock price has dipped about 27 percent, from $64.50 to the $47 range.[4] In the same timeframe, competitor Costco's stock price has appreciated roughly 20 percent, and Target's has climbed more than 70 percent[5] (see Exhibit 1). Analysts are saying Wal-Mart's "glory days are over" and its stock is "dead money."[6] Some observers are speculating that Scott's days as CEO may be numbered if he is unable to get the company back on track soon.

It is a big company to change. From its humble origins 45 years ago as a single shop in the Ozarks, Wal-Mart has grown to 1.8 million employees supporting more than 6,700 stores in 14 countries, serving 175 million customers per week and pulling in an average of $6.6 billion in weekly sales.[7] Over the past decade, Wal-Mart doubled its store count, tripled its revenue, and nearly quadrupled its net income[8] (see Exhibits 2 and 3). Wal-Mart earned more in its first quarter of fiscal 2007 ($78.8 billion)

Exhibit 1 Changes in Stock Price: Wal-Mart, Target, and Costco, January 3, 2000, through May 14, 2007

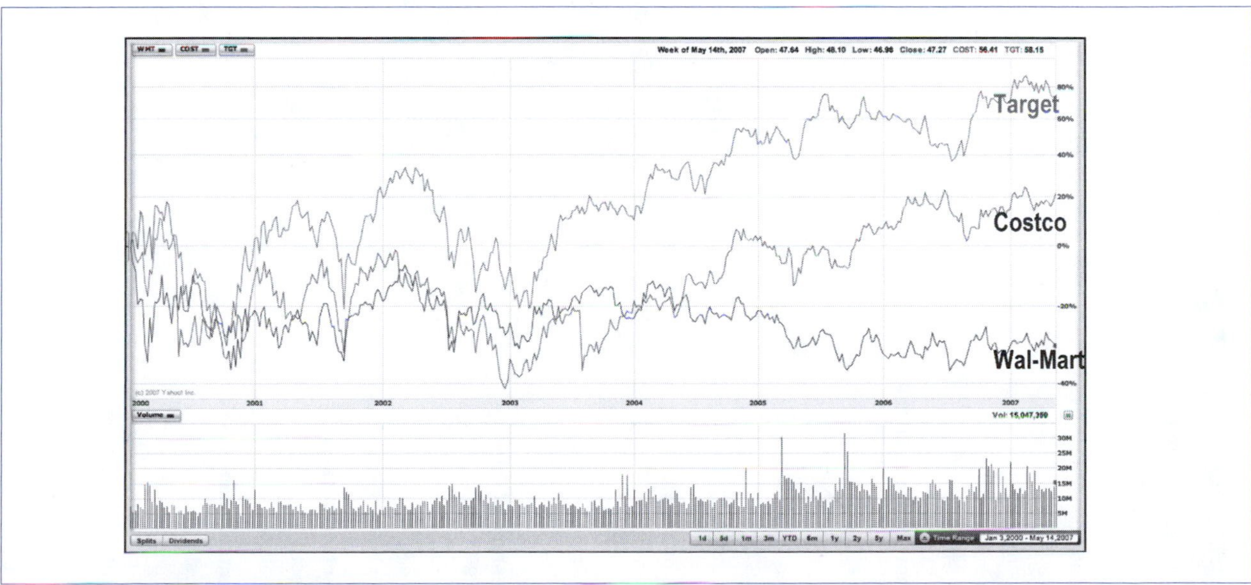

Source: 2007, Yahoo! Finance, http://finance.yahoo.com/charts#chart6:symbol=wmt;range=20000103,20070518;compare=cost+tgt;indicator=volume;charttype=line;crosshair=on;logscale=on;source=undefined, May 17.

Exhibit 2 Wal-Mart Retail Units and Sales, 1997–2007

	2007	2006	2005	2004	2003	2002	2001	2000	1999	1998	1997
Number of retail units											
Wal-Mart Stores	1,074	1,209	1,353	1,478	1,568	1,647	1,736	1,801	1,869	1,921	1,960
Supercenters	2,257	1,980	1,713	1,471	1,258	1,066	888	721	564	441	344
Neighborhood Markets	112	100	85	64	49	31	19	7	4	0	0
SAM'S Clubs	579	567	551	538	525	500	475	463	451	443	436
US Stores Total	4,022	3,856	3,702	3,551	3,400	3,244	3,118	2,992	2,888	2,805	2,740
International Stores	2,760	2,181	1,480	1,248	1,163	1,050	955	892	605	568	314
Total Stores	**6,782**	**6,037**	**5,182**	**4,799**	**4,563**	**4,294**	**4,073**	**3,884**	**3,493**	**3,373**	**3,054**
Percentage of total retail units											
Wal-Mart Stores	26.7%	31.4%	36.5%	41.6%	46.1%	50.8%	55.7%	60.2%	64.7%	68.5%	71.5%
Supercenters	56.1%	51.3%	46.3%	41.4%	37.0%	32.9%	28.5%	24.1%	19.5%	15.7%	12.6%
Neighborhood Markets	2.8%	2.6%	2.3%	1.8%	1.4%	1.0%	0.6%	0.2%	0.1%	0.0%	0.0%
SAM'S Clubs	14.4%	14.7%	14.9%	15.2%	15.4%	15.4%	15.2%	15.5%	15.6%	15.8%	15.9%
International	40.7%	36.1%	28.6%	26.0%	25.5%	24.5%	23.4%	23.0%	17.3%	16.8%	10.3%
Sales by segment											
Wal-Mart	$226,294	$209,910	$191,826	$174,220	$ 157,120	$139,131	$121,889	$108,721	$ 95,395	$ 83,820	$74,840
SAM'S Clubs	$ 41,582	$ 39,798	$ 37,119	$ 34,537	$ 31,702	$ 29,395	$ 26,798	$ 24,801	$ 22,881	$ 20,668	$19,785
International	$ 77,116	$ 59,237	$ 52,543	$ 47,572	$ 40,794	$ 35,485	$ 32,100	$ 22,728	$ 12,247	$ 7,517	$ 5,002
Total	$344,992	$308,945	$281,488	$256,329	$229,616	$204,011	$180,787	$156,250	$130,523	$112,005	$99,627
Percentage of sales by segment											
Wal-Mart	65.6%	67.9%	68.1%	68.0%	68.4%	68.2%	67.4%	69.6%	73.1%	74.8%	75.1%
SAM'S Clubs	12.1%	12.9%	13.2%	13.5%	13.8%	14.4%	14.8%	15.9%	17.5%	18.5%	19.9%
International	22.4%	19.2%	18.7%	18.6%	17.8%	17.4%	17.8%	14.5%	9.4%	6.7%	5.0%
Percentage of sales											
Domestic	77.6%	80.8%	81.3%	81.4%	82.2%	82.6%	82.2%	85.5%	90.6%	93.3%	95.0%
International	22.4%	19.2%	18.7%	18.6%	17.8%	17.4%	17.8%	14.5%	9.4%	6.7%	5.0%
Percentage change in sales											
Domestic	7.3%	9.1%	9.7%	10.6%	12.0%	13.3%	11.4%	12.9%	13.2%	10.4%	2.0%
International	30.2%	12.7%	10.4%	16.6%	15.0%	10.5%	41.2%	85.6%	62.9%	50.3%	25.3%
Percentage sales change											
Domestic	50.4%	75.6%	80.2%	74.6%	79.3%	85.4%	61.8%	59.3%	74.5%	79.7%	
International	49.6%	24.4%	19.8%	25.4%	20.7%	14.6%	38.2%	40.7%	25.5%	20.3%	

Source: 2007, 2002, Wal-Mart Annual Reports.

Exhibit 3 Wal-Mart Income, 1997–2007

	Income Statement (figures in $ millions; fiscal year ends 1/31)										
	2007	2006	2005	2004	2003	2002	2001	2000	1999	1998	1997
Total Operating Revenue	$348,650	$312,101	$284,310	$252,791	$226,479	$201,166	$178,028	$153,345	$129,161	$112,005	$99,627
Cost of Sales	$264,152	$237,649	$216,832	$195,922	$ 175,769	$156,807	$138,438	$ 119,526	$101,456	$ 88,163	$78,897
Gross Operating Profit	**$ 84,498**	**$ 74,452**	**$ 67,478**	**$ 56,869**	**$ 50,710**	**$ 44,359**	**$ 39,590**	**$ 33,819**	**$ 27,705**	**$ 23,842**	**$20,730**
Gross Margins	24.2%	23.9%	23.7%	22.5%	22.4%	22.1%	22.2%	22.1%	21.4%	21.3%	20.8%
Operating, Selling, G&A Exp.	$ 64,001	$ 55,739	$ 50,178	$ 43,877	$ 39,178	$ 34,275	$ 29,942	$ 25,182	$ 21,469	$ 18,831	$16,437
Operating Income	**$ 20,497**	**$ 18,713**	**$ 17,300**	**$ 12,992**	**$ 11,532**	**$ 10,084**	**$ 9,648**	**$ 8,637**	**$ 6,236**	**$ 5,011**	**$ 4,293**
Net Interest Expense	$ 1,529	$ 1,178	$ 980	$ 825	$ 930	$ 1,183	$ 1,194	$ 837	$ 595	$ 716	$ 807
Income Before Taxes	$ 18,968	$ 17,535	$ 16,320	$ 12,167	$ 10,602	$ 8,901	$ 8,454	$ 7,800	$ 5,641	$ 4,295	$ 3,486
Taxes	$ 6,365	$ 5,803	$ 5,589	$ 3,071	$ 2,662	$ 2,183	$ 2,008	$ 2,218	$ 1,432	$ 871	$ 508
Effective Tax Rate	33.6%	33.1%	34.2%	25.2%	25.1%	24.5%	23.8%	28.4%	25.4%	20.3%	14.6%
Net Income from Operations	$ 12,603	$ 11,732	$ 10,731	$ 9,096	$ 7,940	$ 6,718	$ 6,446	$ 5,582	$ 4,209	$ 3,424	$ 2,978
Other Items	$ (894)	$ (177)	$ (215)	$ (42)	$ 15	$ (126)	$ (211)	$ (258)	$188	$ 80	$ 64
Net Income	$ 11,709	$ 11,555	$ 10,516	$ 9,054	$ 7,955	$ 6,592	$ 6,235	$ 5,324	$ 4,397	$ 3,504	$ 3,042
Shareholder Income											
EPS (diluted) ($dollars)	$ 2.71	$ 2.68	$ 2.41	$ 2.07	$ 1.79	$ 1.50	$ 1.44	$ 1.25	$ 0.94	$ 0.76	$ 0.65
Dividend ($dollars)	$ 0.67	$ 0.60	$ 0.52	$ 0.36	$ 0.30	$ 0.28	$ 0.24	$ 0.20	$ 0.16	$ 0.14	$ 0.11

Source: 2007, 2002, Wal-Mart Annual Reports.

than Target made all year ($59.5 billion).[9] Wal-Mart's revenue gave it the No. 1 spot on *Fortune's* April 2007 list of America's largest corporations.[10] By contrast, its profit as a percentage of revenue came in at 3.2 percent, and its total return to investors was 0.1 percent, earning Wal-Mart sub-par ranks by those measures (no. 354 and no. 355, respectively).[11]

Over the past several years, Wal-Mart has stumbled upon a variety of compounding difficulties. Opposition has been mounting against not only Wal-Mart's practices, but also its very presence, due to multiple relationship issues with employees, communities, and governments.[12] It is increasingly challenging for the company to expand at its current rate, both in the United States and abroad. Meanwhile, key competitors have been "growing two to five times faster than Wal-Mart" in same-store sales.[13]

As a result, the company has gradually been losing some of its luster, even in the eyes of its former admirers. In 2004, Wal-Mart had been number one on *Fortune* magazine's list of "America's Most Admired Companies" for the second year running, notwithstanding "a year of bad press and lagging stock price."[14] In 2007, by contrast, Wal-Mart was tied for number 19, behind Costco (no. 18) and Target (no. 13).[15]

What had worked in the past was no longer sustainable in the current competitive environment. Scott wondered whether the change efforts he had started over the past few years would begin to have a positive effect or whether he should somehow adjust Wal-Mart's course.

Company History

Origins

Before founding Wal-Mart, Sam Walton accumulated experience in variety store retailing as a JCPenney management trainee and a franchisee of Ben Franklin stores.[16] Anticipating discount market growth, Walton opened his first Wal-Mart store in Rogers, Arkansas, in 1962, the same year Kmart and Target were founded.[17] Wal-Mart opened 24 more stores by 1967.[18] This start was slow compared with Kmart, which had already opened 162 stores by 1966.[19] Wal-Mart went public in 1970, giving it access to the financial resources needed to begin a decades-long expansion campaign that led to the opening of 3,800 stores by 2005.[20] Wal-Mart opened its first Sam's Club warehouse in 1983 and its first international store in 1991, and the company's national and international multiplatform expansion continues[21] (see Exhibit 4).

Recent History

Wal-Mart's growth soared in recent years, with the company adding nearly one new store every day (since 2006).[22] The company's rapid expansion brought its total retail store presence to 6,782 units worldwide as of February 8, 2007.[23] Wal-Mart spread with a missionary zeal, to "save people money so they can live better."[24] As Wal-Mart's presence continued to grow, so did its sales, to a record $345 billion in the fiscal year ended January 31, 2007 (hereafter referred to as 2007).

The company's massive growth brought with it massive controversies, however. Wal-Mart faced multiple accusations, charges, and lawsuits, many resulting in fines, including environmental violations, child labor law violations, use of illegal immigrants by subcontractors, and allegedly poor working conditions for associates.[25] Side effects of these issues include communities rejecting expansion of Wal-Mart stores into their neighborhoods.[26] Anti-Wal-Mart press is also on the rise, with books such as *How Wal-Mart Is Destroying America and the World: And What You Can Do About It* by Bill Quinn, and Robert Greenwald's film, *Wal-Mart: The High Cost of Low Price.* By one estimate, Wal-Mart's reputation issues have cost it $16 billion in market capitalization and an unknown amount of lost business in each store category or business segment.[27]

Business Segments

Wal-Mart's three business segments are Wal-Mart Stores, Sam's Club, and Wal-Mart International.[28] The Wal-Mart Stores segment includes walmart.com and three retail store formats in all 50 of the United States, including 2,257 Supercenters, 1,074 Discount Stores, and 112 Neighborhood Markets.[29] The Neighborhood Markets have the smallest format, with an average size of 42,000 square feet, and a primary focus on grocery products.[30] Wal-Mart's Discount Stores "offer a wide assortment of general merchandise and a limited variety of food products" within 107,000 square feet of selling space.[31] Supercenters average 187,000 square feet and add a full line of food products to Discount Stores' typical selection.[32] Wal-Mart converted 147 Discount Stores into Supercenters in 2007.[33] Overall, Wal-Mart Stores opened 303 new units in 2007 (276 Supercenters, 15 Discount Stores, and 12 Neighborhood Markets).[34]

Membership-based Sam's Club operates in a retail warehouse format, as well as online at samsclub.com. The segment's 579 clubs average 132,000 square feet, and provide "exceptional value on brand-name merchandise at 'members only' prices for both business and personal use."[35] Sam's Club opened 15 new units in 2007.[36]

Wal-Mart International added 576 (net) new stores in 2006—on its way to doubling its total retail unit count over the past few years.[37] Wal-Mart now operates 2,760 stores outside the United States in various formats, under diverse brand names, in 13 foreign countries and territories.[38] Wal-Mart International includes "wholly owned operations in Argentina, Brazil, Canada, Puerto

Exhibit 4 Wal-Mart Key Events, 1962–2004

1960s	
1962:	*Company founded with opening of first Wal-Mart in Rogers, Arkansas.*
1967:	*Wal-Mart's 24 stores total $12.6 million in sales.*
1968:	*Wal-Mart moves outside Arkansas with stores in Missouri and Oklahoma.*
1969:	*Company incorporated as Wal-Mart Stores, Inc., on October 31.*
1970s	
1970:	*Wal-Mart opens first distribution center and home office in Bentonville, Arkansas. Wal-Mart stock first traded over the counter as a publicly held company. 38 stores now in operation with sales at $44.2 million. Total number of associates is 1,500.*
1971:	*Wal-Mart is now in five states: Arkansas, Kansas, Louisiana, Missouri, and Oklahoma.*
1972:	*Wal-Mart approved and listed on the New York Stock Exchange.*
1973:	*Wal-Mart enters Tennessee.*
1974:	*Wal-Mart stores now in Kentucky and Mississippi.*
1975:	*125 stores in operation with sales of $340.3 million and 7,500 associates. Wal-Mart enters ninth state: Texas.*
1977:	*Wal-Mart enters its 10th state: Illinois.*
1979:	*Wal-Mart is the first company to reach $1 billion in sales in such a short period of time: $1.248 billion. Wal-Mart now has 276 stores, 21,000 associates and is in its 11th state: Alabama.*
1980s	
1981:	*Wal-Mart enters Georgia and South Carolina.*
1982:	*Wal-Mart enters Florida and Nebraska.*
1983:	*First Sam's Club opened in April in Midwest City, Oklahoma. Wal-Mart enters Indiana, Iowa, New Mexico, and North Carolina. For eighth year straight Forbes magazine ranks Wal-Mart No. 1 among general retailers.*
1984:	*Wal-Mart enters Virginia.*
1985:	*Wal-Mart has 882 stores with sales of $8.4 billion and 104,000 associates. Company adds stores in Wisconsin and Colorado.*
1986:	*Wal-Mart enters Minnesota.*
1987:	*Wal-Mart's 25th anniversary: 1,198 stores with sales of $15.9 billion and 200,000 associates.*
1988:	*First Supercenter opened in Washington, Missouri.*
1989:	*Wal-Mart is now in 26 states with the addition of Michigan, West Virginia, and Wyoming.*
1990s	
1990:	*Wal-Mart enters California, Nevada, North Dakota, Pennsylvania, South Dakota, and Utah.*
1991:	*Wal-Mart enters Connecticut, Delaware, Maine, Maryland, Massachusetts, New Hampshire, New Jersey, and New York. International market entered for first time with the opening of two units in Mexico City. Wal-Mart has entered 45 states with the addition of Idaho, Montana, and Oregon. Wal-Mart enters Puerto Rico.*
1993:	*Wal-Mart enters Alaska, Hawaii, Rhode Island, and Washington.*
1994:	*Three value clubs open in Hong Kong. Canada has 123 stores and Mexico has 96.*
1995:	*Wal-Mart Stores, Inc., has 1,995 Wal-Mart stores, 239 Supercenters, 433 Sam's Clubs, and 276 International stores with sales at $93.6 billion and 675,000 associates. Wal-Mart enters its 50th state, Vermont, and builds three units in Argentina and five in Brazil.*
1996:	*Wal-Mart enters China through a joint-venture agreement.*
1997:	*Wal-Mart replaces Woolworth on the Dow Jones Industrial Average.*
1998:	*Wal-Mart enters Korea through a joint venture agreement.*
1999:	*Wal-Mart has 1,140,000 associates, making the company the largest private employer in the world.*
2000s	
2000:	*Wal-Mart ranked 5th by* Fortune *magazine in its Global Most Admired All-Stars list.*
2001:	*Wal-Mart named by* Fortune *magazine as the third most admired company in America.*
2002:	*Wal-Mart ranked #1 on the* Fortune 500 *listing.*
2002:	*Wal-Mart has the biggest single day sales in history: $1.43 billion on the day after Thanksgiving.*
2003:	*Wal-Mart named by* Fortune *magazine as the most admired company in America.*
2004:	Fortune *magazine placed Wal-Mart in the top spot on its "Most Admired Companies" list for the second year in a row.*

Source: 2007, The Wal-Mart Timeline, Wal-Mart Facts, http://www.walmartfacts.com/content/default.aspx?id=3, April 1.

Rico, and the United Kingdom; the operation of joint ventures in China; and the operations of majority-owned subsidiaries in Central America, Japan, and Mexico."[39] In 2006, Wal-Mart divested its operations in Germany and Korea.[40] Mike Duke, vice chairperson of Wal-Mart Stores and head of the International Division, commented that it had "'become increasingly clear that in Germany's [and South Korea's] business environment it would be difficult to obtain the scale and results we desire.' Wal-Mart seeks markets where it feels that there is potential for it to become a top three retailer, an opportunity that did not exist for it in Germany [or South Korea]."[41] Wal-Mart International's U.K.-based Asda subsidiary brings in the largest share of the company's international revenue, at

Exhibit 5 International Wal-Mart Retail Units and Banners, 2007

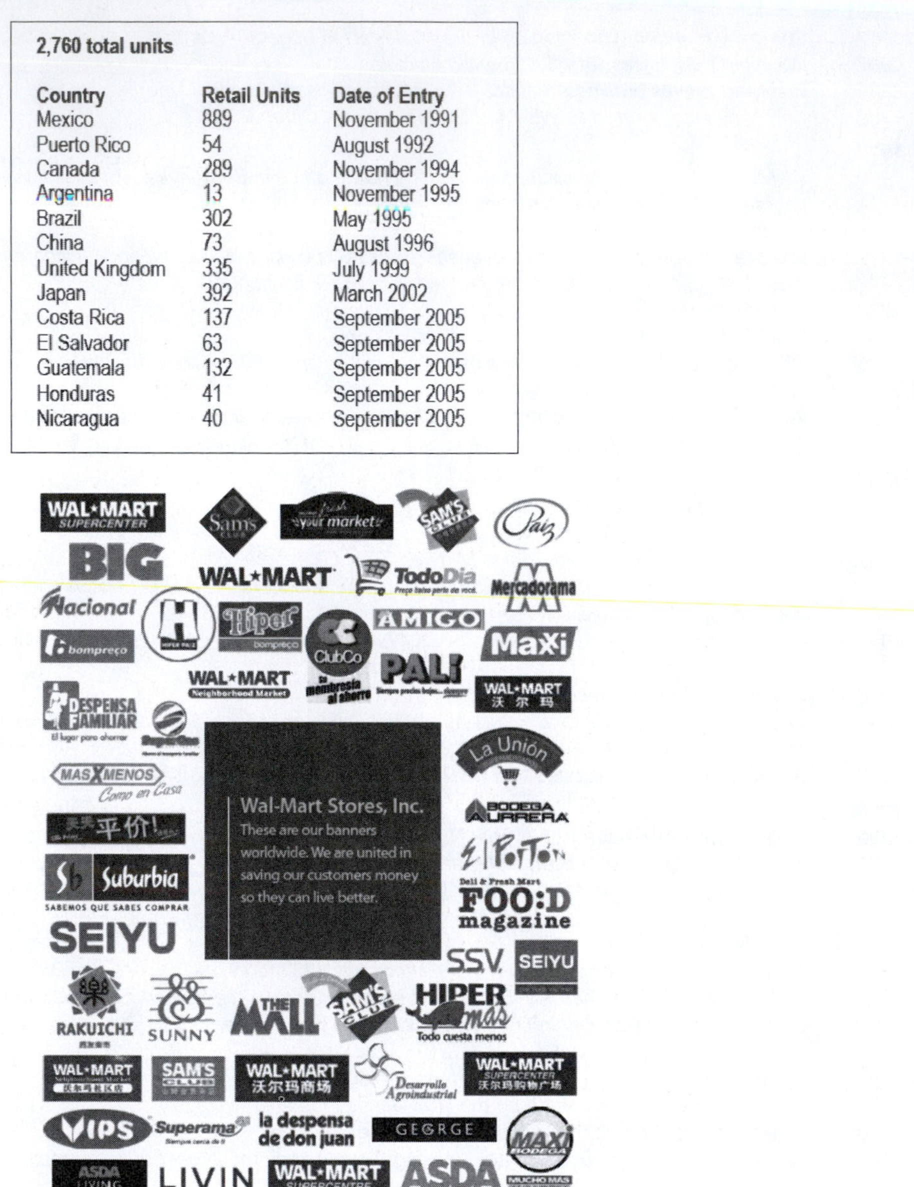

2,760 total units

Country	Retail Units	Date of Entry
Mexico	889	November 1991
Puerto Rico	54	August 1992
Canada	289	November 1994
Argentina	13	November 1995
Brazil	302	May 1995
China	73	August 1996
United Kingdom	335	July 1999
Japan	392	March 2002
Costa Rica	137	September 2005
El Salvador	63	September 2005
Guatemala	132	September 2005
Honduras	41	September 2005
Nicaragua	40	September 2005

Sources: 2007, International Data Sheet, Wal-Mart Stores, http://walmartstores.com/Files/Intl_operations.pdf, February 8; 2007, Wal-Mart Annual Report, 24.

37.4 percent.[42] Wal-Mart de Mexico provides the next largest share, at 23.6 percent of Wal-Mart International sales[43] (see Exhibit 5).

One of the challenges for each of Wal-Mart's segments is determining the appropriate product offerings for each location.

Product/Service Diversification

Wal-Mart continues to build on the discount general-store concept that reflects founder Sam Walton's ideals: "a wide assortment of good quality merchandise; the lowest possible prices; guaranteed satisfaction with what you buy; friendly, knowledgeable service; convenient hours; free parking; [and] a pleasant shopping experience."[44] The company's Neighborhood Market locations provide an average of 29,000 items per store; its Discount Stores offer 120,000 items in each store; and its Supercenters stock more than 142,000 different items. Walmart.com offers customers 1 million SKUs (stock keeping units or items in stock), multiple times the number offered in Wal-Mart's retail stores.[45] Sam's Club features appliances, electronics, furniture, jewelry, and office products, plus healthcare, business, personal and financial services.[46] Interestingly, Wal-Mart "caters heavily to customers with little or no access to banking services, often described as the 'unbanked.'"[47] This category fits 20 percent of Wal-Mart's customer base and, as such, Wal-Mart provides substantial financial services for this customer segment by providing services such as check cashing. It has 170 money centers in its approximately 4,000 U.S. stores.

Product and service offerings are just one of the many complex decisions that Wal-Mart's strategic leaders have to make.

Strategic Leaders

Ultimate leadership control has remained in the Walton family, with chairmanship changing hands only once, from father to son. Successors to the highest executive positions at Wal-Mart have always come from within the company. After eight years as CFO and executive vice president, David Glass succeeded Sam Walton as president and later as CEO.[48] H. Lee Scott joined Wal-Mart in 1979 and was named CEO by David Glass in 2000[49] (see Exhibit 6).

Decision Makers

Twenty-five senior Wal-Mart officers meet via weekly videoconferences "to review the Company's ongoing performance, focus on initiatives to drive sales and customer service, and address broader issues"[50] (see Exhibit 7). Eight of these senior officers currently have the most critical roles.

The most powerful among them is S. Robson (Rob) Walton, first son of Sam Walton and chair of the board of directors since 1992.[51] Rob Walton was initiated into the fledgling family business one night in the early 1960s after he earned his driver's license when Sam recruited him to truck goods from a garage in Bentonville to a Wal-Mart store.[52] Rob officially joined the company in 1969, shortly after graduating from law school, worked his way up to the vice chair position, and became board chair in 1992 after his father died.[53] "We lead when we embrace my dad's vision," according to Rob, "to improve the lives of everyday people by making everyday things more affordable."[54] Rob now lives in Colorado, where he races bicycles and sports cars in his spare time, and flies the company jet to his Bentonville office.[55] He continues to serve as the primary conduit for Walton family input related to company proceedings.[56]

CEO Lee Scott "rose through the ranks by excelling at the mechanical aspects of retailing, playing an indispensable part in Wal-Mart's technology-induced rebound in the latter half of the 1990s."[57] The son of a gas station owner and a music teacher in small-town Kansas, Scott worked factory night shifts to pay for college, while he, his wife, and their baby lived in a mobile home.[58] He put his business degree to use in logistics, first as a dispatcher for Yellow Freight, then as a "headstrong," "aggressive, even abrasive" Wal-Mart transportation manager.[59] His skill in reducing costs helped him ascend to senior logistics jobs, then into the top merchandising post, where he cut billions in excess inventory in the late 1990s.[60] Next Scott ran the 2,300-unit Wal-Mart Stores Division for a year before becoming Wal-Mart's chief operating officer and vice chairperson in 1999.[61] He became CEO in January 2000.[62]

Mike Duke, an industrial engineer who had 23 years of experience with Federated and May Department Stores, followed Scott's path, climbing the distribution and logistics ladder to the leadership of Wal-Mart Stores Division.[63] Now he oversees international operations as vice chairperson.[64]

John Menzer, who joined Wal-Mart in 1995 after 10 years with Ben Franklin Retail Stores, served as Wal-Mart's chief financial officer before becoming CEO of Wal-Mart International in 1999.[65] He led the acquisitions of Seiyu (a majority-owned subsidiary in Japan) and Asda.[66] Now as vice chairperson, Menzer is responsible for Wal-Mart Stores and various corporate functions, including strategic planning.[67]

A native of Ecuador, Eduardo Castro-Wright leads the Wal-Mart Stores Division in the United States after leading Wal-Mart de Mexico from 2001 to 2005, following a distinguished career with Nabisco in the Latin America and Asia-Pacific regions.[68]

Doug McMillon became president and CEO of Sam's Club after a 15-year career with Wal-Mart, first as a buyer, then as a merchandising manager and leader.[69]

Nineteen-year Target veteran John Fleming ascended through Walmart.com in the early 2000s to become Wal-Mart Stores' chief marketing officer, prior to his January 2007 induction as chief merchandising officer for Wal-Mart Stores.[70]

Exhibit 6 History of Leadership Succession at Wal-Mart

History of Leadership Succession at Wal-Mart			
Year	**President**	**CEO**	**Chairman**
1962	Sam Walton	Sam Walton	Sam Walton
1984	David Glass	Sam Walton	Sam Walton
1988	David Glass	David Glass	Sam Walton
1992	David Glass	David Glass	Rob Walton
2000	H. Lee Scott	H. Lee Scott	Rob Walton

Sources: 2007, The Wal-Mart Timeline, Wal-Mart Facts, http://www.walmartfacts.com/content/default.aspx?id=3, April 1; D. Longo, 1998, Wal-Mart hands CEO crown to David Glass, *Discount Store News*, February 15.

Exhibit 7 Wal-Mart Senior Officers, May 2007

Eduardo Castro-Wright
Executive Vice President and President and Chief Executive Officer, Wal-Mart Stores Division

M. Susan Chambers
Executive Vice President of People Division

Patricia A. Curran
Executive Vice President, Store Operations, Wal-Mart Stores Division

Leslie A. Dach
Executive Vice President, Corporate Affairs and Government Relations

Linda M. Dillman
Executive Vice President, Risk Management and Benefits Administration

Michael T. Duke
Vice Chairman, Responsible for International

Johnnie C. Dobbs
Executive Vice President, Logistics and Supply Chain

John E. Fleming
Executive Vice President and Chief Merchandising Officer, Wal-Mart Stores Division

Rollin L. Ford
Executive Vice President, Chief Information Officer

Craig R. Herkert
Executive Vice President and President and Chief Executive Officer, The Americas, International

Charles M. Holley, Jr.
Executive Vice President, Finance and Treasurer

Thomas D. Hyde
Executive Vice President and Corporate Secretary

Gregory L. Johnston
Executive Vice President, Club Operations, SAM'S CLUB

Thomas A. Mars
Executive Vice President and General Counsel

C. Douglas McMillon
Executive Vice President and President and Chief Executive Officer, SAM'S CLUB

John B. Menzer
Vice Chairman, Responsible for U.S.

Stephen Quinn
Executive Vice President and Chief Marketing Officer, Wal-Mart Stores, Inc.

Thomas M. Schoewe
Executive Vice President and Chief Financial Officer

H. Lee Scott, Jr.
President and Chief Executive Officer

William S. Simon
Executive Vice President and Chief Operating Officer, Professional Services and New Business Development

Gregory E. Spragg
Executive Vice President, Merchandising and Replenishment, SAM'S CLUB

S. Robson Walton
Chairman of the Board of Directors of Wal-Mart Stores, Inc.

Claire A. Watts
Executive Vice President, Merchandising, Wal-Mart Stores Division-US

Steven P. Whaley
Senior Vice President, Controller, Wal-Mart Stores Inc.

Eric S. Zorn
Executive Vice President and President, Wal-Mart Realty

Source: 2007, Senior Officers, WalMartStores.com, http://walmartstores.com/GlobalWMStoresWeb/navigate.do?catg=540, May 25.

After 13 years in marketing roles with PepsiCo, Stephen Quinn joined Wal-Mart as senior vice president of marketing in 2005, and then in January 2007 took over Fleming's former position as chief marketing officer for Wal-Mart Stores.[71]

These eight leaders are supported and monitored by the board of directors.

Board of Directors

Wal-Mart has an active, high-caliber, 14-member board of directors that may soon get even more powerful. "The Board has been instrumental in encouraging the company to more quickly address critical issues, and I am extremely pleased that they are not reticent about sharing their opinions," Rob Walton recently wrote, adding: "Today's Board is the furthest thing from a rubber stamp."[72] Two out of three board members have held CEO positions and/or chaired the boards of various companies. Retail turnaround guru Allen Questrom, who overhauled JCPenney, joined the board in June 2007.[73] Questrom recently told *Women's Wear Daily*: "[Wal-Mart is] never going to be a leader in fashion apparel. That's not their calling. But can they improve on that, sure they can."[74] The most famous former board member is New York Senator and Democratic presidential candidate Hillary Rodham Clinton, who served on the Wal-Mart board from 1986 to 1992 as a "loyalist reformer"[75] (see Exhibit 8).

Several board members are among the largest shareholders in the company.

Shareholders

Of the 4.1 billion Wal-Mart shares outstanding, insiders and beneficial owners hold 42 percent, while institutional investors and mutual funds hold 37 percent.[76]

Exhibit 8 Wal-Mart Board of Directors, May 2007

Aida M. Alvarez, 57
Former Administrator of the U.S. Small Business Administration; joined board in 2006

James W. Breyer, 45
Managing Partner of Accel Partners; joined board in 2001

M. Michele Burns, 49
Chairman and CEO of Mercer Human Resources Consulting; joined board in 2003

James Cash, Jr., Ph.D., 59
Retired Professor of Business Administration at Harvard Business School; joined board in 2006

Roger C. Corbett, 64
Retired CEO and Group Managing Director of Woolworths Limited; joined board in 2006

Douglas N. Daft, 64
Retired Chairman of the Board and CEO of The Coca-Cola Company; joined board in 2005

David D. Glass, 71
Former President and CEO of Wal-Mart Stores, Inc.; joined board in 1977

Roland A. Hernandez, 49
Retired Chairman and CEO of Telemundo Group, Inc.; joined board in 1998

Allen I. Questrom, 67
Former Chairman and CEO of JCPenney Company; Barneys New York, Inc.; The Neiman Marcus Group, Inc.; and Federated Department Stores, Inc.; standing for election in June 2007

H. Lee Scott, Jr., 58
President and Chief Executive Officer of Wal-Mart Stores, Inc.; joined board in 1999

Jack C. Shewmaker, 69
Retired Vice Chairman of Wal-Mart Stores, Inc.; joined board in 1977

Jim C. Walton, 58
Chairman of the Board and CEO of Arvest Bank Group, Inc.; joined board in 2005

S. Robson Walton, 62
Chairman of the Board of Directors of Wal-Mart Stores, Inc.; joined board in 1978

Christopher J. Williams, 49
Chairman and CEO of The Williams Capital Group, L.P.; joined board in 2004

Linda S. Wolf, 59
Former Chairman of the Board and CEO of Leo Burnett Worldwide, Inc.; joined board in 2005

Sources: 2007, Board of Directors, WalMartStores.com, http://walmartstores.com/GlobalWMStoresWeb/navigate.do?catg=502, May 25; 2007, Wal-Mart Stores, Inc., Form DEF 14A, Proxy Statement, Notice of 2007 Annual Shareholders' Meeting, U.S. SEC, April 19.

The Walton family owns almost 1.7 billion shares through its holding company, Walton Enterprises, LLC, whose directors were five of America's ten wealthiest individuals in 2005: Sam's three sons, Rob Walton, director Jim C. Walton, and John T. Walton (d. 2005); daughter Alice L. Walton; and widow Helen R. Walton (d. 2007).[77]

Top non-Walton inside shareholders include CEO Lee Scott (1.2 million shares), director David D. Glass (1.2 million shares), director Jack C. Shewmaker (557,674 shares), Mike Duke (413,213 shares), and John Menzer (401,883 shares).[78]

Some 1,127 institutions own Wal-Mart stock.[79] Nearly 536 million Wal-Mart shares are owned by 785 mutual funds.[80]

In total, as many as 312,423 shareholders held common stock in Wal-Mart on March 16, 2007, when the company finalized its annual report for fiscal 2007.[81]

Financial Results

Fiscal 2007 and Recent Years[82]

Over the past 10 years, Wal-Mart's net income has nearly quadrupled, from $3 billion in 1997 to $11.7 billion in 2007. Revenues have more than tripled, from $100 billion to $345 billion. Meanwhile, operating, selling, and general administration expenses have quadrupled, outstripping the increase in revenue and net income, averaging 14.6 percent of sales. Despite the increase in expenses, steadily higher gross margins have boosted operating income (refer to Exhibit 3).

Wal-Mart had assets totaling $151 billion in 2007, up from $39 billion in 1997. Concurrent with the increase in assets, liabilities have grown 319 percent over the same period, from $21.4 billion to $89.6 billion. Shareholder return on equity measured 22 percent in 2007, close to its 10-year average. Total shareholder equity rose from $17.2 billion in 1997 to $61.8 billion in 2007 (see Exhibit 9).

Wal-Mart has improved its profitability over the last several years. Compared with an average operating profit margin of 5.1 percent in the prior three-year period, Wal-Mart has averaged 6.0 percent in the past three years. In 1997, Wal-Mart's operating profit margin was 4.3 percent. From a debt perspective, Wal-Mart has fluctuated up and down, with a debt ratio between 55.1 percent and 61.5 percent over the last 10 years. As of 2007, it measured 59.3 percent, 150 basis points over its 10-year median (see Exhibit 10).

Comparative Revenue[83]

Sales by Region. Of nearly $345 billion in total sales in 2007 (not including Sam's Club fees), domestic U.S. revenues totaled nearly $268 billion, or 77.6 percent of sales, while international revenues were $77 billion, or 22.4 percent of sales. International operations are becoming increasingly important to the company. Driving

Exhibit 9 Wal-Mart Balance Sheet, 1997–2007

	Balance Sheet (all figures in $millions; fiscal year ends 1/31)										
	2007	2006	2005	2004	2003	2002	2001	2000	1999	1998	1997
Assets											
Inventories	$ 33,685	$ 31,910	29,419	26,263	24,098	21,793	20,710	18,961	16,058	16,005	15,556
Other Current Assets	$ 12,903	$ 11,915	$ 8,494	$ 7,285	$ 4,769	$ 4,122	$ 4,086	$ 4,021	$ 3,445	$ 2,584	$ 1,829
Total Current Assets	$ 46,588	$ 43,825	$ 37,913	$ 33,548	$28,867	$25,915	$24,796	$22,982	$19,503	$18,589	$ 17,385
Net Property, Equipment & Leases	$ 88,440	$ 77,865	$ 66,549	$ 57,591	$50,053	$44,172	$39,439	$34,570	$24,824	$23,237	$19,935
Goodwill & Other Long-term Assets	$ 16,165	$ 13,934	$ 12,677	$ 11,316	$11,309	$ 9,214	$10,082	$ 9,738	$ 2,739	$ 2,395	$ 1,251
Total Assets	**$151,193**	**$135,624**	**$117,139**	**$102,455**	**$90,229**	**$79,301**	**$74,317**	**$67,290**	**$47,066**	**$44,221**	**$38,571**
Return on Assets	8.8%	9.3%	9.8%	9.7%	9.6%	9.0%	9.3%	10.1%	9.6%	8.5%	8.0%
Liabilities & Shareholder Equity											
Current Liabilities	$ 51,754	$ 48,348	$ 42,609	$ 37,308	$31,752	$26,309	$28,096	$25,058	$15,848	$13,930	$10,432
Long-Term Debt	$ 27,222	$ 26,429	$ 20,087	$ 17,088	$16,545	$15,632	$12,453	$13,650	$ 6,875	$ 7,169	$ 7,635
Long-Term Leases	$ 3,513	$ 3,667	$ 3,073	$ 2,888	$ 2,903	$ 2,956	$ 3,054	$ 2,852	$ 2,697	$ 2,480	$ 2,304
Other Liabilities	$ 7,131	$ 4,009	$ 1,974	$ 1,548	$ (432)	$ (788)	$ (693)	$ (148)	$ 505	$ 2,123	$ 999
(minority interest, discontinued ops, deferred taxes)											
Total Liabilities	**$ 89,620**	**$ 82,453**	**$ 67,743**	**$ 58,832**	**$50,768**	**$44,109**	**$42,910**	**$41,412**	**$25,925**	**$25,702**	**$21,420**
Shareholder Equity	**$ 61,573**	**$ 53,171**	**$ 49,396**	**$ 43,623**	**$39,461**	**$35,192**	**$31,407**	**$25,878**	**$21,141**	**$18,519**	**$17,151**
Return on Equity	22.0%	22.9%	23.1%	22.4%	21.8%	20.7%	23.0%	24.5%	22.0%	19.6%	13.8%

Source: 2007, 2002, Wal-Mart Annual Reports.

Exhibit 10 Wal-Mart Financial Ratios, 1997–2007

	2007	2006	2005	2004	2003	2002	2001	2000	1999	1998	1997
Stability											
Debt Ratio	59.3%	60.8%	57.8%	57.4%	56.3%	55.6%	57.7%	61.5%	55.1%	58.1%	55.5%
Stockholders Equity to Assets	40.7%	39.2%	42.2%	42.6%	43.7%	44.4%	42.3%	38.5%	44.9%	41.9%	44.5%
Leverage	2.50	2.46	2.36	2.32	2.27	2.31	2.47	2.43	2.30	2.32	n/a
Debt to Equity Ratio	1.46	1.55	1.37	1.35	1.29	1.25	1.37	1.60	1.23	1.39	1.25
Debt to Capitization Ratio	0.38	0.39	0.34	0.33	0.33	0.34	0.32	0.39	0.32	0.39	0.39
Liquidity											
Current Ratio	0.90	0.91	0.89	0.90	0.91	0.99	0.88	0.92	1.23	1.33	1.67
Quick Ratio	0.25	0.25	0.20	0.20	0.15	0.16	0.15	0.16	0.22	0.19	0.18
Profitability											
Operating Profit Margin	5.9%	6.0%	6.1%	5.1%	5.1%	5.0%	5.4%	5.6%	4.8%	4.5%	4.3%
Operating Ratio	18.4%	17.9%	17.6%	17.4%	17.3%	17.0%	16.8%	16.4%	16.6%	16.8%	16.5%
Net Profit Margin	3.3%	3.6%	3.6%	3.6%	3.5%	3.3%	3.5%	3.5%	3.4%	3.1%	3.1%
Total Asset Turnover	2.4	2.5	2.6	2.6	2.7	2.6	2.5	2.7	2.8	2.7	n/a

Source: 2007, 2002, Wal-Mart Annual Reports.

Wal-Mart's overall growth, international sales growth has averaged 33.6 percent over the past 10 years, whereas domestic sales have grown an average of only 11.0 percent in the same period. In the last three years, domestic sales growth has averaged 8.7 percent versus average international growth of 17.8 percent (refer to Exhibit 2).

Wal-Mart has experienced varying rates of growth in international markets. Nonetheless, international revenue has been a constant source of sales growth for Wal-Mart, outpacing the revenue contribution from the Sam's Club segment since 2001.

Sales by Segment. Wal-Mart Stores brought in 65.6 percent of all sales in 2007, down from 75.1 percent of sales in 1997. Wal-Mart International was responsible for 22.4 percent of sales, up from 5.0 percent a decade earlier, while Sam's Club accounted for 12.1 percent of sales in 2007, down from 19.9 percent in 1997 (refer to Exhibit 2).

Sam's Club has suffered against rival Costco for years, losing the battle for comparable-store sales in "64 of the past 73 months," according to one researcher, as well as the battle for membership renewals.[84] Average annual sales per warehouse were $73 million for Sam's Club versus $135 million for Costco in fiscal 2006.[85]

Wal-Mart's online business has not been a significant source of revenue, bringing in an estimated $135 million in sales in 2002, the same year JCPenney.com had sales of $324 million and Amazon.com reached sales greater than $3 billion.[86]

Wal-Mart Supercenters drove 56.1 percent of the company's sales, reflecting the company's competitive strength in traditional nonmembership discount formats.

Results Relative to Competitors

Market Leadership. Wal-Mart is the number one retailer in 77 of the 100 largest general merchandise markets in America, squaring up against Target or Costco in all but 11 of these markets.[87] Either Wal-Mart, Costco, or Target holds the top position in 91 of the top 100 largest general merchandise markets in the United States.[88] Geographically, Wal-Mart is the dominant retailer in the South and throughout midsized and small-town markets, while Costco is the leader in California and Washington.[89] According to ACNielsen, (the world's leading marketing information company), in the United States, Wal-Mart "controls 20 percent of dry grocery, 29 percent of non-food grocery, 30 percent of health and beauty aids, and 45 percent of general merchandise sales."[90] It also controls 45 percent of the retail toy segment.[91] However, Target, Kroger, and Family Dollar Stores are all growing revenue faster than Wal-Mart, threatening its dominance (see Exhibit 11).

Financial Ratios. From a competitive profitability perspective, Wal-Mart's 5.87 percent operating margin and 3.23 percent net margin put it in the middle of the pack relative to its key competitors (refer to Exhibit 11). Target enjoys higher margins, closer to those of JCPenney, while Costco has lower margins, closer to those of Dollar General and Kroger. Wal-Mart's

Exhibit 11 Comparison of Financial Ratios

	Financial Ratios of Select Retailers (sorted by revenue growth, as of May 26, 2007)					
	Quarterly Growth (yoy)		Profitability (ttm)		Management Effectiveness (ttm)	
	Revenue Growth	Earnings Growth	Net Profit Margin	Operating Margin	Return on Assets	Return on Equity
Amazon.com, Inc.	32.30%	117.60%	2.18%	3.74%	10.37%	73.86%
Target Corporation	16.30%	19.20%	4.69%	8.52%	8.93%	18.68%
Kroger Co.	14.50%	36.50%	1.69%	3.47%	7.10%	23.95%
Family Dollar Stores, Inc.	12.20%	66.00%	3.49%	5.70%	9.44%	17.68%
Wal-Mart Stores, Inc.	9.60%	8.10%	3.23%	5.87%	8.81%	21.80%
Costco Wholesale Corp.	7.50%	–15.80%	1.73%	2.55%	6.25%	12.07%
J.C. Penney Corporation	3.10%	13.30%	5.90%	9.73%	9.57%	26.43%
Dollar General Corp.	3.00%	–65.50%	1.50%	2.67%	5.24%	7.96%
Sears Holdings Corporation	1.30%	26.50%	2.81%	4.59%	5.06%	12.25%

Sources: 2007, Key Statistics, Capital IQ, A Division of Standard & Poor's, Yahoo! Finance, http://finance.yahoo.com/q/ks?s=WMT, http://finance.yahoo.com/q/ks?s=TGT, http://finance.yahoo.com/q/ks?s=COST, http://finance.yahoo.com/q/ks?s=KR, http://finance.yahoo.com/q/ks?s=DG, http://finance.yahoo.com/q/ks?s=FDO, http://finance.yahoo.com/q/ks?s=SHLD, http://finance.yahoo.com/q/ks?s=JCP, http://finance.yahoo.com/q/ks?s=AMZN, May 26.

margins are nearest those of Family Dollar Stores and Sears Holdings (Kmart and Sears). Wal-Mart's profit margin may be held down somewhat by its presence in the lower margin grocery business, especially in its Neighborhood Markets format.[92] In Supercenters, groceries serve a larger role of driving store traffic and drawing customers toward higher margin products. From a management effectiveness standpoint, Wal-Mart is creating a return on equity that is higher than Target's and much higher than Costco's and a return on assets that is nearly identical to Target's and higher than Costco's.

First Quarter, Fiscal 2008 (Quarter Ending April 30, 2007)

Wal-Mart had a difficult first quarter. Revenue and earnings "were not where we would have expected [them] to be, nor where we believe they should be," according to CEO Scott.[93] "Quite honestly, we're not satisfied with our overall performance."[94] Wal-Mart increased company sales (not including Sam's Club fees) by 8.3 percent in the first quarter to $85.3 billion.[95] Overall operating income increased 7.9 percent year-over-year, with nearly 53.1 percent of the change coming from Wal-Mart's international operations[96] (see Exhibit 12).

Closing out the first quarter on a down note, Wal-Mart's April same-store sales decrease was the worst ever recorded in 28 years of tracking: an overall U.S. comparable-store sales slide of 3.5 percent for the month, with a 4.6 percent drop at Wal-Mart Stores offset by a 2.5 percent increase at Sam's Clubs.[97] Much of the April decline was blamed on the apparel business, which constitutes 10 percent of Wal-Mart's sales.[98] Recent failed forays into fashion appear to have dragged down overall same-stores sales.[99] Wal-Mart wasn't the only retailer to have a bad April. The International Council of Shopping Centers reported an average 2.3 percent drop in same-store sales across 51 chains.[100] Against the trend, Costco posted a 6 percent same-store sales gain in April (see Exhibit 13).

The financial situation might be better considered with an understanding of the competitive situation in Wal-Mart's industry.

Competitive Situation

We face strong sales competition from other discount, department, drug, variety and specialty stores and supermarkets, many of which are national, regional or international chains, as well as internet-based retailers and catalog businesses. Additionally, we compete with a number of companies for prime retail site locations, as well as in attracting and retaining quality employees ("associates"). We, along with other retail companies, are influenced by a number of factors . . . cost of goods, consumer debt levels and buying patterns, economic conditions, interest rates, customer preferences, unemployment, labor costs, inflation, currency exchange fluctuations, fuel prices, weather patterns, catastrophic events, competitive pressures and insurance costs. Our Sam's Club segment faces strong sales competition from other wholesale club operators, catalogs businesses, internet-based and other retailers."

—***2007 Wal-Mart Annual Report, 28–29***

Exhibit 12 Wal-Mart Fiscal 2008 First Quarter Results versus Target

Wal-Mart Stores, Inc. Fiscal 2008 First Quarter Results Quarters Ending 4/30, all figures in $millions			
Income	**Q1 2008**	**Q1 2007**	**YoY% Chng**
Total Operating Revenue	$86,410	$79,676	8.5%
Cost of Sales	$65,311	$60,237	8.4%
Gross Operating Profit	**$21,099**	**$19,439**	8.5%
Gross Margins	24.4%	24.4%	
Operating, Selling, G&A Exp.	$16,249	$14,944	8.7%
Operating Income	**$ 4,850**	**$ 4,495**	7.9%
Net Interest Expense	$ 392	$ 368	6.5%
Income Before Taxes	$ 4,458	$ 4,127	8.0%
Provision for Taxes	$ 1,532	$ 1,388	10.4%
Effective Tax Rate	34.4%	33.6%	2.2%
Net Income from Operations	$ 2,926	$ 2,739	6.8%
Other Items	$ (100)	$ (124)	
Net Income	**$ 2,826**	**$ 2,615**	8.1%
Shareholder Income *($dollars)*			
EPS (diluted)	$ 0.68	$ 0.63	7.9%
Dividend	$ 0.67	$ 0.60	
Comparable-Store Sales Growth	**0.6%**	**3.8%**	
Wal-Mart Stores	–0.1%	3.8%	
Sam's Club (excl. fuel)	4.7%	4.3%	
Segment Breakdown			
Revenue by Segment			
Wal-Mart Stores	$55,437	$52,499	5.6%
Sam's Club	$10,323	$ 9,775	5.6%
International	$19,627	$16,561	18.5%
Total (excludes other income)	$85,387	$78,835	8.3%
Operating Income by Segment			
Wal-Mart Stores	$ 3,927	$ 3,858	1.8%
Sam's Club	$ 363	$ 303	19.8%
International	$ 903	$ 757	19.3%
Total (excludes other income)	$ 5,193	$ 4,918	5.6%
Operating Margins by Segment			
Wal-Mart Stores	7.1%	7.3%	–3.6%
Sam's Club	3.5%	3.1%	13.4%
International	4.6%	4.6%	0.7%
Total (excludes other income)	6.1%	6.2%	–2.5%
Cash Flows			
Net Income	$ 2,826	$ 2,615	
Change in Inventories	$ (1,280)	$ 259	
Accounts Payable	$ (1,115)	$ (442)	
Accounts Receivable	$ 62	$ 219	
Cash Flows from Operating Activities	**$ 493**	**$ 2,651**	

Sources: 2007, Wal-Mart Stores, Inc., Form 8-K, U.S. SEC, May 15; and 2007, Target Corporation, Form 8-K, U.S. SEC, May 23.

Target Corporation Fiscal 2008 First Quarter Results Quarters Ending 5/5/07 and 4/29/06, all figures in $millions			
Income	**Q1 2008**	**Q1 2007**	**YoY%Chng**
Total Operating Revenue*	$14,041	$12,863	9.2%
Cost of Sales	$ 9,186	$ 8,473	8.4%
Gross Operating Profit	**$ 4,855**	**$ 4,390**	10.6%
Gross Margins	34.6%	34.1%	
Operating, Selling, G&A Exp.**	$ 3,655	$ 3,373	8.4%
Operating Income	**$ 1,200**	**$ 1,017**	18.0%
Net Interest Expense	$ 136	$ 131	3.6%
Income Before Taxes	$ 1,064	$ 886	20.2%
Provision for Taxes	$ 413	$ 332	24.5%
Effective Tax Rate	38.8%	37.5%	3.6%
Net Income from Operations	$ 651	$ 554	17.6%
Other Items	$ –	$ –	
Net Income	**$ 651**	**$ 554**	17.5%
Shareholder Income *($dollars)*			
EPS (diluted)	$ 0.75	$ 0.63	19.6%

**includes sales and net credit card revenues*
***includes SG&A, credit card expenses, depreciation and amortization*

Comparable-Store Sales Growth	**4.3%**	**5.1%**	

Exhibit 13 April 2007 Same-Store Sales Growth

April 2007 Same-Store Sales Growth	
Discounters	
Wal-Mart	–3.5%
Costco	+6.0%
Target	–6.1%
Dollar General	–2.4%
Department Stores	
Federated	–2.2%
JCPenney	–4.7%
Nordstrom	+3.1%
Dillard's	–14.0%
Neiman Marcus	+1.0%
Saks	+11.7%
Apparel	
TJX	–1.0%
Kohl's	–10.5%
Gap	–16.0%
Limited	–1.0%
AnnTaylor	–12.8%
Teen Apparel	
Abercrombie & Fitch	–15.0%
American Eagle Outfitters	–10.0%

Source: J. Covert, 2007, Retail-sales slide fuels concern: Decline of 2.3% in April among worst on record; even Wal-Mart slipped, *Wall Street Journal*, May 11, A3.

Competitors

Target. Target Corporation operates 1,318 general merchandise stores and 182 SuperTarget stores in 47 states, in addition to its online business, target.com.[101] Target describes itself as "an upscale discounter that provides high-quality, on-trend merchandise at attractive prices in clean, spacious and guest-friendly stores."[102] Target has grown revenue from $33 billion in 2001 to more than $59 billion in 2006, a compound annual growth rate of 12.5 percent.[103] Profits have risen as well, as earnings from continuing operations averaged an annual growth rate of 20.4 percent over the same period[104] (see Exhibit 14).

Costco. Costco Wholesale Corporation runs 510 warehouses, averaging 140,000 square feet, in 38 states, six foreign countries (Canada, Mexico, the United Kingdom, Taiwan, Korea, and Japan), and Puerto Rico.[105] Costco offers three kinds of membership and roughly 4,000 products, 10 to 15 times fewer than many competitors, according to the company.[106] Costco benefits from a limited number of products sold in high volumes, high inventory turnover, low costs via purchasing discounts and a no-frills approach, and favorable real estate locations. Gross margins have averaged about 10.6 percent over the past five years, and operating income has increased an average of 10.5 percent over the same period[107] (see Exhibit 15).

Kroger. The Kroger Co. is "one of the nation's largest retailers, operating 2,468 supermarket and multi-department stores under two dozen banners including Kroger, Ralphs, Fred Meyer, Food 4 Less, King Soopers, Smith's, Fry's, Fry's Marketplace, Dillons, QFC, and City Market."[108] Kroger's operating income fell 13.1 percent between 2002 and 2006, from $2.8 billion to $2.2 billion, despite an increase in revenue of 27.7 percent.[109] Operating margins have averaged 24.8 percent over the last three years, up from 15.7 percent in the three years prior[110] (see Exhibit 16).

Other General Discount Competitors. Sears Holdings (Kmart and Sears) offer some additional U.S. competition in general merchandise, while Tesco of Britain and Carrefour of France compete with Wal-Mart internationally. Carrefour is the second-largest retailer in the world

Exhibit 14 Target Performance, 2001–2006

Target	2001	2002	2003	2004	2005	2006
Revenue	$33,021	$ 37,410	$42,025	$46,839	$52,620	$59,940
COGS	$23,030	$25,948	$28,389	$31,445	$34,927	$39,399
Gross Margin	$ 9,991	$11,462	$13,636	$15,394	$ 17,693	$20,541
Gross Margin %	30.3%	30.6%	32.4%	32.9%	33.6%	34.3%
Operating Income/EBIT	$ 2,246	2,811	3,159	3,601	4,323	5,069
		25.2%	12.4%	14.0%	20.0%	17.3%
Net Income	$ 1,101	$ 1,376	$ 1,619	$ 1,885	$ 2,408	$ 2,787
Net Income % chg		25.0%	17.7%	16.4%	27.7%	15.7%

Note: $ in millions

Source: 2006, Target Corporation Annual Report.

Exhibit 15 Costco Performance, 2001–2006

Costco	2001	2002	2003	2004	2005	2006
Revenue	$34,137,021	$37,994,608	$41,694,561	$ 47,148,627	$51,879,070	$58,963,180
COGS	$30,598,140	$33,983,121	$ 37,235,383	$ 42,092,016	$46,346,961	$52,745,497
Gross Margin	$ 3,538,881	$ 4,011,487	$ 4,459,178	$ 5,056,611	$ 5,532,109	$ 6,217,683
Gross Margin %	10.4%	10.6%	10.7%	10.7%	10.7%	10.5%
Operating Income/EBIT	$ 992,267	1,131,535	1,156,628	1,385,648	1,474,303	1,625,632
		14.0%	2.2%	19.8%	6.4%	10.3%
Net Income	$ 602,089	$ 699,983	$ 721,000	$ 882,393	$ 1,063,092	$ 1,103,215
Net Income % chg		16.3%	3.0%	22.4%	20.5%	3.8%

Note: $ in thousands

Source: 2006, Costco Wholesale Corp. Annual Report.

Exhibit 16 Kroger Performance, 2001–2006

Kroger	2001	2002	2003	2004	2005	2006
Revenue	$49,000	$ 51,760	$53,791	$56,434	$60,553	$ 66,111
COGS	$36,398	$ 37,810	$39,637	$42,140	$45,565	$ 50,115
Gross Margin	$12,602	$13,950	$14,154	$14,294	$14,988	$ 15,996
Gross Margin %	25.7%	10.6%	10.7%	25.3%	24.8%	24.2%
Operating Income/EBIT	$ 2,359	$ 2,573	$ 1,374	$ 843	$ 2,035	$ 2,236
		9.1%	–46.6%	–38.6%	141.4%	9.9%
Net Income	$ 877	$ 1,202	$ 285	$ (104)	$ 958	$ 1,115
Net Income % chg		37.1%	–76.3%	–136.5%	$ 1021.2%	$ 16.4%

Note: $ in millions

Source: 2006 The Kroger Co. Annual Report.

(after Wal-Mart) and is probably its closest international competitor from a strategy perspective, as it focuses on hypermarkets (similar to Supercenters), in addition to a variety of other formats.[111] Tesco emphasizes convenience and competes primarily in groceries, but also in general merchandise against Wal-Mart's U.K. subsidiary Asda.[112] Tesco is looking to expand to the West Coast of the United States in 2007.[113] Amazon.com adds another level of global competition for Wal-Mart due to its high number of SKUs and its convenience.

Niche Competitors. Other retailers compete with Wal-Mart at the department level, including Safeway, Best Buy, Circuit City, Home Depot, Ace Hardware, Lowe's, Kohl's, Mervyn's California, Barnes & Noble, and Borders, among others. In order to provide lower prices than its competitors, Wal-Mart has developed a unique relationship with its suppliers.

Suppliers

Wal-Mart's 1,600-member Global Procurement Services team, based in 23 countries, buys merchandise from suppliers in more than 70 countries, including 61,000 suppliers in the United States.[114] Leveraging its size, "Wal-Mart not only dictates delivery schedules and inventory levels but also heavily influences product specifications. In the end, many suppliers have to choose between designing goods their way or the Wal-Mart way."[115] In return, companies with a streamlined product and supply chain can benefit greatly. "If you are good with data, are sophisticated, and have scale, Wal-Mart should be one of your most profitable customers," says a retired consumer-products executive.[116] "Wal-Mart controls a large and rapidly increasing share of the business done by most every major U.S. consumer products company," about 28 percent of the total sales of Dial and almost a quarter of the sales of Del Monte Foods, Clorox, and Revlon.[117]

Customers

Wal-Mart attracts 175 million people to its stores each week.[118] According to ACNielsen (the world's leading marketing information company), the typical Wal-Mart shopper has an annual household income of $10,000 to $50,000.[119] These shoppers account for 54 percent of Wal-Mart's sales.[120] Wal-Mart also attracts an affluent segment (with household incomes of at least $75,000) that accounts for 26 percent of its customer base.[121] The affluent segment cross-shops the most with Costco (27 percent) and Target (28 percent).[122] These upscale shoppers likely have lower price elasticity, a relatively lower switching cost, but a higher sensitivity to brand reputation.

Even though Wal-Mart recently hired some well-known public relations experts and ended its relationship with its Ad Agency of 32 years in hopes of creating a more positive image, according to a 2004 study, "2 to 8 percent of Wal-Mart consumers surveyed have ceased shopping at the chain because of 'negative press.'"[123] Shoppers interviewed by the authors of this case have strong opinions about Wal-Mart (see Exhibits 17 and 18).

Wal-Mart's recent struggles with bad press and lawsuits have created urgency to find a way to protect its market share from potential entrants or substitutes.

Exhibit 17 Wal-Mart Shopper Profile

Income	
	% of sales
<$50,000	54%
$50-$75000	20%
$75,000 +	26%
Education	
	% of sales
Less than a High School Diploma	20%
High School Diploma (incl. some college)	57%
Bachelor Degree and above	23%
Leisure Pursuits—Typical Customer	
	% of customers
Tend Their Garden	43%
Listen to Country Music	30%
Like Auto Racing	17%
Go Fishing	17%
Go Camping	19%
Leisure Pursuits—Affluent Customer	
	% of customers
Listen to Talk Radio	34%
Go to a Theme Park	32%
Listen to Contemporary Music	25%
Go to the Museum	21%
Go to the Zoo	18%

Source: S. Kapinus, 2006, Rollback sushi and discount organics: What Wal-Mart's push to upscale consumers means to you, *ACNielsen Consumer Insight Magazine*, http://us.acnielsen.com/pubs/2006_q2_ci_rollback.shtml, Q2.

Other Sources of Competition

Customers have many alternatives for each of the products and services that Wal-Mart provides, but few alternatives exist for the large-scale discount superstore or warehouse shopping experience. The same products can be purchased at different types of retailers, but it is difficult to replicate the convenience, price, and diversity of merchandise found at a Wal-Mart. Also, new potential market entrants with similar scale would have difficulty competing in any substantial volume on price across a wide array of merchandise. Other large incumbents such as Target and Costco have also built economies of scale that would be difficult for a start-up to replicate. Supply chains must be extensive and very efficient. Product differentiation is usually minor in discount store merchandise. However, switching retailers would be easy for customers in well-served areas.

Beyond these retail industry forces, more general external trends also influence Wal-Mart's competitive situation.

External Trends

Government. Wal-Mart has become a "poster company" on political issues related to trade, health care, the environment, discrimination, worker pay, and general anticorporate sentiment. Many activists even contend that Wal-Mart is breaking antitrust laws by using its "power to micromanage the market, carefully coordinating the actions of thousands of firms from a position above the market."[124] Concerns about Wal-Mart's handling of hazardous waste have prompted local, state, and federal officials in the southwestern United States to initiate official actions. In addition to activists and union groups, U.S. political figures are lashing out against Wal-Mart. Democratic presidential candidates are "denouncing Wal-Mart for what they say are substandard wages and health care benefits."[125] Wal-Mart's political action committee's contributions to candidates (even to a former board member) are being returned as a sign of protest.[126] This sentiment is not only surfacing nationally, but locally as well. Governments in Inglewood, California, Cedar Mill, Oregon, and Vancouver, Canada, have rejected Wal-Mart expansion plans.[127]

Exhibit 18 Interviewee Perspectives on Wal-Mart, 2007

The environment steps are baby steps at the moment. We hope they will take substantive and [significant] action around the critical issues of the environment. Sadly, in the past, much of their efforts have been about publicity and positive spin, not about substance. We will wait to see what level of real commitment they will make around the environment.

—Robert Greenwald, producer/director,
Wal-Mart: The High Cost of Low Price (2007, e-mail interview, May 22)

[Wal-Mart has] a problem with blight. They leave behind in some cases blight by opening a new Supercenter and leaving their old stores empty. They need to have a plan for communities and not leave those huge buildings empty. In Hood River, the community didn't want Wal-Mart to open a Supercenter because they would leave the old store vacant, and Wal-Mart listened. They didn't open the Supercenter.

—Fred G.,
55, suburban Wal-Mart shopper (2007, personal interview, May 21)

[B]eing the low-cost provider loses some of the service, the pleasure of going shopping. Target has wider aisles, and less product on the shelf. In contrast, Wal-Mart bombards you with tons of products.

—Oliver Davis,
Target shopper (2007, personal interview, May 21)

There was a long time I didn't shop at Wal-Mart, and that had to do with the store's image of ruthlessness when it came to destroying the competition. To be honest, I feel a certain amount of shame at shopping there. As a mother, though, I'm afraid budget and convenience rule. In other words, I've sold out.

—Lili N.,
34, affluent shopper (2007, e-mail interview, May 19)

I shop at Wal-Mart for convenience-type items, but if the item I need is over $100 or is something that I need of quality, I will shop elsewhere. . . . I do not believe that Wal-Mart is capable of becoming related to quality items in the near future like Target and I do not believe that they will be successful at both discount and high quality.

—Andre S.,
26, budget-conscious shopper (2007, personal interview, May 20)

The [Wal-Mart] store itself is a little overwhelming—too many people, parking is usually tight, and the lines at the check-out are long. Also, there are so many [unfamiliar] employees working in a single Wal-Mart, that my shopping experience has no personal touch. I enjoy going to my neighborhood HEB [grocery store] because I see familiar faces—both at the check-out and in the aisles. If Wal-Mart would be willing to downsize a bit and have more of a neighborhood feel to it, I might consider stopping in more often.

—Angie R.,
29, affluent shopper (2007, e-mail interview, May 20)

Wal-Mart . . . lets you stay in their parking lot overnight. Friends stay at the "Wally-World" when we go windsurfing in Hood River. You can use their facilities and treat the parking lot like a campground. I like to shop there because of that corporate policy.

—Fred G.,
55, suburban Wal-Mart shopper (2007, personal interview, May 21)

I shop at Wal-Mart very infrequently because I find it hard to find things, [and the store is] often not very clean. There doesn't seem to be well-laid-out aisles like Target; it is more of a jumbled maze. However, one plus is the live fish they have. Kids love to go by and see them! And they usually have better prices. If I am looking for a particular item, like a kids' outdoor toy/sandbox, that is what usually gets me there, because you can find it cheaper.

—Crystal B.,
35, affluent shopper (2007, e-mail interview, May 21)

Wal-Mart neighborhood grocery is OK if you just need staples—it'll be cheap. I won't go into the 24-hour Supercenter down here. I think that was the store that had a stabbing over a Black Thursday laptop deal or something like that. SuperTarget is almost as bad during midday Sunday, but at least the store is cleaner and the meat looks a little better.

—Michael C.,
35, Wal-Mart shopper (2007, e-mail interview, May 21)

(continued)

Exhibit 18 Interviewee Perspectives on Wal-Mart, 2007 *(Continued)*

When I was an Operations Manager for a Fortune 500 *company, we were having a yearly employee appreciation picnic . . . [so] my secretary and I hopped into a company van, shot down to Sam's Club, loaded up four shopping carts of hamburgers, hotdogs, beverages, and all the fixings, got to the checkout, pulled out my Visa, and then found out that Sam's club didn't accept Visa. After a few minutes of arguing with an unhelpful and unsympathetic manager, I left all four carts at the checkout and have never been back since.*

—BRIAN S.,

FORMER SAM'S CLUB MEMBER (2007, DISCUSSION-BOARD POSTING, MAY 22)

Wal-Mart has been such a negative experience that it would be hard for me to go back. I have been hesitant to go to a neighborhood Wal-Mart because of my poor shopping experiences around the country at different big-box Wal-Marts. The Wal-Mart I am closer to is a lower socioeconomic neighborhood, and I drive past it to go to Target because I perceive it as being safer and I feel that I am getting a higher quality product.

—OLIVER DAVIS,

TARGET SHOPPER (2007, PERSONAL INTERVIEW, MAY 21)

[Wal-Mart] will continue to grow, and will make many changes in that time. Some are for the better and some are not. Unfortunately, sometimes plans that are not well [thought-out] are implemented and mandated, which only causes frustration/irritation. Other times workers are stuck in [their] ways and don't want to change.

—ANONYMOUS

WAL-MART MANAGER (2007, E-MAIL INTERVIEW, MAY 21)

[Wal-Mart needs better] price marking, more UPC scanners in the store. I see something and the price is ambiguous. They don't mark the prices. They can also make checkout faster. Why is it so slow? I don't go to Kmart anymore because a lot of times the UPC of something doesn't ring up at the cash register. It isn't in their system. If it is on the shelf, the UPC should be in the computer. Wal-Mart is also getting worse at this.

—FRED G.,

55, SUBURBAN WAL-MART SHOPPER (2007, PERSONAL INTERVIEW, MAY 21)

[Wal-Mart] does offer a big variety [of benefits for associates], some much better than other companies and some not so good in my opinion. Some examples of good discounts are 10% discount on most items (excludes grocery, clearance, and a few other items—biggest complaint on this is that tax in most areas eats up most of the discount), vacation (depends on variety of factors, but generally 2 weeks for full time and 1 week for [part-time] 1st year, and increases thereafter), personnel days (day off with pay—earned up to a certain # each year (average 2)), sick days, holiday pay, etc. On the other side of the coin, [I] think much more needs to be done to provide better health care for its workers, and a goal should be done to improve this every year. Many co-workers I know have dropped [their] coverage or rely on state assistance programs. Wal-Mart also did away with some of its [benefits], such as Christmas bonuses, unless you are grandfathered in (must have been hired before the change was made).

—ANONYMOUS

WAL-MART MANAGER (2007, E-MAIL INTERVIEW, MAY 21)

We have an Associates Fund that everyone chips into in case someone is in critical need. For example, if a cashier were to, heaven forbid, have their house burn down, the fund would immediately come to help out by supplying a place to stay, warm clothes, and food, pretty much everything that the associate would need to get back on her feet, up to and including a replacement house, if that's what it takes. . . . A happy associate is more productive.

SERGIO JIMENEZ,

WAL-MART STORE CO-MANAGER (2007, PERSONAL INTERVIEW, MAY 20)

Wal-Mart takes care of their people in dire situations. When my friend's wife died, they brought them groceries and really took care of them.

—WENDY S.,

46, FRIEND OF WAL-MART ASSOCIATE (2007, PERSONAL INTERVIEW, MAY 20)

One thing the company does . . . every year is [to] hold [grassroots] meetings for associates to come and vent about things they don't like, in the hope that something will change. Sadly, most associates (workers) feel that they are allowed to vent, but not without [retaliation] any more, or at best [their] input will not change anything. I think the company

(continued)

should not just write down the input they are being given, but act on it when possible. If they would do so it would boost morale, and more effort would be given, [causing] customer satisfaction to go up and sales to boost as well.

—ANONYMOUS
WAL-MART MANAGER (2007, E-MAIL INTERVIEW, MAY 21)

If I [were] to change Wal-Mart, I would reduce product on the shelves and change the lighting, and widen the aisles. [T]he bouncing ball for Wal-Mart gives it a cartoon-ish edge, whereas Target does an ad that goes coast to coast, with a heavy CGI aspect that it isn't cartoon-y. It has a big-city feel whereas Wal-Mart has a small-town middle America feel. I am partial to bigger cities. . . . Smaller towns that have limited options [make] me feel constrained, which is one of the reasons I like Target, which has hip trends, whereas Wal-Mart just has the bouncy smiley face. [T]he smiley face reduces [Wal-Mart's] seriousness. I would go to more subtle references to being the low-cost provider, and pitch one-stop shopping, but push the option to have your own personal brand, and reduce the number of SKUs on the walls so you don't feel overwhelmed by the experience there.

—OLIVER DAVIS,
TARGET SHOPPER (2007, PERSONAL INTERVIEW, MAY 21)

I would LOVE a coupon for a certain amount off any item the store. Sort of what Michael's has (40% off any item) or Bed Bath and Beyond has (20% off). I also find Target's returns the most convenient I've ever experienced: they can locate the item you purchased by sliding your credit card through the reader so you don't have to go searching for your receipt. I appreciate that kind of convenience.

—LILI N.,
34, AFFLUENT SHOPPER (2007, E-MAIL INTERVIEW, MAY 19)

Legal. Class-action lawsuits against Wal-Mart have become commonplace. In *Savaglio v. Wal-Mart Stores, Inc.*, the "plaintiffs allege that they were not provided meal and rest breaks in accordance with California law, and seek monetary damages and injunctive relief."[128] A jury ruled in favor of those plaintiffs and awarded them a total of $198 million.[129] In *Dukes v. Wal-Mart Stores, Inc.*, currently pending on behalf of all present and past female employees in all of Wal-Mart's retail stores and warehouse clubs, Wal-Mart is alleged to have "engaged in a pattern and practice of discriminating against women in promotions, pay, training, and job assignments."[130] These lawsuits are providing ample fodder for Wal-Mart opponents to inflict ongoing reputation damage.

Global. The globalization trend that began in the 1990s persists. As trade barriers continue to come down around the world and as technology enables greater access to information, the world is becoming one mega-market of labor, capital, goods, and services. Bilateral and multilateral free trade agreements are continuing to shape markets.

Technology. The development of radio frequency identification (RFID) is expected to play a major part in the next evolution of supply chain management in the retail industry. This technology may better enable retailers to track inventory locations, store shelving status, packages en-route to and from suppliers, warehouses, shelves, and even shoplifting.[131] Recent developments in the technology include a movement toward "common standards and practices that could make RFID as ubiquitous as bar codes," and a push to lower the cost per RFID tag from the current 10-cent mark to the Wal-Mart target of 5-cents.[132] RFID chips are increasingly "able to hold much more information and fit into different shapes and sizes—woven inside clothing, slipped into a paper-thin tag or molded inside a key chain."[133]

Another technology development impacting the retail industry is the unabated growth of electronic commerce, and the increasing pervasiveness of broadband Internet access in most developed countries. As consumers at various socioeconomic levels come to rely more on the Web for information, entertainment, and shopping, retailers are discovering the need to use their online presence not just to spur online sales, but to drive traditional-format sales as well.

Demographics. Americans, like those in many developed nations, are getting older. The Census Bureau estimates the number of those aged 65 and up will rise from approximately 35 million in 2000 to 86.7 million by 2050. The age 65 and up cohort made up 12.4 percent of the total U.S. population in 2000; by 2050, it will make up 20.7 percent of a projected population of nearly 420 million.[134]

The country is also becoming more diverse.[135] Ethnic and gender diversity in the U.S. workforce is on the rise. In 1995, whites/non-Hispanics made up 76 percent of the workforce, but this is projected to decrease to 68 percent in 2020. According to the U.S. Department of Labor, women comprised 46 percent of the labor force in 2006.[136] The percentage of women over the age of 16 in the labor force has risen 23 percent in 44 years to 59 percent in 2004.[137]

The distance in America between the "haves" and the "have-nots" is growing. Increasing returns to education have created a bifurcation in income distribution.[138] The bottom quintile has seen its mean income increase 34.5 percent in real terms from 1967 to 2005, whereas the top income quintile had an increase in mean income of 80.8 percent over the same time period.[139] Average income growth for the bottom three quintiles was only 30.4 percent. The typical Wal-Mart customer is in the middle-income quintiles.

As Wal-Mart's competitive landscape continues to evolve, the company is taking its strategic cues from Sam Walton's words of wisdom: "Everything around you is always changing. To succeed, stay out in front of that change."[140]

Current Strategies

To manage its competitive environment, Wal-Mart is currently deploying a variety of strategies, most of which stem from its relentless core generic strategy of cost leadership, but some of which represent beyond-cost approaches. "Our everyday low price position is the basis for our business," wrote Rob Walton in Wal-Mart's 2006 annual report.[141] He added, "While this core principle is critical to our growth and business strategy, by itself it is not enough anymore."[142] According to Scott in this year's shareholder letter, Wal-Mart is confronting "a period of perhaps the most rapid and profound change in our Company's history. With our transformation plan, we are committed to staying 'Out in Front' of the changes around us."[143] The corporate plan, encompassing previous change initiatives as well as newer ones, rests on "five pillars": "broadening our appeal to our customers, making Wal-Mart an even better place to work, improving operations and efficiencies, driving global growth, and contributing to our communities.[144]

Strategies to Deal with External and Reputational Challenges. Wal-Mart is pursuing two key strategies that will help them overcome external issues affecting the company, including environmental and community-impact issues, among others. These strategies include sustainability efforts and localized charitable giving to help portray it as being a responsible corporate citizen and a good neighbor. Wal-Mart launched its global environmental sustainability initiative in 2004 and has since taken action toward several sustainability goals: sell 100 million compact fluorescent bulbs by 2008; reduce packaging by five percent by 2013; buy fish from certified fisheries; sell "more organic and environmentally friendly products"; and make company facilities and trucks more energy-efficient.[145] The Wal-Mart Foundation in 2006 gave "more than $415 million in cash and in-kind merchandise to 100,000 organizations worldwide," making it the "largest corporate cash contributor in America."[146] The Foundation "gave most of the money at the local level where [it] can have the greatest impact."[147]

Wal-Mart has beefed up pro-community, pro-sustainability, pro-health care information on its Web site, on its television ads, and in its annual report. The company recently launched *In Front with Wal-Mart*, a 30-minute television show airing on the Lifetime and USA networks that "gives [Wal-Mart] a chance to showcase [its] incredible associates and the variety of ways they give back to their communities, bettering the lives of America's working families" and "sheds light . . . on some of [Wal-Mart's] eco-friendly practices."[148] Wal-Mart created an interactive Web site on sustainability, dedicated a page of its 2007 annual report to sustainability, and will soon publish a separate Sustainability Report.[149]

In its public outreach, Wal-Mart also stresses its benefits to suppliers and communities, as well as its commitment to providing affordable health care and competitive wages for its associates.[150] These efforts tie into its supply-chain innovation and people strategies.

Supply-Chain Innovation and People Strategies

As previously mentioned, Wal-Mart creates value for customers with a highly efficient and innovative supply-chain management operation. This operation combines tough, low-cost procurement tactics, leading-edge information systems and "rocket-science" logistics.[151]

There's not much negotiation at all. The manufacturer walks into the room. I've been in these little cubicles, I've seen it happen. The buyer says, "Look, we want you to sell it to us for 5 percent on a dollar—at cost—lower this year than you did last year." They know every fact and figure that these manufacturers have. They know their books. They know their costs. They know their business practices—everything, you know? So what's a manufacturer left to do? They sit naked in front of Wal-Mart. You know, Wal-Mart calls the shots. "If you want to do business with us, if you want to stay in business, then you're going to do it our way." And it's all about driving down the cost of goods.

—*Former Wal-Mart store manager Jon Lehman on Frontline in 2004*[152]

All Wal-Mart suppliers must participate in Retail Link, a computerized system in which they "plan, execute, and analyze their businesses."[153] Along with electronic data interchange, suppliers receive purchase order information and supply invoices electronically, thereby lowering expenses and increasing productivity. Suppliers must meet Wal-Mart's strict lead-time and shipping requirements by using the technology and complying with operating procedures. The Wal-Mart logistics team uses an Internet-based Transportation Link system that complements a Backhaul Betty telephone voice-response system to help them move goods. In one year, Wal-Mart estimated nearly 1 million loads of general merchandise moved to Distribution Centers throughout the country.[154] Store-bound shipments travel by the company's 7,000 trucks, one of the largest fleets in the world.[155] The company relentlessly strives to develop its supply-chain process. For example, "[t]o ensure greater supply chain visibility, satellite-based tracking technology is being installed in the Company's entire fleet of over-the-road trailers. The data generated . . . increases productivity, reduces costs and enhances security."[156]

In the stores, Wal-Mart's legendary inventory management capability is driven by its advanced Texlon barcode system. In addition to tracking the sales price, inventory levels of each product, and a history of quantities sold, Texlon can record trends and predict future needs. Quantities sold can be traced to specific weeks, days, or even hours of each day. Seasonal projections can be documented, and shopping habits are noted. Information is sent daily at midnight to the warehouses, so depleted products are restocked the following night. Reliance on this kind of technology to drive the supply chain enables Wal-Mart's suppliers to use "pull production" instead of "push production." The barcode system will eventually be replaced by an RFID-based system, technology Wal-Mart is driving.

Wal-Mart's technological supply-chain sophistication is intended to provide "value for customers, associates, and shareholders."[157] The system depends on Wal-Mart's 1.8 million associates to provide the final link in the value chain to customers. Wal-Mart's people strategy involves "[g]iving our associates the tools and opportunities they need to be as productive as possible," which has enabled "workforce productivity gains in every quarter of the last two years."[158] Associates who feel overworked may create a weak link in the value chain.

I would say that some customers are happy, but most are not. . . . [M]any workers feel they are being overworked due to mainly understaffing issues, which causes workers to treat the customers worse, then causing customers to become upset. Many customers have at one time been [Wal-Mart] associates and understand how things are handled at each store level and can relate. Personally, [I] believe that overall morale a few years ago was much higher with workers, and that attitude was passed along to the customers. Today many customers feel that [Wal-Mart] only wants them for [their] money, and does not care about them."

—*Anonymous Wal-Mart manager (2007, e-mail interview, May 21)*

Reassuring its "valued long-term associates" that the company "is listening to them," Wal-Mart "again increased [its] average full-time hourly wage in the United States."[159] The company is against unionization of its associates.

Wal-Mart's operational effectiveness goals of improving return on investment, comparable-store sales, and working capital productivity are setting the agenda for its business-segment strategies.[160]

Wal-Mart Stores Segment Strategies

The Wal-Mart Stores segment is in its second year of a three-year strategic plan to improve ROI, people development, and customer relevancy.[161] Customers have become the prime focus since January 2007, when Wal-Mart Stores elevated its new marketing and merchandising chiefs and completed its management reshuffle.

In 2006, Wal-Mart Stores rolled out a $4 generic prescription program, a clear opening-price-point approach. Merchandising has been characterized by the product-focused "opening price point" strategy, which relied on attractive low prices on entry-level items in every category to set the stage for higher-margin prices on more desirable items.[162] This single strategy has served to focus each of the two dozen departments at a typical Wal-Mart Supercenter (see Exhibit 19). Wal-Mart stores often offer retail space to other vendors that provide services, such as nail salons, hair salons, coffee shops, food and beverage vendors (e.g., McDonald's and Subway), full-service banks, and even employment agencies in some locations.

Recently, Wal-Mart Stores "realigned [its] merchandising . . . around five key power categories—entertainment, grocery, health and wellness, apparel, and home."[163] Global Procurement meanwhile is "establishing groups

Exhibit 19 List of Departments in Wal-Mart

Wal-Mart Departments	
Grocery	Pharmacy
Bakery	Health & Beauty
Produce	Vision Center
Deli	Jewelry
Frozen Foods	Lawn & Garden
Apparel	Portrait Studio
Housewares	Photo Lab
Entertainment	Hardware
Electronics	Furniture
Tire & Lube Express	Sporting Goods
Automotive	Toys & Games
School Supplies	Office Products & School Supplies

Source: http://www.walmart.com.

of technical experts—specialists that focus on the many important dynamics of a particular category purchase."[164]

The Wal-Mart Stores customer segmentation and merchandising strategies have been in flux over the past few years, with three different strategies in play to move Wal-Mart Stores toward a more customer-focused position.

The first customer-focused strategy—mimicking Target's upscale, fashion-forward appeal—flopped. "In working to broaden our appeal to our customers, we moved too quickly in the rollout of some of our fashion-forward apparel in the United States," according to Scott.[165] Wal-Mart Stores has at least partially retreated from this strategy.

The second customer-focused strategy—localizing selections based on store-neighborhood demographics—continues to drive various store changes, though it may be waning. In 2006, Wal-Mart "launched six different types of customized stores to attract different demographics, from inner-city residents, to affluent suburbanites, to rural shoppers."[166] With these stores, Wal-Mart attempted to target African-Americans, Hispanics, empty-nesters, suburbanites, rural residents, and the affluent. Wal-Mart expanded and empowered regional marketing teams, moving many executives away from headquarters into regions to better understand Wal-Mart's wide customer base.[167] These changes were inspired by localized merchandizing selection in Wal-Mart de Mexico stores aimed at different mixes of inventory for different income levels.[168] For example, the localization strategy expanded the mix of hip-hop, gospel, and R&B music in a store outside Chicago and led to plans for larger pharmacy sections and fewer children's clothes at a store geared toward empty-nesters.[169] In his March letter to shareholders, Scott wrote, "We continue to strive to make sure every Wal-Mart store is a 'Store of the Community'—one that reflects the individual needs of each neighborhood we serve."[170]

The third customer-focused strategy—appealing to the three universal types of low-price-seeking customers who currently shop at Wal-Mart—now guides merchandising and marketing decisions. According to Fleming and Quinn, the three types are "'brand aspirationals' (people with low incomes who are obsessed with names like Kitchen Aid), 'price-sensitive affluents' (wealthier shoppers who love deals), and 'value-price shoppers' (who like low prices and cannot afford much more)."[171] For these types, the Wal-Mart Stores segment is concentrating on developing unique, innovative products and providing distinguished brands (such as the recently added Dell desktop computers) to better appeal to its core customers as the low-price leader on well-known brands.[172]

This is a much better strategy for Wal-Mart than the store segmentation strategy path . . . they were going down before . . . because it aligns with their basic brand proposition (EDLP) and basic consumer rather than trying to attract a new consumer by adding high-end fashion and complicated assortments. For the same reason, it aligns better with Wal-Mart's supply chain strength. It's far easier to roll out a national brand in stores nationally than it is to ship different assortments to different stores within a region without disrupting the cost efficient supply chain that is Wal-Mart's core competitive advantage. I'm not sure what took them so long but it looks like Wal-Mart is back to a strategy that is sustainable and executable for them.

—**Forrester Research senior analyst Lisa Bradner**[173]

Sam's Club Segment Strategies

Sam's Club, meanwhile, is focused on three areas: "reinvigorating the brand" by broadening products and services; improving inventory management and other performance measures; and optimizing the "in-club experience."[174] Sam's Club stores offer members products such as frozen and dry food goods in bulk, electronics, computer equipment, clothing, books, electronic entertainment, and general merchandise. Sam's Club recently restructured its management layers to give stores additional flexibility and to boost service.[175] Rumors have circulated that Sam's Club may spin off from Wal-Mart, in part to set its own direction in attracting and retaining members and associates, two key groups who are generally less loyal to Sam's Club than to its rival Costco.[176]

Wal-Mart International Segment Strategies

Wal-Mart International's strategy is to prioritize "where the greatest growth and greatest returns exist," what the segment calls "majoring in the majors."[177] The majors appear to include the Americas primarily, followed by the United Kingdom and Japan, as well as China and India over the long term.[178] Wal-Mart International is labeling this strategy "focused portfolio execution."[179] Its second strategy is global leverage, or "taking full advantage of our worldwide assets, including formats, information systems, purchasing organizations, category expertise, and shared best practices."[180] In the past year, it has concentrated on turning around Asda in the United Kingdom through "improved execution in all phases of customer service, differentiation with competitors, and development of new channels and formats."[181] To better compete against U.K. leader Tesco, second-largest Asda reportedly may be considering acquiring the third-largest U.K. retailer, the J. Sainsbury chain of grocery and convenience stores.[182] Wal-Mart's international stores are varied in their mix of products and services, and they stick to the motto of "offering working families the things they need at the prices they can afford."[183]

Just as the business segments are looking to focus on the right challenges for their short- and long-term success in the marketplace, the company must ensure it is applying its greatest resources against its greatest strategic challenges across the enterprise.

Strategic Challenges

The challenges Wal-Mart faces today are actually not much different from what they have been for the past several years. These following quotes come from an article in April 2003: "Even though it is the nation's largest apparel retailer with more than 12 percent of the market, Wal-Mart could be doing better in this category"; "It would like to be a fashion retailer and take on Target with good quality at a low price-point, but it hasn't convinced the American consumer it should be a destination for casual fashion"; "Wal-Mart is . . . looking abroad for future sales growth"; "Wal-Mart will need to struggle against the urge to centralize operations and eliminate decision making from the frontlines where managers have face-to-face contact with customers"; and "The only area in which Wal-Mart has not been able to pummel its competition is against Costco."[184] One of the company's challenges may be to stop proliferating nearly identical sets of challenges each year. Like the stock price, the challenges appear to be stuck in a holding pattern.

One key new challenge is the sluggishness of same-store sales relative to Wal-Mart's competitors. According to *BusinessWeek,* Wal-Mart faces "the diciest conundrum in retailing today . . . can it seduce . . . middle-income shoppers into stepping up their purchases in a major way without alienating its low-income legions in the process?"[185]

Another growing challenge is the difficulty of expanding in the domestic market, whether because of community opposition or geographic saturation (see Exhibits 20 and 21).

These and other strategic challenges are weighing on the minds of Wal-Mart's shareholders, especially on the two with the most responsibility for the company's fate.

Questions Wal-Mart Leaders Must Address

CEO Lee Scott and Chairman Rob Walton are grappling with some vexing questions as they head into the 2007 Wal-Mart Annual Shareholders' Meeting:

- How can Wal-Mart Stores and Sam's Club increase same-store sales?
- How should the company capture share of middle- and upper-income wallets?
- Should Wal-Mart Stores fully retreat from fashion-forward merchandising and marketing? Will its neighborhood-store-localization strategy increase sales enough to offset the associated costs? What should it do to make its new three-types-of-customers segmentation strategy work?
- Should the company spin off Sam's Club? If not, what should it do to compete more effectively against Costco?
- Is Wal-Mart expanding the right kind of new stores at the right pace and in the right places? How and where should the company continue to grow internationally? Should Asda buy J. Sainsbury?
- What will it take to restore the company's reputation in America?
- Should Lee Scott change Wal-Mart's course? If so, how?
- Should Rob Walton replace Lee Scott? If so, when and with whom?

Exhibit 20 Spread of Wal-Mart Stores, 1970–1995

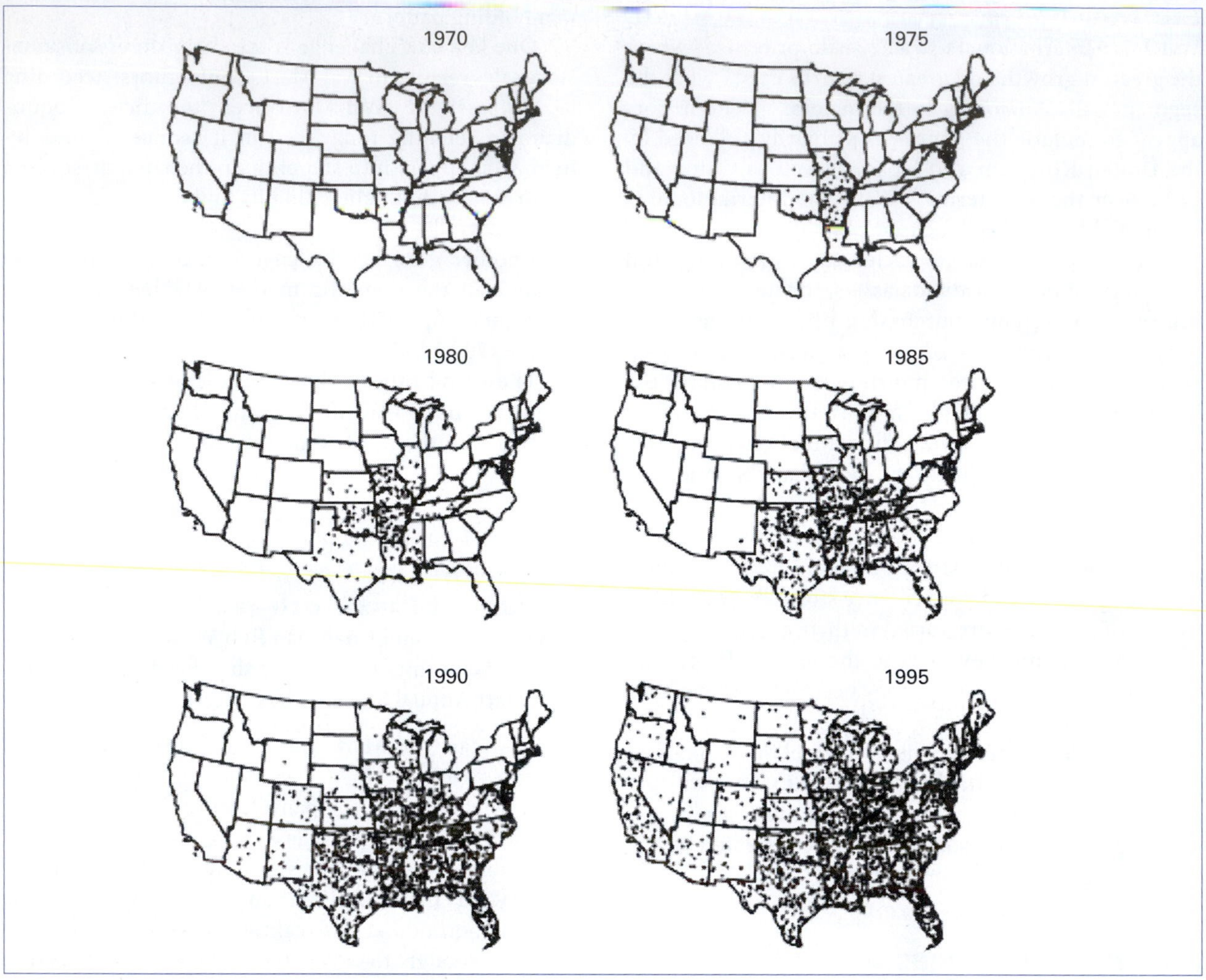

1970

1975

1980

1985

1990

1995

Source: E. Basker, 2004, Job creation or destruction? Labor-market effects of Wal-Mart expansion, University of Missouri, January, Figure 1, 28.

Exhibit 21 Number of Counties Having a Wal-Mart Store, 1963–2006

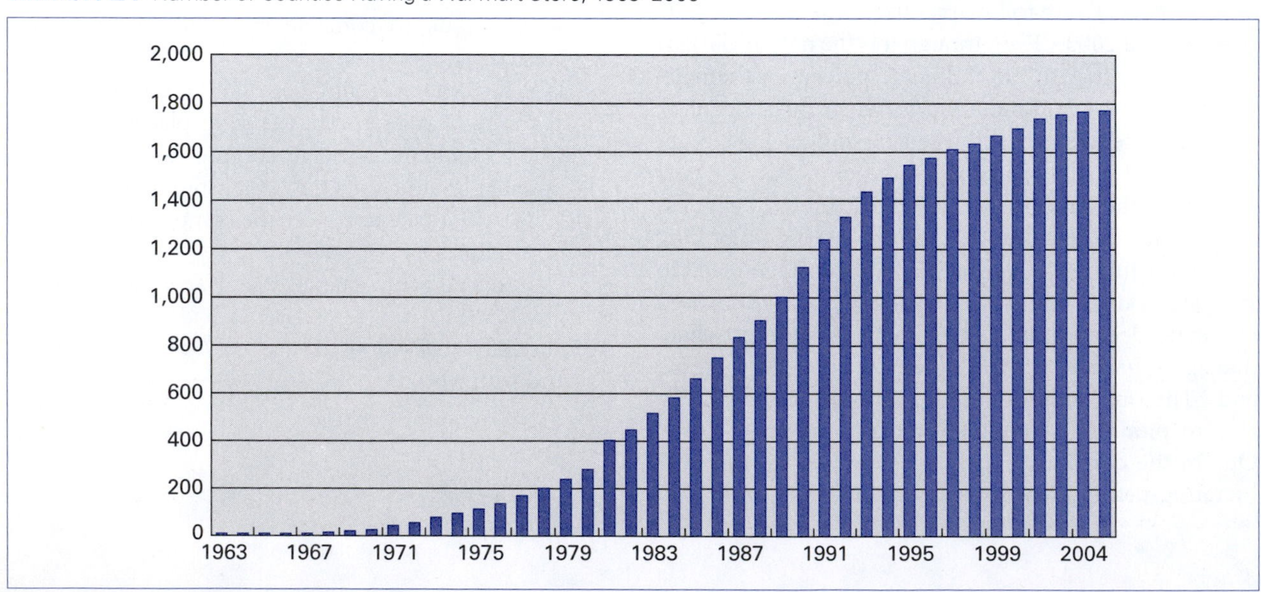

Source: 2005, The economic impact of Wal-Mart, Global Insight, Business Planning Solutions, Global Insight Advisory Services, November 2, Figure 4, 33.

Notes

1. A. Bianco, 2006, *The Bully of Bentonville: The High Cost of Wal-Mart's Everyday Low Prices*, New York: Doubleday Publishing, 1.
2. 2007, 7 demands for change, Against * The * Wal, http://www.againstthewal.net/7demands.html, May 18.
3. 2007, Notice of 2007 Annual Shareholders' Meeting, DEF 14A, Proxy Statement, Wal-Mart Stores, Inc., U.S. SEC, April 19, 52–68.
4. A. Bianco, 2006, *The Bully of Bentonville: The High Cost of Wal-Mart's Everyday Low Prices*, 267; 2007, Yahoo! Finance, http://finance.yahoo.com/charts#chart6:symbol=wmt;range=20000103,20070518;compare=cost+tgt;indicator=volume;charttype=line;crosshair=on;logscale=on;source=undefined, May 17.
5. 2007, Yahoo! Finance, http://finance.yahoo.com/charts#chart6:symbol=wmt;range=20000103,20070518;compare=cost+tgt;indicator=volume;charttype=line;crosshair=on;logscale=on;source=undefined, May 17.
6. A. Bianco, 2007, Wal-Mart's midlife crisis, *BusinessWeek*, April 30, 46–52.
7. 2007, Wal-Mart Data Sheet, http://walmartstores.com/Files/US_operations.pdf, February 8.
8. 2007, Wal-Mart Annual Report.
9. 2007, Wal-Mart Stores, Inc., Form 8-K, U.S. SEC, May 15; and 2007, Company Overview, Target.com, http://investors.target.com/phoenix.zhtml?c=65828&p=irol-homeProfile, May 25.
10. L. Michael Cacace & K. Tucksmith, 2007, *Fortune* 500 largest U.S. corporations, *Fortune*, April 30, F2.
11. Ibid.
12. A. Bianco, 2007, Wal-Mart's midlife crisis, 49–52.
13. A. Bianco, 2007, Wal-Mart's midlife crisis, 46.
14. 2004, Wal-Mart Tops *Fortune*'s List of America's Most Admired Companies, *Fortune*, http://www.timeinc.net/fortune/information/presscenter/fortune/press_releases/02232004AMAC.html, February 23.
15. 2007, America's Most Admired Companies 2007, *Fortune*, CNNMoney.com, http://money.cnn.com/magazines/fortune/mostadmired/2007/top20/, May 18.
16. W. Zellner, 2004, Sam Walton: King of the discounters, *BusinessWeek*, August 9.
17. Ibid.
18. Ibid.
19. A. A. Thompson & A. J. Strickland, *Strategic Management, Concepts & Cases*, 10th ed., New York: Irwin/McGraw-Hill.
20. 2007, The Wal-Mart Timeline, Wal-Mart Facts, http://www.walmartfacts.com/content/default.aspx?id=3, April 1; D. Longo, 1998, Wal-Mart hands CEO crown to David Glass, *Discount Store News*, February 15, 1988.
21. 2007, Wal-Mart Annual Report, 19; 2007, The Wal-Mart Timeline, Wal-Mart Facts, http://www.walmartfacts.com/content/default.aspx?id=3, April 1.
22. A. Bianco, 2007, Wal-Mart's midlife crisis, 46–54.
23. 2007, Data Sheet, Wal-Mart Stores, http://walmartstores.com/Files/US_operations.pdf, February 8, May 25; and 2007, International Data Sheet, Wal-Mart Stores, http://walmartstores.com/Files/Intl_operations.pdf, February 8, May 25.
24. 2007, Wal-Mart Annual Report, 1.
25. A. Biesada, 2007, Wal-Mart Company Overview, Hoovers Online, http://premium.hoovers.com, May.
26. Ibid.
27. P. Engardio, 2007, Beyond the green corporation, imagine a world in which eco-friendly and socially responsible practices actually help a company's bottom line. It's closer than you think, *BusinessWeek Online*, January 29.
28. 2007, Wal-Mart Annual Report, 18-19.
29. 2007, Wal-Mart Annual Report, 31.
30. 2007, Wal-Mart Annual Report , 28.
31. Ibid.
32. Ibid.
33. 2007, Wal-Mart Annual Report, 31.
34. Ibid.
35. 2007, Wal-Mart Annual Report, 28.
36. 2007, Wal-Mart Annual Report, 36.
37. 2007, Wal-Mart Annual Report, 32.
38. 2007, International Data Sheet, Wal-Mart Stores, http://walmartstores.com/Files/Intl_operations.pdf, February 8.
39. 2007, Wal-Mart Annual Report, 32.
40. 2007, Wal-Mart Annual Report, 51-52.
41. 2006, IGD looks at Wal-Mart's decision to pull out of Germany, http://www.igd.com/CIR, March 8.
42. 2007, Wal-Mart Annual Report, 32.
43. 2007, Informe Annual 2006, Wal-Mart de Mexico, http://library.corporate-ir.net/library/19/194/194702/items/231792/AR06.pdf, May 21; and 2007, *CIA World Fact Book*, Mexico, https://www.cia.gov/library/publications/the-world-factbook/geos/mx.html#Econ, May 21.
44. 2007, Wal-Mart Facts: The Wal-Mart Story, http://www.walmartfacts.com/content/default.aspx?id=1, April 1.
45. 2006, CNBC Interview with Carter Cast, http://www.hoovers.com/global/co/interviews/player.xhtml, November 7.
46. 2007, About Sam's Club, Samsclub.com, http://pressroom.samsclub.com/content/?id=3&atg=524, March 1.
47. K. Hundson, 2007, Wal-Mart Pushes Financial-Services Menu, *Wall Street Journal*, June 6, A3.
48. 2007, The Wal-Mart Timeline, Wal-Mart Facts, http://www.walmartfacts.com/content/default.aspx?id=3, April 1; D. Longo, 1998, Wal-Mart hands CEO crown to David Glass, *Discount Store News*, February 15.
49. 2007, The Wal-Mart Timeline, Wal-Mart Facts, http://www.walmartfacts.com/content/default.aspx?id=3, April 1.
50. 2007, Wal-Mart Annual Report, 14; 2007, Senior Officers, Wal-Mart Stores, http://walmartstores.com/GlobalWMStoresWeb/navigate.do?catg=540, May 6.
51. 2007, S. Robson Walton, Wal-Mart Stores, http://walmartstores.com/GlobalWMStoresWeb/navigate.do?catg=540&contId=15, May 6; 2005. Forbes: America's richest 400, MSN Money, http://moneycentral.msn.com/content/invest/forbes/P129955.asp, September 23.
52. A. Bianco, 2006, *The Bully of Bentonville: The High Cost of Wal-Mart's Everyday Low Prices*, 61.
53. 2007, S. Robson Walton, Wal-Mart Stores.
54. 2007, Wal-Mart Annual Report, 13.
55. A. Bianco, *The Bully of Bentonville: The High Cost of Wal-Mart's Everyday Low Prices*, 104.
56. Ibid.
57. A. Bianco, *The Bully of Bentonville: The High Cost of Wal-Mart's Everyday Low Prices*, 79.
58. Ibid.
59. A. Bianco, *The Bully of Bentonville: The High Cost of Wal-Mart's Everyday Low Prices*, 80.
60. A. Bianco, *The Bully of Bentonville: The High Cost of Wal-Mart's Everyday Low Prices*, 81.
61. 2007, H. Lee Scott, Jr., Senior Officers, WalMartStores.com, http://walmartstores.com/GlobalWMStoresWeb/navigate.do?catg=540&contId=17, May 25.
62. Ibid.
63. 2007, Michael T. Duke, Senior Officers, WalMartStores.com, http://walmartstores.com/GlobalWMStoresWeb/navigate.do?catg=540&contId=22, May 25.
64. Ibid.
65. 2007, John B. Menzer, Senior Officers, WalMartStores.com, http://walmartstores.com/GlobalWMStoresWeb/navigate.do?catg=540&contId=19, May 25.
66. Ibid.
67. Ibid.

68. 2007, Eduardo Castro-Wright, Senior Officers, WalMartStores.com, http://walmartstores.com/GlobalWMStoresWeb/navigate.do?catg=540&contId=41, May 25.
69. 2007, C. Douglas McMillon, Senior Officers, WalMartStores.com, http://walmartstores.com/GlobalWMStoresWeb/navigate.do?catg=540&contId=33, May 25.
70. 2007, John E. Fleming, Senior Officers, WalMartStores.com, http://walmartstores.com/GlobalWMStoresWeb/navigate.do?catg=540&contId=42, May 25.
71. 2007, Stephen Quinn, Senior Officers, WalMartStores.com, http://walmartstores.com/GlobalWMStoresWeb/navigate.do?catg=540&contId=6396, May 25.
72. 2007, Wal-Mart Board of Directors, Walmart.com, June 28.
73. M. Halkias, 2007, Questrom nominated to Wal-Mart board, *Dallas Morning News*, http://www.dallasnews.com/sharedcontent/dws/bus/industries/retail/stories/042507dnbusquestrom.36b21ad.html, April 24.
74. Ibid.
75. S. Braun, 2007, At Wal-Mart, Clinton didn't upset any carts, *Los Angeles Times*, http://www.latimes.com/news/nationworld/nation/la-na-hillary19may19,0,5168474.story?coll=la-home-center, May 19.
76. 2007, Morningstar, Wal-Mart Stores (WMT), http://quicktake.morningstar.com/StockNet/powerbrokers.aspx?Country=USA&Symbol=WMT&stocktab=owner, May 6; 2007, Wal-Mart Stores Inc. (WMT), Major Holders, Yahoo! Finance, http://finance.yahoo.com/q/mh?s=WMT, May 6.
77. 2007, Wal-Mart Stores Inc. (WMT), Major Holders, Yahoo! Finance, http://finance.yahoo.com/q/mh?s=WMT; May 6; and 2005, Forbes: America's richest 400, MSN Money, http://moneycentral.msn.com/content/invest/forbes/P129955.asp, September 23; 2002, Proxy, Wal-Mart Stores, http://www.walmartstores.com/Files/proxy_2002/proxy_pg05.htm; M. Weil and M. Barbaro, 2005, John T. Walton, 58; Heir to Wal-Mart Fortune, *The Washington Post*, http://www.washingtonpost.com/wp-dyn/content/article/2005/06/27/AR2005062701471.html, June 28; 2007, Associated Press, *Washington Post*, Helen R. Walton; Philanthropic wife of Wal-Mart chief, http://www.washingtonpost.com/wp-dyn/content/article/2007/04/20/AR2007042002060.html, April 21.
78. 2007, Wal-Mart Stores Inc. (WMT), Insider Roster, Yahoo! Finance, http://finance.yahoo.com/q/ir?s=WMT, May 6.
79. 2007, Wal-Mart Stores Inc. (WMT), Major Holders, Yahoo! Finance, http://finance.yahoo.com/q/mh?s=WMT, May 6.
80. 2007, Morningstar, Wal-Mart Stores (WMT), http://quicktake.morningstar.com/StockNet/powerbrokers.aspx?Country=USA&Symbol=WMT&stocktab=owner, May 6.
81. 2007, Wal-Mart Annual Report, 64.
82. 2007, 2002 Wal-Mart Annual Reports.
83. Ibid.
84. 2007, Sam's Club vs. Costco: Battle of the brands, *BloggingStocks*, AOL Money & Finance, http://www.bloggingstocks.com/2007/04/12/sams-club-vs-costco-battle-of-the-brands/, April 12.
85. T. Otte, 2007, Spinoff in Bentonville revisited, Value Investing, MotleyFool.com, http://www.fool.com/investing/value/2007/05/07/spinoff-in-bentonville-revisited.aspx, May 7.
86. M. Wagner, 2003, Where's Wal-Mart: Wal-Mart's web revenue hardly registers on its ledger, *Internet Retailer*, http://www.internetretailer.com/internet/marketing-conference/70624-wheres-wal-mart.html, April.
87. D. Pinto, 2005, Mass market retailers, http://www.massmarketretailers.com/articles/Every_winner.html, May 16.
88. Ibid.
89. Ibid.
90. A. Bianco, 2007, Wal-Mart's, midlife crisis, 48.
91. D. Pinto, Mass market retailers.
92. M. Holz-Clause & M. Geisler, 2006, Grocery Industry, Grocery Retailing Profile, AgMRC, http://www.agmrc.org/agmrc/markets/Food/groceryindustry.htm, September.
93. 2007, Wal-Mart F1Q08 (Qtr End 4/30/07) Earnings Call Transcript, SeekingAlpha.com, http://retail.seekingalpha.com/article/35633, May 15.
94. Ibid.
95. 2007, Wal-Mart 1st Quarter 2008 Earnings Release, May 10.
96. Ibid.
97. 2007, Wal-Mart April Sales News Release, May 10.
98. R. Dodes & G. McWilliams, 2007, Fashion faux pas hurts Wal-Mart, *Wall Street Journal*, May 21, A8.
99. G. McWilliams, 2007, Wal-Mart net rises as weakness persists, *Wall Street Journal*, May 16, C6.
100. J. Covert, 2007, Retail-sales slide fuels concern: Decline of 2.3% in April among worst on record; even Wal-Mart slipped, *Wall Street Journal*, May 11, A3.
101. 2007, Target Corporation, Form 8-K, U.S. SEC, May 23; 2007, Company Overview, Target.com, http://investors.target.com/phoenix.zhtml?c=65828&p=irol-homeProfile, May 25.
102. Ibid.
103. 2006, Target Annual Report, 2.
104. Ibid.
105. 2007, Company Profile, Costco Wholesale Investor Relations, http://phx.corporate-ir.net/phoenix.zhtml?c=83830&p=irol-homeprofile, May 5.
106. 2006, Costco Annual Report, 9.
107. 2006, 2002, Costco Annual Report.
108. 2007, The Kroger Co., Form 10-K, U.S. SEC, April 4.
109. Ibid.
110. Ibid.
111. 2007, Carrefour profile, Hoovers, Lexis/Nexis Academic, May 8.
112. 2007, Tesco profile, Hoovers, Lexis/Nexis Academic, May 8.
113. Ibid.
114. 2007, Global Procurement, WalMartStores.com, http://walmartstores.com/GlobalWMStoresWeb/navigate.do?catg=337, May 26.
115. A. Bianco & W. Zellner, 2003, Is Wal-Mart too powerful? *BusinessWeek*, http://www.businessweek.com/magazine/content/03_40/b3852001_mz001.htm, October 6.
116. Ibid.
117. Ibid.
118. 2007, Wal-Mart Facts, http://www.walmartfacts.com/FactSheets/3142007_Corporate_Facts.pdf, March 14.
119. S. Kapinus, 2006, Rollback sushi and discount organics, *ACNielsen Consumer Insight*, http://us.acnielsen.com/pubs/2006_q2_ci_rollback.shtml, Q2.
120. Ibid.
121. Ibid.
122. Ibid.
123. Barney Gimbel, 2006, Attack of the Wal-Martyrs, http://money.cnn.com/magazines/fortune/fortune_archive/2006/12/11/8395445/index.htm, November 28.
124. B. C. Lynn, 2006, It's time to enforce antitrust law and break up Wal-Mart, *Harper's Magazine*, July.
125. A. Nagourney & M. Barbaro, 2006, Eye on election, Democrats run as Wal-Mart foe, *New York Times*, August 17.
126. Ibid.
127. 2006, Beaverton council rejects Cedar Mill Wal-Mart plan, *Beaverton Valley Times*, August 8; 2005, No Wal-Mart for Vancouver, *CBC News*, June 29; 2004, Inglewood Wal-Mart proposal defeated, http://www.laane.org/pressroom/stories/walmart/040407CityNewsService.html, April 6.
128. 2007, Wal-Mart Annual Report, 56.
129. Ibid.
130. Ibid.
131. C. Harrison, 2003, Commitment from Wal-Mart may boost tracking technology, *Dallas Morning News*, July 15.
132. Ibid.
133. Ibid.
134. 2004, U.S. Census Bureau, Interim Projections Consistent with 2000 Census, http://www.census.gov/population/www/projections/popproj.html, March.
135. Ibid.
136. 2007, U.S. Department of Labor, Women's Bureau: Statistics & Data, http://www.dol.gov/wb/stats/main.htm, May 14.
137. E. L. Chao & K. P. Utgoff, Women in the labor force: A databook, U.S. Bureau of Labor Statistics, May 2005, 1.

138. G. Becker & K. Murphy, 2007, The upside of income inequality, *The American*, May/June, 24–28.
139. 2007, U.S. Census Bureau, Historical Income Inequality Tables, http://www.census.gov/hhes/www/income/histinc/ineqtoc.html, May 21.
140. 2007, Wal-Mart "Out in Front," Fact Sheets, WalMartFacts.com, http://www.walmartfacts.com/FactSheets/4112007_Wal-Mart__Out_in_Front_.pdf, April 11.
141. R. Walton, 2006, Wal-Mart Annual Report, inside cover.
142. Ibid.
143. H. L. Scott, 2007, Wal-Mart Annual Report, 10.
144. 2007, Wal-Mart "Out in Front."
145. 2007 Wal-Mart Annual Report, 5, 12; and Wal-Mart Stores Overview, http://walmartstores.com/GlobalWMStoresWeb/navigate.do?catg=345, May 25.
146. 2007 Wal-Mart Annual Report, 8, 12.
147. Ibid.
148. 2007, In Front with Wal-Mart, Wal-Mart Stores, Inc., http://www.infrontwithwalmart.com/about.aspx, May 20.
149. 2007, Wal-Mart Annual Report, 5.
150. 2007, Wal-Mart Annual Report, 11.
151. 2003, Knowledge@Wharton, The Wal-Mart Empire: A Simple Formula and Unstoppable Growth, Research at Penn, http://www.upenn.edu/researchatpenn/article.php?631&bus, April 9.
152. 2004, FRONTLINE co-production with Hedrick Smith Productions, Inc., WGBH Educational Foundation, http://www.pbs.org/wgbh/pages/frontline/shows/walmart/etc/script.html.
153. 2007, Wal-Mart supplier requirements and processes, http://walmartstores.com/GlobalWMStoresWeb/navigate.do?catg=331, May 19.
154. Ibid.
155. 2007, Wal-Mart Sustainability, http://walmartstores.com/microsite/walmart_sustainability.html, May 19.
156. 2007, Wal-Mart Annual Report, 16.
157. Ibid.
158. 2007, Wal-Mart Annual Report, 11.
159. Ibid.
160. 2007, Wal-Mart Annual Report, 21.
161. 2007, Wal-Mart Annual Report, 18.
162. S. Hornblower, 2004, Always low prices: Is Wal-Mart good for America? *Frontline*, http://www.pbs.org/wgbh/pages/frontline/shows/walmart/secrets/pricing.html, November 23.
163. 2007, Wal-Mart Annual Report, 18.
164. 2007, Wal-Mart Annual Report, 17.
165. H. L. Scott, 2007, Wal-Mart Annual Report, 11.
166. B. Helm & D. Kiley, 2006, Wal-Mart leaves draft out in the cold, *BusinessWeek*, http://www.businessweek.com/bwdaily/dnflash/content/dec2006/db20061207_540888.htm?campaign_id=rss_innovate, December 7.
167. A. Zimmerman, 2006, To boost sales, Wal-Mart drops one-size-fits-all approach, *Wall Street Journal*, http://online.wsj.com/article/SB115758956826955863.html?mod=hps_us_pageone, September 7.
168. Ibid.
169. Ibid.
170. H. L. Scott, 2007, Wal-Mart Annual Report, 11.
171. M. Barbaro, 2007, It's not only about price at Wal-Mart, *New York Times*, http://www.nytimes.com/2007/03/02/business/02walmart.html?ex=1330491600&en=5a72ddc69030ce62&ei=5088&partner=rssnyt&emc=rss&pagewanted=print, March 2
172. 2007 Wal-Mart Annual Report, 17; P. Svensson, 2007, Dell to sell computers at Wal-Mart, Associated Press, Yahoo! Finance, http://biz.yahoo.com/ap/070524/dell_wal_mart.html?.v=11, May 24.
173. T. Ryan, 2007, From RetailWire: Wal-Mart classifies customers for growth, *Supply Chain Digest*, http://www.scdigest.com/assets/newsViews/07-03-27-2.php?cid=977, March 27.
174. 2007, Wal-Mart Annual Report, 19.
175. 2007, Wal-Mart cutting managers at Sam's Club, Reuters, http://www.reuters.com/article/businessNews/idUSN2628417520070426?feedType=RSS, April 26.
176. T. Otte, 2007, Spinoff in Bentonville revisited, value investing, MotleyFool.com, http://www.fool.com/investing/value/2007/05/07/spinoff-in-bentonville-revisited.aspx, May 7.
177. 2007, Wal-Mart Annual Report, 19.
178. Ibid.
179. Ibid.
180. Ibid.
181. 2007, Wal-Mart F1Q08 (Qtr End 4/30/07) Earnings call transcript, retail stocks, *SeekingAlpha*, http://retail.seekingalpha.com/article/35633, May 15.
182. 2007, Wal-Mart evaluating options in possible bid for the UK's J. Sainsbury chain, *Supply Chain Digest*, http://www.scdigest.com/assets/newsViews/07-03-27-3.php?cid=978, March 27.
183. 2007, Wal-Mart Retail Divisions, http://www.walmartfacts.com/articles/2502.aspx, April 4.
184. 2003, The Wal-Mart Empire: A simple formula and unstoppable growth, *Knowledge@Wharton*, http://www.upenn.edu/researchatpenn/article.php?631&bus, April 9.
185. A. Bianco, 2007, Wal-Mart's midlife crisis, 56.

Case 29

WD-40 Company: The Squeak, Smell, and Dirt Business (A)

Gerry Yemen, Marcia Conner, James G. Clawson

University of Virginia

In the fall of 1999 Garry Ridge, the newly appointed CEO of WD-40 Company, was plowing through his homework. In addition to running the company, Ridge had enrolled in the first class at the University of San Diego's two-year graduate program in executive leadership. The class of 27 included students from Cymer, Kyocera America, Amor Ministries, and the U.S. Marine Corps, working nights and weekends on their master's degrees in leadership. Ridge enrolled in the program in hopes it would help him usher in change to the highly successful but now somewhat static WD-40 Company. He wanted to find ways of rejuvenating the company and stimulating its employees to look beyond the firm's relatively narrow focus of the last 43 years. The nature of WD-40 Company's success in capturing the market had created its own limited growth opportunities.

The Blue and Yellow Can

Norm Larsen and three investors founded Rocket Chemical Company in 1952 to supply rust inhibitors to various customers including aircraft and missile manufacturers. The one-room operation had a three-person staff. Larsen, the lead chemist at the firm, was searching under contract for a formula that could be used to prevent corrosion on airplanes and Atlas missile skins and remove moisture from electrical circuits. After forty tries, Larsen came up with a water displacement (WD) formulation that seemed to work, so he called it WD-40. Although the product seemed to meet the needs of the immediate contracts, over time, engineers at the firm discovered that the creation was equally useful for other difficulties they encountered. They began sneaking it out of the plant to unstick locks and fix sticky doors at home. By 1958, the company had started producing the material in small blue and yellow aerosol cans and marketing it to retail outlets. Sales representatives sold the product directly out of their cars to sporting goods and hardware stores. Rocket Chemical Company grew to include seven employees with sales of about 45 cases a day.

By the mid-1960s, the firm had stopped production of its other products (rust resistors and removers for metal parts and tools) and focused on its most popular product, WD-40. In 1968, sales had reached $1 million, and the firm changed its name to WD-40 Incorporated. The business went public in 1973 (see financial data in Exhibit 1) and was so successful in its market niche that it had no competitors.

Worldwide alternative uses for WD-40 had grown far beyond what Larsen and his cofounders imagined. Letters poured into the company explaining the various and ingenious uses for WD-40. The Denver fire department reported using the product to extract a nude burglar from a café vent. A physician extracted a child's arm from an elevator door. And a python snake was removed from the undercarriage of a city bus in Asia. A veterinarian used WD-40 to remove Cookie, the parakeet, from a sticky mousetrap tray in Vista, California. And although the American Medical Association did not approve WD-40 as a cure, it did have an article that recommended the use of the product for a toe stuck in the bathtub faucet or a finger stuck in a soda bottle (see Exhibit 2 for a list of 50 most novel uses). Dave Barry, a humor columnist at *The Miami Herald,* once advanced the theory that Roman civilization collapsed because it didn't have any WD-40! By 1999, 83 percent of households in the United States owned at least one can. Ridge noted that Americans were more likely to use WD-40 than dental floss. Yet the company's success created an interesting business problem. Because the market was saturated, sales growth was difficult to obtain and the stock price became stagnant.

Exhibit 1 Selected Financial Data

Income Statement

(dollar amounts in millions except per share amounts)	Aug 99	Aug 98	Aug 97
Revenue	$146.3	$144.4	$137.9
Cost of Goods Sold	63.7	62.2	58.4
Gross Profit	82.6	82.2	79.5
Gross Profit Margin	56.5%	56.9%	57.7%
SG&A Expense	46.4	45.9	42.6
Depreciation & Amortization	2.4	2.2	2.2
Operating Income	33.8	34.1	34.7
Operating Margin	23.1%	23.6%	25.2%
Nonoperating Income	0.2	0.1	(1.2)
Nonoperating Expenses	0.0	0.0	0.0
Income Before Taxes	34.0	34.2	33.5
Income Taxes	12.1	12.4	12.0
Net Income After Taxes	21.9	21.8	21.5
Continuing Operations	22.1	21.9	21.4
Discontinued Operations	0.0	0.0	0.0
Total Operations	22.1	21.9	21.4
Total Net Income	22.1	21.9	21.4
Net Profit Margin	15.1%	15.2%	15.5%
Diluted EPS from Continuing Operations ($)	$ 1.41	$ 1.40	$ 1.37
Diluted EPS from Discontinued Operations ($)	0.00	0.00	0.00
Diluted EPS from Total Operations ($)	1.41	1.40	1.37
Diluted EPS from Total Net Income ($)	1.41	1.40	1.37
Dividends per Share	1.28	1.28	1.25

Balance Sheet	Aug 99	Aug 98	Aug 97
Cash	$ 9.7	$ 8.6	$ 10.9
Net Receivables	28.6	27.0	22.6
Inventories	8.0	3.7	5.5
Other Current Assets	5.8	10.4	3.4
Total Current Assets	52.1	49.8	42.4
Net Fixed Assets	3.9	3.6	4.2
Other Noncurrent Assets	35.9	17.6	18.9
Total Assets	92.0	70.9	65.4
Accounts Payable	11.3	6.9	6.7
Short-Term Debt	2.5	0.8	0.8
Other Current Liabilities	6.6	6.2	3.9
Total Current Liabilities	20.4	13.9	11.4
Long-Term Debt	14.1	0.9	1.7
Other Noncurrent Liabilities	1.4	1.1	1.0
Total Liabilities	35.9	15.9	14.1
Preferred Stock Equity	0.0	0.0	0.0
Common Stock Equity	56.2	55.0	51.3
Total Equity	56.2	55.0	51.3
Shares Outstanding (mil.)	15.6	15.6	15.6

(continued)

Exhibit 1 Selected Financial Data (*Continued*)

Cash Flow Statement	Aug 99	Aug 98	Aug 97
Net Operating Cash Flow	$25.8	$23.7	$ 23.3
Net Investing Cash Flow	(18.6)	(6.7)	(1.1)
Net Financing Cash Flow	(6.0)	(19.4)	(18.2)
Net Change in Cash	1.2	(2.3)	4.1
Depreciation & Amortization	2.4	2.2	2.2
Capital Expenditures	(24.6)	(1.3)	(1.5)
Cash Dividends Paid	(20.0)	(20.0)	(19.4)

Source: 2002, Hoover's Company Information, http://hoovers.com, August 2.

Exhibit 2 Fifty Most Novel Uses for WD-40

Spray on trees to prevent beavers from chewing on them	Removes berry stains from patio furniture
Removes tar, sap, and splattered bugs from vehicles	Removes gum stuck to concrete
Cleans surfaces of adhesives, label, tape, and stickers	Cleans heavy dirt from shovels
Removes dirt and grime in kitchens and bathrooms	Cleans dog hair from sliding door rollers
Extracts nude burglar from a café vent	Removes lipstick from fabric
Lubricates dirty or stuck locks and latches	Cleans peanut butter from shoestrings
Cleans and protects tools	Shines wheelbarrow tires
Extracts a child's arm from an elevator door	Spray on trash can lids to keep messes from sticking
Cleans and lubricates bicycle chains	Unkinks gold chains
Extracts a python snake from city bus undercarriage	Helps reclaim rusted plumbing snake
Attracts fish when sprayed on bait	Lubricates table leafs
Cures dog mange	Removes makeup from carpet
Prevents squirrels from climbing into birdhouses when sprayed on metal pole	Lubricates pulley on sump pump
Sprayed on hips and knees to keep joints limber	Frees stuck Lego blocks
Removes toe stuck in bathtub faucet	Lubricates mouse trap machinery
Removes finger stuck in soda bottle	Shines mailboxes
Silences noisy bedsprings	Lubricates cigarette case hinges
Removes crayon from clothes dryer (make sure to unplug dryer first)	Stops squeaks on Tonka trucks
Lubricates hydraulic rams on slide out of 5th wheel	Cleans rust off Santa's sleigh runners
Shines leaves of artificial houseplants	Cleans pigeon droppings from cars
Keeps snow from sticking to shovel	Removes dog slobber from dash and seats in vehicle
Cleans ashtrays	Cleans magazines for an AK-47
Cleans old muffin tins	Cleans bed pans
Cleans doggie doo from tennis shoes	Eases removal of solidified spitballs
Removes gunk when replacing old faucets	Spray WD-40 on plant holders to stop squeaks during wind

In an attempt to fight the stagnation, WD-40 Company acquired Reckitt and Colman's "3-in-One" oil business during 1995. This purchase provided the firm with an existing network of distribution in 17 countries that included several new markets for WD-40.[1] In 1996, WD-40 Company launched a new product, T.A.L. 5, a synthetic lubricant.[2] Management developed a new corporate logo to reflect the integration of the two new products. In 1999, WD-40 bought the Lava brand of heavy-duty hand cleaners from the Block Drug Company. This one-product business and brand consisted of two sizes of soap bar and one size of liquid soap. Management decided to add the Lava Towel, a waterless hand cleaner, and two new sizes of Liquid Lava. Once more, the reason for buying the brand was to increase access to consumers, the brand had high awareness and a common user base to the WD-40 brand, yet it had gaps in its distribution that the WD-40 Company business model could close, expanding distribution channels.

After adding new products, the organization continued to focus on international growth. WD-40 Company opened new manufacturing and sales operations in San Diego, California (near corporate headquarters), and London, and sales offices in Australia, Canada, France, Germany, Italy, Malaysia, and Spain.

Investors bought shares because the company was known to provide high dividends. For almost two decades, WD-40 Company's low cash needs meant it paid out close to 100 percent of earnings to stockholders.[3] Many investors were most comfortable with the company because it delivered a reliable yield that substantially exceeded market averages. Stock was traded at $20.75 in 1998 and paid annual dividends of $1.28 (see Exhibit 3 for average stock prices). Investors were satisfied with yields of 5.2 percent, more than three times that of the S&P 500.

One year after WD-40 Company turned 45 years old in 1999, there were 177 employees around the world: 106 in the U.S. parent corporation, of which six were based in the Malaysian sales office; 10 in the Canadian subsidiary; 52 in the United Kingdom subsidiary, of which nine were in Germany, eight in France, and six in Spain; six in the Australian subsidiary; and three in the company's manufacturing subsidiary (see Exhibit 4 for worldwide sales information). The majority of WD-40 Company employees were engaged in sales and/or marketing activities. With the consolidation of companies in the retail industry, increased portions of WD-40s sales were made to fewer, but larger, clients with greater purchasing power. Despite the firm's new product strategy and steady stock prices, sales remained sluggish, and Garry Ridge, previously traveling salesperson, was called on to lead the company to new growth.

Garry Ridge: The Maniacal Shark

Ridge had first encountered WD-40 Company in Australia as the managing director of a WD-40 licensee. In his role, he developed good relationships with WD-40 Company

Exhibit 3 WD-40 Company Stock Price, 1991–1999

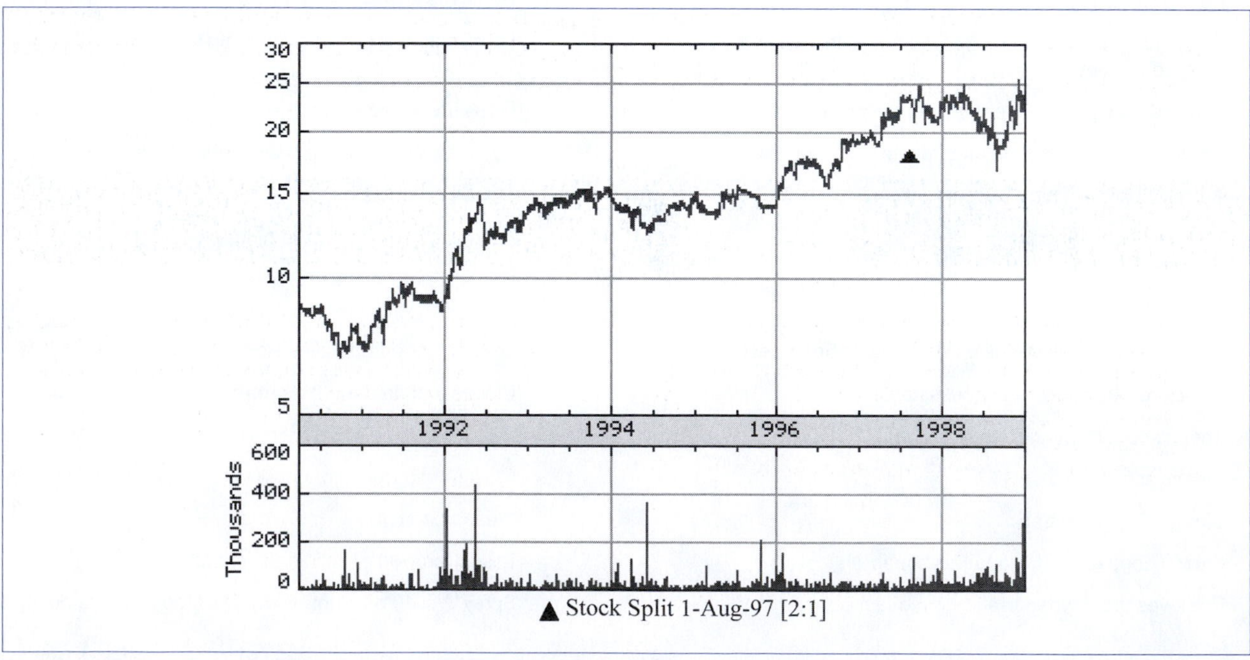

Source: 2000, Yahoo! Finance, http://finance.yahoo.com/q?s=WDFC&d=c&t=my&l=on&z=m&q=l, on September 3.

Exhibit 4 Sales for WD-40's Three Trading Blocs, 1997–1999

	(dollar amounts in millions)					
	August 1999		August 1998		August 1997	
Americas	$ 96.90	66%	$ 98.6	68%	$ 93.4	68%
Europe	37.3	26	34.9	24	32.2	23
Asia/Pacific	12.1	8	10.9	8	12.3	9
Total	$146.30	100%	$144.40	100%	$137.90	100%

Source: 1999, Form 10-K, WD-40 Company, Securities and Exchange Commission, http://web.lexisnexis.com/universe/document?_m=89e5d23a9b3e6cdc8565be08ff036524&_d, August 31.

management, so that when WD-40 Company terminated the license and planned to open a wholly owned subsidiary in Australia to explore the Asian market, Ridge was invited to join the new organization. He recalled:

I loved the brand. My dad was an engineer, and he worked for one company for 50 years, and I went to him for his blessing. I told him, "They've made me an offer to work for WD-40 Company." And he said, "You can't get along without that product, son." I thought, "Well, this is a great opportunity to work for an American company, and start an Australian operation from scratch."

After five years of building the Australian and Asian markets, Ridge began to get bored. He called the vice president of the company and said, "I could have the best job in the world here. I get to play golf and socialize, and have developed a marketing distribution model in Asia. But I'm bored." The VP revealed that WD-40 Company wanted to turn up the volume on their international operations, and he asked Ridge to move to San Diego and take over as vice president of International Operations. Ridge accepted. A little more than three years later the president of the company retired, Ridge threw his hat into the candidacy ring, and got the job.

Ridge felt he was chosen because he knew both the old WD-40 Company and had a desire to create a bridge to a "new" company. He recalled, "We had to change everything from the backroom to the boardroom, and I think I knew enough about what the brand was not to do anything stupid to hurt it. But at the same time, I knew we had to go somewhere else and was willing to run that race."

Now What?

As the new CEO, Ridge was concerned about the flat growth that WD-40 had encountered worldwide. He saw around him people with long tenure in the company who were devoted to the WD-40 brand, yet they seemed to lack a sense of direction or energy. Ridge wondered what he could do to revitalize the company.

1. 1999, Form 10-K, WD-40 Company, Securities and Exchange Commission, Washington, DC 20549, http://web.lexis-nexis.com/universe/document?_m=89e5d23a9b3e6cdc8565be08ff036524&_d August 31. (Accessed on August 5, 2002).
2. Shortly after the Lava purchase in 1999, the company decided to discontinue marketing the T.A.L. 5 lubricant. The product did not produce the revenues management and investors expected.
3. J. Palmer, 2001, The Cult of WD-40: Customers love the product; should investors love the stock? *Dow Jones Capital Market Report,* November 30, http://ptg.djnr.com/ccroot/asp/publib/story_clean_spy.asp?articles=CM0133400172DJFIN.

Case Title	Manu-facturing	Service	Consumer Goods	Food/ Retail	High Tech-nology	Transportation/ Communication	International Perspective	Social/ Ethical Issues	Industry Perspective
3M Cultivating Core Comp.	●		●		●		●		
A-1 Lanes	●						●		●
Abercrombie & Fitch				●				●	●
AMD vs Intel	●				●				●
Boeing	●						●		●
Capital One		●							
Carrefour in Asia				●			●		
Dell	●		●		●				●
Disney		●						●	●
Ford	●		●						●
GE Welch & Immelt	●	●			●			●	
Home Depot		●		●			●		
China's Home Improvement				●			●		
Huawei	●				●		●		
ING Direct		●		●					
JetBlue		●				●	●		●
Corp. Gov. at Knight Trans.		●				●			
Lufthansa		●				●	●		
Microsoft		●			●				
Nestlé	●		●	●				●	
Netflix		●		●					
PenAgain	●		●						
PSA Peugeot Citroën	●		●				●		
Sun Microsystems		●			●		●		
Teleflex Canada	●				●				
Tyco International	●							●	
Vodafone		●			●	●	●		
Wal-Mart Stores				●			●	●	
WD-40	●		●				●		

Case Title	Chapter 1	2	3	4	5	6	7	8	9	10	11	12	13
3M Cultivating Core Comp.			●				●						●
A-1 Lanes								●					●
Abercrombie & Fitch					●					●		●	
AMD vs Intel					●								●
Boeing				●	●			●	●				
Capital One				●		●	●						
Carrefour in Asia		●						●					
Dell		●		●		●							
Disney						●				●		●	
Ford				●	●							●	
GE Welch & Immelt							●					●	●
Home Depot				●	●							●	
China's Home Improvement	●				●			●					
Huawei					●			●					
ING Direct				●								●	●
JetBlue		●		●	●								
Corp. Gov. at Knight Trans.										●		●	
Lufthansa								●	●		●		
Microsoft					●	●							
Nestlé	●						●				●		●
Netflix		●	●		●							●	
PenAgain									●				●
PSA Peugeot Citroën			●						●				
Sun Microsystems	●			●				●					
Teleflex Canada						●						●	●
Tyco International						●				●	●	●	
Vodafone	●		●				●	●					
Wal-Mart Stores	●	●	●	●									
WD-40			●	●				●					●